NEW TRENDS IN SOFTWARE METHODOLOGIES, TOOLS AND TECHNIQUES

Frontiers in Artificial Intelligence and Applications

FAIA covers all aspects of theoretical and applied artificial intelligence research in the form of monographs, doctoral dissertations, textbooks, handbooks and proceedings volumes. The FAIA series contains several sub-series, including "Information Modelling and Knowledge Bases" and "Knowledge-Based Intelligent Engineering Systems". It also includes the biannual ECAI, the European Conference on Artificial Intelligence, proceedings volumes, and other ECCAI – the European Coordinating Committee on Artificial Intelligence – sponsored publications. An editorial panel of internationally well-known scholars is appointed to provide a high quality selection.

Volume 129

Recently published in this series

Vol. 128. J. Zhou et al. (Eds.), Applied Public Key Infrastructure
Vol. 127. P. Ritrovato et al. (Eds.), Towards the Learning Grid
Vol. 126. J. Cruz, Constraint Reasoning for Differential Models
Vol. 125. C.-K. Looi et al. (Eds.), Artificial Intelligence in Education
Vol. 124. T. Washio et al. (Eds.), Advances in Mining Graphs, Trees and Sequences
Vol. 123. P. Buitelaar et al. (Eds.), Ontology Learning from Text: Methods, Evaluation and Applications
Vol. 122. C. Mancini, Cinematic Hypertext –Investigating a New Paradigm
Vol. 121. Y. Kiyoki et al. (Eds.), Information Modelling and Knowledge Bases XVI
Vol. 120. T.F. Gordon (Ed.), Legal Knowledge and Information Systems – JURIX 2004: The Seventeenth Annual Conference
Vol. 119. S. Nascimento, Fuzzy Clustering via Proportional Membership Model
Vol. 118. J. Barzdins and A. Caplinskas (Eds.), Databases and Information Systems – Selected Papers from the Sixth International Baltic Conference DB&IS'2004
Vol. 117. L. Castillo et al. (Eds.), Planning, Scheduling and Constraint Satisfaction: From Theory to Practice
Vol. 116. O. Corcho, A Layered Declarative Approach to Ontology Translation with Knowledge Preservation
Vol. 115. G.E. Phillips-Wren and L.C. Jain (Eds.), Intelligent Decision Support Systems in Agent-Mediated Environments
Vol. 114. A.C. Varzi and L. Vieu (Eds.), Formal Ontology in Information Systems – Proceedings of the Third International Conference (FOIS-2004)

ISSN 0922-6389

New Trends in Software Methodologies, Tools and Techniques

Proceedings of the fourth SoMeT_W05

Edited by

Hamido Fujita

Iwate Prefectural University, Iwate, Japan

and

Mohamed Mejri

Laval University, Quebec, Canada

IOS Press

Amsterdam • Berlin • Oxford • Tokyo • Washington, DC

ISBN 1-58603-556-8
Library of Congress Control Number: 2005930830

Publisher
IOS Press
Nieuwe Hemweg 6B
1013 BG Amsterdam
Netherlands
fax: +31 20 687 0019
e-mail: order@iospress.nl

Distributor in the UK and Ireland
IOS Press/Lavis Marketing
73 Lime Walk
Headington
Oxford OX3 7AD
England
fax: +44 1865 750079

Distributor in the USA and Canada
IOS Press, Inc.
4502 Rachael Manor Drive
Fairfax, VA 22032
USA
fax: +1 703 323 3668
e-mail: iosbooks@iospress.com

PRINTED IN THE NETHERLANDS

New Trends in Software Methodologies, Tools and Techniques
H. Fujita and M. Mejri (Eds.)
IOS Press, 2005

SoMeT 2005
The 4th International Conference on
Software Methodologies,Tools and Techniques

Preface

Software is the essential enabler for the new economy and science. It creates new markets and new directions for a more reliable, flexible, and robust society. It empowers the exploration of our world in ever more depth.

However, software often falls short of our expectations. Current software methodologies, tools, and techniques remain expensive and not yet reliable for a highly changeable and evolutionary market. Many approaches have been proven only as case-by-case oriented methods.

This book presents a number of new trends and theories in the direction in which we believe software science and engineering may develop to transform the role of software and science in tomorrow's information society.

This book is an attempt to capture the essence of a new state of art in software science and its supporting technology. The book also aims at identifying the challenges such a technology has to master. It contains papers accepted at the fourth International Conference on New Trends in Software Methodologies Tools and Techniques, IV, (**SoMeT_05**) held in Tokyo, Japan, from 28th to 30th September 2005, (http://www.somet.soft.iwate-pu.ac.jp/somet_05). This workshop brought together researchers and practitioners to share their original research results and practical development experiences in software science, and its related new challenging technology.

One example we challenge in this conference is Lyee methodology – a newly emerged Japanese software methodology that has been patented in several countries in Europe, Asia, and America, but which is still at an early stage of emerging as a new software style. This conference and the series it continues will also contribute to elaborate on such new trends and related academic research studies and development.

A major goal of this international conference was to gather scholars from the international research community to discuss and share research experiences on new software methodologies, and formal techniques. The conference also investigated other comparable theories and practices in software science, including emerging technologies, from their computational foundations in terms of models, methodologies, and tools. These are essential for developing a variety of information systems research projects and to assess the practical impact on real-world software problems.

SoMeT_02 was held on October 3–5, 2002, in Sorbonne, Paris, France, **SoMeT_03** in Stockholm, Sweden, **SoMeT_04** in Leipzig, Germany and the conference that these proceedings cover, **SoMeT_05**, was held in Tokyo, Japan. These events initiate a forthcoming series that will include the 5th conference, **SoMeT_W06**, to be organized in Quebec, Canada on September 2006 (http://www.somet.soft.iwate-pu.ac.jp/somet_06/).

This book is also in part a means for presenting few selected parts of the results of the Lyee International research project (http://www.lyee-project.soft.iwate-pu.ac.jp), which aims at the exploration and development of novel software engineering methods and software generation tools based on the Lyee framework. This project was sponsored by Catena and other major Japanese enterprises in the area of software methodologies and technologies.

This book participates to provide an opportunity for exchanging ideas and experiences in the field of software technology, opening up new avenues for software development, methodologies, tools, and techniques.

The Lyee framework for example, captures the essence of the innovations, controversies, challenges and possible solutions of the software industry. This world wide patented software approach was born and enriched from experience, and it is time, and again through **SoMeT_W05** to try to let it stimulate the academic research on software engineering, attempting to close the gap that has so far existed between theory and practice. We believe that this book creates an opportunity for us in the software science community to think about where we are today and where we are going.

The book is a collection of **26** carefully reviewed best-selected papers by the reviewing committee.

The areas covered in the book are:

* Requirement engineering and requirement elicitation, and its tools,
* Software methodologies and tools for robust, reliable, non-fragile software design,
* Lyee oriented software techniques, and its legacy systems,
* Automatic software generation versus reuse, and legacy systems, source code analysis and manipulation,
* Software quality and process assessment,
* Intelligent software systems design, and software evolution techniques,
* Software optimization and formal methods,
* Static and dynamic analysis on software performance model, and software maintenance,
* End-user programming environment, User-centered Adoption-Centric Reengineering techniques,
* Ontology, cognitive models and philosophical aspects of software design,
* Software design through interaction, and precognitive software techniques for interactive software entertainment applications,
* Business oriented software application models,
* Software Engineering models, and formal techniques for software representation, software testing and validation,
* Aspect oriented programming,
* Other software engineering disciplines.

All papers published in this book are carefully reviewed and selected by SOMET international program committee. Each paper has been reviewed by three or four reviewers and has been revised based on the review reports. The papers were reviewed on the basis of technical soundness, relevance, originality, significance, and clarity. The acceptance rate for the papers listed in this book is 48% in this year SoMeT.

This book was made possible by the collective efforts of all the Lyee International project collaborators and other people and supporters. We gratefully thank Iwate Prefectural University, University of Laval, Catena Co., ISD, Ltd, SANGIKYO co., and others for their overwhelming support. We are especially thankful to the program committee and others who participated in the review of all submitted papers and thanks also for the hot discussion we have had on the PC meetings to select the papers listed in this book.

This book is another milestone in mastering new challenges on software and its new promising technology, within the SoMeT framework and others. Also, it gives the reader new insights, inspiration and concrete material to elaborate and study this new technology.

We would also like to thank and acknowledge the support of the University of Leipzig, Telematik and e-Business group for allowing us to use the Paperdyne System as a conference-supporting tool during all the phases on this transaction.

The Editors

Conference Organisation

Program Chairs

Hamido (Issam) Fujita, *Iwate Prefectural University, Iwate, Japan,*
e-mail: issam@soft.iwate-pu.ac.jp

Mohamed Mejri, *Laval University, Quebec, Canada*
e-mail: mohamed.mejri@ift.ulaval.ca

Program committee of SoMeT_05

(http://www.somet.soft.iwate-pu.ac.jp/somet_05)

Anna-Maria Di Sciullo, University de Quebec de Montreal, Canada
Ridha Khedri, McMaster University, Hamilton, Canada
Mohamed Mejiri, Laval University, Quebec, Canada
Bechi Ktari, Laval University, Quebec, Canada
Marite Kirikova, Riga Technical University, Latvia
Kasem Saleh, American University of Sharjah, UAE
Remigijus Gustas, Karlstad University, Sweden
Love Ekenberg, Mid Sweden University Sweden,
Benkt Wangler, University of Skovde, Sweden
Rudolf Keller, Zuehlke Engineering AG, Switzerland
Soundar Kumara, The Pennsylvania State University, USA
Margeret M Burnett, Oregon State University, USA
Michael Oudshoorn, Montana State University, Bozeman, USA
Gregg Rothermel, Oregon State University, USA
Bipin Indurkhya, International Institute of Information Technology, Hyderabad, India
Isaac Marks, King's College London, London, UK
Ernest Edmonds, University of Technology, Sydney, Australia
Colette Rolland, University de Paris_1-Pantheon Sorbonne, Paris, France
Souveyet Carine, University de Paris_1-Pantheon Sorbonne, Paris, France
Camille Salinesi, University de Paris_1-Pantheon Sorbonne, Paris, France
Selmin Nurcan, University de Paris_1-Pantheon Sorbonne, Paris, France
Christophe Sibertin-Blanc, Toulouse_1 University, France
Pierre-Jean Charrel, Toulouse_2 University, France
Victor Malyshkin, Russian Academy of Sciences, Russia
Sergei Gorlatch, Muenster.University, Germany
Roberto Poli, Terent University, Italy
Domenico M. Pisanelli, ITBM - CNR, Rome, Italy
Liliana Albertazzi, Mitteleuropa foundation Research Centre, Bolzano, Italy
Samuel T. Chanson, Hong Kong Univ. of Science & Technology, China
Shaoying Liu, Hosei University, Japan
Jun Hakura, Iwate Prefectural University, Iwate, Japan
Masaki Kurematsu, *Iwate Prefectural University, Iwate, Japan*
Yutaka Funyu, *Iwate Prefectural University, Iwate, Japan*

Teruo Higashino, Osaka University, Japan
Norio Shiratori, Tohoku University, Japan
Fumio Negoro, Institute of Software Development (ISD), Tokyo, Japan

Organizing Chairs

Tae Yoneda
Iwate Prefectural University, Iwate, Japan

Hideo Yagihashi
ISD Ltd, Tokyo, Japan

Bechir Ktari
Laval University, Quebec, Canada

Additional Reviewers
David Ramamonjisoa, *Iwate Prefectural University, Iwate, Japan*
Jun Sasaki, *Iwate Prefectural University, Iwate, Japan*

Contents

Preface v

Conference Organisation ix

Chapter 1. Requirement Engineering and Practical Software Models

Modelling Multi-Facetted Purposes of Artefacts 3
Colette Rolland

Reengineering Software: A Case Study 18
Megan Graham and Michael J. Oudshoorn

Advances in AOP with AspectC++ 33
Olaf Spinczyk, Daniel Lohmann and Matthias Urban

The Collatz Problem in a New Perspective: Energy Consumption Analysis 54
Kostas Zotos, Andreas Litke, George Stephanides and Alexander Chatzigeorgiou

Chapter 2. Legacy Systems and Language Conversions

Suggestions of Lyee: A Framework on Software Methodological Thinking 67
Fumio Negoro

LyeeBuilder 83
B. Ktari, M. Mejri, D. Godbout and H. Fujita

Chapter 3. Software Quality and Development Measurement

Approaches to Qualitative Evaluation of the Software Quality Attributes: Overview 103
Kozlov Denis

IT Practitioner's Perspective on Australian Risk Management Practices and Tools for Software Development Projects: A Pilot Study 111
Bee Bee Chua and June M. Verner

Validating Documentation with Domain Ontologies 126
Leonid Kof and Markus Pizka

Co-Developing Model for User Participation in Web Application Development 144
Tae Yoneda, Kohei Mitsui, Jun Sasaki and Yutaka Funyu

A Neuro-Fuzzy Based Approach for the Prediction of Quality of Reusable Software Components 156
Parvinder Singh Sandhu and Hardeep Singh

Chapter 4. Requirement Representation and Formalization

A Gentle Introduction to System Verification 173
Love Ekenberg

Limitation and Possibilities of Automation on the Way from Intention ⇒ Program 194
Victor Malyshkin and Yuri Zagorulko

Chapter 5. Development of Natural Language Based Methodologies

Handling Pronouns Intelligently 207
Anna Maria di Sciullo

About Application and Implementation of Semantic Meta Parsing 224
Gregers Koch

Chapter 6. Software Enterprise Modeling and Component Representation

Inference Rules of Semantic Dependencies in the Enterprise Modelling 235
Remigijus Gustas

A Representation-Theoretical Analysis of the OMG Modelling Suite 252
Cesar Gonzalez-Perez and Brian Henderson-Sellers

Towards Software Development Methodology for Web Services 263
George Feuerlicht and Sooksathit Meesathit

Chapter 7. Configuration Management Software

A Methodology for Deriving the Architectural Implications of Different Degrees of Mobility in Information Systems 281
Matthias Book, Volker Gruhn, Malte Hülder and Clemens Schäfer

Chapter 8. Ubiquitous and Web Related Systems Software

Meme Media for the Federation of Intellectual Resources Over the Web by Clipping and Combining Them 295
Yuzuru Tanaka

Component-Based Grid Programming Using the HOC-Service Architecture 311
Jan Dünnweber and Sergei Gorlatch

Design and Implementation of an Agent-Based Middleware for Context-Aware Ubiquitous Services 330
Hideyuki Takahashi, Yoshikazu Tokairin, Takuo Suganuma and Norio Shiratori

Chapter 9. Software Design for Creative and Interactive Users

Computation, Interaction and Imagination: *Into Virtual Space and Back to Reality* 353
Ernest Edmonds and Linda Candy

GUIDE: Games with UML for Interactive Design Exploration 364
Jennifer Tenzer

A Grounded Theory Study of Programming in Artist-Programmer Collaborations 388
Greg Turner, Alastair Weakley, Yun Zhang and Ernest Edmonds

Acting Interactively in a Digital World 401
Roman Danylak and Ernest Edmonds

Author Index 407

Chapter 1

Requirement Engineering and Practical Software Models

New Trends in Software Methodologies, Tools and Techniques
H. Fujita and M. Mejri (Eds.)
IOS Press, 2005

Modelling Multi-Facetted Purposes of Artefacts

Colette ROLLAND
Université Paris1 Panthéon Sorbonne, CRI, 90 rue de Tolbiac, 75013 Paris, France
rolland@univ-paris1.fr

Abstract. Whereas software variability deals with customisation and adaptability of software, we consider here the issue of modelling variability for Information System artefacts. We view variability in the larger perspective of the system meeting the purpose of many organisations and customer groups. We propose to represent this multi-facetted nature of a purpose through the notion of intentions and strategies organised as a map. The map is a directed, labelled, non-deterministic graph with intentions as nodes, and strategies to achieve intentions, as edges. Its nature allows the capture of different forms of variability through multi-edges between a pair of nodes thereby enabling many traversals of the graph from beginning to end. Besides, using the refinement mechanism of the map, it is possible to represent variability at different levels of detail. We show the power of a map to represent variability and, as an illustration, model the variations of the SAP Materials module as a map. Additionally, we show that variations in process models can also be captured in the map formalism. Again, we apply a multi-facetted process model to customise the SAP materials module.

1. Introduction

Propelled by the failure of systems to meet user expectations, there has been a gathering trend to build ever more purposeful systems, those that achieve specific objectives of organisations. Goal modelling had its early beginnings in 1970s in the definition study of Hice and Turner [7] and context analysis of [16]. It was used in participative analysis in 1980s [12] and was found in a few Object-oriented methodologies of the 1990s [17] but really came into its own in Requirements Engineering in the last decade. Goal modelling is used in RE [1,3,4,10,11,13] to elicit IS requirements that capture the strategic, high level, goals of an enterprise. By linking the rationale behind the system (the *why)* and the functional as well as non-functional requirements (the *what*) goal modelling is helpful in building more purposeful products.

In recent years, a new context in which IS products are developed has emerged. Whereas earlier, an IS product met the purpose of a single organisation and of a single set of customers, a product of today must be conceived in a larger perspective, to meet the purpose of several organisations and to be adaptable to different usage situations/customer sets. The former is typical of an ERP-like development situation whereas the latter is the concern of product-line development [2,18] and adaptable software [8]. In the software community, this leads to the notion of software variability which is defined as the ability of a software system to be changed, customised or configured to a specific context [19].

We believe that variability suggests a move from systems with a *mono-facetted purpose* to those with a *multi-facetted purpose*. Whereas the former concentrates on goal discovery, the multi-facetted nature of a purpose extends it to consider the many different ways of goal achievement. For example, for the goal Purchase Material, earlier it would be enough to know that an organisation achieves this goal by forecasting material need. Purchase material is mono-facetted: it has exactly one strategy for its achievement. However, in the new context, it is necessary to introduce other strategies as well, say the Reorder Point strategy for purchasing material. Purchase Material now is multi-facetted, it has many strategies for goal achievement. These two strategies, among others, are made available in the SAP Materials Management module.

In this paper, we suggest that to model the multi-facetted purpose of an IS product there is a need to balance goal-orientation with the introduction of strategies for goal achievement. Additionally, our position is that the multi-facetted perspective on *products* has implications on the *process* dimension as well. First, there cannot be a mismatch between the process modelling paradigm and the product modelling paradigm. Instead, the former must be aligned to the latter. Thus, the process modelling paradigm should be goal driven. Secondly, it is unlikely that product variability can be discovered with a monolithic way of working. This implies that the process model should provide many different strategies to achieve the same process goal. The foregoing points to the desirability of the process to be looked upon as a multi-facetted purpose process. This multi-facet aspect implies a process model that has the capability to integrate in it the many strategies found in different methodologies for achieving the same process goal. For example, to Elicit a Goal, different methodologies follow different strategies, top-down, bottom-up, what-if, participative etc. These get integrated in one multi-facetted purpose process model.

In this paper, we use a formalism, the *Map* [14], for the representation of multi-facetted purposes. A *map* is a graph, with nodes as *intentions* and *strategies* as edges. An edge entering a node identifies a strategy that can be used for achieving the intention of the node. The map therefore, shows which intentions can be achieved by which strategies once a preceding intention has been achieved. Evidently, the map is capable of expressing goals and their achievement in a declarative manner.

2. Key Concepts of a Map

In this section we introduce the *key concepts* of a map and their relationships and bring out their relevance to model multi-facetted purposes.

A *map* provides a representation of a multi-facetted purpose based on a non-deterministic ordering of intentions and strategies. The key concepts of the map and their inter-relationships are shown in the map meta-model of Fig. 1 which is drawn using UML notations.

- As shown in Fig. 1, a *map* is composed of several sections. A section is an aggregation of two kinds of intentions, *source* and *target*, linked together by a *strategy*.
- An *intention* is a goal, 'an optative' statement [9] that expresses what is wanted i.e. a state that is expected to be reached or maintained. *Make Room Booking* is an intention to make a reservation for rooms in a hotel. The achievement of this intention leaves the system in the state, *Booking made.*

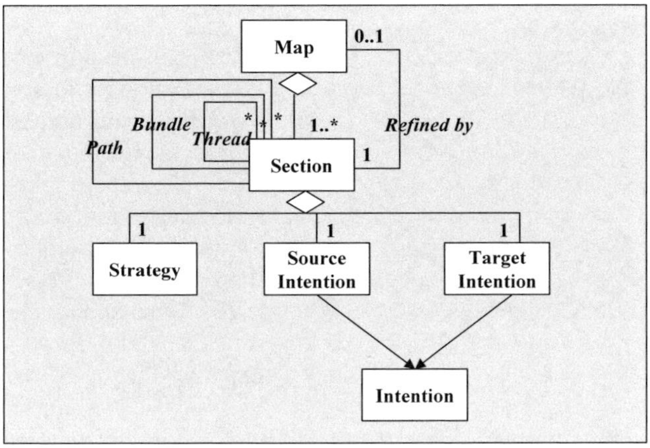

Figure 1. The map meta-model.

Each map has two special intentions, *Start* and *Stop*, associated with the initial and final states respectively.

- A *strategy* is an approach, a manner, a means to achieve an intention. Let us assume that bookings can be made *on the Internet*. This is a means of achieving the *Make Room Booking* intention, and is a strategy. *by visiting a travel agency* is another strategy to achieve the same intention.
- A *section* is an aggregation of the source intention, the target intention, and a strategy. As shown in Fig. 1 it is a triplet $<I_{source}, I_{target}, S_{source-target}>$. A section expresses the strategy $S_{source-target}$ using which, starting from I_{source}, I_{target} can be achieved. The triplet *<Start, Make Room Booking, on the Internet>* is a section; similarly *<Start, Make Room Booking, by visiting a travel agency>* constitutes another section.

A section is the basic construct of a map which itself can be seen as an assembly of sections. When a map is used to model a multi-facetted purpose, each of its sections represents a facet. The set of sections model the purpose in its totality and we will see below that the relationships between sections and between a section and a map lead to the representation of the multi-facetted perspective.

A map is drawn as a directed graph from *Start* to *Stop*. Intentions are represented as nodes of the graph and strategies as edges between these. The graph is directed because the strategy shows the flow from the source to the target intention. The map of Fig. 2 contains six sections MS0 to MS5.

- ***Section relationships***: There are three relationships between sections (Fig. 1), namely the *thread*, *path* and *bundle* which generate *multi-thread* and *multi-path* topologies in a map.

– *Thread relationship*: It is possible for a target intention to be achieved from a source intention in many different ways. Each of these ways is expressed as a section in the map. Such a map topology is called a *multi-thread* and the sections participating in the multi-thread are said to be in a *thread relationship* with one another. MS1 and MS2 are in a thread relationship in Fig. 2. Assume that *Accept Payment* is another intention in our example and that it can be achieved in two different ways, *By electronic transfer* or *By credit card*. This leads to a thread relationship between the two sections shown in Fig. 3.

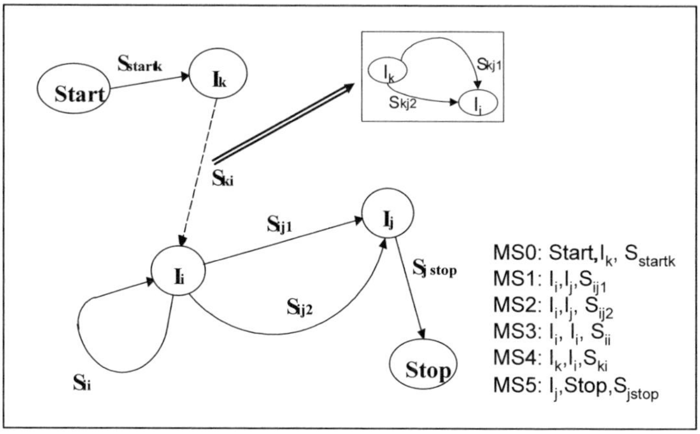

Figure 2. The map as a graph.

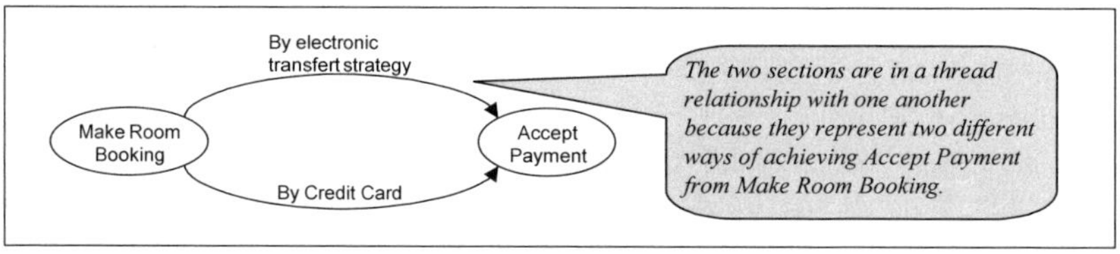

Figure 3. An example of thread relationship.

It is clear that a thread relationship between two sections regarded as facets represents directly the variability associated to a multi-facetted purpose. Multi-faceting is captured in the different strategies to achieve the common target intention.

- *Path relationship:* This establishes a precedence/succedence relationship between sections. For a section to succeed another, its source intention must be the target intention of the preceding one. For example the two sections <*Start, Make Room Booking, On the Internet*>, <*Make Room Booking, Accept Payment, By credit card*> form a path.

From the point of view of modelling facets, the path introduces a composite facet whereas the section based facet is atomic.

Given the thread and the path relationships, an intention can be achieved by several combinations of sections. Such a topology is called a *multi-path*. In general, a map from its *Start* to its *Stop* intentions is a multi-path and may contain multi-threads. MS0, MS4, MS1, MS5 is a path of the map in Fig. 2; MS0, MS4, MS3, MS2, MS5 is another path in the map.

Let us assume in our example that it is possible to *Stop* either because a customer retracts from making the booking (*By customer retraction*) or after payment (*Normally*). Figure 4 shows the entire map with the purpose to *Make Confirmed Booking*. This map contains 6 paths from Start to Stop out of which two are highlighted in the Figure.

Clearly, the multi-path topology is yet another way of representing the multi-facetted perspective. Multi-faceting in this case is obtained by combining various sections together to achieve a given intention of the map. Consider for instance the intention Accept payment in Fig. 4; there are four paths from Start to achieve it; each of

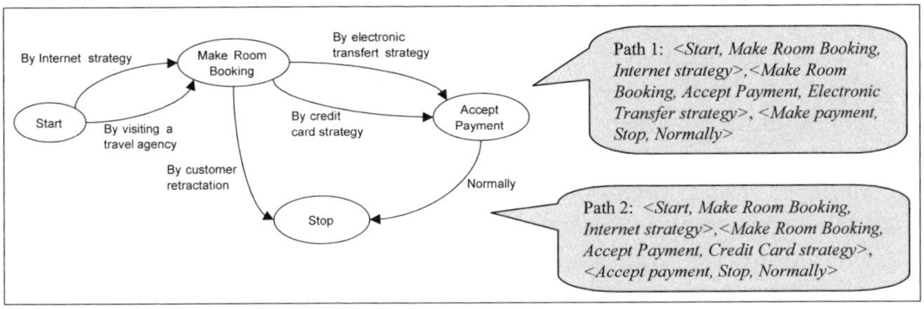

Figure 4. The multi-path of the map *Make Confirmed Booking.*

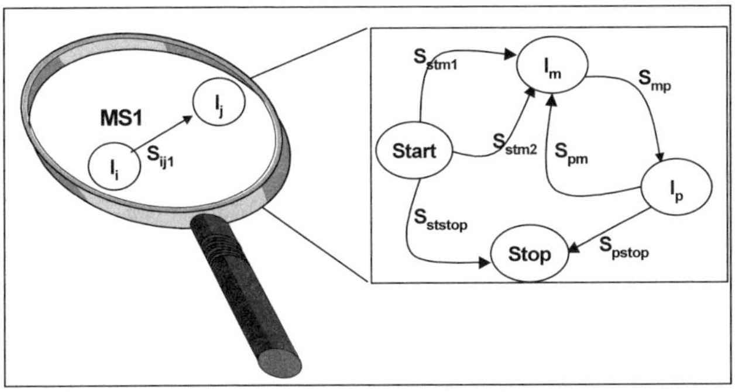

Figure 5. The refinement relationship.

them is a different way to get the intention achieved and in this sense, participates to the multi-faceting. Each path is a composite facet composed of two atomic facets. This can be extended to the full map which can be seen as composed of a number of paths from Start to Stop. This time these paths introduce multi-faceting but to achieve the intention of the map which in our example, is Make Confirmed Booking.

- *Bundle relationship*: Several sections having the same pair $<I_{source}, I_{target}>$ which are mutually exclusive are in a *bundle relationship.* The group of these sections constitutes a *bundle*. Notice that the difference between a thread and bundle relationship is the exclusive OR of sections in the latter versus an OR in the former.

- ***Refinement relationship*:** Fig. 1 also shows that a section of a map can be refined as another map through the *refinement relationship.* The entire refined map then represents the section as shown in Fig. 5. Refinement is an abstraction mechanism by which a complex assembly of sections at level *i+1* is viewed as a unique section at level *i.* As a result of refinement, a section at level *i* is represented by multiple paths & multiple threads at level *i+1.*

From the point of view of multi-faceting, refinement allows to look to the multi-facetted nature of a facet. It introduces levels in the representation of the multi-facetted purpose which is thus, completely modelled through a hierarchy of maps.

To sum up

- The purpose of the artefact is captured in a *hierarchy of maps*. The intention associated to the root map is the high level statement about the purpose. Using the refinement mechanism each section of the root map can be refined as a map and the recursive application of this mechanism results in a map hierarchy. At successive levels of the hierarchy the purpose stated initially as the intention of the root map is further refined.

- At any given level of the hierarchy, the multi-facetted dimension is based on *multi-thread* and *multi-path* topologies. Multi-thread introduces local faceting in the sense that it allows to represent the different ways for achieving an intention directly. Multi-path introduces global faceting by representing different combinations of intentions and strategies to achieve a given map intention. Any path from Start to Stop represents one way of achieving the map intention, therefore the purpose represented in this map.

3. SAP R/3 Materials Management Map

In this section we show the use of the Map to capture the multi-facetted purpose of a product and take the SAP R/3 Materials Management (MM) module to illustrate this.

This module provides automated support for the day-to-day operations of any type of business that entails the consumption of materials. It consists of five key components starting from materials planning (MM-MRP Materials Requirements Planning), through purchasing (MM-PUR Purchasing), managing inventory (MM-IM Inventory Management), managing warehousing (MM-WM Warehouse Management), to invoice verification (MM-IV Invoice Verification). It also includes two support components, MM-IS Information System and MM-EDI Electronic Data Interchange.

In its totality, the MM module can be seen to meet the purpose, *Satisfy Material Need Efficiently.* This is the intention of the root map shown in Fig. 6. The map shows that to meet this purpose two intentions have to be achieved, namely *Purchase Materi*al and *Monitor Stock.* These reflect the conventional view of materials management as "procuring raw material and ensuring effectiveness of the logistics pipeline through which materials flow" [6]. Evidently, there is an ordering between these two intentions: stock cannot be monitored unless it has been procured. This is shown in the Figure by the section *<Purchase Material, Monitor Stock, Out-In strategy>.*

The map of Fig. 6 shows 25 paths from *Start* to *Stop*, 5 following the *Bill for expenses strategy*, 10 following the *Planning Strategy*, and 10 following the *Manual strategy*. Thus, the map is able to present a global perspective of the diverse ways of achievement of the main purpose. When a more detailed view is needed, then it becomes necessary to focus more specifically on the multi-facetted nature of each intention found in the 'global' map. The detailed view of the intentions contained in Fig. 6 is brought out in turn below.

3.1. The Multiple Facets of Purchase Material

The multi-facetted nature of *Purchase Material* is shown in Fig. 6 by including three strategies for its achievement (a) *Planning strategy*, (b) *Manual strategy* and (c) *Reminder strategy*. The three facets are *<Start, Purchase Material, Planning strategy>, <Start, Purchase Material, Manual strategy> and <Purchase Material, Purchase Material, Reminder strategy>.*

Subsumed in the first facet are two mutually exclusive facets, one that allows purchase to be made when stock falls to the reorder point and the other for purchasing as

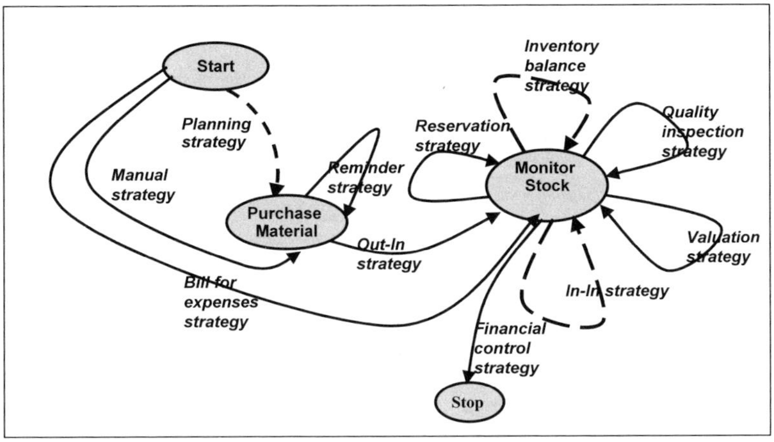

Figure 6. The material management map.

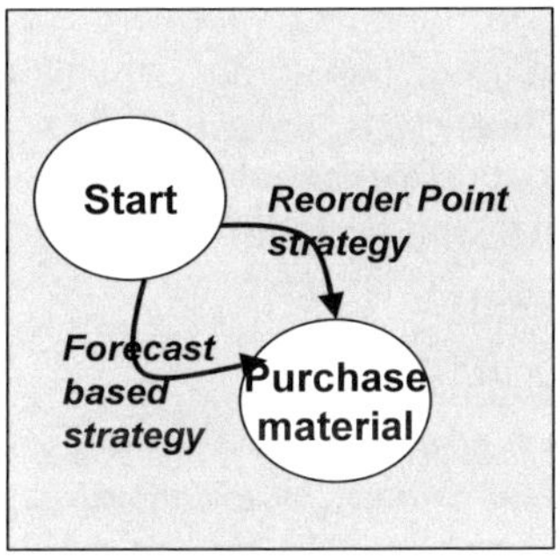

Figure 6a

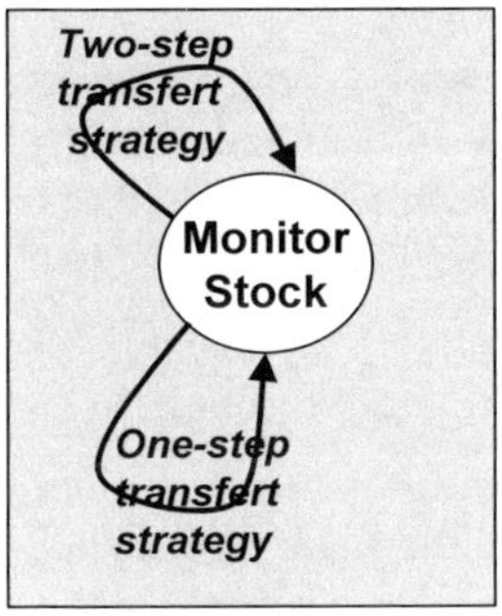

Figure 6b

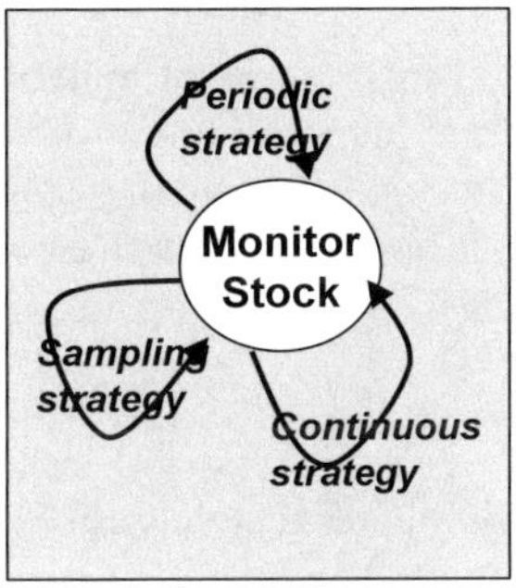

Figure 6c

per the planned material need. As discussed in Section 2, these two are captured in a bundle consisting of the *Reorder point strategy* and *Forecast based strategy* (see Fig. 6a). The second facet, *<Start, Purchase Material, Manual strategy>,* allows the buyer to manually enter a purchase requisition leading to the generation of the purchase order. The third facet is used to remind the vendor to deliver material when the delivery is not made in due time.

The bundled strategies correspond to the SAP functions of MM-MRP Forecast Based Planning and Reorder Point Planning respectively whereas the manual strategy is part of the MM-PUR component. It can be seen that the component structure of SAP does not directly reflect the alternative functionality of achieving the same goal.

3.2. The Multiple Facets of Monitor Stock

Monitor Stock is the second key intention of the material management map. The intention represents the management goal of ensuring proper posting of procured material and effectiveness of material logistics while maintaining financial propriety. This suggests that Monitor Stock has three classes of facets (a) the procurement/posting class, (b) the logistics class, and (c) the financial class. The facets in each class are as follows:

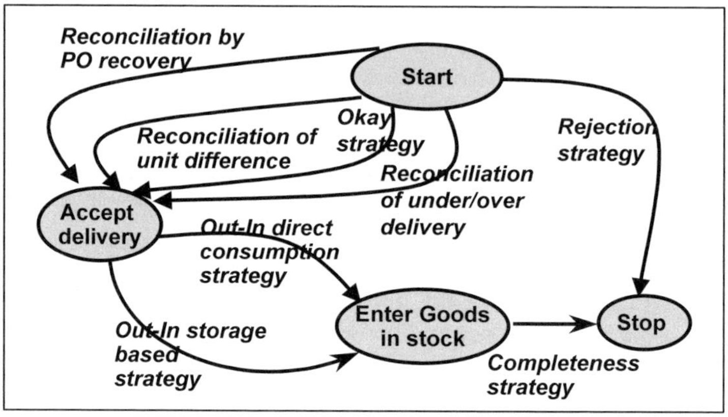

Figure 7. Refinement of <Purchase Material, Monitor Stock, Out-In strategy>.

a) Procurement/posting facets

Procurement of material can be done either against a purchase order or without a formal purchase order, directly from the market. In the latter case, material is immediately ready for posting whereas in the former case, posting is done after delivery is made against the purchase order. Thus, we have two facets of this class:

- Posting of material delivery against a purchase order
- Posting of material procured through direct purchase

These correspond in the map of Fig. 6 to the *Out-in strategy* and *Bill for expenses strategy*, respectively. In SAP, the facet represented by the section *<Purchase Material, Monitor Stock, Out-In strategy>* is covered by functions of the MM-IM and MM-WM components whereas *<Start, Monitor Stock, Bill for expenses strategy>* is a function of MM-IV, the Invoice Verification component.

The facet *<Purchase Material, Monitor Stock, Out-In strategy>* is, in fact, a compound one. It represents the variety of ways in which compliance of delivered material with the purchase order can be ensured and material posting made. Therefore, its refinement reveals a complex assembly of facets that can be represented through a map at a lower level. This refinement is shown in Fig. 7.

Since *<Purchase Material, Monitor Stock, Out-In strategy>* does not permit stock posting unless material delivery complies with the purchase order, its refinement contains an ordering of the two intentions, *Accept Delivery* and *Enter Goods in Stock*. The former has four facets, one for the case where delivery is strictly according to the purchase order and three facets that allow delivery to be accepted within specified tolerances from that in the purchase order. The four facets are as follows:

- The delivery complies with the purchase order
- Reconciliation against the purchase order has to be done
- Reconciliation between the differing units used by the supplier and the receiver has to be done
- Reconciliation of under/over delivery has to be done

These correspond in Fig. 7 to the four multi-threads identified by the strategies *Okay strategy, Reconciliation by PO recovery*, *Reconciliation of unit difference*, and *Reconciliation of under/over delivery*. The nature of the three *Reconciliation* facets is such that one or more can be simultaneously used. Therefore, these strategies do not form a bundle but are each represented as a thread.

Now consider the intention *Enter Goods in Stock*. This displays two facets for entering goods in stock (a) when delivery is made directly to the consumption location and (b) when delivered goods are stored in a warehouse. As shown in Fig. 7, these two ways of achieving *Enter Goods in Stock* correspond to the two strategies, *Out-In direct consumption* and *Out-In storage based strategy*.

The target intention, *Monitor Stock*, of the facet under refinement is achieved in the map of Fig. 7 when the intention *Stop* is achieved. Evidently, this happens when either the material delivered is rejected and no stock entry is made or when, after entering the accepted delivery in stock, all subsequent housekeeping is done to take into account the consequences of entering goods in stock. These two facets of *Stop* are represented in Fig. 7 by *Rejection strategy* and *Completeness strategy* respectively.

b) Material logistics facets

Facets in this class enter the picture only after initial posting of stock has been made by the class of procurement/posting facets of *Monitor Stock*. The interesting question now is about the movement of stock and how this movement is kept track of. That is, *Monitor Stock* has to be repeatedly achieved after each movement to/from warehouses, to consumption points or for quality inspection. This gives us the three facets:

- Control of material movement to/from warehouses
- On-time transfer of material to consumption points
- Quality control of the material transferred

These correspond in the map of Fig. 6 to the *In-In*, *Reservation*, and *Quality inspection strategies*. These strategies have *Monitor Stock* as both their initial as well as their target intentions. This represents the repeated achievement of *Monitor Stock*.

Of the three foregoing facets, the first, represented by the section <*Monitor Stock, Monitor Stock, In-In strategy*> needs further explanation. In fact, subsumed in this facet are two mutually exclusive facets of *Monitor Stock*. These correspond to the cases when the stock to be moved spends a long time in transit or when immediate transfer is possible. As before, the section <*Monitor Stock, Monitor Stock, In-In strategy*> is represented as a bundle of two sections in Fig. 6b having strategies *One-step transfer* and *Two-step transfer*. The former corresponds to immediate transfer and the latter to delayed transfer. In SAP, this bundled section is covered partly by MM-IM and MM-WM and has a relationship with Financial Accounting, Assets Management, and Controlling.

c) Financial propriety facets

The third class of facets of *Monitor Stock* deals with financial propriety. Not only must it be ensured that stock on hand is physically verified but also it should be financially valued. Thus we have two facets in this class

- Physical stock taking of the material
- Valuing the stock for balance sheets

These are represented in the map of Fig. 6 by the *Inventory balance* and *Valuation* strategies respectively. As for the material logistics class of facets, these are also concerned with the repeated achievement of *Monitor Stock*. Therefore, both the source and target intentions of these strategies is *Monitor Stock*.

The facet corresponding to the <*Monitor Stock, Monitor Stock, Inventory balance strategy*> section subsumes three different ways of physical stock taking: by periodic inventory verification, by continuous verification and by verifying a sample of the total inventory. Any of these three can be mutually exclusively deployed. Therefore, we represent it as a bundle of the three strategies, *periodic*, *continuous* and *sampling* strategies as shown in Fig. 6c. This bundle is handled by the MM-IM component in SAP.

The facet represented in Fig. 6 by the section <*Monitor Stock, Monitor Stock, Valuation strategy*> can itself be treated as a bundle of mutually exclusive facets represented by strategies such as LIFO and FIFO. In SAP, only LIFO valuation is available as a function in MM-IM.

3.3. Completing Satisfy Material Need Effectively

The complete fulfilment of *Satisfy Material Need Effectively* requires that the financial aspects of material procurement are properly handled. Thus completion, corresponding to the achievement of *Stop* of Fig. 6 is done by the Financial control strategy allowing the flow from Monitor Stock to Stop. In SAP, this takes the form of the Invoice Verification component, MM-IV.

When a multi-facetted product like the SAP MM is to be adopted, then the task of the adoption process is to select the facets of the MM map that are of relevance. This leads us to the issue of the process dimension considered in the next section.

4. Process Map

In this section we deal with the counterpart of multi-facetted products, namely, multi-facetted processes. As before, these will be represented as maps, but having process intentions and process strategies. Following on with the ERP multi-facetted product of the foregoing section, we consider the process of *aligning organisational requirements to an ERP product*. Thereafter we illustrate this process with the alignment of SAP MM to the requirements of an educational institute.

The process of alignment has been introduced in [15] as a means of mitigating the difficulty of ERP product customising reported for instance by the Partners Group in 1998, where one of the drawbacks found was the difficulty of alignment to specific requirements of the enterprise. This process proposes to move from *functional alignment* of the ERP installation to *requirements alignment* thereby causing the customisation process to focus on requirements rather than on functionality.

As shown in Fig. 8 alignment is essentially a matching process between ERP requirements and organisational requirements both expressed as maps. The former, the *ERP map* specifies the requirements that the ERP product supports (for example, the SAP materials management map of Section 3). The latter is a pair of *As-Is* and *To-Be maps.* The *As-Is* map represents requirements that are currently fulfilled whereas the *To-Be* map projects the new requirements that the organisation would like to satisfy by installing the ERP system. The result of the process is a set of requirements that customisation must meet. This set is also expressed as a map, the *Matched map.* Many of the intentions/strategies of the *Matched Map* are obtained from the *ERP map* and match the To-Be requirements. Others may not be available in the *ERP map* and will require in-house development. In such a case, the *Matched Map* helps in their identification.

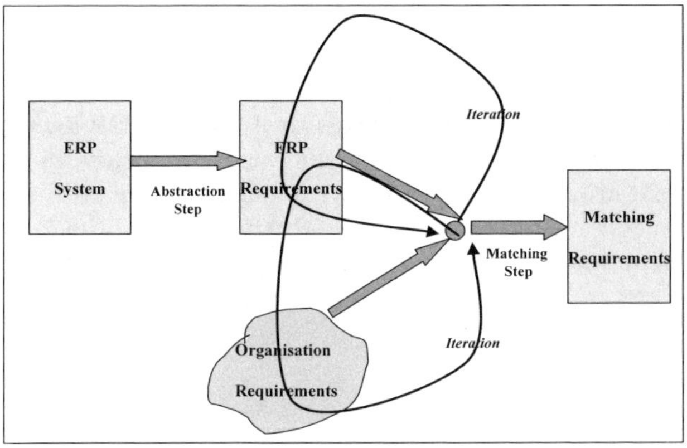

Figure 8. The alignment process.

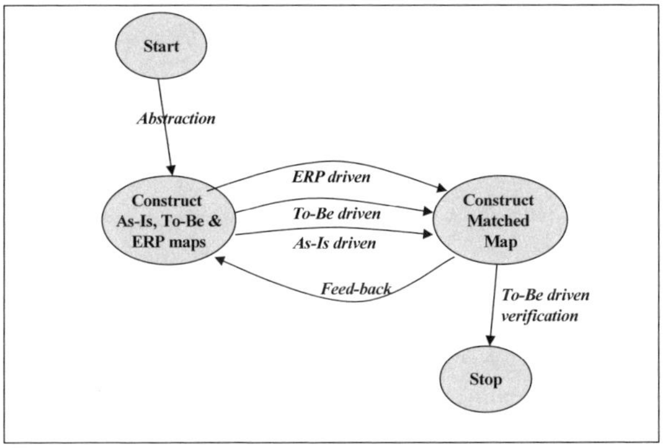

Figure 9. The process model.

Again, all the intentions and strategies of the *ERP map* may not be included in the *Matched Map*. This corresponds to the ERP functionality that is not matching the requirements in the *To-Be map*. Thus, the *Matched Map* is the input to the installation process.

The corresponding *process model* represented as a map is shown in Fig. 9. The root purpose of this map is *Elicit ERP Installation Requirements*. The multi-facetted nature of the process is shown by the sub-purposes embedded in the map, namely the two main intentions *Construct As-Is, To-Be, ERP maps* and *Construct Matched Map* and the various strategies to achieve them. The *Construct Matched Map* process intention is multi-facetted. There are three ways of achieving it by three different strategic drives, *ERP*, *To-Be* and *As-Is* drives. Each drive considers the intentions and strategies of its corresponding map from *Start* to *Stop* in order to decide if these (a) match the requirements exactly and so must be included in the *Matched map,* (b) need adaptation before their inclusion in the *Matched map*, or (c) are irrelevant.

These three strategies have the same initial and target intentions showing that the target intention can be achieved in a non-deterministic way. This reflects the possibility that different organisations may interleave these strategies in different combinations thereby following different processes to *Construct Matched Map*.

Construct As-Is, To-Be, ERP maps is also multi-facetted. It can be achieved in two ways, by the *Abstraction strategy* or the *Feedback strategy*. The latter has *Construct Matched Map* as its source intention and allows an incremental achievement of *Construct As-Is, To-Be, ERP maps*. This extends to *As-Is* and *ERP maps* the view of Anthony Finkelstein and colleagues [5] that starting with complete requirements specification (To-Be) is not always needed in software package requirements engineering. Finally, the *Stop* intention achieves completion of *Elicit ERP Installation Requirements* through the *To-Be driven verification strategy* that verifies the accuracy of the *Matched Map*.

4.1. Applying the Process Map

Now, with the SAP materials management map of Section 3 as our ERP map, we will outline the application of the process model to the Stores and Purchase Department of Netaji Subhas Institute of Technology. This department is the central procurement agency and warehouse of the Institute. The task is to produce the Matched Map that contains a subset of the facets of the SAP materials management map and additional ones, not found in this map.

Since the iteration between *Construct As-Is, To-Be, ERP maps* and *Construct Matched Map* is central to the process model, we will concentrate on illustrating its flow. Let us assume as given the *As-Is*, *To-Be* and SAP materials management map.

- Let us start by following the *As-Is drive* which looks at the *As-Is map* and determines that inventory checking is done periodically, once every year for the entire Institute. This leads to the inclusion of <Monitor Stock, Monitor Stock, Periodic Strategy> in the *Matched Map*.
- Iterating back, the *ERP drive* is now followed and it is seen that the SAP material management map while supporting periodic stock verification also provides a continuous inventory strategy (Fig. 6c). It was realised that the Institute, in fact, needs continuous inventory checking for consumable items. Before this realisation, the focus was completely on solving the periodic check problem. Now, however, attention shifted to the total problem of materials management in the Institute.

Result 1: The two foregoing bullets show that whereas the *As-IS drive* looks for inclusion in the *Matched Map* of *As-Is* requirements, the *ERP drive* may trigger the process of recognising new requirements, clarifying these and identifying new applicable parts of the SAP map. This leads to their inclusion in the *Matched Map*.

As mentioned above, a shift of focus occurred from problem solving to materials management in a holistic sense. As a consequence of this, the working of the entire Stores and Purchase Department was reviewed. Realising that the ERP drive provides useful guidance, this drive was used for the next iteration.

- The ERP drive showed that out of the strategies offered by the SAP materials map offers for purchasing material, the following were useful:
  - The manual strategy is almost always used for purchasing capital goods.
  - Bills for expenses remains necessary for purchases for student projects requiring consumable materials.
  - The Reorder point strategy is needed for purchasing other consumables like stationery.

Result 2: The Institute does not do any forecast based purchasing. However, all the other three strategies are used and these need to be included when customising SAP. The Matched Map was modified to include these.

- The To-Be drive was followed next. It showed the need for automatic purchase order generation because the Department recognized that manual order generation caused many delays which led to complete absence of stock at times. For materials used for teaching this was traumatic. This led naturally to the issue of lot sizing. The Department decided that lot sizes needed to be studied carefully.

Result 3: Iterations help in early identification of critical issues, like lot sizes, needing attention for SAP adoption.

Analysis continued for <*Purchase Material, Monitor Stock, Out-In strategy*> and its refined map was examined. All the *Reconciliation strategies* as well as the *Rejection strategy* offered are indeed useful. Since purchased material is always sent to its buyer from the warehouse after stock entry, the *Out-In direct consumption strategy* is unnecessary. Whereas the *Completeness strategy* envisages update of information in Financial Accounting, Controlling and Assets Management, only Assets management is needed. This is because material management is only by quantity.

Result 4: The construction of the Matched Map helps in identifying SAP cross-module linkages.

Having exhausted the refined map, we move to the main map again. Since there is no reservation of material, the *Reservation strategy* does not apply. Quality inspection is done for all capital goods before they are delivered to the buyer from the warehouse. However, consumer goods do not undergo any inspection. There is no systematic record of purchase of poor quality consumer goods.

Result 5: Procedural issues that organisations must consider before adopting SAP are identified, for example, the issue of quality inspection and record keeping for consumables.

From the *In-In strategy*, it was seen that only the *One-step transfer strategy* is relevant. The *Valuation strategy* is inapplicable because the Institute does not produce a balance sheet showing the value of inventory held. Finally, <*Monitor Stock, Stop, Financial strategy*> was taken up. Automatic invoice verification against purchase orders and goods receipts was found attractive.

The various features are added to the *Matched Map*. The walk-through the SAP map is complete and the *Construct Matched Map* intention is achieved. The process model now suggests a *To-be driven verification* activity to ensure that the *Matched Map* is in accordance with the *To-Be map*. Once this verification is done, the *Matched Map* acts as a specification of the customisation that will be carried out of the SAP MM module.

The foregoing is one possible interleaving of the three drives. However, it would have been possible to produce an equivalent/similar matched map with a different interleaving.

5. Conclusion

A map expression provides a synthetic view of the variability of an artefact in a relatively easy to understand way. Variations are revealed in two ways, by the gradual movement down the different levels of a map, and by the alternative strategies/paths available at a given map level. Product variations express the multi purpose behind systems. Their expression relates more closely to the organisational stakeholders as different from system developers. Yet, this expression acts as a specification of what the new system should achieve. Process variations are a means for developing the multi-facetted product by applying different process strategies and following different process paths.

We are now moving in two directions (a) defining a transformation of the map based specification into a system design and (b) developing an agent based implementation that allows the dynamic selection of the variations depending on the situation of the user of the software.

6. References

[1] Anton A., Potts C., "The use of goals to surface requirements for evolving systems", International Conference on Software Engineering (ICSE '98), Kyoto, Japan, pp. 157–166, 19–25, 1998.
[2] Bosch et al., "Variability issues in Software Product Lines", 4th International Workshop on Product Family Engineering (PEE-4), Bilbao, Spain, 2001.
[3] K.L. Chung, B.A. Nixon, E. Yu, J. Mylopoulos, "Non-Functional Requirements in Software Engineering", Kluwer Academic Publishers, 2000.
[4] Dardenne, A., Lamsweerde, A.v., and Fickas, S., "Goal-directed Requirements Acquisition", Science of Computer Programming, 20, Elsevier, pp. 3–50.
[5] A. Finkelstein., G. Spanoudakis, M. Ryan, Software package requirements and procurement, Proc. of the 8th International Workshop on Software Specification and Design, IEEE Computer Society Press, Washington, DC, pp. 141–145, 1996.
[6] Garg V.K. and Venkitakrishnan N.K., "Enterprise Ressource Planning Concepts and Practice", Prentice Hall of India, 1999.
[7] G.F. Hice, W.S. Turner, L.F. Cashwell, "System Development Methodology", North Holland, 1974.
[8] Hui B, Liakos L., Mylopoulos J., "Requirements Analysis for Customizable software: A Goal-Skills-Preferences Framework", 11th International Requirement Engineering Conference, 2003.
[9] M. Jackson, "Software Requirements & Specifications – A Lexicon of Practice, Principles and Prejudices", ACM Press, Addison-Wesley, 1995.
[10] Kaindl, H., "A design process based on a model combining scenarios with goals and functions", IEEE Trans. on Systems, Man and Cybernetic, Vol. 30 No. 5, September 2000, 537–551.
[11] Lamsweerde, A.v., 2001, "Goal-oriented requirements engineering: a guided tour". Invited mini-tutorial, Proc. RE'01 International Joint Conference on Requirements Engineering, Toronto, IEEE, August 2001, pp. 249–263.
[12] E. Munford, "Participative Systems Design: Structure and Method", Systems, Objectives, Solutions, Vol. 1, North-Holland, 1981, 5–19.
[13] Rolland, C., Souveyet, C., Ben Achour, C., "Guiding goal modelling using scenarios", IEEE Transactions on Software Engineering, Special Issue on Scenario Management, Vol. 24, No. 12, December 1998.
[14] Rolland, C., Prakash, N., Benjamen, A., "A Multi-Model View of Process Modelling", Requirements Engineering Journal, (1999) 4: 169–187
[15] C. Rolland, N. Prakash, "Matching ERP System Functionality to Customer Requirements", Int. Conference on Requirements Engineering, RE'01,Toronto, 2001.
[16] D.T. Ross, K.E. Schoman, "Structured analysis for requirements definition", IEEE Transactions on Software Engineering , Vol. 3, N° 1, 6–15, 1977.
[17] K.S. Rubin, A. Goldberg, "Object Behavior Analysis", Communications of the ACM Vol. 35, No. 9, September 1992.

[18] Svahnberg et al., “On the notion of variability in Software Product Lines”, Proceedings of the Working IEEE/IFIP Conference on Software architecture, 2001
[19] J. Van Gurp “Variability in Software Systems, the key to Software Reuse”, Licentiate Thesis, University of Groningen, Sweden, 2000.

New Trends in Software Methodologies, Tools and Techniques
H. Fujita and M. Mejri (Eds.)
IOS Press, 2005

Reengineering Software: A Case Study

Megan GRAHAM and Michael J. OUDSHOORN
Department of Computer Science, Montana State University, Bozeman MT, USA

Abstract. Optimally software design should be robust enough to handle any future additions or code changes, however it is not always possible to predict the direction a software project will go in. In research projects and in-house projects, where the user and creator are often the same, software design may be overlooked entirely. If software is complex, or has not been designed for its current modifications, it may merit reengineering. The future use and needs of the program must be evaluated. There are many metrics that are used to make this decision, but these metrics only act as a guide. Most of the decision to redesign a software system is subjective, and is often made as the development of the program becomes increasingly difficult. In this paper, the redesign of a complex piece of software is examined. The process of redesign is evaluated to determine if the work put into it was worth the benefits accrued by the new design.

Keywords. Software Reengineering, Software Economics

1. Introduction

If software is to remain useful over its lifespan with a minimal amount of maintenance energy, it must be well engineered. The process of software engineering calls for an overall design before a program is created. This design will affect the ability of the software to be reused, modified and altered for the rest of its life. When considering a design for a project it is often difficult to anticipate all of the uses the software will take on in the future. Even with the best intensions software can become difficult to maintain and unwieldy. This usually occurs as a consequence of unanticipated demands being placed on the software.

1.1. Maintenance of Legacy Software

Software with the characteristics described above falls into the category of legacy software. A legacy system is a system that is typically inherited by a programmer and remains valuable to the organization. Legacy systems are often created by developers who have since left the company and are no longer available for consultation. Often these systems were created using outdated development methods. Additionally, legacy programs [1] regularly have many patches and modifications added to them. They often have outdated or inconsistent documentation, and they are considered monolithic systems as shown in [2] and [3].

When an organization is faced with a legacy system maintenance becomes increasingly difficult. It is not until a perceived level of acceptable maintenance effort is exceeded that an organization considers reengineering the software system. This level of effort is ill defined and poorly understood.

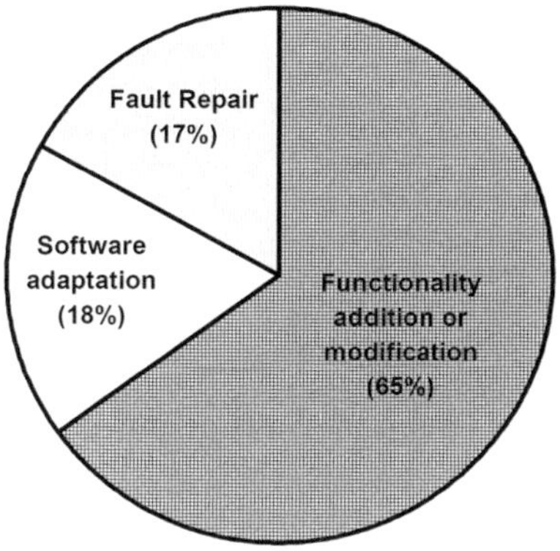

Figure 1. Maintenance effort distribution.

Software maintenance can be broken up into three categories. The first is what people usually think of when they consider maintenance in the general sense and it is the effort needed to repair faults in a software product. These may include coding errors, design errors, and requirement errors. This type of maintenance actually only accounts for about 17% of the total maintenance for most products [4]. The second type of maintenance is adapting software to a different operating environment, which accounts for around 18% of total maintenance [4] during the life of most products. Adapting software to a new environment occurs when some part of the systems operating environment changes such as the hardware platform or the operating system. Finally there is maintenance that is used to add or modify the system's functionality. This type of maintenance is responsible for the majority of the cost in most systems at 65% [3]. When deciding to reengineer a software system, it is a good idea to look at the type of maintenance that is usually performed on the system in question. If a system is continuously being modified then a significant amount of resources are probably going into it and it may need to be reengineered. Adding or modifying the systems functionality is often the most costly overall type of software maintenance. Figure 1 shows the distribution of types of maintenance effort [4].

The high cost of software maintenance is well known. Software maintenance becomes increasingly more expensive over time. As a piece of software gets older more maintenance is needed and each fix or update takes a longer time. This is due to the program becoming increasingly complex, outdated supporting systems, and less knowledge about the program. Research shows that from 50% to 80% of development time is spent on maintenance as quoted in [1,5], and [6]. This may account for upward of 90% of the total cost of the software [7]. Approximately 75% of software maintenance costs have been found to providing adaptive and perfective maintenance [8,9]. As a legacy system grows more difficult to maintain it becomes practical to consider options to reduce the cost of using this system. It has been said that reengineering software as an alternative to maintenance is a "time consuming detour from the clear path to the next maintenance release." [10]. Recently, however, the software community has been focusing more on reengineering as a cost effective approach to dealing with legacy software. It has become increasingly evident that the cost of failing to reengineer a software system in a timely manner can be very large, and the steps involved in reengineering software have been well defined with tools available to assist in the process.

Legacy systems that are being used regularly and are an integral part of an organization are prime candidates for reengineering. If a legacy system is in constant use it probably has a high maintenance cost associated with it due to additions and changes in the software. A piece of software that is used constantly and is accruing high maintenance costs may need to be reengineered. On the other hand if a system is near the end of its life and is relatively static there is a good chance that some maintenance will be more cost effective than reengineering. This is due to the fact that there is probably very little effort that needs to be put into maintaining the program. The key is knowing where the software is within its lifecycle.

The documentation of a system affects the amount of effort that goes into maintenance. It is difficult to maintain a poorly documented system. The time it takes for a new developer to become familiar with a system is very important in code maintenance. This is related to the amount and quality of documentation as well as the overall organization and complexity of the product. High employee turnover when dealing with a legacy system can greatly increase maintenance costs.

Legacy software is an issue that many organizations need to address. It is becoming apparent that reengineering the software is often the best course to take [1]. However, the case must be made to management that reengineering the code is in the best interest of the organization.

This paper presents an actual reengineering effort and the measurements used that support the decision. By collecting data on an actual reengineered project it is possible to become informed as to what actually works and what questions need to be asked (and answered) about a particular program before embarking upon a redesign task. This paper presents an analysis of the process that was used in the system that was reengineered and the lessons that were learned in the process.

1.2. The Option of Reengineering

The options for expensive legacy software include redevelopment, a program of continuous code maintenance, and reengineering the legacy software. When a system becomes very difficult to maintain and understand it can be tempting to a group to just retire the old system and redevelop it from scratch. Although this is not always a bad idea, it is likely that reengineering all or part of the system will sufficiently meet the demands put on the system for less overall cost than completely redeveloping it afresh. Estimates of newly developed code costs have been quoted at \$6–26 per line of code [4], and to reuse software has been estimated to save 80% of the original development effort [4]. If a software project is completely redeveloped it is costly in that a complex system may contain code created by the original developers that is unclear, and this takes time to understand and implement.

After each reengineering effort the maintenance costs drop and slowly increase again until the next reengineering effort as shown in Fig. 2. If the structure of a program has caused it to become sufficiently difficult to understand and maintain, it may be time to reengineer the system. A well-developed and better-engineered piece of software will ideally show a slower rate of cost increase for maintenance. This way a product can be fairly efficient for a longer amount of time before another reengineering effort is necessary. By choosing not to reengineer the code and instead implementing a good maintenance plan the best case for the maintenance is only a 15% savings. The Department of Defence has shown savings of 150% to 200% for reengineering software systems [1].

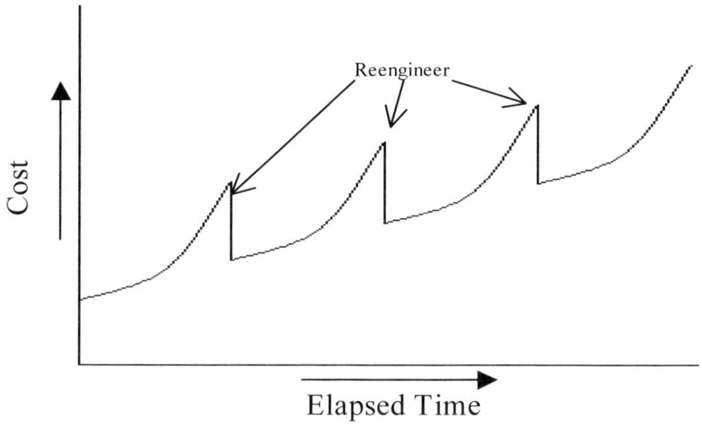

Figure 2. Cost of maintenance over time with three re-engineering efforts.

One should consider the possibility of simply maintaining a system for the remainder of its life especially in cases were the software may not be used for much longer. A complete redevelopment of a system may be useful in a few cases such as when the requirements change drastically. However, common sense dictates in many circumstances, redevelopment would be a waste of all the previous effort put in to a system. Therefore, in systems where a case can be made that an unacceptable level of maintenance is being performed, reengineering the software becomes an acceptable alternative. The remainder of this paper will contain a case study of a significant piece of software that was reengineered.

1.3. Introduction to the Case Study

The design process is often overlooked entirely in research projects and in-house projects. This paper describes the reengineering of a particular software system, which was not designed with any future reuse in mind. The software described in this paper falls into the category of a research project. It is used in academic research for a biology laboratory. Like much of the software used in the academic research community this system was originally created for a specific purpose. When first created it was thought that the software would not become a very complex program. As time went by there were new requirements put on this software. A simple program expanded into ever more complex code, which is now difficult to follow. Ad-hoc design and program growth, such as what occurred in this system, can be very costly in terms of the following items:

- Time it takes to familiarize new employees with a poorly documented and unorganized system.
- Time it takes to add new modules to a system with a poor design and redundant code.
- Time it takes to test code in a system that is difficult to break up into easily testable modules.
- Time it takes to update the system when the old modules are sufficiently difficult to follow.

- Time to it takes fix errors in a system where tracking problems becomes very complex.

The program in this paper is referred to as the Presenter program as it is used to present stimulus to animals. The Presenter program is used to run experiments for a visual neuroscience laboratory. Experiments are conducted on mammals while they are viewing a visual stimulus on a computer monitor. These experiments are performed to contribute to the explanation of how the brain processes visual information. Knowledge of how the brain takes in and acts on visual information is used to give insight into how other parts of our brains are processing and responding to information.

Experiments on the visual system are designed to test ideas about what happens to the information contained in a precise visual stimulus after an animal has viewed it. Experimental designs in a research laboratory are continuously changing and the visual stimuli used in an experiment are being changed along with the design. The Presenter program allows the user to take many types of visual stimuli and enter a variety of parameters to control how the stimulus is presented. The number and types of stimuli are constantly increasing or being altered as new designs are created. The Presenter program has been continuously updated and is in need of modularization.

The Presenter program described above fits the previous description of a legacy system. The maintenance distribution is disproportionately skewed toward adding of functionality. As Fig. 1 indicates, adding and altering functionality is typically a very large portion of the maintenance in a system. In the Presenter program, it can be argued that the nature of experiments causes the addition of functionality to become an even more intricate part of this program.

Prior to completing this project, adding a new stimulus to the Presenter program had become a daunting task. Every time the program requirements changed new code was added to one large module. Errors were introduced and functionality was incorrectly altered. The purpose of this project is to take the Presenter program and pull it apart eliminating duplicate code and creating an object-oriented design. The scientists conducting the experiments need to be able to add new functionality easily without changing the existing Presenter program.

2. Introduction to Experimental System and Presenter

The previous section establishes Presenter as a legacy software artifact in need of reengineering. One of the first steps to reengineering any piece of legacy software is to understand the requirements of the software [11,12]. Neurophysiology is the study of the brain's bioelectric properties [13]. The Presenter program is used by neuroscientists to study the basis of behavior [14] through observations made in the nervous system.

The study of vision is usually done in mammals. This is due to the fact that the visual system of animals, other than mammals, can differ significantly from our own. This project is related to the study of the visual system in rhesus monkeys and cats. Monkeys, like humans have a larger portion of their brain devoted to collecting and processing visual input than any other sensory function. This portion of the brain is known as the primary visual cortex (PVC). Besides being closely related to humans, monkeys are also easily trained to behavioral tasks, which can increase the amount of knowledge we gain from an experiment.

Cats, like monkeys and humans, have a very large primary visual cortex The PVC in cats is possibly better understood than any other cortical area of any other species.

This allows increasingly more in-depth experiments to be performed by using knowledge we have already gained [14].

In visual physiology a concept called a receptive field is used to describe the way the brain processes visual stimuli. A visual receptive field is the "region of the retina which must be illuminated in order to obtain a response in any given fiber" [15]. A fiber refers to the cells carrying information from the retina, however any cell all the way up into the cortex involved in the processing of visual input in the brain can have a receptive field. This report discusses receptive fields of cells in the cortex. The properties of a receptive field include the orientation of a stimulus, light being on or off, color, and direction of motion [14]. These are all attributes of a receptive field in a cell and visual neurons respond preferentially to some or all of these attributes in different combinations. Studies show that most cells in the primary visual cortex respond best to elongated stimuli shown in a specific orientation. These cells do not respond at all to the orthogonal orientation of these bars [13].

There are two main categories of experiment for which the Presenter program is designed. These are experiments in which the animal is behaving and experiments in which the animal is not behaving. In order to use the data collected during a stimulus, it is important that the animal keep its gaze in one spot. This goal is obtained in cats easily as they are paralyzed at the time of the experiments. Such immobilized animals are referred to as non-behaving.

In non-terminal experiments done on monkeys and some cats, a magnetic coil is surgically implanted around the animal's eye and the animal's head is held in place in a magnetic chamber. The coil sends the coordinates of the position on the screen that the animal is viewing to a control computer. This way the animal can be trained to look at specific areas on a screen. The area the animal is trained to look at is usually just a location called the fixation spot. When the animal accomplishes a desired behavior, it is given a juice reward. If an animal shifts its gaze the coils show that the eyes have moved out of the fixation area and this is recorded as an incomplete trial and there is a penalty duration in which no stimulus is shown and there can be no reward.

Once an animal is either trained or anesthetized an experiment can be performed. An array of extra cellular electrodes is placed in the PVC of the animal. The Presenter software is used as a tool to search for cells that respond favorably to visual stimuli. Then the receptive fields of the cells in this area are defined by using Presenter to show a range of stimuli to the animal. All stimuli are shown using 8 bit grayscale to simplify the visual signal being processed. The physiologist estimates the receptive field properties such as orientation and on or off contrast. When a receptive field with certain properties seems to be giving an optimal performance for a cell, it is saved as a particular number and the experimenter can either create more receptive fields or move on with the experiment.

The two types of experiments hold many stimulus parameters in common, however there are extra features that must be contained in the behaving experiments, which the non-behaving experiments do not need to know about.

3. Presenter Program

The Presenter software program is a precise tool used to present experiments and enable a user to take precise measurements. There are many functions in the Presenter program that control what is being shown to an animal and how it is being shown. To understand the specific problems with the current Presenter design one must first understand the details of how the program is functioning. Reengineering the program must not diminish the necessary functionality of Presenter. Understanding the system to be reengineered is an important first step in the process.

3.1. Hardware Setup for Presenter-Control-DataStreamer

The entire system that is used to conduct experiments and record data is the Presenter-Control-DataStreamer Experimental System. Specifically the Presenter part of the system is discussed in this paper. The system is used for presentation and data collection in a visual neurophysiology laboratory.

The hardware for these experiments is fairly specific and extensive. An overview of the Presenter-Control-DataStreamer system is shown in Fig. 3 below. The non-behaving system is similar to the behaving, only not as complex, as it does not require a control computer. The non-behaving system is known as the Presenter-DataStreamer system.

There are three computers involved in the experiment. There is the Presenter computer, which presents a stimulus to a screen. Presenter is discussed in detail in this paper. The stimulus presentation is controlled by the control computer, which acts as the master taking cues from a behaving animal. The control directs the Presenter program and also controls the DataStreamer computer, which collects data from the experiment.

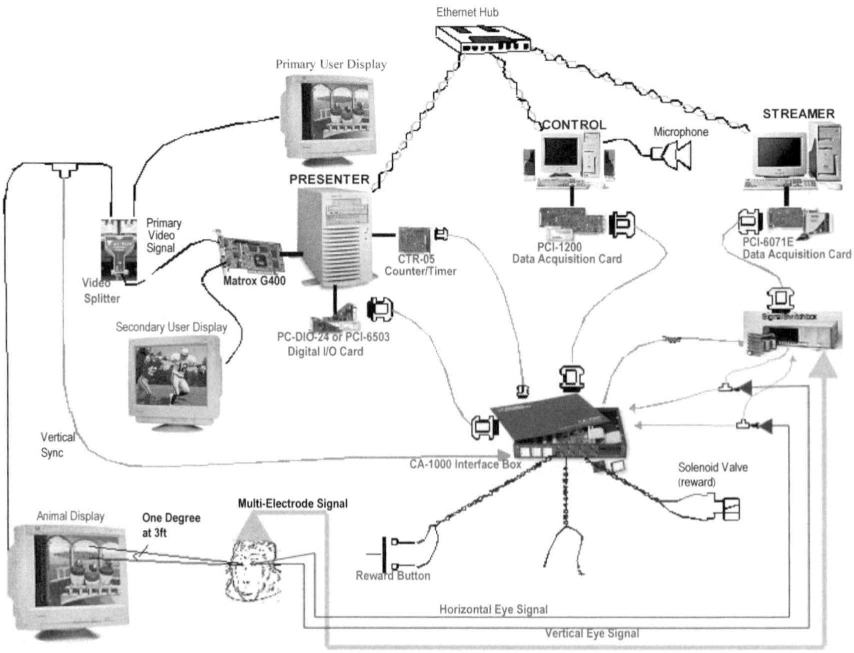

Figure 3. Hardware and experimental set-up for a behaving subject.

3.2. Overview of Presenter

There were several issues to be dealt with while working on the old Presenter. First the software used for development is very specific and not easily updated. The Presenter program is set up and used on three experimental rigs in the lab. Two of the rigs are used for behaving paradigms and have a control computer and one of the rigs is used with non-behaving animals and does not have a control computer. The developer must also deal with updating the hardware and testing the new rigs. Finally, there are several rigs used for experimentation. With different hardware, software, and operating systems on each machine, the versions of the Presenter program being used and developed have diverged from one another.

In the old version of Presenter all the reverse correlation (Sparse Noise, M-Sequence, or Movie) is contained in one long module. The reverse correlation module is unorganized with long functions. The original code is made up of two units called ReverseCorrelation and ReverseCorrelationBG. ReverseCorrelationBG is a smaller module that contains the functionality for mouse events and key events in the reverse correlation module. The large ReverseCorrelation unit contains all the information for the graphical user interface, all the initialization of the stimulus, the idle loop, the code for running and measuring the accuracy of the stimulus and the code used for housekeeping, closing and saving information. Seven of the functions have become very large, measuring from 300 lines of code to over 700 lines of code. Much of the code in the reverse correlation module handles different cases depending on which stimulus is being played. The cases are consistently used over and over in different parts of the ReverseCorrelation module. This indicates one obvious area that can be improved. Each of these cases can be broken off into there own classes that call common functions.

The option of reengineering this program became a possibility when some new functionality was to be added to the Presenter program and it quickly became obvious that continuing to add on to the reverse correlation module would introduce errors into the code that was already being used. This addition would take a very long time with the poor documentation and large amount of code that would need to be changed or written from scratch. The Presenter code was written in a normal lab environment in which different people wrote it and added on to it and it would continue to be utilized in this way. An object oriented design that can keep the code as error free as possible and allow users to add a module without understanding all the code written thus far was necessary. It was decided that the reverse correlation module should be reengineered rather that continue adding to the existing code.

4. Software Reengineering Process

When dealing with legacy software, the first step is to decide to reengineer it or keep the software in its current state. Many times it seems easier to continue to simply maintain rather than investigate whether or not reengineering is appropriate. It needs to be decided if the redesign will be worth the cost or if it is better to continue maintaining the program in its current state. There are several important items that need to be assessed before embarking on a redesign project. The decision making process and some of the general points that need to be addressed in this decision are discussed.

4.1. Criteria for Reengineering

The first step for any group considering reengineering is to examine the system and its current uses to determine if the system being evaluated is a good candidate for reengineering. There are many factors that need to be examined to determine if a system fits the criteria of one that is in need of reengineering.

The decision to reengineer the Presenter program that is discussed in this paper is based on several criteria. The system is an integral part of an academic research laboratory. This program was first created to present an experimental stimulus to an animal in a neuroscience laboratory. Due to the precision needed in the experiments, the program needed to be very precise and reliable. However, an employee with no design experience wrote the original module. After the addition of the first module it became apparent that the reusability was deficient, which led to learning more about object-oriented design. As more functionality was added the new modules implemented some design and used an object-oriented approach. The modules that were being added were also constantly being used and there was high pressure to have a module ready to run experiments with. For these reasons, the program was not reorganized for several years. Although it is only about six years old there are many factors that would make it a legacy system.

The major problem is a lack of object-oriented development in the original program. When the system was first created little thought was given to the future additions that would be made. The system was first developed with almost no use of modern development and object-oriented programming practices. The use of this system requires that program modules be added often and by several different users with varying levels of experience.

The lab has a rapid employee turnover. Many people need to become familiar with the system and this familiarization process was rapidly becoming unacceptable. New modules were needed and the amount of time it would take to add these to the code had grown exponentially. There was also a problem of an increase of errors being introduced in the program due to the high complexity, and difficulty locating the problems in the complex code.

4.2. Steps of Reengineering

Based on the factors discussed in the previous section a system may be considered a good candidate for reengineering. However the effort to reengineer a product comes with many costs of its own. It must be determined if the costs of maintaining a product are going to outweigh the costs of reengineering it. If the cost of maintaining does not seem to be as high as the cost of reengineering then it is best to find a good maintenance program and leave a reengineering for another time.

To determine the cost of reengineering we must look at the various steps in a reengineering process [3]. The steps for reengineering a piece of legacy software are as follows:

- Module capture,
- Problem detection,
- Problem analysis,
- Reorganization, and
- Change propagation.

The first step, module capture, involves documenting and understanding the design of the legacy system. During this step it is important to note problems and duplications with the current system. The cost of this first step should be fairly simple to estimate, as the organization should already have an idea of how long it takes to become familiar with a system. There are also many reverse engineering tools, which can take software and create a diagram of its design. Depending on the time it takes to find and become familiar with a product versus the size of the system to be reengineered, this can help with the cost of reengineering a product by varying amounts.

The next two steps are problem detection and problem analysis. Problem detection is identifying what parts of the current design lack flexibility or are not up to current software design practices. Problem analysis aims to select a design to fix the problems that were identified in the previous step. These steps are very important to the success of the reengineering project and the amount of decrease in maintenance cost is dependent on a good design, which supports future maintenance. Using employees that are already familiar with the system and may have ideas about what would make it more useable can decrease the work that needs to be done in these two steps.

Once the new design is chosen, reorganization must happen. The developers must ensure that the changes that are made are incorporated with the least amount of upheaval in the rest of the organization. A decision can be made on the optimal transformation of the legacy system. There are factors to consider here such as the possibility that the whole system may not need to be transformed at once and it may be beneficial to start with certain modules making the transformation of other modules easier.

Finally, change propagation involves testing once the whole system has been transformed. There also must be a plan to ensure the transition between the old version and the new reengineered version goes smoothly.

There are many tools that can help with the reengineering process [16]. The use of tools to help with different parts of the reengineering process organizations can cut down on their costs.

5. Implementation of New Design

The first part of the horseshoe model involves examining the legacy code to come up with an architecture that accurately describes the code. In doing so, it became apparent that none of the GUI windows show any code reuse or relationships to one another. There are a couple of structures used such as SparseNoiseData and SequenceType, however these are not used in a modern object oriented manner.

5.1. Architecture Recovery/Conformance

In the Presenter system a fairly significant cost was saved in the beginning of the reengineering process. The complexity and need for reengineering became apparent to the group using the software before all the original developers had left. Although unable to take a leading role in the reengineering of this system, the original developer was available for consultation. The lack of documentation and complexity of the program could have been much more costly if the foresight to reengineer had not taken place until after this employee left. Many of the problems with the code were well known as it is in constant use, with new additions being made regularly.

It was decided that the reengineering effort would focus on the oldest part of the program, which is called Reverse Correlation. This is the largest module in the old code. The rest of Presenter uses object-oriented practices and seemed to need substantially less maintenance. This large module is used and depended on more than any other part of the code. Reverse Correlation was created first because it was needed and it continued to be used and added to at a rapid pace. It was decided that the reengineer would be best broken up and the worst module needed to be attacked first. Choosing to only reengineer one module of the program carries a cost of its own. It involves pulling this large module out, reengineering it, and interfacing it properly with the system again. In the case of this system the module being reengineered is fairly independent and the other parts of the system are modularized enough to make this process fairly trivial. The remainder of the discussion focuses on the Reverse Correlation module being reengineered using the horseshoe model.

5.1.1. Problems with Original Design

Once an overall decision to reengineer this module was made, the specific changes that would need to take place had to be decided. This step of the reengineering process involves examining the old code for problems and duplications. First, the original source code of Presenter was examined. It was apparent with this code that much of it was written in C and did not use object-oriented techniques. There were other parts that were written using the functionality of C++, so it was inconsistent and difficult to follow. On a functional level Presenter has very long repetitive functions that could be further broken down into smaller parts. There is also a very large number of case statements in the Reverse Correlation module where each case handles one of the functionalities in the Reverse Correlation Module. The large number of logical branches that occurs can be measured by using cyclomatic complexity.

The original Presenter program makes use of global variables heavily. There are structures in place, which are usually used as global variables. This could easily lead to confusion, as these variables are available throughout whenever this file has been included in other modules of the program. These structures are only used within the module. All these extra global variables need to be dealt with.

The Presenter program consisted of an architecture, which was not designed for reuse. The Reverse Correlation module does not make use of the functionality of other classes. In addition all the functionality is placed in one module, which contains all of the GUI calls along with all of the run time functionality for each of the functional modules. There are several functions, which contain switch statements. These break off into movie, m-sequence, and sparse noise. Sparse noise is further broken into the bar, spot, square, gabor, and grating stimuli. Much of the functionality in these switch statements is repeated for each switch in redundant code. There is also a lack of any reuse in the GUI files. Several of the modules have menus that are common and others would benefit from these same menus, but due to the difficulty of implementing these menu items they have not been added throughout.

5.2. Design Considerations

The major issues with the Presenter program can be separated into two main groups. The first is redundancy. The redundancy in the Presenter program can be removed largely by creating a better design. The second major issue with Presenter is its lack of reusability and this ties in directly with the redundancy. A design without redundancy automatically should be more reusable than redundant code. The presence of a large amount of redundancy suggests that the parts of the program, which are used most often, are not accessible to be reused easily.

5.2.1. Model-View-Controller Implementation in Presenter

When the Presenter program was being redesigned no one working on the project had a strong background in software design and therefore there was a lack of familiarity with specific design patterns. However, some research did turn up information on the Model-View-Controller paradigm. This paradigm was recognized to be applicable to the current program reengineer. Model-View-Controller, or MVC, is considered a useful pattern for making object oriented code with user interfaces quicker to develop and more reusable.

In MVC, the model is the part of the program that represents what lies beneath the surface and is not seen by the user. This is the data and methods, which are used but not displayed to the user. The view is the part that the user sees, and the controller allows the model and the view to remain completely separate from one another. The controller makes sure that any necessary information from the view gets to the model part of the program.

In the Presenter program, the MVC paradigm suggests pulling Reverse Correlation apart so that there is the GUI with its data and methods consisting of the view. The rest of the module controlling the program once all of the user input is complete should be separated into the model part of the program. Using the MVC paradigm the controller would send all necessary information to the model functions along with controlling when they are called.

5.3. Overall Design of Presenter Program

The main goal of this reengineering project is to reduce the cost of Presenter code maintenance. This can be accomplished by improvements on several fronts. First, redundancy can be removed from the original Presenter code. Second, implementing a design that encourages reuse of the code in a way that makes it as simple as possible for future programmers to implement changes. Finally, improvements can be made to the program to account for unforeseen, but (something that is definitely going to happen) changes to the supporting software.

5.3.1. Modularization and Inheritance

The first step in considering a design for Presenter was to find a logical way to break the program into functional parts. The GUI and the methods used for running the program needed to be separated to allow the GUI to be more easily ported. All of the modules containing methods used to interact with the user are placed in classes, which start with the letter 'T'. All of the GUI windows have common elements that are contained within the classes TSimpleBaseGUI and TBaseGUI. To separate the GUI view methods from the model methods, a controller is needed. In the new Presenter design the controller is BaseScreen. All of the information the GUI's is packed up into a structure, which will be sent to the necessary model class by the controller once a runtime method has been requested by the user.

6. Evaluation of New Design and Conclusions

The decision to reengineer the Presenter program was fairly subjective in nature, as are many reengineering decisions for smaller in house projects. The reengineering effort had a certain cost associated with it. This section provides a cost analysis of the reengineering effort using COCOMO II [17] as a tool to measure maintenance cost. By examining the general problems with the original Presenter design and comparing them to another piece of software, which is being considered for reengineering, one may get an idea of the worth of reengineering that software.

6.1. Costs of Reengineering Presenter

During the reengineering effort there was consultation available from one of the original developers, which is not always the case. This was a help in the reengineering process, however the level of experience for the main developer in software design and engineering was very low and the learning curve for anything which was implemented was steep. Even with consultation available the process of understanding the system still took approximately 25% of the total time spent on the project reengineer.

Once the program was well understood a design was developed that would enable future modules to be added to the code with the least amount of effort. Due to the application and dependence on libraries it was decided that the language should remain C++, however current object oriented programming practices were properly applied. The new design increased code reuse and transparency. The major objectives in the redesign include the ability to add new modules seamlessly and the need to decrease the time it takes to become familiar with the program. The redesign also makes testing easier by modularizing the code to allow separation of modules during the testing process.

6.2. Cost Benefit Analysis

In the case study presented here the decision to reengineer the code was based on a growing feeling that the cost of maintaining this system was more than it should be. Knowledge of the original system was quickly disappearing as personnel changed, and it had become difficult to understand and maintain even for those who designed it. There were many areas such as the lack of a good object oriented design that could obviously help improve the maintenance. The amount of improvement in maintenance cost was not known until the project was complete.

There are several maintenance models that can give cost estimates for maintenance on a particular program. The Boehm model is one such model [6]. It is implemented in an updated form in by using COCOMO II. By using the same maintenance model that was used to determine the maintenance cost on a system one could also create a rough estimate of cost savings after a reengineering effort to determine if reengineering justifies the effort.

6.2.1. Lines of Code and Total Man Hours

The module being reengineered was mostly contained in one large class of approximately 4,500 logical lines of code. Many areas of duplicate code were located and repaired. Using object oriented programming tools, such as aggregation, composition,

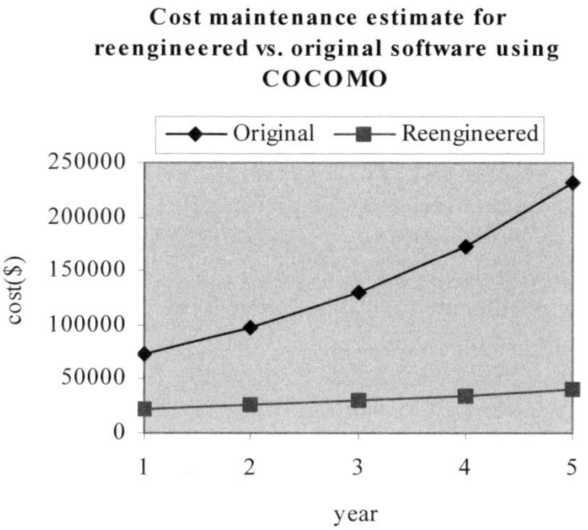

Figure 4. Graph showing cost maintenance estimate for reengineering Presenter Created Using COCOMO II.

and inheritance, while keeping the model-view-controller paradigm in mind the class was broken into 27 different classes. Several new data structures were also created.

Once the reengineering was complete, the new system could be analysed. The new version of Presenter has the addition of a large amount of functionality that was added during the reengineering process. This makes a simple count of total lines of code meaningless as a metric, however by removing all but the original functionality it was found that the new version of Presenter contained approximately the same number of lines of code at about 4,800 lines. The total cost in terms of man weeks for the reengineering of Presenter was 32 man weeks. The number of lines of code in the module before and after the reengineering were almost identical.

In order to create a definitive measurement for the amount of time it takes to create a new module in the old and the new code we would have to add a module to both the old and new code. Due to the size and complexity of the old code it would take a very long time to complete this task. Instead of actually bringing in a developer and creating a new module in the old and new version a lower estimate can be taken on the time it would take to add a new module to the old code. This estimate will be done using MatchToSample, which was added after the implementation of the new design.

Without adding the same module to the old system a lower bound for the number of lines of code that would need to be added was determined. By counting all the reused code that would not have been reused in the original system it was found that there was a savings of well over twice the amount of code needing to be written in the old module. This count is a fairly precise estimate as the new presenter version is modularized sufficiently so that any new functionality was not contained in this count, and the basic functionality which is reused the most was reused the most has not been altered. There are 689 lines in MatchToSample.cpp and in order to get the same functionality as is present in the new code we would need to add an additional 292 lines to the original Presenter code. This is 42% more code, which would be added to just make this run time code module work in the old version. To have the GUI in the same condition as the MatchToSampleGUI, which took 224 lines. The added functionality would take at least 286 more lines, that is 128% more code. For the whole working module, the total is 913 lines added and 578 lines saved this is a savings of 63% less code that needed to be written in the new module.

The amount of time to become familiar with the original code was fairly well known at around 4 weeks. With the new version it is estimated to take approximately 1 week to familiarize a programmer. To arrive at this number three developers were given both versions of the code and asked to estimate the time it would take to become familiar with each. The estimated time to become familiar was normalized to the known time it takes to become familiar with the old model.

The data collected on the module added was used to conduct an analysis on the program. Figure 4 shows the cost comparison of the two versions in graph format. The figure shows a dramatic difference in cost even in the first year of maintenance. The cost of maintenance rises much faster in the original version than in the reengineered version. The difference in cost maintenance between the two versions shows a 78% savings over the next 5 years.

References

[1] R. Seacord, D. Plakosh and G. Lewis, Modernizing Legacy Systems: Software Technologies, Engineering Processes, and Business Practices, Addison-Wesley, 2003.
[2] D.L. Parnas. Software Aging, Proceedings of International Conference on Software Engineering, 1994.
[3] E. Casais. Re-engineering Object-oriented Legacy Systems, Journal of Object-Oriented Programming, 10(8), 1998, pp. 45–52.
[4] J.S. Poalin, An Agenda for Software Reuse Economics, International Conference on Software Reuse, 15 April 2002.
[5] M.A. Waheed, A Practical Approach to Re-engineering Software, Proceedings of the 1992 conference of the Centre for Advanced Studies on Collaborative research, Volume 1, pp. 295–298, 1992, IBM Press.
[6] B.W. Boehm, Software Engineering Economics, Englewood Cliffs, NJ, Prentice-Hall, 1981.
[7] L. Erlikh, Leveraging Legacy System Dollars for E-business, IEEE IT Pro, May/June 2000, pp. 17–23.
[8] J. Martin, Software Maintenance: The Problem and Its Solution, Prentice Hall 1983.
[9] H. van Vliet, Software Engineering: Principles and Practices, Wiley, 2000.
[10] S. Rugaber, L.M. Wills, Creating a Research Infrastructure for Reengineering, 3rd Working Conference on Reverse Engineering, Monterey, CA, 1996, pp. 98–103.
[11] W. Ulrich, Legacy Systems: Transformation Strategies, Prentice Hall, 2002.
[12] S. Valenti, Successful Software Reengineering, IRM Press, 2002.
[13] D.H. Hubel, and T.N. Wiesel, Receptive fields, binocular interaction and the functional architecture on the cat's visual cortex, J. Physiol. 1962, 160, pp. 106–154.
[14] L. Squire, F.E. Bloom, S.K. McConnell, J.L. Roberts N.C. Spitzer, M.J. Zigmond, Fundamental Neuroscience Second Edition, Academic Press, 2003.
[15] F. Ratliff, Studies on Excitation and Inhibition in the Retina. A Collection of Papers from the Laboratories of H. Keffer Hartline, Rockefeller University Press, New York, 1974.
[16] S. Ducasse, Reengineering Object-Oriented Applications, Technical Report, Université Pierre et Marie Curie (Paris 6), TR University of Berne, Institute of Computer Science and Applied Mathematics September 2001, iam-03-008.
[17] E. Horrowidz, USC COCOMO II, Reference Manual, University of Southern California, 1999.
[18] Gartner Group, Forcasting The Worldwide IT Services Industry: 1999, Published on November 2, 1998.
[19] M. Olsem, Reengineering Technology Report, Software Technology Support Center, Hill Airforce Base, 1995.
[20] L.O. Ejiogu, Software Engineering with Formal Metrics, QED Technical Publishing Group, Wellesley, MA, 1991.

New Trends in Software Methodologies, Tools and Techniques
H. Fujita and M. Mejri (Eds.)
IOS Press, 2005

Advances in AOP with AspectC++[1]

Olaf SPINCZYK [a,2], Daniel LOHMANN [a] and Matthias URBAN [b]
[a] *Friedrich-Alexander University Erlangen-Nuremberg*
[b] *pure::systems GmbH, Magdeburg, Germany*

Abstract. Often declared dead or at least dying, C/C++ is still the lingua franca of many application domains. Aspect-Oriented Programming (AOP) is a programming paradigm that supports the modular implementation of crosscutting concerns. Thereby, AOP improves the maintainability, reusability, and configurability of software in general. Although already popular in the Java domain, AOP is still not commonly used in conjunction with C/C++. For a broad adoption of AOP by the software industry, it is crucial to provide solid language and tool support. However, research and tool development for C++ is known to be an extremely hard and tedious task, as the language is overwhelmed with interacting features and hard to analyze. Getting AOP into the C++ domain is not just technical challenge. It is also the question of integrating AOP concepts with the philosophy of the C++ language, which is very different from Java. This paper describes the design and development of the AspectC++ language and weaver, which brings fully-fledged AOP support into the C++ domain.

Keywords. AOP, C++, AspectC++, Programming Languages

1. Motivation

The C/C++ programming language[1] is frequently declared dead or at least dying. Actually, it is still the *lingua franca* in the real world of software industry. There are several reasons for the ongoing success of a language that is often criticized for its complexity. The most important one is the existing code base, which probably is of the dimension of some billion lines of code. Due to its multi-paradigm language design, C++ provides the unique ability to combine modern software development principles with high source-level backward compatibility to this enormous code base. It integrates classical procedural programming, object-oriented programming and, by the means of C++ templates, even generic and generative programming into a single language. Another main reason for the ongoing usage of C/C++ is runtime and memory efficiency of the generated code. For domains, where efficiency is a crucial property, there is still no alternative in sight.

[1] This work was partly supported by the German Research Council (DFG) under grant no. SCHR 603/4.

[2] Correspondence to: Olaf Spinczyk, Martenstr. 1, D-91058 Erlangen, Germany. Tel.: +49 9131 85 27906; Fax: +49 9131 8528732; E-mail: os@cs.fau.de.

[1] Throughout this paper, we use "C/C++" as an abbreviation for "C and C++" and refer to it as a single language. C, as it is used today, is basically a subset of C++ (ignoring some minor differences).

In face of its importance in the real world, C/C++ plays a relatively small role in research activities and tool development related to *Aspect-Oriented Programming (AOP)* [14]. This is surprising, as the most frequently mentioned examples for *aspects* (synchronization, monitoring, tracing, caching, remote transparency...), are particularly important concerns *especially* in the C/C++ dominated domain of (embedded) system software [23].

Probably the biggest problem in research and tool development for C++ is the language itself. On the technical level, one has to deal with the extraordinary complex syntax and semantics. On the conceptual level, one has to be very careful when integrating new concepts like AOP into a language that already supports multiple paradigms. In the following, we discuss some of the peculiarities and difficulties of C++ from the perspective of an aspect weaver.

1.1. Technical Level

Developing a **standard-compliant parser for the C++ syntax** is just a nightmare. It is an extremely hard, tedious and thankless task. Additionally, to support a substantial set of join point types, an aspect weaver has to perform a **full semantic analysis**, and the semantics of C++ is even worse. Pretty basic things, like type deduction and overload resolution, are very complicated due to automatic type conversions and namespace/argument dependent name lookup rules. However, all this gets a most significant raise in complexity if it comes to the **support of templates**. The C++ template language is a Turing-complete language on its own [8]. Template meta-programs are executed by the compiler during the compilation process. To support join points in template code, an aspect weaver has to do the same. It has to perform a **full template instantiation**.

Another problem is the C/C++ **translation model** that is built on the concept of **single translation units**, whereas an aspect weaver typically prefers a **global view** on the project. This and other oddities as the **C preprocessor** make it difficult to integrate aspect weaving into the C++ tool chain. Moreover, even if the language is standardized, in the real world one has to face a lot of **compiler peculiarities**. Proprietary language extensions, implementation bugs and "99% C++ standard conformance" are common characteristics among major compilers.

1.2. Conceptual Level

C++ has a powerful but **complex static type system**, with fundamental and class types, derived types (pointer, array, reference, function), cv-qualifiers (const, volatile) and so on. On the other hand, C++ offers (almost) **no runtime type information** which facilitates a unified access to instances of any type at runtime. This focus on static typing has to be reflected in an aspect language for C++, e.g. in the way type expressions are matched and join point-specific context is provided. Moreover, C++ integrates **multiple programming paradigms** into a single language. Matching and weaving has not only to be supported in classes, but also in **global functions**, **operator functions** and **template code**.

1.3. Our Contribution

AspectC++ is a general purpose aspect-oriented language extension to C++ designed by the authors. It is aimed to bring fully-fledged AOP support into the C++ domain. Since the first language proposal and prototype weaver implementation [21], AspectC++ has significantly evolved. The 1.0 version is going to be released in the third quarter of 2005. While being strongly influenced by the AspectJ language model [16,15], AspectC++ supports in version 1.0 all the additional concepts that are unique to the C++ domain. This ranges from global functions, operators, const correctness and multiple inheritance up to weaving in template code and join point-specific instantiation of templates [18].

This paper describes the design and implementation of the AspectC++ language. On the conceptual level it shows, how we integrated AOP concepts into a language as complex as C++. On the technical level, some interesting details about the weaver implementation are presented. On both levels, the paper focuses on the peculiarities and difficulties discussed in the previous section – and how we solved them in AspectC++.

The paper is organized as follows: In the next section, we discuss related work. Section 3 then describes the primary design goals and rationale of AspectC++. Afterwards in Section 4, we concentrate on the conceptual level by describing the AspectC++ language and how it is integrated into C++. This is followed by two real-world examples in Section 5. Section 6 provides an overview on the weaver and thereby discusses, how we addressed the technical level. Finally, we draw a conclusion from our work in Section 7.

2. Related Work

2.1. Aspect Languages

As already mentioned, AspectC++ adopts the language model introduced by *AspectJ* [16], which is probably the most mature AOP system for the Java language. The AspectJ language model is also used by *AspectC*, a proposed AOP language extension for C. Even though there is no weaver for AspectC available, it was successfully used to demonstrate the benefits of AOP for the design and evolution of system software [5,6].

2.2. Early AOP Approaches

Most of the approaches considered as "roots of AOP", like *Subject-Oriented Programming* [13], *Adaptive Programming* [17] or *Composition Filters* [3] provided a C++ language binding in the beginning. However, with the rising of Java, the C++ support was almost discontinued.

2.3. AOP in Pure C++

A number of attempts have been suggested to "simulate" AOP concepts in pure C++ using advanced template techniques [7], macro programming [9] or *Policy-based Design* [1]. In some of these publications it is claimed that, in the case of C++, a dedicated aspect language like AspectC++ is not necessary. However, these approaches have the common drawback that a class has always to be *explicitly* prepared to be affected by aspects, which makes it hard to use them on existing code. Moreover, aspects have to be *explicitly* assigned to classes, as a pointcut concept is not available. To our understanding, an AOP language should not make any compromise regarding "obliviousness and quantification" [10]. The non-invasive and declarative assignment of aspects to classes is at heart of aspect-oriented programming.

2.4. Other C++ Language Extensions

OpenC++ [4] is a MOP for C++ that allows a compiled C++ metaprogram to transform the base-level C++ code. The complete syntax tree is visible on the meta-level and arbitrary transformations are supported. OpenC++ provides no explicit support for AOP-like language extensions. It is a powerful, but somewhat lower-level transformation and MOP toolkit. Other tools based on C++ code transformation like *Simplicissimus* [20] and *CodeBoost* [2] are mainly targeted to the field of domain-specific program optimizations for numerical applications. While CodeBoost intentionally supports only those C++ features that are relevant to the domain of program optimization, AspectC++ has to support all language features. It is intended to be a general-purpose aspect language.

3. AspectC++ Goals and Rationale

3.1. Primary Design Goals

AspectC++ is being developed with the following goals in mind:

AOP in C++ should be easy. We want practitioners to use AspectC++ in their daily work. The aspect language has to be general-purpose, applicable to existing projects and needs to be integrated well into the C++ language and tool chain.

AspectC++ should be strong, where C++ is strong. Even though general-purpose, AspectC++ should specifically be applicable in the C/C++ dominated domains of "very big" and "very small" systems. Hence, it must not lead to a significant overhead at runtime.

3.2. Design Rationale

The primary goals of AspectC++, as well as the properties of the C++ language itself, led to some fundamental design decisions:

"AspectJ-style" syntax and semantics, as it is used and approved. Moreover, AspectJ was designed with very similar goals (e.g. *"programmer compatibility"* [16]) in mind.

Comply with the C++ philosophy, as this is crucial for acceptance. As different as C++ is from Java, as different AspectC++ has to be from e.g. AspectJ.

Source-to-Source weaving, as it is the only practicable way to integrate AspectC++ with the high number of existing tools and platforms. The AspectC++ weaver transforms AspectC++ code into C++ code.

Support of C++ Templates, even if it makes things *a lot* more difficult. The whole C++ standard library is build on templates, they are a vital part of the language.

Avoid using expensive C++ language features in the generated code, like exception handling or RTTI, as this would lead to a general runtime overhead.

Careful, minimal extension of the C++ grammar, as the grammar of C++ already is a very fragile building, which should not be shaken more than absolutely necessary.

4. The Language

The aim of this section is, to provide an overview of the AspectC++ language and to some of its concepts in detail. The AspectC++ syntax and semantics is very similar to AspectJ. The basics are therefore described only briefly here, which leaves more space to focus on C++-specific concerns and those parts of the language that are intentionally different from AspectJ.

4.1. Overview and Terminology

AspectC++ is an extension to the C++ language. Every valid C++ program is also a valid AspectC++ program[2]. As in AspectJ, the most relevant terms are *join point* and *advice*. A *join point* denotes a specific position in the static program structure or the program execution graph, where some *advice* should be given. Supported advice types include *code advice* (before, after, around), *introductions* (also known as inter-type declaration in AspectJ) and *aspect order* definitions. Join points are given in a declarative way by a join point description language. Each set of join points, which is described in this language, is called a *pointcut*. The sentences of the join point description language are called *pointcut expressions*. The building blocks of pointcut expressions are *match expressions* (to some degree comparable to "Generalized Type Names" (GTNs) and "Signature Patterns" in AspectJ), which can be combined using *pointcut functions* and *algebraic operations*. Pointcuts can be *named* and thereby reused in a different context. While named pointcuts can be defined anywhere in the program, advice can only be given by *aspects*. The aspect

```
aspect TraceService {
  pointcut Methods() = % Service::%(...);
  advice call( Methods() ) : before() {
    cout << "Service function invocation" << endl;
}};
```

gives *before advice* to all calls to functions defined by the pointcut `Methods()`, which is in turn defined as all functions of the class or namespace `Service`, like `void Service::foo()` or `int Service::bar(char*)`. The special `%` and `...` symbols are wildcards, comparable to `*` and `..` in AspectJ. The percent wildcard (`%`) matches any name (or a part of a name) of a C++ entity. The ellipsis (`...`) matches any sequence of argument types (including the C `va_arg` argument type used by functions like `printf`), namespaces or template parameters.[3] More examples for match expressions can be found in Fig. 1-d. A list of the pointcut functions and algebraic operations currently supported by AspectC++ can be found in Fig. 1-e.

---

[2]As long as it does not use one of the AspectC++ keywords `aspect`, `advice`, or `pointcut` as an identifier.

[3]AspectJ supports with "+" a third wildcard for *subtype matching*. In AspectC++ this is realized by the `derived()` pointcut function.

a) Syntax Extensions

The AspectC++ syntax is an extension to the C++ syntax defined in the ISO/IEC 14882:1998(E) standard.

class-key:
  aspect

declaration:
  pointcut-declaration
  advice-declaration

member-declaration:
  pointcut-declaration
  advice-declaration

pointcut-declaration:
  pointcut *declaration*

pointcut-expression:
  constant-expression

advice-declaration:
  advice *pointcut-expression* **:** *order-declaration*
  advice *pointcut-expression* **:** *declaration*

order-declaration:
  order (*pointcut-expression-list* **)**

pointcut-expression-list:
  pointcut-expression
  *pointcut-expression***,** *pointcut-expression-list*

b) Aspects

aspect *A* **{ ... };**
  defines the aspect *A*

aspect *A* : *public B* **{ ... };**
  A inherits from class or aspect *B*

c) Advice Declarations

advice *pointcut* : **before**(...) {...}
  the advice code is executed before the join points in the pointcut

advice *pointcut* : **after**(...) {...}
  the advice code is executed after the join points in the pointcut

advice *pointcut* : **around**(...) {...}
  the advice code is executed in place of the join points in the pointcut

advice *pointcut* : **order**(*high, ...low*);
  high and *low* are pointcuts, which describe sets of aspects. Aspects on the left side of the argument list always have a higher precedence than aspects on the right hand side at the join points, where the order declaration is applied.

If the advice is *not* recognized as being of a predefined kind (i.e. **before**, **after**, **around**, or **order**), it is regarded as an **introduction** of a new method, attribute, or type to all join points in the pointcut.

d) Match Expressions

Type Matching

`"int"`
  matches the C++ built-in scalar type `int`

`"% *"`
  matches any pointer type

Namespace and Class Matching

`"Chain"`
  matches the class, struct or union *Chain*

`"Memory%"`
  matches any class, struct or union whose name starts with "Memory"

Function Matching

`"void reset()"`
  matches the function *reset* having no parameters and returning `void`

`"% printf(...)"`
  matches the function *printf* having any number of parameters and returning any type

`"% ...::%(...)"`
  matches any function, operator function, or type conversion function (in any class or namespace)

`"% ...::Service::%(...) const"`
  matches any const member-function of the class `Service` defined in any scope

`"% ...::operator %(...)"`
  matches any type conversion function

Template Matching

`"std::set<...>"`
  matches all template instances of the class *std::set*

`"std::set<int>"`
  matches only the template instance *std::set<int>*

`"% ...::%<...>::%(...)"`
  matches any member function from any template class in any scope

e) Predefined Pointcut Functions

Functions

call(*pointcut*) $\mathbf{N} \rightarrow \mathbf{C}_C$
  provides all join points where a named entity in the *pointcut* is called.

execution(*pointcut*) $\mathbf{N} \rightarrow \mathbf{C}_E$
  provides all join points referring to the implementation of a named entity in the *pointcut*.

construction(*pointcut*) $\mathbf{N} \rightarrow \mathbf{C}_{Cons}$
  all join points where an instance of the given class(es) is constructed.

destruction(*pointcut*) $\mathbf{N} \rightarrow \mathbf{C}_{Des}$
  all join points where an instance of the given class(es) is destructed.

pointcut may contain function names or class names. A class name is equivalent to the names of all functions defined within its scope combined with the || operator (see below).

Figure 1. AspectC++ Language Quick Reference.

4.2. AspectC++ Grammar Extensions

Figure 1-a shows the AspectC++ extensions to the C++ grammar. Probably the most important design decision for keeping the set of grammar extensions small and simple was to use *quoted match expressions*. By quoting match expressions, pointcuts can be

Control Flow

cflow(*pointcut*) $C \rightarrow C$
: captures join points occuring in the dynamic execution context of join points in the *pointcut*. The argument pointcut is forbidden to contain context variables or join points with runtime conditions (currently cflow, that, or target).

Types

base(*pointcut*) $N \rightarrow N_{C,F}$
: returns all base classes resp. redefined functions of classes in the *pointcut*

derived(*pointcut*) $N \rightarrow N_{C,F}$
: returns all classes in the *pointcut* and all classes derived from them resp. all redefined functions of derived classes

Context

that(*type pattern*) $N \rightarrow C$
: returns all join points where the current C++ `this` pointer refers to an object which is an instance of a type that is compatible to the type described by the *type pattern*

target(*type pattern*) $N \rightarrow C$
: returns all join points where the target object of a call is an instance of a type that is compatible to the type described by the *type pattern*

result(*type pattern*) $N \rightarrow C$
: returns all join points where the result object of a call/execution is an instance of a type described by the *type pattern*

args(*type pattern, ...*) $(N,...) \rightarrow C$
: a list of *type patterns* is used to provide all joinpoints with matching argument signatures

Instead of the *type pattern* it is possible here to pass the name of a **context variable** to which the context information is bound. In this case the type of the variable is used for the type matching.

Scope

within(*pointcut*) $N \rightarrow C$
: filters all join points that are within the functions or classes in the *pointcut*

Algebraic Operators

pointcut **&&** *pointcut* $(N,N) \rightarrow N, (C,C) \rightarrow C$
: intersection of the join points in the *pointcuts*

pointcut **||** *pointcut* $(N,N) \rightarrow N, (C,C) \rightarrow C$
: union of the join points in the *pointcuts*

! *pointcut* $N \rightarrow N, C \rightarrow C$
: exclusion of the join points in the *pointcut*

f) Join Point Types

Code

$C, C_C, C_E, C_{Cons}, C_{Des}$:
: any, *Call*, *Execution*, *Construction*, *Destruction*

Name

N, N_N, N_C, N_F, N_T :
: any, *Namespace*, *Class*, *Function*, *Type*

g) Join Point API

The JoinPoint-API is provided within every advice code body by the built-in object ***tjp*** of class ***JoinPoint***.

Compile-time Types and Constants

That [type]
: object type (object initiating a call)

Target [type]
: target object type (target object of a call)

Result [type]
: result type of the affected function

Arg::<i>::Type, Arg::<i>::ReferredType [type]
: type of the ith argument of the affected function (with $0 \leq i < ARGS$)

ARGS [const]
: number of arguments

JPID [const]
: unique numeric identifier for this join point

JPTYPE [const]
: numeric identifier describing the type of this join point (*AC::CALL* or *AC::EXECUTION*)

Runtime Functions and State

static const char ***signature**()
: gives a textual description of the join point (function name, class name, ...)

That ***that**()
: returns a pointer to the object initiating a call or 0 if it is a static method or a global function

Target ***target**()
: returns a pointer to the object that is the target of a call or 0 if it is a static method or a global function

Result ***result**()
: returns a typed pointer to the result value or 0 if the function has no result value

Arg::<i>::ReferredType ***arg**()
: returns a typed pointer to the argument value with compile-time index *number*

void ***arg**(*int number*)
: returns a pointer to the memory position holding the argument value with index *number*

void **proceed**()
: executes the original code in an around advice

AC::Action **&action**()
: returns the runtime action object containing the execution environment to execute (*trigger()*) the original code encapsulated by an around advice

Runtime Type Information

static AC::Type **type**()

static AC::Type **resulttype**()

static AC::Type **argtype**(*int* i)
: return a C++ ABI V3 conforming string representation of the signature / result type / argument type of the affected function

parsed with the ordinary C++ expression syntax. The real evaluation of the pointcuts itself can be postponed to a separate parser. This clear separation also helps the user to distinguish on the syntax level between ordinary code expressions and match expressions, which are quite different concepts. Additionally, it keeps the match expression language extendable.

4.3. The Join Point Model

4.3.1. Join Point Types

AspectC++ uses a unified join point model to handle all types of advice in the same way. This is different from AspectJ, which distinguishes between *pointcuts* and *advice* on the one hand and *GTNs* and *introductions* on the other. As shown in the example above, in AspectC++ even match expressions are pointcuts and can be named. While such a coherent language design is a good thing anyway, this is particularly useful in combination with aspect inheritance and (pure) virtual pointcuts. In AspectC++, even the pointcuts used for introductions and baseclass introductions can be (pure) virtual and, thus, be defined or overridden in derived aspects. This is demonstrated in the "Reusable Observer" example in Section 5.1.

Regarding the implementation, the unified model requires join points to be *typed* in AspectC++. The basic join point types are *Name* (**N**) and *Code* (**C**). A name join point represents a named entity from the C++ program, like a class, a function or a namespace. It typically results from a match expression. A code join point represents a node in the program execution graph, like the call to or execution of a function. Code join points result from applying pointcut functions to name pointcuts. The basic types are additionally separated into more specialized subtypes like *Class* ($\mathbf{N}_C$) or *Function* ($\mathbf{N}_F$), *Execution* ($\mathbf{C}_E$) or *Construction* ($\mathbf{C}_{Cons}$). The aspect weaver uses the type information to ensure that e.g. code advice (before, after, around) is only given to code join points. Figure 1-f lists all join point types. The subtypes are, however, mostly irrelevant for the user, as most pointcut functions accept the basic types and treat, for instance, a $\mathbf{N}_C$ join point as a the set of $\mathbf{N}_F$ join points describing all member functions.

4.3.2. Order Advice

Besides code advice (before, after, around) and (baseclass-) introductions, AspectC++ supports with *order advice* a third type of advice. Order advice is used to define an partial order of aspect precedences *per pointcut*. This makes it possible to have different precedences for different join points. For example, the order declarations

```
advice "Service" : order("Locking", !("Locking"||"Tracing"), "Tracing");
advice "Client" : order("Tracing", !"Tracing");
```

define that in the context of the class or namespace `Service` all advice given by the aspect `Locking` should be applied first, followed by advice from any aspect but `Locking` and `Tracing`. Advice given by `Tracing` should have the lowest precedence. However, for `Client` the order is different. Advice given by `Tracing` should be applied first. As order declarations are itself advice, they benefit from the unified join point model. They can be given to virtual pointcuts and can be declared in the context of any aspect. Hence, it is possible to separate the precedence rules from the aspects they affect. The AspectC++ weaver collects all partial order declarations for a join point and derives a valid total order. In case of a contradiction, a weave-time error is reported.

Table 1. Matching of C++-specific function signatures.

Expression	Matches	
`"% IntArray::%(...)"`	**1–6**	Any function, operator function, or type conversion function in IntArray
`"% IntArray::%(...) const"`	**1, 5**	Any *const* -function, -operator function, or -type conversion function in IntArray
`"% IntArray::%<...>(...)"`	**3**	Any instance of any *template* -function, -operator function, or -type conversion function in IntArray
`"% IntArray::%<short>(...)"`	**(3)**	Any *<short> instance* of any *template* -function, -operator function or -type conversion function in IntArray
`"...::operator %(...)"`	**5, 6**	Any type conversion function
`"...::operator %*(...)"`	**5, 6**	Any type conversion function that converts to a *pointer type*
`"% IntArray::operator =(...)"`	**4**	Any assignment operator in IntArray

4.3.3. Matching C++ Entities

As already mentioned in Section 1.2, C++ has a rather complex type system, consisting of *fundamental types* (`int`, `short`, ...) and *class types* (`class`, `struct`, `union`), *derived types* (pointer, array, reference, function) and types optionally qualified by *cv-qualifiers* (`const`, `volatile`). Besides *ordinary functions* and *member functions*, C++ also supports overloading a predefined set of *operator functions*. Classes can define *type conversion functions*[4] to provide implicit casts to other types. And finally, classes or functions can be parameterizable with *template arguments*.

The AspectC++ match expression language covers all these elements, because in C++ they are an integral part of a type's or function's name or signature. Hence, they should be usable as a match criteria. The match expression language is defined by an own grammar, which consists of more than 25 rules. We are therefore not going to describe it in detail, but present match expressions for function signatures as one example for AspectC++'s support for matching "C++ specific" entities.

```
class IntArray {
public:
  int count() const;                                        (1)
  void clear();                                             (2)
  template< class T > init( const T* data, int n );         (3)
    IntArray& operator =( const IntArray& src );            (4)
  operator const int*() const;                              (5)
  operator int*();                                          (6)
};
```

The Class `IntArray` consists of members that use cv-qualifiers (1, 5), templates arguments (3), operator overloading (4), and type conversion functions (5, 6). Table 1 demonstrates, how these elements are matched by various match expressions. Additional examples, including match expressions for type and scope, can be found in Fig. 1-d.

[4]Often called type conversion *operators*, too, as they are defined using the `operator` keyword (e.g. "`operator int()`").

4.3.4. Intentionally Missing Features

AspectC++ intentionally does not implement the get() and set() pointcut functions, known from AspectJ to give advice for field access. Even if desirable, they are not implementable in a language that supports free pointers. Field access through pointers is quite common in C/C++ and implies a danger of "surprising" side effects for such advice.

4.4. Join Point API

The join point API (Fig. 1-g) is another part of AspectC++ that is heavily influenced by the "C++ philosophy". Compared to Java, C++ has a less powerful runtime type system, but a more powerful compile-time type system. In Java, basically everything is a Java.lang.Object at runtime, which facilitates the development of generic code, as instances of any type can be treated as Object *at runtime*. In C++ there is no such common root class. C++, by the means of overloading and templates, facilitates the development of generic code that can be instantiated with any type *at compile-time*. In general, Java promotes *genericity at runtime*[5], while the C++ philosophy is to use *genericity at compile time*. For this purpose, we extended the AspectJ idea of a runtime join point API by a *compile-time join point API*, which provides static type information about the current join point at compilation time.

The compile-time join point API is visible to advice code as class JoinPoint. Provided information includes, besides other type information, the sequence of argument types and the result type of the affected function. JoinPoint::Result is an alias for the function's result type. The number of function arguments is available as compile-time constant JoinPoint::ARGS. The function argument types are provided through the template class JoinPoint::Arg<*i*>::Type. We intentionally used an integer template for this purpose, as it makes it possible to iterate at compile time over the sequence of argument types by template meta-programs. Such usage of the compile-time join point API is demonstrated in the "Win32 Errorhandling" example in Section 5.2.

The runtime join point API is visible to advice through the pointer tjp, which refers to an instance of JoinPoint. By using tjp, it is possible to retrieve the dynamic context, like the pointer to the actual result *value* (tjp->result()). Note that the function to retrieve the value of an argument is overloaded. If the index of the argument is known at compile-time, the template version tjp->arg<*i*>() can be used. It takes the index as template parameter and (later at runtime) returns a *typed* pointer to the value. Otherwise, the unsafe version tjp->arg(*i*) has to be used, which takes the index as a function parameter and returns an *untyped* void pointer to the value.

The class JoinPoint is not only specific for each join point, it is furthermore tailored down according to the individual requirements of the actual advice. If, for instance, tjp->result() is never called in the advice code, the function is removed from JoinPoint and no memory is occupied by the reference to the result value at runtime. This "pay only what you actually use" is important for facilitating AOP in the domain of embedded systems, where small memory footprints are a crucial concern.

In AspectC++, the join point API also implements the functionality to proceed to the intercepted original code from around advice (tjp->proceed()). It is also possible

[5] This is even true with Java generics introduced in the upcoming Java 5.0, which are basically a syntactic wrapper around the "treat everything as an object" philosophy.

to *store* the context information of the intercepted function (returned by `tjp->action()`) and *delegate* its execution to another function or thread. This offers a noticeable higher flexibility than in AspectJ, where `proceed()` can only be called from the advice code itself.

4.5. Language Summary

The previous sections presented only a subset of the AspectC++ language features. We left out details about (context binding) pointcut functions, algebraic operations, or the semantics of code advice, as they are very similar to AspectJ. Other elements, like the aspect instantiation, are different from AspectJ, but left out because of space limitations. Nevertheless, these features are available in AspectC++, too.

5. Examples

In the following sections, the expressive power of the AspectC++ language is demonstrated by two real-world examples. The first demonstrates using virtual pointcuts with baseclass introductions for a reusable implementation of the observer pattern. The second example is an aspect that checks the result codes of Win32 API functions and throws an exception in case of an error. It demonstrates how to use the compile-time join point API to exploit the power of C++ template meta-programming in advice code.

5.1. Reusable Observer

Reusable implementations of design patterns are a well known application of AOP [12]. The listing in Fig. 2 shows an AspectC++ implementation of the observer protocol [11]. The abstract aspect `ObserverPattern` defines interfaces `ISubject` and `IObserver` (lines 8–11), which are inserted via baseclass introductions into all classes that take part in the observer protocol (lines 22–23). These roles are represented by pure virtual pointcuts `subjects()` and `observers()`. Thus, their definition is delegated to derived concrete aspects. A third virtual pointcut, `subjectChange()`, describes all methods that potentially change the state of a subject and thereby should lead to a notification of the registered observers (line 17). The pointcut is defined as `execution("% ...::%(...)" && !"% ...::%(...) const") && within(subjects())`. It evaluates to the *execution* of all *non-const methods* that are defined *within* a class from `subject()`. This is a reasonable default. However, it can be overridden in a derived aspect if, for instance, not all state-changing methods should trigger a notification. Finally, the notification of observers is implemented by giving after execution advice to `subjectChange()` (lines 25–28).

The `ClockObserver` aspect is an example for a concrete aspect derived from `ObserverPattern`. To apply the pattern, the developer only has to define the pure virtual pointcuts `subjects()` and `observers()` (lines 41–42) and to write the introduction that inserts `update()` into the observer classes (lines 45–47).

"Reusable Observer" is a typical application of aspects in the world of object-orientation. The `ObserverPattern` implementation is even more generic than the AspectJ implementation suggested by Hannemann [12], where the *derived* aspect has to perform the baseclass introductions for the `Observer` and `Subject` interfaces. Purpose and name of these interfaces are, however, *implementation details* of the protocol and should be

```
File: ObserverPattern.ah

aspect ObserverPattern {
  // data structures to manage subjects and observers
  ...
public:
  // Interfaces for each role
  struct ISubject {};
  struct IObserver {
    virtual void update (ISubject *) = 0;
  };

  // To be defined / overridden by the concrete derived aspect
  // subjectChange() matches execution of all non-const methods
  pointcut virtual observers() = 0;
  pointcut virtual subjects() = 0;
  pointcut virtual subjectChange() =  execution( "% ...::%(...)"
          && !"% ...::%(...) const" ) && within( subjects() );

  // Add new baseclass to each subject/observer class
  // and insert code to inform observers after a subject change
  advice observers () : baseclass( IObserver );
  advice subjects() : baseclass( ISubject );

  advice subjectChange() : after () {
    ISubject* subject = tjp->that();
    updateObservers( subject );
  }
      void updateObservers( ISubject* subject ) { ... }
  void addObserver( ISubject* subject, IObserver* observer ) { ... }
  void remObserver( ISubject* subject, IObserver* observer ) { ... }
};
______________________
File: ClockObserver.ah

#include "ObserverPattern.ah"
#include "ClockTimer.h"

aspect ClockObserver : public ObserverPattern {
  // define the pointcuts
  pointcut subjects()   = "ClockTimer";
  pointcut observers()  = "DigitalClock"||"AnalogClock";

public:
  advice observers() : void update( ObserverPattern::ISubject* sub ) {
    Draw();
  }
};
```

Figure 2. Reusable Observer-Pattern Aspect.

hidden. Moreover, the derived aspect has to define the `subjectChange()` pointcut in any case. In AspectC++ this is not necessary, as it is possible to take advantage from the C++ notion of non-modifying (const) methods in match expressions and thereby find all potentially state-changing methods automatically.

5.2. Win32 Errorhandling

Every program has to deal with the fact that operations might fail at runtime. Today, most developers favor *exceptions* for the propagation of errors. However, especially in the C/C++ world, there are still thousands of legacy libraries that do not support exception handling, but indicate an error situation via the function's *return value*. In the Win32 API, for instance, an error is indicated by returning a special "magic value". The corresponding error code (reason) can then be retrieved using the `GetLastError()` function. The actual "magic value" needed to check the result depends on the *return type* of the function. `BOOL` functions, for instance, return `FALSE`, while `HANDLE` functions return either

```
1  namespace win32 {
2    struct Exception {
3      Exception( const std::string& w, DWORD c ) { ... }
4    };
5
6    // Check for "magic value" indicating an error
7    inline bool IsErrorResult( HANDLE res ) {
8      return res == NULL || res == INVALID_HANDLE_VALUE;
9    }
10   inline bool IsErrorResult( HWND res ) {
11     return res == NULL;
12   }
13   inline bool IsErrorResult( BOOL res ) {
14     return res == FALSE;
15   }
16   ...
17
18   // Translates a Win32 error code into a readable text
19   std::string GetErrorText( DWORD code ) { ... }
20
21   pointcut  Win32API() =  "% CreateWindow%(...)"
22                        || "% BeginPaint(...)"
23                        || "% CreateFile%(...)"
24                        || ...
25 } // namespace Win32
26
27 ____________________
28
29 aspect ThrowWin32Errors {
30
31   // template metaprogram to generate code for
32   // streaming a comma-separated sequence of arguments
33   template< class TJP, int N >
34   struct stream_params {
35     static void process( ostream& os, TJP* tjp ) {
36       os << *tjp->arg< TJP::ARGS - N >() << ", ";
37       stream_params< TJP, N - 1 >::process( os, tjp );
38   } };
39   // specialization to terminate the recursion
40   template< class TJP >
41   struct stream_params< TJP, 1 > {
42     static void process( ostream& os, TJP* tjp ) {
43       os << *tjp->arg< TJP::ARGS - 1 >();
44   } };
45
46   advice call( win32::Win32API() ) : after() {
47     if( win32::IsErrorResult( *tjp->result() ) ) {
48       ostringstream os;
49       DWORD code = GetLastError();
50
51       os << "WIN32 ERROR " << code << ": "
52          << win32::GetErrorText(code) << endl;
53       os << "WHILE CALLING: "
54          << tjp->signature() << endl;
55       os << "WITH: " << "(";
56
57       // Generate joinpoint-specific sequence of
58       // operations to stream all argument values
59       stream_params< JoinPoint,
60                      JoinPoint::ARGS >::process( os, tjp );
61       os << ")";
62       throw win32::Exception( os.str(), code );
63   } }
64 };
```

Figure 3. An Aspect to Throw Win32 Errors as Exceptions.

`NULL` or `INVALID_HANDLE_VALUE`. The aim of the `ThrowWin32Errors` aspect (Fig. 3) is to perform the appropriate check after each call to a Win32 function and thereby transform the Win32 model of error handling into an exception based model. This is actually very useful for developers that have to work with the Win32 API.

The `ThrowWin32Errors` aspect gives after advice for all calls to functions defined by the `win32::Win32API()` pointcut. (Figure 3, lines 21–24) The advice code checks for an error condition using the `win32::IsErrorResult()` helper function. This function performs the check against the type-dependent "magic values". It is overloaded for each return type used by Win32 functions. (lines 6–16). The compiler's overload resolution deduces (at compile-time) for each join point the correct helper function to call. Note that this generic implementation of the advice code is only possible, because `tjp->result()` returns a pointer of the real (static) type of the affected function.

The `win32::Exception` object thrown in case of an error should include all context information that can be helpful to figure out the reason for the actual failure. The most tricky part to solve here is to build a string representation from the actual parameter values. In AspectJ one would iterate at *runtime* over all arguments and call `Object.toString()` on each argument. However, in C++ it is not possible to perform this at runtime, as C++ types do not share a common root class that offers generic services like `toString()`. The C++ philosophy of genericity is based on *static* typing. Retrieving a string representation of any object is realized by overloading the stream operator `ostream& operator <<(ostream&, T)` for each type `T`. Therefore, we have to iterate at *compile-time* over the join point-specific list of argument types to generate a sequence of stream operator calls, each processing (later at runtime) an argument value of the correct type. This is implemented by a small template meta-program (lines 33–44), which is instantiated at compile-time with the `JoinPoint` type (line 39) and iterates, by recursive instantiation of the template, over the join-point-specific argument type list `JoinPoint::Arg<I>`. For each argument type, a `stream_params` class with a `process()` method is generated, which later at runtime will stream the typed argument value (retrieved via `tjp->arg<I>()`) and recursively call `stream_params::process()` for the next argument (lines 35–37, 42–43). Again, the compiler automatically deduces the actual operator to call for a specific argument type during overload resolution.

The "Win32 Errorhandling" example shows, how aspects can be used with the procedural paradigm followed by C-style legacy libraries. It furthermore demonstrates, how advice code can take advantage of the generic and generative programming paradigm offered by C++ templates.[6] A recent paper demonstrates, that this combination of AOP and templates can lead to very generic and efficient aspect implementations [18].

5.3. Examples Summary

The "Reusable Observer" and "Win32 Errorhandling" examples show, how AspectC++ can be used with very different "styles" of C/C++ code, that is, with the different programming paradigms integrated into the C++ language. They also illustrate that certain AspectC++ concepts fits well into the C++ philosophy of static typing, which enables developers to write very expressive aspect code.

6. The Weaver

The AspectC++ weaver `ac++` is a source-to-source front-end that transforms AspectC++ programs into C++ programs[7]. The woven code can then be built with any standard-

[6] It is, of course, inconvenient to use template meta-programming to build just a string of argument values. However it is the only way of doing this in C++ *at all.*

[7] The `ac++` weaver and documentation are available from `http://www.aspectc.org/`.

conforming C++ compiler, like g++ or VisualC++. AspectC++ programs have already been executed on a broad variety of platforms, ranging from the smallest 8 bit micro-controllers to 64 bit servers. The following sections provide some details about the weaver implementation.

6.1. Translation Process

A C++ program consists of a set of self-contained[8] translation units. The translation process is performed in two steps. First, the compiler transforms each translation unit into an object file, which contains binary code augmented by symbol information that describes all externally visible and unresolved symbols. Then, the linker binds all object files and creates the executable code by resolving all dependencies.

Various development tools like IDEs or program builders like `make` strongly rely on this two-step translation process. Thus, for the sake of easy integration, the `ac++` command is called for each translation unit and produces C++ code that can be directly fed into the C++ compiler. On the one hand this design decision facilitates the implementation of wrapper programs, which hide `ac++` from the build environment. On the other hand this significantly restricts the knowledge of the aspect weaver to single translation units. To overcome this limitation the following problems had to be solved.

6.1.1. Visibility of Aspects

Aspects should be able to affect code in any translation unit. Therefore, a mechanism is needed to include the definition of an aspect in all translation units. Programmers should not be forced to include the definition by hand using the C++ preprocessor directive `#include`. This would violate the "obliviousness" goal. Therefore, we adopted the "forced include" mechanism known from many C++ compilers for that purpose. In practice, this means that aspect definitions are stored in "aspect header files" (`*.ah`). The location of these files is provided on the command line and the weaver automatically includes all aspect headers in the currently processed translation unit.

6.1.2. Link-Once Code

Traditionally, a C/C++ linker does not accept two externally visible symbols with the same name to be defined in two different translation units. This is problematic for a C++ aspect weaver, because there are many situations, in which global objects have to be generated. Examples are the instances of singleton aspects and introductions of static attributes or non-inline functions. As the `ac++` weaver always processes only a single translation unit, there is no global knowledge, which would help to find the right place for inserting the generated code. To solve this problem, `ac++` exploits the so-called COMDAT feature of state-of-the-art C++ compilers. A standard-compliant C++ compiler sometimes has the same problem as `ac++`. For example, non-inline member functions or static attributes of template classes are allowed to be defined in header files. To avoid the problem of duplicate symbols the compiler and linker use "vague linkage". Thus, by using certain code generation patterns COMDAT can also be used by the weaver. In most cases, generated global code is transparently wrapped by a template class.

[8]Anything that is used either has to be defined or declared.

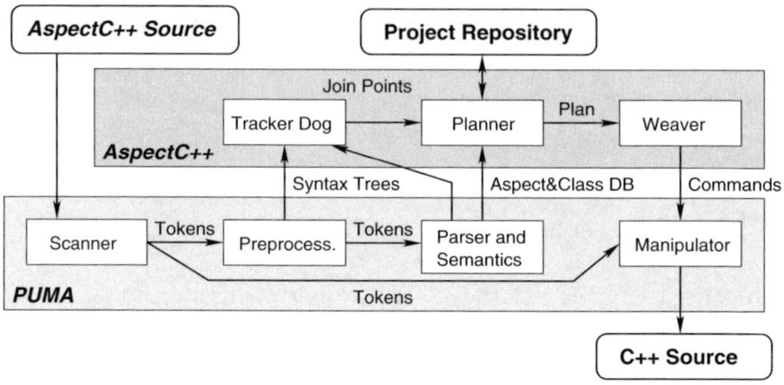

Figure 4. Architecture of the AspectC++ Weaver.

6.1.3. Information Sharing

To provide at least a "partial global" knowledge `ac++` accesses a global project repository. This is a file, which describes processed translation units by listing join points, aspects, and advice. It can be used by one `ac++` incarnation to save information for other `ac++` incarnations running later. For example, it would be impossible to provide a project-wide unique ID (Fig. 1-g) for each join point without the project repository. As a side-effect the project repository can also be used by IDEs, like the Eclipse ACDT[9], to visualize join points.

6.2. Architecture and Implementation

Figure 4 illustrates the architecture of `ac++` by showing the main building blocks and the data flow during a program transformation from AspectC++ to C++. The weaver implementation is based on PUMA, a framework for C++ code analysis and transformation. PUMA is developed in-line with AspectC++ by our group. It contains a complete C++ front-end, which supports standard ISO C++ 98 as well as several g++ and VisualC++ language extensions. The `ac++` weaver has a weight of 85 ksloc, from which are 70 ksloc used solely by the PUMA framework, that is for analyzing and manipulating C++ code.

The weaving process starts in PUMA with scanning, preprocessing, parsing, and a full semantic analysis of the source code. The semantic analysis includes complete function call resolution, necessary to implement call advice, and full template instantiation, needed for matching and weaving in template instances.

The `ac++` level first processes the resulting syntax tree. The *Tracker Dog* is responsible to find all points in the code, which might be affected by advice. The resulting potential join points are passed to the *Planner*, which also uses the *Aspect&Class Database* from the *Parser and Semantics* (PUMA level). The planner internally parses and analyses pointcut expressions (including pointcut type checks) and calculates the sets of matching join points. For each join point the planner sets up a plan that is later used by the *Weaver* to generate a sequence of code manipulation commands. The code manipulation is performed again on the PUMA-level by the *Manipulator*.

The PUMA framework itself is implemented in AspectC++. Aspects are, for instance, used to adapt the system to compiler-specific peculiarities. The PUMA core im-

[9]Available from `http://acdt.aspectc.org/`.

plements only the standard C++ grammar. All additional compiler-specific grammar extensions are woven in by aspects. Currently such grammar extensions are implemented for VisualC++ (10 aspects, 12 introductions, 13 execution advice) and g++ (1 aspect, 15 introductions, 15 execution advice).

6.3. Code Generation

6.3.1. JoinPoint Structure

AspectC++ generates a C++ class with a unique name for each join-point that is affected by advice code. By performing static code analysis on the advice and templates instantiated by advice (with `JoinPoint` as a template parameter) `ac++` avoids to generate unneeded elements in this class. The following code fragment shows a part of the `JoinPoint` structure for a call join point in the "Win32 Errorhandling" example.

```
struct TJP_WndProc_1 {
  ...
  template <int I> struct Arg {
    typedef void Type;
    typedef void ReferredType;
  };
  template <> struct Arg<0> {
    typedef ::HWND Type;
    typedef ::HWND ReferredType;
  };
  ...
  void **_args;
  inline void *arg (int n) {return _args[n];}
  template <int I> typename Arg<I>::ReferredType *arg () {
    return (typename Arg<I>::ReferredType*)arg (I);    }
};
```

6.3.2. Advice Transformation

Advice code is transformed into a member function of the aspect, which in turn is transformed to a class. If the advice implementation depends on the `JoinPoint` type, it is transformed into a template member function and the unique join point class is passed as a template argument to the advice code. Thus, in this case the advice code is generic and can access all type definitions (C++ typedefs) inside the join-point class with `JoinPoint::`*Typename*, as described in Section 4.4. The following code fragment shows `JoinPoint` dependent advice code after its transformation into a template function.

```
class ThrowWin32Errors {
  // ...
  template< class JoinPoint>
  void __a0_after( JoinPoint *tjp ) {
    if( win32::IsErrorResult( *tjp->result() ) ) {
      // ...
  }
};
```

6.3.3. Weaving in Regular Code

Weaving of call or execution advice is based on inlined wrapper functions. For instance, in the "Win32 Errorhandling" example the after call advice for `BeginPaint()` is implemented by replacing the call expression `BeginPaint(NULL,&ps)` by `__call_WndProc_1_0(NULL,&ps)`. The wrapper function calls `BeginPaint()` first and invokes the advice afterwards.

```
inline ::HDC __call_WndProc_1_0 (::HWND arg0,
                                  ::LPPAINTSTRUCT arg1) {
  ::HDC result;
  void *args_WndProc_1[] = { (void*)&arg0, (void*)&arg1 };
  TJP_WndProc_1 tjp_WndProc_1 = { args_WndProc_1, &result };
  result = ::BeginPaint(arg0, arg1);
  AC::invoke_ThrowWin32Errors_ThrowWin32Errors_a0_after<
             TJP_WndProc_1> (&tjp_WndProc_1);
  return (::HDC) result;
}
```

Although generating a wrapper function seems straightforward, call advice weaving is a complex transformation. For example, a call can syntactically be expressed a numerous ways in C++. Specific transformation patterns are needed for unary and binary operator calls. Even invisible calls by implicitly called conversion functions have to be considered.

6.3.4. Weaving in Template Code

AspectC++ supports advice for join points associated with individual template instances. Therefore, the weaver has to perform a full template instantiation analysis to distinguish template instances and to compare their signatures with match-expressions. To be able to affect only certain instances on the code generation level, our weaver uses the explicit template specialization feature of C++. For example, if advice affects only the instance `container<int>` the template code of `container` is copied, manipulated according to the advice and the instantiation, and declared as a specialization of `container` for `int` as shown here:[10]

```
template <class ElementType> class container {
public:
  void insert (ElementType elem) {...}
};
...
namespace AC{ typedef int t_container_0; }
template <> class container<AC::t_container_0> {
public:
  inline void __exec_old_insert(AC::t_container_0 elem){...}
  void insert (AC::t_container_0 arg0) {
    AC::invoke_MyAspect_a0_before ();
    this->__exec_old_insert(arg0);
  }
};
```

[10]C++ does not support the explicit specialization for template functions. However, we can work around this problem by defining a helper template class. Furthermore, some compilers do not support explicit specialization in non-namespace scope. We handle this problem by using partial specialization with an extra dummy argument.

Table 2. Code Sizes of "Hello World" implementations (Bytes).

[g++ 3.3.3]	plain	before	around
no opt. (-o0)	108	234	437
full opt. (-o6)	37	43	172

6.4. Overhead

The code generated by `ac++` is quite efficient in most cases and does not lead to a significant overhead. AspectC++ counts, however, on inlining of the generated wrapper functions by the compiler. As demonstrated in [18], the runtime overhead of code advice is in the range of just a few CPU clock cycles. It mainly depends on the amount of state that is requested by the advice code using e.g. the join point API. Table 2 illustrates the overhead regarding code size for certain types of advice. The depicted numbers show the code sizes of a simple "Hello World" application, if using no aspect ("plain", `printf`-statement in `main()`), before execution advice (empty `main()`, `printf`-statement given by advice), and around execution advice, respectively. In the optimized case the size of "before" is almost the same as of "plain". The code generated for around advice, however, does not accommodate optimization, as it calls the original function through an extra function pointer, which prevents inlining. This gives room for further improvements of `ac++`.

7. Summary and Conclusions

In this paper, we described our work on the design and development of AspectC++, an AOP language extension and weaver for C++. We motivated our work with the ongoing significance of C++ in software industry. Research and tool development for C++ is hard. We examined, from the perspective of an AOP language designer, some of the major peculiarities of C++ and categorized them into a conceptual level (language) and a technical level (tools).

On the conceptual level, we emphasized that an AOP extension for C++ has to fit into the philosophy of C++. Multi-paradigm programming, the focus on static typing and compile-time genericity, as well as backward compatibility to existing code are the fundamental elements of this philosophy. In AspectC++, this is addressed in many places, but particularly by the match expression language, the (static) join point API and the code generated by the weaver. AspectC++ thereby integrates AOP well into the C++ language, which was also demonstrated in the examples.

On the technical level, we discussed some of the major difficulties regarding tool development for C++. We pointed out that an aspect weaver benefits from a fully-fledged syntax/semantics analysis, which is, however, a very tedious task to implement. The complexity of the language and the (anachronistic) translation model put a heavy burden on the weaver implementation. We presented some details of the implementation and demonstrated, how the weaver transforms AspectC++ code into C++ code.

Today, AspectC++ is already used by researchers from academia and industry. Currently, 156 people, most of them from companies in the telecommunications or embedded systems area, are subscribed on the `ac++` user mailing list. The most prominent academic applications can be found in the domain of tailorable embedded databases [24], namely the Berkeley DB, and operating systems, which is our main field of research. We use AspectC++ in our PURE and CiAO operating system product lines [19,22].

We can already carefully conclude that AspectC++ does not lead to a significant run-time and memory overhead. However, more investigations are necessary on this topic, as this depends significantly on the interaction of the generated code with the optimization capabilities of the back-end compiler.

Regarding future work, we will continue working on the template support. This has evolved a lot over the last months, however, is still considered "experimental". We also plan to extend weaver in order to support plain C applications[11]. Weaving in macro-generated code is another feature that will be addressed in near future, as well as improving the code generation for around advice. However, AspectC++ is almost feature-complete. We are convinced that it is now ready for a broad adoption.

References

[1] Andrei Alexandrescu. *Modern C++ Design: Generic Programming and Design Patterns Applied.* AW, 2001.

[2] Otto Skrove Bagge, Karl Trygve Kalleberg, Magne Haveraaen, and Eelco Visser. Design of the CodeBoost transformation system for domain-specific optimisation of C++ programs. In Dave Binkley and Paolo Tonella, editors, *Third International Workshop on Source Code Analysis and Manipulation (SCAM 2003)*, pages 65–75, Amsterdam, The Netherlands, September 2003. IEEE.

[3] L. Bergmans. *Composing Concurrent Objects.* PhD thesis, University of Twente, 1994.

[4] Shigeru Chiba. Metaobject Protocol for C++. In *10th ACM Conf. on OOP, Systems, Languages, and Applications (OOPSLA '95)*, pages 285–299, October 1995.

[5] Yvonne Coady and Gregor Kiczales. Back to the future: A retroactive study of aspect evolution in operating system code. In Mehmet Akşit, editor, *2nd Int. Conf. on Aspect-Oriented Software Development (AOSD '03)*, pages 50–59, Boston, MA, USA, March 2003. ACM.

[6] Yvonne Coady, Gregor Kiczales, Michael Feeley, and Greg Smolyn. Using AspectC to improve the modularity of path-specific customization in operating system code. In *ESEC/FSE '01*, 2001.

[7] Krysztof Czarnecki, Lutz Dominick, and Ulrich W. Eisenecker. Aspektorientierte Programmierung in C++, Teil 1–3. *iX, Magazin für professionelle Informationstechnik*, 8–10, 2001.

[8] Krysztof Czarnecki and Ulrich W. Eisenecker. *Generative Programming. Methods, Tools and Applications.* AW, May 2000.

[9] Christopher Diggins. Aspect-Oriented Programming & C++. *Dr. Dobb's*, 408(8), August 2004.

[10] Tzilla Elrad, Robert E. Filman, and Atef Bader. Aspect-oriented programming. *CACM*, pages 29–32, October 2001.

[11] Erich Gamma, Richard Helm, Ralph Johnson, and John Vlissides. *Design Patterns: Elements of Reusable Object-Oriented Software.* AW, 1995.

[12] Jan Hannemann and Gregor Kiczales. Design pattern implementation in Java and AspectJ. In *17th ACM Conf. on OOP, Systems, Languages, and Applications (OOPSLA '02)*, pages 161–173. ACM, 2002.

[13] William Harrison and Harold Ossher. Subject-oriented programming—a critique of pure objects. In *8th ACM Conf. on OOP, Systems, Languages, and Applications (OOPSLA '93)*, pages 411–428, September 1993.

[14] G. Kiczales, J. Lamping, A. Mendhekar, C. Maeda, C. Lopes, J.-M. Loingtier, and J. Irwin. Aspect-oriented programming. In M. Aksit and S. Matsuoka, editors, *11th Eur. Conf. on OOP (ECOOP '97)*, volume 1241 of *LNCS*, pages 220–242. Springer, June 1997.

[15] Gregor Kiczales, Erik Hilsdale, Jim Hugunin, Mik Kersten, Jeffrey Palm, and William G. Griswold. Getting started with AspectJ. *CACM*, pages 59–65, October 2001.

[11] Actually, `ac++` is already able to weave in C code, but the generated code has always to be compiled with a C++ compiler.

[16] Gregor Kiczales, Erik Hilsdale, Jim Hugunin, Mik Kersten, Jeffrey Palm, and William G. Griswold. An overview of AspectJ. In J. Lindskov Knudsen, editor, *15th Eur. Conf. on OOP (ECOOP '01)*, volume 2072 of *LNCS*, pages 327–353. Springer, June 2001.

[17] Karl J. Lieberherr. *Adaptive Object-Oriented Software: The Demeter Method with Propagation Patterns*. PWS, 1996.

[18] Daniel Lohmann, Georg Blaschke, and Olaf Spinczyk. Generic advice: On the combination of AOP with generative programming in AspectC++. In G. Karsai and E. Visser, editors, *3rd Int. Conf. on Generative Programming and Component Engineering (GPCE '04)*, volume 3286 of *LNCS*, pages 55–74. Springer, October 2004.

[19] Daniel Lohmann and Olaf Spinczyk. Architecture-Neutral Operating System Components. *19th ACM Symp. on OS Principles (SOSP'03)*, October 2003. WiP session.

[20] Sibylle Schupp, Douglas Gregor, David R. Musser, and Shin-Ming Liu. Semantic and behavioral library transformations. *Information and Software Technology*, 44(13):797–810, 2002.

[21] Olaf Spinczyk, Andreas Gal, and Wolfgang Schröder-Preikschat. AspectC++: An aspect-oriented extension to C++. In *40th Int. Conf. on Technology of OO Languages and Systems (TOOLS Pacific '02)*, pages 53–60, Sydney, Australia, February 2002.

[22] Olaf Spinczyk and Daniel Lohmann. Using AOP to develop architecture-neutral operating system components. In *11th SIGOPS Eur. W'shop*, pages 188–192, Leuven, Belgium, September 2004. ACM.

[23] A. Tešanović, D. Nyström, J. Hansson, and C. Norström. Aspects and components in real-time system development: Towards reconfigurable and reusable software. *Embedded Computing*, February 2004.

[24] A. Tešanović, K. Sheng, and J. Hansson. Application-tailored database systems: a case of aspects in an embedded database. In *8th Int. Database Engineering and Applications Symp. (IDEAS '04)*, Coimbra, Portugal, July 2004. IEEE.

H. Fujita and M. Mejri (Eds.)
IOS Press, 2005

The Collatz Problem in a New Perspective: Energy Consumption Analysis

Kostas ZOTOS, Andreas LITKE, George STEPHANIDES and Alexander CHATZIGEORGIOU
Dept. of Applied Informatics, University of Macedonia,
54006 Thessaloniki, Greece
{zotos, litke, steph, achat} @uom.gr

Abstract. The importance of low power consumption is widely acknowledged due to the increasing use of portable devices, which require minimizing the consumption of energy. Energy dissipation is heavily dependent on the software used in the system. In this paper we analyze the energy consumption of the Collatz Problem and draw some useful conclusions.

Keywords. Analysis of Software Algorithms, Perfomance Evaluation, Software Engineering, Energy Consumption

1. Introduction

The vast majority of microprocessors being produced today are incorporated in embedded systems, which are mainly included in portable devices. The later ones require the lowest power operation achievable, since they rely on batteries for power supply. Furthermore, high power consumption raises other important issues, such as the cost associated with cooling the system, due to the heat generated. A lot of optimization efforts have been made, regarding the hardware used, to decrease power consumption [1]. However, recent research has proved that software is the dominant factor in the power consumption of a computing system [5].

Even though most of Embedded and Realtime programming is now carried out in high level languages, a good understanding of the generated assembly code really helps in debugging, performance analysis and performance tuning. Here we present a description of C++ to assembly translation. We will be analyzing the code generated by a compiler targeting the ARM processor family [7]. The concepts learnt here can easily be applied to understand the generated code for any other processor-compiler combination. We draw some useful conclusions regarding whether the energy consumption is increased with the use of different algorithms.

The rest of the paper is organized as follows: Section 2 provides a general overview of power consumption, while Section 3 explains important issues about the Collatz Problem. In Section 4 we describe the experimental framework setup. Next (Section 5), the results are presented and discussed whereas in the final section (Section 6) some conclusions are drawn.

2. Energy Consumption

In this section, we describe basic elements that characterize the energy consumption in a system. To clarify the reasons why energy consumption of a program varies, it is necessary to name the main sources of power consumption in an embedded system. The system power falls into mainly two categories, each of which is described in the following paragraphs.

2.1. Processor Power

When instructions are fetched, decoded or executed in the processor, the nodes in the underlying CMOS digital circuits switch states. For any computing system, the switching activity associated with the execution of instructions in the processing unit, constitutes the so-called base energy cost. The change in circuit state between consecutive instructions is captured by the the overhead or inter-instruction cost. To calculate total energy, which is dissipated, all that is needed is to sum up all base and overhead costs for a given program.

2.2. Memory Power

We assume that the system architecture consists of two memories, namely the instruction memory and data memory (Harvard architecture). Having presumed that, the energy consumption has to be calculated on a twofold basis, one for each memory. The energy consumption of the instruction memory depends on the code size and on the number of executed instructions that correspond to instruction fetches, whereas that of the data memory depends on the volume of data being processed by the application and on how often the later accesses data.

3. The Collatz Problem

We are trying to implement one very easy, but interesting problem, the Collatz problem, by using different programming techniques. The most interesting thing about this problem is that the algorithm of this problem is not classified for all possible input until now, although it is very simple to state it. This problem is also known as the hailstone problem, 3n+1 problem, Hasse's algorithm, Kakutani's algorithm, syracuse problem, or the Thwaites Conjecture or Ulam's problem. This problem was posed by L. Collatz in 1937.

In their words, it is a very simple problem. Take any number as an input, and divide it by 2 if the number is even, or multiply by 3 and add 1 if the number is odd. The conjecture is that, no matter which no you take as an input, you will come to 1. However, this is still an open problem and no one can prove it until it is true for all values of n, although it has been checked for quite large numbers through a computer. This might be a challenging task for those who want to solve open problems and gain popularity.

Total the numbers of elements in the sequence until it reaches 1, including input number and 1; this is called the cycle of the sequence of that given input number. For example, if user inputs 5, the sequence will be something like this:

5 16 8 4 2 1

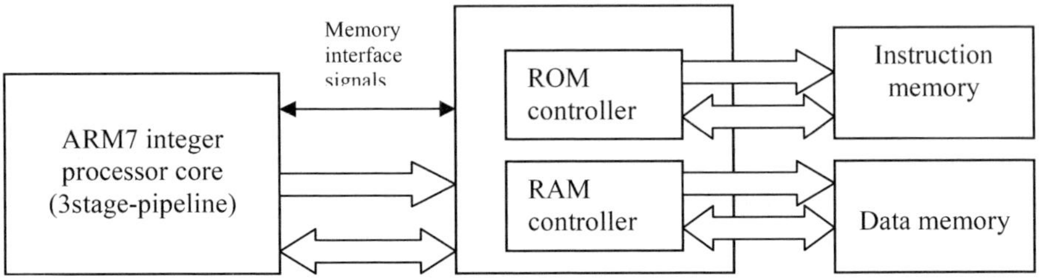

Figure 1. Target Architecture.

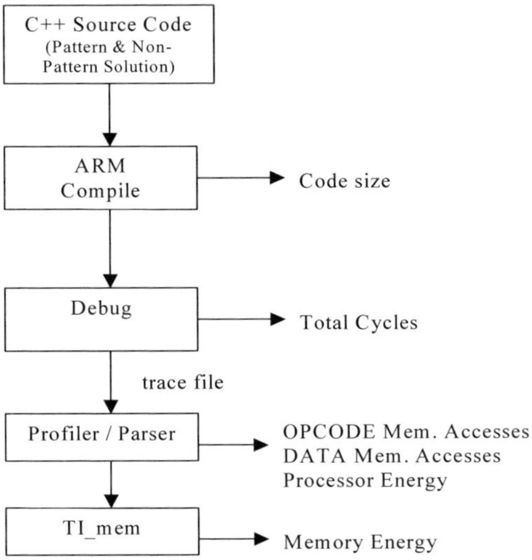

Figure 2. Framework steps.

The cycle of this sequence is 6. This sequence is also called the hailstone sequence. The algorithm to generate this sequence is very simple.

4. Framework Setup

To evaluate the energy cost of software design decisions a generalized target architecture was considered (Fig. 1). It was based on the ARM7 integer processor core [6], which is widely used in embedded applications due to its promising MIPS/mW performance [4]. The process that has been followed during the conduction of the aforementioned experiments (Fig. 2) begins with the compilation of each C++ code with the use of the compiler of the ARM Developer Suite [2]. At this stage, we were able to obtain the code size. Next and after the debugging, a trace file was produced which logged instructions and memory accesses. The debugger provided the total number of cycles. A profiler was specially developed for parsing the trace file serially, in order to measure the memory accesses to the instruction memory (OPCODE accesses) and the memory accesses to the data memory (DATA accesses). The profiler calculated also the dissipated energy (base + interinstruction energy) within the processor core. Fi-

Table 1. Measurement results for different programming styles (Energy measurements in mJ).

Programming style:	*No Structured*	*Structured*	*Recursive*	*OO*	*Generic*
#Cycles	1234	1290	1056	2088	2094
Opcode Mem. Accesses	1063	1260	1044	1692	1692
Data Mem. Accesses	112	18	6	272	284
Processor Energy	0,001283301	0,001228216	0,00107924	0,00216191	0,002194
Instr. mem. Energy	0,003496	0,004146	0,003434	0,005142	0,005139
Data mem. Energy	0,000282	0,000045	0,000015	0,000686	0,000716
Total Energy	0,005061301	0,005419216	0,00452824	0,00798991	0,008049

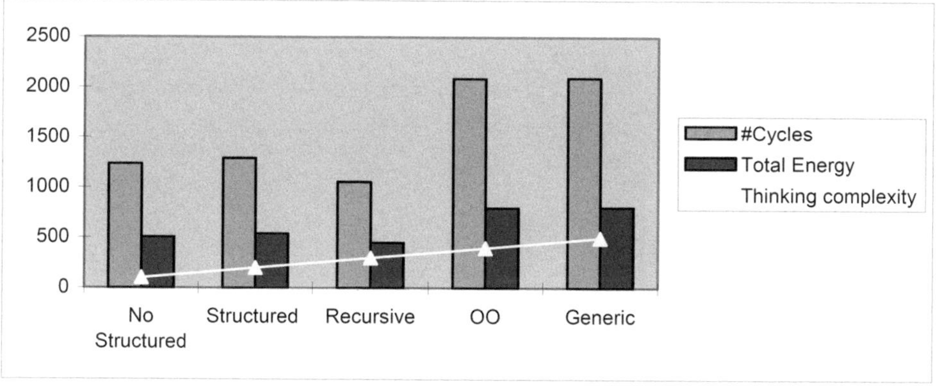

Figure 3. Programming styles versus total energy and cycles.

nally, with the use of an appropriate memory simulator (provided by an industrial vendor), the energy consumed in the data and instruction memories was measured. The results we will present in the following section regard the number of cycles, the OP-CODE Memory Accesses, the DATA Memory Accesses, the energy consumed in the processor, the data memory energy and the instruction memory energy.

5. Solving a Problem

In the following example we examine how energy is altered using different programming techniques. As we realize from the results (Table 1, Fig. 3) the change of the programming technique increases the energy complexity. The following algorithm was posed by L. Collatz in 1937.

5.1. The Algorithm (for 3n+1 Sequence)

A1. [Input n]
A2. [Termination] If n = 1 then exit
A3. [Check number] If n is even then n := n / 2 else n := n * 3 + 1
A4. [Next number] Go to A2.

5.2. No Structured Programming

This is perhaps the first technique of programming the computer, without any procedure or anything else. The most problematic thing about this style is its management and reusability because there is almost no abstraction layer in this style of programming. Therefore, it is quite difficult to handle a large-scale program using this technique.

```
#include <iostream>
using std::cout;
using std::endl;

int main(int argc, char* argv[])
{  int iCount = 1;
   int iNo    = 22;
   int iTemp  = iNo;
   while (iTemp != 1)
   {
      // if number is even
      if (iTemp % 2 == 0)
      {  iTemp /= 2;  }
      // if number is odd
      else
      { iTemp = iTemp * 3 + 1; }
      ++iCount;
   }
   cout << "Cycle length of " << iNo << " is " << iCount << endl;
  return 0;
}
```

5.3. Structured Programming

We can break down the program into small modules (functions), so it will become more manageable and more reusable than the non-structured version. Logically, one function of the program should do the unit work of the algorithm, but it is quite subjective to describe the unit work. This programming style will increase the abstraction level by dividing the problem into small pieces and solving those pieces one by one.

```
int NextTerm(int iNo)
{ if (iNo % 2 == 0)
   {
      iNo /= 2;
   }
    else
   {
      iNo = iNo * 3 + 1;
   }
   return iNo;
}

int CalculateCycle(int iNo)
{  int iCount = 1;
   while (iNo != 1)
```

```
   {
      iNo = NextTerm(iNo);
      ++iCount;
   }
   return iCount;
}

int main(int argc, char* argv[])
{  const int iNo = 22;
   cout << "Cycle length  of " << iNo << " is "<<
CalculateCycle(iNo) << endl;
   return 0;
}
```

5.4. Recursive Programming

This is a simple example of recursion. In other words, a more typical definition may be something like this: "Recursion is a way to specify a process by repeating a means of itself." In programming language context, recursion means a function that calls itself. Typical examples of recursion are factorial, Fibonacci number, Tower of Hanoi, and so forth.

```
int CalculateCycle(int iNo, int iCount)
{  ++iCount;
   if (iNo == 1)
   { return iCount; }
   else
   { if (iNo % 2 == 0)
      {
         iNo /= 2;
         iCount = CalculateCycle(iNo, iCount);
      }
      else
      {
         iNo = iNo * 3+ 1;
         iCount = CalculateCycle(iNo, iCount);
      }
   }
   return iCount;
}

int main(int argc, char* argv[])
{  const int iNo = 22;
   cout << "Cycle length of " << iNo << " is = "<<
CalculateCycle(iNo, 0) << endl;
   return 0;
}
```

5.5. Object-Oriented Programming

Object-oriented programming is a programming style in which you make classes and create instances of those classes, called objects. Technically, a class is a prototype that defines the variables and methods of one kind. This problem is very small, so that you can not get the full advantage of object-oriented programming. This program is technically object based but not object oriented.

```
class Collatz
{
private:
   int m_iCycle;
   int m_iNo;
   int NextTerm(int p_iNo);
public:
   Collatz(int p_iNo = 0);
   void CalculateCycle();
   int GetCycle() const;
};

Collatz::Collatz(int p_iNo) : m_iNo(p_iNo), m_iCycle(1)
{  if (m_iNo < 1)
      throw std::out_of_range("Number should be greater than 0");
}

int Collatz::NextTerm(int p_iNo)
{ if (p_iNo % 2 == 0)
   {
      p_iNo /= 2;
   }
   else
   {
      p_iNo = p_iNo * 3 + 1;
   }
   return p_iNo;
}

void Collatz::CalculateCycle()
{ while (m_iNo != 1)
   {
      m_iNo = NextTerm(m_iNo);
      ++m_iCycle;
   }
}

int Collatz::GetCycle() const
{return m_iCycle;}

int main(int argc, char* argv[])
{ const int iNo = 22;
  try
   {
      Collatz objCollatz(iNo);
      objCollatz.CalculateCycle();
      cout << "Cycle length of "<< iNo << " is "<<
objCollatz.GetCycle() << endl;
   }
   catch(std::out_of_range& ex)
   {
      cout << ex.what() << endl;
```

```
    }
    return 0;
}
```

5.6. Generic Programming

Generic means general or common. Technically, generic programming refers to a program written in such a way that it should work independent of data type. A generic program should work on all data types that satisfy the required concepts use in the program. In C++, a template is used for generic programming.

```
template <typename T>
class Collatz
{
private:
    T m_iCycle;
    T m_iNo;
    int NextTerm(T p_iNo);
public:
    Collatz(T p_iNo = 0);
    void CalculateCycle();
    T GetCycle() const;
};

template <typename T>
Collatz<T>::Collatz(T p_iNo)  : m_iNo(p_iNo), m_iCycle(1)
{   if (m_iNo < 1)
        throw std::out_of_range("Number should be greater than 0");
}
template <typename T>
int Collatz<T>::NextTerm(T p_iNo)
{   if (p_iNo % 2 == 0)
    { p_iNo /= 2; }
    else
    { p_iNo = p_iNo * 3 + 1; }
  return p_iNo;
}

template <typename T>
void Collatz<T>::CalculateCycle()
{  while (m_iNo != 1)
   {  m_iNo = NextTerm(m_iNo);
      ++m_iCycle;
   }
}

template <typename T>
T Collatz<T>::GetCycle() const
{ return m_iCycle; }

int main(int argc, char* argv[])
{ const int iNo = 22;
   try
   {  Collatz<int> objCollatz(iNo);
```

```
      objCollatz.CalculateCycle();
      cout << "Cycle length of " << iNo << " is "<<
objCollatz.GetCycle() << endl;
   }
   catch(std::out_of_range& ex)
  {  cout << ex.what() << endl; }
    return 0;
}
```

5.7. Template Metaprogramming

In this programming style, we use the compiler to do the program's work for us. In other words, it is something like writing a program about a program. In template metaprogramming, we use a C++ compiler as an interpreter; the compiler expands the template and generates the code, which can be executed at run time by the compiled code. Execution speed of this program is very fast because the compiler has already resolved it at compile time. Nothing comes without price, and here the price is compilation time. Compilation time of the program may increase drastically; the length of times depends on the nature of the algorithm implemented by using this technique.

```
template<int N>
class CalculateCycle
{public:
   enum { count = CalculateCycle&< N % 2 ? (N * 3 + 1) : (N / 2)
>::count + 1 };
};

template <>
class CalculateCycle<1>
{public:
   enum { count = 1 };
};

int main(int argc, char* argv[])
{  const int iNo = 22;
   cout << "Cycle length of " << iNo << " is = "<<
CalculateCycle<iNo>::count << endl;
  return 0;
}
```

6. Conclusions

The power consumption of an embedded system depends heavily on the executing code. The necessity to consider low energy consumption arises from the wide use of portable devices, which obviously require low power operation. In this paper, we have explored the energy consumed using the example of the Collage problem. We have observed that function calling causes high energy consumption. However, further research is required in order to investigate accurately the degree of this effect.

References

[1] Chandrakasan, A., and R. Brodersen, "Low Power Digital CMOS Design", Kluwer Academic Publishers, Boston, 1995.

[2] Chatzigeorgiou, A., D. Andreou, and S. Nikolaidis, Description of the software power estimation framework, IST-2000-30093/EASY Project, Deliverable 24, February 2003, URL: http://electronics.physics.auth.gr/easy.

[3] Deitel, H.M., and P.J. Deitel, "C++: How to Program", Prentice Hall, Upper Saddle River, 2001.

[4] Furber, S., "ARM System-on-Chip Architecture", Addison-Wesley, Harlow, UK, 2000.

[5] Tiwari, V., S. Malik, and A. Wolfe, *Power Analysis of Embedded Software: A First Step Towards Software Power Minimization*, IEEE Transactions on VLSI Systems, vol. 2 (1994), 437–445.

[6] http://www.arm.com/armtech/ARM7TDMI?OpenDocument.

Chapter 2

Legacy Systems and Language Conversions

New Trends in Software Methodologies, Tools and Techniques
H. Fujita and M. Mejri (Eds.)
IOS Press, 2005

Suggestions of Lyee: A Framework on Software Methodological Thinking

Fumio NEGORO
ISD Institute, 3-11-3 Takanawa, Minato-ku, Tokyo 108-0074 Japan
E-mail: f-negoro@lyee.jp

Abstract. This study considers our thinking is comprised of the set of something. Something in this study is cited as existences resident in our mind. This study considers the existences can be defined by certain rules. What are they? In this study, they are what cannot be negated, nor affirmed. The rules are introduced to the limits of our thinking, by using Whole, Part, Static, Dynamic, Synchronous, Asynchronous, Memory, Assimilation, Awareness and Mind, as axiom. In this study, these concepts are defined but their rationality cannot be verified by humans. This study proposes a hypothesis of the world comprised of such rules. By the rules of this world, how Software is introduced by human intelligence is observed theoretically.

"Lyee" is meant to be this theoretical axiomatic observation. With this theoretical observation, we expect a new awareness of software is established.

With this effect, for example, we can obtain universal algorithm independent of programming languages and programs. With this algorithm, we can realize automatic programming language conversion and program's diagnosis.

In this paper, a theoretical observation of Lyee is proposed. Other rules and examples of concrete cases not discussed herein can be referred to other papers.

1. Awareness of Software

This study considers the being of internal and external existences can be defined by awareness. Awareness itself is 'internal existences'. For example, an apple on the table – this is an external existence. Awareness recognizes it. With this awareness, it becomes an internal existence. Which is the first to come? Lyee considers an internal exis-tence as the first, in principle. For more details on Lyee please refer to http://www.lyee-project.soft.iwate-pu.ac.jp/ and http://www.lyee.jp/.

1.1. Rules

This study considers the rules suggest the natural providence that we cannot be aware of. It is hypothesized that our thinking establishes awareness with the influence of the rules.

The following descriptions with three-digit serial numbers mean the rules in this study.

001: Closing feature is an action to determine the contour of existence.
002: Dividing feature is to divide existence into parts.

003: The closing feature shall not derive a boundary problem among divided units that were caused by the division.
004: Objectifying feature is to conclude awareness.
005: Efficiency feature is an intent to perform all above features optimally.
006: No-error feature is to obey the rules.

We, humans, cannot satisfy all above rules. Counter reactions caused by the contradiction of such awareness produce all kinds of the thing to solve humanly.

007: Static feature is an anch-llogical mode.
008: Dynamic feature is a collection of static features.
009: Dynamic feature (= Attribute) is a shadow of static feature (= Substance).
010: The set (= Attribute) is also a shadow of the element of the set (=Substance).
011: Dynamic feature becomes a logical mode.

In this study, an equation, for example, is an anch-llogical mode and its meaning is a logical mode. That is, an equation is a static feature and the meaning of the equation is a dynamic feature. The equation reflects a certain meaning but it is not the same as the deep meaning itself. Therefore, the equation cannot become a real entity, although it is a static feature (= Substance).

012: Awareness is a dynamic feature.
013: The structure is the rule that puts a dynamic feature closer to a static feature.

Buildings, equation, writing, etc. are all Attributes (not Substance). But, they are the means to approach to the substance, which are a static feature that has a real meaning. That is, it is a universal existence. To recognized substance is what we desire.

Is the discussion likewise useful for software and us?

1.2. Static and Dynamic Features of Programs

This study considers that, if we can match the static and dynamic features of the same existence, it can grasp the existence closest to the Substance of the existence that cannot be grasped usually. This is one of the important theoretical observations of this study.

014: Dynamic feature is a track of a static feature.

In order to confirm the meaning of the structure of programs and the meaning of its dynamic feature, programs are defined respectively by the traditional structure and the structure of this study with the same requirements. And their dynamic features are obtained by using the exclusive program (referential document 1). Results are shown in Fig. 1. The left side of Fig. 1 is the dynamic feature of program of the traditional method.

Particles in the Fig are the unitized functions of the program. The linear pattern in the background is a track of the program's EXECUTE statements that execute those functions. If the particles of unitized functions are expressed in gray shaded pattern on Fig. 1 (for more details on Lyee please refer to http://www.lyee.jp/), this pattern looks

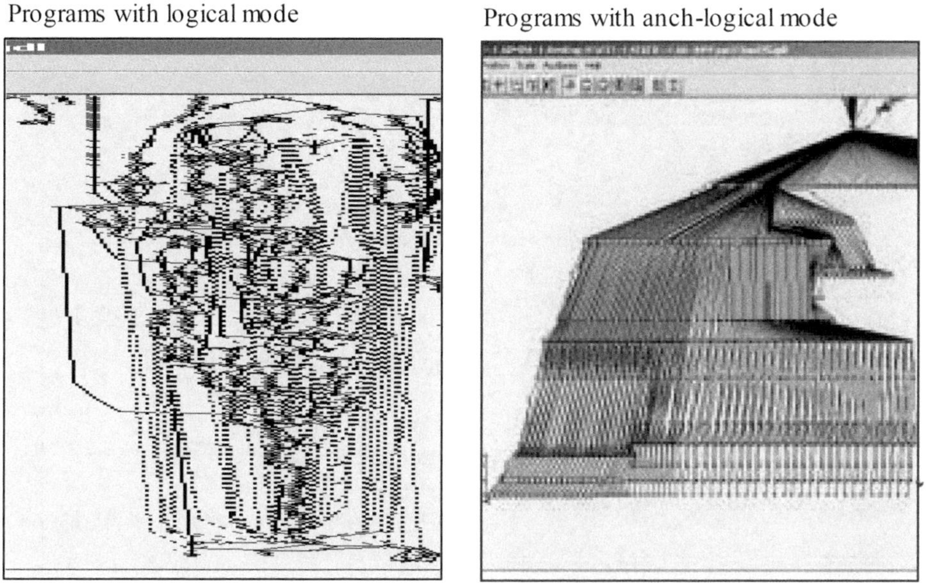

Analysis of program by SamCOTS (Static Analyser of Malicious COTS) Laval University

Figure 1. Example of the dynamic feature of programs.

like the shape of corn, for example. This is the common shape appearing with programs of the traditional method.

The right side of the Fig. 1 is the dynamic feature of the structure of this study. It is obvious that it is different from the pattern of the traditional method. The structure of this study feature looks like the shape of comb, for example. With the structure of the traditional program, both the static feature and the dynamic feature take the same logical mode of thinking. For more details on this analysis please refere to the document on reference 1. The details on Fig. 1 is also given in better quality at reference [1].

But, in contrast, the static feature and the dynamic feature of the structure of this study do not tale the same logical mode. The dynamic feature of the structure of this study becomes a shape of comb and expresses the appearance of the static feature without limits. The meaning of the dynamic feature's approaching to the static feature unlimitedly is the existence of this program is closer to the Substance unlimitedly.

Impossible with the traditional thinking, but as obvious from the Fig. 1, a thinking of this study is trying to grasp Substance. It looks to grasp the essence of software more deeply. Is the right? It suggests an entirely new thinking approach to software, doesn't it?

2. System of Application Concept

The system of the concepts introduced from this study is shown in Fig. 2. In this chapter, each of the concepts is discussed. By using these concepts, a new knowledge of software can be obtained. That knowledge can be used to obtain approaches for solving the problems related to software.

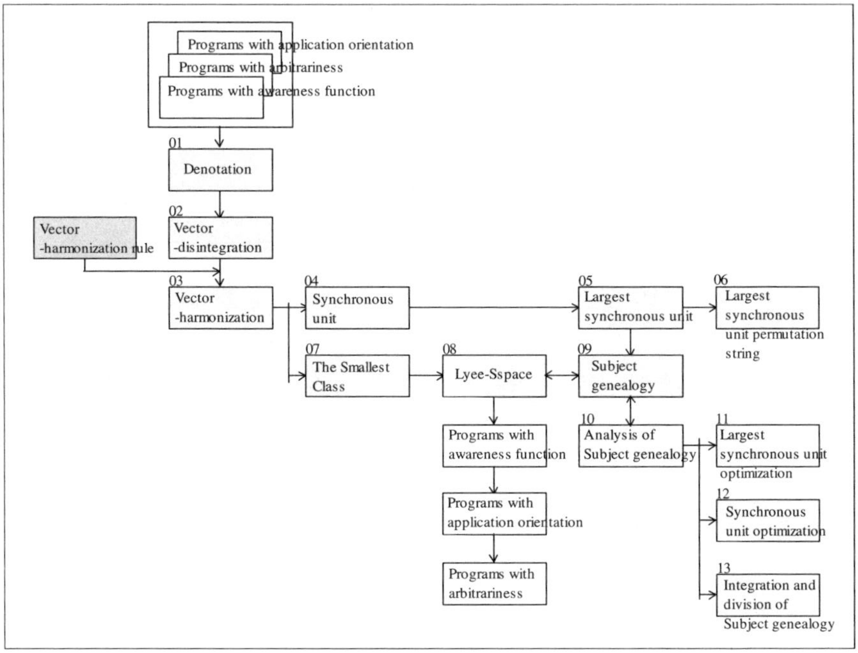

Figure 2. System of application concept.

2.1. Vector

With this study, a structure that materializes awareness is observed theoretically. In this paper details are omitted but the structure to be obtained is named 'Vector'.

015: The Vector is defined based on Subject.
016: The Subject belongs to Requirement or programs.

The relationship of the classification of Vector's Subjects and the Vector classification is shown in Table 1, the kinds of Vector in Table 2, and the concept of Subject and the classification in Table 3.

017: The role of Vector is to determine predication of the definition of Subject. In other words, the predication of Requirements or programs is divided and classified in accordance with the predicate structure.

This study considers programs become a set of the ordering set of Subjects. Statically, programs are a set of Subjects. The structure to predicate Subjects concludes to a universal structure, regardless of the classification of Subject. The traditional method doesn't use the concept of Subject.

018: Vectors possess static and dynamic features.
019: The classification of Vector shows 17 kinds and it expands to 23 kinds. The definition rules of the 23 kinds are referred to other papers, if interested.

Table 1. Relationship of Vectors' Subject classification and Vector classification.

No.	Classification of Subjects	Classification of Vectors																
		L2	L3	L4	I2	O4	SI2	SO4	SL2	SL3	SL4	R4	R2	R3R	R3E	R3C	R3D	R3M
1	Normal		O	O						O	O							
2	Boundary	O	O	O					O	O	O							
3	INPUT	O							O									
4	INPUT logical unit				O		O											
5	OUTPUT logical unit					O		O										
6	Coordinates Yi											O						
7	Coordinates Xi												O					
8	Coordinates Zi													O	O	O	O	O

Table 2. Relationship of Vector classification and coordinates of Existence.

No.	Classification	Coordinates of the existence of Vectors			Names of Vectors		Definition
		Yi	Xi	Zi			
1	L2		O		Siginification Vectors		To set Noun information defined by I2 or the preset value into the process area.
2	L3			O			To define conditions of Subject to materialize.
3	L4	O					To materialize the Subject area.
4	I2		O		INPUT Vectors		To intake INPUT information into the process area.
5	O4	O			OUTPUT Vectors		To output OUTPUT information.
6	SI2	O	O		Structural Vectors		To initialize I2's Subject area.
7	SO4	O					To initialize O4's Subject area.
8	SL2	O					To initialize L2's Subject area.
9	SL3	O					To initialize L3's Subject area.
10	SL4	O					To initialize L4's Subject area.
11	R4	O			Connection Vectors	CONTINUE	To connect coordinates Yi and Xi.
12	R2		O			CONTINUE	To connect coordinates Xi and Zi.
13	R3R			O		REBOOT	To connect coordinates Zi and Yi.
14	R3E			O		END	END of coordinates function.
15	R3C			O		CONTINUE	To connect coordinates Zi and neighbored lower Yi.
16	R3D			O		MULTIPLEX	To connect coordinates Zi and neighbored upper Zi.
17	R3M			O		DUPLICATE	To Connect Zi and neighbored-neighbored upper Yi.

Table 3. Relationship of Subjects.

No.	World of software		World of TDM
	Subjects	Definition of Subjects	
1	Normal	1. Nouns used by other Vectors 2. Nouns possessing the different 2nd protocol (equivalent)	Subjects of PS3 and PS4
2	Boundary	1. Nouns not belonging to I2's Subjects 2. Nouns not belonging to O4's Subjects 3. Nouns to become Subjects of L-12	Subjects of PS-12
3	INPUT	1. Nouns belonging to I2's Subjects 2. Nouns possessing preset value	Subjects of PS2
4	INPUT logical unit	1. Nouns possessing INPUT attribute	A set of actual Harmonize Links belonging to a partial set of Harmonize Structure
5	OUTPUT logical unit	1. Nouns possessing OUTPUT attribute	A set of actual Harmonize Links belonging to a partial set of Harmonize Structure
6	Coordinates Yi	NONE	1. An action to remove Harmonize Links materializing assimilation that belongs to Harmonize Structure. 2. An action to wave to Coordinates Function and Consciousness Function.
7	Coordinates Xi	NONE	
8	Coordinates Zi	NONE	

2.2. SF (Scenario Function)

This study observes structure to grasp awareness. In this paper details are omitted but the structure to be obtained is named 'SF'. Refer to Fig. 3.

020: Vectors belong to Coordinates of SF.
021: Coordinates of SF is shown by X, Y and Z.
022: Both static and dynamic features co-exist in SF.
023: If a static feature resides in a dynamic feature, that dynamic state possesses synchronicity.
024: If static and dynamic features can be defined by the same structure, the structure possesses synchronicity.

The structure of Vector is the case that is the closest to this rule. The discovery of this structure is one of the most featured outcomes of this study.

025: If static and dynamic features can be defined by the same structure, the structure doesn't possess synchronicity.
026: Because of the effect of Vector, SF possesses synchronicity unlimitedly.

Why is synchronicity in thinking so important? We cannot be aware of the static existence (Substance) as our fate. So, we obtain an existence in which our alternative awareness can be attained. However, that existence always concludes to what possesses the dynamic feature. Consequently, we behave to obtain synchronicity in existence. It is though insufficient, a countermeasure to cope with rules 001–006. [Refer to Fig. 1.]

027: The static feature of Vector jointly works with the static feature of SF.
028: The dynamic feature of Vector jointly works with the dynamic feature of SF.

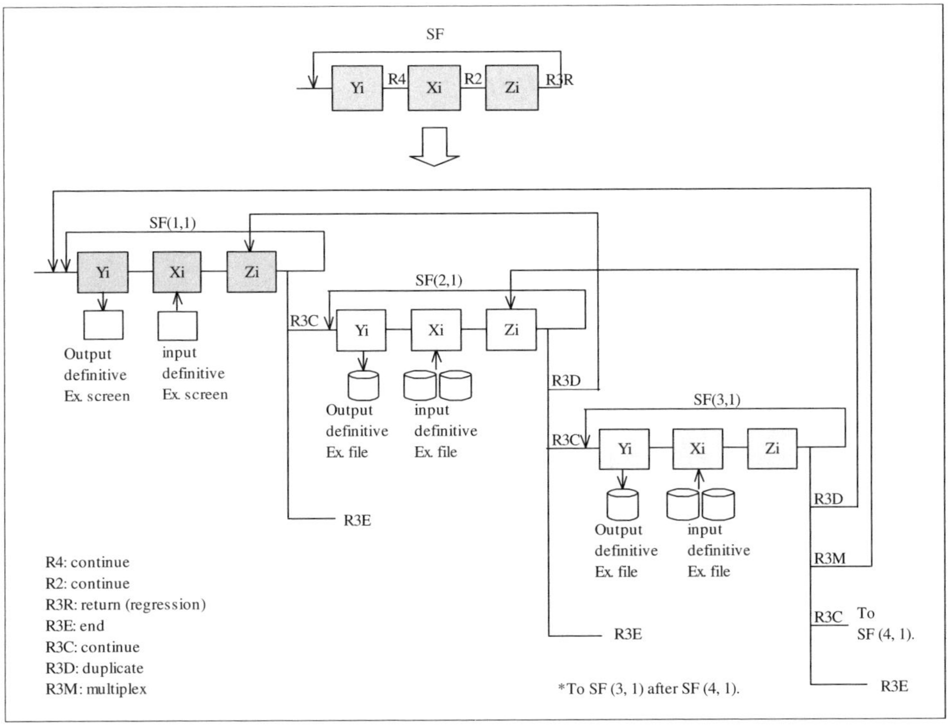

Figure 3. SF (Scenario Function).

029: Subject is defined by the static feature of Vector.
030: Subject is materialized by the dynamic feature of Vector.
031: Vector can be extracted from the static feature of programs.
032: Programs possess both dynamic and static features.
033: Dynamic and static features of programs are asynchronous.
034: The dynamic feature of programs and the dynamic feature of SF are asynchronous.

SF is defined functionally. The type diagram is shown in Fig. 2. Details can be referred to other papers mentioned on the web site [2].

2.3. Requirements

Rules regarding the conceptual meaning of Requirement on this study are listed below.

035: Requirements are awareness or a set of awareness.
036: Whole is a static feature
037: Part is a dynamic feature.
038: A partial set consisted of existences of the dynamic feature is a dynamic feature.
039: The whole set consisted of existences of the dynamic feature is a dynamic feature.
040: The rule to claim Part as whole is a closing feature.
041: The closing feature is the rule to change a dynamic feature to a static feature.

042: The rule to express Part and the dynamic feature is an opening feature.
043: Requirements is an opening feature.
044: The boundary of Parts becomes Part.
045: Our memory is awareness with the closing feature. It is called Knowledge.
046: Knowledge possesses the dynamic feature.
047: Requirements cannot be materialized by Knowledge only.
048: Requirements possesses both the opening and closing features.

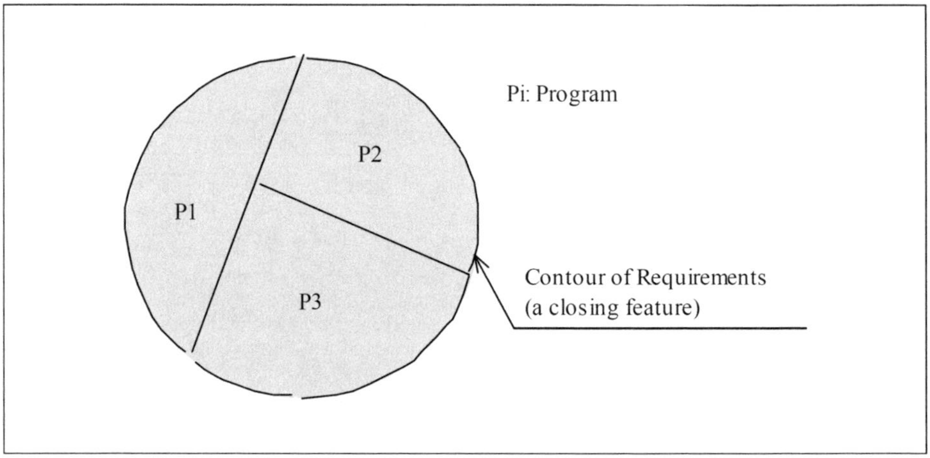

Figure 4. Impression of program's Requirements.

2.3.1. Nature of Requirements

Refer to Fig. 5.

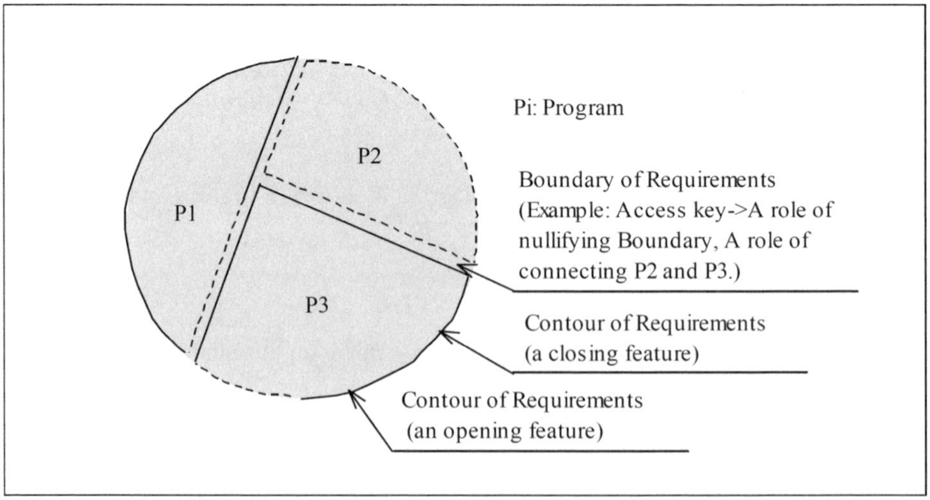

Figure 5. Nature of Requirements.

049: Requirements are Part.
050: The Part is a set of Parts.

051: Requirements is a set of Parts.
052: There is a boundary between neighboring Parts.
053: The Boundary is Part.
054: Part is a dynamic feature.
055: Access keys assume a role to define the Boundary.

2.3.2. Relationship of Requirements and SF

056: Requirements can be divided into plural SFs.
057: Requirements and SF jointly work.
058: SF can be divided.

Refer to Fig. 6.

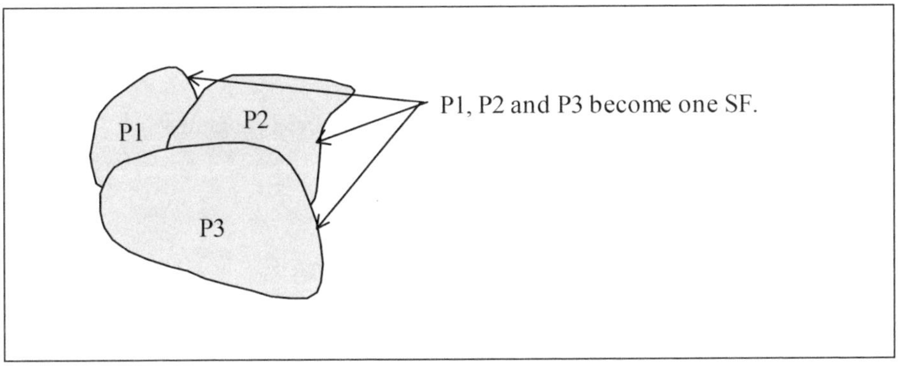

Figure 6. Relationship of Requirements and SF.

2.4. Programming Languages

Programming languages are discussed from the viewpoint of this study, conceptually based on the below rules definitions:

059: Vectors, Subjects and SF can be defined by the programming language.
060: Source statements of programming languages (Protocol Statements, hereinafter) can be classified into 7 kinds as below:
- *a. Remarks statement*
- *b. Directive statement*
  The Directive statement, herein said, belongs to programming languages and issues direction to compiler.
- *c. Area definition statement*
- *d. EXECUTE command statement*
- *e. CONTROL statement*
  Loop statement, for example.
- *f. IO statement*
  READ, WRITE and SQL statements, for example.
- *g. CALL statement*

A command statement to activate a program not existing in the related program, for example.

061: Terms used in compiler are called Reserved terms.

062: There are following modes of the structure of one protocol statement.

a. One protocol statement is comprised of one start reserved term and one end reserved term.

b. One protocol statement is comprised of plural start reserved terms and one end reserved term.

063: Other terms than the start reserved term and the end reserved term belong to one protocol statement.

064: One or more area names belong to one protocol statement.

065: There is a protocol statement of area name not belonging to .

066: Area names are not reserved terms.

067: The Area name becomes Subject of Vector.

2.5. Synchronization

Herein discussed is the method to obtain Synchronicity from programs.

2.5.1. Denotation

068: Programs become a set comprised of Denotations.

069: Denotation is the smallest functional unit in the program.

070: Denotation is a closing feature.

For example, the range of CONTROL statements are an example of Denotation.

071: Protocol statements belonging to Denotation can be replaced by one or more Vectors. This is called Vector-disintegration of Denotation.

2.5.2. Harmonization

Herein, the harmonization of Vector is discussed. Please refer to Fig. 7.

072: Vector has a nature of closing Requirements.

073: With Vectors, the Vector-harmonization is established.

074: Programs without the Vector-harmonization possess flaws.

075: By adding new Vectors, the program can be closed.

Details of the Vector-harmonization are discussed below.

076: Nouns belonging to I2's Subject become Subject of L2.

077: There are L2's Subjects that materialize with a static feature.

078: Subjects of L3 and L4 always form a pair.

079: If L3 of the same Subject as L4 does not exist, L3 of the different Subject fulfills its substitute.

080: Nouns belonging to Subject of O4 become Subject of L3 and L4.

081: With Subjects of L3 and L4, there are Nouns not belonging to Subject of O4.

082: There are Subjects common to L2, L3 and L4.

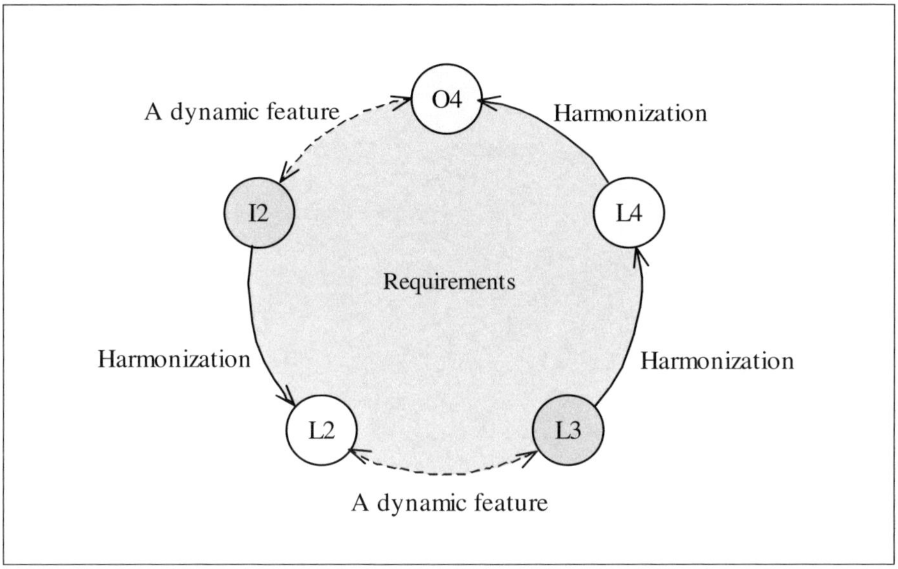

Figure 7. Relationship of Requirements and Vectors.

083: There is O4 that materializes I2.
084: There is I2 that materializes O4.
085: Harmonization between Subjects of I2 and O4 is indefinite.
086: Against one O4, I2 becomes one or more.
087: Against more than one O4, I2 becomes more than one.
088: The harmonization of Subjects of L2 and L4 is indefinite.
089: The harmonization of Subjects of O4 and I2 is indefinite.

Fig. 7 shows the limits of the closing feature by the Vector-harmonization.

2.5.3. Structural Vectors

Refer to Fig. 8. The definition of Structural Vectors can be referred to Table 2.

090: Structural Vectors are Vectors that complement the Vector harmonization feature.
091: Structural Vectors assume a role to put the opening to the closing of Requirements occurring between L2 and L3.

2.5.4. Connection Vectors

Refer to Fig. 8. The definition of Connection Vectors can be referred to Table 2.

092: Connection Vectors are Vectors that complement the Vector harmonization feature.
093: Connection Vectors assume a role to put the opening to the closing of Requirements occurring between I2 and O4.

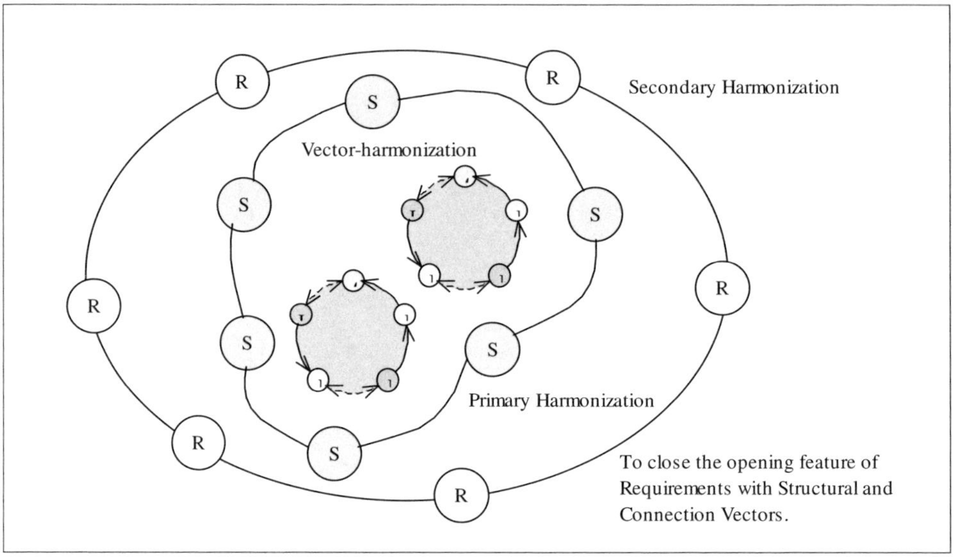

Figure 8. Harmonizing structure of Requirements.

2.5.5. Synchronous Unit

094: The synchronous unit of programs means a Protocol statement string to materialize OUTPUT command that is fetched from the program.

095: With the program, synchronous units with the same number of OUTPUT commands belonging to the program materialize.

096: The synchronous unit expresses the closing feature of Requirements.

2.5.6. Largest Synchronous Unit

097: The largest synchronous unit of programs means the largest Protocol statement string to materialize OUTPUT command that is fetched from the program.

098: With the program, the largest synchronous units with the same number of synchronous units materialize.

099: The largest synchronous unit expresses the closing feature of Requirements.

100: One largest synchronous unit jointly works with one SF.

2.5.7. Coordinates of the Largest Synchronous Unit

101: The synchronous unit belonging to the largest synchronous unit becomes the factor to determine coordinates of the largest synchronous unit.

102: SF possesses coordinates.

103: By using the coordinates, SF expresses a static structure that jointly works with programs. This structure is shown as SF.

2.5.8. The Smallest Class

Refer to Fig. 9.

<table>
<tr><th colspan="13">A definition standard of the smallest class</th></tr>
<tr><th rowspan="2">Typeof Vector</th><th colspan="2">Vector</th><th rowspan="2">Noun</th><th colspan="4">Data attribute of Noun</th><th rowspan="2">Subject</th><th rowspan="2">Cllassification of Subject</th><th colspan="3">Coordinates of Subject</th></tr>
<tr><th>The 2nd rule</th><th>The 4th rule</th><th>2nd</th><th>4th</th><th>6th</th><th>7th</th><th>X</th><th>Y</th><th>Z(n)</th></tr>
</table>

Figure 9. The Smallest Class.

104: This is the structure to make Protocol statement belonging to protocol statement independent.

105: Information defined by Vectors and their coordinates is called the Smallest Class.

2.5.9. Lyee-Space

106: Lyee-Space is a set of the Smallest Classes belonging to programs.

107: Lyee-Space is created from the program source.

108: Programs can be edited from Lyee-Space.

2.5.10. Genealogy of Subjects

Refer to Fig. 10.

<table>
<tr><td rowspan="4">First Subject</td><td rowspan="4">Typeof Vector</td><td rowspan="4">The 2nd rule</td><td rowspan="2">Noun</td><td rowspan="2">X coordinate of Noun</td><td colspan="2">Data attribute of Noun</td><td colspan="2">Data attribute of Subject</td><td rowspan="2">Subject</td><td rowspan="2">Cllassification of Subject</td><td colspan="3">Coordinates of Subject</td></tr>
<tr><td>2nd</td><td>4th</td><td>2nd</td><td>4th</td><td>X</td><td>Y</td><td>Z(n)</td></tr>
<tr><td rowspan="2">Noun</td><td rowspan="2">X coordinate of Noun</td><td colspan="2">Data attribute of Noun</td><td colspan="3">Coordinates of L3</td><td colspan="4" rowspan="2">Noun is a input subject?</td></tr>
<tr><td>2nd</td><td>4th</td><td>X</td><td>Y</td><td>Z(n)</td></tr>
</table>

Figure 10. Elements of the genealogy of Subjects.

109: The Subject genealogy is created from Lyee-Space.

110: The Subject genealogy is the context range which is defined by tracking down reversibly on Lyee-Space from Subject 1 (Noun belonging to OUTPUT command-Subject) to Subject 2 (Noun(s) belonging to INPUT command-Subject).

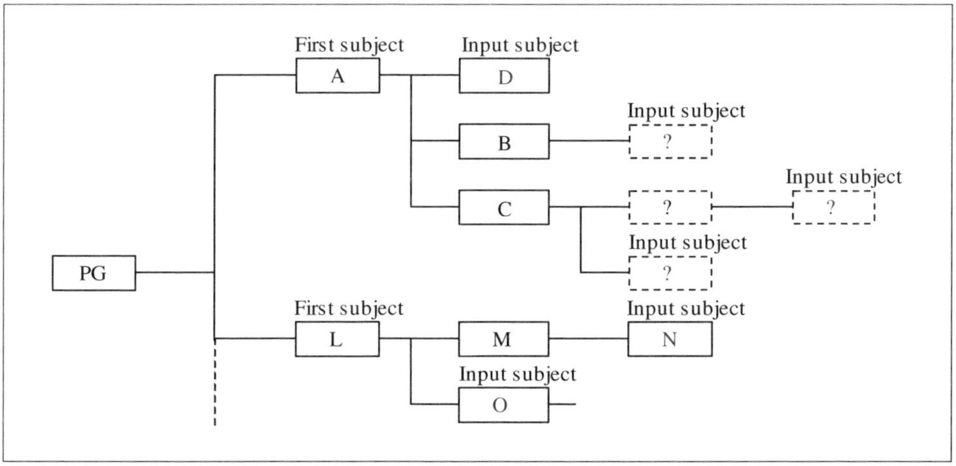

Figure 11. A conception of Subject genealogy.

111: The Subject genealogy is the ordering set comprised of Subjects.

112: With the Subject genealogy, the closing feature materializes.

113: The OUTPUT Subject means Subjects that belongs to O4's Subject and become L4's Subject.

114: The INPUT Subject means Subject that belongs to O4's Subject and become L4's Subject.

115: The pre-set value on the program source that becomes L2's Subject is INPUT Subject.

116: If the closing feature is not established in the Subject genealogy, the program source that causes its Lyee-Space has flaws with itself. The program source with flaws does not become an object for this theoretical observation.

117: The Subject genealogy is a unit of synchronization.

Example of Subject genealogy: Refer to Fig. 11 and Fig. 12.

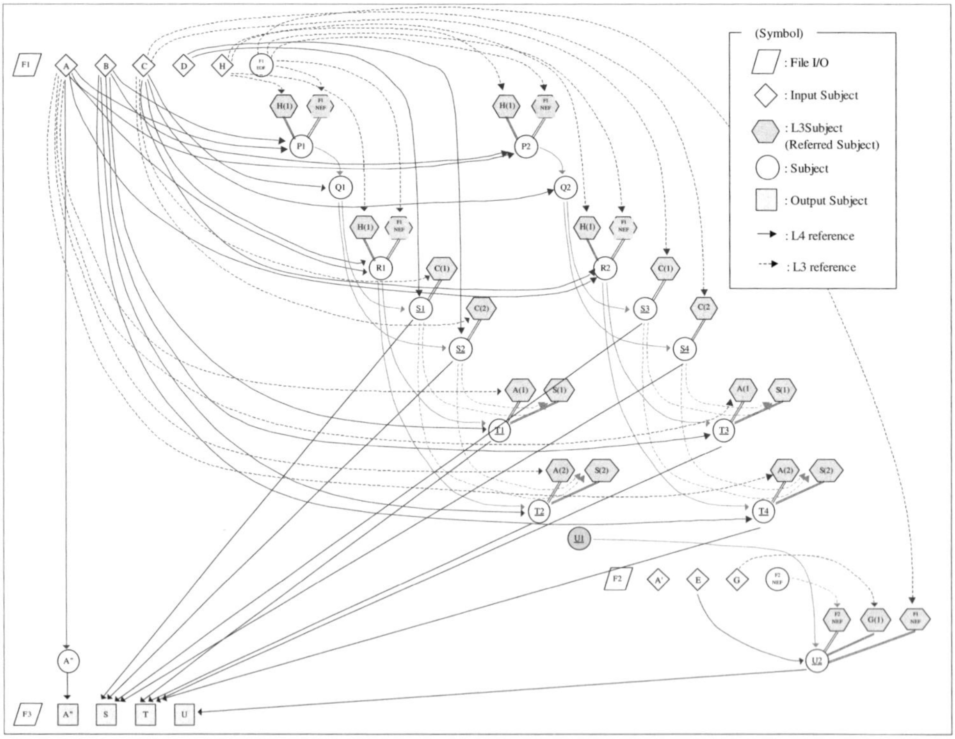

Figure 12. A type of Subject genealogy.

118: If the same Subject, even one piece, co-exists in plural Subject genealogies that are obtained from the same Lyee-Space, those Subject genealogies can be integrated. The Subject genealogy before integration is called Simple Genealogy, and the integrated Subject genealogy is called Integrated Genealogy.

119: The Simple Genealogy cannot be divided.

120: The number of the Simple Subject genealogy to materialize is the number of OUTPUT Subjects belonging to the origin Lyee-Space.
121: With the Simple Genealogy and the Integrated Genealogy, the number of Subjects and the number of context lines belonging thereto respectively can be minimized. This is called the optimized structure of the Subject genealogy. Lyee-Space can be redefined from the Subject genealogy with the optimized structure, and a source program can be obtained from that Lyee-Space. It is an optimized software.
122: The Simple Subject Genealogy is equivalent to SF.
123: The complex Subject genealogy is a set of SFs.
124: The set of SFs becomes the ordering set. The ordering set of SFs is called PRD.

2.5.11. Analysis of Subject Genealogy

The analysis of the Subject genealogy means the algorithm to discover logical FALSE resident in the program source.

125: The logical closing feature means the logical TRUE.
126: If the factor to negate the closing feature of the ordering set belongs to that set, the factor is an error.
127: If the logical closing feature is negated by the error, the logical closing feature becomes the logical opening feature.
128: The logical opening feature means logical FALSE.
129: We define Requirements we are aware of as TRUE and, on that basis, define program source we are aware of as TRUE. To define Requirements means to put dynamic awareness to be a static feature. To define program source means to put the dynamic feature of Requirements to be a static feature.
130: Requirements are an origin to define program source.
131: Requirements to be defined and program source to be defined are not the same existence.
132: In the program source to be defined, logical FALSE is resident, which surpasses the awareness of Requirements that become its origin.

3. Conclusion

The theme of this study can be positioned as a theoretical observation to obtain software's third-party recognizing method. This paper is a part of it. In this study, software can be positioned to be an existence resident in us. To that effect, a rule called the law is hypothesized, and by using the system of the rule, the being of the existence of programs we intend can be discussed. This paper presents the concept of it.

With this study, the law can choose definitions that are impossible to demonstrate or are unable to negate. And, by using that system, programs are placed in that world and the being of the existence of programs is observed by that law.

If the collection of the matters that can be demonstrated is called a scientific world, the being of this recognizing method cannot be called scientific. However, if the law cited by this study cannot be negated, the world of this study might be positioned to be the imaginary number versus the real number. As the role of the imaginary number demonstrates and along with the time the research of this study will deepen, it may be able to form an order enabling this world can communicate with the scientific world.

With the essence of software, many a phenomenon can be seen which foretell matters that cannot be grasped by the view to date. The outcome of this study has already contributed to the actual society. With this fact as a theoretical foothold, the deepened study and the clue to another look at the present software are the additional theme in the future. Separate from the merits and demerits of our world ruled by information processing machinery, to handle software as science is an important matter to achieve.

Acknowledgment

I am thankful to Wittgenstein, Spinoza and Masani, whose thinking modes have given important suggestions on this work.

The Lyee program was visualized by the analysis system (Sam COTS), which was developed at the Laval University, Quebec, Canada. A sincere gratitude is expressed to those who undertook such development.

References

[1] Analysis of program by SamCOTS (Static Analyser of Malicious COTS) Laval University. http://www.lyee-project.soft.iwate-pu.ac.jp/en/refarence/laval.pdf (copyright by the university of Laval, Malcots group).

[2] Papers and research report on Lyee Research work can be referred at http://www.lyee-project.soft.iwate-pu.ac.jp, and also at http://www.lyee.jp.

New Trends in Software Methodologies, Tools and Techniques
H. Fujita and M. Mejri (Eds.)
IOS Press, 2005

LyeeBuilder

B. KTARI [a], M. MEJRI [a], D. GODBOUT [a] and H. FUJITA [b]
[a] *Faculty of Software and Information Science,*
Department of Computer Science and Software Engineering,
Laval University, Québec, G1K 7P4, Canada
[b] *Faculty of Software and Information Science,*
Iwate Prefectural University,
152-52 Sugo, Takizawa, Iwate, 020-0193 Japan

Abstract. The Lyee methodology allows the development of a software by simply defining its requirements. More precisely, a developer has only to provide words, calculation formulae, calculation conditions and layout of screens and printouts, and then leaves in the hands of the computer all subsequent troublesome programming process, i.e. control logic aspects. The formalization of Lyee methodology led to the definition of Lyee-Calculus, a formal process algebra, that easily and naturally supports the basic concepts of the Lyee methodology. Moreover, we provided an implementation of the constructs of the Lyee-Calculus in Java language in order to concretely show the efficiency of this calculus and its suitability for the Lyee methodology. In other words, this Java implementation of the Lyee-Calculus provides a means of bridging the gap between Lyee requirement specifications and their implementations.

In this paper, we present a new software development environment, LyeeBuilder, that allows to automatically generate applications from specifications using a GUI interface. This software aims to give to programmers an environment that allows them to automatically generate applications from screens and word definitions.

1. Introduction

Producing easily and quickly software with high qualities is the basic concern of the software development research field. Over the last years, various methodologies and techniques have been elaborated and proposed to improve one or many aspects related to the software development life cycle. However, despite the great effort in this research field, the production of clearly understood and modifiable systems still an ambitious goal and far from reached. Recently, a new and very promising methodology, called Lyee [1] (governementaL methodologY for softwarE providencE), has been proposed. Intended to deal efficiently with a wide range of software problems related to different fields, Lyee allows the development of software by simply defining its requirements. More precisely, a developer has only to provide words, calculation formulae, calculation conditions (preconditions) and layout of screens and printouts, and then leaves in the hands of the computer all subsequent troublesome programming process (e.g., control logic aspects). In spite of its recentness, the results of the use of Lyee have shown it good potential. Nevertheless, since both the semantics of Lyee generated software together with the process of automatic generation of software from requirements are described using informal language, difficulties and confusions may arise when trying to understand and study this methodology. For that reason, we proposed, in [2], a formalization of the process of automatic generation of software together with the semantics of Lyee generated software using process algebra. This formalisation led to the definition of Lyee-Calculus, a formal process algebra, that easily and naturally supports the basic concepts of the Lyee methodology. In fact, a Lyee generated software is basically made of small components (called vectors in Lyee terminology), where each one has an atomic goal, that collaborate together by interaction in order to produce the desired results (global goal). In the other hand, it is commonly known that a process algebra naturally supports concurrency and communication.

Moreover, we proposed, in [3], an implementation of the constructs of the Lyee in Java language in order to concretely show the efficiency of this calculus and its suitability for the Lyee methodology. In other words, this Java implementation of the Lyee-Calculus provided a means of bridging the gap between Lyee requirement specifications and their implementations.

This paper provides a new formalization, using the Lyee-Calculus, of the Lyee methodology. This new version takes into consideration some details needed to write real programs. Moreover, we present a new software development environment, LyeeBuilder, that allows to automatically generate applications from specifications using a GUI interface. This software allows end-user generate his software without programming.

The remainder of this paper is organized as follows. In Section 2, we present the syntax and the semantics of the Lyee-calculus. In Section 3, we present a new formalization of the Lyee methodology using our calculus. In Section 4, we present our implementation in Java of the constructs required by the Lyee-Calculus. In Section 5, we present a new software development environment, LyeeBuilder, that allows to automatically generate applications from specifications using a GUI interface. In Section 6, we present one case study that concretely shows how a Java program is generated from simple Lyee-like requirements. Finally, Section 7 discusses some future work.

2. Lyee-Calculus

In this section, we give the syntax and the semantics of Lyee-calculus that we have specially define to formalize the Lyee methodology [2].

2.1. Syntax

Lyee-calculus programs are systems composed of independent and parallel processes that communicate using hand-shake technique on named channels. The syntax of processes is described below in terms of processes P, Q:

$$P, Q \ ::= \ [K].P \ \mid \ (P \mid Q) \ \mid \ P + Q \ \mid \ P \rhd Q \ \mid \ P/L \ \mid \ A(\overrightarrow{X}) \stackrel{def}{=} P \ \mid \ nil$$

The intuitive meaning of each syntactic construction is as follows:

- *Sequence*: $[K].P$, where K is a set of actions, is a process that has to perform all the action in K and then behaves as the process P. The order in which the actions in K have to be executed is not important. Notice that for the sake of simplicity we write $[\kappa_1, \ldots, \kappa_n]$ instead of $[\{\kappa_1, \ldots, \kappa_n\}]$. A process can send a value v through a channel ι by doing the action $[\iota!e]$ (v corresponds to the valuation of e). Similarly, a process can receive a value from a channel by doing the action $[\iota?e]$. A processus can also performs a silent action τ.
- *Parallel composition*: $P \mid Q$ behaves as processes P and Q running in parallel. Each one of them may interact with the other on channels known to both, or with the outside word (environment or the end-user) independently from the other. When two processes synchronise on the same channel, the whole process will perform an action τ and behaves as the remaining process.
- *Choice*: $P + Q$ behaves as P or as Q. The choice is deterministically (made by the environment) if both P and Q do not begin with a silent action, otherwise the choice is not deterministically.
- *Guarded choice*: $P \rhd Q$ is the process that behaves as P until process Q is activated. Whenever the latter is activated, the former is stopped and cleared from memory.
- *Restriction*: P/L is the process that behaves as P except that it can communicate with the environment using channels given in L only.
- *Definition*: $A(\overrightarrow{X}) \stackrel{def}{=} P$ is a defining equation where A is a process identifier, $\overrightarrow{X}$ are variables (parameters), and P may recursively involve A.
- *nil process*: nil is the process that cannot perform any action.

2.2. Operational Semantics

Hereafter, we give the formal operational semantics of the Lyee-calculus. This semantics is defined by the interaction relation $\stackrel{\kappa}{\rightarrow}$, where $P \stackrel{\kappa}{\rightarrow} Q$ means that there is a reaction amongst the subprocesses of P such that the whole can execute the atomic action κ and becomes Q. The relation $\stackrel{\kappa}{\rightarrow}$ is the least relation that satisfies the rules given by Table 1.

Notice that :

- $\looparrowright$ is a relation that simplify processes by eliminating the nil process as follows:

$$P \mid nil \looparrowright P \qquad nil + P \looparrowright P \qquad nil \rhd P \looparrowright P \qquad nil/L \looparrowright nil$$
$$nil \mid P \looparrowright P \qquad P + nil \looparrowright P \qquad P \rhd nil \looparrowright P$$

- We denote by $[\![e]\!]$ the set of values containing the result of the evaluation of the expression e. If e is a variable, it evaluation will be its domain (int, real, etc.). For the sake of simplicity, we consider that all variables belong to the real set.
- $\kappa_\lfloor$ is the name of the channel used by the action κ, i.e:

$$\tau_\lfloor = \emptyset$$
$$(\iota!e)_\lfloor = (\iota?e)_\lfloor = \{\iota\}$$

Table 1. Operational Semantics of Lyee-Calculus.

$$(R^l_+)\ \frac{P \xrightarrow{\kappa} P'}{P + Q \xrightarrow{\kappa} P'} \qquad (R_{\nrightarrow})\ \frac{P \xrightarrow{\kappa} Q' \quad Q' \nrightarrow Q}{P \xrightarrow{\kappa} Q} \qquad (R^r_+)\ \frac{Q \xrightarrow{\kappa} Q'}{P + Q \xrightarrow{\kappa} Q'}$$

$$(R_!)\ \frac{v \in [\![e]\!]}{[\iota!e].P \xrightarrow{\iota!v} P} \qquad (R_?)\ \frac{v \in [\![e]\!]}{[\iota?e].P \xrightarrow{\iota?v} P[v/e]} \qquad (R_\tau)\ \frac{v \in [\![e]\!]}{[\tau].P \xrightarrow{\tau} P}$$

$$(R_{[\,]})\ \frac{[K_1].P \xrightarrow{\kappa} P'}{[K_1 \cup K_2].P \xrightarrow{\kappa} [K_2]P'}\ K_2 \neq \emptyset$$

$$(R^\tau_\rhd)\ \frac{P \xrightarrow{\iota?v} P' \quad Q \xrightarrow{\iota!v} Q'}{P \rhd Q \xrightarrow{\tau} Q'} \qquad (R^l_\rhd)\ \frac{P \xrightarrow{\kappa} P'}{P \rhd Q \xrightarrow{\kappa} P' \rhd Q} \qquad (R^r_\rhd)\ \frac{Q \xrightarrow{\kappa} Q'}{P \rhd Q \xrightarrow{\kappa} Q'}$$

$$(R^\tau_|)\ \frac{P \xrightarrow{\iota?v} P' \quad Q \xrightarrow{\iota!v} Q'}{P \mid Q \xrightarrow{\tau} P' \mid Q'} \qquad (R^l_|)\ \frac{P \xrightarrow{\kappa} P'}{P \mid Q \xrightarrow{\kappa} P' \mid Q} \qquad (R^r_|)\ \frac{Q \xrightarrow{\kappa} Q'}{P \mid Q \xrightarrow{\kappa} P \mid Q'}$$

$$(R_=)\ \frac{P[\overrightarrow{Y}/\overrightarrow{X}] \xrightarrow{\kappa} P'}{A(\overrightarrow{Y}) \xrightarrow{\kappa} P'}\ A(\overrightarrow{X}) = P \qquad (R_/)\ \frac{P \xrightarrow{\kappa} P'}{P/L \xrightarrow{\kappa} P/L}\ \kappa_\downarrow \in L$$

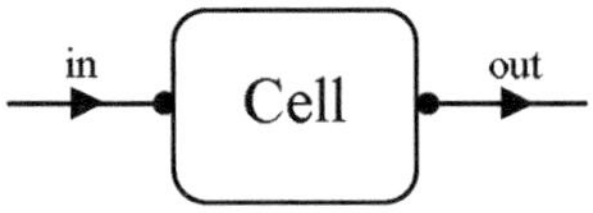

Figure 1. Cell formalized as a process.

2.3. Example

In this section, we show how to model a cell of memory as a process that interacts with its environment through its communication channels. As shown by Fig. 1, we consider that the cell has two ports (channels) of communication, *in* and *out*. The basic task of this cell is to infinitely wait a value on channel *in* and to make it available on channel *out*. The same value may be outputted as mush as necessary until a new value is imputed.

We write the process cell $C^x(v)$, meaning that the memory cell x holds the value v, as follows:

$$C^x(v) \stackrel{def}{=} [in^x?y].C^x(y) + [out^x!v].C^x(v)$$

By capturing a memory cell as a process, we can add intelligence to it. For instance, we can write a cell that it does not allow the access to its content until it will be initialized. This smart cell can be defined as follows:

$$Cell(x) \stackrel{def}{=} [in^x?y].C^x(y)$$

Now, giving two processes defined as follows:

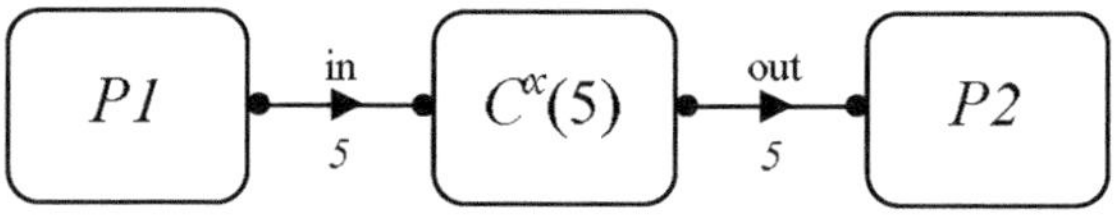

Figure 2. Example of interacting processes.

$$P1 \stackrel{def}{=} [in^x!5].nil$$
$$P2 \stackrel{def}{=} [out^x?y].nil$$

it is easy to write a program where these two processes communicate through a cell x:

$$P1 \mid Cell(x) \mid P2$$

The Fig. 2 shows the interaction between all the involved processes. Here are the different steps of that program execution:

$$\begin{aligned} P1 \mid Cell(x) \mid P2 = & \ [in^x!5].nil \mid [in^x?y].C^x(y) \mid [out^x?y].nil \\ \stackrel{\tau}{\rightarrow} & \ C^x(5) \mid [out^x?y].nil \\ = & \ (\,[in^x?y].C^x(y) + [out^x!5].C^x(5)\,) \mid [out^x?y].nil \\ \stackrel{\tau}{\rightarrow} & \ C^x(5) \end{aligned}$$

3. Formalization: Beyond the Lyee Methodology

The implemented version of the Lyee Calculus within the LyeeBuilder software is slightly different from the one given in [2]. This new version takes into consideration some details needed to write real programs. However the initial version was given in an abstract level to show the main ideas behind the calculus. It is important to know that this new version can be considerably simplified so that we can obtain more efficient generated programs.

Let Use(e) denotes the set of words used in the expression e. For instance, $Use(a * b + 1) = \{a, b\}$. Also, let $\mathcal{F}(S)$ be the following function:

$$\mathcal{F}(\emptyset) = \emptyset$$
$$\mathcal{F}(\{x\} \cup A) = \{\iota_4^x?x\} \cup \mathcal{F}(A)$$

Now let's see how to automatically generate software from simple user requirement using the Lyee-calculus. Suppose that the user requirement contains k screens $\{s_1, \ldots, s_k\}$. Suppose also that each screen contains a set of statements where each one of them has the following form: $(w, e, c, InOut, type)$ where w is a word, e its definition, c its condition, $InOut$ to specify if it is input, output, both or neither input no output (the value i is used for input word, o for output, io for both input and output and empty filed for neither input nor output) and $type$ is its type (the type B is reserved for bouton). To define the program $\mathcal{P}(s_1, \ldots, s_k)$ associated with this requirement, we need to formalize the following vectors (processes):

Signification Vectors

$$
\begin{array}{ll}
L4(x,e) & = [\jmath_4^c?true].[\mathcal{F}(Use(e))].L4'(x,e) \\
L4'(x,e) & = [\jmath_4^c?true].[\jmath_4^x!eval(e)].\mathsf{fresh}(\mathcal{F}(Use(c)), \jmath_4^c).L4'(x,e) \\
& \quad + \\
& \quad [\jmath_4^c?false].[\jmath_4^x!\bot].L4(x,e)
\end{array}
$$

$$
L2(x) = [\imath_2^x?z].[\jmath_4^x!z].L2(x)
$$

$$
\begin{array}{ll}
L3(x,c) & = \mathsf{fresh}(\mathcal{F}(Use(c))).[\jmath_4^c!eval(c)].L3(x,c) \\
Var(c) = \emptyset & \Rightarrow L3(x,c) = [\jmath_4^c!eval(c)].nil
\end{array}
$$

$$
\begin{array}{ll}
L3_e(x,c_e) & = \mathsf{fresh}(\mathcal{F}(Use(c_e))).[d_e^x!eval(c_e)].L3_e(x,c) \\
Var(c_e) = \emptyset & \Rightarrow L3_e(x,c_e) = [d_e^x!eval(c_e)].nil
\end{array}
$$

$$
\begin{array}{ll}
L3_{I2}(x,c_{I2}) & = [\imath_{I2}'^3?x].(\ Ready(Use(c_{I2})).[\mathcal{F}(Use(c_{I2}))].[\imath_{I2}^3!eval(c_{I2})] + \\
& \qquad \neg Ready(Use(c_{I2})).[\imath_{I2}^3!false]\ ).L3'_{I2}(x,c_{I2}) \\
L3'_{I2}(x,c_{I2}) & = \mathsf{fresh}(\mathcal{F}(Use(c_{I2})).[\imath_{I2}^3!eval(c_{I2})].L3'_{I2}(x,c_{I2}) \\
& \quad + \\
& \quad [\imath_{I2}'^3?x].[\mathcal{F}(Use(c_{I2}))].[\imath_{I2}^3!eval(c_{I2})].L3'_{I2}(x,c_{I2})
\end{array}
$$

$$
\begin{array}{ll}
L3_{O4}(x,c_{O4}) & = \mathsf{fresh}(\mathcal{F}(Use(c_{O4}))).[\imath_{O4}^4!eval(c_{O4})].L3_{O4}(x,c_{O4}) \\
Var(c_{O4}) = \emptyset & \Rightarrow L3_{O4}(x,c_{O4}) = [\imath_{O4}^4!eval(c_{O4})].nil
\end{array}
$$

Action Vectors

$$
\begin{array}{ll}
I2(x) & = [d_x?x].[\imath_{I2}'^3!x].(\ [\imath_{I2}^3?true].[\imath_2^x!x]\ +\ [\imath_{I2}^3?false].Error().[d_x!""].[\imath_2^x!\bot]\ ).I2(x) \\
& \quad + \\
& \quad [\imath_{I2}^3?false].Error().[d_x!""].[\imath_2^x!\bot].I2(x)
\end{array}
$$

$$
\begin{array}{ll}
O4(x) & = [\imath_{O4}^4?true].[\imath_4^x?x].[d_x!x].O4(x) \\
Var(c_{O4}) = \emptyset & \Rightarrow O4(x) = [\imath_{O4}^4?true].O4'(x) \\
& \quad O4'(x) = \mathsf{fresh}([\imath_4^x?x]).[d_x!x].O4'(x)
\end{array}
$$

$$
\begin{array}{ll}
S4(x) & = [\jmath_4^x?y].S_4^x(y) \mid MC_4^x() \\
S4^x(y) & = [\jmath_4^x?z].[mc_4^x!true].S_4^x(z) + [\imath_4^x!y].S_4^x(y)
\end{array}
$$

$$
MC_4^x() = [mc_4^x?true].[l[0]!true, \ldots, l[n]!true].MC_4^x() + [mc_{reg}^x?c].(c :: l).MC_4^x()
$$

$$
\begin{array}{ll}
R3(b,e,s) & = [d_b?clik].[\jmath_4^b!true].(\ e.f = 'open' \Rightarrow [\imath^{e.s}!true]\ + \\
& \qquad e.f = 'close' \Rightarrow [\imath^{e.s}!false]\ ).R3(b,e,s)
\end{array}
$$

Pallet: The three pallets W_{02}, W_{03} and W_{04} of a given screen s are formalized as follows:

$$
\begin{array}{l}
W_{02}(s) = |_{(w,*,*,\{i,i/o\},\overline{B})\in s}\ I_2(w)\ |_{(w,*,*,\{i,i/o\},\overline{B})\in s}\ L_2(w)\ |_{(w,*,*,*,*)\in s}\ L3_e(w) \\
\qquad\quad |_{(w,*,*,\{i,i/o\},\overline{B})\in s}\ L3_{I2}(w) \\
W_{03}(s) = |_{(w,*,c,\overline{i},\overline{B})\in s}\ L_3(w,c)\ |_{(w,*,c,\overline{i},\overline{B})\in s}\ S_4^{L3}(w,c)\ |_{(w,e,c,*,*,B)\in s}\ R_3(w,c,e) \\
W_{04}(s) = |_{(w,*,*,*,*)\in s}\ S_4(w)\ |_{(w,e,*,\overline{i},\overline{B})\in s} L_4(w,e))\ |_{(w,*,*,\{o,i/o\},\overline{B})\in s}\ O_4(w) \\
\qquad\quad |_{(w,*,*,\overline{i},\overline{B})\in s}\ L3_{O4}(w)
\end{array}
$$

where $\overline{B}$ denotes any type except B (complementary of B), where $\overline{i}$ denotes any type except i (complementary of i) and $*$ denotes anything.

Scenario Function: The scenario function, $SF(s)$, attached to the screen s is formalized as follows:

$$SF(s) = W_{04}(s) \mid W_{03}(s) \mid W_{02}(s)$$

Control Function: The control function attached to a screen s, is formalized as follows:

$$\Phi(s) = SF(s).\Phi'(s)$$
$$\Phi'(s) = ([\iota^{s_k}?true].s_k.open() + [\iota^{s_k}?false].s_k.hide()).\Phi'(s)$$

The control function attached to a set of screens is formalized as follows:

$$\Psi(s_1, \ldots, s_k) = (|_{s \in \{s_1,\ldots,s_k\}} [\iota^s?true.]\Phi(s)) \rhd [\iota^{s_0}?false].nil$$

We suppose that s_0 is the screen that we find when we exit the program (exit screen that does not belongs to the screens of the program itself).

Lyee Program: Finally, the Lyee program $\mathcal{P}(s_1, \ldots, s_k)$ associated with the requirement containing the screens $s_1, \ldots, s_k$ is as follows:

$$\mathcal{P}(s_1, \ldots, s_k) = \Psi(s_1, \ldots, s_k)/\mathcal{L}(s_1, \ldots, s_k) \mid \mathit{VisualDebugger}$$

where the set $\mathcal{L}(s_1, \ldots, s_k)$ contains all the input and output channels and it is defined as follows:

$$\mathcal{L}(s_1, \ldots, s_k) = (\bigcup_{(w,*,*,i/o,*) \in s_k} \{d_w\}) \cup \{\iota^{s_1}\}$$

The meaning of i/o is that this field has to contains the value i, o or io. We suppose also that s_1 is the first screen that appears when the user runs this program.

4. The Lyee-Calculus Implementation in Java

A mapping from Lyee-Calculus to Java has been implemented. Our implementation inherits from JCSP [4] since the later provides all the necessary classes to program concurrent processes. Moreover, a mapping from the Lyee formalization, with Lyee-Calculus, to Java classes has been implemented as shown within this section.

4.1. Lyee-Calculus to Java

The corresponding Java classes and methods of Lyee-Calculus constructs are defined in Table 2.

Since there is no direct mapping from $[K].P$ and $P \rhd Q$ to the constructs provided JCSP, we have defined two new classes `ArrayChannel` and `GuardedProcess` [3].

4.2. A Special Case: Cell Implementation

We recall the definition of a cell with Lyee-Calculus (Section 2.3 in page 86):

$$C^x(v) \stackrel{def}{=} [in^x?y].C^x(y) + [out^x!v].C^x(v)$$

Since the implementation of choice, $P + Q$, in JCSP in restricted to input channels, we have implemented a Cell as following:

Table 2. Mapping from LyeeCalculus to Java code.

Description	*Lyee-Calculus*	*Mapping*
Sequence	$[K].P$	`ArrayChannel` class
Sequence	$P \mid Q$	JCSP `Parallel` class
Sequence	$P + Q$	JCSP `Alternative` class
Sequence	$P \rhd Q$	`GuardedProcess` class
Sequence	P / L	Identifier scope of Java language
Sequence	$A(\overrightarrow{X}) \stackrel{def}{=} P$	`while` (true) { ... }
Sequence	nil	Empty statement (;)

Table 3. Mapping from Lyee Formalization to Java code.

Description	*Lyee Requirement Formalization*	*Mapping*
Program	$\mathcal{P}(s_1, \ldots, s_k)$	`Program` class
Control Function (1)	$\Psi(s_1, \ldots, s_k)$	`Psi` class
Control Function (2)	$\Phi(s)$	`Phi` class
Scenario Function	$SF(s)$	`SF` class
Pallet functions	W_{02}, W_{03}, W_{04}	`W02`, `W03` and `W04` classes
Action Vectors	I_2, O_4, S_4, R_3	`I2`, `O4`, `S4` and `R3` classes
Signification Vectors	L_4, L_3, L_2	`L4`, `L3` and `L2` classes

$$
\begin{aligned}
C^x(v) &\stackrel{def}{=} P_1^x \mid P_2^x(v) \\
P_1^x &\stackrel{def}{=} [in^x?y].[buf!y].P_1^x \\
P_2^x(v) &\stackrel{def}{=} P_2^{x\prime}(v) \rhd [buf?y].P_2^x(y) \\
P_2^{x\prime}(v) &\stackrel{def}{=} [out^x!v].P_2^{x\prime}(v)
\end{aligned}
$$

where *buf* is a private `One2OneChannel` shared between processes P_1^x and P_2^x. Hence a cell is implemented as two processes running in parallel, the first one is intended to wait, from channel *in*, for a new value y, and the second is intended to send, through the channel *out*, the current value of the cell. Whenever the former receives a new value, the latter is killed and a fresh instance is started with the received value.

4.3. From Lyee Requirement to Java

For each function used to formalize the Lyee methodology, we define a class in Java that implements it. The correspondence between these Java classes and the function used in the Lyee Formalization are given in Table 3.

The code of almost all the classes is very closed to the definition of the functions that they implement (Section 3, page 87) [3].

5. LyeeBuilder

In this section, we present a user-friendly GUI builder, called LyeeBuilder, allows end-user generate his software without programming. The end-user has just to create screen

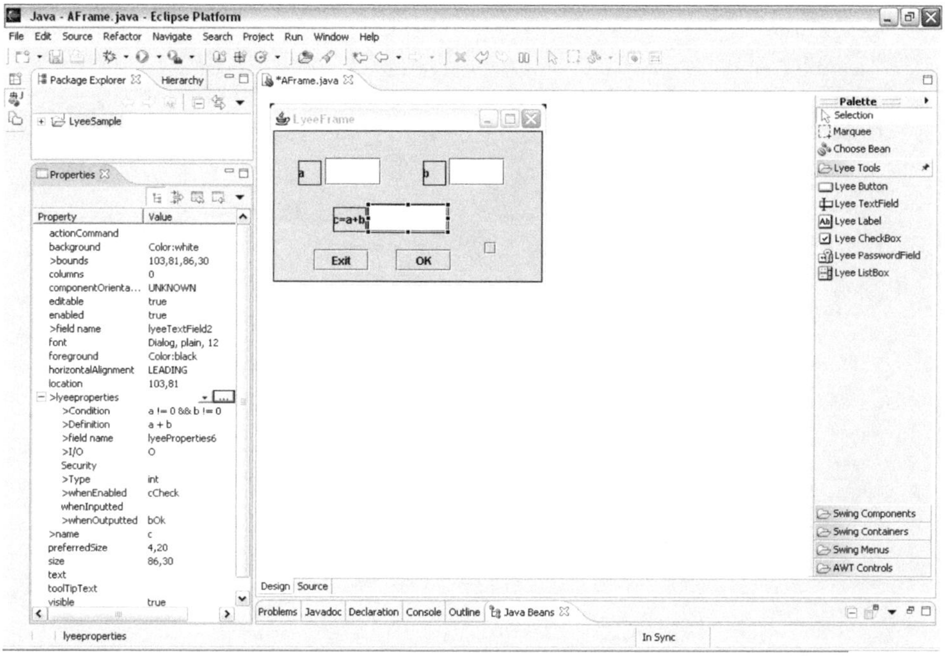

Figure 3. LyeeBuilder.

to put the desired fields (the definition of words, texts, and button) in each screen and then the code will be automatically generated. When the user insert an object (button, edit-field, etc.) in a screen, then in the left hand side of the builder he will see a list of properties among them those related to the Lyee methodology so he can write the definition of his word, the calculation condition, etc. (see Fig. 3). The connection between a screen can be done via button. When the user insert a connection button he will see the name of all his created screen and he has just to tell what screen has to be visualized when the button is pressed by the end-user.

5.1. Lyee Properties

The main fields found in the LyeeProperties area are the following (see Fig. 4):

- Condition: this is a boolean expression that specify when the definition of a word is computed.
- Definition: this is an arithmetic or a boolean expression that define a word.
- I/O: this field specifies whether a word is an input, output or both input and output.
- Security: this field specifies the security level (secret, public) attributed to the word.
- Type: this specifies the type (int, float, string, boolean, button) of the word.
- whenOutputted: this is a boolean condition that says when a word could be outputted. An output word can be outputted only when this condition become true.
- WhenInputted: This is also a boolean condition saying when an input word could be accepted. Whenever this condition is false, the inputted value is rejected.

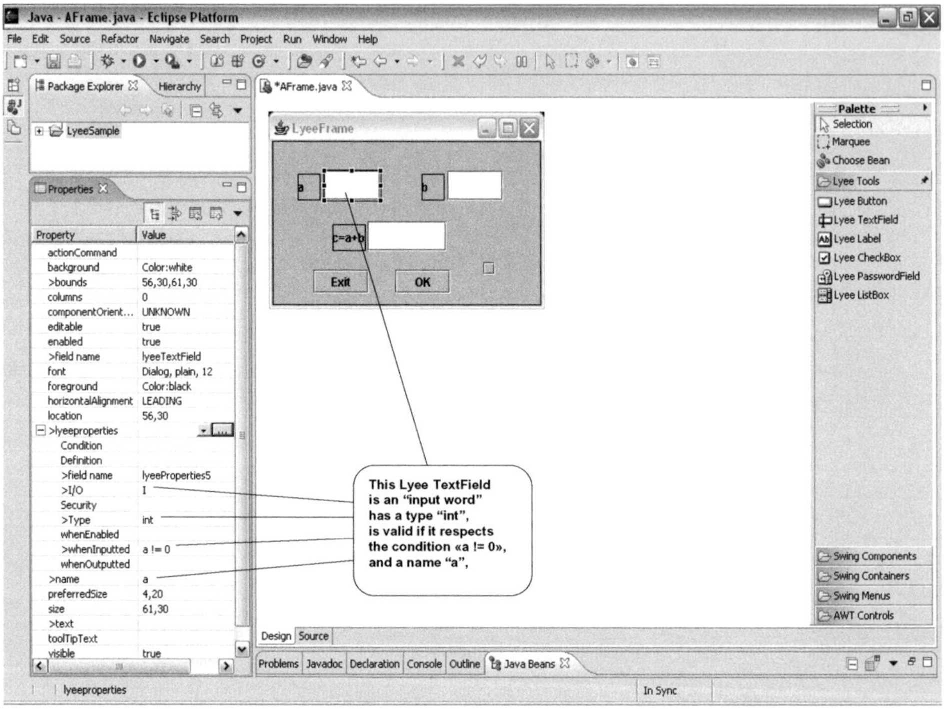

Figure 4. Example of Word Attributes.

- whenEnabled: an input area or a button can be available only if a specific condition become true. This boolean condition is given by this field.

The new fields whenOutputted, WhenInputted and whenEnabled give more possibilities within software development. For the next version of LyeeBuilder, we want to associate with each kind of action (input, output, compute, etc) a condition that trigger (activate) it.

5.2. Syntax

The language used to give definitions to different fileds has the following syntax given in a BNF format by Table 4 (see also Fig. 5).

5.3. Components and Properties

As shown in the figures of the last section, in a typical LyeeBuilder screen, we have on the left side the different components that can be used to build a screen, on the right side the "Properties" attached to these components and on the middle we have the frame that we want to build.

In this section, we present the typical values of the different properties related to the available components (see Fig. 6).

- *LyeeTextField*: This kind of component is typically used to input values from user or to output results to user. Consequently, the I/O properties could be I, O, or

Table 4. Syntax.

Syntax of Arithmetic Expressions: $a ::= v \mid Id \mid (a) \mid a_1 + a_2 \mid a_1 - a_2 \mid a_1 * a_2 \mid a_1 / a_2$ Id= Identifier of a word v= An integer or flat value
Syntax of String Expressions: $s ::= Constant\ String \mid s_1 \hat{}\, s_2$ The operator "^" allows to concatenate two strings.
Syntax of Boolean Expressions: $b ::= true \quad \mid false \quad \mid (b)$ $\mid \quad b_1 == b_2 \mid b_1 != b_2 \mid b_1 \&\& b_2 \mid b_1 \mid\mid b_2$ $\mid \quad s_1 == s_2 \mid s_1 != s_2$ $\mid \quad a_1 == a_2 \mid a_1 != a_2$ $\mid \quad a_1 < a_2 \mid a_1 \leq a_2 \mid a_1 > a_2 \mid a_1 \geq a_2$
Syntax of Screen Actions: $ScreenAction ::= ScreenName.open \mid ScreenName.close$ $\mid \quad ScreenAction \&\& ScreenAction$

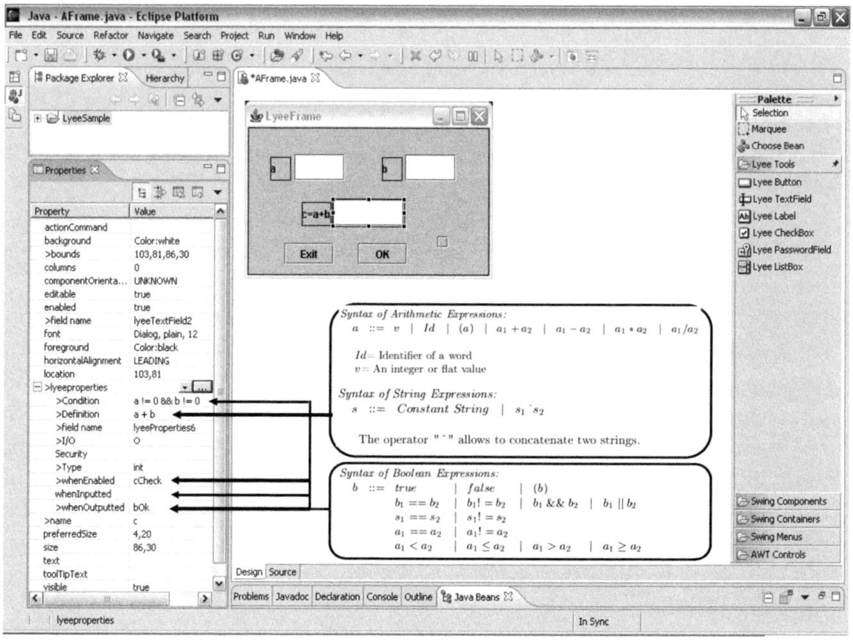

Figure 5. Screen Elements.

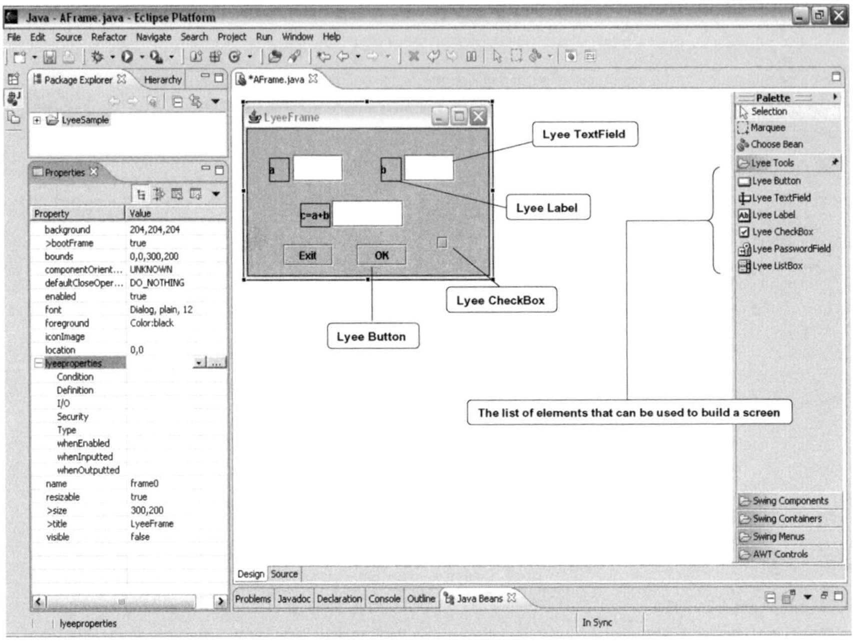

Figure 6. Components.

I/O. When it's an input, the *whenInputted* property could be defined to specify a condition that will be used to validate user inputs. When it's an output, the *Condition*, *Definition* and *whenOutputted* fields could be defined. In both cases, the *Type* field could be used to specify the type of value inputted or outputted. By default, the type int is considered.

- *LyeePasswordField*: This kind of component is very close to the last one except that it's not very convenient to use it as an output (O) or input/output (I/O). Usually, we use it as an input (I).
- *Label*: This kind of component is typically used to output results. Consequently, the I/O field should be set to O and *Condition*, *Definition* and *whenOutputted* fields could be defined.
- *Button*: This kind of component is typically used to activate the computation of some words, to allow the output of other words, and/or to open/close frames (screens). In case of we want to open/close frames, this has to be specified in the *Definition* field of this button. For instance, if the definition of a button B1 is "s0.close", then when this Button is pushed it will close the frame s0 which is the program, i.e. s0.close is equivalent to exit. Now, if the *Definition* field of the button B1 is "s1.close && s2.open", then when this Button is pushed it will close the frame s1 and open the frame s2.
  It is important to know that that the Type field associated to button has to be set to the value "Button".
- *ListBox*: This is a special component that is typically used as an I/O word. The input value of such component corresponds to the user-selected item (from the list). The output part corresponds to an expression whose value is added to the com-

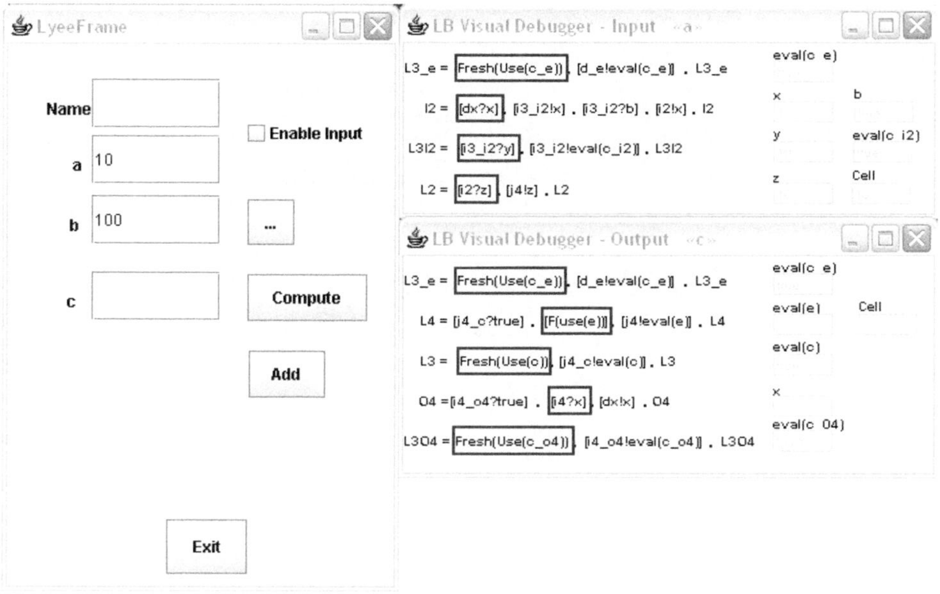

Figure 7. VisualDebugger in action.

ponent (a new item will be added to the list). Consequently, even if it is typically used as an I/O, the user can use it as an O. *Condition* and *Definition* fields could be defined.

- *CheckBox*: This kind of component is typically used as an input.
  It is important to know that that the I/O field associated to CheckBox has to be set to the value "I". No other fields should be defined.

Note that for all the Lyee components, the whenEnabled property could be defined. Also, note that in this version of LyeeBuilder, the Security property could be defined but it is not considered by LyeeBuilder engine. Finally, for a given component, if no Lyee properties are defined, no behavior (LyeeCalculus processes) will be attached to that component.

5.4. *VisualDebugger*

We have added to LyeeBuilder tool a new kind of tool named VisualDebugger. This new tool offers to the user the ability to follow the different internal steps executed through the computation of q word definition for instance (see Fig. 7).

In order to show the step-by-step behaviors of the different processes (pallets) related to a specific word, the user has simply to push the Ctrl button and to right click on the corresponding screen component. But before that, he has to activate, at the Lyee generation code step, the VisualDebugger option. This activation is made by adding to the program parameters the following expression: -debug n where the constant n corresponds to the idle (specified in ms) that has to be taken into account between each step.

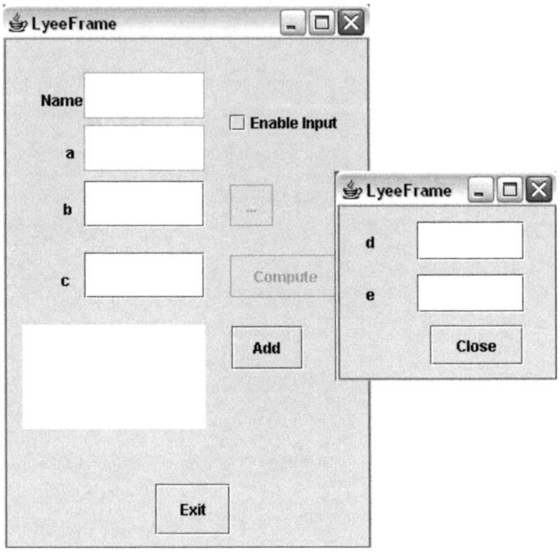

Figure 8. Screen Elements.

5.5. *Implementation*

To implement the LyeeBuilder, we decided to build it over the Eclipse Platform [5] as it is an extensible IDE. Our implementation can be divided into 2 core parts, the visual editor and the code generator.

The editor was built as a plug-in over the Visual Editor Project (VE) [6] which eases the creation of visual Java application. The palette was adapted to show Lyee components instead of the usual Java components. These Lyee components are mostly standard Java components to which were added communication channels and the Lyee properties to suit the developer's specifications. VE is also responsible to generate the Java code to display the visual components such as Lyee text fields and buttons.

Additional Java code needs to be generated to have an application corresponding to the specifications made by the developer. The Java Emitter Templates of the Eclipse Modelling Framework (EMF) [7] was used to produce it. When activated, it generates additional code into the Java classes that allow Lyee objects to use the Lyee calculus package. First, it scans the Java source files to get every Lyee components attached to a screen. Then it generates code to create channels for these components and to launch the processes required. Finally, it also adds calls in the main method of the program to initialize every Lyee frames as needed.

6. Case Study

In this section, we give a concrete example to show how a Java program is generated from simple requirement using LyeeBuilder.

The example that we present contains two screens illustrated by Fig. 8. The requirements are given in Table 5.

The Figs 9 and 10 illustrate respectively how to generate the Java code from requirements and the generated code.

Table 5. Requirements

	Condition	Definition	Type	I/O	Security	whenInputted	whenOutputted	whenEnabled
name			string	I				cInput
a				I		a != 0		
b		(a*e)-d		O				
c		b*b					bCompute	
list		name^" "^c	string	IO			bAdd	
selected		list		O			bAdd	list != ""
cInput				I				
bNext		frame2.open	Button					a != 0
bCompute			Button					a!=0 && b!=0
bAdd			Button					
bExit		s0.close	Button					
d				I				
e				I		d!= 0		
bExit		frame2.close	Button					

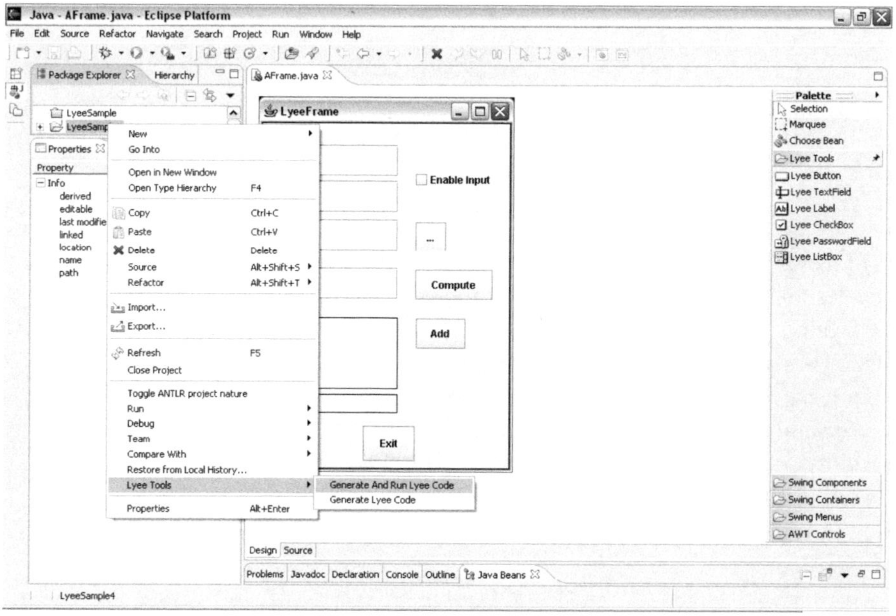

Figure 9. Generation of code.

7. Future Work

As future work, we want to more improve our implementation and to test it on real big system described in terms of Lyee requirement. We want also to connect this implementation to other user-friendly tools, that we have developed, in order to automatically generate, from Lyee requirements, reliable and optimized Java codes. More precisely, we plan to plug to LyeeBuilder LyeeAnalyzer tool which is based on classical static analysis techniques that were presented in [8] to improve many aspects of the Lyee methodology.

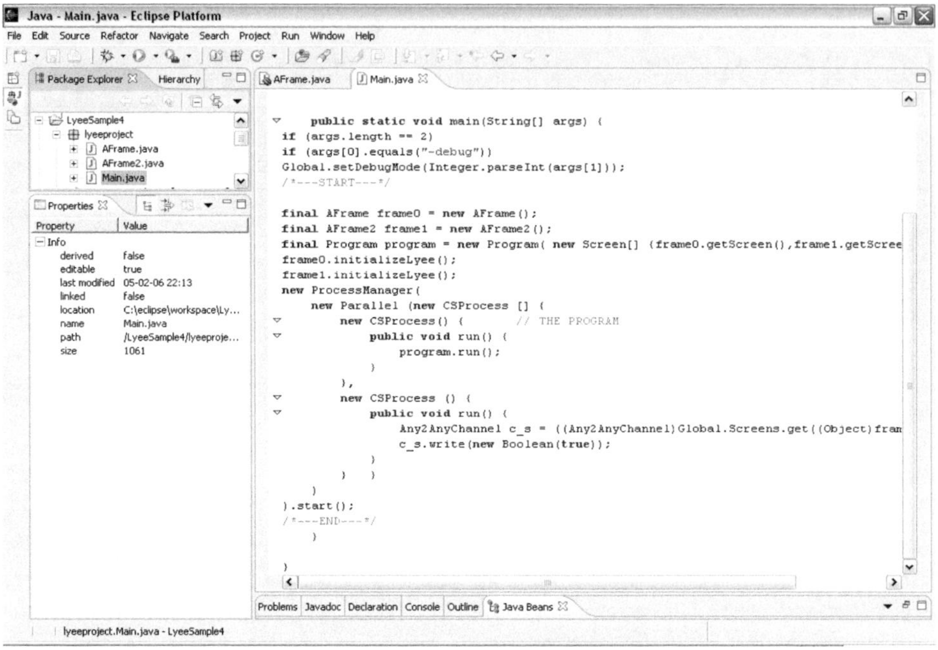

Figure 10. Java generated code.

In the long-term, we view LyeeBuilder as a new and a very user-friendly tool that generates automatically different kind of code (Java, Cobol, etc.) from high level user specification given in a the metalanguage. The development and especially the maintenance of software have to be as simple as possible. We want also, to connect this tool with a legacy translation tool so that we can transform, for example, a Cobol software to LyeeBuilder specification and update it. Finally, we want to give the LyeeBuilder the possibility of interaction or interpretability with the different existing tools.

References

[1] F. Negoro, I. Hamid, A proposal for intention engineering, 5th East-European Conference Advances in Databases and Information System (ADBIS'2001) .

[2] M. Mejri, B. Ktari, H. Fujita, Lyee-calculus: A formalization of lyee methodology, in: H. Fujita, P. Johannesson (Eds.), New Trends in Software Methodologies, Tools and Techniques, IOS Press, 2003, pp. 235–261, proceedings of the 2nd International Workshop on Lyee Methodology, Stockholm, Sweden.

[3] B. Ktari, M. Mejri, H. Fujita, From lyee-calculus to java code, in: H. Fujita, P. Johannesson (Eds.), New Trends in Software Methodologies, Tools and Techniques, IOS Press, 2004, pp. 235–261, proceedings of the 3nd International Workshop on Lyee Methodology, Leipzig, Germany.

[4] P. Welch, Communicating Sequential Processes for Java (JCSP), http://www.cs.kent.ac.uk/projects/ofa/jcsp/ (2004).

[5] Eclipse Foundation, eclipse.org, http://www.eclipse.org (2005).

[6] Eclipse Foundation, The Eclipse Visual Editor Project, http://www.eclipse.org/vep/ (2005).

[7] Eclipse Foundation, Eclipse Tools – EMF, SDO, XSD – Home, http://www.eclipse.org/emf/ (2005).

[8] M. Mejri, B. Ktari, M. Erhioui, Static analysis on lyee-oriented software, in: H. Fujita, P. Johannesson (Eds.), New Trends in Software Methodologies, Tools and Techniques, IOS Press, 2002, pp. 375–394, proceedings of 1st International Workshop on Lyee Methodology, Paris.

[9] R. Milner, A calculus of communicating systems, Lecture Notes in Computer Science 92, Springer-Verlag, Berlin, 1980.

[10] C.A.R. Hoare, Communicating Sequential Processes, Prentice Hall International Series in Computer Science, Prentice Hall, 1985.

[11] J.A. Bergstra, J.W. Klop, Algebra of communicating processes with abstraction, Theoretical Computer Science 37 (1) (1985) 77–121.

[12] F. Negoro, Principle of Lyee software, 2000 International Conference on Information Society in 21st Century (IS2000) (2000) 121–189.

[13] F. Negoro, Introduction to Lyee, The Institute of Computer Based Software Methodology and Technology, Tokyo, Japan, 2001.

[14] M. Woitaszek, Introduction to Occam, `http://www.cs.rit.edu/~msw4585/occam/` (2004).

[15] G. Berry, G. Boudol, The chemical abstract machine, in: Proceedings of the 17th ACM SIGPLAN-SIGACT symposium on Principles of programming languages, POPL'90, San Francisco, California, United States, 1990.

[16] G. Boudol, Some chemical abstract machines, Lecture Notes in Computer Science (LNCS) 803 (1994) 92–123.

Chapter 3

Software Quality and Development Measurement

New Trends in Software Methodologies, Tools and Techniques
H. Fujita and M. Mejri (Eds.)
IOS Press, 2005

Approaches to Qualitative Evaluation of the Software Quality Attributes: Overview

Kozlov DENIS
University of Jyväskylä, Finland

Abstract. An overview of three most frequently used methods for qualitative evaluation of entities is presented in the paper, namely Overall Integral Index, Fuzzy Analytic Hierarchy Process and Consensus Relation. The implementation of these approaches to the measurement of the software quality attributes is discussed.

Keywords. Software quality attributes, evaluation

1. Introduction

The requirements for software quality are nowadays very high. The high level of software quality gives a guarantee to its user that the software is error free and effective in use. As a result of such a quality orientation, the software measurement has become extremely popular.

The primarily goal of the software measurement is to measure software quality attributes – measurable physical or abstract properties of an entity [1], as precisely as possible. The most accurate measurement of the software quality can be reached only, if it is performed in terms of the interval scale. However, there are only few software attributes that can be evaluated using the interval scale. The majority of the attributes is to be measured in the ordinal scale. In this case the measurement is usually performed based on the experts' judgment.

The most frequently used approach to the qualitative measurement of complex entities and systems is considered to be Overall Integral Index. However, there are also some other methods for qualitative evaluation of entities that can be applied for the case of the software measurement, for instance, Fuzzy Analytic Hierarchy Process and Consensus Relation.

The aim of the paper is to highlight the main points of the above approaches and to make a tentative comparative analysis of them. Some issues of the application of the approaches for the software measurement are discussed.

2. Overall Integral Index

Many authors attempted to transform the approach Overall Integral Index for different fields. For instance P. Faratin et all implemented it for the case of qualitative evaluation of the service-oriented negotiations between autonomous agents [2].

The main points of the approach have been developed in 1980s by the Russian scientist – founder of the qualitative measuring in Russia G.G. Azgaldov [3].

According to this approach the entity or system to be evaluated should be characterized by a number of attributes, each of which is to be evaluated by experts. In case of the entity named "software" such attributes can be e.g.: understandability, learnability, operability, attractiveness and compliance [4].

The evaluation process consists of several phases:

1. The tree of criteria (attributes) is to be developed. The tree of attributes should reflect all the attributes and sub-attributes to be evaluated.
2. Weights of each attribute are to be defined. Each attribute should be evaluated from the viewpoint of its importance for the end-user. The sum of the weights for sub-attributes of an attribute should be 100% or 1.
3. The generalized criteria is defined according to the formula

   $$W = \sum m_i \times X_i \quad (1)$$

   where m_i is weight of each attribute; X_i is individual quality attribute
4. If $W_1 > W_2$ then the entity (software) corresponding to the generalized criteria W_1 is of higher quality than the second one.

A concrete example for the above attributes has been given in the part 6 of the paper.

3. Fuzzy Analytic Hierarchy Process

One more approach that can be also applied for the case of the software quality evaluation is Analytic Hierarchy Process and its fuzzy variety.

Analytic Hierarchy Process is described in details in [5] and is widely used in other areas, for instance, [6,7].

The method is a regular procedure for hierarchical representation elements (a tree of criteria), determining features of any complex object (in our case – software attributes). Paired comparison is the way to determine importance factors. The result of comparison is like in the above approach is estimated in scores. On the basis of such comparison factors of criteria importance, evaluation of alternatives are calculated and general estimation as the weighted sum of criteria estimations is determined.

In order to establish relative importance of elements in hierarchy, the scale of relations is used. Value 1 is given to the relation of the objects, which have identical importance when compared in pairs. Value 9 is given to the relation of the objects when one object is superior to the other. Values 3, 5, 7 are used in interim situation when compared in pairs. In case when the compromise is necessary, values 2, 4, 6, 8 can be used. The given scale enables a Decision Maker to bring some numbers to conformity with the degrees of preference of one object under comparison to another. The method provides estimation of rejection degree from consistency. When such deviations exceed the established limits, the decision maker should recheck them in a matrix of pair comparisons.

The above main point of Analytic Hierarchy Process will be accompanied by an example in the part 6 of the paper.

At this point we would like to stress that in spite of its simplicity and transparency, the Analytic Hierarchy Process is often criticized for its inability to adequate handle the inherent uncertainty and imprecision associated with the mapping of the decision maker's perception to exact numbers [8]. In the traditional formulation of the Analytic Hierarch Process, human's judgments are represented as exact numbers, however, in many practical cases the human preference model is uncertain and the decision maker might be reluctant or unable to assign exact numerical values to the comparison judgments [7]. In case of qualitative evaluation of the software attributes it is very difficult for the decision maker to express the strength of his preferences and to provide exact pairwise comparison judgment.

Due to this disadvantage of the Analytic Hierarchy Process in its pure form, we would like to mention briefly some basic principles of the Fuzzy Analytic Hierarchy Process, which can be found in greater details in [7].

In case of the Fuzzy Analytic Hierarchy process the comparison ratios are expressed as fuzzy sets or fuzzy numbers, which incorporate the vagueness of the human thinking. When comparing any two objects E_i and E_j at the same level of the decision hierarchy, the uncertain comparison judgement can be represented by the fuzzy number $\tilde{a}_{ij}$ [7].

$\tilde{a}_{ij} = (l_{ij}; m_{ij}; u_{ij})$, where l_{ij}, m_{ij} and u_{ij} – the lower, mean and upper bounds, respectively

It is assumed that $l_{ij} < m_{ij} < u_{ij}$.

Fuzzy priorities $\hat{w}_i$ approximate the fuzzy ratios $\tilde{a}_{ij}$ so that $\tilde{a}_{ij} \approx \hat{w}_i / \hat{w}_j$.

The membership function that represents the decision-maker's satisfaction with different crisp solution ratios $\hat{w}_i / \hat{w}_j$:

$$\mu_{ij}\left(\frac{w_i}{w_j}\right) = \begin{cases} \dfrac{\left(\dfrac{w_i}{w_j} - l_{ij}\right)}{m_{ij} - l_{ij}}, & \dfrac{w_i}{w_j} \le m_{ij} \\[2ex] \dfrac{\left(u_{ij} - \dfrac{w_i}{w_j}\right)}{u_{ij} - m_{ij}}, & \dfrac{w_i}{w_j} \ge m_{ij} \end{cases} \tag{2}$$

The maximum prioritization problem can be represented in the following way:

Maximize λ subject to $(m_{ij} - l_{ij})\lambda w_j - w_i + l_{ij} w_j \le 0,$ (3)

$$(u_{ij} - m_{ij})\lambda w_j + w_i - u_{ij} w_j \le 0,$$

$$\sum_{k=1}^{n} w_k = 1, w_k > 0, k = 1,2,...n$$

$i=1,2,\ldots,n-1$, $j=1, 2, \ldots n$, $j > 1$

4. Consensus Relation

Let some n software products will be characterized by m criterion (attributes). Let a set $A = \{a_1, a_2, ..., a_n\}$, $|A| = n$, be a set of software products. By every criterion (attribute), the software product can be ranked in order of preference. We have the relation set A =

$\{\alpha_1,\ldots,\alpha_m\}$, where $|A| = m$. Every *ranking* (preference relation $\succsim$) $\alpha = \{a_1 \succ a_2 \succ \ldots\sim a_s \sim a_t \ldots\sim a_n\}$ includes $\succ$, a strict preference relation π, and $\sim$, an indifference relation ν, so that $\alpha = \pi \cup \nu$. The relation π is complete, transitive, irreflexive, and antisymmetric, and the relation ν is reflexive and symmetric. Such the relation α is known to be called *preorder*. How to obtain preorder relations describing many properties of objects is discussed in greater detail in [8]. The relation set A can be titled a *preference profile* for the given m properties.

A single preference relation can be determined that would give an integrative characterization of the software products. Let a space Π be a set of all $n!$ strict (linear) order relations $\succ$ on A. Each linear order corresponds to one of permutations of first n natural numbers $\mathbf{N_n}$. We will consider a permutation $\beta \in \Pi$ of the software products $a_1, \ldots, a_n$ to represent the preference profile A and will call it *consensus ranking*. It is desirable that, in some sense, β would be nearest to the every of rankings $\alpha_1, \ldots, \alpha_m$.

It is clear that the problem described above is very similar to the problem of rating of competitors for quality awards where A is a set of enterprises to be evaluated or ranked by group of m experts [6].

For a profile, finding the consensus ranking is possible due to measure of distance between pairs of rankings firstly introduced by Kemeny and discussed in many papers, see, for instance, in [8,9]. The ranking α can be represented by an (n×n) relation matrix $[a_{ij}]$ whose rows and columns are labeled by the software products and properties of the relation matrix are connected to those of the corresponding relation.

$$a_{ij} = \begin{cases} 1 & \text{if } a_i \succ a_j \\ 0 & \text{if } a_i \sim a_j \\ -1 & \text{if } a_i \prec a_j \end{cases} \tag{4}$$

The Kemeny distance function $d(\alpha_k, \alpha_l)$ between two rankings α_k and α_l is defined by formula [6]

$$d(\alpha_k,\alpha_l) = \frac{1}{2}\sum_{i,j=1}^{n}\left|a_{ij}^k - a_{ij}^l\right| = \sum_{i<j}\left|a_{ij}^k - a_{ij}^l\right| \tag{5}$$

It can be then defined a ‘distance’ between a ranking α and a profile A as follows:

$$D(\alpha, A) = \sum_{k=1}^{m} d(\alpha,\alpha_k) = \sum_{i<j}\sum_{k=1}^{m}\left|a_{ij}^k - a_{ij}\right| = \sum_{i<j}\sum_{k=1}^{m} d_{ij}^k \tag{6}$$

Like in the case of the relation matrix, we can define an $(n\times n)$ *profile matrix* $P = |pij|$ which can represent in compact form all the rankings. In the profile matrix

$$p_{ij} = \sum_{k=1}^{m} d_{ij}^k \qquad \text{i,j} = 1,\ldots,\text{n} \tag{7}$$

where $d_{ij}^k = \begin{cases} 0 & \text{if } a_i^k \succ a_j^k \\ 1 & \text{if } a_i^k \sim a_j^k \\ 2 & \text{if } a_i^k \prec a_j^k \end{cases}$

In sense of the measure (6), the consensus linear ranking β is the closest relation (so called *median*) to the preference profile, i.e.

$$\beta = \arg\min \sum_{k=1}^{m} d(\alpha, a_k)$$

These generally defined principles of the Consensus Relation will be accompanied by the concrete numerical example in the part 6 of the paper.

5. Comparison of Approaches

Some basic ideas for comparison of the above approaches are represented in [6]. The comparison was conducted based on the characteristics of the methods. By taking into account the characteristics of the Fuzzy Analytic Hierarchy Process the table of the comparative characteristics of the methods given in [6] will be represented in the following way:

Characteristic of the method	Analytic Hierarchy Process	Fuzzy Analytic Hierarchy Process	Overall Integral Index	Consensus Relation
Scaling	Ratio; priorities	Ratio; fuzzy defined priorities	Order; priorities	Order
Preference elicitation	Pairwise comparison	Pairwise comparison of fuzzy numbers	Pairwise comparison	Distance between rankings
Weighting of particular attributes	Normalized ratio via eigenvalues	Normalized ratio via fuzzy eigenvectors	Normalized relative attributes	No
Synthesis of resulting estimation	Additive, eigenvectors	Additive, fuzzy eigenvector	Additive, multiplicative	Linear order relation as consensus
Description of structure of objects in question	Hierarchic	Hierarchic	Hierarchic	Not important

6. Numerical Example

It is reasonable to accompany the above approaches by a simple example that would model a real situation of evaluation. Let 4 software products be evaluated by 5 criteria: understandability, learnability, operability, attractiveness and compliance. For this purpose a group of 3 experts was organized.

6.1. Overall Integral Index

Each of the 3 experts sets weights for attributes with the help of [n x n] matrix of attributes pair comparison. For instance, the matrix for group of the above attributes (let define them as x_1, x_2, x_3, x_4 and x_5) has been made by the first expert:

	X_1	X_2	X_3	X_4	X_5
X_1	10	8	7	6	5
X_2		10	9	7	6
X_3			10	8	6
X_4				10	7
X_5					10

Then, relative estimation of weight for each attribute are usually calculated by means of the matrix of pair comparisons in several ways:

	X_2/ X_1	X_3/ X_2	X_4/ X_3	X_5/ X_4
X_1	0,800	0,875	0,857	0,833
X_2		0,900	0,778	0,857
X_3			0,800	0,750
X_4				0,700
Average value	0,800	0,888	0,812	0,785

All the average values presented in the bottom row of the table are used to calculate normalized weight factors. For instance, $m_{x3/x1} = 0.7$; $m_{x3/x2/x1} = 0.888*0.8=0.71$, etc.

The average relative weights: $M_{x3/x1} = (m_{x3/x1}+ m_{x3/x2/x1})/2 = 0.705$; $M_{x4/x1}= (0.6+0.577)/2 = 0.589$; $M_{x5/x1}=(0.5+0.453)/2=0.477$. The obtained values are normalized.

Further procedure is repeated for each of the quality attributes. Other experts make the same procedure in parallel. Average estimations of weights of indexes are normalized by division of each into the sum of estimations. For every attribute the average value is calculated by three experts. Normalized final weights of indexes made by three experts are as follows:

$$m_{x1} = 0.27;\ \hat{m}_{x\,2} = 0.24;\ \hat{m}_{x\,3} = 0.19;\ \hat{m}_{x\,4} = 0.16;\ \hat{m}_{x\,5} = 0.13.$$

A value of the quality attribute W_1 for the first software is

$$W_1 = 10\times 0.27+8\times 0.24 + 7\times 0.19+6\times 0.16+ 5\times 0.13 = 7.56$$

The same procedure should be repeated also for the other quality attributes and software products. A software product with a higher value of a quality attribute is assumed to be best from the point of view of this attribute.

6.2. Consensus Relation

Using this method, experts have determined the following rankings for the software products.

In this case the preference profile matrix is as follows:

$$[p_{ij}] = \begin{bmatrix} 0 & 0 & 5 & 0 & 4 \\ 6 & 0 & 6 & 4 & 6 \\ 1 & 0 & 0 & 0 & 1 \\ 6 & 2 & 6 & 0 & 6 \\ 2 & 0 & 5 & 0 & 0 \end{bmatrix}$$

The search of the optimum linear order according to criterion function with the help of special algorithm [12] on this matrix has given the following distribution of places between the software products: 1, 2, 3, 4, 5.

6.3. Fuzzy Analytic Hierarchy Process

For the purpose of simplicity let's consider that only three quality attributes are measured.

The fuzzy comparison judgments are shown in the table:

	Understandability	Learnability	Operability
Understandability	1	(2, 3, 4)	(1, 2, 3)
Learnability	(1/4, 1/3, ½)	1	(1/3, 1/2, 1)
Operability	(1/3, 1/2, 1)	(1, 2, 3)	1

From the table it is seen that Understandability is considered as the most important attribute, since all the fuzzy numbers in the first row are greater than one. For example, Understandability is assessed as being about two times more important than Learnability and about two times more important than Operability. Since the fuzzy pairwise comparison matrix is reciprocal, only the elements of the upper right part are used for the calculation of weights. The weights can be obtained by resolving a non-linear equation (3). A practical example how to calculate it can be found, e.g., in [12].

7. Conclusion

In conclusion it is reasonable to point out the following main principles for choosing an approach for a qualitative evaluation:

1. If a group of experts is reliable (i.e. experts have been working long in the area) and homogeneous (i.e. the difference between the experts' knowledge is not considerable) and accuracy of the results is not a critical issue, so the Overall Integral Index approach can be chosen;

2. Of a group of experts is not reliable or heterogeneous, and accuracy of the results is not critical issue, the Consensus Relation can be chosen;
3. Finally, if a group of experts is not reliable or heterogeneous and accuracy is important, the Fuzzy Analytic Hierarchy Process can be chosen.

The most accurate approach from the above ones is the Fuzzy Analytic Hierarchy Process; however, this is also the most complex method.

In many cases the sub-optimal approach to be chosen for the qualitative evaluation seems to be the Consensus Relation, since it gives an acceptable level of accuracy.

Finally, we would like to stress that one of the considerable disadvantages of the above approaches is that they all require at least two software products to be evaluated. If there is only one software product available for evaluation, these approaches can not be implemented. In this case it is reasonable to use other methods like Heuristic Analysis etc. However, due to the high competition among the software developers in the market there are no many areas (except several very ad hoc fields), where only a software product of the only software developer exists.

8. Future Research

In the future we plan to implement the above approaches to evaluation of a real software project. For this purpose we chose the software development project Korppi, whose outcome is supposed to be a web-based application for tracking of students' studying progress at the University of Jyväskylä, Finland. The results of the research are supposed to be published.

References

[1] IEEE, "IEEE Std. 1061–198, Standard for a Software Quality Metrics Methodology, revision". Piscataway, NJ., IEEE Standards Dept., 1998.
[2] P. Faratin, C. Sierra and N. Jennings: Negotiation decision functions for autonomous agents. Robotics and Autonomous Systems, 24 (1998), 159–182.
[3] G.G. Azgaldov: The Foundations of Quality, Moscow, Economics, 1982.
[4] ISO 9126 – Software Engineering. Product Quality.
[5] T.L. Saaty. The Analytic Hierarchy Process, McGraw – Hill, New York, 1980.
[6] V. Artemenko, P. Martyusheva, S. Muravyov and N. Znamenschikova: Methods of Rating Competitors for Quality Awards: Tentative Comparative analysis, Proceedings of the 10th IMEKO TC7 International Symposium, June 30–July 2, 2004, Saint-Petersburg, Russia, 491–496.
[7] L. Mikhailov, P. Tsvetinov: Evaluation of Services using a Fuzzy Analytic Hierarchy Process.
[8] H. Deng: Multicriteria analysis with fuzzy pairwise comparison. International Journal of Approximate Reasoning, 21 (1999), 215–231.
[9] H.P. Young, a. Levenglick: A Consistent Extension of Condorset's election principle, SIAM Journal of Applied Mathematics, 35(2), 1978, 285–300.
[10] S.V. Moravyov, V. Savolainen: Recursive Brunch and Bound Algorithm for Multiple Properties Measurement on Ordinal Scale. In: Callaos N., Guo Q., Pierre S., Muravyov S. (Eds.).
[11] S.V. Muravyov, V. Savolainen: Special Intepretation of formal measurement scales for the case of multiple heterogeneous properties, Measurement 29, 2001, 209–223.
[12] C.K. Kwong, H. Bai. A Fuzzy AHP approach to the determination of importance weights of customer requirements in quality function deployment. Journal of Intelligent Manufacturing, 13, 2002, p. 367–377.

New Trends in Software Methodologies, Tools and Techniques
H. Fujita and M. Mejri (Eds.)
IOS Press, 2005

IT Practitioner's Perspective on Australian Risk Management Practices and Tools for Software Development Projects: A Pilot Study

Bee Bee CHUA [a] and June M. VERNER [b]
[a] *Department of Information Systems, University of Technology, Sydney*
[b] *Empirical Software Engineering, National ICT Australia, Sydney*

Abstract. The focus of this paper is a pilot study of IT practitioners regarding risk management practices and tools used in Australian software development projects. Our previous work [1] explained the method used for investigating whether there were differences in the practices and procedures relating to projects with 1) internal customers, 2) external customers and 3) both internal and external customers. For a comprehensive view to enable understanding the method use for data analysis in this pilot study 1) we explain the approach to what we have undertaken; 2) we discuss data collection for the survey and 3) describe our data analysis from the survey. Our respondents were from software development organizations in Australia and all had previously been involved with at least one software development project. Overall, we found that 1) risk management practices were used more frequently for projects involving external customers, 2) risk management is taken more seriously when external customers are involved, 3) the people who were responsible for risk management practices had senior positions within the organization, 4) there was no difference in the type of customer for projects where simulation and predictive tools were used, 5) external customers were more satisfied with simulation and predictive tools than internal customers.

Keywords. Risk management practices, risk management tools, risk assessment and tools satisfaction

1. Introduction

IT practitioners face many different types of challenges when developing software projects. One potential challenge is to know the right methodologies, tools and techniques to use for the various project tasks. IT practitioners who manage software development projects usually have good risk management [22], as inadequate risk management is likely to cause project failure. It has been suggested that good requirements are significantly related to software project outcomes [2] and that poor requirements are a major reason for project failure.

In many cases both practitioners and users lack a good understanding of the importance of requirements. Associated with incomplete, ambiguous, and unverifiable requirements, which not only make it very difficult for the developers to deal with any changes, are many other problems such as poor schedule estimation, cost overruns and project late delivery [10,18,21].

Risk management, coupled with the use of risk tools, has been suggested as useful in managing requirements. While a large number of risk management practices and tools are described in the literature [3–10] only a few risk management practices and tools have been successfully introduced into general use in the software development community. In reality, many organizations that develop software, either for external customers or for in-house users do not use risk management practices or tools to identify and assist with the control of requirements risks. This is possibly because most risk management tools and practices have a project cost, time and quality focus, rather than an explicit requirements focus.

Over the past many years, various types of software metrics and risk metrics have been suggested [11–13]. These metrics were specifically introduced to help the software development team identify and measure goals associated with risks with software processes and software products. There has been some criticism that these metrics do not sufficiently address risks particularly requirement risks. There are many types of risks related to requirements including: incomplete requirements [14], ambiguous requirements, unclear requirements and each of these has an impact on cost, time and quality. This is exacerbated when requirements become volatile. Such problems are likely to hamper the project managers' ability to manage software projects successfully.

Poor requirements can lead to serious problems in any type of software development project. The Standish Group [15] found that one third of projects were never completed and one half were challenged, i.e., were delivered with only partial functionality, had major cost overruns and significant delays. When IT practitioners were asked to identify the causes of project failure, 50% of the respondents mentioned that they were due to the lack of user involvement (13%), incomplete requirements (12%), changing requirements (12%), unrealistic expectations (6%) and unclear objectives (5%). In order to cross-validate the survey findings, the European Software Institute conducted a survey to investigate software practitioners' perceptions of software problems. They concluded that the majority of problems were similar to the problems found by the Standish group, i.e., in the areas of requirements specification (more than 50%) and requirements management (50%) [16].

Other software project risks include the lack of top management commitment, unclear or misunderstood project scope or objectives [17] and a large number of requirements problems [18]. May [19] mentioned common software problems were poor user input, stakeholder conflicts, vague requirements, poor cost and schedule estimation, skills that do not match the job and failing to plan. These problems were related to both organizational and technical complexity. Technical complexity increases when projects are exposed to inadequate feasibility studies, budget and scheduling. This results in significant risk. Another empirical research study conducted by Zowghi et al. [20] found that requirements volatility (RV) was an independent variable that significantly impacted project cost and time during software development. Although these researchers proposed a conceptual framework to support their hypotheses they did not consider the impact that risk management tools and practices had on the project outcomes. While they found that inherent complexities (organizational complexity, technical complexity, people relationship complexity and requirements complexity) are likely to cause project failure they did not investigate risk management practices and tools.

To investigate what risk management practices and tools were used by IT practitioners in Australian software organizations, we developed a questionnaire as the basis of a pilot study. This questionnaire contained questions related to the risk impact of requirements changes and was developed through a broad literature study.

Our primary objective is to examine what risk management practices and tools are used in Australia within the context of requirements risk management in software development projects. We are particularly interested to discover what tools and methods are used for software developed for both internal and external customers.

Although risk management practices are significantly associated with good requirements [21]. However, Glass [22] noted that most developers and project managers perceive risk management activities as extra work and expense. He also suggests that risk management is the least practiced discipline amongst the different project management areas. Although we are interested to discover who is using tool support to manager requirements risks and for what type of customer, we do not expect to find much tool support for this type of risk management in practice.

The remainder of this paper is organized as follows. In Section 2, we report on the development of our questionnaire and the questionnaire responses. In Section 3, we present our analysis of the results. In Section 4, we discuss our main findings and conclude by making some recommendations for future research.

2. Questionnaire Responses

We developed a questionnaire for our pilot study based on a broad study of the literature, that contained questions related to the risk impact of requirements changes. We distributed the questionnaire by post to 25 recipients who were randomly chosen from Australian Stock Exchange website[1]. We later distributed copies of the questionnaire to 17 Sydney software companies via email. Our questionnaire is based on the literature that addresses risks related to requirements changes and their impact on software development projects. We were specifically concerned that our respondents should have software development experience. A survey was chosen because of its simplicity and because we wanted to find the frequencies of tool and technique usage as well as identify relationships amongst variables.

The questionnaire is divided into seven sections: (1) respondents software development experience, (2) organization details, (3) characteristics of software projects, (4) functional requirements changes, (5) non-functional requirements changes, (6) factors affecting requirement changes, and (7) risk management. We began the questionnaire by asking for some details about the respondents' software development background. In addition we asked if they developed software for 1) internal customers, 2) external customers or 3) the software was for customers who were both internal and external.

We received completed questionnaires from 16 IT practitioners (mainly directors, project managers, project leaders, developers and consultants) who worked in software development for Australian business organizations. Nine out of 25 respondents (36%) answered the survey that was posted to the local software companies. Because the respondents who were sent questionnaire by post were very slow respond we decided to use an alternate approach and to send an email survey, with the questionnaire attached, to software companies listed on the Australian Stock Exchange website. This was more successful with 7 out of 17 (41%) replying within two weeks.

---

[1] Website address: www.ferret.com.au.

Our sample size of 16 is fairly small but large enough for a pilot study and sufficient for us to test the relationships between some of the variables. Moser and Kalton [23] comment, that the results of a postal survey can be considered as unbiased if the response rate is more than 30%.

Almost 99% of our respondents had been involved in the development of more than one software development project (Electronic Commerce, Mobile Commerce, Banking, Financial, Healthcare, Shipping, Telecommunication, Information Technology, Information Systems, Engineering, Education, Import and Export, Transportation, Property and Construction, Airlines etc.). We infer from this that our respondents have adequate software development knowledge and that they should have some knowledge of risks associated with software development projects.

For the purpose of analysis we have divided our respondents into groups based their customers, 1) internal customers 2) external customers 3) both internal and external customers.

3. Results and Analysis

Due to the impact that poor requirements have on project outcomes, we wished to investigate the types of risk management practices and tools used to deal with requirements risks.

Our goal is to investigate the types of risk tools and risk management practices used by the respondents in Australia for their 1) internal customers 2) external customers and 3) internal and external customers.

With this goal in mind, we have classified the following questions into three sections. In Section 1, the respondents involevment in software development organisations is shown. In Section 2, we provide organizational details. In Section 3, we address the respondents involved in risk management practices and in Section 4, we present the respondents viewpoint on risk management tools. In order to reduce invalid responses from respondents, we provided instructions on how to complete the survey. If respondents answered either 'no' or 'not sure' to question 1 and 2 they were not required to proceed with the survey. Sixteen respondents indicated that their organiza-tion developed software projects and that they were involved in the development of software projects.

3.1. Section 1: Respondents' Involved in Software Development Organizations

1. Has your organization developed software development projects? [Yes = 16, No = 0, Not Sure = 0]
2. Were you involved in the development? [Yes = 16, No = 0, Not Sure = 0]
3. Indicate the types of software development project areas you worked in previously. [A. Electronic Commerce = 7, B. Mobile Commerce = 4, C. Banking = 4, D. Financial = 8, E. Healthcare = 4, F. Shipping = 4, G. Telecommunication = 7, H. Information Technology = 5, I. Information Systems = 8, J. Engineering = 3, H. Education = 4, I. Import and Export = 0, J. Transportation = 6, K. Property and Construction = 2, L. Airlines = 1, M. Others = 1].

Not suprisingly, software development companies in Australia offered a broad range of business solutions to their customers. In the responses we observed that there was more than one type of software project selected. Also, based on the results we concluded that commonly found projects developed in Australia are Electronic Commerce, Financial, Telecommunication and Information Systems.

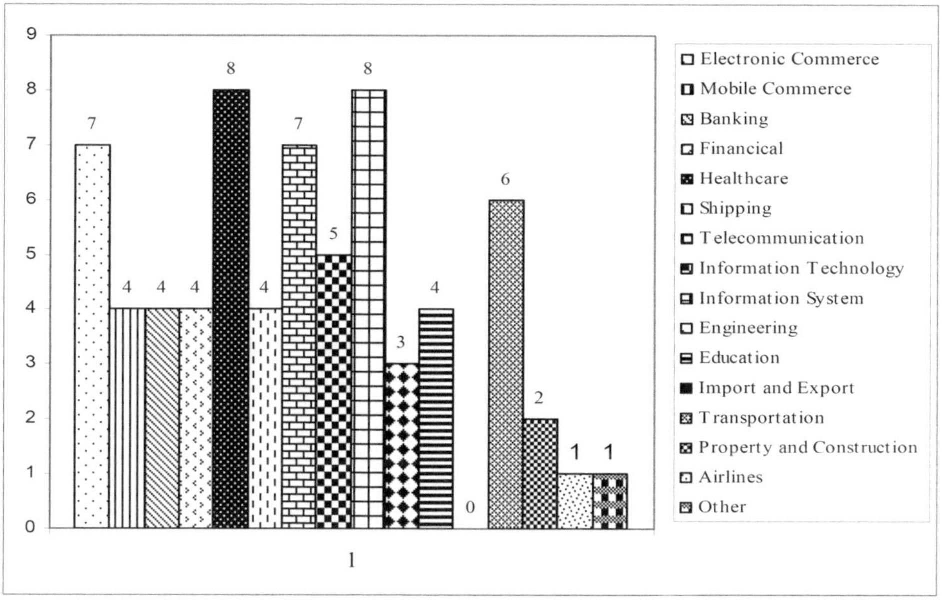

Figure 1. Types of software development projects.

3.2. Section 2: Organization Details

This section investigated the industry type of the respondent's organization, respondents' type of work, and the type of customers they worked with. The aim is to investigate and evaluate the relationship between group sizes effectively and provide some idea of how the size of an IT company impacts the development of software projects for different types of customers.

4. What type of industry does your organization belong to? [Consumer Business = 1, Energy Resources = 0, Financial Resources = 1, Healthcare = 1, Property and Construction = 0, Public sector = 1, Information Technology = 3, Airline = 0, Travel Industries = 1, Telecommunication = 1, Media = 2, Software Solutions = 2, Education = 1, Shipping =1 and Other = 1]
5. How many staff involved in the project? [less than 10 staff = 8, more than 10 staff but less than 40 staff = 8, more than 40 staff but less than 70 staff = 0, more than 70 staff but less than 110 staff = 0, more than 110 staff = 0]

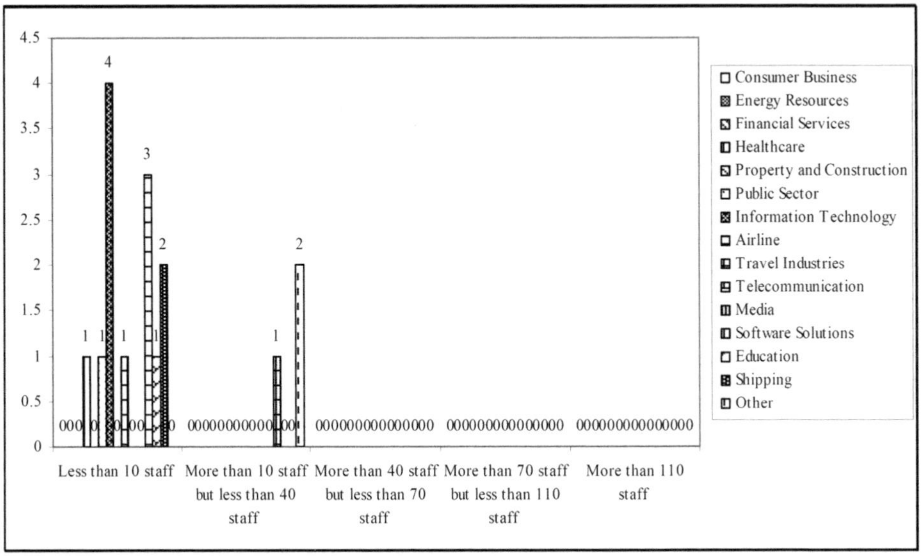

Figure 2. The size of IT companies participated in the survey.

The majority of the companies surveyed has less than 10 staff working on their projects. The organization were based in Information Technology (4), Software Solutions (3), Public Sector (1), Healthcare (1), Travel industries (1), Education (1) and Shipping (2).

6. What was the project-estimated cost? [less than 1 million = 9, more than 1 million but less than 5 million = 6, more than 5 million but less than 1 billion = 1, more than 1 billion = 0]

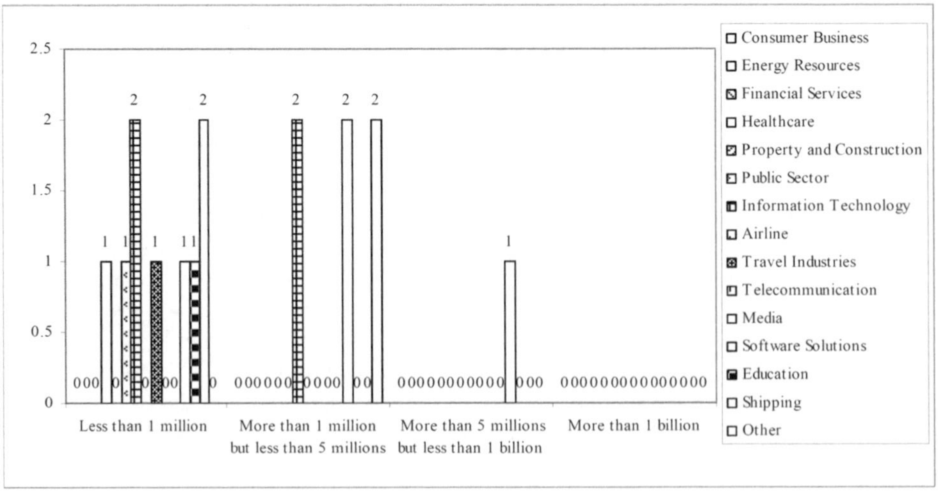

Figure 3. Project cost from different industries.

7. Indicate your position in the organization. [Managing director = 3, Project Director = 1, Project Manager = 3, Software Development Manager = 2, Software Quality Assurance manager = 0, Project Leader = 1, Developer = 1, Tester = 1, Technical Support = 1 and Other = 3]

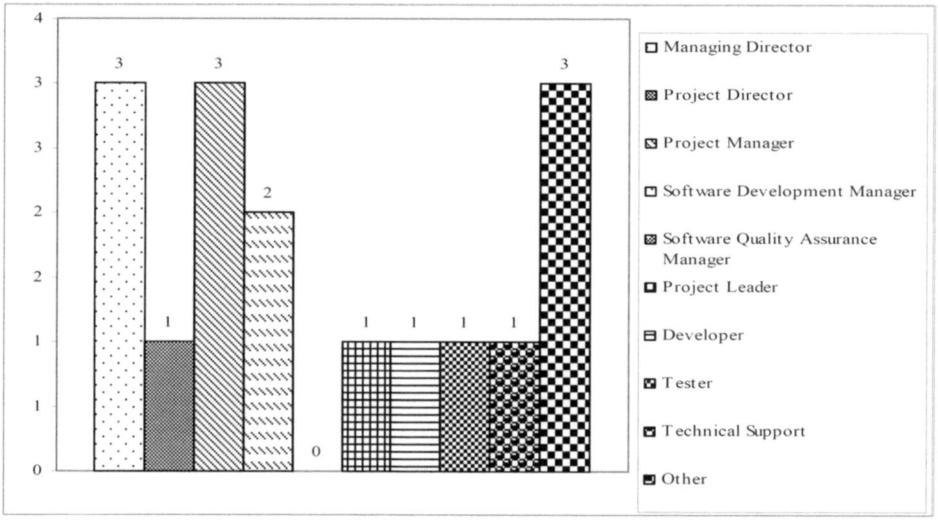

Figure 4. Types of positions in the organization.

8. Who are your customers? [Internal customers= 4, External customers = 9, Internal and external customers = 3]

From Fig. 5, we can see that 4 respondents replied that projects they developed are for internal customers, 9 respondents replied that their projects are developed to support external customers and 3 respondents replied that the projects are developed to support internal and external customers.

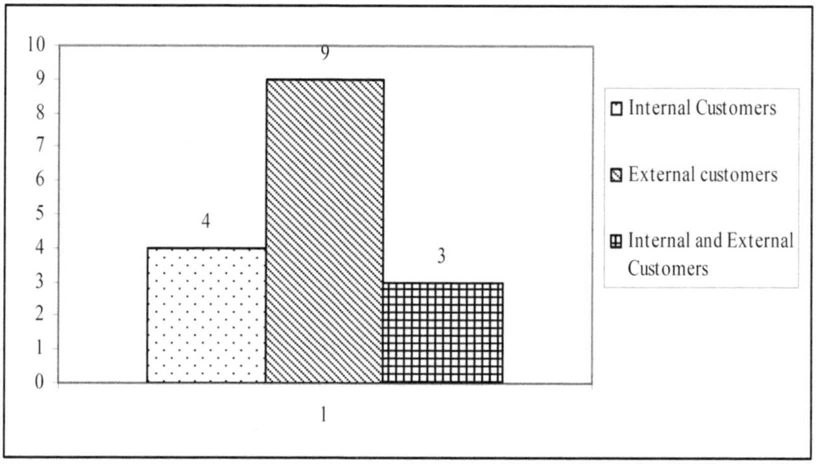

Figure 5. Types of customers.

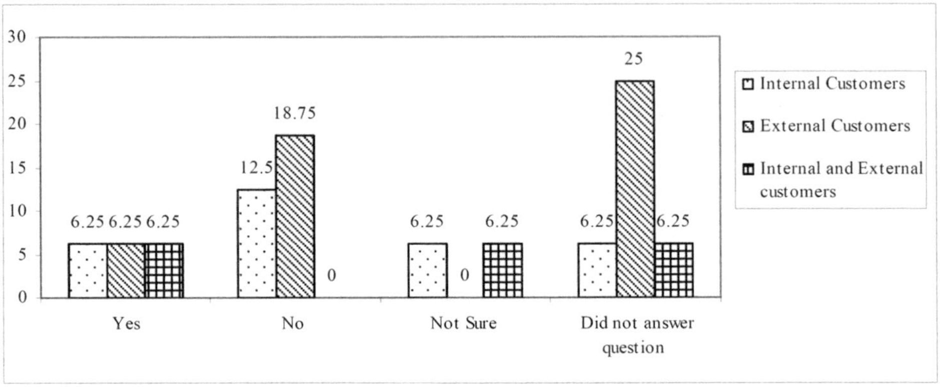

Figure 6. Organizations use risk assessment.

3.3. Section 3: Risk Management Practices

Many guidelines and standards have been defined for different approaches to risk management. In particular, the Project Management Institute standards [24], UK Office of Government Commerce, and the Australian and New Zealand standard AS/NZ 4360. These standards include many different types of risk ranging from corporate governance through strategic portfolio management to projects and tasks. However, there is no single risk management standard or guideline considered as best practice. This is because most risk management processes follow the same basic procedures although the terminology may differ [25]. We next review questions from 9 to 15 in detail to find out whether organizations assess risks and the types of risk management practices that are used for their customers.

9. Does your organization use risk assessment to identify the risk impact of requirements changes? [Yes = 3, No= 5, Not Sure = 2, Did not answer the question = 6]

Analysis of this question showed some minor differences between different groups of employees. Three (18.75%) respondents (including one managing director, one project manager and one software development manager) answered "Yes". In contrast, 5 (31.25%) respondents answered "No". This group included one developer, one from tester, one from Technical Support and two from the "other" group who worked as a consultant. These results may be due to differences in interests of the two groups. We suggest that the management team is probably interested to know the "how and why" of requirements changes and their impact on project variables such as cost, time and effort. The more technical group is probably interested to know "what" these requirements changes are. In fact, according to the technical respondents, requirements changes by type, are updated into change control software that monitors all the changes that are made.

Figure 6 shows that a large proportion of respondents (50%), including groups who are 'not sure' and 'did not answer the question', did not respond to the question. We suspected that the organizational size may be a factor and that risk assessment may not be used commonly in small and medium organizations but is more likely to be used in large software organizations.

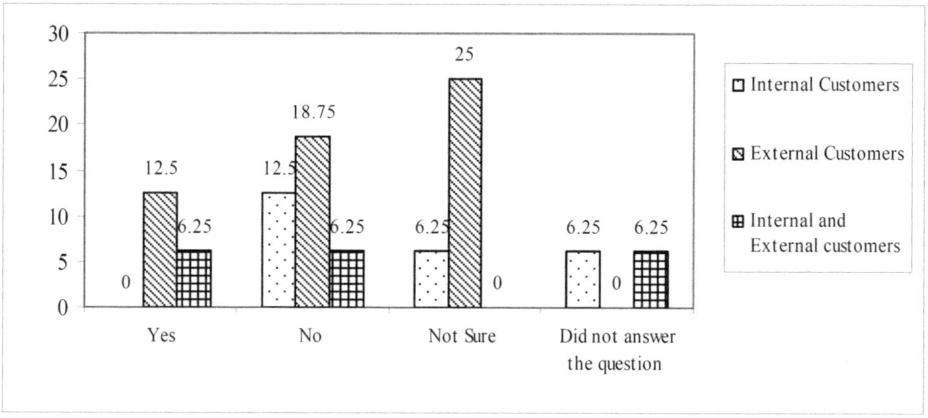

Figure 7. Risk models used by types of customers.

In summary, respondents with a higher position in the organization is likely to have better knowledge of exactly what risk assessment procedures are used within the organization.

10. Does your organization use a risk assessment model? [Yes = 3, No = 6, Not Sure = 5, Did not answer the question = 2]

This question was asked in relation to the previous question. Surprisingly, though the Australian risk standard has been in place for some time, few organizations take risk management seriously. Based on Fig. 7, we see that only 2 (12.5%) organizations dealing with external customers use risk assessment models. Three organizations (18.75%) without a risk assessment model deal with external customers. Four respondents (25%) reported they did not know if a risk assessment model was used when dealing with their external customers.

We suspect the reason is that many risk assessment models are inappropriate or are difficult to use. Nogueira [25] made the comment that the main weakness of the current models is their human dependency. Risk assessment models produce inconsistent results with different experts achieving different conclusions from the same scenario.

11. What risk management strategies were used to help control the number of requirement changes? [Risk Analysis = 7, Risk Identification = 7, Risk Assessment = 7, Risk Evaluation = 4 and others = 1]

We were also interested to find out what risk management strategies were used to control the number of requirement changes. Figure 8 shows risk practices for all groups. In the survey, a respondent was allowed to tick more than one choice for risk management strategies. We discovered that organizations adopted risk analysis, risk identification and risk assessment more commonly for use on external projects rather han internal projects. These results also indicate that these strategies give external customers a structured mechanism to provide visibility into threats to project success. Importantly, the visible threats such as ambiguous wording of government guidelines and polices, rapid technological changes and stakeholders' continuous requirements changes make it difficult to control project risk and to prioritize each risk appropriately.

The risk management life cycle begins with a first stage of risk identification and is followed by other stages in subsequent risk cycles. However, risk analysis is not yet

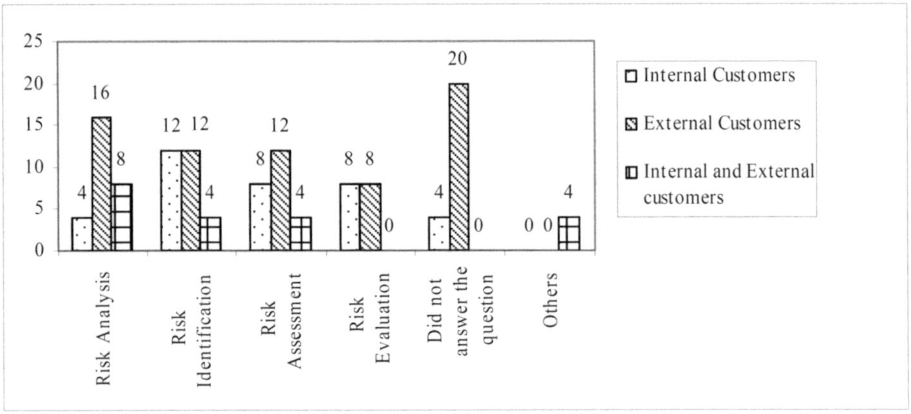

Figure 8. Risk management strategies used by customers.

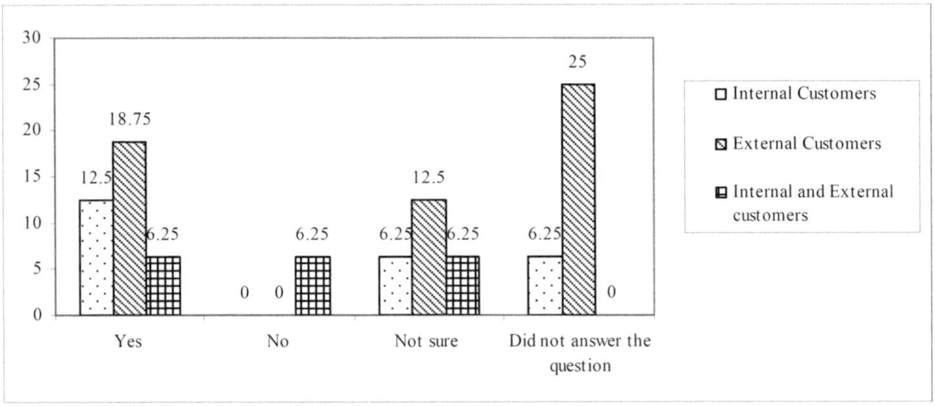

Figure 9. Customers accept risk analysis.

commonly used as a strategy to manage requirements changes. Even Hillson [26] claimed that the current level of risk analysis appears to be rather shallow and is largely driven by the capabilities of the tools and techniques used.

In Fig. 8, we see that 24% of the respondents did not attempt to answer this question. Perhaps they did not have enough risk management training to be familiar with the strategies asked, they were not involved in any risk management, or they could have used strategies other than the ones we mentioned in the questionnaire, though we find this unlikely.

12. Did your customers accept requirement changes based on risk analysis? [Yes = 6, No = 1, Not sure = 4 and Did not answer question = 5]

We are particularly interested to find out which groups accepted the respondents' risk analysis. Basically, 3 (18.75%) respondents agreed that their risk analysis was accepted by external customers compared to 2 (12.5%) responces for internal customers and 1 (6.25%) for both internal and external customers in Fig. 9. The data suggests that risk analysis is taken more seriously when the customers are external. These external projects may have legal agreements and the organizations could incur

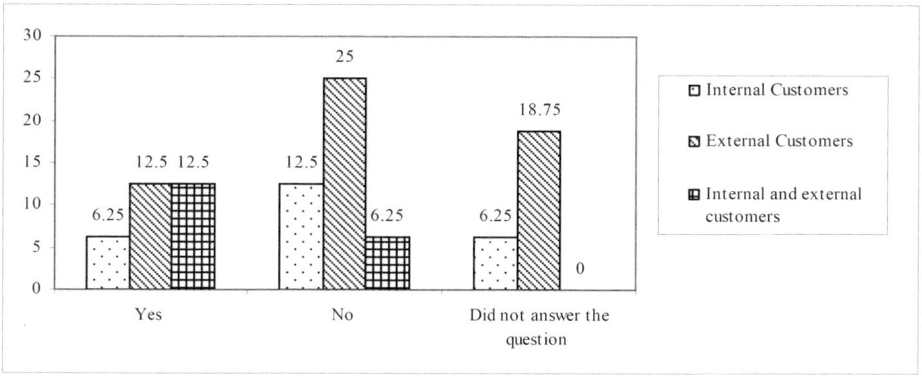

Figure 10. Respondents involved in conducting requirement changes.

heavy penalties for failure or late delivery. As a result, risk for external customer projects is taken seriously.

Having established that some of the respondents use risk management practices, we are interested to know the types of tools they use for 1) internal customers, 2) external customers and 3) internal and external customers. In addition, we are also interested to find out how satisfied they are with these tools and if their level of satisfaction is colored by the type of customer.

3.4. Section 4: Risk Management Tools

Risk management is used in many different disciplines e.g., Health and Safety, Business and Finance, Construction, Engineering and other related disciplines. The process of risk management is divided into five steps: risk identification, risk assessment, risk response development, control and capitalization. Generic tool support enables project managers to deal with different types of risk and supports different risk management processes. Use of a simulation tool can provide important insights into project costs, time and effort when requirement changes take place.

Although automated risk tools promise greater reliability when used to predict project parameters such as cost, time and effort, they are considered weak with respect to the control of requirements risks. The tools may be good in some situations but not all.

13. Does your role in the organization involve you in conducting requirements changes risk assessment? [Yes = 5, No = 7, Did not answer the question = 4]

We were also interested to discover if our respondents were themselves actually involved with requirement changes and with which types of clients. Figure 10 shows that a large number of respondents did not respond. From Fig. 10 we see that 2 respondents (12.5%) for each group of customers 1) external and 2) internal and external answered that they have used risk assessment to conduct requirement changes. There is a high percentage (43.75%) of respondents who saidthey did not use risk assessment when conducting requirement changes. We wondered if the main reason was lack of risk assessment, or lack of adequate risk assessment tools that could display data in a meaningful fashion. Also most of the projects that our respondents discussed were of fairly short duration (under six months). Again, this finding agrees with a

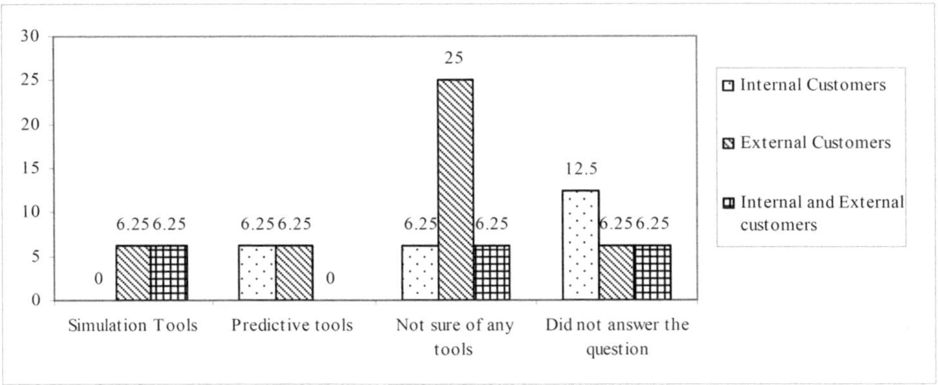

Figure 11. Different types of tools.

project management and techniques report by Thomsett [28] that risk assessment tools are in active use in fewer than 12,000 organizations worldwide.

14. What types of tools were used to control the risk impact of requirement changes? [Simulation = 2, Predictive = 2, Not sure of any tools = 6, Did not answer the question = 4]

Kaindl et al. [27] suggests that the requirements engineering (RE) literature is based on the assumption that commercial RE tools are well suited for managing large requirements sets written in natural language but not for engineering requirements. We expected that some projects would begin with incomplete requirements and would need to use both quantitative and qualitative risk tools to assess what the impacts of changes would be. Therefore, we felt that this question would give us some idea of which tools are popular.

Figure 11 shows that only one (6.25%) organization used simulation tools for 1) external customers and 2) internal and external customers. No respondent mentioned using simulation tools for internal customers. For predictive tools, there is no difference on type of customers. However, there was a difference when we look at respondents who were not sure of the tools used to control the impact of requirement changes. For example, 4 (25%) of the respondents were not sure what types of tools were used for external customers, 1 (6.25%) respondent was not sure about tools for internal customers and 1 (6.25%) respondent for tools for both internal and external customers.

We also suspected that simulation and predictive tools are not very useful for risk analysis as they do not provide enough information. Surprisingly, our result contrasts with a report [28] that risk tools have been widely developed for the software industry as it appears that there may not be enough benefit gained by using them.

15. Are you generally satisfied with the risk assessment tools that you use? [Yes = 4, No = 2, Not Sure = 6, Did not answer the question = 4]

Our initial assumption was that there would be a high percentage of respondents who were satisfied with the tools they use. The results, shown on Fig. 12 did not support this assumption. From Fig. 12, we see that only 1 (6.25%) respondent is satisfied with the tools used to support projects for internal customers. Most satisfaction were found on 3 (18.75%) respondents with tools support for external

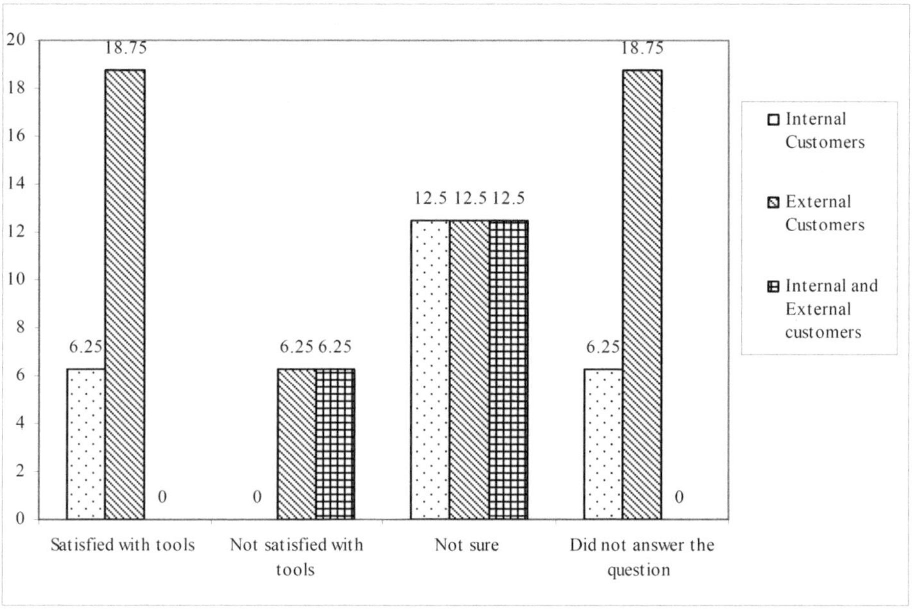

Figure 12. Satisfaction levels of using risk tools.

customers. A large proportion of 6 (37.5%) respondents were uncertain about their satisfaction with the tools used. More respondents who deal with external customers are satisfied with tools they use (mainly simulation and prediction tools). These results suggest that we need to improve the effectiveness of the tools, both for ease of use and functionality offered.

The questions we asked in the survey instrument are designed to gain a better understanding of the types of tools and practices used within the Australian organizations. One limitation of this pilot study stems from the unique characteristics of Australian culture, which may affect the personal understanding that our respondents have of risk management practices and tools within the organisations. It will be interesting to see if there are differences across different organisational cultures.

4. Conclusion and Future Works

In this pilot study, we reviewed risk management practices and risk tools for the development of software projects for 1) internal customers, 2) external customers and 3) internal and external customers and found in some cases that they were different.

We review our findings from two perspectives: 1) Australia's organizations and 2) Australia's IT practitioners.

From an organizational perspective, the people in the organization who govern software projects are at a senior level of management. These are the people who are more likely to know what is going on with risk management, and to know if it is done or not. Organization size may make a difference in the use of risk management practices.

From the IT practitioners' perspective, risk management practices are used for all projects no matter what type of customer. Practitioners tended to be more satisfied with the tools used if they have external customers and simulation are tools are more likely to be used for these external customers. Type of customer does not affect the use of predictive tools.

Our data suggests that risk is taken more seriously when the customers are external that such projects are also more likely to have 1) a defined risk model and 2) greater use of risk management strategies.

This work provides a partial overview of risk management practices and provides some pointers to the direction of future research. We intend to continue this work by investigating:

- what other tools are used for risk management,
- are the tools used for more than an assessment of the degree of risk,
- are they really useful for risk management,
- do they provide good value,
- how useful are these tools and where are they used, and
- what are their shortfalls?
- What type of risk management practices and tools used in US, Europe and India market?

The pilot study is a first step in our empirical research. This will allow us to develop an understanding of the Australian software development community and how they deal with rerquirements risks. In subsequent studies we intend to design a more comprehensive questionnaire and distribute it more extensively in order to eventaully develop a predictive tool for IT practitioners so that they may assess impacts of requirement changes more effectively.

Acknowledgement

The authors wish to thank the companies who actively participated in this study and provided on and off the record information.

References

[1] B.B. Chua and J. M. Verner, "Risk Management practices and tools: A pilot study of Australian Software development projects", *SWDC-REK International Conference for Software Development*, May, 2005.

[2] J.M. Verner, K. Cox, S. Bleistein, and N. Cerpa, "Requirement Engineering and Software Project Success: An Industrial Survey in Australia and the U.S," *in Proceedings of AWRE, Adelaide, Australia*, 2005.

[3] B.W. Boehm, *Software Risk Management: Principle and Practice*, IEEE Software, Vol. 8, No. 1, 1991.

[4] T. Demarco and L. Lister, *Managing Risk on Software Projects,* Dorset House Publishing Company, 2003.

[5] C.B. Chapman and S.C. Ward, Project *Risk Management – Processes, Techniques and Insights,* John Wiley and Sons, 2003.

[6] Project Management Institute, A *Guide to the Project Management Body of Knowledge (PMIBOK@Guide) 2000 Edition,* Project Management Institute Publications, 2001.

[7] T. Kendrick, *Identifying and Managing Project Risk: Essential Tools for Failure-Proofing Your Project,* American Management Association, 2003.

[8] S. Grey, *Practical Risk Assessment for Project Management,* John Wiley & Sons, 1995.
[9] L.J. Nogueria, "A Risk Assessment Model for Evolutionary Software Projects," [Verified: 05 Jan 2005], http://www.disi.unige.it/person/ReggioG/PROCEEDINGS/luqi.pdf, 2005.
[10] A. Tiwana and M. Keil, "The one minute risk assessment tool." in Proceedings to Communications of the ACM, Vol. 47, No. 11, 2004.
[11] F. Norman and N. Martin, "*Software Metrics and Risk*". in Proceedings of 2nd European Software Measurement Conference, 1999.
[12] L. Rosenberg and L. Hyatt, "*A Software Quality Model and Metrics for Identifying Project Risks and Assessing Software Quality,*" in Proceedings of 8th Annual Software Technology Conference in Utah, 2002.
[13] F. Norman and L.S. Pfleeger, *A Rigorous and Practical Approach, Second* Edition, PWS Publishing Company, 2002.
[14] H. Krasner, "Requirements Dynamics in Large Software Projects." in Proceedings of the 11th World Computer Congress (IFIP'89), Amsterdam, the Netherlands, 1989.
[15] Standish, "The Scope of Software Development Project Failures; The Standish Group": Dennis MA; [verified 20th Dec 2004], http://www.standishgroup.com/choas.html, 1995.
[16] European Software Institute, "European User Survey Analysis." Report USV_EUR 2.1, ESPITI Project, 1996.
[17] M. Christel and K. Kang, "Issues in Requirements Elicitation", Carnegie Mellon University, Pittsburgh, 1992.
[18] A.V. Lamsweerede, "Requirement Engineering in the Year 00: A Research Perspective," in Proceedings of ACM. 2000.
[19] J.L. May, "*Major Causes of Software Project Failures,*" Crosstalk Journal, [Verified 05th Jan 2005] http://www.stsc.hill.af.mil/crosstalk/1998/07/causes.pdf.,1998.
[20] D. Zowghi and N. Nurmuliani, "A study of the Impact of Requirement Volatility on Software Project Performance," in Proceedings of the Ninth Asia-Pacific Software Engineering Conference (APSEC'02), 2002.
[21] T. Addison and S. Vellabh, "Controlling Software Project Risks – an Empirical Study of Methods Used by Experienced Project Managers, " in Proceedings of SAICSIT, pp. 129–140, 2002.
[22] J.M. Verner and W. Evanco, "In–house Software Development: What Software Project Management Practices Lead to Success? " IEEE Software Jan/Feb, Vol. 22, No. 1, pp. 86–93, 2005.
[23] C.A. Moser and G. Kalton, *Survey methods in social investigation*. Heinemann Educational, UK, 1971.
[24] Project Management Institute, PMBOK – *A Guide to the Project management Body of Knowledge*, PMI Standards Committee, 2001.
[25] J.C. Nogueira, N. Nada and V. Berzins, "A Formal Risk Assessment Model for Software Evolution," [Verified 05 Jan 2005] http://www.disi.unige.it/person/ReggioG/PROCEEDINGS/luqi.pdf, 2000.
[26] D. Hillson, *Project risk management: Future developments.* International Journal Project & Business Risk Management, Vol. 2, No. 2, pp. 181–195, 1998.
[27] H. Kaindl, S. Brinkemper, A.J. Bubenko, B. Farbey, S.J. Greenspan, C.L. Heitmeyer, L.J. Prado Leite, C.S.D.P, R.N. Mead, J. Mylopoulos and J. Siddiqi, "Requirements Engineering and Technology Transfer: Obstacles, Incentives and Improvement Agenda." in Proceedings of Requirement Engineering, Springer-Verlag London Limited, 2002.
[28] Thomsett, *Thomsett project management and techniques.* [Verified 05 Jan 2005] http://www.isaca.org/Template.cfm?Section=Home&CONTENTID=16222&TEMPLATE=/ContentManagement/ContentDisplay.cfm, 2004.

New Trends in Software Methodologies, Tools and Techniques
H. Fujita and M. Mejri (Eds.)
IOS Press, 2005

Validating Documentation with Domain Ontologies

Leonid KOF [1] and Markus PIZKA
Fakultaet fuer Informatik, Technische Universitaet Muenchen, Munich, Germany

Abstract. Do we always use the same name for the same concept? Usually not. While misunderstandings are always troublesome, they pose particularly critical problems in software projects. Requirements engineering deals intensively with reducing the number and scope of misunderstandings between software engineers and customers. Software maintenance is another important task where proper understanding of the application domain is vital. In both cases it is necessary to gain (or regain) domain knowledge from existing documents that are usually inconsistent and imprecise.

This paper proposes to reduce the risk of misunderstandings by unifying the terminology of the different stakeholders with the help of an ontology. The ontology is constructed by extracting terms and relations from existing documents. Applying text mining for ontology extraction has an unbeatable advantage compared to manual ontology extraction: Text mining detects terminology inconsistencies before they are absorbed in the ontology. In addition to this, the approach presented in this paper also introduces an explicit validation of ontology gained by text mining.

1. Documents are Always Inconsistent

Usually, some kind of requirements document is written in the beginning of a software project. After requirements elicitation, one of the first tasks of the software developer is to understand the requirements document which includes trying to understand the terminology used. But practical experiences show that apart from being imprecise, requirements documents also use inconsistent terminology.

A simple steam boiler specification [1], written for a formal methods contest, for example, looked extremely precise at first glance. However, the document called the same measuring unit in different places "water level measurement device", "water level measuring unit", "device to measure the quantity of water", ... Obviously, this unwanted obfuscation hampers understanding of the domain. The reader can not be sure whether there is just one unit or two or three different devices. And of course, real life specifications, not written for an academic formal methods contest, are very likely even less consistent. Furthermore, real life documents are usually much longer rendering manual detection and resolution of such inconsistencies virtually impossible.

[1] Correspondence to: Leonid Kof, Fakultaet fuer Informatik, Technische Universitaet Muenchen, Boltzmannstr. 3, D-85748, Garching bei Muenchen, Germany Tel.: +49 89 289-17834; Fax: +49 89 289-17307; E-mail: kof@in.tum.de.

The consequences of this confusion grow with the progress of a software system through the software life cycle. At the later maintenance stage not only the documentation is inconsistent, but also the terminology used in the code does not necessarily coincide with the documentation. Sneed concludes in [2] that in many systems "*procedures and data are named arbitrarily*". Clearly, this strongly contributes to the fact that software maintenance consumes 80% of all costs for software and 50% out of these 80% must be devoted to program comprehension [3].

The goal of the approach presented in this paper is to detect and eliminate terminology inconsistencies by building consistent ontologies. The ontology extracted from documents and code are themselves validated either via prototyping (in requirements engineering) or by comparison with the implemented domain model (in the case of re-engineering). After validation by the stakeholders, this ontology will then be used as a consistent conceptual basis in the development or maintenance process.

Outline

The reminder of this paper is organized as follows: Section 2 gives an overview of existing text analysis methods. Section 3 shows how ontologies can be extracted in general, whereas Section 4 introduces an ontology extraction approach based on text analysis. In 5 we will show how ontology extraction can be embedded in the process of requirements engineering (or software re-engineering) and how the extracted ontology becomes validated, though validation is performed differently for requirements engineering and re-engineering. Finally, Section 7 summarizes the results of the proposed approach.

2. Related Work on Text Analysis

Document analysis for itself is neither a completely new problem nor a new solution in software engineering. There have already been various attempts to apply text analysis to requirements documents. In [4] Ben Achour classifies the linguistic methods of requirements engineering as either syntactic, lexical, or semantic.

Before giving an overview of the related approaches, we want to pose a set of criteria making a text analysis approach suitable for requirements documents analysis:

- The approach should not rely on any firm expression patterns. This is necessary due to extremely poor quality of requirements documents and practical impossibility to enforce any writing style.
- The approach should be interactive and not completely automatic. This is necessary to detect inconsistencies in the analyzed document. As praxis shows, inconsistencies are inevitable in requirements documents, which makes a completely automatic approach unfeasible. As Aussenac-Gilles [5] and Goldin & Berry [6] state, completely automated technique is not desirable as it potentially results in wrong extraction or information loss. Obviously, the human interaction should be limited to validation activities and should be unnecessary, for example, for pure term extraction.
- The approach should not rely on any previous domain knowledge. It is mostly the case in requirements engineering, that software at project beginning engineers have little superficial knowledge about the application domain, which causes difficulties in understanding the customer.

- The approach should extract not only terms relevant for the application domain, but also relations between these terms (i.e., ontology extraction instead of glossary extraction).

Among the three classes of existing approaches (lexical, syntactical, and semantical), lexical approaches are the most robust ones. Lexical methods, as proposed by Goldin & Berry [6], extract terms on the basis of common character sequences occurring in different sentences: any character sentence appearing in at list two sentences is a potential domain term. The decision whether the character sequence is really a term is made manually by the analyst. This simplicity is also the reason for the robustness of the lexical techniques. However, lexical approaches are limited to term extraction, they do not provide any term classification.

Syntactic methods are the oldest and the best known ones: Abbott suggested in [7] a method of terminology extraction based on an analysis of substantives, verbs, etc. (substantives become classes, verbs become actions, etc.) A similar proposal was made by Chen in [8]. Abbott states,

> Although the process we follow in formalizing the strategy may appear mechanical, it is not (given the current state–of–the–art of computer science) an automatable procedure.

The techniques proposed by Abbott and Chen could certainly be automated, today, using modern "Part–of–Speech" taggers (see for example Ratnaparkhi [9]). However, even if they were automated, these techniques would not produce a complete ontology but only the bare terminology.

A number of syntactic approaches were proposed for ontology extraction was proposed for other (not software engineering) applications. For example, Hearst [10] suggests a heuristics for extraction of the "is-a" relation from text. Berland and Charniak [11] extend the idea of Hearst to the extraction of the "part-of" relation. Degeratu and Hatzivassiloglou [12] use ideas similar to Hearst to extract the 'terms and relations from legal documents. The three above approaches, although sensible in the domains they were developed for, have common drawbacks making them barely applicable to requirements engineering:

- they rely on certain firm expression patterns,
- they are completely automated and do not give the user a validation possibility.

Other existing syntactical techniques, like those by Lame [13] and Zhou et al. [14] do not rely on firm expression patterns, but they require a-priori knowledge of domain terminology to become applicable.

Semantic techniques like those by Fuchs [15], Gervasi and Nuseibeh [16] or Ambriola and Gervasi [17] translate every sentence into a logical formula. This is surely even more than ontology extraction, but they rely on firm predefined expression patterns, which makes these approaches barely applicable to real life requirements documents. Furthermore, they *use* a given ontology to work, but they do not produce one.

The summary of this overview on related work on text analysis is obvious: there is no ontology extraction approach *satisfying the above requirements* in software engineering, yet! One could object that text mining was not necessary for ontology extraction. But, the only alternative would be purely manual ontology design (as in [18]) which would immediately lead into the troubles that we aim to overcome. Manual design does not reliably detect terminology inconsistencies but rather is a major source for inconsistencies.

The remainder of this paper describes our proposed ontology extraction approach and its embedding into software engineering process. In the context of the presented work an ontology is defined as a taxonomy enriched with associations. The taxonomy itself consists of a set of terms and the "is-a"–relation.

3. Ontology Construction Basics

The concept of an "ontology" was introduced in artificial intelligence as a means for communication between intelligent agents (see for example [19]). Today, it is regarded as a generally useful concept to communicate concept dependencies. As software development involves communication between "intelligent agents", here called software engineers and domain experts, an ontology can be a valuable instrument to establish a common language within a software project.

3.1. Do We Actually Need an Ontology?

At first it might seem that an ontology is unnecessary because a common language could also be established with a simple glossary. However, a brief example by Zave and Jackson [20] shows that a simple glossary quickly falls short in establishing a common understanding. The context of this example is a hypothetical university information system with a definition of the term "student", the binary relation "enrolled", and a conversation between the two agents Able and Baker:

> Able: Two important basic types are *student* and *course*. There is also a binary relation *enrolled*. If the basic types and relations are formalized as predicates, then it holds that
>
> $$\forall s\ \forall c\ (enrolled(s, c) \Rightarrow student(s) \wedge course(c)).$$
>
> Baker: Do only students enroll in courses? I don't think that's true.
> Able: But that's what I mean by *student*!

Although they *do* agree that the term "student" is an important domain concept, they disagree on the meaning of this concept.

3.2. Basics of Ontology Construction During Requirements Engineering

The usefulness of an ontology as a requirements engineering product has already been recognized. For example, Breitman and Sampaio do Prado Leite [18] regard an application ontology as one of the products of the requirements engineering activity. All methodologies for ontology construction listed in their work share the same basic steps as shown in Fig. 1. Apart from validation and verification, these steps include identification of information sources, identification of the list of terms, classification of the terms and their description.

Besides these common steps, the various methodologies listed by Breitman & Sampaio do Prado Leite remain rather abstract in the sense that they do not specify *how* to identify information sources, *how* to classify terms, and so on.

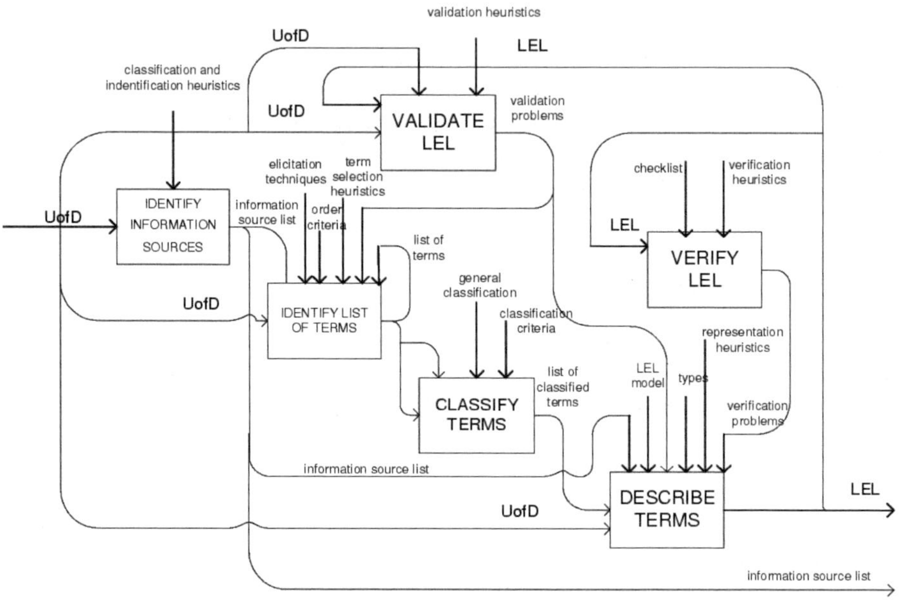

Figure 1. Ontology Construction Process (source: [18]).

However, if we consider ontology construction as an activity within the requirements engineering process, the identification of the sources of information seems rather obvious: the primary source of information are the requirements documents. For our second example for employing ontologies in software engineering, i. e. re-engineering, two sources of information have to be regarded: documentation of the software system and its code itself.

The next section shows how we extract a domain ontology from textual documentation.

4. Ontology Extraction via Text Analysis

Text analysis can easily be introduced into the general ontology construction process presented above. Figure 2 depicts the activities needed to produce an ontology starting from some documents[1].

"Parsing and subcategorization frames extraction" corresponds to the "identification of the term list step" of Fig. 1, "term clustering & taxonomy building" as well as "association mining" correspond to "term classification". Term validation and verification will be addressed later (see Section 5).

Note, that we define ontology as a taxonomy enriched with associations. The taxonomy itself consists of a set of terms and the "is-a"–relation. The overall process of ontology construction consists of four steps: term extraction, term clustering, taxonomy building (as cluster hierarchy) and relation (aka association) mining.

[1] See [21] for further details.

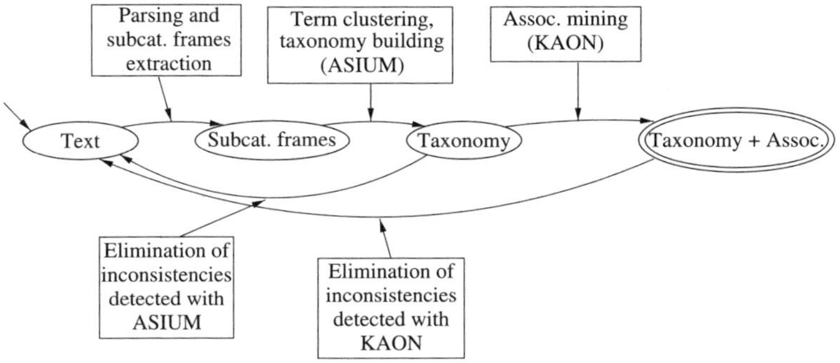

Figure 2. Ontology Extraction Procedure [21].

Extraction of terms from requirements documents: To extract terms, each sentence is parsed and the resulting parse tree is decomposed. Noun phrases that are related to the verb of the sentence are extracted as domain concepts. For example, from the sentence "`The control unit sends an alarm message in a critical situation`" "`send`" is extracted as the main verb, "`control unit`" as the subject and "`alarm message`" as the direct object.

Term clustering: The second step clusters related concepts. Two concepts are considered as related and put into the same cluster if they occur in the same grammatical context. I.e., two terms are related in the following cases:

- They are subjects of the same verb.
- They are direct objects of the same verb.
- They are indirect objects of the same verb and are used with the same preposition.

For example, if the document contains two sentences like

1. "The control unit sends an alarm message in a critical situation"
2. "The measurement unit sends measurements results every 5 seconds",

the concepts "`control unit`" and "`measurement unit`" are considered as related, as well as "`alarm message`" and "`measurements results`".

Taxonomy building: Concept clusters constructed in the previous step are used to build the taxonomy by joining overlapping concept clusters. The emerging larger clusters represent more general concepts. For example, the two clusters {`alarm message, measurements results`} and {`control message, measurements results`} are joined into the larger cluster

{`alarm message, control message, measurements results`}

because they share the common concept {`measurement results`}. The new joint cluster represents the more general concept of possible messages.
This step also aids in identifying synonyms[2] because synonyms are often contained in the same cluster. For example, if a cluster contains both "`signal`" and

[2]Different names for the same concept.

"`message`", the domain analyst performing the ontology construction can identify them as synonyms.
Since manual construction of the taxonomy would be both cumbersome and error-prone we use the tool ASIUM [22] for term clustering and taxonomy building.

Associations/relations mining: There is a potential association between two concepts if they occur in the same sentence. Each potential association then has to be validated by the requirements engineer before being recorded as an association between concepts.
Note, that the validation of the association proposed by the association mining tool automatically implies a validation of the requirements document. If the tool suggests an association that *can not* be valid (i.e., a pair containing completely unrelated concepts), then we have detected an evidence that the requirements document contains some inconsistent noise that must be eliminated (see [23] for an in–depth treatment of association mining).
We use the tool KAON [23] during this step.

All techniques introduced but term extraction were developed separately from each other for other purposes than requirements documents analysis. However, chaining these separate techniques into a proper process and enriching them with term extraction results is of great benefit for ontology extraction from requirements documents. The feasibility of the approach described above was proven on two case studies, presented in [21].

5. Applying Ontology to Document Validation

The method introduced above extracts an ontology from natural language documents. It is applicable to different kind of texts, such as requirements documents in new projects, or user and developer documentation of existing software.

5.1. Dealing with Inconsistencies

One key feature of the introduced text analysis method is its interactivity. In each step the analyst receives feedback allowing him to steer the construction. During the construction of concept clusters or overlaps the analyst may identify the content of the resulting clusters as inconsistent. This indicates that some unrelated concepts were put into the same cluster. Since such defects are not introduced by the extraction and clustering steps themselves, the inconsistencies detected can and should be corrected in the original text before the analysis continues, as illustrated in Fig. 2[3].

5.2. Terminology Validation after Extraction

The idea of iterative ontology extraction perfectly fits the Volere requirements engineering (RE) process [24]. According to [24] virtually every RE process is built in a similar way and runs through knowledge acquisition, writing the requirements document, requirements validation and prototyping. Figure 3 depicts a simplified Volere RE process. Solid arrows stem from the original process, dashed arrows are the transitions that we add in our approach to improve the validation phase.

[3]See [21] for details on inconsistency detection and correction.

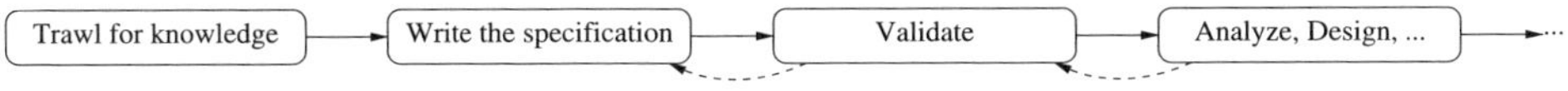

Figure 3. Volere Requirements Engineering Process.

According to the Volere RE–Process, the RE process starts out with a brainstorming and refinement of the requirements until the requirements are ripe enough to be written down. Obviously, the results of the brainstorming sessions must be validated after writing them down. Robertson & Robertson [24] list several validation goals, such as

- Completeness of each requirement
- Traceability
- *Consistent terminology*

The ontology extraction described in the previous section facilitates checking for consistent terminology because inconsistent terminology becomes exposed in the text mining phase as implausible concept clusters and associations.

As stated above, the standard Volere–Process had to be extended to accommodate this kind of document validation: When inconsistent terminology is detected during text mining, it has to be corrected before the construction of the ontology continues. This feedback loop is marked by a dashed arc from "Validate" to "Write the specification" in Fig. 3. As a result of this iteration the requirements document will only contain consistent terminology by the moment ontology construction is finished. One could argue that this iteration could go on for a long time which is correct from an abstract point of view. In practice, applying this process has the pleasant side-effect to quickly teach writers of requirements documents how to use consistent terminology.

Obviously, the same idea of document analysis and validation can be applied in the case of software re-engineering. The only difference is that not the requirements documents but any existing documentation can be analyzed.

5.3. Validating the Taxonomy and Associations

Obviously, the extracted ontology itself must also be validated. In contrast to the validation of the terminology, this validation step depends on the goal (requirements engineering vs. re-engineering) of the analysis.

In the case of requirements engineering there is no reference domain model for the extracted domain ontology to be compared with. Thus, the ontology can only be validated via manual examination by a domain expert or via prototyping. Prototyping and validation in the case of requirements will be discussed in Section 6.1.

In the case of re-engineering or software maintenance there are more sources of information than just the RE documentation. Another domain model can be extracted from the existing code. In virtually any realistic situation, the implemented and the documented domain model will differ. Section 6.2 shows how the domain model extracted from code can be compared with the ontology deduced from additional documentation and how the results of this comparison can be used to improve both documentation and code.

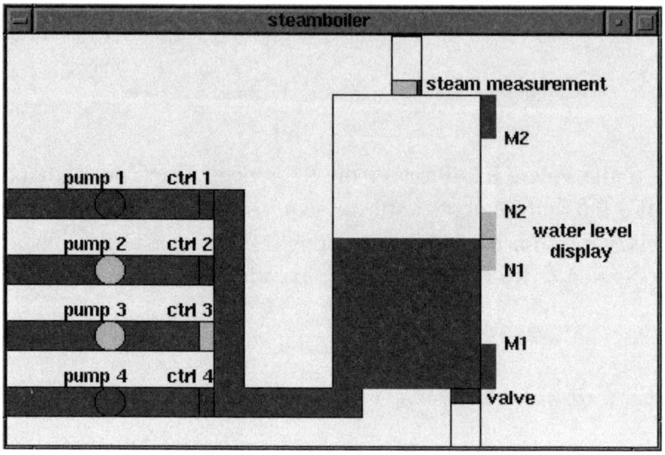

Figure 4. The steam boiler system [25].

5.4. Ontology as a Document Validation Means: A Case Study

In one of our case studies we analyzed the steam boiler specification [1] to extract an ontology form it. This specification describes a control application whose aim is to support required water level in a steam boiler. The steam boiler system consists of the following units (see also Fig. 4, taken from [1]):

- the steam-boiler
- a device to measure the quantity of water in the steam-boiler ("water level display" in Fig. 4)
- four pumps to provide the steam-boiler with water
- four devices to supervise the pumps (one controller for each pump) ("ctrl" in Fig. 4)
- a device to measure the quantity of steam which comes out of the steam-boiler ("steam measurement" in Fig. 4)
- an operator desk (missing in Fig. 4)
- a message transmission system (missing in Fig. 4)

The system should provide the required water level even despite failures of some components. Depending on the functioning components the system works in different operation modes.

Figure 5 shows a manually constructed ontology for the steam boiler system.[4] It shows the concepts introduced in the specification and a classification of these concepts. The classification is explicitly introduced in the requirements document as well. The concept classes are:

- sent messages (messages sent by the control program)
- received messages (messages received by the control program)

[4]Rectangular boxes represent concepts and hexagonal boxes represent relations between concepts. The very common "is-a"–relation is shown by means of variable-width lines, the thin end pointing to the more general concept and the thick end pointing to the less general one.

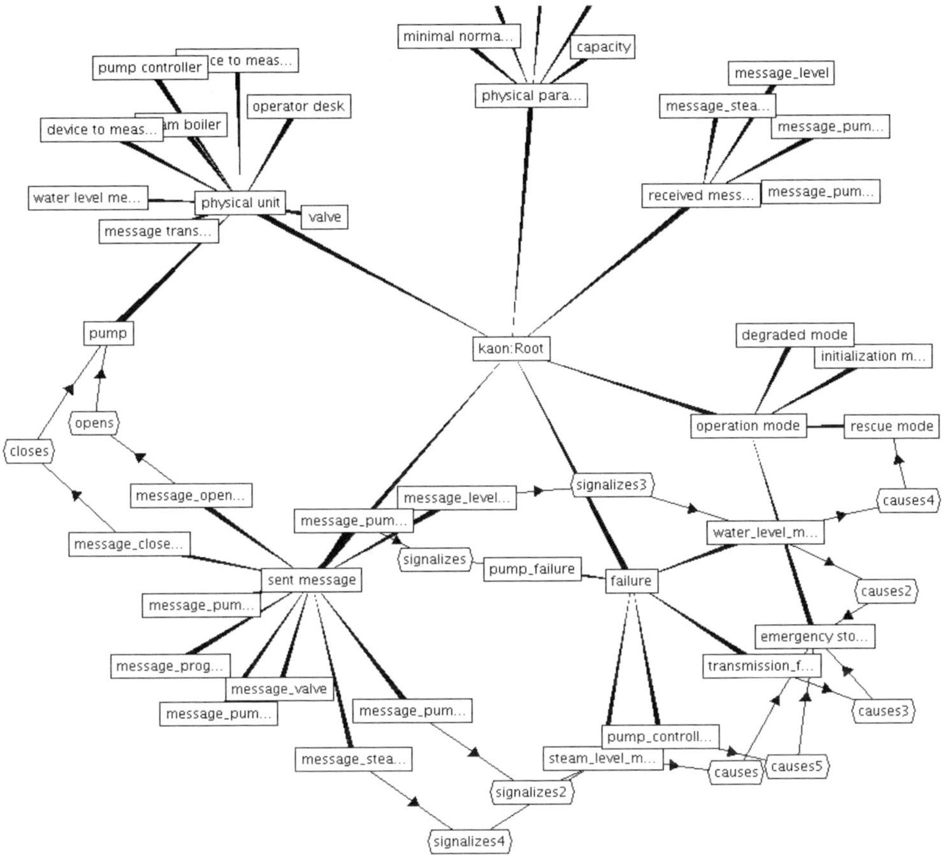

Figure 5. Steam boiler ontology, manually constructed.

- failures
- operation modes
- physical units
- physical parameters

Only few associations are explicitly stated in the requirements document. Figure 5 shows three classes of them:

"signalizes" is an association between a hardware failure and a message signalizing this failure.

"causes" is an association between a hardware failure and the operation mode caused by this failure.

"opens/closes" are associations between messages controlling the pumps and the pumps themselves.

Figure 6 shows a part of the ontology produced by the means of text analysis. The diagram shows the ontology root (`kaon:Root`), four top-level concepts (`operation mode`, `failure`, `physical unit` and `message`) with some of their subordi-

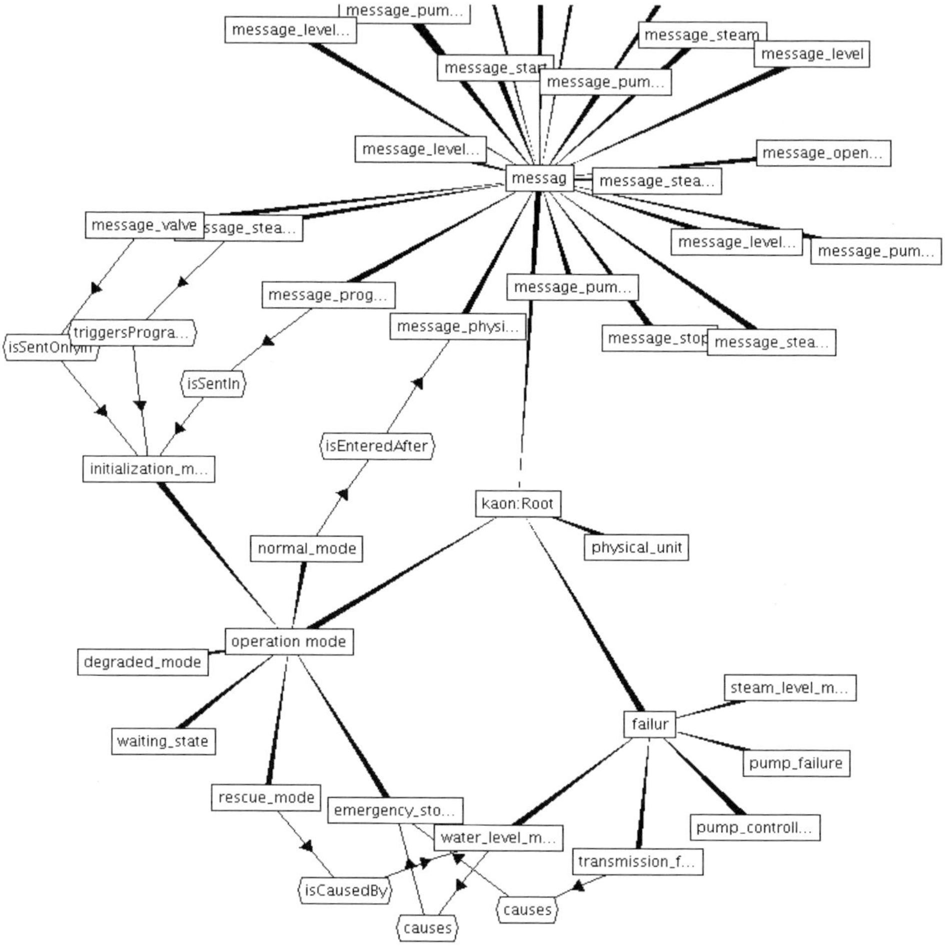

Figure 6. Steam Boiler: part of the produced ontology.

nate concepts and relations between them. For example, there are associations "Transmission_failure causes emergency_stop_mode" and "Rescue_mode is_caused_by water_level_measuring_unit_failure".

When compared to the manually constructed ontology in Fig. 5, the extracted ontology contains all the concept classes but "physical parameters". The names of physical parameters were not extracted as they occur solely in incomplete phrases (enumerations). Extraction of concepts from incomplete phrases is not possible yet. For the same reason two of the physical units were not extracted: "operator desk" and "message transmission system". These concepts are mentioned only once in the document and their role is not further specified. A human reader would extract these two concepts, but would have to guess how they interact with other components. This point can be seen both as a weakness of the extraction technique and as an omission in the document: these two components are also missing in the steam boiler simulator (Fig. 4), programmed for the participants of the formal methods contest, whose goal was to provide a formal steam boiler specification. As for other concept classes (messages, operation modes and failures), the approach succeeded in extracting all the concepts belonging to these classes.

Additionally to the concepts present in the original requirements document, operation mode "waiting state" was extracted from the revised document version. This concept was added during document revision, as the original document contained some abstract "state", which was treated exactly in the same way as operation modes. The extracted ontology contains also additional relations, like "message_program_ready isSentIn initialization_mode" and "message_steam_boiler_waiting triggersProgramStart_in initialization_mode". These relations are sensible, but missing in the manually constructed ontology.

To summarize, the presented approach to ontology extraction by the means of text analysis is a powerful method, able to find flaws in requirements documents, to correct them, and then to produce an application domain ontology.

6. Use Cases for Ontology Validation

6.1. Requirements Engineering: Ontology Validation via Prototyping

Is ontology extraction sufficient for document validation? Not really, because the ontology itself could be flawed. It therefore has to be validated by a domain expert, first. For this purpose, we convert the ontology into a domain specific model. "Domain specific" means that the modelling technique is tailored to the needs of the application domain.

In one of our case studies [21] we used the formal method and tool AutoFOCUS [26] to build the model domain for a distributed embedded control systems. AutoFOCUS offers the following modelling concepts for distributed embedded systems specification:

- hierarchically structured components
- messages
- typed channels (for message exchange)
- automatons (as a component implementation) including states and state transitions

The mapping of the ontology extracted from documents onto an AutoFOCUS domain model consists of two steps:[5]

1. Complete subtrees of the extracted taxonomy are mapped on AutoFOCUS concepts. For example, one of the taxonomies extracted in the case study contained the subtree "hardware". Each leaf concept of this subtree was mapped to an AutoFOCUS "Component". The taxonomy also contained the subtree "failures", which was mapped to AutoFOCUS "States", etc.
   If two branches are non disjoint, one either has to map both of them onto the same modelling concept or to descend to finer subtrees. The decision on which concept to use for what subtree is context dependent and has to be made by the analyst.
2. The associations existing in the ontology are mapped onto the corresponding connection concepts available in the formal model. These are communication channels for components and transitions between states for subtrees that were mapped onto states.

[5]Mapping to AutoFOCUS is presented in more detail in [27].

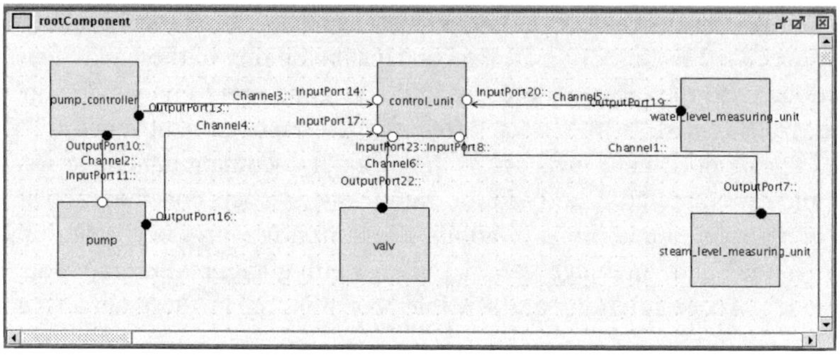

Figure 7. Component network, converted from the steam boiler ontology in Fig. 6.

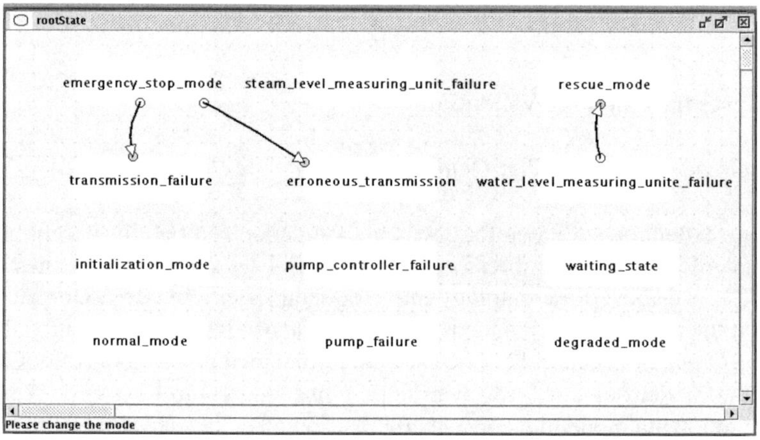

Figure 8. The automaton for "control_unit", converted from the steam boiler ontology in Fig. 6.

The result of this modelling is a formal model of the system specified by the requirements document. Note, that due to the automated terminology extraction and the mechanical construction of the ontology, this formal model resembles the system specified by the requirements documents without being biased from misinterpretations of the software engineer or forgotten resp. ignored statements in the documents.

In case of AutoFOCUS, this model is even executable representing a prototype of the target system. This prototype in turn is an excellent means to validate the ontology itself because it allows a domain expert to check whether all the intended states, components, transitions, etc. are in place and behave as expected. A failure of this validation represents a flaw in the ontology which is most likely due to an inconsistency or incompleteness of the original requirements document!

For example, consider Figs 7 and 8. The former one represents the components and channels generated from the ontology shown in Fig. 6, while the latter represents the generated states and state transitions for the "control_unit". The state transition diagram is obviously incomplete. This is due to the fact that the relations between corresponding states are missing in the ontology. The associations, in turn, are missing just because the state are never explicitly mentioned in the same sentence. Thus, missing state transitions in the resulting AutoFOCUS model indicate lack of explicitness in the requirements document.

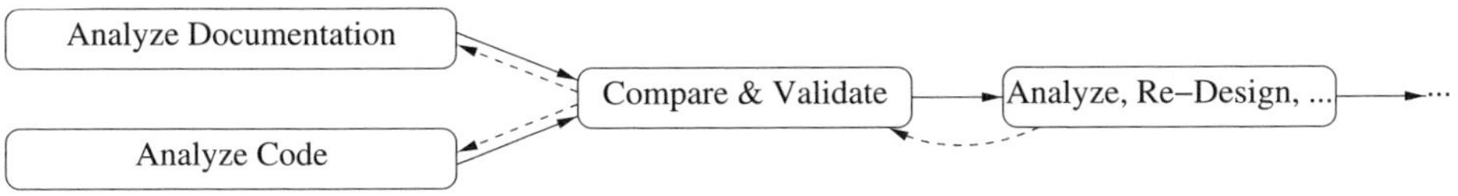

Figure 9. Knowledge acquisition process, adapted to several information sources.

6.2. Re-Engineering: Ontology Comparison

Similar to requirements engineering, software re-engineering can usually only be accomplished after a sound domain knowledge has been gained. However, in opposite to requirements engineering there is more than one relevant source of information. In addition to the documentation, the program code is another, an even more important source of domain information. As the code and the documentation are frequently changed independently after roll-out, the documented and the implemented domain model are hardly ever consistent but differ from each other. Thus, to validate the ontology extracted from the documentation, it is necessary to compare it to the ontology implemented in program code or vice versa.

The availability of more than one source of information entails minor changes to the process of knowledge acquisition. Figure 9 shows ontology extraction from two different sources. Now, validation is done by comparing different ontologies and not via prototyping.

To compare the documented and the implemented domain model, it is necessary to extract a domain model from the program code. In the case of object-oriented (OO) code, a significant portion of the concept hierarchy is explicitly coded with the class hierarchy induced by inheritance and associations. In non-OO code other structural dependencies, such as modules, file and directory structure, and `#include` directives must be taken into concern. For simplicity, we assume an OO programming model, here.

In [28], we have shown, how concise and consistent naming within the program code can be achieved and preserved during software development and maintenance. Here, require concise naming of identifiers within the code and continue this line of thought by using the names of the identifier as the starting point for term extraction. The associations between the concepts – i.e. classes – are extracted from the inheritance hierarchy and associations among classes.

Note, that the ontology build from code will comprise domain concepts as well as technical concepts, as for example classes used for file or database access. To be able to compare this ontology with an ontology build from domain only documentation, the domain concepts must be separated from the technical concepts. Ontology comparison metrics, such as introduced by Maedche and Staab [29], can cater for such "add-ons" when measuring ontology similarities. The defined metrics are asymmetric, so it is possible to see whether the documented ontology is covered by the implemented ontology.

The following list defines ontology similarity measures adapted to the comparison of ontologies extracted from documentation and program code.

Lexical comparison: Lexical comparison is based on the edit distance [30] measuring the minimal number of insertions, deletions and substitutions necessary to convert one string into another. For example, the edit distance between "toy example" and "toy-examples" is 2. On the basis of the edit distance Maedche and Staab define string similarity of the two strings L_i and L_j:

$$StrSim = \max\left(0, \frac{\min(|L_i|, |L_j|) - EditDistance(L_i, L_j)}{\min(|L_i|, |L_j|)}\right)$$

The string similarity measure *StrSim* returns values between 0 and 1; 0 meaning completely different, 1 for match. Lexical ontology similarity of two ontologies built on lexicons $\mathcal{L}_1$ and $\mathcal{L}_2$ is defined as

$$LexSim(\mathcal{L}_1, \mathcal{L}_2) = \frac{1}{|\mathcal{L}_1|} \sum_{L_i \in \mathcal{L}_1} \max_{L_j \in \mathcal{L}_2} (StrSim(L_i, L_j))$$

The lexical similarity measure *LexSim* is asymmetric, which is necessary for comparison of the documented and the implemented ontology: *LexSim*(*DocumentedLexicon*, *ImplementedLexicon*) measures whether every documented concept is implemented. Surely, one should expect that the implemented ontology contains more concepts. However, it is suspicious, if the documented concepts are missing in the implementation.

Taxonomy comparison: Taxonomy similarity measures whether the sub- and superconcepts of a certain concept coincide in two ontologies. Let $\mathcal{H}$ denote the taxonomic (hierarchical) part of the ontology and let $SupSub(L, \mathcal{H})$ be the set of sub- and superconcepts of L in the hierarchy $\mathcal{H}$. Taxonomic overlap of two hierarchies with respect to the term L is defined as

$$TO(L, \mathcal{H}_1, \mathcal{H}_2) = \frac{|SupSub(L, \mathcal{H}_1) \cap SupSub(L, \mathcal{H}_2)|}{|SupSub(L, \mathcal{H}_1) \cup SupSub(L, \mathcal{H}_2)|}.$$

The average value measures the extent to that the documented and the implemented hierarchies agree.

$$\overline{TO}(\mathcal{H}_1, \mathcal{H}_2) = \frac{1}{|\mathcal{L}_1|} \sum_{L \in \mathcal{L}_1} TO(L, \mathcal{H}_1, \mathcal{H}_2)$$

This metric is asymmetric, just like the lexical similarity metric. $\overline{TO}$(*DocumentedHierarchy*, *ImplementedHierarchy*) measures whether the documented concept hierarchy (extracted as cluster hierarchy) is correctly implemented.

Relation comparison: The relation similarity metric defined by Maedche and Staab [29] is rather complicated though this complexity is dispensable for ontologies extracted from code. It caters for relations with arbitrary domain and range but the relationships at the class level of OO code are restricted: Each relation connects just two classes. Note, that the relations extracted from the text are binary as well (see Section 4 or [21] for details). Thus, to compare relations, a simpler metric can be used.

Let $\mathcal{L}_1$ and $\mathcal{L}_2$ be two lexicons and let the lexicons be sorted in such a way that for all i the concept L_{1i} corresponds to the concept L_{2i}. This correspondence can be established for example by the means of the lexical similarity measure. Given the sets of non-taxonomic relations $\mathcal{R}_1$ and $\mathcal{R}_2$ as parts of the extracted ontologies, it is easy to determine the coinciding relations, i. e. the relations connecting the corresponding terms. With this the relational overlap of two ontologies can be computed as follows:

$$\overline{RO}(\mathcal{R}_1, \mathcal{R}_2) = \frac{\textit{Number of coinciding relations}}{|\mathcal{R}_1|}$$

Again, this metric is asymmetric.
$\overline{RO}$(*DocumentedRelations*, *ImplementedRelations*) exposes whether all the documented relations are implemented.

These ontology similarity metrics deliver valuable information to software maintainers by giving an estimate on how large the discrepancies between documentation and code are. In other words, these numbers reflect the reliability of the information contained in the documentation.

In the case that the similarity measures are high enough (it is up to the analyst to define what "high enough" means) they also validate the extracted domain ontology.

7. Summary

The ontology based validation method presented in this paper tackles a crucial tasks in various software engineering activities: validation of the terminology. Two example scenarios that could benefit from this approach are requirements engineering and software maintenance.

The starting point of this ontology construction is an analysis of the available documents. However, as experience shows, the documents, especially the requirements documents, are usually inconsistent. Thus, detection of inconsistencies has predominant importance if the ontology is to provide any value.

The iterative text analysis approach presented in this paper performs both tasks: it extracts the terminology and gives feedback to the analyst, enabling him to discover inconsistencies. After elimination of these inconsistencies the domain ontology is built and can be used as *the* common language for all the stakeholders in further project phases.

In order that become actually useful, the ontology gets validated. In the case of requirements engineering the validation is performed via prototyping, in the case of reengineering the ontology extracted from documents is validated by comparing it with another ontology extracted from the actual program code.

Term extraction, ontology construction and validation all together are combined into an integrated process that delivers a valuable tool to counter inconsistencies in documentation and code which are a frequent source of misunderstandings during software development and subsequent errors in the resulting products.

References

[1] Abrial, J.R., Börger, E., Langmaack, H.: The steam boiler case study: Competition of formal program specification and development methods. In Abrial, J.R., Borger, E., Langmaack, H., eds.: Formal Methods for Industrial Applications. Volume 1165 of LNCS., Springer–Verlag (1996) `http://www.informatik.uni-kiel.de/~procos/dag9523/dag9523.html`.

[2] Sneed, H.M.: Object-oriented cobol recycling. In: WCRE '96, IEEE Computer Society (1996) 169.

[3] Pigoski, T.M.: Practical Software Maintenance. Wiley Computer Publishing (1996).

[4] Ben Achour, C.: Linguistic instruments for the integration of scenarios in requirement engineering. In Cohen, P.R., Wahlster, W., eds.: Proceedings of the Third International Workshop on Requirements Engineering: Foundation for Software Quality (REFSQ'97), Barcelona, Catalonia (1997).

[5] Aussenac-Gilles, N.: Supervised Learning for Ontology and Terminology Engineering. In Kushmerick, N., Ciravegna, F., Doan, A., Knoblock, C., eds.: Machine Learning for the Semantic Web, Dagstuhl seminar, Dagstuhl (Germany) (2005).

[6] Goldin, L., Berry, D.M.: AbstFinder, a prototype natural language text abstraction finder for use in requirements elicitation. Automated Software Eng. **4** (1997) 375–412.

[7] Abbott, R.J.: Program design by informal English descriptions. Communications of the ACM **26** (1983) 882–894.

[8] Chen, P.: English sentence structure and entity-relationship diagram. Information Sciences **1** (1983) 127–149.

[9] Ratnaparkhi, A.: Maximum Entropy Models for Natural Language Ambiguity Resolution. PhD thesis, Institute for Research in Cognitive Science, University of Pennsylvania (1998).

[10] Hearst, M.A.: Automatic acquisition of hyponyms from large text corpora. Technical Report S2K-92-09 (1992).

[11] Berland, M., Charniak, E.: Finding parts in very large corpora. In: Proceedings of the 37th annual meeting of the Association for Computational Linguistics on Computational Linguistics, Morristown, NJ, USA, Association for Computational Linguistics (1999) 57–64.

[12] Degeratu, M., Hatzivassiloglou, V.: Building automatically a business registration ontology. In: The Second National Conference on Digital Government (dg.o 2002), LA, CA. (2002).

[13] Lame, G.: Using nlp techniques to identify legal ontology components: Concepts and relations. In: Law and the Semantic Web. (2003) 169–184.

[14] Zhou, L., Booker, Q., Zhang, D.: Toward rapid ontology development for underdeveloped domains. In: HICSS '02: Proceedings of the 35th Annual Hawaii International Conference on System Sciences (HICSS'02)-Volume 4, Washington, DC, USA, IEEE Computer Society (2002) 106.

[15] Fuchs, N.E., Schwertel, U., Schwitter, R.: Attempto Controlled English (ACE) language manual, version 3.0. Technical Report 99.03, Department of Computer Science, University of Zurich (1999) `http://www.ifi.unizh.ch/attempto/publications/papers/ace3_manual.pdf`, accessed 21.05.2004.

[16] Gervasi, V., Nuseibeh, B.: Lightweight validation of natural language requirements: a case study. In: 4th International Conference on Requirements engineering, IEEE Computer Society Press (2000) 140–148.

[17] Ambriola, V., Gervasi, V.: Experiences with domain-based parsing of natural language requirements. In Fliedl, G., Mayr, H.C., eds.: Proc. of the 4th International Conference on Applications of Natural Language to Information Systems. Number 129 in OCG Schriftenreihe (Lecture Notes) (1999) 145–148.

[18] Breitman, K.K., Sampaio do Prado Leite, J.C.: Ontology as a requirements engineering product. In: Proceedings of the 11th IEEE International Requirements Engineering Conference, IEEE Computer Society Press (2003) 309–319.

[19] Russell, S., Norvig, P.: Artificial Intelligence: A Modern Approach. 2nd edition edn. Prentice-Hall, Englewood Cliffs, NJ (2003).

[20] Zave, P., Jackson, M.: Four dark corners of requirements engineering. ACM Trans. Softw. Eng. Methodol. **6** (1997) 1–30.

[21] Kof, L.: An Application of Natural Language Processing to Domain Modelling – Two Case Studies. International Journal on Computer Systems Science Engineering **20** (2005) 37–52.

[22] Faure, D., Nédellec, C.: ASIUM: Learning subcategorization frames and restrictions of selection. In Kodratoff, Y., ed.: 10th European Conference on Machine Learning (ECML 98) – Workshop on Text Mining, Chemnitz Germany (1998).

[23] Maedche, A., Staab, S.: Discovering conceptual relations from text. In W.Horn, ed.: ECAI 2000. Proceedings of the 14th European Conference on Artificial Intelligence, Berlin, IOS Press, Amsterdam (2000) 321–325.

[24] Robertson, S., Robertson, J.: Mastering the Requirements Process. Addison–Wesley (1999).

[25] Abrial, J.R., Börger, E., Langmaack, H.: Formal Methods for Industrial Applications: Specifying and Programming the Steam Boiler Control. Volume 1165 of LNCS. Springer–Verlag (1996).

[26] The AutoFocus Homepage: (2004) `http://autofocus.in.tum.de/index-e.html`, accessed 21.02.2004.

[27] Klitni, A.: Textanalyse für Requirements Engineering: Konvertierung der Analyseergebnisse nach AutoFOCUS (2004) Technische Universität München, Fakultät für Informatik, Systementwicklungsprojekt.
[28] Deißenböck, F., Pizka, M.: Concise and consistent naming. In: Proceedings of the 13th International Workshop on Program Comprehension, St. Louis, Missouri, USA, IEEE CS Press (2005).
[29] Maedche, A., Staab, S.: Measuring similarity between ontologies. In: EKAW '02: Proceedings of the 13th International Conference on Knowledge Engineering and Knowledge Management. Ontologies and the Semantic Web, Springer-Verlag (2002) 251–263.
[30] Levenshtein, V.I.: Binary codes capable of correcting deletions, insertions, and reversals. Cybernetics and Control Theory **10** (1966) 707–710.

New Trends in Software Methodologies, Tools and Techniques
H. Fujita and M. Mejri (Eds.)
IOS Press, 2005

Co-Developing Model for User Participation in Web Application Development

Tae YONEDA[a], Kohei MITSUI[b], Jun SASAKI[a] and Yutaka FUNYU[a]
[a]*Iwate Prefectural University, Faculty of Software and Information Science*
Sugo 152-52, Takizawa-mura, Iwate-ken, Japan
[b]*Nara Institute of Science and Technology, Graduate School of Information Science*
1896-5, Takayama-cho, Ikoma-city, Nara-ken, Japan

Abstract. As a first step to resolve the assignments of an end user development environment, this paper proposes a co-developing model for the participation of users in web application development. First, the procedure for a simple web application is arranged from the view points of "screen" and "screen transition" so that an end user can easily take part in the development. These can be classified into two parts; one that an end user can define and the other that an end user cannot. Using the definition items in these two parts, an operational model for co-developing is proposed, and the procedures for co-development are shown. A collaboration model that can be developed by a user and a system engineer is proposed; then, based on the proposed model, a tool supporting co-developing is built.

1. Introduction

With the recent progression of the information society, the various requirements expected of information systems have increased. To develop high quality information systems rapidly, many development methodologies and technologies have been proposed and put into practice. However, most projects developing information systems have not been felt to have achieved the user requirement, and so they have failed [1]. The causes have been recognized as existing in the software development phases, the requirement definition phase or in the design phase of the software development process. Especially, the difficulty to obtain the end user's requirements has been pointed out as the most important cause.

However, a new software development paradigm in which an end user develops an information system by him or herself has received much attention. In this paradigm, because the developer is the end user who understands their own requirements for the system, it might be possible that the system can satisfy the end user's requirements. The "Cyber Framework developed by Cyber Laboratory Inc." is one such end user oriented development environment [2]. In this environment, engineers make software components and the end users can construct a required system by combining the components. Even though users can develop a system comparatively easily by using the Cyber Framework, it is still difficult to use the parts and develop a system for an end user who has no systems development experience to use the components and develop an actual system.

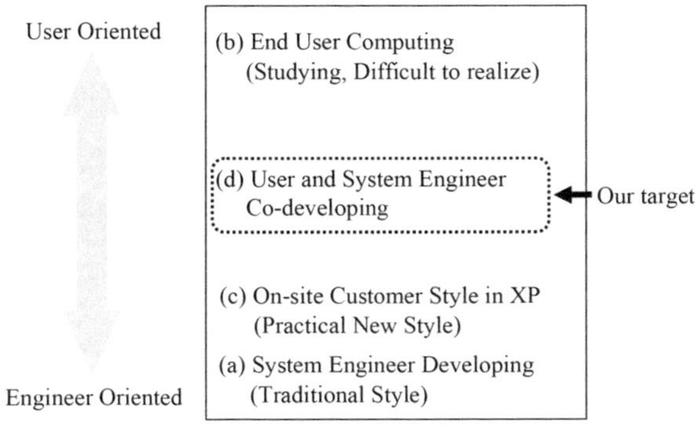

Figure 1. Target of Proposed Model.

Lyee (Governmental Methodology for Software Providence) is a development methodology based on human thinking processes. It has been proved both axiomatically [3] and mathematically [4,5]. The characteristics of Lyee software are that "it can be designed using word definitions which an end user can define easily" and "it has realized automatic coding" [6]. Thus, Lyee is expected to realize software systems developed by end users. Though much research has been reported on it [7–10], the environment of system being developed only by an end user is not yet practical; therefore, many problems remain to be resolved.

On the other hand, the Internet is a recent phenomenon, one that has spread rapidly and widely. Thus, a lot of web based network systems are in use in many societies. Especially, web applications that use WWW (World Wide Web) technology have been focused on.

In this paper, as a first step to resolve assignments of an end user development environment, a Co-developing model for the participation of the user in web application development is proposed. First, the procedure for a simple web application is arranged from the view point of "screen" and "screen transition" in which an end user can easily take part in the development. Next, the procedures are classified into two parts; one that an end user can defined and the other one that the end user cannot define. Using the definition items in these two parts, an operational model for co-developing is proposed, and the procedures for co-development are shown. A collaboration model that can be developed by an end user and a system engineer is proposed. As well, based on the proposed model, a tool supporting Co-developing is built.

2. Target and Aspects of the Proposed Model

Traditionally, the person involved in system development is a system engineer (Fig. 1(a)). In this style of development, it is difficult to provide a system that satisfies the user's requirements. However, a new style in which the end user develops a system has been researched (Fig. 1(b)); though, it is still difficult to realize the style and apply it widely in practice. There is also another new style; "On-site Customer" in XP (eXtreme Programming) of agile development (Fig. 1(c)). In the on-site customer style, the customer (user) sits down together with the systems engineer in the same work space, and answers questions from developers about the user requirements for the system. Thus, the user requirements can be comparatively more satisfied by the system. However, even in this style, a user doesn't develop the system subjectively, and so it is difficult to develop a system that flexibly reflects the user requirements.

In this research, our target is a co-developing style involving user and system engineer (Fig. 1(d)). The system requirements are defined by the user as if the system is developed by that user and so the description is friendly for user. A system engineer then programs according to the definition and develop the required system. Thus, user can positively contribute to the development. To realize this style, a model is needed that can extract parts from user participants for system development. In the Section 4, such a model is proposed.

Definitions are as follows.

User: The person who will use a developed system. One who has the basic handling skills to use a computer; however, one who has not developed a system.

Scale of system: A mid or small sized system is considered. In the first model we propose, we suppose that there is one user who can participate in the development project. However, in the next step, we propose a model in which more than one user can participate.

Development environment and application: the development environment to be provided to the user is a web application. A user can develop a system as a web application using the environment.

3. Co-Developing Frame

3.1. Analysis of a Simple Feature of a Web Application

To propose a model that has parts in which a user can be a participant in a development of a system as a web application, we first analyze "user registration".

The user registration feature is as follows (Fig. 2):

(1) User name and user ID are input.
(2) If the user ID overlaps that of another user ID, an error alert occurs.
(3) If the user ID does not overlap that of another user ID, the registration is confirmed.
(4) When the registration button is pushed, the User ID and User Name are registered.

From this feature, those parts that a user can easily express or understand are extracted as follows:

- Composition of screen for inputting User ID and User Name
- Composition of screen for outputting error when the User ID overlaps that of another
- Composition of screen for confirming registration
- Composition of screen for notifying registration success
- Screen after pushing the confirmation button
- Screen after pushing the return button
- Screen after pushing the registration button

In short, the parts that a user can easily express or understand are summarized to "screen" or "screen transition." Thus, we focused on "screen" and "screen transition" to extract parts for user participants in the development of a web application system.

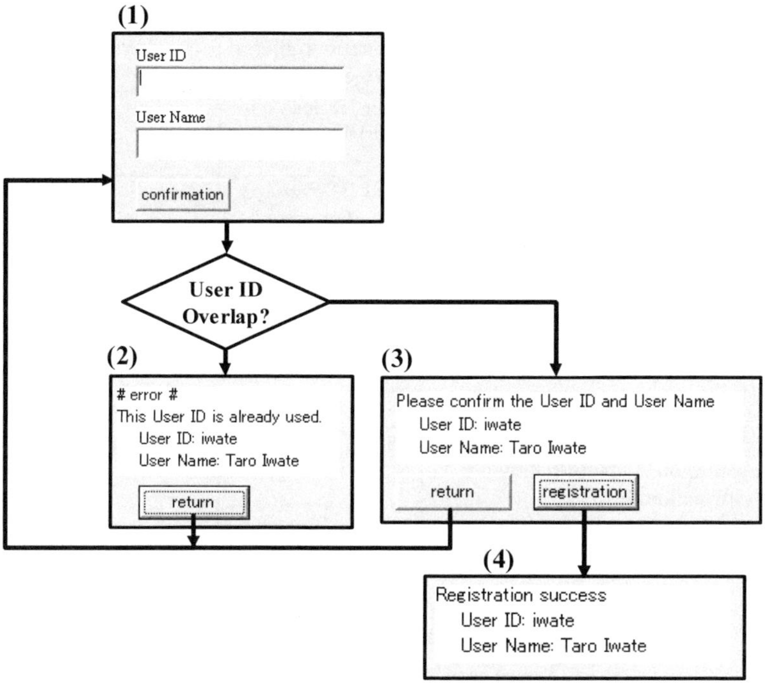

Figure 2. Flowchart of the User Registration Feature.

Table 1. Definitions of Screens in the User Registration Feature.

Screen Name	Screen Composition
Registration screen	Fields for inputting User ID and User Name, confirmation button
Error screen	Text for notice of User ID overlapped, return button
Registration Confirmation screen	Text for notice of input contents, registration button, return button
Registration Completion screen	Text for notice of input contents

Next, the user registration feature is summarized from the view point of screen and screen transition; Tables 1 and 2, respectively. Then, a screen can be defined by screen name and screen composition, while a screen transition can be defined by pre-screen name, condition, transaction and post-screen name.

3.2. Frame for Co-Developing by a User and a System Engineer

The user can easily define the screen name in the definition items for the screens and for the pre-screen and post-screen names in the definition items of screen transitions. On the other hand, screen composition, condition and transaction in the definition items have to be implemented using a programming language. Generally, it is difficult for a user to describe the logic and conditions using programming language. However, the meaning of the logic and conditions in the required system are distinctive for the user, and so the user can describe these using natural language.

Table 2. Definitions of Screen Transitions in the User Registration Feature.

	Pre-screen Name	Condition(button)	Condition(others)	Transaction	Post-screen Name
(A)	Registration screen	Registration button	User ID does not overlap other IDs	–	Registration Confirmation screen
(B)	Registration screen	Registration button	User ID overlaps that of another	–	Error screen
(C)	Error screen	Return button	–	–	Registration Confirmation screen
(D)	Registration Confirmation screen	Registration button	–	User ID and User Name are added to User List	Registration Confirmation screen
(E)	Registration Confirmation screen	Return button	–	–	Registration screen

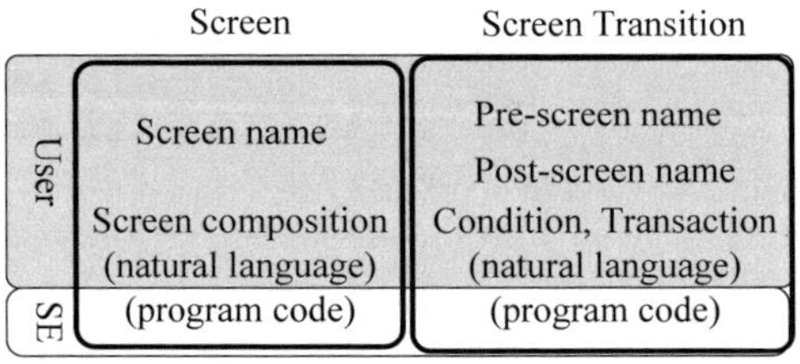

Figure 3. Frame of Co-developing.

In this paper, we suppose Co-developing by an end user and a system engineer. The user defines the screen, pre-screen and post-screen names. The user can also define the screen composition, condition and transaction in natural language. Then, a system engineer defines the screen composition, condition and transaction in programming language. (Fig. 3) Consequently, the user can define the skeleton of the system and the system engineer supports this by realizing it as a system. In this frame, the user positively participates in system developing.

4. Co-Developing Model

In Section 3, we proposed a frame enabling the user to aggressively participate in system development, by focusing on screens and screen transitions and using natural language definitions for a user. In this section, a model is proposed in which the definition of items in the proposed frame can be constructed, and then can act smoothly as a system.

The actions in a web application are discussed in two steps from the view points of screen and screen transition.

Step 1) decisions in respect of the screen displayed (screen transition)
Step 2) display of the screen (screen display)

The role and features of each step are described to smoothly construct and act on the definition items in each step.

4.1. Screen Transition

The role of the screen transition is to facilitate the decision for the display of the post-screen. The definition items of screen transition are pre-screen name, condition, transaction and post-screen name. A transition to the post-screen is decided by these definition items. The transition often involves some transactions.

Some of definition items in the screen transition can only be defined by a user, and the others have to be defined by a system engineer. To smoothly construct and modify a system using these definitions, the features of screen transition can be clarified into two parts: (a) a part to be realized only by user definition (called the selection part) and (b) a part needing definitions to be defined by a system engineer (called the evaluation and transaction part).

(a) Selection
In screen transition, the definition items defined only by a user are pre-screen and post-screen names. A feature of using these definitions is the picking up of the screen transitions based on pre-screens. A screen transition is decided by an evaluating process (described in (b)). This part is called a "selection."
Example:

> Select transitions from the transitions in the user registration feature shown in Table 2. For example, when the pre-screen is the registration screen, two transitions, (A) and (B) in Table 2, are picked up. In addition, one transition decided by an evaluating process is selected.

(b) Evaluation and Transaction
The definition items in the screen transition needing to be defined by a system engineer are condition and transition. Features of using these definitions are the evaluation of the conditions of the extracted conditions of selected transitions, and choosing a transition. The chosen transition is then reported to the selection part (described in (a)). If the transition involves some transactions, these are then carried out. This part is called "evaluation and transaction."
Example:

> Decide one transition from the extracted transitions in the selection example, (a). If the condition is that the registration button is pushed and the User ID input has already been registered, those conditions are evaluated. Then a transition (B) in Table 2 is chosen and is reported to the selection part.

4.2. Screen Display

The role of the screen display is to display of the screen decided in the screen transition part. The definition items of screen display are screen name and screen composition. Though the screen name is defined by the user, it is not directly concerned with the action of displaying the screen. Most parts of the screen display have to be defined by a system engineer. Thus, features in the screen display are simply classified by the functions.

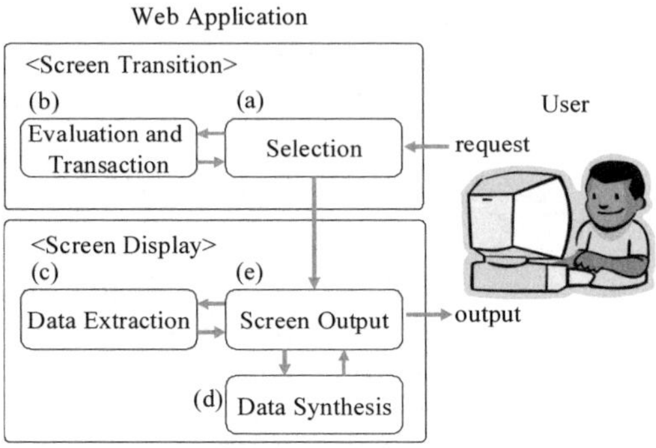

Figure 4. Operation Model.

The features in the screen display can be realized by using a template technique. Screen composition in a web application consists of parts that depend on transactions and parts that are independent of transactions. The latter parts are made as a template. The other parts, called data variables, are applied when the values are transacted.

(c) Data Extraction

In this part, data to be substituted for the template variables is extracted from the database, and is selected or modified from the information given from the screen transition. This part is called data exaction.

Example:

In the screen (2) shown in the flowchart of the user registration feature in Fig. 2, User ID and User name are selected from the information input in the pre-screen.

(d) Data Synthesis

In this part, data extracted in the data extraction part are substituted for the data variables in the template. All of the extracted data are substituted.

Example:

In the screen (2) shown in the flowchart of the user registration feature in Fig. 2, User ID and User name selected from the information of the screen transition are substituted for each of the data variables in the template of the screen (2).

(e) Screen Output

In this part, the screen contents generated in the data synthesis are transmitted to the client and are output.

4.3. Operation Model

In Section 4.1 and 4.2, to smoothly construct a system from the definitions in the frame proposed in Section 3.2, features to make good usage of the definitions were described. In this section they are summarized as an operation model.

The operation model for co-developing is shown in Fig. 4. In this model, we clarified five operation modules as follows. When a web application receives a request from a user, the selection module (Fig. 4(a)) is called and executed. In the selection module, some screen transitions that have a coincidence precondition are selected from the table of the screen transitions. Next, the evaluation and transaction module (Fig. 4(b)) is

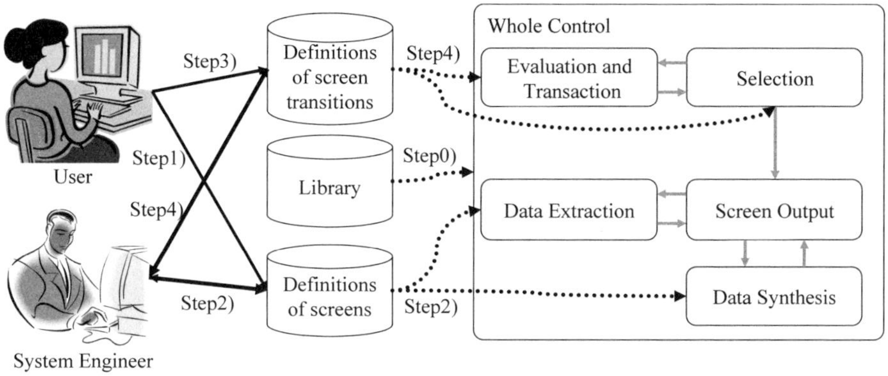

Figure 5. Co-development procedures.

called and executed. The conditions of the selected screen transitions are evaluated and one transition is chosen. If the chosen transition has transactions, they are processed. Then, the chosen transition is reported to the selection module. The selection part then executes the screen output module (Fig. 4(e)) and gives the next screen. If the screen has some template variables, the data extraction module (Fig. 4(c)) is called and executed. The data extraction part extracts data needed for the screen. The data synthesis module (Fig. 4(d)) substitutes the data for the data variables in the template. Finally, the screen output module outputs the generated screen.

Procedures for the co-development with a user and a system engineer based on the operation model are shown in Fig. 5.

The work flow of the model is as follows:

Step 0) The library to control the whole model is given beforehand. This is a fixed form.

Step 1) A user defines the screen name, and then defines the screen composition by natural language.

Step 2) A system engineer programs based on the screen composition defined in natural language. Then, templates of screens that include data variables are produced. These are mainly used in the data extraction and synthesis modules in the operation model.

Step 3) A user defines the pre-screen and post-screen names, and defines also the condition and transaction by natural language. In the model, these results are used in the selection module.

Step 4) A system engineer programs based on the condition and the transaction defined in natural language by the user. In the model, these are mainly used in the evaluation and transaction module.

Repeat from Steps 1) to 4) until all the screens and screen transitions are defined.

Step 5) Build all the components, construct a system.

5. Tool

Based on the proposed model, a tool to realize co-developing is constructed. This tool is a web application developed by using PHP language. The interface consists of User

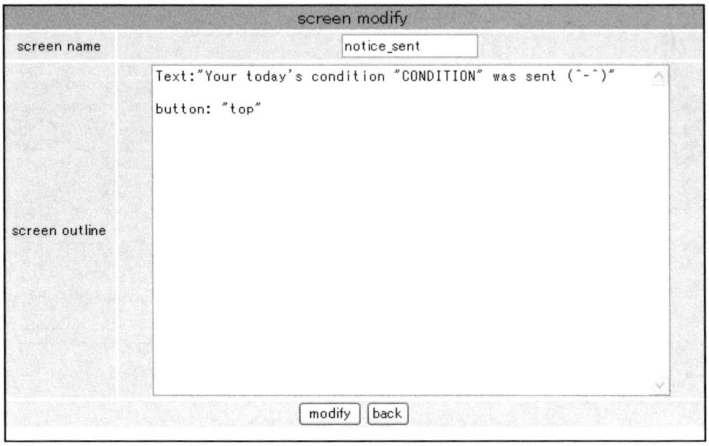

Figure 6. Definition of a Screen in the User Mode.

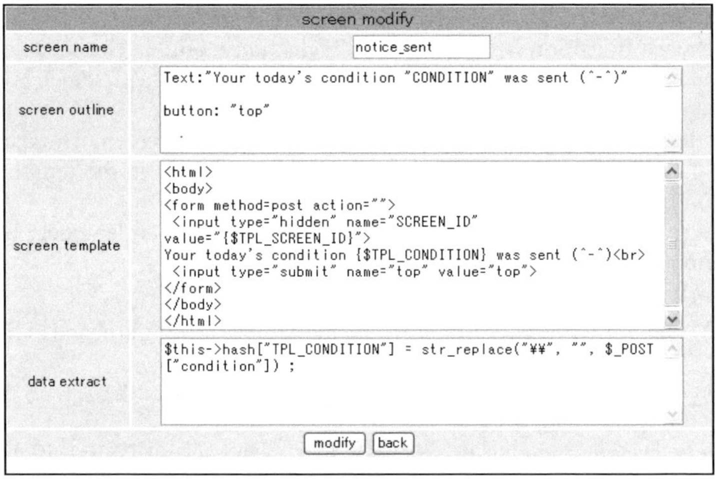

Figure 7. Program for a Screen in the System Engineer's Mode.

and System Engineer's modes. In the User mode, a user defines screens and screen transitions individually by natural language. In the System Engineer's mode, a System Engineer programs each of the components of screens and screen transitions based on the natural-language definition described by the user.

Some examples of screen shots in this tool are shown in the following figures.

In Step 1), a user defines screens of the developing system. The user individually defines the screen name and the screen composition of each screen. Figure 6 is an example of a screen definition; the screen name is "notice_sent." In the area of screen composition, text and buttons which are placed in the screen are described.

In Step 2), a system engineer programs based on the screen composition defined by the user. First, data items which can be treated as variables are extracted from the screen composition as defined, and they are defined as variables in the area of data extraction. Then, using the variables, the screen composition is programmed in the area of the screen template. Figure 7 shows the System Engineer mode of the "notice_sent" screen.

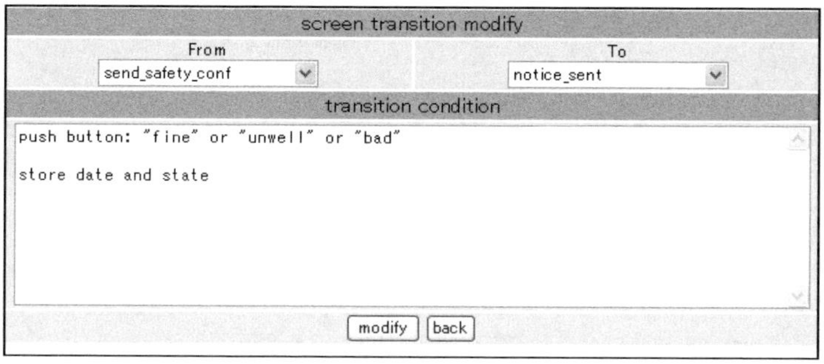

Figure 8. Definition of a Screen Transition in the User Mode.

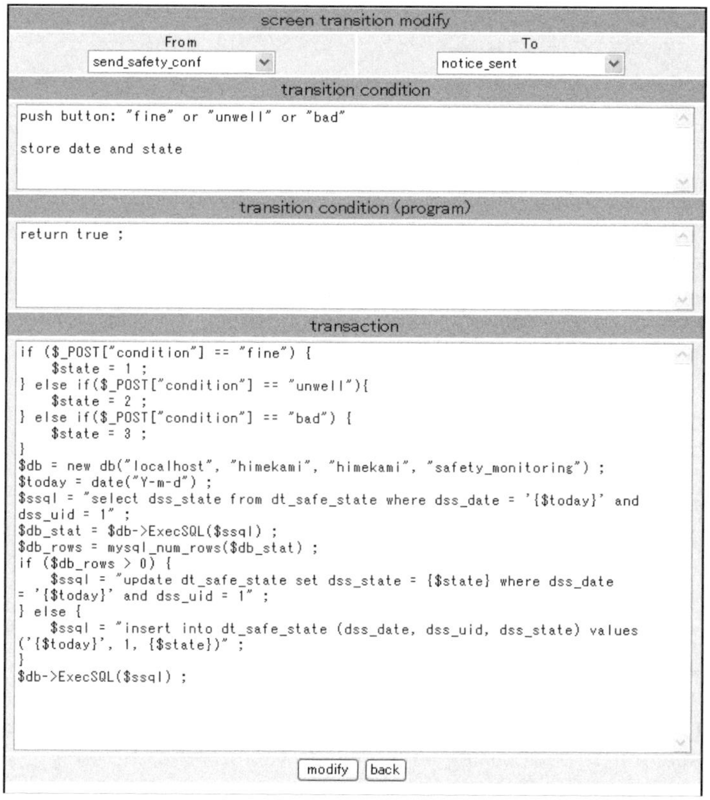

Figure 9. Program of a Screen Transition in the System Engineer's Mode.

In Step 3), a user defines screen transition, pre-screen name, post-screen name, condition and transaction in natural language. First, the user selects a pre-screen and a post screen from the screen name list defined in the screen definition pages. Then, condition and transaction in the screen transition are described in each area. Figure 8 shows an example of definition of the transition from send_safety_conf screen to notice_sent screen in the User mode.

In Step 4), a system engineer programs based on the condition and transaction defined in natural language. Figure 9 shows the program of the transition from send_safety_conf screen to notice_sent screen in the System Engineer's mode.

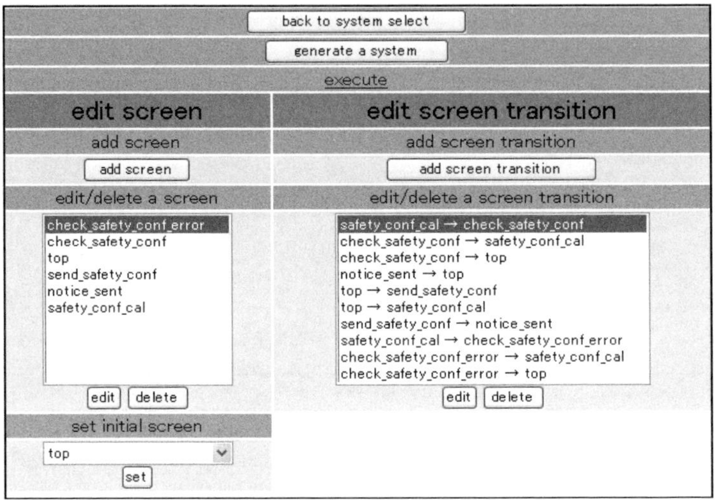

Figure 10. Construction and Execution of a System.

In Step 5), after building all the components, a system is constructed. In the screen shown in Fig. 10, components are listed on the screen and screen transitions in the developing system are represented. After all of the components are defined and programmed, the "generate a system" button will be clicked. Then, the source files of the system being developed are generated. Next, when the "execute" button is clicked, the developed system can be executed.

By using this tool, a simple system, here a "Safety Monitoring System to support a Senior Citizen's Life", could be developed. The Outline of the system is: every day, a senior living alone sends information on their condition as one of "fine", "unwell" or "bad" by using a web page. Then, his or her family confirms receipt of the senior's sent information by using a web page. We are able to confirm that this system can be developed.

6. Conclusions

In this paper, a co-developing model for user participation in the development of a web application is proposed by focusing on screens and screen transitions.

- A frame is described in which a user can aggressively participate in system development.
- An operation model for smoothly constructing a system from the definitions in the proposed frame is presented. This is a model engine to realize the co-developing model.
- Procedures for co-development by users and system engineers based on the operation model are presented.
- Based the proposed model, a tool to realize co-developing is constructed. In addition, using this tool, a simple system, a Safety Monitoring System, could be developed. Then, we confirmed that this system could be completely developed by our proposed method.

Consequently, by using the proposed model, an end user without any programming knowledge can actively participate in system development. In other words, even if a user does not know how to program, he or she can develop a system with the efficient support of a systems engineer.

However, there are some considerations;

- A user has to be able to image what screens are needed for the system as it develops.
- There is not enough support to create dynamic pages in the web application.
- There is not enough support to set up a database.

Finally, our future works will include;

- To evaluate this model; thus, it will be necessary to apply it to real user system developments.
- A visual interface for the user will be required.
- The creation of a mechanism to reuse the defined and programmed components.

Reference

[1] The Standish Group, *The Chaos Report*, http://www.standishgroup.com, 2003.

[2] Cyber Laboratory Co., Ltd., *Cyber Framework*, http://www.cyberlab.co.jp/cf_info.html, 2001.

[3] F. Negoro, "Lyee's Hypothetical World," Proceeding of SoMeT02: New Trends in Software Methodologies, Tools and Techniques, pp. 3–22, 2002.

[4] O. Arai and H. Fujita, "A Word-unit-based Program: Its Mathematical Structure Model and Actual Application," Proceeding of SoMeT02: New Trends in Software Methodologies, Tools and Techniques, pp. 63–74, 2002.

[5] S. Gorlatch, "Declarative Programming with Lyee for Distributed Systems," Proceeding of SoMeT04: New Trends in Software Methodologies, Tools and Techniques, pp. 129–137, 2004.

[6] CATENA Corporation, *Lyee system development*, http://www.catena.co.jp/english/e-contents/elyee/lyeedevelop2.htm#top, 2004.

[7] Y. Funyu, J. Sasaki, T. Nakano, T. Yamane and H. Suzuki, "An Experiment on Software Development of Hospital Information System," Proceeding of SoMeT02: New Trends in Software Methodologies, Tools and Techniques, pp. 328–340, 2002.

[8] T. Yamane, H. Suzuki, T. Yoneda, J. Sasaki and Y. Funyu, "A User Requirement Acquisition Method based on Word-units for a User Development," Proceeding of SoMeT03: New Trends in Software Methodologies, Tools and Techniques, pp. 137–144, 2003.

[9] H. Suzuki, T. Yamane, T. Yoneda, J. Sasaki and Y. Funyu, "A framework for user accessible boundary software," Proceeding of SoMeT03: New Trends in Software Methodologies, Tools and Techniques, pp. 157–166, 2003.

[10] K. Mitsui, K. Fujisawa, T. Yoneda, J. Sasaki and Y. Funyu, "HIMEKAMI: an End-user System Development Environment Based on Lyee Theory," Proceeding of SoMeT04: New Trends in Software Methodologies, Tools and Techniques, pp. 157–166, 2004.

H. Fujita and M. Mejri (Eds.)
IOS Press, 2005

A Neuro-Fuzzy Based Approach for the Prediction of Quality of Reusable Software Components

Parvinder Singh SANDHU[a] and Hardeep SINGH[b]
[a]*Guru Nanak Dev Engineering College, Ludhiana (Punjab) India*
[b]*Guru Nanak Dev University, Amritsar (Punjab) India*

Abstract. The requirement to improve software productivity has promoted the research on software metric technology. There are metrics for identifying the quality of reusable components. These metrics if identified in the design phase or even in the coding phase can help us to reduce the rework by improving quality of reuse of the component and hence improve the productivity due to probabilistic increase in the reuse level. A suit of metrics can be used to obtain the reusability in the modules. And the reusability can be obtained with the help of Neuro-fuzzy based approach where neural network can learn new relationships with new input data, can be used to refine fuzzy rules to create fuzzy adaptive system. An algorithm has been proposed in which the inputs can be given to Neuro-fuzzy system in form of Cyclometric Complexity, Volume, Regularity, Reuse-Frequency & Coupling, and output can be obtained in terms of reusability.

Keywords. Fuzzy System, Sugeno Fuzzy Model, Neural Network

Introduction

The aim of Object Oriented Metrics is to predict the quality of the object oriented software products. Various attributes, which determine the quality of the software, include maintainability, defect density, fault proneness, normalized rework, understandability, reusability etc. The requirement today is to relate the quality attributes with the metrics. To achieve both the quality and productivity objectives it is always recommended to go for the software reuse that not only saves the time taken to develop the product from scratch but also delivers the almost error free code, as the code is already tested many times during its earlier reuse.

A great deal of research over the past several years has been devoted to the development of methodologies to create reusable software components and component libraries, where there is an additional cost involved to create a reusable component from scratch. That additional cost could be avoided by identifying and extracting reusable components from the already developed large inventory of existing systems. But the issue of how to identify good reusable components from existing systems has remained relatively unexplored. The Literature suggests that the identification of reusable components within existing software systems is expensive and yield only limited benefits since the identified reusable components are not truly useful [6], which is quite discouraging fact. Our approach to identification of reusable software is based on software models and metrics. As the exact relationship between the attributes of the reusability is difficult to establish so a Neural Network approach could serve as an economical, automatic tool to generate reusability ranking of software [1,2] by formulating the relationship based on its training. When one designs with Neural Networks alone, the network is a black box that needs to be defined; this is a highly compute-intensive process. One must develop a good sense, after extensive experimentation and practice, of the complexity of the network and the learning algorithm to be used. Neural nets and fuzzy systems, although very different, have close relationship: they work with impression in a space that is not defined by crisp, deterministic boundaries [15]. Neural network can be used to define fuzzy rules for the fuzzy inference system. A neural network is good at discovering relationships and pattern in the data, so neural network can be used to preprocess data in the fuzzy system. Furthermore, neural network that can learn new relationships with new input data can be used to refine fuzzy rules to create fuzzy adaptive system. With the objective of taking advantage of the features of the both [8], we used Neuro-Fuzzy approach to economically determining quality of reusable components in existing systems as well as the reusable components that are in the design phase.

In the second section we have given a brief overview of previous attempts to identify reusable components described in the literature. Third section is devoted to the measures or metrics used by the proposed inference systems. Fourth section describes the approaches used. Next section discusses the results obtained.

1. Background

It was Selby [14] tried to identify a number of characteristics of those components, from existing systems, that are been reused at NASA laboratory and reported that the developers there has achieved a 32 percent reusability index. Dunn and Knight in 1991 [9] also experimented and reported the usefulness of reusable code scavenging. Chen, Nishimoto and Ramamoorty briefly discuss the idea of subsystem extraction by using code information stored in a relational database [17]. They also describe a tool called the C Information Abstraction System to support this process. Esteva and Reynolds [7] describe the use of Inductive Learning techniques based on software metrics used to identify reusable modules. Their system was able to learn to recognize reusable components. Caldiera and Basili [3] describe a tool called Care, that helps identify reusable components according to a set of "reusability attributes" based on software metrics. These attributes include measurement of how useful the component is in the problem domain, how much it would cost to reuse it, and its quality. The idea behind Care is that it will do the initial identification of the components that have strong reusability characteristics, and then a domain expert will do a further examination of these components to determine their appropriateness to the domain, and package them to reuse. Mayobre [4] describes how these techniques can be extended and used to help in identifying data communication components a Hewlett-Packard.

Arnold [11,12] mentions a number of heuristics that can used for locating reusable components in the Ada source code. The heuristics are counting the number of references to a particular procedure, identifying the loosely coupled modules and identifying modules that carry high cohesion.

2. Approach Used to Determine Quality of Reusable Components

Following major steps taken to determine the quality of Reusable parts from the existing software systems:

- Selecting the software system that needs to be processed.
- Parsing of the software system to generate the Meta information related to that Software.
- Meta information will act as input to reusability model that uses certain metrics that generates the values which is given input to the inference Engine.
- Neuro-Fuzzy system, which is already trained using the training data, will get the metric values from the earlier stages and determines the reusability value of the software components. Considering the reusability value the component can be extracted and put into the Reusable Software Reservoir for future reuse.

2.1. Metric Suit Used by Reusability Model

2.1.1. Cyclometric Complexity Using Mc Cabe's Measure

According to Mc Cabe, the value of Cyclometric Complexity can be obtained using the following formula [16]:

$$\text{Cyclometric Complexity} = \text{Number of Predicate nodes} + 1 \quad (1)$$

Where predicate nodes are the nodes of the directed graph, made for the component, where the decisions are made i.e. predicate nodes should have more than one arrow coming out of it.

If the complexity is low then reuse of component will not repay the cost. Otherwise high value of complexity indicates poor quality, high development cost, low readability, poor testability and prone to errors i.e. high rate of failure [5].

Hence the value of Cyclometric Complexity of a software component should be in between upper and lower bounds as an contribution towards reusability.

If Cyclometric complexity is high with high regularity of implementation then there exists high functional usefulness.

2.1.2. Regularity

The notion behind Regularity is "How well we can predict length based on some regularity assumptions". As actual length (N) is sum of N1 and N2. The estimated length is:

$$\text{Estimated Length} = N' = \eta_1 \log_2 \eta_1 + \eta_2 \log_2 \eta_2 \quad (2)$$

The closeness of the estimate is a measure of the Regularity(r) of Component coding is

$$\text{Regularity} = 1 - \{(N - N')/N\} = N'/N \quad (3)$$

The above derivation indicates that Regularity is the ratio of estimated length to the actual length. High value of Regularity indicates the high readability, low modification cost and non-redundancy of the component implementation [3].

Hence there should be some minimum level of Regularity of the component to indicate the reusability of that component.

2.1.3. Halstead Software Science Indicator

According to this metric volume of the source code of the software component is [10]:

$$\text{Volume} = (N_1 + N_2) \log_2 (\eta_1 + \eta_2) \tag{4}$$

Where n_1 = the number of distinct operators that appear in the program
n_2 = number of distinct operands that appear in the program
N_1 = The total number of operator occurrences
N_2 = The total number of operand occurrences

If the volume is high means that software component needs more maintenance cost, correctness cost and modification cost. On the other hand less volume increases the extraction cost, identification cost from the repository and packaging cost of the component. So the volume of the reusable component should be in between the two extremes.

2.1.4. Reuse Frequency

Reuse frequency is calculated by comparing number of static calls addressed to a component with number of calls addressed to the component whose reusability is to be measured. Let N user defined components are X_1, X_2 ... X_N in the system, where S_1, S_2 ... S_M are the standard environment components e.g. printf in C language.

$$\text{Reuse Frequency} = \frac{\eta(C)}{\left[\frac{1}{M}\sum_{i=0}^{M}\eta(S_i)\right]} \tag{5}$$

The equation (5) shows that the "Reuse frequency" is the measure of function usefulness of a component. Hence there should be some minimum value of "Reuse Frequency" to make software component really reusable [3].

2.1.5. Coupling

Functions/methods that are loosely bound tend to be easier to remove and use in other contexts tan those that depend heavily on other functions or non-local data.

Different types of coupling effects reusability with different extent. Depending on the type of interface between two functions coupling can be classified in following categories [13].

2.1.5.1. Data Coupling

Data coupling exists between two functions when functions communicate using elementary data items that are passed as parameters between the two.

2.1.5.2. Stamp Coupling

When two functions communicate using composite data item e.g. structure in C language then that kind of coupling is called Stamp Coupling.

2.1.5.3. Control Coupling

If data from one function is said to direct the order of instruction execution in another function then Control Coupling is there between those functions. In other words functions share data items upon which control decisions are made.

2.1.5.4. Common Coupling

In case of Common Coupling the two functions share global data items.

Weight of coupling increases from "a" to "d" means Data coupling is lightest weight coupling, whereas Content Coupling is the heaviest one. Let

a_i = number of functions called and Data Coupled with function "i"
b_i = number of functions called and Stamp Coupled with function "i"
c_i = number of functions called by function "i" and Control Coupled with function "i"
d_i = number of functions Common Coupled with function "i"
Then total lack of coupling measure m_c for function "i" can be calculated as:

$$m_c = \frac{K}{(w_1 * a_i + w_2 * b_i + w_3 * c_i + w_4 * d_i)} \tag{6}$$

As lack of coupling(m_c) decreases, there is decrease in understandability and maintainability, so there should be some maximum value of the coupling associated with a software component, beyond which the component becomes non-reusable i.e. there should be minimum value for the lack of coupling measure (m_c).

2.2. Neuro-Fuzzy System's Architecture

The fuzzy logic approach is beneficial for measuring the reusability of a software component as the conventional model based approaches are difficult to be implemented. Unfortunately, with the increase in the complexity of the problem being modeled and unavailability of the precise relationship among various constituents for measuring the reusability, has led to rely on another approach which is mostly known as neuro-fuzzy or fuzzy-neuro approach. It has the benefits of both neural networks and fuzzy logic. The neuro-fuzzy hybrid system combines the advantages of fuzzy logic system, which deal with explicit knowledge that can be explained and understood, and neural networks, which deal with implicit knowledge, which can be acquired by learning.

A fuzzy system can be considered to be a parameterized nonlinear map, called *f*, which can be expressed as:

$$f(x) = \frac{\sum_{l=1}^{m} y^{l} \left(\prod_{i=1}^{n} \mu_{A_i^l}(x_i) \right)}{\sum_{l=1}^{m} \left(\prod_{i=1}^{n} \mu_{A_i^l}(x_i) \right)} \tag{7}$$

where y^l is a place of output singleton if Mamdani reasoning is applied or a constant if Sugeno reasoning is applied. The membership function $\mu_{Ai}^{l}(x_i)$ corresponds to the input $x=[x_1, x_2, x_3,\dots x_m]$ of the rule l. The *"and"* connective in the premise is carried out by a product and defuzzification by the center-of-gravity method. Consider a Sugeno type of fuzzy system having the rule base

Rule1: If x is A1 and y is B1, then $f1= p_1x + q_1y + r1$
Rule2: If x is A2 and y is B2, then $f2= p_2x+ q_2y + r2$
Let the membership functions of fuzzy sets Ai, Bi, i=1,2, be , μ_{Ai}, μ_{Bi}.
1. Evaluating the rule premises results in

$w_i = \mu_{Ai}(x) * \mu_{Bi}(y)$ where i = 1,2 for the rule rules stated above.

2. Evaluating the implication and the rule consequences gives equation:

$$f(x,y)=\frac{w_1(x,y)f_1(x,y)+w_2(x,y)f_2(x,y)}{w_1(x,y)+w_2(x,y)}$$

Or

$$f=\frac{w_1f_1+w_2f_2}{w_1+w_2}$$

Let

$$\overline{w_i}=\frac{w_i}{w_1+w_2}$$

then f can be written as

$$f=\overline{w_1}f_1+\overline{w_2}f_2$$

These all computations can be presented in a diagram form as shown in the Fig. 1(a) and 1(b).

In the Adaptive neuro-fuzzy inference system using a given input/output data set, we have constructed a fuzzy inference system (FIS) whose membership function parameters are tuned (adjusted) using a hybrid method consisting of back-propagation form of the steepest descent method for the parameters associated with the input membership functions, and least squares estimation for the parameters associated with the output membership functions. As a result, the training error decreases, at least locally, throughout the learning process. Therefore, the more the initial membership functions resemble the optimal ones, the easier it will be for the model parameter training to converge. Before training, the initial rule section and setting up of initial membership function parameters in the FIS, is done using human expertise about the target system to be modeled. This allows fuzzy systems to learn from the data they are modeling. We are using the Sugeno type Fuzzy Inference System with five metric value Inputs & one output as shown in Fig. 2.

In the fuzzy Inference system Linguistic variables are then assigned to the input parameters based on their values. The assignment of the linguistic variables depends on the range of the input measurement.

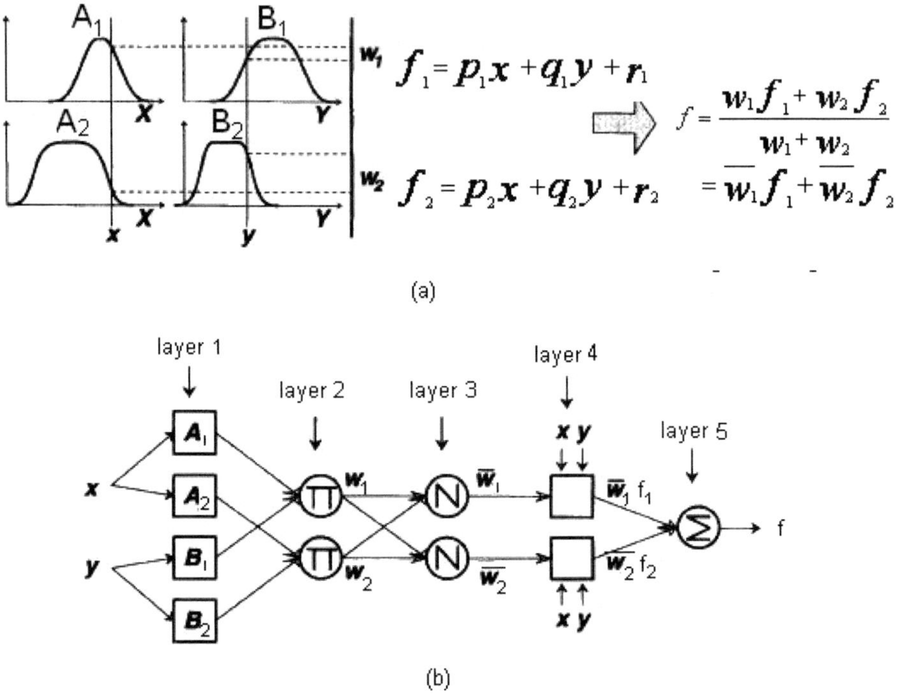

Figure 1. (a) A two-Input First-Order Sugeno Fuzzy Model with to rules. (b) Equivalent Neuro-Fuzzy System.

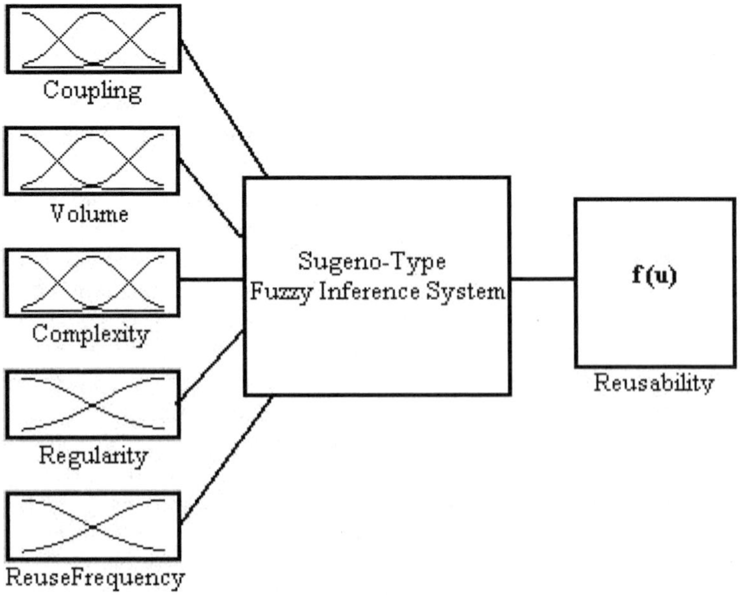

Figure 2. Fuzzy System with 5 Inputs & one Output.

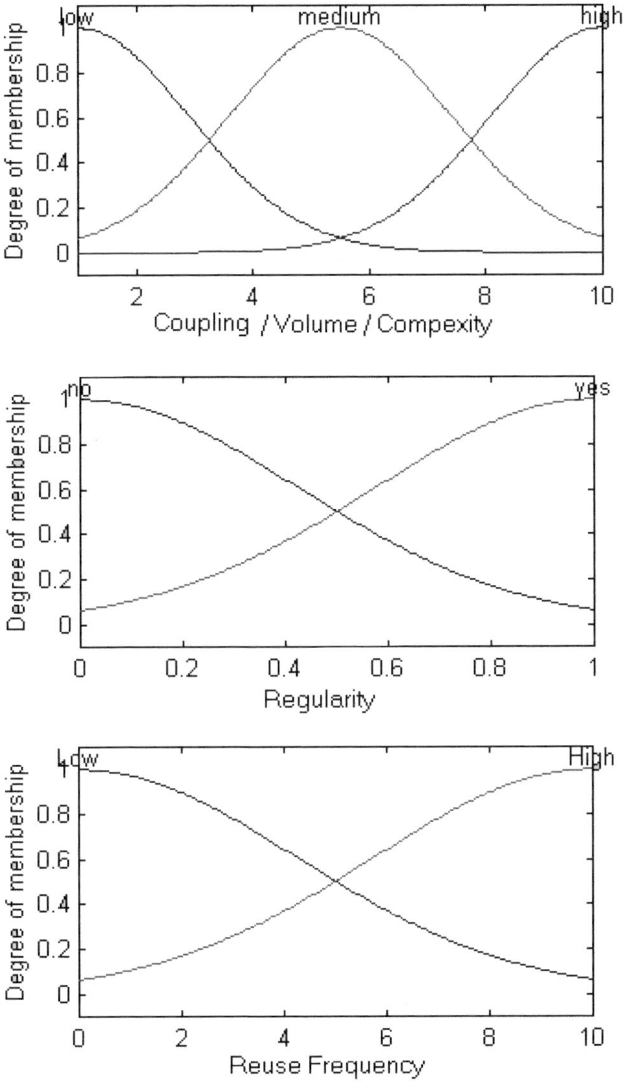

Figure 3. Initializing membership- functions for Fuzzy System.

Values to the linguistic variables of Complexity are assigned in terms of complexity of the software component. Cyclometric Complexity is assigned three linguistic variables "low", "medium" and "high" in the range of 0 to 10. The plot is also shown in Fig. 3.

Values to the linguistic variables of Regularity are assigned in terms of level of regularity for the software component under consideration. Regularity is assigned two linguistic variables "yes" and "no" in the range of 0 to 1. The plot is also shown in Fig. 3.

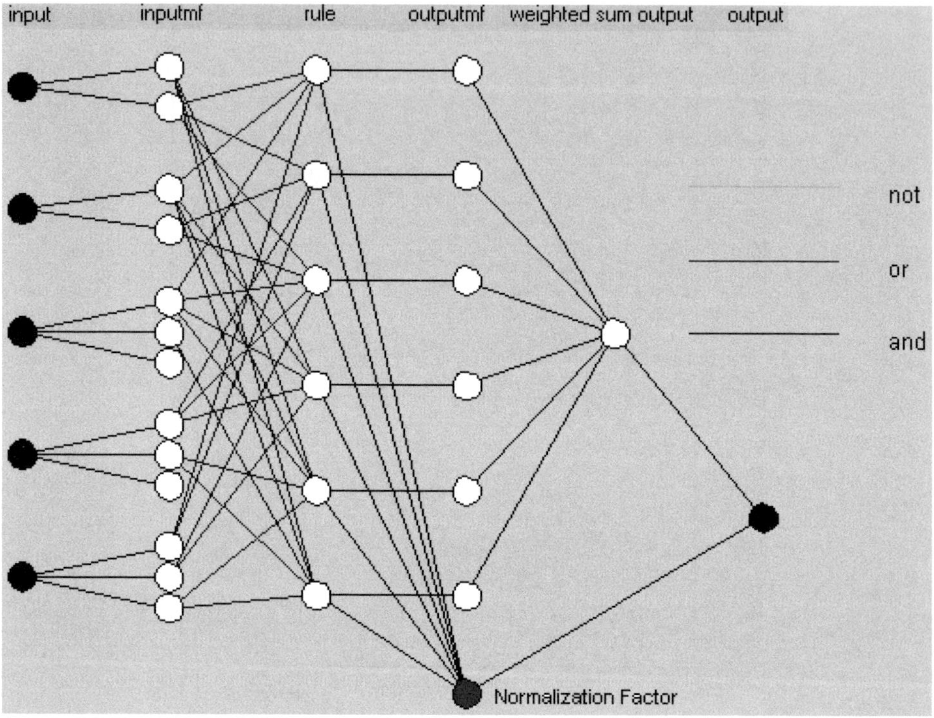

Figure 4. Neural Network incorporating the Fuzzy inference system.

Values to the linguistic variables of Volume are assigned in terms of volume of the software module. Quality attribute Volume is assigned three linguistic variables "low", "medium" and "high" in the range of 0 to 10. The plot is also shown in Fig. 3.

Values to the linguistic variables of Reuse-Frequency are assigned in terms of number of times the software module is reused. Reuse-Frequency is assigned two linguistic variables "Low" and "High" in the range of 0 to 10. The plot is also shown in Fig. 3.

Values to the linguistic variables of coupling are assigned in terms of level of coupling of the software module with other modules or the level of dependency of the software module on other modules. Coupling is assigned three linguistic variables "low", "medium" and "high" in the range of 0 to 10. The plot is also shown in Fig. 3.

Values to the linguistic variables of Reusability are assigned in terms of "how reusable the software module is?" As the output membership functions are only linear or constant for Sugeno-type fuzzy inference. Reusability is assigned six linguistic variables PERFECT, HIGH, MEDIUM, LOW, VERY-LOW and NIL as constants in the range of 0–100.

A network-type structure similar to that of a neural network, which maps inputs through input membership functions and associated parameters, and then through output membership functions and associated parameters to outputs, can be used to interpret the input/output map is shown in the Fig. 4.

The parameters associated with the membership functions will change through the learning process. The computation of these parameters (or their adjustment) is facilitated by a gradient vector, which provides a measure of how well the fuzzy inference

1. If (Coupling is low) and (Volume is medium) and (Complexity is mediur
(Regularity is yes) and (Reuse-Frequency is High) then (Reusability is PERF!
2. If (Coupling is low) and (Volume is medium) and (Complexity is higl
(Regularity is yes) and (Reuse-Frequency is High) then (Reusability is HIGH
3. If (Coupling is medium) and (Volume is high) and (Complexity is higl
(Regularity is yes) and (Reuse-Frequency is High) then (Reusability is MEDI
4. If (Coupling is medium) and (Volume is high) and (Complexity is higl
(Regularity is no) and (Reuse-Frequency is Low) then (Reusability is LOW)
5. If (Coupling is high) and (Volume is high) and (Regularity is no) and (I
Frequency is Low) then (Reusability is NIL)
6. If (Coupling is high) and (Complexity is high) and (Regularity is ye:
(Reuse-Frequency is Low) then (Reusability is VERY-LOW)

Figure 5. Initial Rules Being used by Fuzzy Inference.

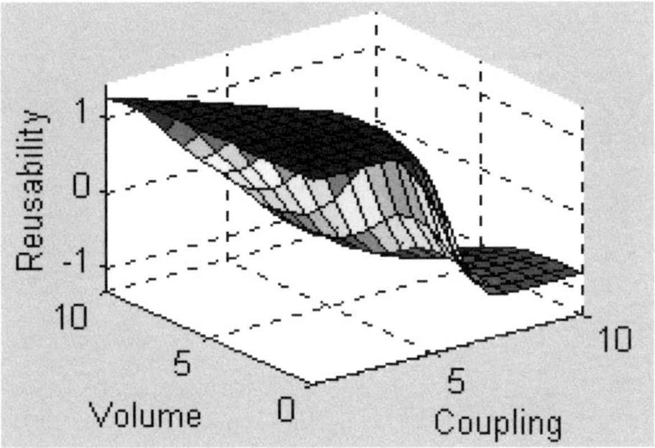

Figure 6. Surface plot between Coupling, Complexity and Reusability.

system is modeling the input/output data for a given set of parameters. Once the gradient vector is obtained, any of several optimization routines could be applied in order to adjust the parameters so as to reduce some error measure. The Error Tolerance is used to create a training stopping criterion, which is related to the error size. The training will stop after the training data error remains within this tolerance. This is set to 0 as we don't know how training error is going to behave.

The initial rules selection is shown in Fig. 5 and the initial 3D surface plot in between Coupling, Complexity and Reusability is shown in Fig. 6. The Training of the NEURO-FUZZY SYSTEM is performed using Training Data for 2000 iterations and the training error reduces after each iteration as shown by the Fig. 7 and stabilities at the error value of 0.33591, so at this point the network is said to be converged.

3. Conclusion

During the testing phase, when NEURO-FUZZY SYSTEM is tested against the data of Annexure-II Average Testing error 0.41318 is obtained. The plot between the actual output and the expected output is shown in Fig. 8. The plot between the actual output and the expected output for the testing data of Annexure-I is shown in Fig. 9. As the

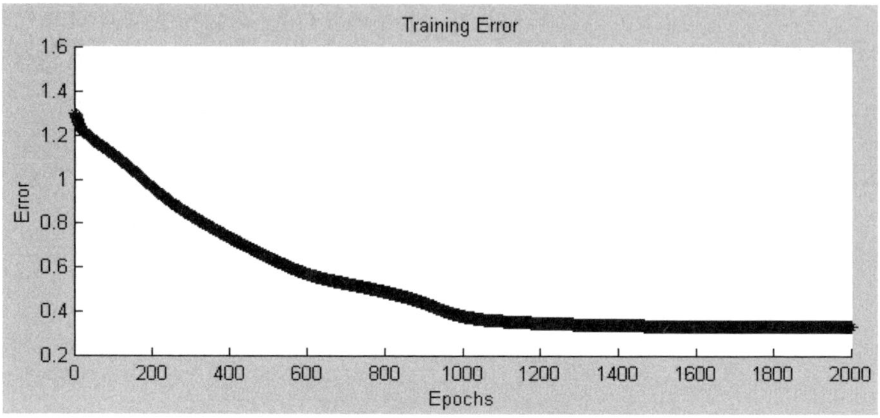

Figure 7. Plot of Training error V/s Epochs.

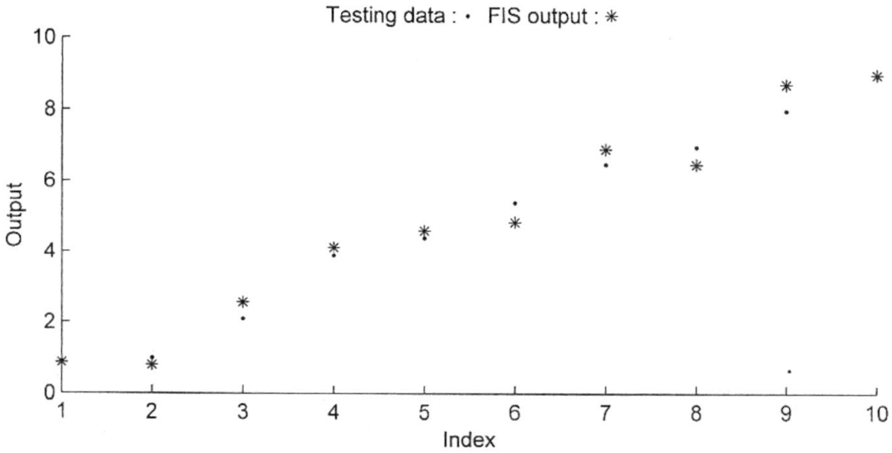

Figure 8. Plot between the actual output and expected output.

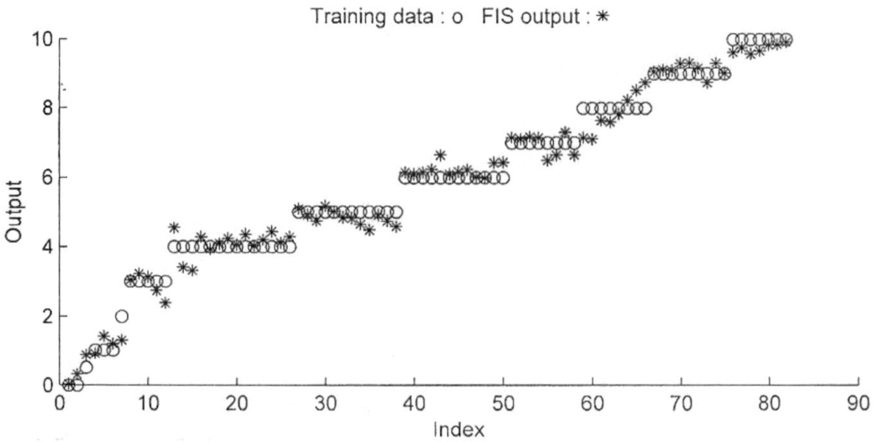

Figure 9. Plot between the actual output and expected output for testing data.

actual output produced by the Adaptive neuro-fuzzy inference system is close to the expected output by the experienced so the above system can be recommended for Automating the identification of Reusable Components in existing software systems.

References

[1] G. Boetticher, K. Srinivas, and D. Eichmann, *A Neural Net-based Approach to Software Metrics*, Proceedings of the 5th International Conference on Software Engineering and Knowledge Engineering, San Francisco, CA, 14–18 June 1993, pp. 271–274.
[2] G. Boetticher and D. Eichmann, *A Neural Network Paradigm for Characterizing Reusable Software*, Proceedings of the Australian Conference on Software Metrics, 18–19 November 1993.
[3] G. Caldiera and V.R. Basili, *Identifying and Qualifying Reusable Software Components*, IEEE Computer, February 1991.
[4] G. Mayobre, *Using Code Reusability Analysis to Identify Reusable Components from Software Related to an Application Domain*, Proceeding of the Fourth Workshop on Software Reuse, Reston. VA, November, 1991.
[5] Guttorm Sindre, Reidar Conradi, Even-André Karlsson, "*The REBOOT approach to software reuse*", *Journal of Systems and Software*, 30(3): 201–212, September 1995.
[6] J.C. Esteva, *Automatic Identification of reusable Components*, IEEE Seventh International Workshop on Computer-Aided Software Engineering – CASE '95, 1995.
[7] J.C. Esteva and R.G. Reynolds, *Identifying Reusable Components using Induction*, International Journal of Software Engineering and Knowledge Engineering, Vol. 1, No. 3 (1991) 271–292.
[8] J.-S.R. Jang and C.T. Sun, *Neuro-fuzzy Modeling and Control*, Proceeding of IEEE, March 1995.
[9] M.F. Dunn and J.C. Knight, *Software reuse in Industrial setting: A Case Study*, Proceeding of the 13th International Conference on Software Engineering, Baltimore, MA, 1993.
[10] M.H. Halstead, *Elements of Software Science*, Elsevier North-Holland, New Tork, 1977.
[11] R.S. Arnold, *Heuristics for Salvaging Reusable Parts From Ada Code*, SPC Technical Report, ADA_REUSE_HEURISTICS-90011-N, March 1990.
[12] R.S. Arnold, *Salvaging Reusable Parts From Ada Code: A Progress Report*, SPC Technical Report, SALVAGE_ADA_PARTS_PR-90048-N, September 1990.
[13] R.S. Pressman, *Software Engineering: A Practitioner's Approach*, McGraw-Hill, 2004.
[14] R.W. Selby, *Empirically Analyzing Software Reuse in a Production Environment*, Software Reuse: Emerging Technology, W. Tracz, ed., IEEE Computer Society Press, 1988.
[15] S.V. Kartalopoulos, *Understanding Neural Networks and Fuzzy Logic-Basic Concepts and Applications*, IEEE Press, 1996, pp. 153–160.
[16] T. MaCabe, *A Software Complexity measure*, IEEE Trans. Software Engineering, vol. SE-2, December 1976, pp. 308–320.
[17] Y.F. Chen, M.Y. Nishimoto and C.V. Ramamoorty, *The C Information Abstraction System*, IEEE Transaction on Software Engineering, Vol. 16, No. 3, March 1990.

ANNEXURE I
Training Data for the Adaptive Neuro-Fuzzy System

Coupling	Volume	Complexity	Regularity	Reuse Frequency	Reusability
10.0000	10.0000	10.0000	0	0	0
10.0000	1.0000	1.0000	0	0	0
9.0000	9.0000	9.0000	0	0	0.5000
9.0000	1.0000	1.0000	0	0	1.0000
9.0000	9.0000	8.0000	0.4000	1.0000	1.0000
9.0000	9.0000	2.0000	0.4000	1.0000	1.0000
9.0000	8.0000	7.0000	0.3000	1.0000	2.0000
8.0000	7.0000	7.0000	0.5000	2.0000	3.0000
8.0000	2.0000	3.0000	0.5000	2.0000	3.0000

8.0000	3.0000	3.0000	0.5000	2.0000	3.0000
8.0000	7.0000	6.0000	0.4000	2.0000	3.0000
8.0000	7.0000	2.0000	0.4000	2.0000	3.0000
7.0000	8.0000	6.0000	0.6000	2.0000	4.0000
8.0000	2.0000	6.0000	0.5000	2.0000	4.0000
8.0000	3.0000	6.0000	0.5000	2.0000	4.0000
7.0000	2.0000	6.0000	0.5000	2.0000	4.0000
7.0000	2.0000	2.0000	0.5000	2.0000	4.0000
7.0000	2.0000	3.0000	0.5000	2.0000	4.0000
7.0000	3.0000	6.0000	0.5000	2.0000	4.0000
7.0000	3.0000	3.0000	0.5000	2.0000	4.0000
7.0000	6.0000	7.0000	0.5000	3.0000	4.0000
7.0000	6.0000	2.0000	0.5000	3.0000	4.0000
7.0000	6.0000	3.0000	0.5000	3.0000	4.0000
7.0000	3.0000	7.0000	0.5000	3.0000	4.0000
7.0000	3.0000	2.0000	0.5000	3.0000	4.0000
7.0000	3.0000	3.0000	0.5000	3.0000	4.0000
6.0000	7.0000	6.0000	0.5000	3.0000	5.0000
6.0000	7.0000	3.0000	0.5000	3.0000	5.0000
6.0000	7.0000	2.0000	0.5000	3.0000	5.0000
6.0000	3.0000	6.0000	0.5000	3.0000	5.0000
6.0000	3.0000	3.0000	0.5000	3.0000	5.0000
6.0000	3.0000	2.0000	0.5000	3.0000	5.0000
6.0000	7.0000	6.0000	0.5000	2.0000	5.0000
6.0000	7.0000	3.0000	0.5000	2.0000	5.0000
6.0000	7.0000	2.0000	0.5000	2.0000	5.0000
6.0000	3.0000	6.0000	0.5000	2.0000	5.0000
6.0000	3.0000	3.0000	0.5000	2.0000	5.0000
6.0000	3.0000	2.0000	0.5000	2.0000	5.0000
3.0000	4.0000	6.0000	0.6000	2.0000	6.0000
3.0000	6.0000	6.0000	0.6000	2.0000	6.0000
3.0000	5.0000	6.0000	0.6000	2.0000	6.0000
3.0000	4.0000	4.0000	0.6000	2.0000	6.0000
3.0000	4.0000	4.0000	0.6000	3.0000	6.0000
3.0000	6.0000	6.0000	0.6000	2.0000	6.0000
3.0000	6.0000	4.0000	0.6000	2.0000	6.0000
3.0000	5.0000	4.0000	0.6000	2.0000	6.0000
4.0000	4.0000	6.0000	0.6000	2.0000	6.0000
4.0000	6.0000	6.0000	0.6000	2.0000	6.0000
2.0000	5.0000	6.0000	0.6000	2.0000	6.0000
4.0000	5.0000	4.0000	0.6000	3.0000	6.0000
2.0000	4.0000	6.0000	0.7000	2.0000	7.0000
2.0000	6.0000	6.0000	0.7000	2.0000	7.0000
2.0000	5.0000	6.0000	0.7000	2.0000	7.0000
2.0000	4.0000	6.0000	0.7000	2.0000	7.0000
2.0000	6.0000	4.0000	0.6000	2.0000	7.0000
3.0000	5.0000	4.0000	0.6000	3.0000	7.0000
3.0000	4.0000	6.0000	0.7000	3.0000	7.0000
3.0000	5.0000	4.0000	0.6000	3.0000	7.0000
2.0000	4.0000	6.0000	0.7000	2.0000	8.0000
2.0000	6.0000	6.0000	0.7000	2.0000	8.0000
1.0000	4.0000	6.0000	0.7000	2.0000	8.0000
1.0000	6.0000	6.0000	0.7000	2.0000	8.0000
2.0000	4.0000	6.0000	0.8000	2.0000	8.0000
2.0000	6.0000	6.0000	0.8000	3.0000	8.0000
1.0000	6.0000	6.0000	0.8000	3.0000	8.0000
1.0000	6.0000	4.0000	0.8000	3.0000	8.0000
1.0000	4.0000	5.0000	0.9000	3.0000	9.0000
1.0000	5.0000	5.0000	0.9000	3.0000	9.0000

1.0000	6.0000	5.0000	0.9000	3.0000	9.0000
0	4.0000	5.0000	0.9000	3.0000	9.0000
0	6.0000	5.0000	0.9000	3.0000	9.0000
1.0000	6.0000	4.0000	0.9000	3.0000	9.0000
1.0000	6.0000	4.0000	0.8000	3.0000	9.0000
0	6.0000	4.0000	0.8000	4.0000	9.0000
1.0000	6.0000	4.0000	0.8000	4.0000	9.0000
0	5.0000	5.0000	1.0000	4.0000	10.0000
0	4.0000	4.0000	1.0000	5.0000	10.0000
4.0000	5.0000	5.0000	0.9000	4.0000	10.0000
0	5.0000	4.0000	0.9000	5.0000	10.0000
1.0000	4.0000	4.0000	0.9000	7.0000	10.0000
1.0000	4.0000	4.0000	1.0000	6.0000	10.0000
0	5.0000	4.0000	1.0000	7.0000	10.0000

ANNEXURE II
Training Data for the Adaptive Neuro-Fuzzy System

Coupling	Volume	Complexity	Regularity	Reuse Frequency	Reusability
9.0000	8.0000	9.0000	0	0	0.9000
9.0000	2.0000	1.0000	0	0	1.0000
8.0000	8.0000	7.0000	0.4000	1.0000	2.1000
8.0000	7.0000	7.0000	0.7000	2.0000	3.9000
7.0000	7.0000	6.0000	0.6000	2.0000	4.4000
6.0000	3.4000	2.0000	0.5000	3.0000	5.4000
4.0000	5.0000	4.5000	0.6000	4.0000	6.5000
2.0000	6.0000	4.0000	0.6000	2.0000	7.0000
1.0000	6.0000	4.0000	0.8000	3.0000	8.0000
1.0000	6.0000	4.0000	0.8000	4.0000	9.0000

Chapter 4

Requirement Representation and Formalization

New Trends in Software Methodologies, Tools and Techniques
H. Fujita and M. Mejri (Eds.)
IOS Press, 2005

A Gentle Introduction to System Verification

Prof. Love EKENBERG
Department of Computer and Systems Sciences, Stockholm University and KTH,
Forum 100, SE-164 40 Kista, Sweden

Abstract. Verification is an important instrument in the analysis of systems. Roughly, this means that requirements and designs are analyzed formally to determine their relationships. Various candidates for formalizing system development and integration have been proposed. However, a major obstacle is that these introduce non-standard objects and formalisms, leading to severe confusion. This is because these models often are unnecessarily complicated with several disadvantages regarding semantics as well as complexity. While avoiding the mathematical details as far as possible, we present some basic verification ideas using a simple language such as predicate logic and demonstrate how this can be used for defining and analyzing static and dynamic requirement fulfillment by designs as well as for detecting conflicts. The formalities can be found in the appendix.

Motivation

Assume that we have 100 switches in an interlocking system and where the switches can be either on or off. If we want to, e.g., check that some very undesirable state really is impossible; then there are 2^{100} (=1,267,650,600,228,229,401,496,703,205,376) possible states to check.

Assuming that we can test one billion states per second (quite a lot), the check takes about 40,196,936,841,331 years to perform. The age of the universe is about 10–20,000,000,000 years. So the calculation takes roughly 2–4,000 times the age of the universe. Few people can wait that long.

Thus, the number of states might be many, in most real life cases indefinitely many. Consequently, ordinary state-space exploration, for instance using simulations, is usually meaningless to perform.

Components

For being able to tackle problems of these magnitudes, we must use some kind of formal analysis. In general, at least three components are necessary for this:

1. A suitable reality
2. A representation format
3. A verification mechanism

Obviously, we cannot model everything. Without a suitable reality these activities are quite uninteresting. This also includes various assumptions on an object having certain properties. For instance, objects must be considered to be perceived in one or another way and having relationships to each others. Furthermore, some kind of systematical procedures should be assumed. Totally chaotic behaviors are usually intractable.

Moreover, given a decent reality, the format for representing this must be rich enough. At the same time, it should be computationally meaningful. This means that the representation language must have the capability to express meaningful knowledge of the world in a tractable format.

A Representation Format

There are two aspects of a language designed for knowledge representation:

1. Syntax, i.e., a structure for determining whether a sentence is allowed in the representation.
2. Semantics, i.e., a structure to give a (precise) meaning to a sentence.

Syntax

Syntax just means that the sequences of symbols representing a system – the alphabet – must follow certain rules. It is like a grammar for a natural language including an alphabet and formation rules. Obviously, it is important how symbols are combined.

To illustrate this, compare the following sentences.

- Am I a hungry dog
- I am a hungry dog
- Dog hungry a am I

The first one is a question, the second is a statement and the third is meaningless. So normally, the combination rules are worth to consider.

Important components in an alphabet are predicate symbols, connectives, quantifiers, and other operators:

- **Predicate symbols**
  correspond to relations and properties:
  e.g. x *is larger than* y
- **Connectives**
  are used for combining sentences:
  e.g. I have a dog *and* a cat
- **Quantifiers**
  quantify:
  e.g. *There are some* dogs that are larger than *all* cats
- **Other operators and signs**
  are used for expanding the expressibility of the language in various ways:
  e.g. 1 + 1 = 2

Semantics

Semantics, on the other hand, stipulate the meaning of sentences in a language and is what actually defines what kind of sentences that can meaningfully be handled in a model. Various strengths of expressibility require representation languages with various properties. For instance, the following sentences require different kinds of logics to be meaningfully represented.

1. All lions are dangerous.
2. Lions must be dangerous.
3. Lions are always dangerous.
4. Most lions are dangerous.
5. Lions are quite dangerous.

Sentence 1 above requires predicate logic for being meaningfully represented. Similarly, sentence 2 requires modal logic, sentence 3 requires temporal logic, sentence 4 requires 2nd order logic and sentence 5 requires fuzzy logic.

Whatever the semantics is for a formal language, it must be exactly defined. This is not always the case with natural languages. Consider for instance the following sentences.

- It is raining cats and dogs!
- My children are killing me!
- The weather is terrible!
- I am starving!
- I hate Mondays!

All of the sentences are meaningful in a natural language, but their normal meanings do not coincide with how they are formally interpreted.

In principle, the semantics for predicate logic is based on the truth concept and could be (informally) stated as the following:

- $A \wedge B$
  Both A and B are true
- $A \vee B$
  A or B is true or both are true
- $\neg A$
  A is not true
- $A \rightarrow B$
  If A is true, then B is true
- $A \leftrightarrow B$
  A is true if and only if B is true
- $\forall x\, A(x)$
  All x have the property A
- $\exists x\, A(x)$
  At least one x has the property A

One way of expressing the semantics of a simple language, such as propositional logic, is by using truth tables.

	B	**A ∧ B**
True	True	True
True	False	False
False	True	False
False	False	False

A and B denote arbitrary (but syntactically permitted) sentences in a language.

Assuming set of sentences Γ and introducing a truth function t: Γ → {true, false}, the straightforward interpretation of the table is that t(A ∧ B) iff t(A) and t(B) etc.

Specifications in Logic

We can use these simple truth tables to illustrate formal properties of systems.

Consider the following example. Assuming that it is not broken, a light bulb is on (L) precisely when the power switch is closed (S) and there is a functional battery connected (B).

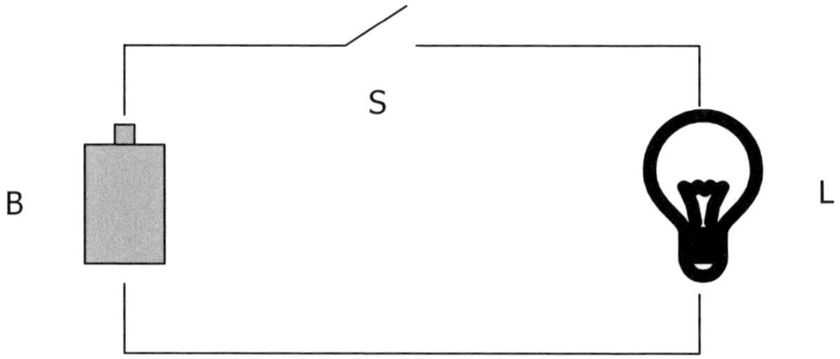

Figure 1. A model.

This can be represented by the sentence (B ∧ S) ↔ L. The corresponding truth table is shown below.

B	**S**	**L**	**(B ∧ S) ↔ L**
True	True	True	True
True	True	False	False
True	False	True	False
True	False	False	True
False	True	True	False
False	True	False	True
False	False	True	False
False	False	False	True

Note that only four of the rows represent possible states in this model, i.e., when the model is true. When a model is false, it does not represent anything meaningful (except the empty set). Therefore the "false rows" are meaningless for our purposes.

B	**S**	**L**	**(B ∧ S) ↔ L**
True	True	True	True
True	False	False	True
False	True	False	True
False	False	False	True

Another simple example is an ordinary relation in a database.

Car_owner	Name	Soc. sec. no.	Car reg. no.	Manufacturer
	L. Smith	10101010	AAA111	Toyota
	M. Jones	21212121	BBB222	Volvo

Then entries can be represented as instantiated predicate symbols, such as

- Car_owner(L_Smith,10101010,AAA111,Toyota) and
- Car_owner(M_Jones,21212121,BBB222,Volvo)

Ordinary predicate logic can then be used for posing questions to such a database, for instance,

List all persons owning a Toyota, i.e., ∃y∃zCar_owner(x,y,z,Toyota).

Inference

As we have seen, logic can be used for representing systems such as the above. This is in itself a good thing, since such models can be articulated and communicated. However, the most important thing is that formalized models can be analyzed in a variety of respects. First we look at one important concept – logical inference.

Consider the following inferences:

- All cats are happy. Leonardo is a cat. Therefore, Leonardo is happy.
- All rabbits eat carrots. Manuela is a rabbit. Therefore, Manuela eats carrots.
- All elephants are wise. Arnold is an elephants. Therefore, Arnold is wise.

A main observation is now that the logical correctness of these is not a matter of cats, rabbits, or elephants. It is the format of the reasoning that gives it its logical form.

- All cats are happy: ∀x(C(x) → H(x)), Leonardo is a cat: C(a), Leonardo is happy: H(a). Here *C(x)* means that *x* is a cat and *H(x)* means that x is happy. The symbol *a* denotes the object *Leonardo*.
- All rabbits eat carrots: ∀x(C(x) → H(x)), Manuela is a rabbit: C(a), Manuela eats carrots: H(a). Here *C(x)* means that *x* is a rabbit and *H(x)* means that x eats carrots. The symbol *a* denotes the object *Manuela*.
- All elephants are wise: ∀x(C(x) → H(x)), Arnold is a elephant: C(a), Arnold is wise: H(a). Here *C(x)* means that *x* is a elephant and *H(x)* means that x is wise. The symbol *a* denotes the object *Arnold*.

The important thing here is the form, i.e., assuming that ∀x (C(x) → H(x)) and C(a) are valid, then we can deduce H(a).

Let us see how this applies to formal verification. Reconsider Fig. 1 again and assume the lamp is not on (¬L). We would like to find the problem.

- Our system design is (B ∧ S) ↔ L.
- We also know that ¬L, i.e., L is not the case.
- But then ¬(B ∧ S) follows logically, i.e., ¬(B ∧ S) is not the case. Otherwise, L would be the case.
- This, in turn, is the same as ¬B ∨ ¬S, because if not both of B and S are true, at least one of them must be false.

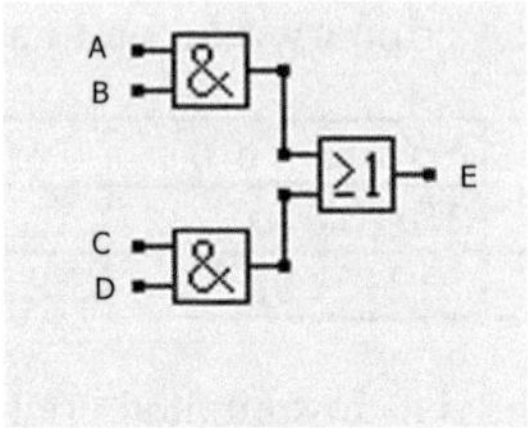

Figure 2. Modeling using circuits.

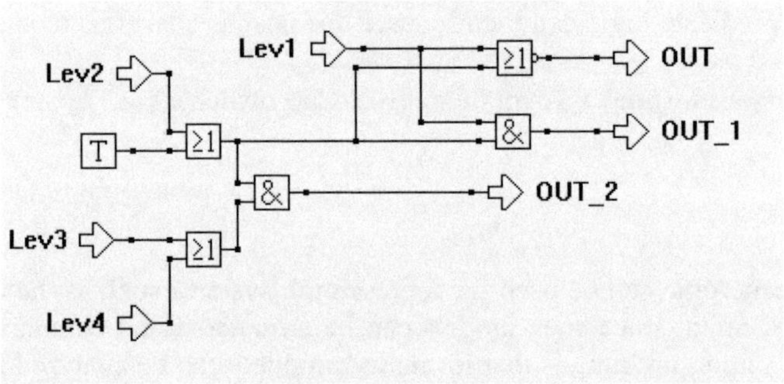

Figure 3. Another circuit.

Thus, we have deduced the following:

The lamp is not on because the power switch is not closed or there is not a functional battery connected.

This was not a big surprise in this case, but the reasoning applies to systems of arbitrary size. And then it might be of highest importance.

Again, it is the logical form that is important. Consider the following:

The nuclear power plant has a meltdown (L) precisely when the supply of internal electricity does not work (S) and the backup systems are dysfunctional (B).

Also here, our system design is $(B \wedge S) \leftrightarrow L$ and an analysis of why the plant does not have a nuclear meltdown would look exactly the same.

Thus, the reasoning has nothing to do with nuclear power plants, lamps, batteries, power switches, etc. Nevertheless and therefore, it is highly useful and widely applicable.

Other Representation Formats

A multitude of representation formats have been suggested. One common is circuit representation. The circuit in Fig. 2 has the same meaning as the sentence $[(A \wedge B) \vee (C \wedge D)] \leftrightarrow E$. Figure 3 shows a larger circuit with some other components as well.

Another modeling language is UML that has received a lot of industry support from IT suppliers as well as users and has been effectively standardized. In the figure below, two UML class diagrams are shown. The first diagram represents that an owner can own CAR. An owner has a social security number and a car has a registration

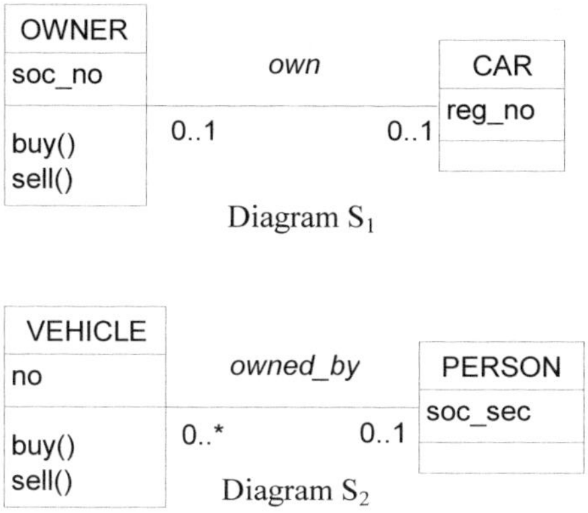

Figure 4. Sample UML diagrams S_1 and S_2.

number. Furthermore, all owners must own at most one car and one car can be owned by at most one owner.

In the second diagram, a similar situation is depicted. However, an owner can have more than one car. Otherwise, the diagram is very similar to the first one.

One reasonable translation of the first class diagram is

- $\forall x \forall y[\text{own}(x,y) \rightarrow \text{owner}(x) \wedge \text{car}(y)]$
- $\forall x \forall y[\text{soc\_no}(x,y) \rightarrow \text{owner}(x)]$
- $\forall x \forall y[\text{reg\_no}(x,y) \rightarrow \text{car}(x)]$
- $\forall x \forall y \forall z[(\text{own}(x,y) \wedge \text{own}(x,z)) \rightarrow y = z]\}$
- $\forall x \forall y \forall z[(\text{own}(y,x) \wedge \text{own}(z,x)) \rightarrow y = z]\}$

Similarly, the translation of the second class diagram is:

- $\forall x \forall y[\text{owned\_by}(x,y) \rightarrow \text{vehicle}(x) \wedge \text{person}(y)]$
- $\forall x \forall y[\text{no}(x,y) \rightarrow \text{vehicle}(x)]$
- $\forall x \forall y[\text{soc\_sec}(x,y) \rightarrow \text{person}(x)]$
- $\forall x \forall y \forall z[(\text{owned\_by}(x,y) \wedge \text{owned\_by}(x,z)) \rightarrow y = z]$

Similarly, more general UML specifications can readily be translated to predicate logic and, consequently, be represented in a verifiable format.

Tractability

In a general UML schema, the potential state-space is infinite – or at least enormous. Consequently, we need more instruments for the analysis. Fortunately, the concepts of satisfiability, validity and logical consequence provide many of these.

The definitions of these concepts are very natural:

- A sentence is satisfiable iff (if and only if) there is a state where it is true.
- A sentence is valid iff it is true in all possible states.
- A sentence A follows logically from (or is a logical consequence of) a sentence B and C iff A is true in the states where B and C are true.

In the first two cases, the analogy between process descriptions and semantics is apparent. Logical consequence can be described by the following simple sequence.

If
P is true
And
$P \rightarrow Q$ *is true*

Then
Q is true

If any of the first two sentences are false, we do not bother about the result. Logical consequence only concerns what is the case when we have valid preconditions. If a system representation contains a sentence saying, e.g., that *one* is not equal to *one*, we would not be able to use this representation in any reasonable contexts anyway.

A nice feature of the concepts validity, satisfiability, and logical consequence is that they can be checked for within standard logics. This means that we can systematically check whether a state is impossible for a system, whether all possible states are acceptable, or whether a specification fulfills a set of requirements.

Dynamics

So far, so good. However, the reality is not a static entity. It consists of a continuum of state changes – some more important than others. Furthermore, events cause changes in the state-space. This must consequently be addressed in a framework for system verification.

For example, assume that we have a set of sentences $\{\neg r(a) \vee r(b), r(c) \leftrightarrow r(a)\}$. Then the possible models (states) are (if we adopt the notion that *r(a)* means that *r(a) is true*, etc.)

$$\sigma_1 = \{r(a), r(b), r(c)\}$$
$$\sigma_2 = \{\neg r(a), r(b), \neg r(c)\}$$
$$\sigma_3 = \{\neg r(a), \neg r(b), \neg r(c)\}$$

Now, the treatment of a dynamic system requires some concept of event rules which is given its semantics through the event concept. Intuitively, an event is an instance of an event rule, i.e. a transition from one state to another one. Formally, it could look like this:

An event rule is a structure $\langle P(z), C(z) \rangle$. $P(z)$ and $C(z)$ are first-order formulae, and z is a vector of variables in an alphabet. In terms of conceptual modeling, $P(z)$ denotes the precondition of the event rule, and $C(z)$ the post-condition.

To concretize a bit, consider the event rules

$$Er_{1a} = \langle r(a), r(b) \rangle$$
$$Er_{1b} = \langle \neg r(a), (\neg r(b) \wedge \neg r(c)) \rangle$$
$$Er_{1c} = \langle (\neg r(a) \wedge r(b)), r(a) \rangle$$

Informally, a transition occurs when a precondition in a rule is satisfied. In that case, the post-condition is obtained. More formally, the set of *events* for a system representation is a relation over the state-space. A pair of sentence sets (σ, ρ) belongs to this relation iff there is an event rule $\langle P(\mathbf{z}), C(\mathbf{z})\rangle$, and a vector **e** of constants in the language, such that $P(\mathbf{e}) \in \sigma$ and $C(\mathbf{e}) \in \rho$.

Figure 5 illustrates this. The arrows in the figure represent basic events and the circles represent the states of the system $\{\neg r(a) \vee r(b), r(c) \leftrightarrow r(a)\}$.

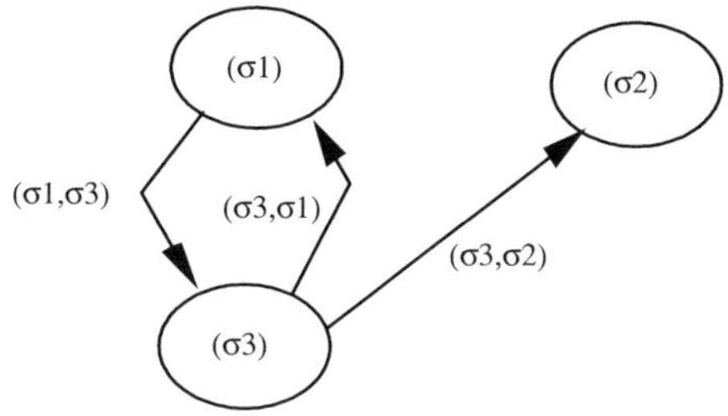

Figure 5. A state-space for the system $\{\neg r(a) \vee r(b), r(c) \leftrightarrow r(a)\}$.

For another example, consider the UML diagrams again.

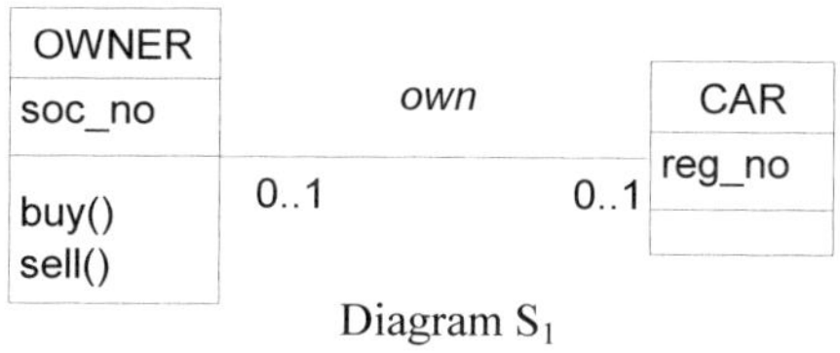

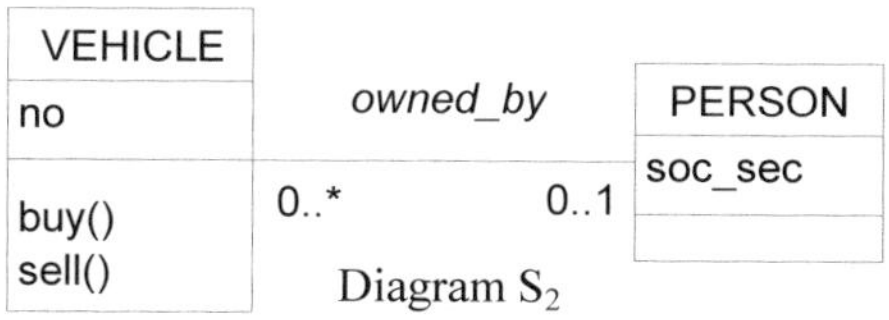

Figure 6. Sample UML diagrams S_1 and S_2.

The (essential) states for diagram S_1 (the upper one in the figure) basically are:

$\sigma_1 = \{own(a,c)\}$

$\sigma_2 = \{own(a,d)\}$

$\sigma_3 = \{own(b,c)\}$

$\sigma_4 = \{own(b,d)\}$

$\sigma_5 = \{own(a,c), own(b,d)\}$

$\sigma_6 = \{own(a,d), own(b,c)\}$

$\sigma_7 = \{\ \}$

The states for diagram S_2 (the lower one in the figure) are:

τ_1 = {owned_by(c,a)}
τ_2 = {owned_by(d,a)}
τ_3 = {owned_by(c,b)}
τ_4 = {owned_by(d,b)}
τ_5 = {owned_by(c,a), owned_by(d,b)}
τ_6 = {owned_by(d,a), owned_by(c,b)}
τ_7 = { }
τ_8 = {owned_by(c,a), owned_by(d,a)}
τ_9 = {owned_by(c,b), owned_by(d,b)}

Now, Fig. 7 illustrates the state-space of diagram S_1. The arrows in the figure represent basic events and the circles represent the possible states of the diagram.

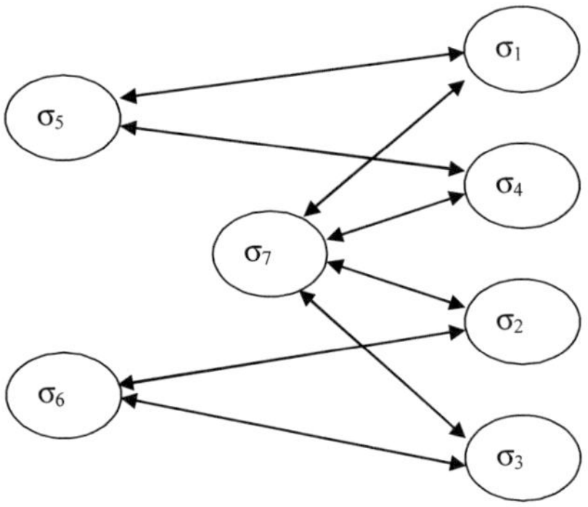

Figure 7. The state-space of diagram S_1.

Similarly, the state-space of diagram S_2 is depicted in Fig. 8.

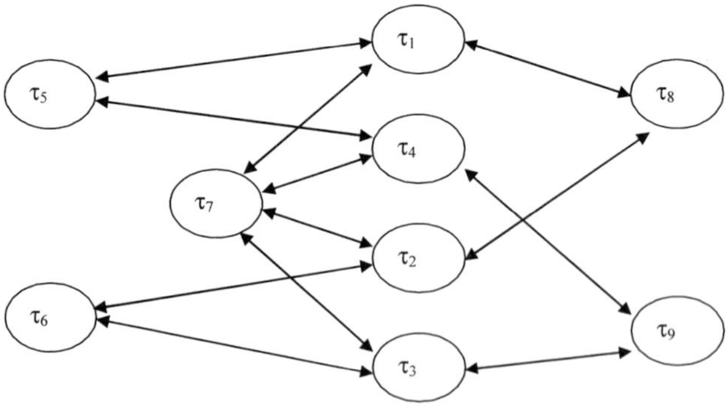

Figure 8. The state-space of diagram S_2.

Checking Properties of Systems

Having these mechanisms defined, various properties can be checked. For instance, the diagram S_1 is consistent, since there is a state that is consistent with the diagram, e.g., {own(a,c)}. On the other hand, the static diagram $S_1 \cup \{\exists x \exists y \exists z[own(x,y) \wedge$

own(x,z) $\wedge$ $\neg$y = z]} is inconsistent, since it is false in all states. Thus, in the former case, the representation might be meaningful. In the latter case, we can see that the system representation must be erroneous.

Systems in Conflict

Other types of analyses that can be performed include whether diagrams are conflicting with respect to some global semantics. The basic idea is that if two system representations are non-conflicting, then neither system obstructs the other. This can also be used for characterizing situations in which two systems could be meaningfully integrated.

For instance, assume each of two systems to be represented by a specification. Intuitively, they are in conflict with respect to a set of static integration assertions, expressing concepts of one system in terms of the other system, if the static rules of one of the systems, in union with the integration assertions, restrict the set of states to the empty set for the other, or vice versa.

In principle, freeness of conflicts means that all states that were reachable before two schemas are integrated will still be reachable after the schemas are integrated, i.e., no information is lost by integrating the schemas. This property is essential in system design.

Static Verification

A requirement specification should define a proper behavior of a design, i.e., it should define adequate system properties. A reasonable and minimal formal meaning of requirement fulfillment seems to be that every state that a system might be in should also be a state that is valid for the requirement specification. Otherwise, something is erroneous. Consequently, this is a kind of soundness requirement, requiring every design state to not contradict the requirements. This is normally captured by requiring that the requirements follow logically from the system specification. Thus, formally checking that a design specification fulfils a set of requirements is just a matter of calculations in logic.

Dynamic Verification

Typically, a design should fulfill its requirement specification. However, it might still be the case that despite a design not fulfilling a requirement specification, it is still perfectly adequate for an application. Figure 9 shows the description of a system represented by a non-connected graph. For instance, if the system starts in S_1, then there is no possibility that it would enter a state in the right sub-graph starting in S_2.

The crucial issue here is that if a system starts in a state that is consistent with the requirements, every state that it possible to reach from this state might be consistent with the requirements. Thus, even if the design does not fulfill the requirements in the sense above, it might be the case that the requirements are fulfilled in every feasible state, given a particular start state.

Informally, a checking algorithm could look like this:

1. Check that the start state fulfills the requirements.
2. Prove that if a state fulfills the requirements, then all possible consecutive states fulfill the requirements.

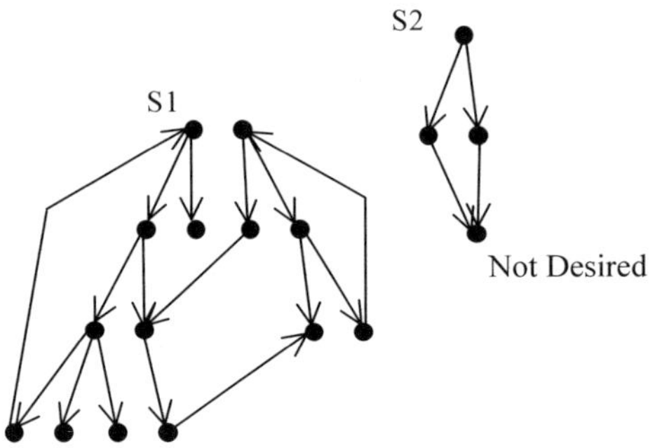

Figure 9. A state-space of a system represented by a non-connected graph.

3. Then, we can deduce that all states following the start state fulfill the requirements.

In other words, if a system starts in an start state that fulfills the requirement specification and step 3 above is reached, the system cannot end up in an undesired state.

Concluding Remarks

In this paper, we have informally demonstrated how static and dynamic system analyses can be performed using a simple logic. In particular, we have seen that static analyses quite straightforwardly can be applied, but dynamic analyses need some extensions to be adequately performed .This type of analyses are needed when the state-space is large and when we do not have a probability distribution over the possible states. There are several approaches to these issues and some commonly used methods, such as ER-modeling and UML is usually applied in system development. These are often loosely used, but can effectively be translated to a logical format and the above described machinery can be applied efficiently as well. However, as is the case with most methodologies, logical approaches as the ones presented are not the single truth and should be applied with some care and be combined with other tools as well as some heuristics.

Appendix
Formalities

Formal Verification in Logic

Specification languages have been extensively treated in the literature and the approaches to this can basically be sorted into four basic categories.

1. Development for particular purposes, such as Z, Z++, Object-Z, etc., [DDKS91, L91].
2. Semi-formal languages, [CD94].
3. Integration of an informal technique with a formal one, e.g., FuZed [BF98] or Fusion [C93].
4. Approaches for using or modifying more standard formal languages like logic or algebra. For instance, [RG98] discuss BDI logic for the target language.

Also, [DKR00] suggests an object-based temporal logic, for specifying dynamic and static properties of object-based systems.

In particular, UML and similar modelling languages belongs to category 2 above. These are not yet precise modelling techniques and some translations to such have been proposed. [KC00], provide a translation and mapping of UML to Object-Z, restricted to UML class constructs and class diagrams. [FBL97] converts UML class diagrams to Z specifications. [DLC97] develops an Object-Z specification and [EK99] has focused on defining the semantics of core UML modelling concepts. However, one main problem with these approaches is that they do not transform the specifications into a format where logic verification techniques can be applied in a computationally meaningful way.

On the other hand, schema integration and simple first-order integration conflicts have, for some years, occurred in distributed database management for investigating the issue of combining one or more database systems into an integrated system, e.g., [BBJW97, BHP94, SK92]. More elaborated approaches to verification problems are presented, e.g., in [CS88, DFW98, RG98, BE04]. More object-oriented approaches to conceptual modelling has also been suggested e.g., in [FSM92, SF91, DKR00]. Modal transition systems, e.g., [L89, H99], and probabilistic specification techniques [JL91] have also prevailed. However, these approaches do not discuss the problem of conflict detection with respect to a broader class of conflicts [PSG93, SP94].

A general problem with the latter ones is that unnecessarily complicated machineries often are introduced. In our work, following the general philosophy of [BB95], we have strived to fulfil two basic requirements: that the target language should be executable; and that it have clear semantics.

The approach presented here is based on the approach on a logic formalism earlier developed in [EJ02, AEP03, EJ95, EJ96, EJ04], where various aspects of conflict detection and formal verification were discussed. It has also been applied to integration of multi-agent architecture designs [DEJ00, BE00], formalised in [E00].

Translating UML Specifications

A translation of a UML specification results in a conceptual schema as defined below. Essentially, classes are mapped to unary predicates, attributes and associations to binary predicates, and methods to events.

Definition 1. Translating class diagrams

Given a set C of class diagrams in a UML specification, where the strings *agg* and *lex* do not occur. R_C is the least set of first order formulae defined by the following clauses.[1]

A. Alphabet

- If r is a name of a class definition in C, then r is a predicate symbol of arity one in $L(R_C)$.
- If t is a name of an association in C, then t is a predicate symbol of arity two in $L(R_C)$ (for simplicity, we assume uniqueness of association and attribute names).

[1] In the definitions below, we assume an underlying *language* L of first-order formulae.

- If *t* is a name of an attribute in C, then *t* is a predicate symbol of arity two in $L(R_C)$.
- *agg* is a predicate symbol of arity two in $L(R_C)$.
- *lex* is a predicate symbol of arity one in $L(R_C)$.

B. Constraint generation

B.1. Typing constraints for associations

If *r* and *s* are names of class definitions in C, and *t* is a name of an association from *r* to *s* in C, then $\forall x\forall y(t(x,y)\rightarrow(r(x)\wedge s(y)))$ is in R_C.

B.2. Typing constraints for attributes

If *r* is a name of a class definition in C and *t* is a name of an attribute of *r* in C, then $\forall x\forall y(t(x,y)\rightarrow(r(x)\wedge lex(y)))$ is in R_C.

B.3. Aggregation constraints

If *r* and *s* are names of class definitions in C, and *t* is a name of an aggregation from *r* to *s* in C, then $\forall x\forall y(t(x,y)\rightarrow(r(x)\wedge s(y)\wedge agg(x,y)))$ is in R_C.

B.4. ISA constraints

If *r* and *s* are names of class definitions in C, and the statement *r ISA s* belongs to C, then $\forall x(r(x)\rightarrow s(x))$ is in R_C.

B.5. Subclass constraints

Assume that *p, r* and *s* are names of class definitions in C, and that *p ISA s* and *r ISA s* belong to C. If *p* and *r* are disjoint in C, then $\forall x\neg(p(x)\wedge r(x))$ is in R_C. If *p* and *r* are exhaustive with respect to *s* in C, then $\forall x(s(x)\rightarrow(p(x)\vee r(y)))$ is in R_C.

B.6. Cardinality constraints

If *r* and *s* are names of class definitions in C, and *t* is a name of an association from *r* to *s* in C, with cardinality $((\min_r .. \max_r), (\min_s .. \max_s))$, then the formulae below are in R_C.

Minimum number of associations for the domain

$$\forall y\exists x_1 ... \exists x_{\min_r} ((s(y)) \rightarrow (t(x_1, y) \wedge ... \wedge t(x_{\min_r}, y))) \wedge$$
$$\neg(x_1 = x_2) \wedge ... \wedge \neg(x_1 = x_{\min_r}) \wedge$$
$$\neg(x_2 = x_3) \wedge ... \wedge \neg(x_2 = x_{\min_r}) \wedge ... \wedge$$
$$\neg(x_{\min_{r-1}} = x_{\min_r})$$

Maximum number of associations for the domain

$$\forall y \forall x_1 ... \forall x_{\max_r} \forall x_{\max_r+1}[((t(x_1, y) \wedge ... \wedge t(x_{\max_r}, y) \wedge t(x_{\max_r+1}, y))$$
$$\rightarrow$$
$$((x_1 = x_2) \vee ... \vee (x_1 = x_{\max_r}) \vee (x_1 = x_{\max_r+1}) \vee$$
$$(x_2 = x_3) \vee ... \vee (x_2 = x_{\max_r}) \vee (x_2 = x_{\max_r+1}) \vee ... \vee$$
$$(x_{\max_r} = x_{\max_r+1}))]$$

Minimum number of associations for the range

$$\forall y \exists x_1 ... \exists x_{\min_s} ((r(y)) \rightarrow (t(y, x_1) \wedge ... \wedge t(y, x_{\min_s}))) \wedge$$
$$\neg(x_1 = x_2) \wedge ... \wedge \neg(x_1 = x_{\min_s}) \wedge$$
$$\neg(x_2 = x_3) \wedge ... \wedge \neg(x_2 = x_{\min_s}) \wedge ... \wedge$$
$$\neg(x_{\min_{s-1}} = x_{\min_s})$$

Maximum number of associations for the range

$$\forall y \forall x_1 ... \forall x_{\max_s} \forall x_{\max_s+1}[((t(y, x_1) \wedge ... \wedge t(y, x_{\max_s}) \wedge t(y, x_{\max_s+1}))$$
$$\rightarrow$$
$$((x_1 = x_2) \vee ... \vee (x_1 = x_{\max_s}) \vee (x_1 = x_{\max_s+1}) \vee$$
$$(x_2 = x_3) \vee ... \vee (x_2 = x_{\max_s}) \vee (x_2 = x_{\max_s+1}) \vee ... \vee$$
$$(x_{\max_s} = x_{\max_s+1}))]$$

Definition 2. Translating methods

Given a set of methods *M* in a UML specification, where the string *inv* does not occur. ER_M is the least set of expressions defined by the following clauses.

A. Alphabet

If g(y) =<pre(x), post(x)> is a method in *M*, then the corresponding predicate symbols with the same arities are in L(ER_M).

inv is a predicate symbol of arity one in L(ER_M).

B. Methods

Let *k* be a class and g(y) =<pre(x), post(x)> a method in *k*. If g(y) is a method in *M*, then $<\text{inv}(g(y)) \wedge \text{pre}(x)\ ,\ \text{post}(x) \wedge \neg\text{inv}(g(y))>_k$ is in ER_M, where pre(x) and post(x) are as above. (inv(g(y)) means that the method g(y) has been invoked.)

Definition 3. State diagram for a class

A *state diagram for a class k* is a triple <N, A, G>, where

- N is a set of nodes
- A is a set of directed arcs, i.e. pairs over N
- G is a set of quadruples <a, ue(x, **y**), guard(x, **y**), p(x, **y**)>

In G, a is an arc. ue(x, **y**) is a UML event, where x is an object (reference) of class k and **y** is a vector of objects and values. guard(x, **y**) is an open first order formula. p(x, **y**) is a set of formulas, where each formula has one of the following forms

insert(a(x, y_i)), delete(a(x, y_i)), or *invoke(umlev(z)).*

Here, x is an object (reference) of class C, y_i is a member of **y** and **z** is a vector of objects and values.

Definition 4. Translating state diagrams

Given a set *S* of state diagrams $<N, A, G>_k$ in a UML specification, where the string *state* does not occur. A *schema* for S is constructed as follows.[2]

A. Alphabet

If $<<t_i, t_j>$, ue(x, **y**), guard(x, **y**), p(x, **y**)$> \in G$, then the corresponding predicate symbols and constants in t_i, t_j, ue(x, **y**), guard(x, **y**), and p(x, **y**) with the same arities are in $L(ER_S)$ and $L(R_S)$.

state is a predicate symbol of arity two in $L(ER_S)$ and $L(R_S)$.

B. Rules for an object in a state

$R_S = \{\forall x(\text{state}(x, t_i) \rightarrow \neg\text{state}(x, t_j)) \mid t_i, t_j \in N \wedge i \neq j\} \cup \{\forall x \exists t(\text{state}(x, t)\} \cup \{\forall x(\text{state}(x, t_i) \rightarrow k(x)) \mid t_i \in N\}$, where t_i is a state in a class *k*.

C. Arcs

If $<<t_i, t_j>$, ue(x, **y**), guard(x, **y**), p(x, **y**)$>$ is an arc in *G*, $<\text{inv}(\text{ue}(x, \mathbf{y})) \wedge \text{state}(x, t_i) \wedge \text{guard}(x, \mathbf{y}), \text{state}(x, t_j) \wedge \neg\text{inv}(g(y)) \wedge (\bigwedge a(x, y_i) \mid \text{insert}(a(x, y_i)) \in p(x, \mathbf{y})) \wedge (\bigwedge \neg a(x, y_i) \mid \text{delete}(a(x, y_i)) \in p(x, \mathbf{y})) \wedge (\bigwedge \text{inv}(\text{umlev}(\mathbf{z}) \mid \text{invoke}(\text{umlev}(\mathbf{z}) \in p(x, \mathbf{y}))>_k$ is in ER_S.

D. Schema

The *schema for S* is the structure $<R_S, ER_S>$.

Definition 5. Collaboration diagram

A collaboration diagram for a UML specification is a pair $<B, M>$, where

- B is a set of classes.
- M is an ordered set of quadruples $m_i = <a, \text{ue}(\mathbf{x}), b, i>$, where a and b are classes, ue(**x**) is a UML event and *i* is a natural number.[3]

Definition 6. Translating collaboration diagrams

Given a collaboration diagram $D = <B, M>$ in a UML specification, where the string *sent* and method does not occur. A *schema* for D is constructed as follows.

---

[2] A variety in modal logic is found in [BE04].

[3] We assume that all methods have unique names. Furthermore, each method is assigned a new name for all times it is called. Since a collaboration diagram is finite, this does not imply a loss of generality.

A. Alphabet

If <a, $ue(x)_k$, b, i> $\in$ M, then the corresponding predicate symbols and constants with the same arities are in $L(R_D)$.

sent is a predicate symbol of arity two in $L(R_D)$.

B. Static rules

- $\{\forall x(inv(x) \rightarrow sent(x))\} \in R_D$
- If <y1, $ue_i(x)$, y2, i>, <z1, $ue_j(x)$, z2, j> $\in$ M, and $i < j$, then $\forall x \forall y(sent(ue_j(x)) \rightarrow sent(ue_i(x))) \in R_D$

C. Schema

The *schema for D* is the structure $<R_D, \varnothing>$.

Definition 7. A schema for a UML specification

Let *C* be a set of class diagrams, *M* a set of methods, *S* a set of state diagrams, and D a collaboration diagram of a UML specification *U*. Furthermore, let R_C, R_S, R_D, ER_S and ER_M be as in the definitions above regarding these components. A schema for *U* is the structure <R, ER>, where

- $R = R_C \cup R_S \cup R_D$, and
- $ER = ER_M \cup ER_S$.

Schemas and their Semantics

Definition 8.

A *schema* S is a structure $\langle R, ER \rangle$ consisting of a *static part* R and a *dynamic part* ER. R is a finite set of closed first-order formulae in a language L. ER is a set of *event rules*. Event rules describe possible transitions between different states of a schema and will be described below.

Definition 9.

L(R) is the *restriction of L to R*, i.e. L(R) is the set $\{p \mid p \in L$, but p does not contain any predicate symbol, that is not in a formula in R$\}$. The elements in R are called *static rules* in L(R).

Definition 10.

An *event rule* in L is a structure $\langle P(\mathbf{z}), C(\mathbf{z}) \rangle$. $P(\mathbf{z})$ and $C(\mathbf{z})$ are first-order formulae in L, and **z** is a vector of variables in the alphabet of L.[4] In terms of conceptual modeling, $P(\mathbf{z})$ denotes the precondition of the event rule, and $C(\mathbf{z})$ the post condition.

Definition 11.

The set of *basic events* for a schema $\langle R, ER \rangle$ is a relation $E \subseteq D \times D$, where D is the set of diagrams for R. An element (σ, ρ) belongs to E iff

---

[4] The notation A(x) means that x is free in A(x).

- there is a rule $\langle P(\mathbf{z}), C(\mathbf{z})\rangle$ in ER, and a vector $\mathbf{e}$ of constants in L, such that $P(\mathbf{e}) \in \sigma$ and $C(\mathbf{e}) \in \rho$. In this case we will also say that the *basic event* (σ, ρ) *results* from the event rule.[5]

Definition 12.

By a *diagram* for a set R of formulae in a language L, we mean a Herbrand model of R, extended by the negation of the ground atoms in L that are not in the Herbrand model. Thus, a diagram for L is a Herbrand model extended with classical negation.[6]

The *description of a schema S* is a digraph $\langle D, E\rangle$, where D is the set of diagrams for S, and E is the set of basic events (i.e. arcs in the digraph) for S.

Definition 13.

Let S = <SR, ER> be a schema, $V = V_1 \nabla \ldots \nabla V_k$ be a sequence of event rules in ER.

(i) The *event path extension for V*, $\Pi(S, V)$, is the set of sequences of diagrams for S, $(\sigma_1, \sigma_2, \ldots, \sigma_{k+1})$, such that $(\sigma_i, \sigma_{i+1}) \in \Lambda(S, V_i)$.

(ii) The *event path extension for S*, $\Pi(S)$, is the union of $\Pi(S, V)$ for all sequential combinations V of event rules in ER.

Definition 14.

Let S = <SR, ER> be a schema, $V=V_1 \nabla \ldots \nabla V_k$ be a sequence of event rules in ER.

- The set of *connecting events in S for V, $\Lambda(S, V)$* is $\{(\sigma_1, \sigma_{k+1}) \mid$ there is a sequence of diagrams $(\sigma_1, \sigma_2, \ldots, \sigma_{k+1}) \in \Pi(S, V)\}$.
- The set of *events in S for V, $\Lambda(S, V)$* is $\{(\sigma_1, \sigma_{k+1}) \mid$ there is a sequence of diagrams $(\sigma_1, \sigma_2, \ldots, \sigma_{k+1}) \in \Pi(S, V)\}$.
- The *connecting event extension of S, $\Lambda(S)$* is the union of $\Lambda(S, V)$ for all sequential combinations V of event rules in ER.
- The set of *event extension of S, $\Lambda(S)$* is the union of $\Lambda(S, V)$ for all sequential combinations V of event rules in ER.
- The *event extension of S, $\Lambda(S)$* is the union of $\Lambda(S)$.
- An *event for S,* is a pair $(\sigma, \rho) \in \Lambda(S)$.

The elements of $\Lambda(S)$ will be called *lambda pairs.*

Consistency and Conflict

The definitions below use sets IA of static integration assertions as equivalences that given two schemata, expresses formulae in one schema in terms of formulae in the other. An integration assertion specifies what extra constraints that are imposed when schemata are integrated (merged) to a combined specification. The choice of this set is depending on what actual correspondences between the schemata.

[5] In [EJ96] an approach using event messages is described. However this concept is not necessary in a model not presupposing a particular information processor.

[6] For our purposes, this is no loss of generality by the well-known result that a closed formula is satisfiable iff its Herbrand expansion is satisfiable. For a discussion of this expansion theorem and its history, see, e.g. [DG79].

Definition 15.

Let S be a schema. S is *consistent* iff its description is nonempty. Otherwise S is *inconsistent.*

Definition 16.

Let IA be a set of static integration assertions expressing S_2 in S_1, and let the schemata be described as connected digraphs $\langle D_i,E_i \rangle$, *Conflict(S_1,S_2,IA) is false* iff $\forall\sigma\in D_1\ \exists\tau\in D_2\ \sigma R\tau$, where $\sigma R\tau$ iff $\sigma \cup \tau \models$ IA. Otherwise S_2 and S_1 are in conflict with respect to IA and vice versa.

Definition 17.

Let IA and $\langle D_i,E_i \rangle$ be as above. Further, let G_i denote a specific subset of the D_i, fulfilling some required property and let Prob be a probability distribution over a subset of $D_1 \cup D_2$. S_2 and S_1 are *free of risk conflicts* iff $\forall\sigma\in G_1\ \exists\tau\in G_2\ \text{Prob}(\sigma \wedge \tau) < \alpha$, for some $\alpha\in[0,1]$.

Definition 18.

Let S_1 = <R_1, ER_1> and S_2 = <R_2, ER_2> be two schemata. An *identifying dynamic integration assertion expressing the schema S_2 in the schema S_1* is an expression ([V], [U_1, …, U_n]), where V is an event rule in ER_2 and U_1, …, U_n are event rules in ER_1.

Definition 19.

Let S_1 = <R_1, ER_1> and S_2 = <R_2, ER_2> be two schemata, and ID = ([V], [U_1, …, U_n]) be an identifying dynamic integration assertion expressing the schema S_2 in S_1. *ID is adequate for S_1, S_2, and IA*, if:

(i) For all $(\sigma', \rho') \in \Lambda(S_2, V)$, there is a sequence of events $(\sigma_1, \sigma_2, \ldots, \sigma_n, \sigma_{n+1}) \in \Pi(S_1, U_1 \nabla\ldots\nabla U_n)$, such that $\sigma_1 \cup \sigma'$ and $\sigma_{n+1} \cup \rho'$ are both diagrams for IA.

(ii) For all $(\sigma_1, \sigma_2, \ldots, \sigma_n, \sigma_{n+1}) \in \Pi(S_1, U_1 \nabla\ldots\nabla U_n)$, there is an event $(\sigma', \rho') \in \Lambda(S_2, V)$, such that $\sigma_1 \cup \sigma'$ and $\sigma_{n+1} \cup \rho'$ are both diagrams for IA.

If only (i) above is fulfilled, then we will say that ID is *semi-adequate* for S_1, S_2 and IA. When $(\sigma_1, \sigma_2, \ldots, \sigma_n, \sigma_{n+1})$ and (σ', ρ') correspond in the way described in (i) or (ii), they are called *compatible* with ID.

Definition 20.

Let S_1 = <R_1, ER_1> and S_2 = <R_2, ER_2> be two schemata. Also, let IA be a set of static integration assertions expressing the schema S_2 in S_1, and let D be a set of IDs. S_1 and S_2 are *dynamically non-conflicting* with respect to IA and D, if:

(i) Conflict(S_1,S_2,IA) is false.
(ii) Conflict(S_2,S_1,IA) is false.
(iii) All the IDs in D are semi-adequate for S_1, S_2, and IA.

Requirement Fulfilment

Definition 21.

A *requirement specification*, K, is a conjunction of first-order formulae.

Definition 22.

A *schema* S = ⟨R,ER⟩ *fulfils* a requirement specification, K, iff R |= K.

Definition 23.

A *schema* S = ⟨R,ER⟩ *fulfils* a requirement specification, K, from state σ iff

$\sigma \models K$

$\sigma_i \models K$, for all σ_i in $(\sigma, \sigma_2, \ldots, \sigma_n)$ in $\Pi(S)$.

References

[AEP03] B. Amon, L. Ekenberg, P. Johannesson, M. Munguanaze, U. Njabili and R. M. Tesha, "From First-Order Logic to Automated Word Generation for Lyee," Knowledge-Based Systems, vol. 16, pp. 413–429, 2003.

[BB95] J.v. Benthem and J. Bergstra, "Logic of Transition Systems", Journal of Logic, Language and Information, vol. 3, pp. 247–283, 1995.

[BBJW97] M. Boman, J. Bubenko, P. Johanesson, B. Wangler, Conceptual Modelling, Prentice-Hall, Englewood Cliffs, NJ, 1997.

[BE00] M. Boman and L. Ekenberg, Risk Constraints in Agent Conflicts, Proceedings of LUMIS'2000, IEEE Computer Society Press, 2000.

[BE04] V. Boeva and L. Ekenberg, "A Transition Logic for Schemata Conflicts," Journal of Data and Knowledge Engineering 51/3, pp. 277–294, 2004.

[BF98] J. Bruel, R.B. France, Transforming UML models to formal specifications, in: Proceedings of International Conference on the Unified Modelling Language (UML): beyond the notation, 1998.

[BHP94] M.W. Bright, A.R. Hurson, S.H. Pakzad, Automated resolution of semantic heterogeneity in multidatabases, ACM Transactions of Database Systems 19 (2), 1994, 212–253.

[C93] D. Coleman, Object-oriented Development: The Fusion Method, Prentice-Hall, Emglewood Cliffs, MA, 1993.

[CD94] S. Cook, J. Daniels, Let's get formal, Journal of Object-Oriented Programming (JOOP) 22–24 (1994) 64–66.

[CS88] J. Carmo and A. Sernadas, A Temporal Logic Framework for a Layered Approach to Systems Specification and Verification, in: C. Rolland, F. Bodart, M.Leonard, ed., Temporal Aspects of Information Systems (North-Holland, 1988) 31–46.

[DEJ00] G. Davies, L. Ekenberg and P. Johannesson, Detecting Temporal Conflicts in Integrated Agent Specifications, Computational Conflicts, Eds. Mueller and Dieng, pp. 103–124, Springer Verlag, 2000.

[DFW98] C. Dixon, M. Fisher and M. Wooldridge, Resolution for Temporal Logics of Knowledge, Journal of Logic and Computation 8 (1998) 345–372.

[DG79] B. Dreben and W. D. Goldfarb, The Decision Problem: Solvable Classes of Quantification Formulas: Reading, Mass, Addison-Wesley, 1979.

[DKR00] D. Distefano, J. Katoen and A. Rensink, On a Temporal Logic for Object-Based Systems, in: S.F. Smith, C.L. Talcott, ed., Fourth International Conference on Formal Methods for Open Object-based Distributed Systems (Kluwer Academic Publishers, Stanford, California, USA, 2000) 305-326.

[DKRS91] R. Duke, P. King, G.A. Rose, G. Smith, The Object-Z specification language, in: Timothy D. Korson, Vijay K. Vaishnavi, Bertrand Meyer (Eds.), Technology of Object Oriented Languages and Systems: TOOLS 5, Prentice- Hall, Englewood Cliffs, NJ, 1991, pp. 465–483.

[DLC97] S. Dupuy, Y. Ledru, and M. Chabre-Peccoud. Integrating OMT and Object-Z. In K. Lano (eds.) A. Evans, editor, Proceedings of BCS FACS/EROS ROOM Workshop, technical report GR/K67311-2, Dept. of Computing, Imperial College, 180 Queens Gate, London, UK, June 1997.

[E00] L. Ekenberg, " The Logic of Conflicts between Decision Making Agents," Journal of Logic and Computation, vol. 10, No. 4, pp. 583–602, 2000.

[EJ95] L. Ekenberg and P. Johannesson, "Conflictfreeness as a Basis for Schema Integration," Proceedings of CISMOD-95, pp. 1–13, LNCS, Springer-Verlag, 1995.
[EJ96] L. Ekenberg and P. Johannesson, "A Formal Basis for Dynamic Schema Integration," Proceedings of 15th International Conference on Conceptual Modelling ER'96, pp. 211–226, LNCS, 1996.
[EJ02] L. Ekenberg and P. Johannesson, "UML as a Transition Logic," Proceedings of 12th European-Japanese Conference on Information Modelling and Knowledge Bases, 2002.
[EJ04] L. Ekenberg and P. Johannesson, "A Framework for Determining Design Correctness," *Knowledge-Based Systems* 17, pp. 249–262, 2004.
[EK99] A. Evans, S.Kent, Core Meta-Modelling semantics of UML: The pUML approach, Proc. 2nd IEEE Conference on UML: UML'99, LNVCS, No. 1723, pp. 140–155, 1999.
[FBL97] R.B. France, J.-M., Bruel, M.M. Larrondo-Petrie and M. Shroff. Exploring the semantics of Uml type structures with Z. Proc. 2nd IFIP conference, Formal methods for Open Object-Based Distributed Systems9FMOODS'97). pp. 247–260, Chapman and Hall 1997.
[FSM92] J. Fiadeiro, C. Sernadas, T. Maibaum and A. Sernadas, Describing and Structuring Objects for Conceptual Schema Development, in: P. Loucopoulos, R. Zicari, ed., Conceptual Modelling, Databases and CASE: An Integrated View of Information Systems Development (John Wiley, 1992) 117–138.
[H99] M. Huth, A Unifying Framework for Model Checking Labeled Kripke Structures, Modal Transition Systems, and Interval Transition Systems, in: FST\&TCS99 (Chennai, India, 1999).
[JL91] B. Jonsson and K.G. Larsen, Specification and Refinement of Probabilistic Processes (IEEE Computer Society Press, 1991) 266–277.
[KC00] S-K. Kim and D. Carrington A Formal Mapping between UML Models and Object-Z Specifications, ZB'2000, International Conference of B and Z Users, York,
[L89] K.G. Larsen, Modal Specifications, in: J. Sifakis, ed., Automatic Verification Methods for Finite State Systems, number 407 in Lecture Notes in Computer Science, International Workshop (Grenoble, France, Springer Verlag, 1989) 232–246.
[L91] K. Lano, Z++ an object-oriented extension to Z, in: J.E. Nichols (Ed.), Z User Workshop, Oxford 1990, Workshops in Computing, Springer-Verlag, Berlin, 1991, pp. 151–172.
[PSG93] F. Polat, S. Shekhar and H.A. Guvenir, Distributed Conflict Resolution Among Cooperating Expert Systems, Expert Systems, 10(4) (1993) 227–236.
[RG98] A.S. Rao, M.P. Georgeff, Decision procedures for BDI logics, Journal of Logic and Computation 8 (1998) 293–342.
[SF91] C. Sernadas and J.L. Fiadeiro, Towards Object-Oriented Conceptual Modelling, Data and Knowledge Engineering 6 (1991) 479–508.
[SK92] A.P. Sheth, V. Kashyap, So Far (Schematically) yet So Near (Semantically), DS-5, 1992, pp. 283–312.
[SP94] S. Spaccapietra and C. Parent, View Integration: A Step Forward in Solving Structural Conflicts, IEEE Transactions on Knowledge and Data Engineering, 6(2) (1994) 258–274.

New Trends in Software Methodologies, Tools and Techniques
H. Fujita and M. Mejri (Eds.)
IOS Press, 2005

Limitation and Possibilities of Automation on the Way from Intention ⇒ Program

Victor MALYSHKIN [a] and Yuri ZAGORULKO [b]
[a] *Supercomputer Software Department (SSD), Institute of Computational Mathematics and Mathematical Geophysics, Russian Academy of Sciences, 630090, Novosibirsk, Russia*
malysh@ssd.sscc.ru, http://ssd.sscc.ru
[b] *AI Laboratory, A.P. Ershov Institute of Informatics Systems, Russian Academy of Sciences, 630090, Novosibirsk, Russia*
zagor@iis.nsk.su, http://www.iis.nsk.su

Abstract. The paper is devoted to the discussion of the limitations and possibilities of the automation of the process of program construction from an informal specification

1. Introduction

Shortly the idea of the paper is to go carefully the way from general intention/dream/idea via ontology up to the synthesized program that implements this intention. This way is divided in several stages. Every next stage is one of the possible elaborations of the current stage. Different researchers did this way earlier many times. Now the possibilities of automation on all the stages are discussed from the viewpoint of the current state of Computer Science.

2. Basic Stages

User's intention can be formulated as informal or formal expression depending on the user's knowledge. Therefore, the process of the program construction that implements an intention is divided at least in two stages: informal formulation of the intention and formal one. Methods of artificial intelligence (AI) [1] support the process of informally formulated intention transformation into the formal specification. Methods of Computer Science support the transformation of the formal specification into the desirable program. As usual specification is considered as formulated intention. Formal specification is considered as intention formulated in the frame of a theory. Process of program construction is considered as the sequence of successive elaborations (transformation) of initial intention into the desirable program. Certainly, all the successively done elaborations should reflect the peculiarities of an object domain.

This list of the basic stages discussed here is: $\texttt{Chaos} \rightarrow \texttt{Philosophy}_{\texttt{i}} \rightarrow \texttt{Concepts}_{\texttt{ij}} \rightarrow \texttt{Ontology}_{\texttt{ijk}} \rightarrow \texttt{Theory}_{\texttt{ijkl}} \rightarrow \texttt{Specification}_{\texttt{ijklm}} \rightarrow \texttt{Algorithmation}_{\texttt{ijklmn}} \rightarrow \texttt{Program}_{\texttt{ijklmns}}$.

2.1. Chaos

The initial period of the investigation in any object domain is characterized by the chaos of knowledge organization. "*And the earth was without form, and void; and darkness [was] upon the face of the deep. And the Spirit of God moved upon the face of the waters*" [Gen.1:1–31]. On the first stage of knowledge creation and organization some basic conceptualizing notions should be developed. This might be enough in order to formulate an initial user's dream/intention.

2.2. Philosophy$_i$

"*In the beginning was the Word, and the Word was with God, and the Word was God*" [Jn.1:1–51]. This is absolutely right from the viewpoint of program construction. On this stage some conceptualization of object domain in the general form should be done.

2.3. Concepts$_{ij}$

On this stage the abstract simplified viewpoint to the whole object domain is developed.

2.4. Ontology$_{ijk}$

The panhuman ontology is understood here as description, i.e., conceptual specification (schema) for organization of the knowledge system and the ways of knowledge use (operationalism[1]) [3,4,13,14]. For our goals the ontology should be represented in the form of some type of semantic net. This should provide the pass to such implementable [2] representation of ontology as computational model [5].

2.5. Theory$_{ijkl}$

Development of ontology provides the creation of the axiomatic theory that describes the object domain.

2.6. Specification$_{ijklm}$

Formulation of the intention in the frame of the **Theory$_{ijkl}$**.

2.7. Algorithmation$_{ijklmn}$

If implementable specification [2] is formulated then an algorithm is constructed that compute the desirable intention. Not implementable specification can also be formulated. In this case the backtracking might be done or some other way should be taken in order to develop an implementable specification.

Panhuman ontology and theory correspond to each notion, to each term, the set of its permitted values (interpretation). This is also included into the basis for dream/

[1] Operationalism is the philosophical doctrine. It demands that the value of any notion or term can be assigned by the operations only. In Computer Science this doctrine is embodied in the structural program synthesis approach [5].

intention representation. If this correspondence is not determined then the dream is *absolutely Not_Implementable*, the dream belongs to the chaos. Merely, in this case nobody knows what this dream is (including the person who has produced this dream). Otherwise the dream is *potentially implementable*. Obviously, all the sets should be recursively countable sets. Here the line between Not_Implementability and Implementability is really drawn. Certainly, we must recognize the notion of the technological implementability, that includes the requirement of the polynomial complexity of the algorithm [2].

2.8. $Program_{ijklmns}$

Clearly defined stage. On this stage the technological implementability is in the first priority. Formal specification provides all the necessary info in order to construct desirable program. On the basis of ontology implementable specification is finally constructed in the form of semantic net. This generally provides the program synthesis that possesses the necessary properties.

3. Analysis of the Stages

The term "ontology" is borrowed from philosophy and now actively exploited in computer science and artificial intelligence.

3.1. Ontology and Functional Specification

There are many interpretations of what the ontology is. In the paper of Thomas R. Gruber[2] the ontology is defined as "explicit specification of conceptualization". This is the most general definition of ontology where the conceptualization is an abstract, simplified view to the world that we wish to represent for some purpose. Conceptualization includes objects, concepts and other entities which are assumed to exist in given object domain, and also relationships among them. From this viewpoint every knowledge base, knowledge-based system, or knowledge-level agent is defined by some conceptualization, explicitly or implicitly.

In the context of AI, the base of ontology is a set of representational terms. In such ontology, definitions associate the names of entities of the object domain (e.g., classes, relations, functions, or other objects) with a human-readable text describing what the names mean, and formal axioms that constrain the interpretation and well-formed use of these terms.

3.2. Definitions

Summing up, the ontology represents explicit detailed description (model) of some part of world with respect to a given object domain.

Thus, the ontology is the structure <E, D, R, A, P >, where

E – set of concepts;

[2] Gruber, T.R. Towards Principles for the Design of Ontologies Used for Knowledge Sharing. In Inter. Journal of Human-Computer Studies, 1994, 43 (5/6): 907–928.

D – set of definitions of concepts;
R – set of relations between concepts;
A – set of a axioms;
P – set of rules of use of concepts and relations.

In such a way, ontology is the system, which consists of the set of concepts associated with the relations, their definitions, and assertions (axioms and rules), which allow to constrain (restrict) meaning of concepts within given object domain.

As an example of ontology, let us consider the ontology of science. This ontology includes the ontology of scientific activities, the ontology of scientific knowledge and the ontology of a subject domain that describes a certain branch of science.

Ontology of scientific activities includes the following classes of concepts related to the organization of research activities:

- *Scientist*. Concepts of this class correspond to persons of scientific activity: researchers, employees and members of the organizations, outstanding scientists and others.
- *Organization*. Concepts of this class describe the various organizations, scientific communities and associations, institutes, research groups and other associations.
- *Event*. These notions include meetings, seminars, conferences, research trips and expeditions.
- *Publication*. This class serves to describe various types of publications and the materials represented in printed or electronic format (such as monographs, articles, reports, proceedings of conferences, periodicals, photo and video data, etc.).
- *Activity*. This class includes the notions that describe organization of research activities (projects, programs, etc.).

Ontology of scientific knowledge contains the metanotions which specify structures for the description of considered subject domain:

- *Subdivision of science*. This class allows one to structure a science, i.e., to identify its significant parts and subparts.
- *Research method*. This class serves to describe the various methods of research used in a specific scientific discipline.
- *Object of research*. Notions of this class classify the objects of research and introduce a structure for their description. For example, the object of research in the humanities can be a person, the society or a nation, as well as the various objects created by the persons as a result of they activity.
- *Scientific result*. This class contains the notions such as discoveries, new laws, theories and methods of research. Usually scientific results are presented in publications.

Ontology of a subject domain describes a certain scientific discipline as a field of science and includes the formal and informal description of its concepts and relations between them. These concepts are implementations of meta-notions of the ontology of scientific knowledge.

Thus, if such a discipline as "Computer Science" (see Fig. 1) is considered, then the implementations of the meta-notion "subdivision of science" will be *Computer Science, Program Design,* etc. The relations "generic-specific" and "whole-part" will order these concepts in a hierarchy. For the Computer Science, the methods and objects

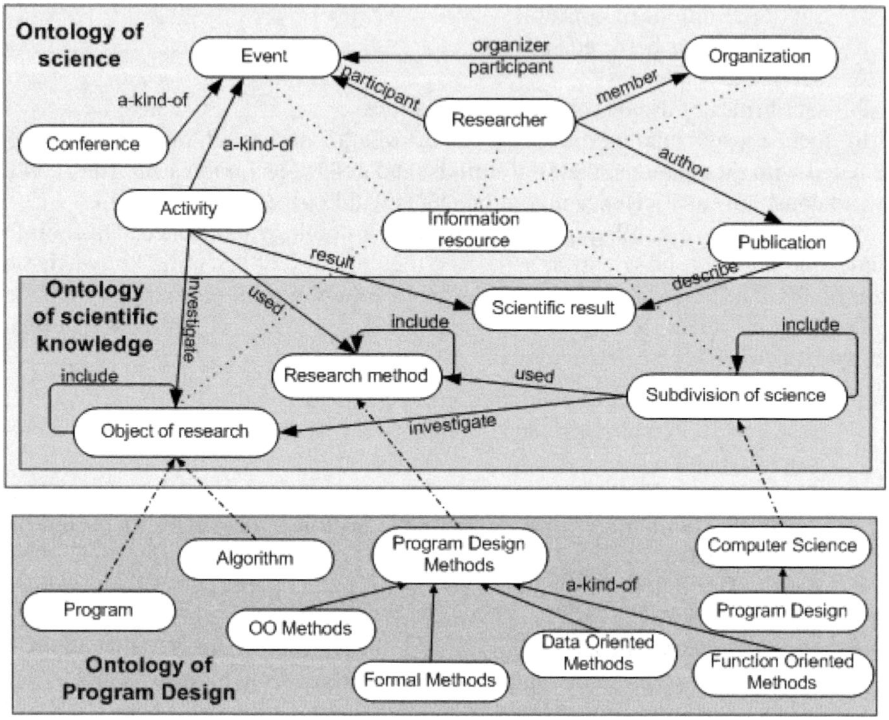

Figure 1. An example of ontology representation.

of research are very important. In particular, the *Research methods* in *Program Design* are *Formal methods, Object Oriented methods, Data Oriented Methods* and *Function Oriented methods*, while the *Objects of research* are *Algorithms* and *Programs*.

Ontology which specifies description of object domain "Program Design" has such basic concepts as *task (problem), subtask, algorithm, program, module, procedure, function, parameter*, and the like. Each of these concepts has the own set of attributes served for description of its properties, and set of constraints (restrictions) on values of attributes. Additionally, the set of synonyms is connected with each concept, i.e. words and expressions of one or more natural languages. These synonyms specify a vocabulary, which is used to express concepts of the ontology in the texts.

On the lowest level of hierarchy there are identifiers of structural components (i.e. elements of repository), which are presented in the system at the given moment. Such structural components may be both algorithms or functions and larger units like modules and even programs.

All concepts of ontology are built in two hierarchies: the class–subclass and the part- the whole. The former serves for implementation of the property's inheritance. The letter allows us to represent the structure of aggregative entities; in particular, it can serve for reduction of a task to subtasks. Moreover, the other relations on the concepts may be defined in order to specify the associative and structural relations, which both constitute the links of tasks (subtasks) with algorithms implementing them and express the ways of connection of structural components of a program.

The object domain ontology is constructed with the help of the software systems like Semp-Tao system [8,9]. This is software environment for the development of the knowledge-based system. The SemP-Tao is based on an integrated knowledge representation model that unifies such classic means as frames, semantic networks, production rules, as well as apparatus of subdefinite data types and the methods of constraint programming. The SemP-Tao offers a powerful collection of tools and methods, including

- high-level tools to define the semantics of objects of the subject domain by specifying constraints on the values of their attributes;
- hierarchical semantic network with definable properties of relations;
- facilities for manipulating imprecise (i.e., subdefinite) values of numerical, symbolic, and set-valued types;
- ability to specify expert knowledge and inference and information processing by means of production rules.

Since integration of these tools and methods is based on the object-oriented approach, the main elements of the technology are presented to the user in the form of a single knowledge representation and processing language. In fact this language is a powerful object-oriented production language with two-level dynamic control facilities. The interactive graphic interface founded on the basic structural units of language (classes, relations etc) allows one to build the knowledge base (the ontology) in a natural manner and with high-level tools. Once the system of needed notions has been defined, the engineer can manipulate the objects in a production-oriented style, ignoring their internal semantics and focusing mostly on the relations between them. Also special module is built in the system, which allows to attach and to use constructed ontologies in various applications.

3.3. Formal Specification

A user expresses his/her intention in the form of problem specification with some limited natural language in terms of concepts specified in ontology. The required program can be principally built/derived from this specification.

3.4. Basic Idea

On the first stage the problem specification is transformed into formal representation. Linguistic processor using subject vocabulary and the ontology implements this transformation. The linguistic processor is created with the help of the Alex [10] like systems. This is the software environment supporting the text-processing technology based on a hierarchical system of lexical templates. This environment was approved for development of several applied system [11,12].

The dictionary of Alex system represents information about words and word combinations necessary to process texts. This information is stored as a library of named templates linked to concepts of the subject domain ontology. Dictionary template is represented by a dictionary entry that includes the following information:

- *Template name* corresponds to the normalized form of the word or word combination representing a concept.

- *Template definition* (string definition of the template) is a construction in a certain formal language; it describes a set of language expressions of arbitrary complexity (disjoint in the general case) that can represent the concept in the text. Thus, the template presents all of the possible synonymous or "almost synonymous" language expressions of the concept.
- *Template class* is the name of a certain group of templates, reflecting the essence of the corresponding class of concepts.
- *Attributes* represent internal parameterized characteristics of the concept represented by the template or the details of its lexical and semantic compatibility with other concepts.

The string definition of a template can contain one of the following:

1. A set of different forms of one word,
   [resource] = resourc**...**
   where the ellipsis sign represents an inflection of arbitrary length (possible zero);
2. A set phrase (a term) represented by a string of templates and/or word forms, for example,
   [computational resource] = computational_**[resource]**
   where the template definition refers to an existing dictionary template;
3. A set of equivalent (synonymous) string definitions, for example,
   [rise in wages] = **[rise]**_(in)_**[wages]**
   [rise]_(in)_**[salary]**
   [rise]_(in)_**[pay]**
   where the parentheses denote that the element is optional in the corresponding text line.

The most numerous group in the dictionary contains the templates associated with the subject domain, or domain templates. The name of a template represents a concept and corresponds to the normalized form of a word or word combination from the synonymic set. The hierarchy of classes of domain templates corresponds to the hierarchy of classes representing the subject domain in the ontology, and covers all the words and phrases that express the key concepts needed for analysis of the specification.

The linguistic processor of the Alex system using the constructed dictionary templates extracts all concepts of ontology and semantic relations between them from the text in two steps. From the beginning the linguistic processor determines all concepts, attributes of concepts and its values (for instance, for concept "Task" these may include its input and output parameters, its values, etc.). After that, based on the knowledge about possible links between concepts of ontology, the linguistic processor reconstructs presented in the text semantic associations between concepts.

Final result of this phase is the semantic network, in which concepts and relations between them extracted from text are presented. If it doesn't succeed to create semantic network on the basis of informal description or it proved that obtained semantic network is confluent, the system asks the user to refine used terms or to change their others terms from list which is proposed.

Then obtained description (semantic network) is tested for consistency and completeness by verification module using ontology. (This module is implemented also by Semp-TAO system.) In case of detection of violation (collision) the user is informed about it and the processing of specification is stopped. In case of incompleteness of the task specification it is attempted to complete specification by concepts and association from ontology. The complement of specification is performed by production module, which includes the set of production rules. As result of this stage the semantic network representing functional description of task is obtained.

Then, this description is optimized, starting from available repository of structural components, and the transformation from functional description into functional scheme of program is performed. In the course of this transformation, the concepts of ontology presented in the scheme are replaced by certain structural components from the repository. Final result of this stage is functional scheme of a program, which solves the specified problem.

Transformation of functional description into functional scheme of program is performed by one more production module also using ontology.

3.5. Implementable Specification

If implementable specification is constructed, then there are different methods and tools for program construction.

Dream ⇒ software. It was already said above that on the trail from the intention to its implementation in software a suitable representation of the intention should be found. It means, that the general diagram intention ⇒ software should be reduced to the diagram

Implementable_ specification ⇒ Algorithm⇒ Program

One of the possible implementable treatment of the idea "dream⇒good_program" is given in the paper by Zohar Manna [6], where the dream is represented as functional specification from which a desirable algorithm is derived (problem algorithmation). Unfortunately, this approach did not meet and could not meet good success because it does not provide derivation of an algorithm and construction of the implementing program of the required quality [2].

3.6. Language of Mathematics

Another example gives the idea that the best programming language is the language of mathematics. The project for implementation of this idea was formulated in 1963 in the paper by I.B. Zadykhailo [7]. This very attractive idea is also far not fully implementable. Even low-level mathematical specification can be technologically Not-Implementable [2].

Different notions of specification implementabily should be now considered. *Potential implementability* means that there exists an algorithm, may be unknown for now. *Dynamic implementability* means that a proper algorithm exists and can be chosen/constructed in the course of execution only (matrices multiplication). *Static implementability* provides the choice of an algorithm in the course of compilation (traditional programming languages are statically implementable). The cases of potential implementability and dynamic implementability can be called as *technologically Not_Implementable* specifications because high quality of a program cannot be reached in general case.

3.7. Structural Synthesis of Programs

Method of structural synthesis of programs [5] provides the pass from formal implementable specification formulated in the form of semantic net to a desirable program. The key technological idea of the method is to replace random search in logic programming by the associative search [2]. Semantic net is very suitable representation of the knowledge that is close to ontology and ontological knowledge can be well transformed into semantic net.

Program synthesis problem is considered in static formulation. Given:

- computational model *C* (a set of dependances shown in Fig. 3),
- set of input variables *V*,
- set of output variables *W*.

A problem *s* is formulated as:

on *C* **compute** *W* **from** *V* (1)

An algorithm, solving the specified problem *s* should be derived and an implementing program *P* should be constructed. Certainly this problem formulation can be used in dynamic case too.

Contrary to logic programming functional specification is not given here, the desirble function is defined by the structure of the computational model *C* (the term *semantic net* is also in use). Actually, for problem specification (1) the final set of algorithms solving a problem is defined by the computational model *C*. If *C* contains well implemented dependances (good modules or procedures) then there are good chances that the final program will be of good quality too. From technological viewpoint, the structural synthesis of program [3] is the model that exploits the idea of the module reuse. If there is a set of good programs, then, under proper conditions, new program, assembled out of good modules can be also of good quality.

A dream is represented here as very attractive tuple (C,V,W). List of input data *V*, list of desirble results *W* are given and implementing software is automatically constructed. But finite model of structural synthesis of program is very restricted model. Certainly, the specified algorithm is well derived on computational model.

3.8. Steps of Software Construction from the Dream

Thus, we can see that actually most of the above listed stages can be supported by special software. The first stages of application software development $\mathtt{Chaos} \rightarrow \mathtt{Philosophy}_{\mathtt{i}} \rightarrow \mathtt{Concepts}_{\mathtt{ij}} \rightarrow \mathtt{Ontology}_{\mathtt{ijk}} \rightarrow \mathtt{Theory}_{\mathtt{ijkl}} \rightarrow \mathtt{Specification}_{\mathtt{ijklm}}$ are supported far less (and with far less success) then the stages $\mathtt{Specification}_{\mathtt{ijklm}} \rightarrow \mathtt{Algorithmation}_{\mathtt{ijklmn}} \rightarrow \mathtt{Program}_{\mathtt{ijklmns}}$, where, by the way, also there are no outstanding successes in automatic program construction. Practically, databases and compilation techniques are now well developed. All the other stages are supported not sufficiently.

References

[1] Genesereth, M.R. and Nilsson, N.J. Logical Foundation of Artificial Intelligence. Morgan Kaufmann, Los Altos, California, 1987.

[2] V. Malyshkin. Concepts and Operationalism, Turbulence and Ontology, Specification and Implementation in Software Engineering. – In series New Trends in Software Methodologies, Tools and Techniques, Vol. 111, pp. 49–54. Proceeding of the SoMeT'04 Int. conference, 28–30 September 2004, Leipzig, Germany.

[3] N. Guarino, Formal ontology, conceptual analysis and knowledge representation. Int. J. of Human Computer Studies. 1995, V. 43, No. 5/6, pp. 625–640.

[4] M. Uschold. A.Tate. Knowledge level modeling: concepts and terminology. The Knowledge Engineering Review. 1998, V. 13, No. 1, pp. 5–29.

[5] V.A. Valkovskii, V.E. Malyshkin. *Synthesis of Parallel Programs and Systems on the Basis of Computational Models*. Nauka, Novosibirsk, 1988. (In Russian, Sintez parallel'nykh programm i sistem na vychislitel'nykh modelyakh).

[6] Z. Manna, R. Waldinger. Synthesis: dreams⇒programs. IEEE Tr. On SE, 1979, Vol. SE-5, pp. 294–398.

[7] I.B. Zadykhailo. Sostavlenie tsiklov po parametricheskim zapisyam spetsialnogo vida. Zhurnal vychislitelnoi mathematiki I mathematicheskoi physiki. 1963, Vol. 3, No. 2, pp. 337–357 (in Russian).

[8] Yu.A. Zagorulko, I.G. Popov. A Software Environment based on an Integrated Knowledge Representation Model. Perspectives of System Informatics (Proc. of Andrei Ershov Second International Conference PSI'96). Novosibirsk, June 25–28, 1996, pp. 300–304.

[9] Yu.A. Zagorulko, I.G. Popov. Knowledge representation language based on the integration of production rules, frames and a subdefinite model. Joint Bulletin of the Novosibirsk Computing Center and Institute of Informatics Systems. Series: Computer Science, 8 (1998), NCC Publisher, Novosibirsk, 1998. pp. 81–100.

[10] Zhigalov V.A., et al. The Alex system as a tool for multi-purpose automated text processing. In: Proc. of the International Workshop Dialog'2002: Computer linguistics and intelligent technologies, Vol. 2, Protvino, Russia, 2002, pp. 192–208.

[11] I. Kononenko, S. Kononenko, I. Popov, Yu. Zagorul'ko. Information Extraction from Non-Segmented Text (on the material of weather forecast telegrams). Content-Based Multimedia Information Access. RIAO'2000 Conference Proceedings, v. 2, 2000, pp. 1069–1088.

[12] E. Sidorova, I. Kononenko, Yu. Zagorulko. A Knowledge-Based Approach to Intelligent Document Management // Proceedings of the 7th International Workshop on Computer Science and Information Technologies CSIT'2005, Ufa, Russia, 2005.

[13] Kleshchev A.S. Artemjeva I.L. Mathematical models of domain ontologies. Technical report 18-2000. Vladivostok, IACP of FEBRAS, p. 43. Available at http://www.iacp.dvo.ru/es/.

[14] Kleshchev A.S., Artemjeva I.L. A structure of domain ontologies and their mathematical models. In The Proceedings of the Pacific Asian Conference on Intelligent Systems 2001 (PAIS 2001), November 16–17, 2001. pp. 410–420.

Chapter 5

Development of Natural Language Based Methodologies

New Trends in Software Methodologies, Tools and Techniques
H. Fujita and M. Mejri (Eds.)
IOS Press, 2005

Handling Pronouns Intelligently*

Anna Maria DI SCIULLO
Département de linguistique, Université du Québec à Montréal
Montréal, Québec, H3C 3P8, Canada

Abstract. Intelligent information processing systems, including search, question answering, and summarization systems, must be able to handle pronouns, i.e. elements that do not have independent reference. We thus, focus on pronominal anaphora resolution (Mitkov [20], Kennedy and Boguraev [18], Lappin and Leass [19]), and identify the main features of an intelligent software design that includes the identification of minimal domains of interpretation based on asymmetric relations. We show that the identification of domains of interpretation based on asymmetric agreement (Di Sciullo [9]) opens new avenues in intelligent systems design.

1. Minimal Domains and Asymmetric Relations

Linguistic expressions are composed of minimal domains of interpretation. These domains have been recently thought of in terms of the notion of syntactic phases (Chomsky, [5,6], Uriagereka [23]). A phase is a unit of the computation: it has an internal structure, it is subject to impenetrability, and it is isolable at the semantic and at the sensorimotor interfaces. We argued elsewhere that phases are also part of the derivation of morphological objects (Di Sciullo [7,8,10]), and that morphological phases have similar, even though not identical, properties to syntactic phases. We will not discuss the derivational properties of phases, or minimal domains here, but concentrate on their formal and interpretative properties and their relevance for pronominal anaphora resolution.

Minimal domains of interpretation are part of linguistic expressions cross-linguistically. In Japanese, some elements that function as question markers can also act as universal and existential quantifiers (see Hagstrom [14], Gil [13], Dornish [11]). For example, the particle *-ka* in (1a) is in the illocutionary force domain (CP), and the linguistic expression it is part is interpreted as a question. In (1b) *-ka* is in the morphological domain, and the expression it is part is interpreted as an indefinite pronoun.

(1) a. *John-*wa ***nani****-o tabe-masi-ta* ***ka****?*
John –Top what-Acc eat-Past Q-part
'What did John eat?'

b. *Dare-mo ga* ***nani-ka*** *o tabe-te-ir*u
Everyone Nom something Acc eating
'Everyone is eating something'.

---

* I thank the anonymous reviewers for their comments on an earlier version of this paper. This work is supported in part by funding from the Social Sciences and Humanities Research Council of Canada to the Major Collaborative Research on Interface Asymmetries, grant number 214-2003-1003, awarded to professor Anna Maria Di Sciullo, of the Département de Linguistique at Université du Québec à Montréal. www.interfaceasymmetry.uqam.ca.

A minimal domain of interpretation is the smallest domain with a complete interpretation. A proposition (TP) is a minimal domain of interpretation, since it is the minimal domain that may be interpreted as true or false with respect to a world. A nominal constituent (DP) is a domain of interpretation, since it is the minimal domain that may denote sets of individuals. A word, i.e., a morphological object, is also a domain of interpretation, since it is a minimal domain with an isolable interpretation.

We define a minimal domain of interpretation in terms of relations. Moreover, we take the relations in a domain of interpretation to be asymmetric.

In set theory, asymmetry is a property of a relation. A relation is a set of ordered pairs and asymmetry is the property of a relation such that there is no pair in which the same coordinates are in the inverse order. Thus, in the set $A = \{a, b, c\}$, the relation R_1 is asymmetric: $R_1 = \{\langle a, b\rangle, \langle b, c\rangle, \langle a, c\rangle\}$. Asymmetry is not symmetry or antisymmetry. A symmetric relation includes pairs in which the same coordinates occur in the inverse order. So for example, given the set A, the relation R_2 is symmetric: $R_2 = \{\langle a, b\rangle, \langle b, c\rangle, \langle b, a\rangle, \langle c, b\rangle, \}$. Finally, an antisymmetric relation is an asymmetric relation which may include a pair in which the first and the second coordinates are the same. Thus, given the set A, the relation R_3 is antisymmetric: $R_3 = \{\langle a, b\rangle, \langle b, c\rangle, \langle a, a\rangle\}$, (see see Wall [24]).

In linguistic theory, the structure of linguistic expressions is expressed in terms of oriented graphs, and asymmetric relations are defined in terms of the relations between the nodes of the graphs (trees), see (2). The relations of precedence, dominance, and asymmetric c-command relations are asymmetric in the sense that they hold from X to Y and not from Y to X. In a tree, a node α c-commands β, iff each γ that dominates α dominates β, and α does not dominate β, and a node α asymmetrically c-commands β, iff α c-commands β, and β does not c-command α. (see Chomsky [3–5], Kayne [17]). Thus, in (2), X asymmetrically c-commands Y.

(2) a.

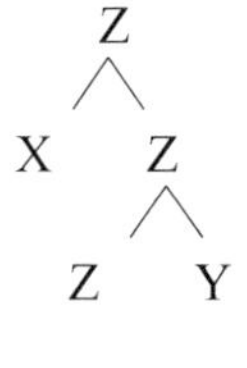

b. $[_Z \text{ X } [_Z \text{ Z Y}]]$

It has been shown that asymmetry is part of the properties of syntactic relations (see Chomsky [6], Kayne [17], Moro [21]), morphological relations (see Di Sciullo [8], Hale and Keyser [15]), and phonological relations (see Dresher [12], Raimy [22]). This property of relations is crucial because the alteration of the asymmetric relations brings about a difference in semantic interpretation or information structure. Thus in English, the interpretation of expressions including a quantifier such as *everyone*, and a definite pronoun, such as *he* or *him*, depends on their relation, see (3). The simplified trees in (4) illustrate that the first pronoun does not only precede the other, but also asymmetrically c-commands it. The copy of the pronouns is overlined.

(3) a. Everyone saw him. ~~∀~~y | ∃x y saw x

b. He saw everyone. ∃x | ~~∀~~y x saw y

(4) a.

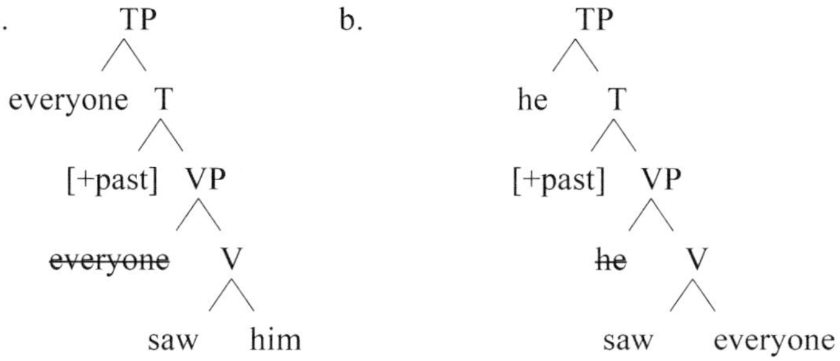

However, the relation between pronouns and their binders cannot be reduced to precedence relations, as the examples in (5) illustrate.

(5) a. Who saw him?

b. Who did he see?

In the examples in (5) the interrogative expression *who* precedes the pronoun *him*; however, in (5a), *who* quantifies over individuals that are the experiencer(s) of the event denoted by the verbal predicate *see*, whereas in (5b), the individuals bear the role associated with the object of the event denoted by the verbal predicate. Thus in the examples in (5) the interrogative expression occupies the same position in the linear string; however, its syntax-semantic role differs. The simplified structures in (6) illustrate this point.

(6) a.

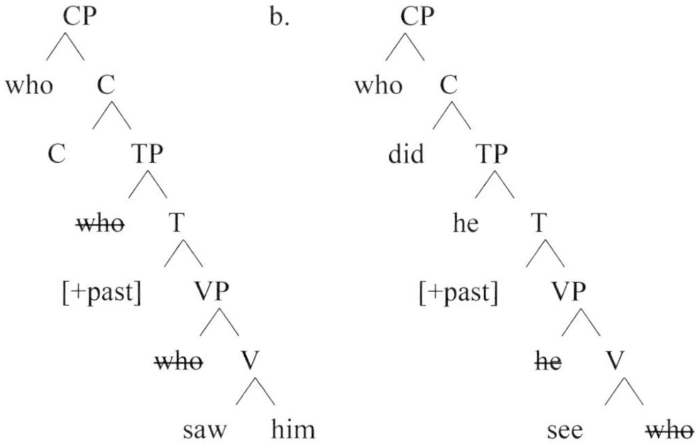

The examples in (7) further illustrate that precedence is not sufficient to determine the antecedent of a pronoun.

(7) a. John respects himself.

b. John's friend respects himself.

In (7a) the antecedent of the reflexive pronoun *himself* is *John*, whereas in (7b), the antecedent of *himself* is the constituent [*John's friend*]. The simplified structure in (8a) illustrates that *John* asymmetrically c-commands himself, whereas in (8b) it does not.

(8) a. b.

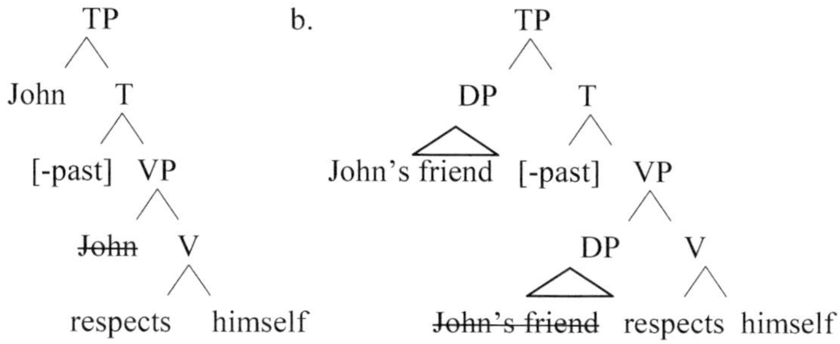

The relation of a pronoun be it indefinite, interrogative, reflexive or personal, to its antecedent cannot be set independently from the asymmetric relation of its minimal domain of interpretation.

2. Pronominal Anaphora Resolution

Pronominal anaphora resolution is generally treated in terms of preference conditions (e.g., frequency of occurrence in the discourse, proximity, preference of the subject over the object for the antecedent) rather than in terms of fine-grained syntax-semantic conditions. This is typically the case in so-called knowledge-poor approaches, including non-linguistic knowledge (see Kennedy and Boguraev [18], Mitkov [20]). We develop the view that pronominal anaphora resolution is determined by fine-grained linguistic knowledge (see Beaver [1], Carter [2], Hobbs [16], Lappin and Leass [19], for richer approaches to pronominal anaphora resolution than linguistic-knowledge-poor approaches).

Pronominal anaphora resolution systems based on preference scores, proximity, and on string-linear preference constraints are not optimal. For example, Mitkov's [20] MARS algorithm correctly identifies the antecedent of *him* as *the president* in the expression in (9). See the appendix. However, it fails to identify the correct antecedent for a pronoun *him* in (10). See the appendix.

(9) The president wants the chief officer to trust him.
(10) The chief officer trusts him.

The incorrect result is due to the fact that MARS did not analyze *chief officer* as being a minimal morphological domain. The expression *chief officer* qualifies as a morphological domain, since it is impenetrable and it has a complete interpretation: a *chief officer* is an officer who occupies a predominant position in a hierarchy. The internal structure of a morphological domain is not visible in a propositional domain, as depicted in (11), where the elements in the morphological domain are in square brackets. The constituents of a morphological domain (i.e. a morphological phase) cannot be the antecedent of a pronoun.

(11)

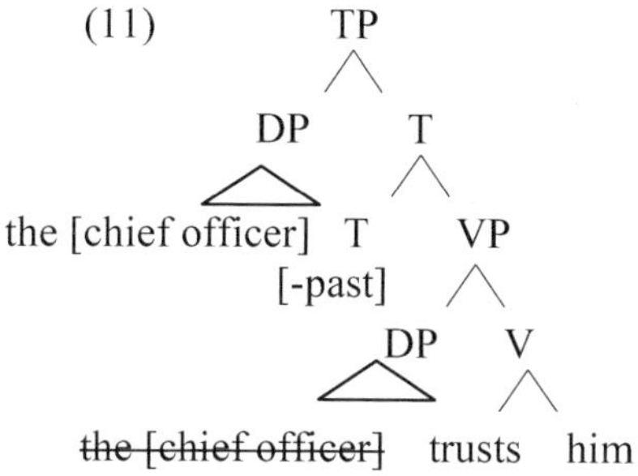

Likewise, the correct antecedent of the pronoun *him* in (12), that is, *the chief officer's lawyer*, is not found. Instead, the closest DP, that is, *the president*, is picked up. See the appendix. This shows that MARS does not rely on fine-grained syntax-semantic properties.

(12) The chief officer's lawyer wants the president to trust him.

Furthermore, MARS picks up the same antecedent for the pronoun in the examples in (13) and (14). See the appendix. Here again, MARS fails to analyze the syntax-semantic properties of the minimal domain of interpretation of the pronoun.

(13) The president and the CLO came in. He was confident about the outcome of the meeting as was the CLO.

(14) The president and the CLO came in. He was confident about the outcome of the meeting as was the president.

These results show that anaphora resolution based on linguistic-poor knowledge and on string-linear preference relations is not optimal.

3. Handling Pronouns

Pronominal anaphora is a clear case where the identification of minimal domains of interpretation is crucial for the handling of pronouns. A proposition and a discourse share formal properties, including asymmetric c-command between their constituents share formal properties (see Di Sciullo [9]). Propositions are minimal domains of interpretation where relations are established between predicates and arguments, as well as between arguments. Given the Binding Theory (15) (see [3]), a pronominal must be free and an anaphor must be bound in their binding domain (BD). Binding is asymmetric, and local.

(15) Binding Theory
A. An anaphor is bound in its BD.
B. A pronominal is free in its BD.

α is bound by β iff α and β are co-indexed
and β asymmetrically c-commands α
α is free iff α is not bound.

Binding determines the necessary antecedent for an anaphor and a possible antecedent for a pronoun in a local BD. Binding contributes to the interpretation of arguments, be they nominal expressions, reflexives, or pronouns. When two arguments are related through binding, they have the same referent. We will not use co-indexing to indicate a binding relation between two arguments, rather the arguments involved in binding relation will be in italics, and arguments that are not bound will not be. Thus in (16a), *himself* is bound by *the chief officer*, whereas in (16b), *him* is not bound by *the chief officer*. These examples illustrate the effect of the Binding Theory in the propositional BD. A proposition (TP) is a minimal domain of interpretation.

(16) a. [$_{TP}$ [$_{DP}$*The chief officer*] trusts [*himself*]]]
b. [$_{TP}$ [$_{DP}$The chief officer] trusts [him]]]

A nominal expression (DP) may also constitute a BD, i.e., a minimal domain of interpretation, for anaphors and pronouns, as the examples in (17) and (18) illustrate.

(17) a. [[$_{TP}$ The chief officer expects [$_{TP}$ [$_{DP}$ *Bill*'s picture of *himself*] to be on sale]]
b. [$_{TP}$ The chief officer expects [$_{TP}$ [$_{DP}$ Bill's picture of him] to be on sale]]

(18) a. #[$_{TP}$ [$_{DP}$*The chief officer*] expects [$_{TP}$ [$_{DP}$ Mary's picture of *himself*] to be on sale]]
b. [$_{TP}$ [$_{DP}$*The chief officer*] expects [$_{TP}$ [$_{DP}$ Mary's picture of *him*] to be on sale]]

In (17a) the antecedent of *himself* is in the DP subject of the embedded clause and in (17b) the antecedent of the pronoun *him* is outside of this DP. In (18a), the antecedent of the anaphor *himself* is not within the DP, as there is no compatible antecedent within the DP, and the structure contravenes to the condition A of the Binding Theory. In (18b), *him* is free within the DP, which is its BD, i.e., its minimal domain of interpretation.

While pronouns must be free in their BD, they must be bound by an antecedent outside of their BD, since they lack independent reference. The example in (19a) shows that the antecedent of the pronoun *him*, may be located in the matrix clause, outside of the embedded TP containing the pronoun. The example in (19b) illustrates that the antecedent of *him* may be located in a non-adjacent proposition within the Discourse Domain (DD).

(19) a. [$_{TP}$ [$_{DP}$*The president*] thinks [$_{CP}$ that [$_{TP}$ the chief officer] trusts [*him*]]]]
b. [$_{DD}$ [$_{TP}$ [$_{DP}$*The president*] talked to the members of the company today.] [$_{TP}$ The reactions of the shareholders were unequal.] [$_{TP}$ The minutes of the meeting indicate [$_{CP}$ that[$_{TP}$ [the chief officer] trusts [*him*]]]]]

The identification of the BD cannot be reduced to the proposition (TP) however, given structures such as (20a) where the BD of *himself* is the DP of which it is part, and (20b) where *himself* is bound outside of the TP. It has been proposed in Chomsky [3] that the BD be defined in terms of the notion of SUBJECT, that is, in terms of the presence of a functional structure including Inflection (Tense and subject-verb agreement).

This allows for a unified account of structures such as (20) as well as structures such as (21). The structure in (21a) is marginal (#) because the anaphor *himself* does not have an antecedent within its BD, the embedded tensed clause. The structure in (21b) is fine because *himself* is in an infinitival clause and its BD is the matrix clause, where its antecedent is located.

(20) a. $[_{TP}$ $[_{DP}$ The president] expects $[_{TP}$ $[_{DP}$*Bill*'s picture of *himself*] to be on sale]]

b. $[_{TP}$ $[_{DP}$T*he president*] expects $[_{TP}$ $[_{DP}$ pictures of *himself*] to be on sale]]

(21) a. #$[_{TP}$ $[_{DP}$ *The president*] expects $[_{CP}$ that $[_{TP}$ [*himself*] would win]]]

b. $[_{TP}$ $[_{DP}$*The president*] expects $[_{TP}$ [*himself* to win]]

The facts show that the identification of the BD for a pronoun or an anaphor is dependent on the internal structure of TPs and DPs. The BD cannot be defined in terms of a fixed category, but rather in terms of the syntax-semantic properties of the configurations. The minimal domain of interpretation of pronouns and anaphors can be defined in terms of a relation of a certain kind. We propose that this relation is asymmetric agreement.

4. Asymmetric Agreement

According to Asymmetry Theory [10], the operations of the grammar apply under asymmetric Agree, (22). This is the case for the operation Link, (23), that featurally relates two objects. Thus, if X and Y are linked, their features must be in a subset relation.

(22) Agree (φ_1, φ_2)
Given two sets of features φ_1 and φ_2, Agree (φ_1, φ_2) applies if and only if φ_1 properly includes φ_2.

(23) *Link (α, β)*
Given two objects α and β, Link *(α, β)* creates a new object where α and β are featurally related.

Asymmetric Agree applies in movement and in binding. In the case of movement, there is a subset relation between the displaced constituent and its copy, since the copy has all the features of the displaced constituent except for the uninterpretable features. In the case of binding, the features of the binder and the bindee are also in a subset relation.

In Di Sciullo [9], the DD-Linking condition was proposed for discourse pronominal anaphora, (24), in terms of the Link operation extended to the Domain of the Discourse (DD). Like the other operations of this theory, Link, (23), applies under asymmetric Agree, (27). Agree is an asymmetric relation, since proper inclusion is asymmetric. A pronoun (DPro) is linked to the closest antecedent (nominal expression (DP), or a pronoun (DPro)) it asymmetrically c-commands and agrees with. Pronominal anaphora resolution is essentially the identification of the closest DP/DPro with respect to which a pronoun stands in a proper inclusion relation.

(24) DD-Linking (Discourse Domain Linking)
A pronominal must be linked in its DD.

Asymmetric agreement also holds for Binding, since the feature structure of anaphors and antecedents are in proper inclusion relation. An antecedent properly includes the set of features of an anaphor, since without the antecedent the reference of an anaphor cannot be interpreted. The grammatical features, i.e., phi-features of anaphors and pronouns, must also be part of the linking relation along with the semantic features: no linking relation would hold, say in the examples (17), if the number feature of the pronouns were different from the number feature of the DP antecedents. There are three sorts of interpretable features that play a role in pronominal anaphora: phonetic, formal, and semantic. The phonetic features are legible at the phonetic interface, the formal and the semantic features are legible at the semantic interface and are determinant in anaphora resolution. I focus on the formal and the semantic features in what follows.

The elements that enter into anaphoric relations have the formal feature D (Determiner) and the phi-features Person (Per), Number (Num), Gender (Gen), as well as morphological case (e.g., nominative, accusative, dative, oblique) which we will not consider here. Both pronouns (DPro) and definite determiners are D, but differ in their phi-features, definite determiners not being specified for person, gender, and for morphological case. DPs differ from DPros, Ns are inherently 3rd pers. Argument DPs and DPros have semantic features that participate in anaphoric relations. DPs have independent reference [+Ir], whereas DPros do not [–Ir]. An anaphoric relation has only one [+Ir] feature, the [–Ir] feature of DPros is linked by the [+Ir] feature of the antecedent DPs. Given the Binding Theory, an anaphoric pronoun, such as *himself*, must be bound by an antecedent in its BD, whereas pronouns must be free. Given D-Linking, a pronoun such as *him* must be linked in its DD.

The formal and semantic features that are necessary for pronominal anaphora resolution based on asymmetric agreement are specified in (25). The feature specifications are provided for both strong and week DPros, such as the pronominal clitics of Romance languages, e.g., *le CLO le voit* (Fr.) 'the CLO sees him'. We will not discuss week pronominal anaphora here, which properties also follow from asymmetric agreement [10]. The semantic features include the independent reference feature ([±Ir]), along with the animate ([±ani]) feature and the part-whole ([±w]) feature. The [±ani] feature differentiates *he* from *it*, and the [±w] feature differentiates anaphoric pronouns, such as *himself*, from non-anaphoric pronouns, such as *he* and *him*, anaphoric pronouns are [+w], non-anaphoric pronouns are [–w].

(25) DPros and DPs formal and semantic features

		Formal: pers, num, gen	Semantic: Ir, ani, w
DPro			
strong		+ + +	+/– +/– +/–
week		– + +	+/– +/– +/–
DP		3rd pers. + +	+ +/– +/–

5. Predictions

5.1. Propositions and Discourse

Given asymmetric agreement, the set of features of the antecedent must be a superset of the set of features of the anaphor. This makes the correct predictions within the propositional domain, BD. It also makes correct predictions in the domain of the discourse, DD, as the examples in (26) and (27) illustrate.

(26) a. [$_{TP}$ [*the chief officer*] trusts [*himself*]].

{ +Ir, +ani, +w } {$-$Ir, +ani, $-$w}
{+3^{rd}pers,+ sing, +masc} {+3^{rd}pers,+ sing, +masc}

b. [$_{TP}$ [the chief officer] trusts [him]].

{+Ir, +ani, +w } {$-$Ir, +ani, +w}
{+3^{rd}pers,+ sing, +masc} {+3^{rd}pers,+ sing, +masc}

c. [$_{TP}$ [*the president*] thinks [$_{CP}$ that [$_{TP}$ [the chief officer] trusts [*him*]]]].

{ +Ir, +ani, +w} {$-$Ir, +ani, +w}
{3^{rd}pers,+ sing, +masc} {+3^{rd}pers,+ sing, +masc}

In (26a), the BD is the proposition, and the features of the pronominal anaphor *himself* are properly included in the set of features of its asymmetrically c-commanding antecedent John. In (26b), the BD of the pronoun *him* is also propositional, and the pronoun is not bound by the local antecedent with which it asymmetrically agrees. In (26c), the pronoun *him* is free in its BD, as predicted by the Binding Theory, and it must be bound outside of that domain, in its DD, given D-Linking. A possible antecedent for this pronoun is the DP in subject position [the president] in the matrix clause. Consider now (27):

(27) [$_{DD}$ [$_{TP}$ [*the president]* talked to [the members of the company] today].

{+Ir, +ani, +w} {+Ir, +ani, +w}
{+3^{rd}pers,+ sing, +masc} {3^{rd}pers,+ plur, +masc}

[$_{TP}$ [The reactions of the shareholders] were unequal].

{+Ir, -ani, +w }
{+3^{rd}pers,+ plur, +masc}

[$_{TP}$ [The minutes of the meeting] indicate [$_{CP}$ that [$_{TP}$ [the CLO] trusts [*him*]]]]].

{+Ir, -ani, +w} {+Ir, +ani, +w} {$-$Ir, +ani, +w}
{+3^{rd}pers, + plur, +neut} {+3^{rd}pers,+ sing, +masc) {+3^{rd}pers,+ sing,+masc}

In (27), the pronoun *him* is not bound by its local antecedent [the CLO] with which it asymmetrically agrees in its BD, as predicted by the Binding Theory. Given D-Linking, the pronoun must be linked in its DD. The antecedent of the pronoun is the DP [*the president*] in the first proposition of the discourse, since it is the closest DP with which the features of the pronoun may enter into a proper inclusion relation. The intermediate DPs do not share the same set of phi-features with the pronoun. Thus, no superset relation can be established between the set of features of the intermediate DPs and the set of features of the pronoun. Thus, the facts are correctly predicted by the proposed approach to pronominal anaphora based on asymmetric agreement.

5.2. Syntax-Semantic Knowledge

The syntax-semantic properties of the DPs and DPros that are part of anaphoric relations provide further evidence that pronominal anaphora resolution operates on minimal domains of asymmetric relations. Consider the examples in (28) to (31) which are telling with respect to the role of the internal syntax-semantic properties of minimal domains of interpretation.

(28) a. [$_{DD}$ [$_{TP}$ The president bought [*a Mercedes*]]. [$_{TP}$[*They]* are solid cars].]
b. [$_{DD}$ [$_{TP}$ I need [*a rewritable CD*]]. [$_{CP}$ Where did you put [*them*]]?]

(29) a. #[$_{DD}$ [$_{TP}$ I saw [*the president's Mercedes*]]. [$_{TP}$[*They*] are solid cars].]]
b. #[$_{DD\ TP}$ I need [*the rewritable CD*]]. [$_{CP}$ Where did you put [*them*]]?]]

(30) a. [$_{DD}$ [$_{TP}$ The Mercedes is [*a nice car*]]. [$_{TP}$ [*They*] sell well]].]
b. [$_{DD}$ [$_{TP}$ [*The rewritable CD*] is popular]]. [$_{TP}$ [*They* sold well this year].]

(31) a. [$_{DD}$ [$_{TP}$ The Mercedes is [*a nice car*]]. [$_{TP}$ [*It*] sells well].]
b. [$_{DD}$ [$_{TP}$ [*The rewritable CD*] is popular]. [$_{TP}$ [*It*] sold well this year].]

The examples in (28) show that an indefinite DP, [*a Mercedes*], [*a rewritable CD*], can be the antecedent of a plural pronoun. The examples in (29) show that this is not the case for a definite singular DP, [*the president's Mercedes*], [*the rewritable CD*]. The examples in (30) and (31) show that a definite DP that denotes a type can be the antecedent of a plural or a singular pronoun.

Interestingly, MARS does not identify any antecedent for the pronoun *they* in (28a), and it also wrongly identifies [*a nice car*] as the antecedent of the pronoun *it* in (31a). See the appendix.

Pronominal anaphora resolution crucially relies on the semantic features of the antecedent and the pronoun. Indefinite DPs, like plural DPs, denote sets of individuals. They can thus be the antecedents of plural pronouns. Similarly, the set of individuals denoted by conjunct DPs can be the antecedent of a plural pronoun, as the example in (32a) illustrates, even though only one of the conjuncts can be the antecedent of a singular pronoun, as the example in (32b) illustrates.

(32) a. [*The president and the CLO*] came in. [*They*] were confident about the outcome of the meeting.
b. [*The president]* and the CLO came in. [*He*] was confident about the outcome of the meeting as was the CLO.

The examples above illustrate that pronominal anaphora resolution cannot be established without the identification of the syntax-semantic properties of the whole domain of interpretation. In the case of (32a), the coordination structure must be taken into account, and in the case of (32b), the VP deleted structure in the adjunct clause must be taken into account. The syntax-semantic properties of the verbal predicates must also be taken into account, as shown in (33) with propositions including an expletive pronoun, such as *it* and *there*, occupying the subject position. In English and in French, the formal features of an expletive pronoun are {+3rdpers, –ani}, since *it* is not specified for number and gender.

(33) [*The company X*] was making progresses. [*It*] seemed as if the market was not ready for a breakthrough. However, the new X-software sold very well.

The expletive *it* in the second sentence in (33) will not be part of an asymmetric agreement relation with the phi-compatible DP in the subject position in the preceding sentence if expletives differ semantically from pronouns and full DPs. Expletives do not denote sets of individuals, contrary to pronouns and DPs. Thus a DP cannot be the antecedent of an expletive, since the former cannot be a subset of the latter.

The expletive *it* and the pronoun *it* have the same form, they can only be differentiated by the lexical properties of the predicate on which they are dependent. Thus, the pronoun *it* in (34) is an expletive, because the predicate *seem* does not have an external argument, and is a raising verb (see (34b), whereas the pronoun *it* in (35) is not an expletive, as the predicate *indicate* selects an external argument, and thus the verb is not a raising verb (see 35b).

(34) a. It seems that the market is ready for a breakthrough.
b. The market seems to be ready for a breakthrough.

(35) a. It indicates that the market is ready for a breakthrough.
b. *The market indicates to be ready for a breakthrough.

The examples in (36) further illustrate that the syntax-semantic properties of the predicates play a role in pronominal anaphora resolution.

(36) a. The president congratulated [*the CLO*]. [*He*] was not expecting such a reaction.
b. [*The president*] frightened the CLO. [*He*] was not expecting such a reaction.

In the case of *congratulate*, the internal argument (object) is the experiencer, and in the case of *frighten*, the experiencer is the external argument. The external argument (subject) of *expect* is also an experiencer, consequently the DPro in the local argument structure domain of *expect* will take as its antecedent the object of *congratulate* in (36a), i.e., *the CLO*, and the object of *fear* in (36b), i.e., *the president.* The fact that the properties of the predicates play a role in pronominal anaphora resolution does not come as a surprise, since predicate argument structure domain is a minimal domain of interpretation.

In sum the syntax-semantic properties of the minimal domain of interpretation must be analyzed for the efficient processing of pronouns.

5.3. Linguistic Knowledge and Real-World Knowledge

Linguistic knowledge determines the core properties of discourse pronominal anaphora, whereas real-world knowledge is parasitic on the linguistic knowledge. The examples in (37) and (38) illustrate this point.

(37) a. [*The President's party*] was a success. [*They]* celebrated until 2 AM.
b. They talked about the [*President's party*]. [*They*] celebrated until 2AM.

(38) [*The CEO*] talked to the CLO. [*He*] became a millionaire within a time-frame of four years.

In (37a) and (37b), the antecedent of the pronoun *they* is the DP [the President's party] in the preceding c-commanding proposition, since *party* is a group noun including several members. Real-world knowledge, e.g., one property of a successful party is that it lasts a long time, enforces the anaphoric relation based on the linguistic knowledge. In (38), the pronoun *he* has two possible DP antecedents: the DP subject [the CEO] and the DP object [the CLO], and asymmetric agreement holds between each one of the DPs and the pronoun *he*. Given that CEOs are more likely to become millionaires than CLOs, real-world knowledge enforces the linguistic knowledge that, all things being equal, the subject rather than the object is the antecedent of an anaphor. Real-world knowledge is not basic in pronominal anaphora resolution. Independent results point to the same conclusion. Lappin and Leass [19] report that real-world relations marginally improve the syntax-based RAP algorithm's performance (by 2%).

Interestingly, MARS provides inconsistent results with the examples in (37a) and (37b). See the appendix. It does not rely on real-world knowledge, and it does not rely on the syntax-semantic properties of the minimal domains of interpretation.

In the next section, we sketch part of the design of a pronominal anaphora interpreter based on rich linguistic knowledge, including the identification of minimal domains of interpretation.

6. Intelligent Pronominal Anaphora Resolution

Information processing systems are generally based on poor linguistic knowledge. This is the case for most operating search engines and question answering systems. The performance of these systems is also poor, the reason being that most systems rely on keyword search, Boolean operators and probabilistic methods instead of syntax-semantic properties. By doing so, they fail to take into consideration the properties of the object to which they apply: natural language. Intelligent natural language software design must include the notion of minimal domain of interpretation defined in terms of asymmetric relations for pronominal anaphora resolution. The parts of the architecture of a system for intelligent pronominal anaphora resolution are identified in (39). The system includes a Sentence Delimiter (SD) that sequentially identifies each sentence of a discourse, preserving the asymmetric irreversible relation between the propositions. It includes a Syntax-Semantic Parser (SSP) that analyzes each proposition from left to right, recovering the internal structure and the asymmetric relations between the constituents, including DPs and DPros, and identifying their formal and semantic feature structure. The Domain Identifier (DI) recovers the minimal domains of interpretation for pronouns and anaphors. The Pronoun Linker (PL) implements the operations of Asymmetry Theory including the Link operation, applying under asymmetric agreement. The output yields an annotated discourse with pronominal anaphora resolution.

(39) **Partial architecture of a system for intelligent pronominal anaphora resolution**

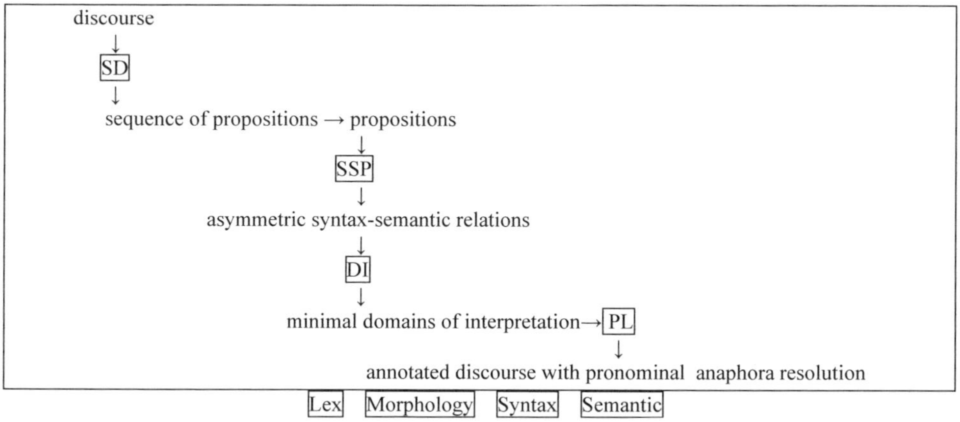

Intelligent pronominal anaphora resolution relies on morphological-syntax-semantic properties and asymmetric relations, including asymmetric agreement. It identifies necessary and possible antecedents for pronouns in linguistically motivated minimal domains of interpretation. The recovery of minimal domains of interpretation based on asymmetric relations, instead of domain-independent preference constraints, constitutes a step forward in intelligent software design. If it is true that conceptual processing of linguistic expressions is based on irreversible relations of Universal Grammar, incorporation of these relations in information processing systems can only improve their performance and bring these artificial systems closer to human performance.

7. Summary

The Binding Theory is an interface legibility condition of the interpretation of anaphors and pronouns within propositions. The Discourse Domain Linking is a legibility condition that requires a pronoun, i.e., an element that lacks independent reference, to be linked to the closest antecedent, a nominal expression or another pronoun, with which it asymmetrically agrees within its minimal domain of interpretation. Both Discourse Domain Linking and Binding are bounded conditions; they apply to minimal domains of interpretation, morphological, syntactic and discursive. Pronominal anaphora resolution crucially relies on the identification of these domains, where asymmetric agreement holds between pronouns and their antecedents.

8. Appendix

Results from Mitkov's Anaphora Resolution System (MARS)

(9) The president wants the chief officer to trust him.
(40) Result from MARS for (9):

him appears in paragraph 2, sentence 1, from position 9 to position 9. It is singular. The antecedent is indicated to be The president in paragraph 2, sentence 1, from position 1 to position 2.

Candidates were:

Candidates	Sent	Pos	Def	Given	I-V	F-Cand	Rei	Sect-Hdg	N-PP-NP	Col-Pat	Im-Ref	Seq-Inst	Ref Dist	Term Pref	Syn_Par	B_P	TOTAL SCORE
The president	1	1 - 2	0	2	0	0	0	1	0	0	0	0	2	0	0	0	5
chief	1	5 - 5	-1	-1	0	0	0	1	0	0	0	0	2	0	0	0	1

(10) The chief officer trusts him.
(41) Result from MARS for (10)

him appears in paragraph 1, sentence 1, from position 5 to position 5. It is singular. The antecedent is indicated to be chief in paragraph 1, sentence 1, from position 2 to position 2.

Candidates were:

Candidates	Sent	Pos	Def	Given	I-V	F-Cand	Rei	Sect-Hdg	N-PP-NP	Col-Pat	Im-Ref	Seq-Inst	Ref Dist	Term Pref	Syn_Par	B_P	TOTAL SCORE
chief	1	2 - 2	-1	-1	0	0	0	1	0	0	0	0	2	0	0	0	1

(12) The chief officer's lawyer wants the president to trust him.
(42) Result from MARS for (12):

him appears in paragraph 1, sentence 1, from position 10 to position 10. It is singular. The antecedent is indicated to be the president in paragraph 1, sentence 1, from position 6 to position 7.

Candidates were:

Candidates	Sent	Pos	Def	Given	I-V	F-Cand	Rei	Sect-Hdg	N-PP-NP	Col-Pat	Im-Ref	Seq-Inst	Ref Dist	Term Pref	Syn_Par	B_P	TOTAL SCORE
the chief officer's lawyer	1	1 - 4	0	2	0	0	0	0	0	0	0	0	2	0	0	0	4
chief officer's	1	2 - 3	-1	-1	0	0	0	0	0	0	0	0	2	0	0	0	0
chief	1	2 - 2	-1	-1	0	0	0	0	0	0	0	0	2	0	0	0	0
the president	1	6 - 7	0	1	0	0	0	0	0	0	0	0	2	0	1	0	4

(13) The president and the CLO came in. He was confident about the outcome of the meeting as was the CLO.

(43) Result from MARS for (13):

He appears in paragraph 2, sentence 2, from position 1 to position 1. It is singular. The antecedent is indicated to be The president in paragraph 2, sentence 1, from position 1 to position 2.

Candidates were:

Candidates	Sent	Pos	Def	Given	I-V	F-Cand	Rei	Sect-Hdg	N-PP-NP	Col-Pat	Im-Ref	Seq-Inst	Ref Dist	Term Pref	Syn_Par	B_P	TOTAL SCORE
The president and the CLO	1	1 - 5	-1	2	0	0	0	0	0	0	0	0	1	0	1	0	3
The president	1	1 - 2	0	2	0	0	0	0	0	0	0	0	1	0	1	0	4

(14) The president and the CLO came in. He was confident about the outcome of the meeting as was the president.

(44) Result from MARS for (14):

He appears in paragraph 2, sentence 2, from position 1 to position 1. It is singular. The antecedent is indicated to be The president in paragraph 2, sentence 1, from position 1 to position 2.

Candidates were:

Candidates	Sent	Pos	Def	Given	I-V	F-Cand	Rei	Sect-Hdg	N-PP-NP	Col-Pat	Im-Ref	Seq-Inst	Ref Dist	Term Pref	Syn_Par	B_P	TOTAL SCORE
The president and the CLO	1	1 - 5	-1	2	0	0	1	0	0	0	0	0	1	0	1	0	4
The president	1	1 - 2	0	2	0	0	1	0	0	0	0	0	1	0	1	0	5

(28a) The president brought a Mercedes. They are solid cars.

(45) Result from MARS for (28a):

They appears in paragraph 2, sentence 2, from position 1 to position 1. It is plural. The antecedent is indicated to be !!NOTHING!! in paragraph, sentence, from position to position.

Candidates were:

Candidates	Sent	Pos	Def	Given	I-V	F-Cand	Rei	Sect-Hdg	N-PP-NP	Col-Pat	Im-Ref	Seq-Inst	Ref Dist	Term Pref	Syn_Par	B_P	TOTAL SCORE

(30a) The Mercedes is a nice car. It sells well.

(46) Result from MARS for (30a):

It appears in paragraph 2, sentence 2, from position 1 to position 1. It is singular. The antecedent is indicated to be a nice car in paragraph 2, sentence 1, from position 4 to position 6.

Candidates were:

Candidates	Sent	Pos	Def	Given	I-V	F-Cand	Rei	Sect-Hdg	N-PP-NP	Col-Pat	Im-Ref	Seq-Inst	Ref Dist	Term Pref	Syn_Par	B_P	TOTAL SCORE
a nice car	1	4 - 6	-1	-1	0	0	0	0	0	0	0	0	1	0	0	0	-1

(44a) The president's party was a success. They celebrated until 2 AM.
(47) Results from MARS for (44a):

They appears in paragraph 2, sentence 2, from position 1 to position 1. It is singularplural. The antecedent is indicated to be The President's party in paragraph 2, sentence 1, from position 1 to position 3.

Candidates were:

Candidates	Sent	Pos	Def	Given	I-V	F-Cand	Rei	Sect-Hdg	N-PP-NP	Col-Pat	Im-Ref	Seq-Inst	Ref Dist	Term Pref	Syn_Par	B_P	TOTAL SCORE
The President's party	1	1 - 3	0	2	0	0	0	0	0	0	0	0	1	0	1	0	4

(37b) They talked about the President's party. They celebrated until 2 AM.
(48) Result from MARS for (37b):

They appears in paragraph 2, sentence 1, from position 1 to position 1. It is plural. The antecedent is indicated to be !!NOTHING!! in paragraph , sentence , from position to position.

Candidates were:

Candidates	Sent	Pos	Def	Given	I-V	F-Cand	Rei	Sect-Hdg	N-PP-NP	Col-Pat	Im-Ref	Seq-Inst	Ref Dist	Term Pref	Syn_Par	B_P	TOTAL SCORE

References

[1] D. Beaver, "The Optimization of Discourse Anaphora", *Linguistics and Philosophy 27(1)*, pp. 3–56. 2004.

[2] D. Carter, *Interpreting Anaphora in Natural Language Texts*, Chichester: Ellis Horwood, 1987.

[3] N. Chomsky, *Lectures on Government and Binding,* Dordrecht: Foris, 1981.

[4] N. Chomsky, *The Minimalist Program*, Cambridge, Mass.: The MIT Press, 1995.

[5] N. Chomsky, "Minimalist Inquiries", in R. Martin, D. Michaels and J. Uriagereka eds. *Step by Step. Essays on Minimalist Syntax in Honor of Howard Lasnik*, Cambridge, Mass.: The MIT Press, 2000, pp. 89–155.

[6] N. Chomsky, "Derivation by Phase", in M. Kenstowicz, ed. *Ken Hale: A Life in Language*, Cambridge, Mass.: The MIT Press, 2001.

[7] A.M. Di Sciullo, "Morphological Phases", in H.-J. Yoon, ed. *Proceedings of the 4th GLOW in Asia 2003, Generative Grammar in a Broader Perspective. The Korean Generative Grammar Circle*, 2003, pp. 113–136.

[8] A.M. Di Sciullo, "Morphological Relations in Asymmetry Theory", in A.M. Di Sciullo, ed. *Asymmetry in Grammar, volume 2: Morphology, Phonology and Acquisition,* Amsterdam: John Benjamins, 2003, pp. 11–38.
[9] A.M. Di Sciullo, "Domains of Argument Structure Asymmetries", in *SCI 2005*.
[10] A.M. Di Sciullo, *Asymmetry in Morphology*, Cambridge, Mass.: The MIT Press, 2005.
[11] E. Dornish, Overt Quantifier Raising in Polish: The Interaction of WH-Phases and Clitics, Doctoral dissertation, Cornell University, 1998.
[12] E. Dresher, "Contrast and asymmetries in inventories", in Anna-Maria di Sciullo, ed., *Asymmetry in grammar, Volume 2: Morphology, phonology, acquisition,* Amsterdam: John Benjamins, 2003, pp. 239–257.
[13] D. Gil, "Quantifiers", in M. Haspelmath, E. Köning, W. Oesterreicher and W. Raible, eds., *Language Typology and Language Universals, vol. II*, Berlin New York: Walter de Gruyter, 2001, pp. 1257–1294.
[14] P. Hagstrom, Decomposing Questions, Doctoral dissertation, MIT, 1998.
[15] K. Hale and J. Keyser, *Prolegomena to a Theory of Argument Structure*. Cambridge, Mass.: The MIT Press, 2002.
[16] J. Hobbs, "Resolving Pronouns Reference", *Lingua 44*, 1987, pp. 339–352.
[17] R. Kayne, *The Antisymmetry of Syntax*, Cambridge, Mass.: The MIT Press, 1994.
[18] C. Kennedy and B. Boguraev, "Anaphora for Everyone: Pronominal Anaphora Resolution without a Parser", *Proceedings of the 16th International Conference on Computational Linguistics (COLLING'96)*, Copenhagen, Denmark, 1996, pp. 113–118.
[19] S. Lappin and H. Leass, "An Algorithm for Pronominal Anaphora Resolution". *Computational Linguistics*, vol. 4, 1994, pp. 535–561.
[20] R. Mitkov, *Anaphora Resolution*, Edinburgh, London, Pearson Education, 2002.
[21] A. Moro, *Dynamic Antisymmetry*, Cambridge, Mass.: The MIT Press, 2000.
[22] E. Raimy, "Asymmetry and Linearization in Phonology", in Anna Maria Di Sciullo, ed. *Asymmetry in Grammar. Volume 2: Morphology, Phonology and Acquisition,* Amsterdam/ Philadelphia: John Benjamins, 2003, pp. 129–146.
[23] J. Uriagereka, "Multiple Spell-Out", in S.D. Epstein and M. Hornstein, eds. *Working Minimalism*, Cambridge, Mass.: MIT Press, 1999, pp. 251–283.
[24] R. Wall, *Introduction to Mathematical Linguistics*, New Jersey: Prentice Hall, 1972.

New Trends in Software Methodologies, Tools and Techniques
H. Fujita and M. Mejri (Eds.)
IOS Press, 2005

About Application and Implementation of Semantic Meta Parsing

Gregers KOCH
Department of Computer Science, Copenhagen University, DIKU, Universitetsparken 1, DK-2100, Copenhagen, Denmark, Tel.: (+45) 35 32 14 00, Fax.: (+45) 35 32 14 01
Email: gregers@diku.dk

Abstract. This paper contains a description of our method of semantic meta parsing, and the method is implemented as a Prolog program. For comparison, we present briefly Johnson and Kay's method of semantic abstraction [9]. The two methods are compared by application on a sample problem from Hans Kamp's Discourse Representation Theory (DRT) [10].

1. Introduction

The previous paper dealt with interpretation and semantic abstraction, with special attention to semantic meta parsing. [13].

The paper by Johnson and Kay also deals with interpretation and semantic abstraction [9]. They present a complicated but rather general parser which, by means of different interpretations, is capable of implementing essential parts of various semantic theories. An example is chosen for comparison.

2. Johnson and Kay's System

Before discussing our own system, in this part of the paper we give a brief description of Johnson and Kay's way of making semantic abstraction. [11–13,9]

They show how the same rules construct formulae in the style of Montague grammar, or representations similar to DRT [10]. The idea is that semantic representations are specified indirectly using semantic construction operators, which enforce a barrier between the grammar and the semantic representations themselves. Different operations can be associated with these operators and, depending on the set in force at a given time, the effect of interpreting the expression will be to construct a representation in one semantic formalism or another. The set of operators contains members corresponding to such notions as composition, conjunction, etc. The set is small and independent of the semantic formalism, but no claims are made for their general sufficiency.

Their grammar generates simple transitive clauses and subject-relative clauses. It is based on the Montague-style grammars as presented in Covington's book.[4]

```
:- op(950, xfy, ^).
:- op(300, xfy, =>).
parse(String,ExtSem) :-
  external(IntSem,ExtSem), s(IntSem,String,[]).
s(S) --> np(VP^S), vp(VP).
np(NP) --> det(N1^NP), n1(N1).
n1(N) --> n(N).
n1(X^S) --> n(X^S1), rc(X^S2), {conjoin(S1,S2,S)}.
vp(X^S) --> v(X^VP), np(VP^S).
rc(VP) --> [that], vp(VP).
v(X^Y^S) --> [Verb], {verb(Verb,X^Y^Pred), atom(Pred,S)}.
n(X^S) --> [Noun], {noun(Noun,X^Pred), new_index(X,S1),
                    atom(Pred,S2), compose(S1,S2,S)}.
det((X^Res)^(X^Scope)^S) --> [Det],
                    {determiner(Det,Res^Scope^S)}.
np((X^S1)^S) --> [Pronoun],
  {pronoun(Pronoun), accessible_index(X,S2), compose(S1,S2,S)}.

pronoun(it).
verb(beats, X^Y^beat(X,Y)).
verb(owns, X^Y^own(X,Y)).
noun(man, X^man(X)).
determiner(a, Res^Scope^S) :- conjoin(Res,Scope,S).
determiner(every, Res0^Scope^S) :-
  compose(S1, S2, S), subordinate(Res, ResName, S1),
  compose(Res0, Res1, Res), subordinate(Scope, ScopeName, Res1),
  atom(ResName => Scopename, S2).
```

The semantics of VP and N are represented by terms of the form $X \hat{} S$, where X represents a referential index and S represents the semantics of a sentence. NP meanings are represented by terms of the form $VP \hat{} S$, where S represents a sentential meaning. [3,1]

2.1. *An Application to Discourse Representation*

The representations built by the following constructors are inspired by Hans Kamp's "box representations" [10]. A discourse representation "box" is represented by the list of items that constitute its contents. A representation is a difference-pair of the lists of the representations of the currently open boxes (i.e. the current box and all superordinate boxes). In Prolog, we use the binary '-' operator to separate the two members of the pair.

```
atom(P,[B|Bs]-[[P|B]|Bs]).

compose(B0s-B1s,B1s-B2s,B0s-B2s).

conjoin(P1,P2,P) :- compose(P1,P2,P).

subordinate([[]|B0s]-[B|B1s],B,B0s-B1s).

new_index(Index,C) :- atom(i(Index),C).

accessible_index(Index,Bs-Bs) :- member(B,Bs), member(i(Index),B).

external([[]]-[S],S).
```

With these constructors, the parser yields the following semantic value for an example sentence.

```
?- parse([every,man,that,owns,a,donkey,beats,it],S).
S = [[own(X,Y),donkey(Y),i(Y),man(X),i(X)] => [beat(X,Y)]]
```

This representation is true just in case for all individuals X and Y such that X is a man and Y a donkey and X owns Y, it is also true that X beats Y.

Given the smart but complex system by Johnson and Kay for interpretation and semantic abstraction, the question is, could the same objectives be obtained in a simpler way, or at least in such a way that the resulting parser typically will get a considerably simpler structure, when implementing most existing semantic theories?

This question will be answered affirmatively by referring to our system for semantic meta parsing, briefly described in some earlier papers [11–13].

Here we extend the description with several details of a specific implementation in the programming language Prolog.

As an example for comparison we choose to present simple implementations of Hans Kamp's Discourse Representation Theory (DRT) in both systems [10].

3. A System for Semantic Meta Parsing

Here we present an application of our system for semantic meta parsing. It deals with the automated generation of logical parsers or translators.

A logical parser is a logical formula describing a translation process into some logical notation. More precisely, we add the requirement to the meta system that the logical description is capable of producing by deduction a feasible description of the translation process. The translation takes place from a specified language fragment L, typically from a fragment of a natural language like English or French, but a programming language like Pascal may also be used. The target language of the translation is an appropriately chosen logic Log1. As to the logical host language, the meta level translation takes place in one logical language Log2, and the object level translation takes place in a possibly different logical language Log3. Here we shall confine ourselves to discussion of the situation where both logical host languages coincide with the Horn Clause Logic HCL. Other possibilities for Log2 and Log3 can certainly also be dealt with, but here we confine ourselves to Log2 = Log3 = HCL.

As target logic Log1 our system can accomodate virtually any possible logic, and this flexibility seems to be one of the really strong features of this approach. In that particular sense we may consider it a system with high semantic generality. In the style of Johnson & Kay [9] and as an illustration we can exemplify with a variant of Montague's intensional logic or with a sort of discourse representation structures like Kamp and Reyle.[10]

3.1. The System

In this section we shall describe the method by means of an example. The method presupposes that a context-free grammar has been created, including a lexicon, and it performs semantic induction for a pair of text and semantic structure. The result of the induction is a definite clause grammar (DCG) corresponding to the grammar and it will be annotated with variables.[2] Our example uses the following little grammar

```
s -> np vp.   np -> det n.   vp -> v np.
```

The sample text is “a horse eats an apple” and the intended semantic structure is

```
a(x, horse(x), a(y, apple(y), eats(x,y)))
```

representing the predicate-logic formula

$$\exists x[horse(x) \wedge \exists y[apple(y) \wedge eats(x, y)]]. \qquad (1)$$

First step:

Reformulate the intended semantic structure into a functional tree structure where each functor has a label or a number attached.

Second step:

Create a syntax tree through parsing of the sample text in accordance with the grammar.

Third step:

Label the terminals of the syntax tree with the same labels or numbers as under step one in such a way that each functor in step one constitutes an element from the category of the syntax tree carrying the corresponding label. More precisely, make a connection from a numbered functor in the result structure to the lexical category in the syntax structure to which the word (lexical or syncategorimatic) belongs.

Fourth step:

Here we want to create one referential index (sometimes called a focus variable), for each noun phrase, and we shall construct a flow between the focus variable and certain other constituents. The referential indices correspond to those variables (here x and y) being part of the semantic structure.

The aim is to obtain that during parsing the resulting DCG must create a variable (a referential index) as an identifier for one of the semantic objects occuring in the semantic structure (here horse, apple etc.).

Fifth step:

Here the lexical flow is constructed as a flow connecting each textual word with an element of the semantic structure. In the example a lexical flow connects the word “horse” with the arguments of the noun category.

Sixth step:

Each edge in the semantic structure of step one can be designated by the labels of the two ends of the edge. Connect the nodes with the same labels in the syntax tree through a flow following the edges of the syntax tree.

Seventh step:

In this step we control that the arity is the same for each occurrence of a functor and we control the consistency of the local flow. This means that each nonterminal function symbol has the same number of arguments in every occurrence, and these arguments are connected to the surrounding nodes in the same way for every occurrence of the same syntax rule.

In our example the method will give us the following DCG:

```
s(A) --> np(B,C,A),vp(B,C).
np(D,E,F) --> det(D,G,E,F), n(D,G).
vp(H,I) --> v(H,J,K), np(J,K,I).
```

A slightly more complicated example could be the text “the reader undoubtly hopes Pilcher comes home to the typewriter soon” and here the intended semantic structure may be

```
undoubtly(the(x,reader(x)
              & the(y,typewriter(y)
                    & hopes(x,soon(to(y,home(comes(pilcher))))))))
```

(the resulting parser has been excluded due to space limitations).

3.2. An Application to Discourse Representation

Let us build upon the following little grammar

```
s -> np vp
np -> det n | det n rc | pron
vp -> v np
rc -> that vp
```

and let our system exploit the following pair of sample text and intended semantic representation

```
every man that owns a donkey beats it

[[i(x)&man(x)&i(y)&donkey(y)&own(x,y)] => [beat(x,y)]]
```

Then we get the following program generated automatically by means of our semantic meta parsing system

```
s(Z) --> np(X,Y,Z),vp(X,Y).
np(X,Z,W) --> det(X,Y,Z,W),n(X,Y).
np(X,Z,W) --> det(X,Y,Z,W),n(X,U),rc(X,U,Y).
np(X,Y,Y) --> pron(X).
vp(X,W) --> v(X,Y,Z),np(Y,Z,W).
rc(X,Y,Z) --> that(Y,W,Z),vp(X,W).
det(X,Y,Z,[i(X)&Y]=>[Z]) --> [every].
det(X,Y,Z,i(X)&Y&Z) --> [a].
pron(X,pron(X)) --> [it].
n(X,man(X)) --> [man].
v(X,Y,own(X,Y)) --> [owns].
that(X,Y,X&Y) --> [that].
```

If we augment this program with a simple and commonplace pronoun resolution program, it seems to be a feasible translator into the relevant discourse representation, comparable to Section 1.1. Notice that the construction of this part of the system is not automated.

3.3. Implementing Semantic Meta Parsing

Here follows a brief description of an implementation of semantic meta parsing as a Prolog program. More material is available in two theses with me as the supervisor [8, 14].

The topmost predicate of our Prolog program is the predicate 'inductor/2' defined in the following way

```
inductor(Readfile,Writefile) :-
    read_parametres(Readfile),
    sample_text(ES),
    sem_rep(RS),
    dataflow_structure(ES,RS,DF),
    generate_rules(DF,PR),
    postedit(PR,ER),
    write_program(ER,Writefile).
```

It includes a call of the predicate 'dataflow-structure/3' that implements the described method by automated construction of dataflow structures, with the seven steps built in like this

```
dataflow-structure(ES, RS, DF) :-
    variables(VA),
    numbering(RS, NR),                          % step one
    syntaxstructure(ES, SS),                    % step two
    binding(NR, SS, NS),                        % step three
    focusstream(NS, FS, VA, VA1),               % step four
    lexicalstream(FS, LS),                      % step five
    connection(NR, LS, FB, VA1),                % step six
    consistency(FB, DF),                        % step seven
    write('Dataflow-structure:'), write(DF), nl.
```

Many more details may be found in the appendix and in the two reports [8,14].

3.4. Discussion

In purely technical terms it is possible to follow Johnson and Kay's recommendation to operate with one and only one parsing program, irrespective of which kind of analysis you want. But as is apparent in the examples, the coupling to the individual applications tends to be rather complicated, even in utterly simple cases as the one described in Section 2.1. So it seems to be far more practically sensible to work with a meta system that for each individual application has the ability to produce automatically the intended corresponding translator. How this can be done was described rather briefly in Section 3.1, and the essential parts of an implementation in Prolog is given in Section 3.3 and the appendix.

It is considerably more pragmatically reasonable to avoid abstraction as far as possible and so to speak to express matters in as concrete a form as possible. The method of semantic meta parsing follows that principle. Any reader can convince himself that the resulting parsing program becomes more comprehensible and easier modifiable in this way. So in this respect we could be said to recommend semantic concreteness and generality in contrast to semantic abstraction.

Acknowledgements are due to the anonymous referees for their criticism and demands leading to a strongly improved paper.

References

[1] T. Andreasen, P.A. Jensen, J.F. Nilsson, P. Paggio, B.S. Pedersen, H.E. Thomsen, Content-based text querying with ontological descriptors, 199–219, *Data & Knowledge Engineering 48 (2)*, 2004.
[2] C.G. Brown and G. Koch (eds.), *Natural Language Understanding and Logic Programming III*, North-Holland, 1991.
[3] J. van Benthem and A. ter Meulen (eds.), *Handbook on Logic and Language*, North-Holland, 1997.
[4] M. A. Covington, *Natural Language Processing for Prolog Programmers*, Prentice Hall 1994.
[5] Hamido Fujita and Paul Johannesson (eds.), *New Trends in Software Methodologies, Tools and Techniques*, IOS Press, 2002.
[6] Hamido Fujita and Paul Johannesson (eds.), *New Trends in Software Methodologies, Tools and Techniques*, IOS Press, 2003.
[7] Hamido Fujita and Volker Gruhn (eds.), *New Trends in Software Methodologies, Tools and Techniques*, IOS Press, 2004.
[8] John Hansen, *Semantic Induction in Visual Prolog*, thesis (in Danish), DIKU, 1996.
[9] M. Johnson & M. Kay, Semantic abstraction and anaphora, in *COLING Proceedings* (1990) 17–27.
[10] H. Kamp and U. Reyle, *From Discours to Logic*, Kluwer, 1993.
[11] G. Koch, A linguistic method relevant for Lyee, 88–95, in [4], 2002.
[12] G. Koch, Some applications of a linguistics method related to Lyee, 112–119, in [5], 2003.
[13] G. Koch, On interpretation and abstraction in semantic meta parsing, 231–240, in [6], 2004.
[14] M. Vesterager and P.A. Jacobsen, *Induktor – a Translator Generator Based on Logico-Semantic Induction*, thesis (in Danish), DIKU, 1999.

4. Appendix

Here follows a listing of the essential parts of the semantic meta parser Inductor.

The main program is called inductor/2:

```
inductor(INDFIL, UDFIL) :-
   indlaes_parametre(INDFIL),
     listing,
   eksempelsaetning(ES),
   resultatstruktur(RS),
   dataflow_graf(ES, RS, DF),
   generer_regler(DF, PR),
   efterbehandling(PR, ER),
   udskriv_program(ER, UDFIL).
```

A procedure to read in the input file is

```
indlaes_parametre(INDFIL) :-
   consult(INDFIL),
   grammatik_ok.
```

grammatik_ok tests that the grammar is not left recursive (to avoid infinite loops).

The seven steps described in Section 3.1 are triggered by the procedure dataflow_graf/3:

```
dataflow_graf(ES, RS, DF) :-
   variabler(VA),
   nummerering(RS, NR),                       % step one
   syntaksstruktur(ES, SS),                   % step two
   binding(NR, SS, NS),                       % step three
   fokusstroem(NS, FS, VA, VA1),              % step four
   leksikalstroem(FS, LS),                    % step five
   forbinding(NR, LS, FB, VA1),               % step six
   konsistens(FB, DF),                        % step seven
   write('Dataflow-graf: '), write(DF), nl.
```

nummerering enumerates the objects in the intended result structure.

```
syntaksstruktur(ES, SS) :-
   startsymbol(S),
   e1_tilhoerer_e,
   opbyg_syntakstrae(S, ES, [], SS).
```

The procedure opbyg_syntakstrae builds a syntax tree in accordance with the given context-free grammar:

```
opbyg_syntakstrae([], ES, ES, []).
opbyg_syntakstrae(NT, ES1, ES2, [p(NT, DELSS)]) :-
   produktion(NT, LNT),
   opbyg_syntakstrae(LNT, ES1, ES2, DELSS).
opbyg_syntakstrae(NT, ES1, ES2, [p(NT, [LT])]) :-
   leksikon(NT, LT, _),
   select(LT, ES1, ES2).
opbyg_syntakstrae([DELLNT|RESTLNT], ES1, ES3, DS) :-
   opbyg_syntakstrae(DELLNT, ES1, ES2, DELDS),
   opbyg_syntakstrae(RESTLNT, ES2, ES3, RESTDS),
   append(DELDS, RESTDS, DS).
```

The procedure binding creates a correspondance between the corresponding parts of the intended result structure and the syntax structure:

```
binding([], SS, SS).
binding(T, SS, SS) :-
   atom(T).
binding(n(TAL, ST), p(NT, [LT]), p(n(TAL, NT), [LT])) :-
   atom(NT),
   leksikon(NT, LT, ST).
binding(n(TAL, ST), p(NT, LIST1), p(NT, LIST2)) :-
   binding(n(TAL, ST), LIST1, LIST2).
binding(n(TAL, ST), [DELSS|RESTNS], [DELNS|RESTNS]) :-
   binding(n(TAL, ST), DELSS, DELNS).
binding(n(TAL, ST), [DELNS|RESTSS], [DELNS|RESTNS]) :-
   binding(n(TAL, ST), RESTSS, RESTNS).
binding([DELNR|RESTNR], SS, NS) :-
   binding(DELNR, SS, NS1),
   binding(RESTNR, NS1, NS).
```

The new discourse referents (variables) are spread over the syntax structure by call of the predicates fokusstroem and fokusvariabler:

```
fokusstroem(NS, FS, VA1, VA2) :-
   fokusvariabler(VA1, NS, VA2, FV),
   konstruer_stroem(FV, FS).

fokusvariabler(VA, [], VA, []).
fokusvariabler(VA, T, VA, T) :-
   atom(T).
fokusvariabler(VA1, p(NT, NL), VA2, p(NT, [], FL)) :-
   not navnefrase(NT),
   fokusvariabler(VA1, NL, VA2, FL).
fokusvariabler(VA1, p(NT, NL), VA3, p(NT, [V], FL)) :-
   navnefrase(NT),
   select_variabel(V, VA1, VA2),
   fokusvariabler(VA2, NL, VA3, FL).
fokusvariabler(VA1, [DELNS|RESTNS], VA3, [DELFS|RESTFS]) :-
   fokusvariabler(VA1, DELNS, VA2, DELFS),
   fokusvariabler(VA2, RESTNS, VA3, RESTFS).
```

The remaining parts of the data flow are constructed by activation of the following procedure:

```
konstruer_stroem([],[]).
konstruer_stroem([T], [T]) :-
   atom(T).
konstruer_stroem(p(NT, VL, PL1), p(NT, VL, PL4)) :-
   udbred_ned(NT, VL, PL1, PL2),
   udbred_horisontalt(PL2, PL3),
   konstruer_stroem(PL3, PL4).
konstruer_stroem([DELFV|RESTFV],[DELFS|RESTFS]) :-
   konstruer_stroem(DELFV, DELFS),
   konstruer_stroem(RESTFV, RESTFS).
```

Chapter 6

Software Enterprise Modeling and Component Representation

New Trends in Software Methodologies, Tools and Techniques
H. Fujita and M. Mejri (Eds.)
IOS Press, 2005

Inference Rules of Semantic Dependencies in the Enterprise Modelling

Remigijus GUSTAS
Department of Information Systems, Karlstad University, 651 88 Karlstad, Sweden
Remigijus.Gustas@kau.se

Abstract. Enterprise models should have a capacity to describe consistently business processes across organisational and technical system boundaries. It would help system designers to understand why the technical system components are useful and how they fit into the overall organisational system. The implementation bias of many information system methodologies is a big problem for inconsistency and integrity control. The same implementation oriented foundations are often used in system analysis and design phase, without rethinking these concepts fundamentally. Common repository of most CASE tools does not guarantee the consistency of enterprise architectures for a reason that interplay among static and dynamic dependencies is not available. Enterprise modelling and integration should stick to the basic conceptualisation principle that prescribes analysis of only conceptually relevant aspects. It cannot be influenced by any implementation details. The consistency problems are best detectable and traceable at the conceptual layer. In this study on semantic dependencies, we demonstrate how various fundamental concepts from different classes of models can be interlinked and analysed together. An important result of this study is a set of inference rules. The inference capability is an intrinsic feature of logical approaches, but the conventional methods of system analysis have not yet dealt in sufficient detail with the inference principles.

Keywords. Enterprise Modeling, Integration of static and dynamic dependencies, inference rules

Introduction

The term of Enterprise Architecture (EA) has been used for many years within information system engineering community. It refers to various types of graphical representations that define how business, data, technology and software application structures (Spewak, 1992) are perceived from different points of view. The concept of enterprise in the context of information system development denotes a limited area of activity in organisation (Bubenko, 1993) that is of interest by a planner, owner, designer or builder (Zachman, 1996). In the Nineties, the term of enterprise architecture started to be used even by business managers, especially those involved in business process reengineering, to refer to the graphical descriptions of organizational processes. Today, enterprise models (yet another name of EA) denote a comprehensive graphical description of the syntactic, semantic and pragmatic relations across organizational and technical system boundaries (Gustas & Gustiene, 2004). For instance, when managers are talking about the alignment of information technology (IT) systems and applications with respect to business processes, they define graphical enterprise models, which demonstrate how the alignment should be achieved. US Government agencies are required by law to maintain EA, because of congressional legislation (Raines, 1997).

There are many approaches to define components of enterprise architecture. The Zachman framework (Zachman, 1996) is considered as a comprehensive guide of documents or blueprints that comprise any enterprise architecture. Typically, EA is defined in various perspectives such as the "what", "who", "where", "when" and "how". Various actors involved in the enterprise modelling usually concentrate on one of the following layers: the strategic layer (planner view), the conceptual (implementation independent) layer (owner view) and the implementation-oriented layer (designer and builder views). An integrated conceptual representation of the organisational and technical system is necessary to develop a holistic understanding of EA and to plan orderly transitional processes from the current to the target enterprise architecture. There are two basic challenges facing the overall enterprise engineering process: enterprise modelling and integration (Vernadat, 1996). Modelling involves visualisation or externalisation of EA from different points of view such as planner, owner, designer, builder and subcontractor. It involves representation and population of various cells of the Zachman Framework with instances of diagrams that represent the strategic (pragmatic), conceptual (across organisational and technical system boundaries) and the implementation dependent (logical, physical) system development perspectives. Nevertheless, views and perspectives do not make the enterprise architecture. To obtain value from the graphical representations, these documents must be integrated. The developers of enterprise engineering tools usually rely on a common repository. Since the interplay among semantic dependencies is not completely clear, the existence of a common repository does not guarantee the consistency and integrity of enterprise models.

Fragmented representations of EA are difficult to maintain even for very experienced system analysis and design specialists, not just for a reason that they deal with the same semantic details on different levels of abstraction, but because these representations are huge. Many experts have been building information systems for years, but just few of them have actually learned how to keep track of interdependencies among various diagram types. The difficulty resides in the implementation bias of many information system methodologies. The implementation-oriented diagrams are much more complex than conceptual models and thus they are difficult to trace. Sometimes, similar semantic constructs are applied in different perspectives without rethinking them fundamentally. These deficiencies of EA results in a difficulty to integrate views of two subcultures: business management and IT development personnel. The traditional information system analysis and design methods are not working well enough for the achievement of that purpose. For example, the UML (Booch et al., 1999) provides twelve standard diagram types for representation of a technical system solution. Nevertheless, it is very little known how to control consistency and integrity of these diagrams. To our knowledge, the UML foundation is not provided by any inference or reasoning rules. Another weakness is the focus on the technical system (logical) part and very little possibilities to define the organisational (would it be conceptual or strategic) system part. The underlying modelling foundation of the conventional information system modelling approaches is too weak for development of the semantic reasoning rules on EA. Inference rules at the conceptual layer (not the logical rules) are crucial to enable reasoning about organisational and technical process consistency.

This paper is organised as follows. The second and third section defines the basic elements and dependencies that are used for modelling of EA at the conceptual layer. In the fourth next section, the importance of critical quality aspects is discussed. The

Figure 1. The Action and Flow dependency.

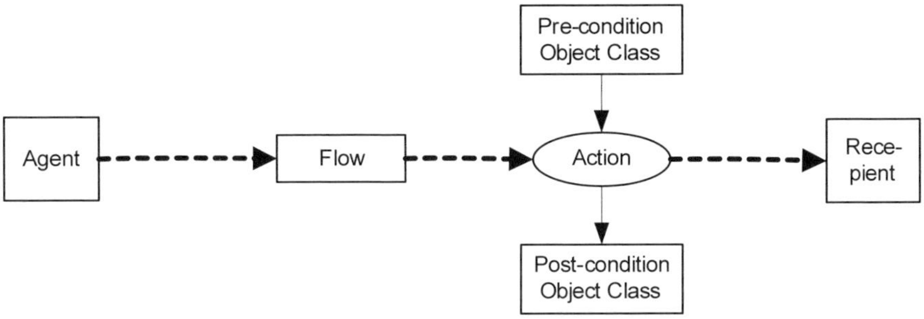

Figure 2. Extended graphical notation of the communication action.

inference rules are introduced in the fifth section. The conclusion section outlines the perspective of enterprise modelling in other areas and discusses the future work.

1. Basic Dynamic Dependencies in the Enterprise Modelling Approach

Understanding the strategic dependencies (Yu & Mylopoulos, 1994) is essential for reaching a consensus on how the current or future situation of enterprise architecture looks like. The dependencies between various technical and organisational components involved describe the "who" perspective. A strategic dependency link between two actors (agent and recipient) indicates that one actor depends on another actor. An instance of actor can be an individual, a group of people, an organisation, a machine, software or hardware component. The dependent actors in a diagram can be related by the actor dependency link (·····►). The actor dependency is usually seen as a physical, information or a decision flow between two participants. Graphical notation of the actor dependency between an agent and a recipient is presented in Fig. 1.

A strategic flow dependency link between actors at the conceptual level is defined as a communicative action. Thus, it is considered at the same time to be an action and a communication flow (Goldkuhl, 1995). An agent A initiates a flow F by using action C to achieve his goal (Gustas & Gustiene, 2004). If another actor B is a recipient of the same flow F, then such dependency is defined as (A ·····► B) /C(F). An ellipse notation is used to distinguish actions. The flow dependency represents a communication channel for transferring information or physical flow between agent and recipient. For instance, (Company ·····► Person) /Employ(Contract).

An action is typically changing a state of affairs, i.e. a state of an object that is instantiated in some class. Otherwise, the action is not purposeful. In other words, any action should be interpreted as an object transition. Cohesion of a transition dependency and communication dependency results into a more complex abstraction that defines two perspectives of action: static and behavioural. We will use an extended graphical notation to describe such a twofold nature of action. The extended communication action dependency between two states of the same object is represented Fig. 2.

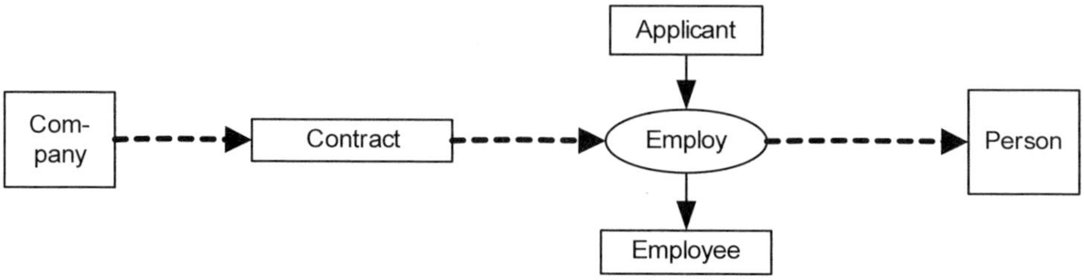

Figure 3. Communication action of Employ.

Actions are carried out by actors. At the same time, any action can be defined as a transition (—►) from the precondition state to the postcondition state. If an object is instantiated in a precondition class D, then, by using action C, the transition to the postcondition class E can be performed. This is represented by (D —► E) /C(F). For instance, (Applicant —► Employee) /Employ(Contract). Graphical example of the transition dependency is illustrated in Fig. 3.

The transition dependency typically defines a semantic relationship between two states of the same object. Such transitions are normally considered as the "how" perspective. Both the transition and communication dependencies describe a very important part of knowledge about business processes. Unfortunately, many communication-based approaches often neglect some behavioural aspects of the state transition and vice versa, many software engineering approaches disregard the dependencies of communication (Action Technologies, 1993), (Winograd & Flores, 1986), (Gustas, 2000).

A simple description of an object's state, for example, in terms of a finite-state machine, would mean definition whether an object exist or not in some state. However, an individual that just exists in a particular state, without relating it to other objects is not very useful. Analysts need to know how and why the associations of object classes are going to be changed and what are the static dependencies among them. Fundamentally, two kinds of changes occur during any transition: declassification of object from the current class and classification of the same object to the next class. Sometimes, it is referred as a reclassification event (Martin & Odell, 1998). A declassification event typically removes an existing object and classification event creates an object. Different classes of objects are characterised by at least one entirely new attribute. The importance of such noteworthy difference is essential to understand semantics of communication action.

2. Interplay among the Basic Static and Dynamic Dependencies

The static concept dependencies define the "what" perspective. These dependencies are stemming from various semantic models that are introduced in the area of information system analysis and design. For instance, semantics of static dependencies in object-oriented approaches are defined as cardinality constraints, which represent a minimum and maximum number of one set of objects that can be associated to another set of objects. Graphical notation (Hoffer et al., 2004), (Martin & Odell, 1998) of typical associations is represented in Fig. 4.

Note: the meaning of '*' is 'many' (i.e. more than one), the meaning of '?' is 'undefined', which corresponds to a constraint less link (0,*) or to a link with unspecified

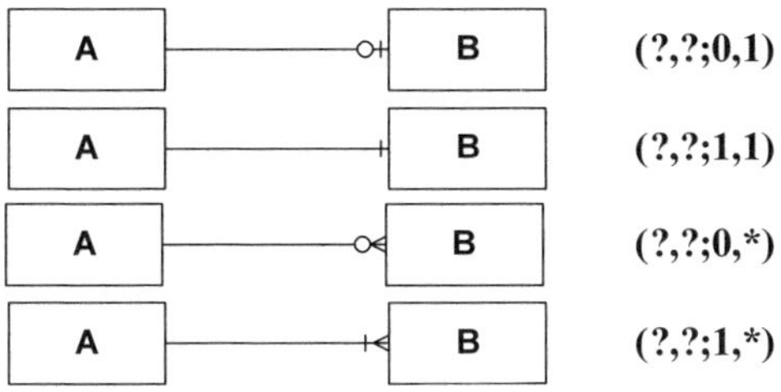

Figure 4. Graphical notation of cardinality constraints.

cardinality constraints. Notations that are commonly used at the initial phase of concept modelling have to provide a clear understanding of cardinality constraints in both directions. The common static dependencies that may be specified between any two concepts A and B are as follows:

1. (0,1;1,1) – Injection dependency which will be denoted by A ===> B,
2. (1,1;1,1) – Bijection dependency (A ←→ B),
3. (0,* ;1,1) – Total Functional dependency (A ⟶ B),
4. (1,1;1,*) – Surjection dependency (A ⟵⟶> B),
5. (0,1;1,*) – Surjective partial functional dependency (A ==>> B),
6. (1,*;1,*) – Mutual multivalued dependency (A ≪⟶≫ B),
7. (0,* ;1,*) – Total multivalued dependency (A ⟶≫ B),
8. (0,1;0,1) – Partial injection dependency, (A |==> B),
9. (0,* ;0,1) – Functional (partial) dependency (A ⟼ B),
10. (0,*;0,*) – Multivalued (partial) dependency (A|⟶≫ B).

In the final phase of enterprise modelling, only first five dependencies, from a total number of ten, are used. These totally applicable links are considered as basic concept attribute links. The remaining five dependencies can be expressed in terms of more primitive ones. It should be noted that not basic dependencies are used without any limitations in the conventional approaches of system analysis and design, except cases No 6, 7 and 10. Many-to-many associations in the design phase are normally converted to a new aggregated concept, which can be defined as an aggregation or composition of concepts A and B. The other relations, such as No 8 and 9 as a rule are easily transformable to one of the basic dependencies, by using the inheritance link. This process is entitled as eliminating of semantic holes (Gustas, 1994).

Dependencies can be shared by extracting and attaching them to a more general concept. Inheritance (⟶▸) is as a core link to connect a specific concept to more general one. It enables evolution of the specialisation hierarchy without information loss and is similar to the dynamic specialisation (Leonard, 2004). Therefore, the inheritance dependency in the enterprise modelling is richer than the classical inheritance. Graphical notations of the basic static dependencies are presented in Fig. 5.

Composition is a conceptual dependency link (multivalued —< and singlevalued —<▸), which is used to relate a whole to other concepts that are viewed as parts. The composition dependency in the enterprise modelling is a more restricted link as compared to other methodologies. It is characterised by the following properties: 1) a part cannot simultaneously belong to more than one whole. If it does belong – then it must be the same whole, 2) a part and a whole are created at the same time, 3) once a part is created, it is terminated at the same time the whole is terminated. This definition is

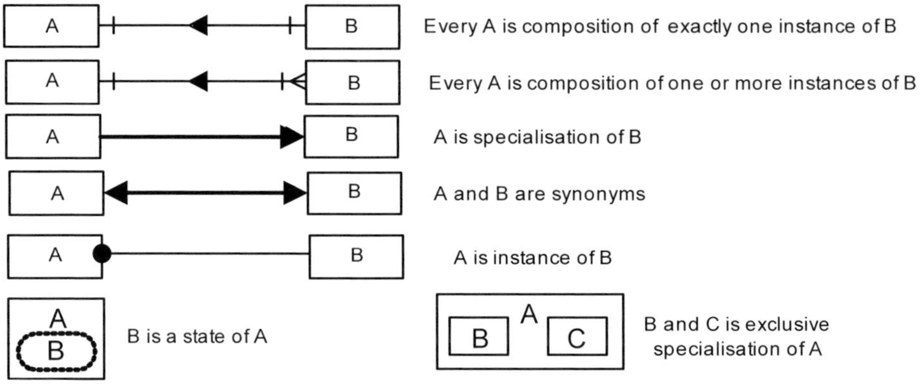

Figure 5. Graphical notation of the basic static dependencies.

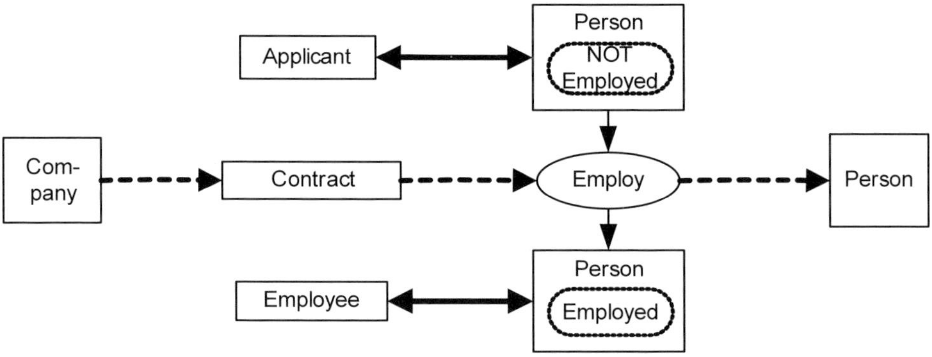

Figure 6. Communication action of Employ with synonymous concepts.

more strict as compared to a composition that is used in the object – oriented approach (Maciaszek, 2001), (Stumpf & Teague, 2005). Not just a part, but also a whole is dependent on a part as well. Therefore, the cardinality is never equal to zero. This difference is significant, since it has an impact on update operations (see inference rules). The creation and removal of objects is always propagated to its parts and vice versa.

The introduced set of dependencies is used together with the transition dependency that was defined in the previous section. The transition dependency can be used to specify semantics of a possible state change. An actual state always persists until the action terminates. Termination of action causes a transition to the next state. The graphical notation of transition dependency Employ (Person [NOT Employed]) —▸ Person [Employed] is represented in Fig. 6.

Since every transition represents reclassification of an object (from one class to another), the transition dependency in the enterprise modelling is not linking explicitly two states like in Object-Process methodology (Dori, 2002). Instead, the object transition dependency connects two classes of objects. For instance, two states such as 'NOT Employed' and 'Employed' are attached to a concept of Person by using an operation of restriction (Gustas, 1994). It results in two new compound names such as Person [NOT Employed] and Person [Employed] that are representing more specific subclasses of Person.

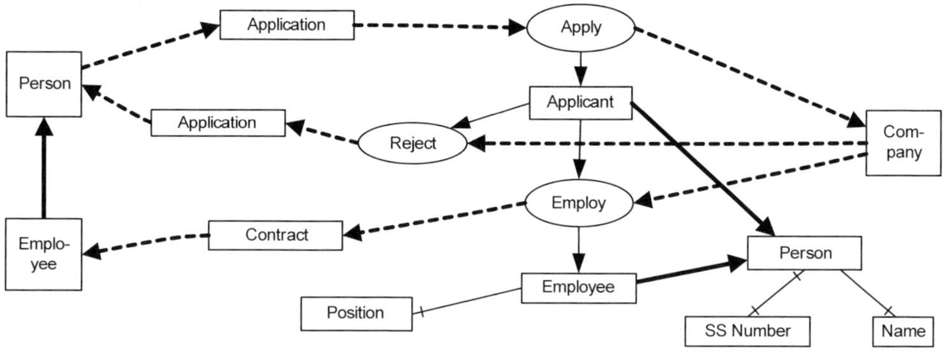

Figure 7. Graphical example of the integrated static and dynamic description.

In the object oriented-approach (Martin & Odell, 1998) fundamentally two kinds of changes may occur: creation and removal of an object in a class. Sometimes, objects are passing several states, and then are destroyed. An action of object removal will be specified as follows: **(PRECONDITION CLASS → ⊥) /ACTION( )**. Here: ⊥ is an empty element that indicates the initial or final state in a life cycle of object. A graphical notation of dependency between a final state and action, that defines the deletion operation of object, can be viewed as a special case of a state-transition dependency, which is not provided by a next state. Removal of an object terminates all its associations. And visa versa, a creation of an object must bring all its pre defined static dependencies into existence. The creation action of an object in a particular class can be specified by the following expression: **(⊥ → POSTCONDITION CLASS) /ACTION( )**.

The basic dependencies are very important to understand the semantics of any communication action. A typical action workflow loop (Action Technologies, 1993) can be defined in terms of two or even three communicative action dependencies between actors. By matching the actor dependencies from agents to recipients, one can explore opportunities that are available to these actors. We shall illustrate the basic semantic dependencies in one action workflow loop between two actors (Person and Company) together with the creation, destruction and transition actions, which are represented in Fig. 7.

This diagram illustrates that a person is authorised to apply for a job by sending an application to a company. If a company accepts the application, then an object of applicant is created. According to the business definition that prescribes the diagram, a company is obliged either to employ or to reject the application. If company decides to reject, then the object of applicant is destroyed (Reject action is triggered by Company), otherwise it is reclassified to employee (Employ action is triggered). Please note that object of Employee (the same as Applicant) is a specialisation of a Person concept, but it is characterised by the additional attribute of Position. The two other attributes (Name and SS Number) must be instantiated at the time when the applicant is created. Otherwise, the Apply action is rejected. In this diagram, the attribute of Position is essential to characterise the semantic difference between two concepts such as Applicant and Employee. If employee is terminated by the next action, then the association to position will be removed. In such a way, sequences of communicative actions prescribe sequences of the update operations, which should be defined at the implementation dependent layer. The object oriented way of interpretation of enterprise models was demonstrated in the other paper (Gustas & Jakobsson, 2004). Additionally, such diagrams at the conceptual layer may serve as a basis to analyse obligations and authorisations of the actors involved. For instance, if (Person ┈┈► Company) /Apply (Application) then (Company ┈┈► Employee)/Employ (Contract) or (Company ┈┈► Person)/ Reject (Application).

3. Semantic Consistency and Integrity

Information system quality (Gustiene, 2003) is essential for understanding of the organisational and technical system fitness. Nevertheless, it is very little known on how the semantic quality problems might be treated in a systematic way. Surely, various diagrammatic descriptions that humans employ for representation of enterprise architectures on different levels of abstraction should be evaluated by certain quality criteria. Lindland, Sindre and Solvberg (Lindland et al., 1994) have proposed a framework for understanding the syntactic, semantic and pragmatic quality. The syntactic quality can be characterised by correctness of modelling language. A better pragmatic quality of system specification would mean agreement on what is going to be achieved. The pragmatic quality is build upon the semantic quality. Two characteristic features of the semantic quality are validity and completeness (Krogstie, 2003). Validity means that all statements in the model are consistent and relevant to the problem. Completeness means that the enterprise model contains all relevant statements. It is not easy to apply these two criteria in practice, because we do not know how the semantic quality can be controlled. The semantic quality criteria are still poorly analysed in the literature.

The most difficult part of enterprise modelling is arriving at a coherent, complete and consistent semantic description of a new system that is defined across organisational and technical boundaries. The ability to describe essential system solutions in a clear and sufficiently rich way is acknowledged as crucial in many areas including software requirements engineering, object oriented system design (Booch et al., 1999), structured analysis (Yourdon, 1989), conceptual modelling, e-service composition (Hull et al., 2003), semantic web (Daconta et al., 2003), knowledge management and information system modelling (Hoffer et al., 2004). One of the major difficulties using conventional system engineering approaches is that very little support for semantic consistency control is available. Such needs are especially acute for teams, which are operating in a collaborative enterprise modelling environment or they are involved in joint information system development sessions, where different perspectives (e.g. static and dynamic), different points of view and system descriptions on different levels of abstraction are used.

The semantic consistency criterion refers to whether or not conceptual descriptions are compatible. Violation of compatibility gives rise for inconsistency. CASE tools have analysis facilities that typically control some type of inconsistency in a single perspective. For example, when designer is drawing a data flow diagram (Hoffer et al., 2004) and decomposition of process takes place, most CASE tools will automatically place the inflows and outflows on the lower level of abstraction. Deleting such flows would cause the diagrams out of balance. CASE tools that typically support methods for identification of discrepancies during the process of database view integration (Batini et al., 1986) are concentrating just on consistency of the static perspective. None of the information system modelling approaches is dealing with the semantic

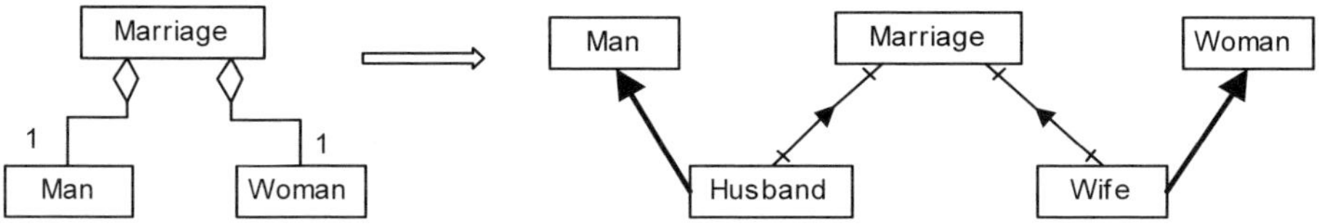

Figure 8. Interpretation of aggregation through the basic dependencies.

consistency in few perspectives at the same time. The difficulty lies that interplay between static and dynamic dependency types is not clear.

The usefulness of great number of semantic dependencies in the area of information system analysis and design is another open problem. For instance, many dependencies that are introduced in database theory encounter problems with missing attribute values. These problems result from the fact either that the instance of the attribute is temporally unknown, but applicable, or that its value can never be known, because the attribute is not applicable. For unambiguous specification of system semantics, in the final phase of enterprise modelling, only basic dependencies are used. These dependencies are totally applicable. Not basic dependencies can be eliminated in various ways. This process is entitled as semantic normalisation. It is achieved by defining alternative courses of actions or defining more precise semantics of the static links. Semantic normalisation of dependencies helps analysts to improve the semantic quality of diagrams and to use a full power of inference rules. Normalisation of concept diagrams is performed through appropriate transformations. Some methods call this process as elimination of semantic holes (Gustas, 1994), strengthening or restricting (Borgida, 1984), (Brachman & Schmolze, 1985). In object-oriented approach, the transformation process is called sharpening the meaning of concepts (Martin & Odell, 1998). The diagrams, which are defined in terms of the basic dependencies, have ability to communicate unambiguously the semantics of enterprise models. This idea is illustrated in Fig. 8. We are not going any further into this subject for the reason of space limitations.

Aggregation and composition that is used in object oriented system design is a weaker form of the enterprise modelling composition dependency, which was defined in the previous chapter. For example, the concept of Marriage can be defined as an aggregation of Man and Woman. It is interpreted in terms of the basic dependencies as the composition of Husband and Wife that are specialisations of Man and Woman. Composition and specialisation dependencies are very useful semantic relations, because they clearly represent how destruction and creation operations are propagated in the corresponding hierarchies. For instance, if an object of Wife is removed then the object of Marriage and Husband will cease to exist. Despite of that, the same object is not declassified (Leonard, 2004) as an instance of Woman.

Enterprise modelling approach has no implementation bias (Gustas & Gustiene, 2002), (Gustas & Gustiene, 2004) like many other information system methodologies. It follows the basic conceptualisation principle (Griethuisen, 1982). Enterprise modelling and integration is dealing exceptionally with the conceptually relevant aspects and it is not influenced by the possible implementation decisions. Many information system methodologies are not following the basic conceptualisation principle. Consequently, the information system modelling quality suffers significantly. Consistency control at the conceptual layer is critical, because it is a driving force for a change management in a systematic way. Since conceptual models define system semantics, they help designers to understand why the technical system components are useful and how they fit into the overall organisational system. The traditional methods of information system analysis are based on the idea of dividing the technical system representations into three major parts that are known as data architecture, application architecture and technology architecture. Although there is a great power in separation of different technical architectures, there is also a deep fallacy in such orientation. One consequence is the difficulty to apply the automated reasoning rules for inconsistency analysis of the isolated views. Such system development tradition is not taking into account interdependencies that are crucial to glue the static and dynamic aspects of the enterprise models.

4. Inference Rules of Semantic Dependencies

System analysts and designers may concurrently perceive and represent concept dependencies in a number of ways. Similarities and differences are not difficult to identify, if just the basic set of the static and dynamic dependencies is used. Discrepancies among various views can be automatically detected by using a specific set of inference rules. Not all structural differences of enterprise models are interpreted as semantic conflicts. Some dependencies can be viewed as weaker and some of them as stronger. A set of the weaker dependencies can be derived according to the following inference rules:

1) **if A ===> B then A ⟶ B,**
2) **if A ===> B then A ==>> B,**
3) **if A —<▶ B then A —< B,**
4) **A ===> B, B ===> A if and only if A ⟷ B,**
5) **A ==>> B, B ⟶ A if and only if A ⟵⟶> B,**
6) **A —▶ B, B —▶ A if and only if A ◀▶ B.**

A generalisation hierarchy consists of interconnected concepts by inheritance links on different levels of abstraction. In the enterprise modelling, not like in object-oriented methods, all kind of the basic dependency links could be inherited (Gustas, 1998) according to the special inference rules:

1) **if A —▶ B, B —▶ C then A —▶ C,**
2) **if A —▶ B, B ===> C then A ===> C,**
3) **if A —▶ B, B ⟶ C then A ⟶ C,**
4) **if A —▶ B, B ==>> C then A ==>> C,**
5) **if A —▶ B, B —< C then A —< C,**
6) **if A —▶ B, B →▸ C then A →▸ C.**

The object – oriented tools take advantage of inheritance just for attributes and operations. The presented six inference rules demonstrate the inheritance capability of the communication and transition dependencies. Such dependencies are going together with the communication action. For instance, if Manager —▶ Employee, Employee →▸ Person[NOT Employed] /Terminate(Employee.SS number) then Manager →▸ Person[NOT Employed] /Terminate(Employee.SS number). Graphical illustration of the same dependency is given in Fig. 9.

Clearly, the derived transition dependency link is redundant and, therefore, it can be removed by using an appropriate semantic normalisation procedure.

The semantic quality of diagrams can be improved by eliminating ambiguity of concepts. It can be achieved by the following inference rules:

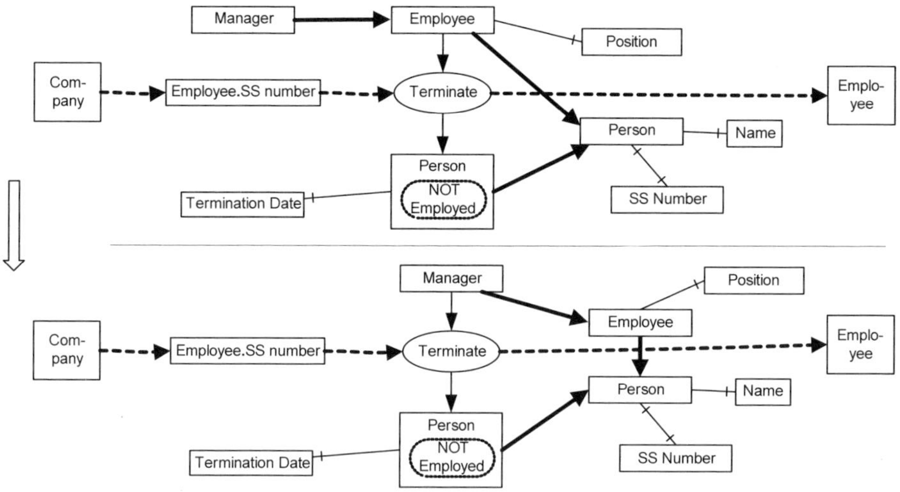

Figure 9. Graphical illustration of the inherited transition dependency.

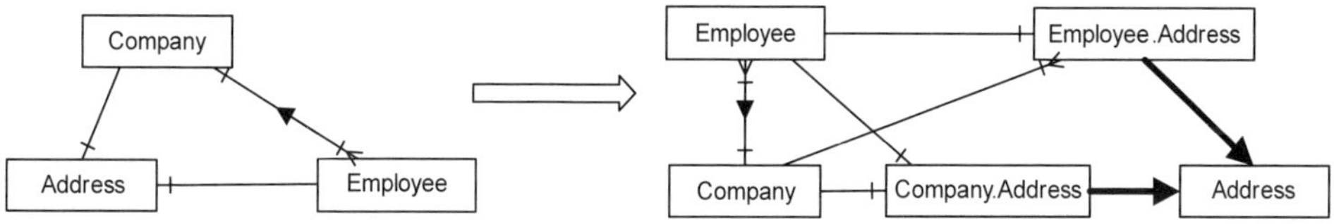

Figure 10. Inference rules with the prefixing operation.

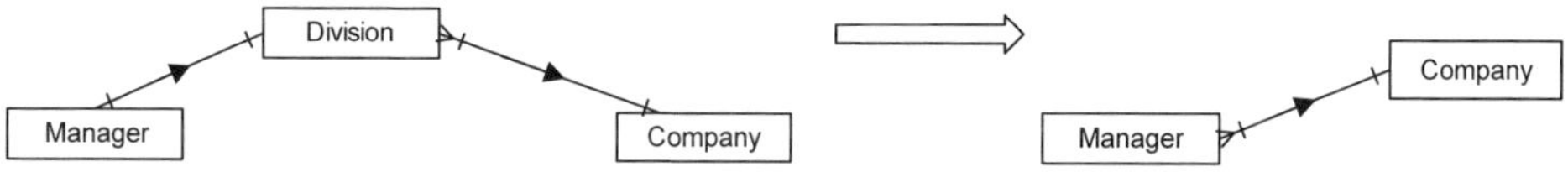

Figure 11. Transitiveness of the composition dependency.

1) **if A ===> B, B ===> C then A ===> B.C, B.C ➞ C,**
2) **if A ⟶ B, B ⟶ C then A ⟶ B.C, B.C ➞ C,**
3) **if A ==>> B, B ==>> C then A ==>> B.C, B.C ➞ C.**

Here **B.C** is the operation of prefixing C in the context of concept B (Gustas, 1994).

The prefixing rules are useful to resolve ambiguity of concepts. Since Address is considered as an attribute of two concepts, it may be perceived in two ways as a company address or as an employee address. The prefixing rules is an important technique for resolving ambiguity of concepts that are used in different contexts. Conceptual representations of ontologies (Daconta et al, 2003) have not yet dealt with the concept of context. Illustration of the prefixing operation is presented in Fig. 10.

The composition dependency is transitive. It is characterised by the following property: **if A ≻— B, B ≻— C then A ≻— C**. Graphical illustration of the inference rule is presented in Fig. 11.

A composition hierarchy is quite useful to analyse how various transition dependencies are propagated along the operations.

The basic communication dependencies together with the composition and inheritance links constitute a formal basis for inconsistency analysis and view integration in

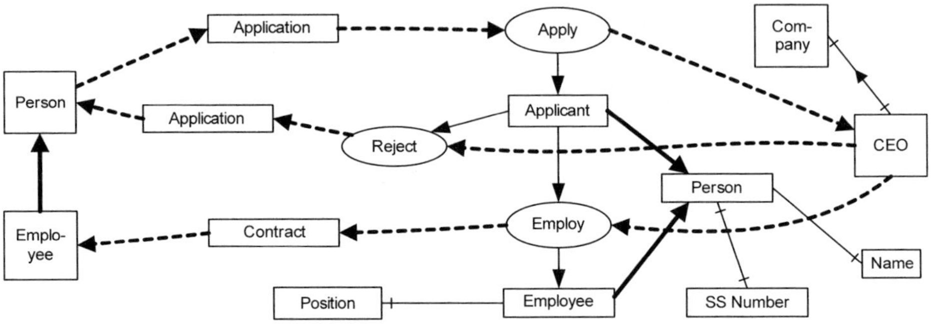

Figure 12. Illustration of propagation and inheritance of the communication links.

enterprise modelling. It should be noted that the communication dependency between two actors might be refined in terms of the object transition between two concepts. New concept is always characterised in terms of a different set of the static dependencies, which define the contents of change in the receiving organisational or technical component. The actor communication links are inherited by the more specific concepts and are propagated along the singlevalued composition hierarchy. The inference rules are as follows:

1) **if A ·····▶ B, B ◀▷— C then A ·····▶ C,**
2) **if A ◀▷— B, A ·····▶ C then B ·····▶ C,**
3) **if A ──▶ B, B ·····▶ C then A ·····▶ C,**
4) **if A ──▶ B, C ·····▶ B then C ·····▶ A.**

For instance, if Employee ──▶ Person, (Person ·····▶ Company) /Apply (Application) then (Employee ·····▶ Company) /Apply(Application). Illustration of how the communication dependencies are propagated along with the composition hierarchy is represented in Fig. 12.

According to the presented inference rules, the communication actions of Apply, Reject and Employ are relevant for CEO, but at the same time they are propagated to Company (see the graphical representation in Fig. 7).

An instantiation dependency (≤) indicates that an object is an instance of a concept. The instantiation is the reverse side of the classification dependency (see the notation in chapter 3). The classification dependency is characterised by the following inference rules:

1) **if A ≤ B, B ──▶ C, then A ≤ C.**
2) **if C ≤ A, B ──▶ A, ~ (C ≤ B) then C ≤ ¬B, ¬B ──▶ A,**
3) **if C ≤ A, B ──▶ A, ~ (C ≤ ¬B) then C ≤ B.**

Here: ¬ is the operation of concept negation (Gustas, 1994), ~ is the logical negation.

For instance, if IBM ≤ Company, Company ──▶ Organisation then IBM ≤ Organisation, if John Smith ≤ Employee, Manager ──▶ Employee, ~ (John Smith ≤ Manager) then John Smith ≤ ¬Manager, ¬Manager ──▶ Employee (note that ¬Manager concept in a natural language corresponds to 'NOT Manager'). Since precondition and postcondition class object sets are exclusive, the last two inference rules have some important consequences for system model evolution and integration. The rules can be implemented by the CASE tools to generate hidden semantic details in the dynamic

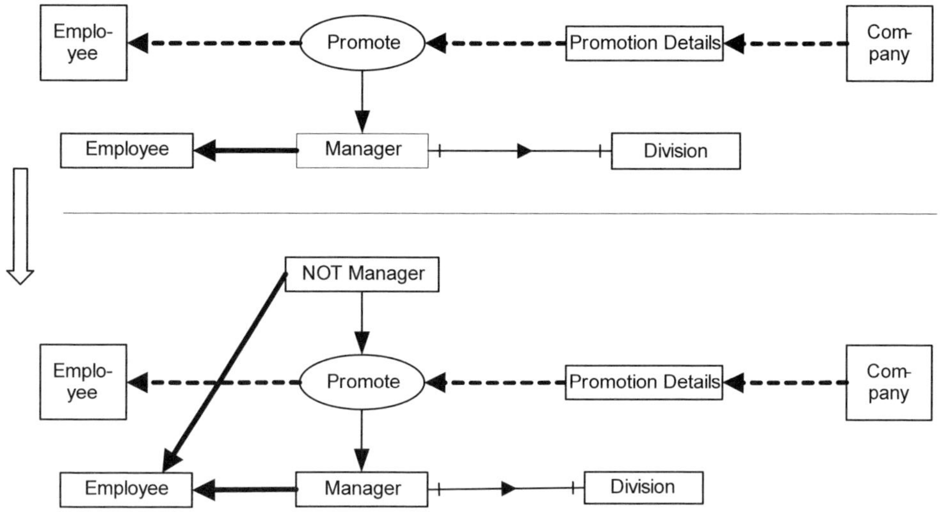

Figure 13. Generation of the negated concept and inheritance dependency.

part of a diagram. Example of automatic generation of the new concept (NOT Manager) together with the transition and inheritance dependency is graphically represented in Fig. 13.

It is not difficult to prove validity of the following rule:

(⊥→ E) /A( ), E ⟶ G if and only if (¬E → E) A( ), ¬E ⟶ G, E ⟶ G.

According to the presented graphical example, for an employee object to be promoted to a Manager (see the Promote action), he must be instantiated first as a NOT Manager. Automatic generation and visualisation of hidden semantic links is useful for conceptual integration of communication actions from semantically similar, but structurally differently defined interaction loops. For instance, inference rules justify integration of two diagrams that are represented in Fig. 14.

Instances of concept identifiers are viewed as objects of the same concept class. These objects are defined according to the following rule:

if X ≤ A.B, A ⟷ A.B then X ≤ A[B = X], A[B = X] ⟶ A.

Here: A[B = X] is the operation of concept A restriction by the condition [B = X].

Inference rules of instances might remind inferences in the predicate logic. The logical inferences such as, **if X is A and A has C, then X has C**, can be derived from the previous rule in combination with inference rules of the inheritance dependency. For instance: if IBM ≤ Company, Company[Name = IBM] ⟶ Company, Company ⟶ Address then Company[Name = IBM] ⟶ Address.

5. Concluding Remarks and Outlook

Organizational or technical system components in the enterprise modelling approach are viewed as actors. The organizational system part might consist of humans, departments, companies, etc., and the technical system part is typically composed of software or hardware components. Communication flow dependencies among actors of various

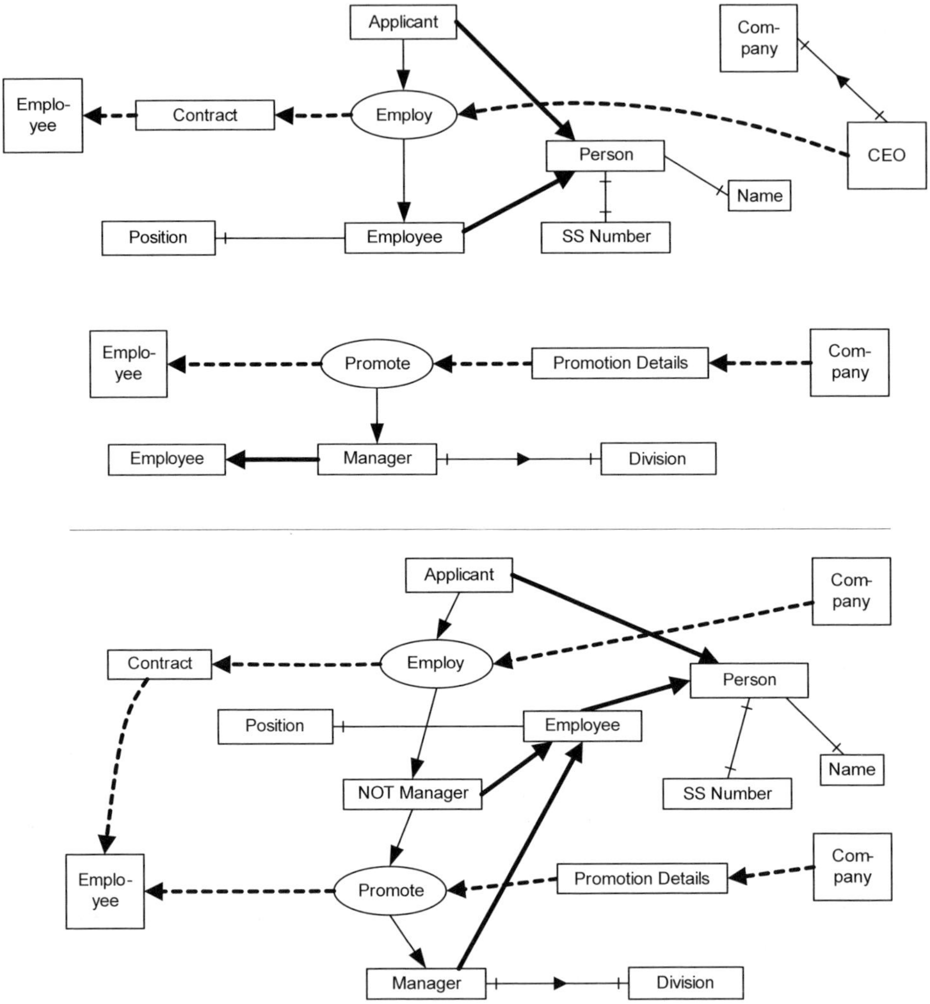

Figure 14. Integration of communication actions from different interaction loops.

types together with the actor composition and generalization links are used to refine enterprise architectures. The inference rules of semantic dependencies are critical for inconsistency detection between more specific and more general levels on various levels of abstraction. Therefore, integrity among dependencies, which are specified by various people such as information technology planners, business owners, system designers, users and builders, can be controlled in a more systematic way. The key issue of enterprise modelling is graphical description and motivation of the true information needs from the point of different actors involved.

A starting point of the enterprise modelling is implementation independent. It is introduced for the purpose of describing information system architectures across technical and organisational boundaries. Currently, we aim at the extended enterprise modelling approach with reasoning rules and engineering process that is similar to what architects use when constructing buildings. The graphical models are useful for visualisation and reasoning about the semantic consistency of information system at the implementation independent layer of abstraction. Since UML is a de facto industry standard, using it is quite reasonable on the implementation dependent layer of abstraction (Gustas & Jakobsson, 2004). Nevertheless, UML is not provided by any automatic reasoning or inference rules. The presented set of inference rules is critical for inconsistency control on the conceptual layer, because it makes possible to use just one diagram type for semantic definition of the entire system.

Various studies of enterprise engineering problems in different companies and in the public sector have demonstrated that a consistent and integrated conceptual representation is necessary to understand orderly transitional processes from the current to the target enterprise architecture. Information system requirements need to be captured, visualised and agreed upon. Just as the complex buildings or machines require explicit representations of their design structures, so does overall enterprise architecture. The static and dynamic dependencies are not analysed in isolation. Therefore, the semantic modelling process can have some assistance for the integrity and consistency control across various views and perspectives.

Enterprise models can be represented as ontological descriptions that are defined and published using XML artefacts. Graphical descriptions of various services on the Internet are subject for search, change, analysis and integration (OASIS BCM, 2003) across technical and organisational boundaries. Service representations should include not just software components, but definition of interoperation details among various business actors involved. A self-describing nature of services on the Internet and particularly the ability to define requirements for business collaborations in terms of enterprise models would provide significant competitive advantages. Recent developments in the area of semantic web (Berners-Lee et al., 2001) give us indication that enterprise modelling can provide the automated support needed for e-business integration at the strategic and conceptual layer. It has the potential to reduce web-based system development complexity and costs, to increase e-business re-engineering efficiency and to identify new revenue streams. However, before the collaborative enterprise engineering becomes reality, there are a number of challenging problems that need to be solved. The most important fundamental issues include e-service composition and integration.

The term of ontology is used in many different senses. Many researchers of semantic web would use the notion of ontology to call a diagram, which represents a specification of a conceptualisation. The most typical ontology for the semantic web has quite simple static structure and a set of inference rules. Additionally, e-service architecture should define its actors, concepts, actions and business relationships. Enterprise modelling can be applied as an approach for definition of service oriented architectures. The model is sufficiently rich to express the static and dynamic structure of available services. A communication action is fundamental enterprise modelling construct. It defines a linkage between transitions of objects and physical actors, who typically initiate or are affected by object transitions. Therefore, this construct helps to cross a boundary between two completely different types of conceptual representations. Definition of a communication action in such a way is critical for the ontological definition of services, because the semantic diagrams are complemented with a capacity to define the actor interoperation details.

References

[1] Action Technologies, (1993), Action Workflow Analysis Users Guide, Action Technologies.
[2] Batini, C., Lenzerini, M. & Navathe, B.L. (1986), A Comparative Analysis of Methodologies for Database Schema Integration, ACM Computing Surveys, Vol. 18, No. 4, 323–363.
[3] Berners-Lee, T., Hendler, J. & Lassila, O. (2001), The semantic Web, Scientific American, May 2001.
[4] Booch, G., Rumbaugh, J. & Jacobsson, I. (1999), The Unified Modelling Language User Guide, Addison Wesley Longman, Inc., Massachusetts.
[5] Borgida, A.T. (1984), "Generalisation/Specialisation as a Basis for Software Specification. On Conceptual Modelling", M. Brodie, J. Mylopoulos, J.W. Schmidt (eds.), On Conceptual Modelling, Springer-Verlag, New York, pp. 87–112.
[6] Brachman, R. & Schmolze, J.G. (1985), An Overview of the KLONE Knowledge Representation System, Cognitive science, 9(2), pp. 171–212, 1985.
[7] Bubenko, J.A. (1993), "Extending the Scope of Information Modelling", Fourth International Workshop on Deductive Approach to Information Systems and Databases, Polytechnical University of Catalonia, 73–97.
[8] Daconta, M.C., Obrst, L.J. & Smith, K.T. (2003), The semantic Web: A Guide to the Future of XML, Web Serwices, and Knowledge Management, Wiley, Indianapolis.
[9] Dori, D. (2002), Object-Process Methodology: A Holistic System Paradigm, Springer, Berlin.
[10] van Griethuisen, J.J. (1982), Concepts and Terminology for the Conceptual Schema and Information Base, Report ISO TC97/SC5/WG5, No 695.
[11] Goldkuhl, G. (1995), Information as Action and Communication, in Dahlbom, B. (ed.), The Infological Equation – Essays in Honor of Börje Langefors, Göteborg University, Sweden, pp. 63–79.
[12] Gustas, R. (1994), Towards Understanding and Formal Definition of Conceptual Constraints. Information Modelling and Knowledge Bases VI, IOS Press, pp. 381–399.
[13] Gustas, R. (1998), "Integrated Approach for Modelling of Semantic and Pragmatic Dependencies of Information Systems", Conceptual Modelling – ER'98, Springer, pp. 121–134.
[14] Gustas, R. (2000), Integrated Approach for Information System Analysis at the Enterprise Level, Enterprise Information Systems, Kluwer Academic Publishers, pp. 81–88.
[15] Gustas, R. and Gustiene, P. (2002), Extending Lyee Methodology using the Enterprise Modelling Approach, Frontiers in Artificial Intelligence and applications, IOS Press, Amsterdam, pp. 273–288.
[16] Gustas, R. & Gustiene, P. (2004), Towards the Enterprise Engineering Approach for Information System Modelling across Organisational and Technical Boundaries, Enterprise Information Systems V, Kluwer Academic Publisher, Netherlands, pp. 204–215.
[17] Gustas, R. & Jakobsson, L. (2004), Enterprise Modelling of Component Oriented Information System Architectures, New Trends in Software Methodologies, Tools and Techniques, IOS Press, pp. 88–102.
[18] Gustiene, P. (2003), On Desirable Qualities of Information System Specifications, 10th International Conference On Concurrent Engineering: Research and Applications, Madeira Island, Portugal, pp. 1279–1288.
[19] Hoffer, J.A., George, J.F. & Valacich J.S. (2004), Modern System Analysis and Design, Pearson Prentice Hall, New Jersey.
[20] Hull, R., Christophides, V. & Su, J. (2003), E-services: A look Behind the Curtain, ACM PODS, San Diego, CA.
[21] Krogstie, J. (2003), Evaluating UML Using a Generic Quality Framework, UML and Unified Process, IDEA Group, ISBN: 1-931777-44-6.
[22] Leonard, M. (2004), IS Engineering Getting out of Classical System Engineering, Enterprise Information Systems V, Kluwer Academic Publishers, pp. 35–45.
[23] Lindland, O.I., Sindre, G. and Solvberg, A. (1994), Understanding Quality in Conceptual Modelling, IEEE Software, (11, 2).
[24] Martin, J., Odell, J.J. (1998), Object-Oriented Methods: A Foundation (UML edition), Prentice-Hall, Englewood Cliffs, New Jersey.
[25] Maciaszek, L.A. (2001), Requirements Analysis and System Design, Addison Wesley.
[26] OASIS BCM (2003), Business-Centric Methodology Specification, Version 0.10. Available: http://www.businesscentricmethodology.com [accessed June 9, 2005].
[27] Raines, F.D. (1997), Memorandum for the Heads of Executive Departments and Agencies. Available: http://www.whitehouse.gov/omb/memoranda/m97-16.html [accessed June 9, 2005].
[28] Spewak, S.H. (1992), Enterprise Architecture Planning: Developing a Blueprint for Data, Applications and Technology, John Wiley & Sons.
[29] Storey, V.C. (1993), Understanding Semantic Relationships, VLDB Journal, F Marianski (ed.), Vol. 2, pp. 455–487.

[30] Stumpf, R. & Teague, L. (2005), Object Oriented System Analysis and Design with UML, Pearson Prentice Hall, New Jersey.
[31] Vernadat, F.B. (1996), Enterprise Modeling and Integration: principles and applications, Chapman & Hall.
[32] Winograd, T. & Flores, R. (1986), Understanding Computers and Cognition: A New Foundation for Design, Ablex Norwood, N.J.
[33] Yourdon, E. (1989), Modern Structured Analysis, Prentice-Hall, Englewood Cliffs, N.J.
[34] Yu, E. & Mylopoulos, J. (1994), "From E-R to 'A-R' – Modelling Strategic Actor Relationships for Business Process Reengineering", 13th International Conference on the Entity – Relationship Approach, Manchester, U.K.
[35] Zachman, J.A. (1996), "Enterprise Architecture: The Issue of the Century", Database Programming and Design Magazine.

New Trends in Software Methodologies, Tools and Techniques
H. Fujita and M. Mejri (Eds.)
IOS Press, 2005

A Representation-Theoretical Analysis of the OMG Modelling Suite

Cesar GONZALEZ-PEREZ and Brian HENDERSON-SELLERS
Department of Software Engineering, Faculty of Information Technology, University of Technology, Sydney, Australia

Abstract. Conceptual modelling in software engineering is dominated by the implicit semantics of UML, some other OMG products, and a bunch of related modelling tools. Although other alternatives to modelling are seen in academic circles, industry is dominated by this single approach. With no room to improve and no freedom to experiment, stagnation is guaranteed. The paper claims that a technology-free, purely theoretical analysis of models and modelling is necessary in order to find what real models are about, what the real modelling mechanisms behind software engineering are, and what kind of modelling infrastructure should serve as a foundation for future modelling technologies.

Keywords. Conceptual modelling, Representation theory, UML, Metamodelling

Introduction

Modelling is usually linked to representing, describing and explaining concepts and systems. Similarly, the idea of a model is often related to the notions of reproduction, specification and description. Although these instinctive connections are useful for many every-day activities, software engineers often need to go beyond them and into a more formal understanding of models and modelling. Current trends such as Model-Driven Architecture (MDA, [9]) or other model-centric approaches are positioning modelling under the spotlight more than ever before.

This paper delves into what models are and what modelling means, approaching it from a technology-agnostic perspective so that unnecessary constraints are avoided. Works such as (Seidewitz, 2003) are valuable in their analyses, but their heavy reliance on specific solutions (the OMG suite of standards in the cited case) makes their value a small fraction of what it could have been. In our work, we present a purely theoretical discourse that establishes a basic conceptual set and a collection of modelling needs and, as an example of its application, analyse the OMG suite.

1. Models and Modelling

From a simplistic point of view, we could say that a model is *a statement about a given subject under study (SUS), expressed in a given language*. This definition is similar to that given by (Seidewitz, 2003) ("a set of statements about some system under study"), but it incorporates an explicit reference to the language the model is expressed in. If we

Figure 1. A model and the SUS that it represents. The arrow can be read as "represents".

Figure 2. A model must be homomorphic with its SUS so the operations that are possible on the SUS are also possible on the model.

accept this definition, then the sentence "today it's raining" would be a model of the real world, since it is a statement about a given subject (my perceived real world), expressed in a given language (English). Since today it's raining (I can verify it looking through the window), the statement expressed by the sentence is true, and so the prospective model would be a *valid* model. Figure 1 shows a model and the SUS that it represents.

We could call the sentence "today it's raining" a model, but it would be of little use. The value of models usually resides in our ability to reason about the SUS by looking at the model only; this is sometimes called *abstraction*. At the same time, we need to acknowledge that modelling is often performed to fight complexity, which usually appears in the form of SUS that are not simple monolithic entities but intricate composites. This applies to function (e.g. different tasks in a workflow description, transaction against an online shop) as well as structure (e.g. the parts of a car, the hierarchy in an organisation). Therefore, we can say that the major reason why we need models is to reason about the complexity of the SUS without having to deal with it directly. As a result, a suitable model would have to exhibit the appropriate structure for it to be useful. For this reason, we prefer to say that, for a statement about an SUS (expressed in a given language) to be a real model, it needs to be homomorphic with the SUS that it represents. This means that the structure of the model and the structure of the SUS must coincide to some degree, and the operations that are possible on the SUS are also possible on the model. For example, consider a car and the parts it is made of. This is the subject under study. By looking at it, we can (albeit with a big effort) enumerate all its parts, sub-parts, etc. recursively in a tree-wise fashion. A model that represents a car and its parts should exhibit the same structure and allow for the same operation, i.e. enumerate parts and sub-parts recursively (Fig. 2).

We have established that models represent SUS. This statement, however, raises two additional questions. First of all, what kind of entities are the model and the SUS? Secondly, what is the nature of this "representation"? In order to answer the first question, we need to take into account that the usual depiction of modelling activities that is found in most software engineering works suffers from a very peculiar problem: they show the model as being a representation of a fragment of reality (whatever "reality" means) and *external* to it. A very good example can be found in (Martin and Odell, 1992), Figure 5.1. Although this may seem a simple matter of notation, it reveals the underlying assumption that a model is somehow different to its SUS. However, even the most simplistic thought experiment would show that, if a SUS is part of reality, then a model of it is also part of reality, as vividly explained by (Meyer, 1997),

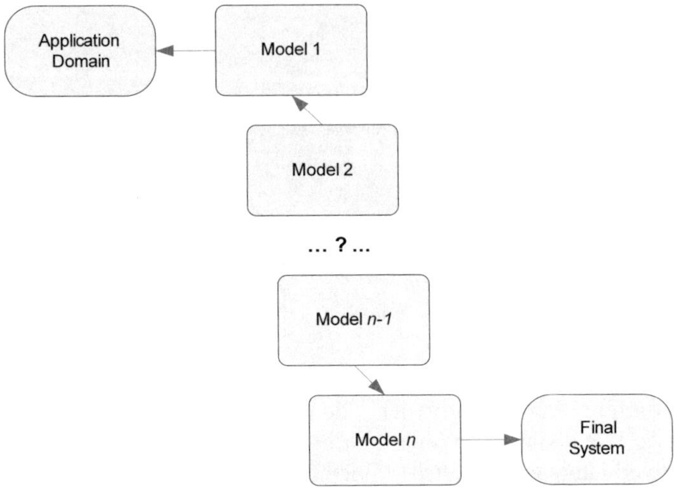

Figure 3. Backward- and forward-looking models in a software development project. At some point during the project, focus shifts from looking back to the application domain into looking forward to the final system to build.

p. 230–231. Therefore, models are not external to reality but components of it. Precisely because of this, we can create models that represent other models, thus creating a model chain, as will be discussed later.

Answering our first question, we can conclude that anything can be a SUS, and that a model, once created, becomes part of reality and, therefore, is a potential SUS for further models. With regard to our second question (what is the nature of the connection between a model and its SUS), two different scenarios are often found, as described by (Seidewitz, 2003). Sometimes a model is created to describe an existing SUS and enable reasoning about the SUS in its absence. For example, a training flight simulator is a model of a real aeroplane that is better suited for training pilots than the SUS it models. Some other times, a model is created to specify a SUS that does not exist. For example, blueprints of a building are created to define how the building will look like and how it will be built. We will call the former backward-looking models since they look backward (as far as temporality is concerned) to the SUS they model, and we will call the latter forward-looking models since they look forward into the future.

Software engineering makes use of both kinds of models. At the beginning of a software development project, models of an application domain are created. These models try to represent an existing reality, and for this reason they are backward-looking models. However, the last stages of a project involve models that specify the final system to be built and help us create it by detailing every single aspect of it. These are forward-looking models. At some point during the project, focus shifts from backward-looking to forward-looking (Fig. 3). We can observe this by realising that the main reason for creating backward-looking models is to get rid of unnecessary detail so that the resulting model is simpler than (but, hopefully, homomorphically equivalent to) the real thing; on the other hand, the main reason why we create forward-looking models is to explicitly document as much detail as possible about a SUS that we intend to create. Detail is actively removed when looking back, but actively added when looking forward. We may assume that the nature of these two kinds of details is not the

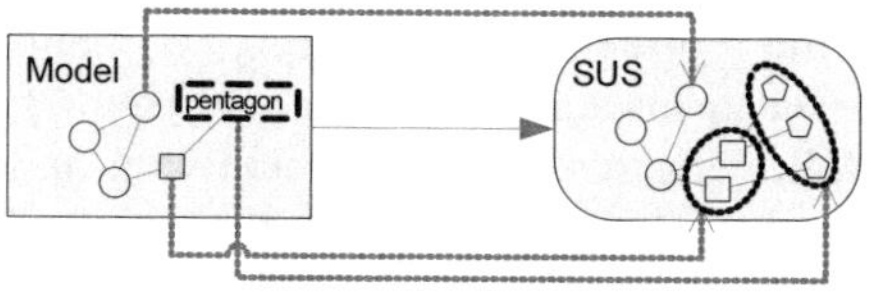

Figure 4. Examples of isotypical, prototypical and metatypical interpretive mappings. A circle is shown to have an isotypical mapping. The shaded square on the model is an example (prototype) for any square in the SUS. The declaration of "pentagon" in the model is metatypically mapped to all possible pentagons in the SUS.

same. This issue, together with the mechanisms by which the back-to-forward shift happens, are certainly interesting topics by themselves, and will be considered as the theme for further research.

For both types of models (backward- and forward-looking), homomorphism dictates that the structure of the model must match the structure of the SUS at some relevant level of detail; in other words, for each relevant entity in the SUS there must be an entity in the model that plays the same structural roles. What is the nature of the connection between a relevant entity inside the SUS and its "surrogate", homomorphic entity inside the model? We will use the term "interpretive mappings" to refer to the collection of information that allows finding out these connections when necessary.

Interpretive mappings are not always one-to-one relationships. In fact, the "cardinality" of the mappings depends on the characteristics of the representation process employed to create the model. For example, an architectonic scale model of a building usually contains a simplified, small-scale version of each room of the real building. In this case, each small room in the model is mapped to a real room in the real building; the cardinality is one to one. If the same model contains a figurine to exemplify how people would interact with the building in the real world, this figurine does not correspond to any particular person in the SUS, but to the prototypical idea of a person in the SUS interacting with the building. A number of persons in the SUS can play the structural role that the figurine plays in the model and, therefore, the interpretive mapping between the figurine and the persons it represents is one-to-many. There is a second way in which an interpretive mapping can be one-to-many; consider a label attached to the above mentioned architectonic scale model that reads something like "persons walk through this way". Rather than incorporating a prototype of potential SUS entities, this model entity *declares* what kind of entities in the SUS are suitable for interpretive mapping. Summarising, we can identify three different kinds of interpretive mappings:

- **Isotypical** mappings are those that map one model entity to one SUS entity. The model entity straightforwardly represents the SUS entity.
- **Prototypical** mappings are those that map one model entity to a set of SUS entities given by example, i.e. the model entity exemplifies the kind of SUS entities that can be mapped to it.
- **Metatypical** mappings are those that map one model entity to a set of SUS entities given declaratively, i.e. the model entity is a description of the properties that SUS entities must comply with in order to be mapped to it.

Figure 4 shows examples of the three kinds. Notice that, in principle, there is nothing that prevents the three kinds to coexist within the same model. Also notice that the cardinality on the side of the model is always one, meaning that for a given SUS entity, at most one model entity will be mapped to it.

We must clarify that these three kinds of interpretive mappings are disjoint. This is usually clear, but some scenarios can result in confusion. For example, imagine a model that includes the following sentence "the cats living in 3/21 Walker Street, Lavender Bay". This sentence fragment is a metatypical representation of a collection of cats, since it declares what kind of object it refers to (cats) and the properties that objects of this type must exhibit in order to comply with the description (i.e. living at 3/21 Walker Street, Lavender Bay). However, our knowledge says that only one cat lives at that address, so we could interpret the statement as an isotypical representation. This, however, is not correct, since the statement is not portraying a cat living at that address but declaring cats living at that address. The fact that only one cat happens to comply with the representation is circumstantial and does not change the kind of interpretive mapping.

2. OMG's Suite

2.1. UML Class Diagrams

We can find these three kinds of mappings in software engineering. Consider a UML class diagram, for example. This diagram depicts a model and, as such, can be thought of as a model of that model. Each box in the class diagram that a UML-aware expert identifies as "a class" is really a representation of a class in the class model. The box on the paper is just a visual artefact that represents a conceptual construct (the class). We must emphasise here that boxes on the paper are *not* classes but *represent* classes. Therefore, each box on the diagram is isotypically mapped to the corresponding class in the model. Because this is an isotypical mapping, the cardinality is one to one, and we often equate the box on the paper to the class in the model, thus confounding the model and its representation. This is convenient but does not mean that the box and the class are the same thing. Now, each class in the model is a declaration of what kinds of objects can appear in the system being modelled; therefore, each class in the model is metatypically mapped to a number of objects in the running system. At the same time, we could argue that each class in the model is isotypically mapped to a class in the source code. Finally, let's consider what UML 1.5 (OMG, 2003b) calls object diagrams, i.e. structural diagrams in which objects can appear. A box drawn on a piece of paper that is identified by an expert as "an object" is an ambiguous thing. Some people would interpret it as a representation of a particular object in the running system (an isotypical mapping) while others would interpret it as an example of an object that may occur in the running system (a prototypical mapping). Since the cardinalities of these two mappings, as well as their semantics, are different, we claim that UML 1.5 is ambiguous in relation to object diagrams. UML 2 (OMG, 2003c) removes the concept of Object as a model entity and introduces InstanceSpecification. The term "object" has driven some people to believe that the "objects" in UML 1.5 object diagrams are real objects (and the associated confusion related to objects being in the same layer together with their classes), when they are just a *representation* of objects. In this sense, the term "instance specification" is much better suited, since it clearly reflects that the model element is just a specification (i.e. an entity in a forward-looking model) of an instance in the SUS. However, the same ambiguity that we found in UML 1.5 remains, since the definition, description and semantics of InstanceSpecification in UML 2 (see (OMG, 2003c), p. 62–64) allow for both isotypical ("An instance specification may specify the existence of an entity in a modeled system.") and prototypical ("An instance specification may provide an illustration or example of a possible entity in a modeled system.") mappings. Whether this open definition enhances expressiveness or hinders interpretation in practice is something that only time will tell.

2.2. Layering

In general, we can say that OMG standards use metatypical mappings between layers with only one exception: InstanceSpecification in UML 2 (or Object in UML 1.5) can exhibit isotypical and prototypical mappings to user models, as explained in the previous section. In all the remaining cases, OMG's products not only use metatypical mappings but they choose a very special kind of metatypical mapping, namely, instance-of relationships. As we said in the previous section, a metatypical mapping is one in which the set of SUS entities that can be mapped to a given model entity is specified declaratively, i.e. the model entity is a description of the properties that SUS entities must comply with in order to be mapped to it. A type (in the UML sense) is definitely a declaration of its instances, so an instance-of relationship between a type and its instances can well be seen as a valid way to implement a metatypical mapping. However, other ways exist, and OMG's line of products ignores them: a subtype-of relationship between a subtype and its supertype also implements a metatypical mapping, since the supertype can be seen as a specification of what properties SUS entities must exhibit so they can be mapped to it. There is therefore no reason why software engineering modelling structures should not use it.

Furthermore, not only instance-of and subtype-of relationships are valid implementations of metatypical mappings; "exotic" relationships such as deep instantiation (Atkinson and Kühne, 2001) and powertype instantiation (Gonzalez-Perez and Henderson-Sellers, 2005b; Henderson-Sellers and Gonzalez-Perez, 2005) have been recently defined in the literature. The need for these new, "exotic" relationships is very clear: the concept of representation is transitive, meaning that a model of a model of a SUS is also a model of the same SUS. However, the instance-of relationship, the only one adopted by OMG, not only is not transitive, but is also *representation-blind*, i.e. it is not aware of the representation process. This means that an instance-of relationship allows us to describe the properties of an instance from the perspective of its type, but it cannot take into account further chained representation processes that may involve the specified SUS entity in a forward-looking model. For example, consider the class Class in (the latest draft of) UML 2 (OMG, 2003c). Class has a name attribute (inherited from NamedElement) as well as an isAbstract attribute. Together with the semantics of Class as described by the UML 2 specification, this is enough to metatypically map Class to any class in a user model (the SUS of UML 2, see Fig. 5). However, from the perspective of UML, a class in the user model (such as Book) is just an instance-of Class, and therefore an object (since Class is a class). As an object, it will have a value for the name attribute ("Book" in our example) and a value for the is Abstract attribute (*false* in our example). This object cannot be the class Book (since it is an object and not a class, to start with), but is a *representation* of the class Book. However, the purpose of creating a Book class is to instantiate it into book objects in the running system, but since UML can only generate an object that represents the Book class, and not the Book class itself, this cannot be done. Of course, software engineers are well accustomed to do the mental trick of automatically navigating the isotypical mapping between the object that represents the Book class, generated from UML, and the real

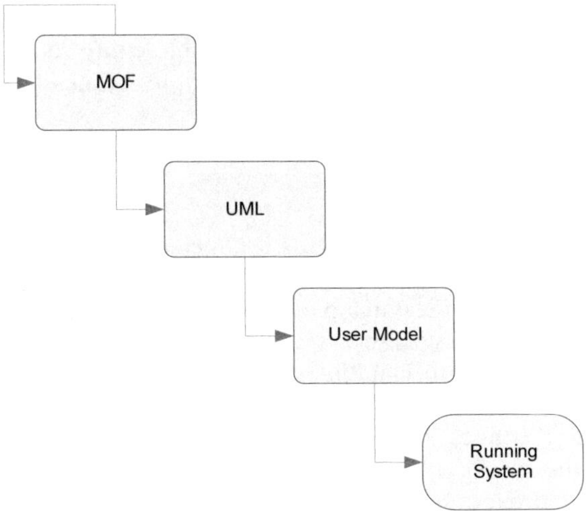

Figure 5. The four-layer OMG approach to model chaining. The top layer, MOF, is a self-model.

Book class (its SUS entity, synthesised on the fly). However, and from a formal modelling perspective, this is only a trick and, in our view, far from acceptable in an engineering discipline. The reasons are twofold: first of all, UML (or any other approach that is limited to instance-of relationships as a means of implementing metatypical mappings) can only generate objects that represent classes, as explained above. The real classes are not derived from UML but from the objects derived from UML, by developers that use their subjective judgement to synthesise them as necessary. For example, when a developer creates the Book class by instantiating the Class class in UML, an object representing the Book class is created. The box on the paper labelled "Book", strictly speaking, represents an object which can be isotypically mapped to a class that doesn't yet exist. This class is created by the developer (or, even worse, separately by each developer that reads the diagram) when necessary. For example, when some code needs to be written from the diagram, a real class (for example, a C# class) is created. This class, as we have explained, is not an instance of UML's Class but an isotypical partner of an instance of UML's Class. In some scenarios (e.g. mapping classes to database schemata), model transformation technologies such as QVT (Query, View, Transformation) (OMG, 2002b) or MDA (Model-Driven Architecture) (OMG, 2003a) can help with this issue by providing a means of implementing the isotypical mapping between the specific class and object; however, this means that UML is not a self-contained modelling language since it needs assistance from external technologies to achieve formal completeness. The second reason is that modelling tools implemented as software systems (as most are) need to implement a fully formalised modelling infrastructure in order to support the necessary functionality. In our experience, modelling tool implementers know that using instance-of relationships only is not enough to achieve this, and additional workarounds must be added to traverse the "hidden" isotypical mapping that we have described.

2.3. Integrating Process and Product Metamodels

In the context of software development methodologies, metamodels are simply forward-looking models that represent any possible methodology that can be created. Like their model-oriented cousins (see first meaning of "metamodel", above), methodology metamodels can be seen also as languages that can be used to express, in this case, methodologies. In any case, the content of a methodology metamodel depends on what the metamodel authors understand by "methodology". We will adopt the definition given by (Gonzalez-Perez and Henderson-Sellers, 2005a): a methodology is *a specification of the process to follow and the work products to be generated, plus consideration of the people and tools involved, during a software development effort*. Since a methodology needs to consider both process and product aspects, and a methodology metamodel must be able to represent any possible relevant methodology, then process and product aspects must be integrated within the metamodel. The philosophy underpinning such integration is a linguistic simile: meaningful messages are built by applying actions to objects or, more specifically, complete sentences are constructed by combining verbs and nouns. Verbs specify the actions that are performed, while nouns denote the authors and receivers of the said actions. Verbs without nouns can only specify actions, but an action needs a noun on which to be performed; similarly, nouns without verbs can only specify receivers or authors of actions, but not the actions themselves. Translating this into the methodology field, a software development process defines the actions to be performed when developing software, but these actions are meaningless without a detailed definition of the producers that execute the actions and the products that are involved. Similarly, products of software development (such as models or documents) alone are not enough; an indication of the process appropriate to create and employ them is necessary.

The Australian standard metamodel for software development methodologies, AS 4651 (SA, 2004), is intended to be used by a methodologist in creating a specific, tailored methodology. On the process side, AS 4651 offers classes that allow the methodologist to define activities, tasks, techniques and phases, among others. This falls within the same scope as OMG's SPEM (Software Process Engineering Metamodel) (OMG, 2005). From the product side, AS 4651 offers classes that allow the methodologist to define models, languages and model unit kinds. This falls within the same scope as OMG's MOF (Meta-Object Facility) (OMG, 2002a). AS 4651 defines associations between process-related classes and product-related classes. Consequently, the appropriate links can be defined between process and product elements in the methodology. AS 4651 is the only standard metamodel, as far as we know, to fully support product/process integration. The capability of AS 4651 to allow the methodologist to define both process and product aspects does not imply that both must be defined every time a methodology is needed; a method engineering approach (Brinkkemper, 1996) guarantees that a significant repository of pre-defined methodology components is maintained and re-used as necessary.

In order to achieve a similar degree of power, the OMG suite of products would need to be integrated at the most abstract level possible. MOF would seem to be an appropriate candidate for such as integration but, unfortunately, MOF mixes together two different concerns: on the one hand, MOF tries to define the infrastructure necessary to define modelling languages (such as UML); on the other hand, it tried to be an auto-model so it can fulfil its role at the top of the hierarchy (Seidewitz, 2003; Smith, 1999). Our claim here is that a true auto-model should be minimal since, if the auto-

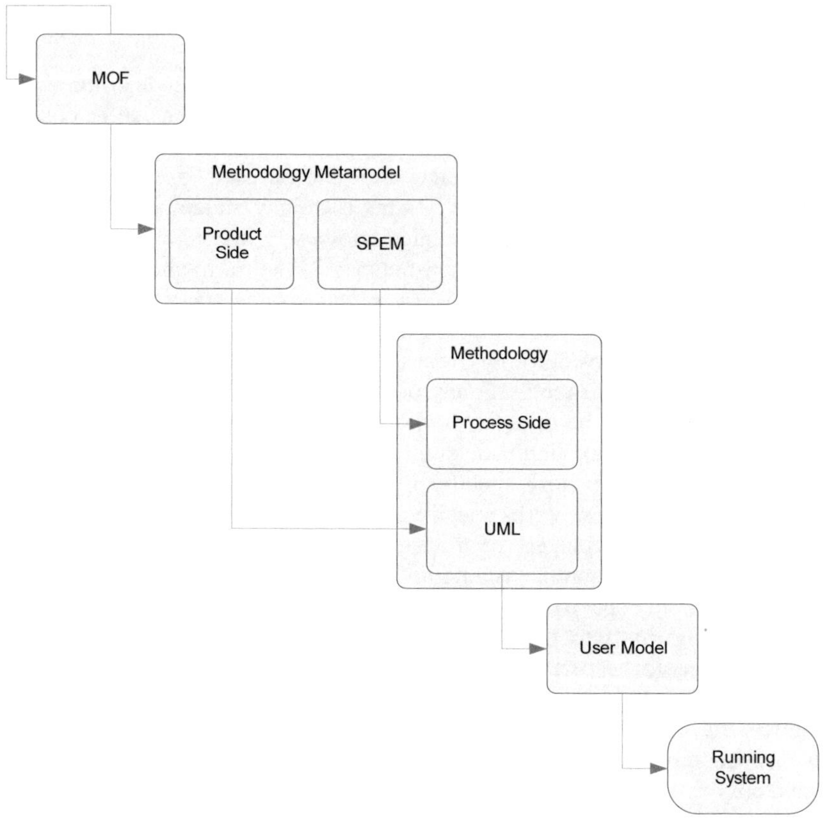

Figure 6. Reorganising OMG's product suite into a meaningful hierarchy. Notice how SPEM and UML reside at different conceptual levels.

model is not minimal (i.e. contains entities that are not used by the auto-model itself), then these entities would not have any interpretive mappings to any SUS entities, which violates one of the premises in our theory (see Section 1). From this perspective, every class in MOF should have instances that are part of MOF in order for MOF to be a valid auto-model. Since MOF is a language specification, structural by nature, classes such as Operation and Exception cannot have instances that are part of MOF. Therefore, we must conclude that it contains more classes than it would need to define itself. Of course, this may well be a consequence of trying to offer the necessary infrastructure to represent modelling languages. A possible solution to this paradox would be to reduce the MOF to a minimal auto-model, perhaps along the lines of the CDIF meta-metamodel, and then create a methodology metamodel as an instance of MOF. Such a metamodel would justifiably focus on defining the language elements necessary to specify methodologies, addressing both process and product aspects. In this scenario, UML would be the product side of any methodology, while SPEM would comprise the process side of the above mentioned metamodel (Fig. 6). The recent Australian standard, while outside of the OMG suite of products, already offers such support.

Finally, we note that, currently, UML is a direct instance of MOF, but it should not be; this becomes clear if we realise that UML is one of many possible modelling languages, while SPEM in not one of many possible process specifications but a metamodel to build process specifications. UML and SPEM, therefore, are not at the same conceptual level, having different foci and level of abstraction, so integration cannot be performed between them simply in the way intended by the OMG.

3. Conclusions

This paper presents a technology-agnostic analysis of the concepts of model and modelling in software engineering. It has been shown that a model is always homomorphic with its subject under study (SUS), and that interpretive mappings (either isotypical, prototypical or metatypical) are required in order to trace model entities back to the SUS entities that they represent. The difference between forward- and backward-looking models has been explained, and the issue of focus shift identified. The need of product and process integration in methodologies has also been addressed in the context of the OMG's suite of models. Furthermore, UML has been determined to be ambiguous with relation to its Object or InstanceSpecification (depending on the UML version) class, and a "hidden" isotypical mapping has been identified that prevents software developers from deriving real class models from UML. Also, OMG's process standard (SPEM) and modelling standard (UML) are identified as being incompatible as far as an integral process plus product methodology metamodel is concerned. The Australian Standard AS 4651, however, is considered valid and suggested as an alternative.

Acknowledgements

We wish to thank the Australian Research Council for providing funding towards this project. This is contribution number 05/09 of the Centre for Object Technology Applications and Research.

References

Atkinson, C. and Kühne, T. 2001. The Essence of Multilevel Metamodelling. In *«UML» 2001: Modeling Languages, Concepts and Tools*, Vol. 2185 (Eds., Gogolla, M. and Kobryn, C.), Springer-Verlag, Berlin, pp. 19–33.

Brinkkemper, S. 1996. Method Engineering: Engineering of Information Systems Development Methods and Tools. *Information and Software Technology,* **38**(4), 275–280.

Gonzalez-Perez, C. and Henderson-Sellers, B. 2005a. A Powertype-Based Metamodelling Framework. *Software and Systems Modelling,* [in press].

Gonzalez-Perez, C. and Henderson-Sellers, B. 2005b. Templates and Resources in Software Development Methodologies. *Journal of Object Technology,* **4**(4).

Henderson-Sellers, B. and Gonzalez-Perez, C. 2005. The Rationale of Powertype-Based Metamodelling. In *Second Asia-Pacific Conference on Conceptual Modelling*, Vol. 7, number 6, Australian Computer Society, pp. 7–16.

Martin, J. and Odell, J.J. 1992. *Object-Oriented Analysis and Design,* Prentice-Hall, Englewood Cliffs, NJ.

Meyer, B. 1997. *Object-Oriented Software Construction,* Prentice-Hall, Upper Saddle River, NJ.

OMG. 2002a. *Meta Object Facility (MOF) Specification,* formal/2002-04-03, Object Management Group.

OMG. 2002b. MOF 2.0 Query / Views / Transformations RFP. Object Management Group.

OMG. 2003a. MDA Guide. (Eds., Miller, J. and Mukerji, J.), Object Management Group.

OMG. 2003b. *Unified Modelling Language Specification,* formal/03-03-01, Object Management Group.

OMG. 2003c. *Unified Modelling Language Specification: Infrastructure,* ptc/03-09-15, Object Management Group.

OMG. 2005. *Software Process Engineering Metamodel Specification,* formal/05-01-06, Object Management Group.

SA. 2004. *Standard Metamodel for Software Development Methodologies,* AS 4651-2004, Standards Australia.

Seidewitz, E. 2003. What Models Mean. *IEEE Software,* **20**(5), 26–31.

Smith, J. E. 1999. UML Formalization and Transformation. PhD Thesis. Northeastern University, USA.

New Trends in Software Methodologies, Tools and Techniques
H. Fujita and M. Mejri (Eds.)
IOS Press, 2005

Towards Software Development Methodology for Web Services

George FEUERLICHT[a] and Sooksathit MEESATHIT[b]
Faculty of Information Technology, University of Technology, Sydney,
PO Box 123 Broadway Sydney NSW 2007 Australia
[a]*jiri@it.uts.edu.au,* [b]*smeesath@it.uts.edu.au*

Abstract. The emergence of Web services represents a shift from component-based architectures that have proved successful in the context of enterprise computing to service-oriented architectures that are more suited to the highly distributed Internet-based applications. This trend towards service-oriented computing necessitates the re-evaluation of software development methodologies that are used in the construction of distributed applications. With growing acceptance of service-oriented computing and increasing number of large-scale Web Services projects there is some evidence that practitioners involved in implementing these solutions are paying only limited attention to how such applications should be designed. Frequently, the design of Web Services applications is driven by performance and scalability considerations, rather than any sound software engineering principles. A comprehensive methodological framework is required to guide designers and developers of service-oriented applications through the various phases of software development life cycle with specific emphasis on producing stable, reusable and extendable services.

In this paper we discuss design of service-oriented applications from a software engineering perspective, and propose a software development framework for Web Services based on identification of elementary business function using business function decomposition and mapping these functions to service operations. We apply interface design principles adapted from object-oriented design as guidelines for the design of services.

Keywords. Software development, Methodology for service-oriented applications, Web Services

Introduction

Web Services are being increasingly used as an application development and integration platform within enterprises and to implement e-business applications in various industry sectors. Examples range from relatively simple Web Services designed to provide programmatic access to popular websites such as Google (www.google.com), Amazon (www.amazon.com), eBay (www.ebay.com) and Yahoo (www.yahoo.com), to comprehensive Web Services solutions provided by travel industry companies such as Galileo (www.galileo.com) and Sabre (www.saber.com). While Web Services are becoming the preferred platform for implementing Internet applications and sophisticated Web Services development tools are becoming widely available, there is some evidence that practitioners involved in Web Services projects are paying only limited attention to how such applications should be designed. This can lead to project failures as the overall quality of service-oriented applications depends largely on the quality of their design that in terms determines reusability, extensibility and reliability of the applications.

Web Services design is an active research area and although there is some agreement about the basic design principles there are no comprehensive software development methodologies for Web Services at present. Many existing approaches focus on designing Web Services from components using object-oriented methods or component-based techniques. Web services development tools that support development and deployment of Web Services applications are widely available and simplify the coding and deployment phases of the software development life cycle using code generation techniques to produce WSDL and deployment files. However, software development tools can only assist developers by reducing the programming effort, and in general transform existing components by directly mapping component methods into Web Services operations, without providing much scope for making design decisions based on methodological support. Although there are similarities between software components and services, mapping existing components directly to Web Services can lead to suboptimal design and results in poor performance, reduced scalability, and complex interdependencies between services. It is evident that existing object-oriented and component-based design and development methodologies are not directly applicable to Web Services.

In this paper we discuss design of service-oriented applications from a software engineering perspective, and propose a software development methodology for Web Services. We first review existing literature on design of Web Services (Section 1), and then describe a software development framework based on identification of elementary business function and mapping these functions to service operations (Section 2). Using a travel example scenario based on the Open Travel Alliance specification (OTA, http://www.opentravel.org) we illustrate how the methodology can be used to develop a consistent set of Web Services from an industry-domain specification of XML message structures. In conclusion (Section 3) we compare our methodology to document-centric and message-oriented Web Services approaches, discussing relative advantages of the proposed methodology.

1. Related Work

In this section we review literature on the available methods for Web Services design, grouping these methods into approaches based on object-oriented and component design (Section 1.1), methods for transformation of industry domain specifications (Section 1.2), and business process transformation approaches (Section 1.3).

1.1. Object-Oriented and Component-Based Approaches

Ambler [1] proposed a methodology for deriving Web Services specifications from UML class diagram of existing object-oriented applications. The methodology identifies five types of classes: user interface classes, business/domain classes, process classes, persistence classes, and system classes. The first step in this methodology involves eliminating persistence classes and system classes from the class diagram. Persistence classes are classes that encapsulate access to persistent stores, while system classes are classes that encapsulate technical features; as these types of classes do not relate to business methods they do not need to be considered as candidates Web Services. Next step involves the simplification of hierarchies (both inheritance and aggregation hierarchies) of the remaining classes. Two simplification rules are defined: the rule for inheritance hierarchy involves the elimination of subclasses that do not add new contracts (i.e. public method), and the rule for aggregation hierarchy is to ignore classes that are not associated with other classes outside of the aggregation hierarchy. This step is followed by the identification of class contracts, i.e. public methods that can be called by objects in other classes, and removing all operations that are not class contracts (i.e. private operations). Then potential domain packages (groups of highly coupled classes) are identified using rules based on the types of messages received by the client and server components of the system, and their interfaces exported as Web Services. This is followed by identifying class contracts (i.e. public methods) that are used by classes outside a domain package. The contracts are then combined to reduce the number of candidate Web Services. The final set of service contracts are mapped to Web Services operations, and the input and output parameters of the operations defined using XML schemas. Ambler's method is an example of a bottom-up Web Service design approach that defines Web Services on top of existing components or objects and is useful for migration to service-oriented architectures. The main focus of this method is grouping of highly coupled classes into coarser components called domain packages, and refining the resulting component interfaces to produce larger grained services that are exported as Web services.

Levi and Arsanjani [2] proposed component-based Web Services design method based on identifying business processes and dividing the problem domain into functional areas based on departmental boundaries, business process boundaries and value chains. The functional areas (i.e. major business areas) are mapped to enterprise components which are then decomposed to identify their constituent business processes creating a goal model using Goal-Service Graphs. The objective of this step is to identify high-level business goals, their sub-goals and services required to achieve the goals. The main benefit of the goal model is that it allows designers to define services based on business needs. The services identified in the Goal-Service Graphs are then assigned to enterprise components that are responsible for providing the services. Service identification involves making decisions about granularity of the services. Next, specifications for enterprise components are created defining the pre and post-conditions for each service and an abstract specification of component behavior. The main focus of this methodology is on designing enterprise components suitable for transformation into Web Services by exporting their interfaces.

Luo et al. [3] proposes a methodology for designing Web Services to support enterprise integration projects. The first phase of this method is domain decomposition that identifies relevant functional areas within the problem domain by identifying and modeling business processes. The resulting model is then mapped to Component Business Modeling (CBM) map of the relevant industry domain. Next candidate services are identified based on the inter-component interactions and by grouping business tasks according to components based on the selected CBM. This step is followed by business process realization to ensure that the identified services and components can realize the required business processes. Then the identified services are mapped to the business components that implement the services and business processes, and the service model is created. Identification of services for externalization is based on business alignment, transparency, and service granularity. Finally, the resulting services are fully specified including definition of data input and outputs, interaction models (i.e. synchronous or asynchronous mode of communication), messaging and transport protocols, service composition requirements and non-functional requirements, expressing the specifications using BPEL and WSDL.

Finally, in this category of methods we include the application of Design by Contract (DBC) [4] to the problem definition of service interfaces. Design by Contract is a widely used object-oriented design approach that involves defining interface contracts including pre and post-condition for object methods. DBC is a highly suitable methodology for specifying the Web Services at design time reducing the potential for errors and improving the overall quality of the software development process [5].

1.2. Transformation of Industry Domain Specifications Approaches

Existing industry domain specifications as represented by industry standards (e.g. RosettaNet, http://www.rosettanet.org) embody the domain model for a given industry domain (e.g. travel, healthcare, etc) and provide a good starting point for the design of Web Services. Masud [6] gives guidelines for the definition of Web Services interfaces using WSDL, and Web Services interaction flows using BPEL from existing RosettaNet standards. The methodology describes how relevant information can be extracted from RosettNet PIP (Partner Interface Process) specifications and the corresponding document schemas, and used to define Web Service interfaces and choreography descriptions of the interaction semantics between business partners. Designing Web Services from existing e-business standards enables design of interfaces and interaction dialogues based on industry-wide standard business processes and vocabularies. This avoids the need to define Web Services for individual partner organizations and results in significantly improved interoperability. RosettaNet standard consists of specifications that include dictionaries, Implementation Framework, and PIP specifications. Masud focuses on deriving Web Services interface and choreography descriptions from corresponding PIP specifications and associated Message Structure definitions. The initial phase of the methodology involves definition of Web Services operations and their input and output messages using WSDL. Relevant messages are identified from choreography diagrams and PIP specifications. Next, WSDL message elements based on RosettaNet message definition are defined and corresponding operations specified by mapping messages into operations. The second phase of the methodology deals with creating BPEL descriptions for interactions between trading partners using Web Services defined during the first phase. The methodology uses business process definitions and choreography information defined using UML diagrams and associated tables within the PIP specification as the basis for BPEL specifications. Partner roles defined in PIP are mapped into BPEL, and then the PIP choreography is implemented as choreography of abstract and executable business processes in BPEL.

1.3. Business Process Transformation Approaches

Papazoglou and Yang [7] propose a Web Services development methodology that serves as a framework for business process analysis and service design, and produces service specifications expressed in Web Services Flow Language (WSFL) [8] and service usage interfaces expressed in WSDL. The WSFL service specification describes interaction flows between a set of constituent Web Services that implement a business process (e.g. the travel reservation service provided by airlines), and WSDL service usage interface describes the interface of high-level Web Services that represent the overall business processes. A key component of this methodology is a business process analysis framework used to model constituent services and to define high-level services. During the first phase, the objectives and structure of business processes are identified, grouping and describing activities that implement the corresponding business processes, and defining usage interfaces and relationships between constituent services in WSFL. The second phase is concerned with mapping the constituent services to service provider roles and defining WSDL for the usage interfaces. Another key component of the methodology are service design principles that define guidelines for functional and non-functional aspects of service design. The functional service design considerations include service coupling and service cohesion. Minimization of coupling involves avoiding representational coupling, identity coupling and communication coupling. Increasing service cohesion involves maximizing functional service cohesion, communicational service cohesion, and logical service cohesion [9]. The non-functional service design guidelines identify key design consideration that relate to non-functional aspects of Web Services design and include service provisioning strategies, service policy management models, service programming style (i.e. document centric and RPC centric), and authorization design considerations. The methodology uses both top-down and bottom-up approaches to design interfaces for composite Web Services. Top-down approach is used to analyze business processes and to identify service invocations required to implement each activity within the scope of the process, and the bottom-up approach is used to map existing services provided by external service providers to usage interfaces of the business processes.

Radeka [10] proposes a Web Services design methodology for intra-enterprise Web Services-based application development. The starting point for the method is writing scenarios in plain text to describe the user experience. Then high level business process models are developed based on these scenarios. The process flows help to describe the steps needed to be executed to deliver high-level services. Refining the business model involves maximizing the number process steps that are reused across individual business process diagrams and replacing process steps with corresponding services. Information flows between services are then specified, providing basis for defining service interfaces. The main objective of this methodology is design of sharable component services that can be reused in multiple application contexts.

In summary, while Web Services design and development is an active research area at present there are no widely accepted software development frameworks that can guide designers and developers of Web Services applications. In particular, most methodologies focus on identifying Web Services given a set of application requirements, but do not address the details of definition of service interfaces. We regard service interface design as the key determinant of interoperability and robustness (i.e. application stability when requirements change) of service-oriented applications and we focus on this aspect of Web Services design in our methodology.

2. Web Services Software Development Framework

Similar to the methodology described in Section 1.2 above [6] we base our approach on an existing domain standard, the Open Travel Alliance specification (OTA, http://www.opentravel.org). OTA standard provides a comprehensive specification of business processes, interaction semantics, and data formats for the travel industry domain and avoids the need to perform detailed requirements analysis, providing a starting point for Web Services design. As is the case with most e-business industry domain standards, OTA is a document-oriented specification that relies on document interchange as the basic interoperability mechanism. Such document-oriented standards suffer from a number of important limitations when used directly (i.e. shipping OTA XML documents as SOAP payloads) for the implementation of Web Services applications. These limitations include poor interoperability, limited reuse and extendibility of services [11,12]. The approach described in this paper transforms the document-oriented OTA specification of message structures into a set of well-defined services using interfaces design principles described in Section 2.1 below.

2.1. Web Services Interface Design Principles and Guidelines

The focus of the proposed methodology is on design of service interfaces based on design principles derived from literature on software design, ranging from structured methodologies to more recent object-oriented and component design approaches. We briefly discuss each design principle and how it relates to design of services in the following sections.

Completeness: Application domain functionality should be fully covered by the specified set of services. Incomplete functionality coverage necessitates additional application development, resulting in increased complexity of applications and poor interoperability as additional functionality is not explicitly defined using core services [13].

Minimality: Services should be designed and developed for common (core) functions that provide opportunity for reuse; additional services should be implemented using composition of core services and operations [14], whenever possible. Specialized functions should be supported via an extendibility mechanism [15]. Ensuring minimality of services leads to less complex, more cohesive, and more consistent services.

Orthogonality: Orthogonality is a fundamental software design requirement and requires that the functionality of individual software modules (i.e. services) does not overlap, i.e. each service interface defines a distinct function within the application domain. Orthogonality ensures that redundancy is minimized maximizing reuse, and generally leads to well-defined and cohesive services. As a consequence, service composition can be used to define higher-level services without duplicating functionality.

Coupling and Cohesion: Coupling is a measure of the strength of interconnection between software modules [7,9,16]. Using services, coupling occurs via a service interface, and the level of interface coupling determines interdependencies between services. Service interfaces should be designed to minimize coupling in order to avoid invalidating client applications that use the service [12]. Cohesion refers to the level of interrelationships between the elements of a software module [7,9,16]. High level of service cohesion increases application stability as cohesion limits the impact of changes to a limited number of services (ideally, a single service operation).

Clarity Uniformity and Elegance: Services should have well-defined semantics and should be easy to understand to improve usability. Web Service interface should explicitly describe operations that the service performs, including the semantics of the parameters. Clarity can be improved using a suitable naming convention [15], and by including additional documentation that describes the semantics of each service and its operations [17]. Uniformity of naming services, operations, and parameters can significantly improve usability of interfaces and at the same time minimize ambiguity [18].

Universality, Evolution and Extendibility: The universality principle dictates that all service providers should implement the standard set of services; this is a key requirement to ensure application interoperability as lack of universality necessitates extensive translation or run-time resolution of service semantics. Once externalized, service interfaces must be maintained to ensure continuous support for existing applications. Support for evolution as user requirements change over time is of utmost importance in any large-scale application system. Using services, evolution is supported in a controlled manner via interface versioning ensuring that existing interfaces are maintained for *legacy* applications. Extendibility is supported via definition of non-standard services that support specialized functions. Web Services versioning strategies have been the subject to extensive research recently Hammond [19], Brown and Ellis [20], Browne et al. [21], and Peltz and Anagol-Subbarao [22].

To illustrate the proposed design framework, we use an airline flight booking example scenario based on the OTA specifications. For simplicity, we limit the scope of the example to a single pair of OTA messages and corresponding XML documents: OTA_AirBooking_RQ (airline flight booking request message) and OTA_AirBooking_RS (airline flight booking response message). The design framework consist of a number of steps described in the following sections.

2.2. Design Scope

The first step in the methodology is to define the scope of business processes to be considered for analysis. This helps to clarify the goals and focus of the analysis and provides the basis for verification of completeness of the design [23]. The following tasks need to be performed:

1. Identification of relevant business processes and participants
2. Identification of relevant use cases
3. Identification of relevant document schemas

In our example the flight booking process involves only two participants: a travel agent, and an airline, and two OTA documents (OTA_AirBook request and response messages). Note that we do not model the initial planning stage of the booking process that involves gathering of flight availability and pricing information. For more complex scenarios UML use case diagram would be used to represent the interaction; the relative simplicity of the business process under consideration does not justify drawing a use case diagram.

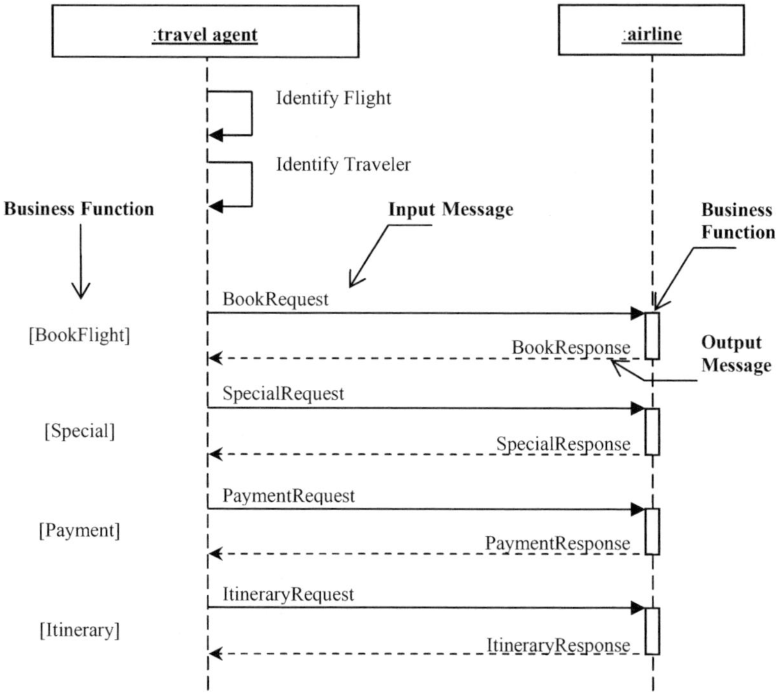

Figure 1. Sequence Diagram of Airline Booking Process.

2.3. Business Function Decomposition

Next step involves decomposition of the airline booking process into elementary (atomic) business functions. Business function decomposition identifies sub-functions, activities, and actions [23] and when applied recursively leads to discovery of elementary business functions (i.e. functions that can not be further decomposed). This approach is consistent with maximizing method cohesion as elementary business functions typically accomplish a single conceptual task and exhibit high levels of cohesion. Document schemas alone are not sufficient as an input for business function decomposition, and comprehensive knowledge of business function semantics is required to perform this task. We use information provided by the OTA specification, and the documentation embedded in the XML schema definitions of the relevant messages for this purpose.

UML sequence diagrams can be used to model the logic of usage scenarios, and at the same time to perform business function decomposition. The sequence diagram illustrated in Fig. 1 identifies elementary business functions for the airline booking process that are implicit in the OTA_AirBook RQ/RS message pair and described in corresponding documentation. Figure 1 shows sequential flow of actions in the flight booking process. The agent gathers relevant information from the customer, and sends a booking request to the airline. The airline responds with a confirmation message if the booking operation was successfully completed. The agent may then submit special requests (e.g. for seating or a special meal). This is followed by supplying payment details and processing of the payment. Finally the agent requests travel itinerary from the airline.

Table 1. Airline Booking Services and its Operations.

Service	Operation	Message Type	Message Name
AirBook	Book Flight	Input	BookRequest
		Output	BookResponse
	Special	Input	SpecialRequest
		Output	SpecialResponse
AirPayment	Payment	Input	PaymentRequest
		Output	PaymentResponse
AirItinerary	Itinerary	Input	ItineraryRequest
		Output	ItineraryResponse

The sequence diagram in Fig. 1 shows input and output message pairs that represent a business function, with the name of the function indicated on the left-hand side of the diagram. The sequence diagram identifies four business functions: BookFlight, Special, Payment, and Itinerary.

2.4. Definition of Services

The goal of this step is to define a set of services that correspond to the elementary business functions identified in Section 2.3 above. We map the business functions into four corresponding operations: BookFlight, Special, Payment, and Itinerary. The operations are then grouped into services, with input and output messages forming the service interface as shown in Table 1.

Grouping of operations into services is performed based on design principles stated in Section 2.1; for example, operations Payment and Itinerary are allocated to a separate services to ensure reusability, as these operations are used in a number of different contexts.

2.5. Definition of Service Interfaces

Following the specification of services and operations we define the service interfaces assigning input and output parameters to individual operations. We identify the parameters based on corresponding OTA XML messages, as indicated in Table 1, adopting OTA naming standard with some minor simplifications. Table 2 shows the interface specification for the AirBook service. CabinType is used to specify the type of cabin (i.e. economy, business, and first class), and TravelerName and PassportNumber are attributes of the passenger. The operation Special is used to request seating and meal preferences, and returns Acknowledgement to confirm the success of this operation.

Table 3 shows the interface specification for the AirPayment service that includes CreditCareID, and BookingReferenceID, and Amount in the input message and ReceiptNumber in the output message to indicate that the payment was processed.

And finally, Table 4 contains the specification for the AirItinerary service with input message containing the identifier BookingReferenceID, and output message a list of parameters that describe the passenger itinerary where Equipment describes the type of aircraft used and BookingStatus indicates if the flight is booked or on a waiting list.

Table 2. Interface definition for AirBook service.

Operation	Message Type	Message Name	Message Content
BookFlight	Input	BookRequest	FlightNumber DepartureAirport ArrivalAirport DepartureDate CabinType TravelerName PassportNumber
	Output	BookResponse	BookingReferenceID
Special	Input	SpecialRequest	BookingReferenceID Seat Meal
	Output	SpecialResponse	Acknowledgement

Table 3. Interface definition for AirPayment service.

Operation	Message Type	Message Name	Message Content
Payment	Input	PaymentRequest	BookingReferenceID CreditCardID Amount
	Output	PaymentResponse	ReceiptNumber

Table 4. Interface definition for AirItinerary service.

Operation	Message Type	Message Name	Message Content
Itinerary	Input	ItineraryRequest	BookingReferenceID
	Output	ItineraryResponse	FlightNumber PassengerName DepartureDate DepartureTime ArrivalDate ArrivalTime Equipment OperatingAirline BookingStatus

2.6. Refining Web Service Interface Specification

Having defined the input and output parameters for service operations we can now consider if the design of the interfaces is consistent with design principles of minimal coupling and maximum cohesion as outlined in Section 2.1. These principles have been used as important design considerations in various software development methodologies, including object-oriented design [9], and structured programming [16].

Table 5. Interface definition for SpecialMeal and SpecialSeat operations.

Operation	Message Type	Message Name	Message Content
SpecialMeal	Input	MealRequest	BookingReferenceID Meal
	Output	MealResponse	MealAcknowledgement
SpecialSeat	Input	SeatRequest	BookingReferenceID Seat
	Output	SeatResponse	SeatAcknowledgement

Consider for example the operation Special of the AirBook service defined in Table 2. On closer inspection, the operation performs two separate tasks: special meal request, and a seating request, and consequently the operation cannot be regarded as fully cohesive. When the operation Special is used for a seating request only, the Meal input parameter remains undefined and this impacts on the clarity of the semantics of the operation. Similarly, the semantics of the output parameter Acknowledgement are confusing as it is not clear which input parameter Acknowledgement refers to (i.e. Meal or Seat). Table 5 shows special requests implemented as two separate operations, resulting in improved cohesion and clarity of the interfaces. Reducing granularity (i.e. the level of aggregation) of operations can improve orthogonality and cohesion, and at the same time reduce coupling. Finding the optimal level of granularity for services and individual service operations requires careful examination. Coarse-grained operations tend to lack cohesion and suffer from increased coupling, while fine-grained operations increase the number of service interfaces, and consequently the number of runtime evocations with corresponding increase in application complexity. We examine design tradeoffs that involve fine-tuning granularity of service operations in the conclusion (Section 3) and in more detail in a recent publication [24].

2.7. Finalizing Design of Services

The design steps described in the above sections are primarily concerned with maximizing the cohesion of services and service operations. We have considered cohesion and coupling of service operations in more detail elsewhere and developed a technique for minimization of service coupling based on data engineering principles [24]. As the final step in the Web Services design process we should verify that the service definitions are consistent with all the design principles and guidelines detailed Section 2.1, ensuring the orthogonality, completeness, minimality, and uniformity of the specification. Given the limited scope of the example scenario presented here such considerations cannot be meaningfully discussed in the context of this paper. We are currently working on a comprehensive case study based on the OTA specification that will allow such an examination and establishing conformance of the resulting service specifications with the design principles stated in Section 2.1.

2.8. WSDL Specification

The resulting design of service interfaces can be implemented in the form of WSDL specifications as described in our earlier publication [28]. We illustrate the process here for the AirBook service defined in Table 1. Columns in Table 1 are mapped to WSDL

```
1  <?xml version="1.0" encoding="UTF-8"?>
2  <wsdl:definitions
3                                   :
4  <wsdl:message name="SpecialResponse">
5                                   :
6  </wsdl:message>
7  <wsdl:message name="SpecialRequest">
8                                   :
9  </wsdl:message>
10 <wsdl:message name="BookResponse">
11                                  :
12 </wsdl:message>
13 <wsdl:message name="BookRequest">
14                                  :
15 </wsdl:message>
16 <wsdl:portType name="AirBookPortType">
17   <wsdl:operation name="BookFlight">
18     <wsdl:input message="tns:BookRequest"/>
19     <wsdl:output message="tns:BookResponse"/>
20   </wsdl:operation>
21   <wsdl:operation name="Special">
22     <wsdl:input message="tns: SpecialRequest"/>
23     <wsdl:output message="tns:SpecialResponse"/>
24   </wsdl:operation>
25 </wsdl:portType>
26                                  :
27 <wsdl:service name="AirBook">
28 <wsdl:port binding="tns:fligthBookingBinding" name="AirBookPort">
29 <soap:address location="http://localhost:8000/ccx/fligthBooking"/>
30 </wsdl:port>
31 </wsdl:service>
32 </wsdl:definitions>
```

Figure 2. Partial WSDL description of AirBook Web services.

data elements as shown in Fig. 2 for the AirBook operation. The Service column is mapped to <service> (line 27). The Operation column is mapped to <portType> (line 16), and each operation name is mapped to <operation> (lines 17 and 21). The Message Type column is mapped to <input> and <output> (lines 18–19 and 22–23), and each cell in the Message column becomes the name of a message (lines 4–15).

3. Conclusions

We have described a software development methodology for Web Services in this paper. The proposed design framework specifies a set of steps that can be used to transform an industry domain specification of business processes and related data requirements, to a set of corresponding service definitions.

In contrast with document-centric approaches, the method produces relatively fine-grained service operations, and this can lead to higher network overheads and more complex interactions between services. Proponents of document-centric and message-oriented approaches generally recommend the use of coarse-grained service interfaces that allow a single request to perform a complete high-level business function (e.g. airline flight booking) improving performance of applications and avoiding issues related to high latency and poor reliability of the existing Internet infrastructure [25,26]. However, using services with coarse-grained interfaces externalizes complex data structures creating interdependencies, and impacting on service reusability [27,28]. For example, embedding the Payment and Itinerary operations within the flight booking service (approach adopted by OTA) without explicitly defining separate operations for these atomic business functions makes the operations unavailable in different application context (e.g. payment for hotel or car rental). Furthermore, coarse-grained service operations are less flexible and more difficult to evolve as a number of business functions are typically combined and implemented as a single operation. Frequently, such services exhibit overlapping functionality (i.e. lack of orthogonality) and require that a number of operations are modified when requirements change, making application maintenance difficult in practice. Another important consideration for service design is application complexity, and some argue that low-granularity operations lead to complex interaction semantics for distributed applications. In our travel example we use four separate operations (BookFlight, Special, Payment, and Itinerary) to perform flight booking; using the OTA message-oriented approach a single pair of messages is used to achieve similar functionality. Using separate services and operations provides more flexibility, and closely models the interaction between the parties (i.e. travel agent and airline). Defining operations explicitly avoids the need to use complex message structures with implied functionality, and implicit business semantics.

Another frequently used argument in favor of the coarse-granularity, document-centric approach is that it allows validation of XML documents [29]. Document validation can be important for complex XML documents to ensure schematic correctness, but it is of lesser importance for simple parameters that characterize low-granularity operations.

Stability of service interfaces is another important design consideration. It is often claimed that the document-centric approach is associated with less rigid (i.e. more flexible) interfaces as changes or enhancements are made to the message schemas, not the method signatures [29,30]. Using the document-centric approach, the Web Services method signature has the simple form of service.operation (XML in, XML out), and does not need to be modified when requirements change [31]. Changes can be accommodated using XML extendibility mechanism (i.e. via the use of <xsd:any> element that allows the definition of data elements with untyped, imprecise content). However, while the interface signature does not need to change, the document structure has to be modified, breaking the interface contract, and forcing the modification of all dependent applications.

The above design issues will the subject of continuing debate. The main benefit of the software development methodology proposed in this paper is that it allows discussion of design tradeoffs such as the service granularity in the context of methodological framework, rather than making such decisions based on performance considerations only without any regard to software engineering issues.

We have used a simple travel domain scenario based on the OTA specification to illustrate the proposed methodology, but the approach is not domain-specific and should be equally applicable to other e-business domains such as global trade, healthcare, etc. The main focus of the software development framework described in this paper is on Web Services design. We do not address the problem of service-oriented analysis directly and rely on the availability of document-centric specification as the input into the design process. We are currently working on applying the methodology to Web Services design in other industry domains and enhancing the analysis component of the software development framework.

References

[1] S.W. Ambler. *Deriving Web Services from UML Models, Part 2: Establishing the Process*, 2002. http://www-106.ibm.com/developerworks/webservices/library/ws-uml2/.

[2] K. Levi and A. Arsanjani. A Goal-driven Approach to Enterprise Component Identification and Specification. *Communications of the ACM,* 45(10):45–52, 2002.

[3] M. Luo, et al. *Service-oriented Business Transformation in the Retail Industry Part 1: Apply SOA to Integrate Package Solutions and Legacy Systems*, 2005. http://www.ibm.com/developerworks/webservices/library/ws-retail1/.

[4] B. Meyer. *Object-oriented Software Construction.* 2nd ed. Prentice Hall, Upper Saddle River, N.J., 1997.

[5] R. Smith. *Modeling in the Service Oriented Architecture*, 2003. http://archive.devx.com/javasr/articles/smith1/smith1-1.asp.

[6] S. Masud. *Use RosettaNet-based Web Services, Part 2: BPEL4WS and RosettaNet*, 2003. http://www-106.ibm.com/developerworks/webservices/library/ws-rose2/.

[7] M.P. Papazoglou and J. Yang. Design Methodology for Web Services and Business Processes. In *Proceedings of the 3rd VLDB-TES Workshop*, pp. 54–64, Hong Kong, August 2002. Springer.

[8] F. Leymann. *Web Services Flow Language (WSFL 1.0)*, 2001. http://www-306.ibm.com/software/solutions/webservices/pdf/WSFL.pdf.

[9] B. Venners. *What's Method to Do?*, 1998. http://www.javaworld.com/javaworld/jw-05-1998/jw-05-techniques.html.

[10] K. Radeka. Designing a Web Services Project for Maximum Value: the 90 Day Challenge. In *Proceedings of Conference on Object Oriented Programming Systems Languages and Applications archive (OOPSLA 2002) Practitioners Reports*, Seattle, Washington, November 2002. ACM Press New York, NY, USA. ISBN:1-58113-471-1.

[11] G. Feuerlicht and S. Meesathit. Design Framework for Interoperable Service Interfaces. In *Proceedings of the 2nd International Conference on Service Oriented Computing*, pp. 299–307, New York, NY, USA, November 2004. ACM Press. ISBN:1-58113-871-7.

[12] G. Feuerlicht and S. Meesathit. Design Framework for Domain-Specific Service Interfaces. In *Proceedings of The Second International Workshop on Web Services: Modeling, Architecture, and Infrastructure (WSMAI-2004)*, pp. 109–15, Porto, Portugal, April 2004. INSTICC Press.

[13] M. Segal and K. Akeley. *The Design of the OpenGL Graphics Interface*, 1994. http://www.sun.com/software/graphics/opengl/OpenGLdesign.pdf.

[14] B. Venners. *Designing Contracts and Interfaces A Conversation with Scott Meyers, Part II*, 2002. http://artima.com/intv/mincomp3.html.

[15] R. Vallee-Rai. *Sable API Design Guidelines*, 1998. http://www.sable.mcgill.ca/publications/technotes/sable-tn-1998-1.ps.

[16] E. Yourdon and L.L. Constantine. *Structured Design: Fundamentals of a Discipline of Computer Program and Systems Design.* Prentice-Hall, Englewood Cliffs, N.J., 1979.

[17] S. Loughran. *Making Web Services that Work*, 2002. http://www.hpl.hp.com/techreports/2002/HPL-2002-274.pdf.

[18] E. Berk. *Manager of Developer Relations*, 2000. http://armadillosoft.com/api.pdf.

[19] J. Hammond. *Introducing Web Services into the Software Development Lifecycle*, 2002. http://www3.software.ibm.com/ibmdl/pub/software/rational/web/whitepapers/2003/TP033.pdf.

[20] K. Brown and M. Ellis. *Best Practices for Web Services Versioning: Keep Your Web Services Current with WSDL and UDDI*, 2004. http://www-106.ibm.com/developerworks/webservices/library/ws-version/.

[21] J. Browne, P. Higgins, and I. Hunt. E-business Principles, Trends and Vision, In J. Gasos and K.D. Thoben, J. Gasos and K.D. Thoben editors, *E-business Applications: Technologies for Tomorrow's Solutions*. Springer, 2002.

[22] C. Peltz and A. Anagol-Subbarao. *Design Strategies for Web Services Versioning: Adapting to the Needs of the Business*, 2004. http://sys-con.com/story/?storyid=44356&DE=1.

[23] H.-E. Eriksson and M. Penker. *Business Modeling with UML: Business Patterns at Work.* John Wiley & Sons, New York, USA, 2000.

[24] G. Feuerlicht. Designing Service-Oriented E-Business Applications Using Data Engineering Techniques. In *Proceedings of the Third Workshop on e-Business, in conjunction with ICIS 2004*, Washington D.C., USA, December 2004. ISBN:957-01-9161-9.
[25] B. Lublinsky and D. Tyomkin. Dissecting Service-Oriented Architectures. *Business Integration Journal*, October 2003, pp. 52-58.
[26] Sun Microsystems. *Designing Web Services with the J2EE(TM) 1.4 Platform: JAX-RPC, SOAP, and XML Technologies*, 2004. http://java.sun.com/blueprints/guidelines/designing_webservices/html/.
[27] L. Wilkes and R. Veryard. *Service-Oriented Architecture: Considerations for Agile Systems*, 2004. http://msdn.microsoft.com/architecture/soa/default.aspx?pull=/library/en-us/dnmaj/html/aj2service.asp.
[28] G. Feuerlicht. Implementing Service Interfaces for e-Business Applications. In *Proceedings of the Second Workshop on e-Business (WeB 2003)*, Seattle, USA, December 2003. ISSN: 1617-9846.
[29] J. McCarthy. *Reap the Benefits of Document Style Web Services*, 2002. http://www-106.ibm.com/developerworks/webservices/library/ws-docstyle.html.
[30] C. Peltz. *Applying Design Issues and Patterns in Web Services*, 2003. http://devresource.hp.com/drc/technical_articles/WSsuccess1.pdf.
[31] B. Lublinsky. *Unifying Data, Documents, and Processes*, 2004. http://www.ftponline.com/ea/magazine/summer2004/features/blublinsky/.

Chapter 7

Configuration Management Software

New Trends in Software Methodologies, Tools and Techniques
H. Fujita and M. Mejri (Eds.)
IOS Press, 2005

A Methodology for Deriving the Architectural Implications of Different Degrees of Mobility in Information Systems

Matthias BOOK, Volker GRUHN, Malte HÜLDER and Clemens SCHÄFER [1]
Chair of Applied Telematics / e-Business, University of Leipzig, Germany [2]

Abstract. When building information systems that can be accessed through desktop and mobile devices, developers often face the same basic design decisions that depend on a number of still unstructured criteria. Going through the whole decision-making process for every project is inefficient and error-prone, however, a comprehensive set of best practices has not yet been established. We therefore present the foundations of a classification scheme for mobile commerce systems that helps developers to categorize applications according to high-level requirements. After a discussion of the criteria, we suggest implications that can be drawn from it and present examples for their application.

Keywords. Mobile Computing, Software Architecture

1. Introduction

Recent years have brought an increasing demand of users to be able to do business very flexibly – ideally, any service should be available on any device, anywhere, anytime. The wide-spread presence of wireless networks and the availability of a diverse range of terminal devices has enabled the development of mobile applications that take us a step closer to accomplishing Weiser's vision of ubiquitous computing [1]. As this field is maturing, there is a need for collecting characteristics and principles of mobile systems. Considering that this is still a relatively young field, with most of the enabling technologies introduced into markets in the 1990s (such as GSM, GPRS and IEEE 802.11 WLAN) or just becoming available around this time (such as UMTS), the development methods for mobile applications are still unrefined and bear potential for optimization.

We are focusing on the architecture of mobile information systems with distinct client-server characteristics here since a large base of such information systems, albeit

[1] Correspondence to: Clemens Schäfer, Chair of Applied Telematics / e-Business, University of Leipzig, Klostergasse 3, 04109 Leipzig, Germany. Tel.: +49-341-97-32334; Fax: +49-341-97-32339; E-mail: schaefer@ebus.informatik.uni-leipzig.de.

[2] The Chair of Applied Telematics / e-Business is endowed by Deutsche Telekom AG.

without mobile capabilities, already exists today. Many organizations (e.g. in the insurance sector) are currently evaluating the business processes supported by these legacy applications for efficiency optimizations that may be gained through mobile access. Consequently, the architectural implications of enabling mobile access to information systems are an important issue in the industry.[1]

We consider it likely that some aspects of the development of mobile information systems are very similar to the development of traditional information systems, while other aspects may be more specific to mobile use, yet still independent of concrete, individual applications. Therefore, we hypothesize that a classification of information systems' mobile aspects will yield insights into their characteristics that support an efficient design process. Concrete measures to support architectural, technical, and process design decisions based on the proposed classification scheme are subject to further research in order to reach an ambitious goal: Using such a classification scheme, developers would not have to make fundamental design decisions on architectural, technical and process aspects from scratch during the development of each individual application, but could deduce some of the required design patterns, methods and processes from the class that an application belongs to.

While applications can certainly be classified quite exactly according to technical criteria, we believe that this should not be done *a priori* since the technical characteristics should be determined by the tasks the user needs to perform with the application, not vice versa. Also, the technical criteria are more prone to become outdated, while a classification on a higher level of abstraction remains applicable to a wide spectrum of technologies [2]. In fact, our motivation is to classify applications by non-technical criteria, as far as possible, so we can deduce the necessary technical implications from them.

In the following sections, we will give a brief overview of existing classification schemes that have been proposed (Section 2). Next, we present our definitions of different aspects of mobility and connectivity, which are pivotal criteria of our classification methodology (Section 3). After showing technical implications of our classification methodology (Section 4) and depicting some examples of its use, we finally conclude with a discussion of the criteria introduced so far, and present opportunities for further research on additional criteria that can contribute to refining the classification scheme (Section 5).

2. Related Work

Classification schemes for mobile computing applications that can be found in the literature are usually based on business criteria, i.e. they classify applications by the tasks and processes the user can perform with them. For example, Varshney and Vetter [3] discern mobile or wireless financial, advertising, inventory management, product locating and

[1] Obviously, other classes of mobile computing applications without explicit client-server characteristics also exist (e.g. peer-to-peer applications based on mobile ad-hoc networks). However, for the sake of clarity of the classification scheme, we restrict ourselves to mobile information systems for now. An extension of the classification scheme to include other types of applications will be an important aspect of further research (see Section 5).

shopping, service management, auctioning, entertainment and office applications, among others.

However, the criteria for associating specific applications with these classes are not explicitly stated, and the classes themselves do not seem to be disjoint, which renders the association ambiguous and thus makes it hard to draw precise conclusions from the classification. Varshney and Vetter do present a list of networking requirements that need to be fulfilled for applications of certain classes (such as location management, multicast support, network dependability, quality of service, and roaming across networks). However, since quite a few of these requirements are listed for every class, they do not really seem to be correlated to the class characteristics, but are actually basic requirements for any mobile application to a stronger or lesser degree.

Classification approaches that employ technology-centric criteria, such as the underlying network protocols, may seem helpful at first glance since the selected technology can have far-reaching consequences for the application design. For example, the decision to use a web-based user interface based on HTTP implies that the browser must use the pull paradigm to communicate with the server, while the server cannot initiate any communication with the client. This imposes restrictions on the interaction patterns that users can perform within the application [4]. For another example, developers of GPRS-based applications need to bear in mind latencies of about 25 seconds for setting up a connection and about two seconds for a request-response cycle in addition to the actual data transmission time [5]. For an application that relies on many request-response cycles (e.g. piecing a web page together from various elements), this technical characteristic from a low level of the protocol stack may severely diminish usability.

From yet another perspective, we can distinguish different types of mobility and use them for the classification of applications. In this context, Pandya [6] discerns device mobility, user mobility and service mobility: According to his definition, device mobility is given when the device remains connected to a network while it is moved physically. User mobility means that the user is not restricted to a single device, but can rather use different devices in order to use a service. Finally, a user experiences service mobility when he can access the same service from anywhere, independently of his location.

This approach of abstracting from concrete business and technology characteristics seems to be a step in the right direction. However, we believe that the concept of device mobility needs to be refined to encompass different degrees of mobility, as described in Section 3. Pandya's user mobility, in contrast, should always be given in today's mobile applications: A device that is tied so inseparably to one user that it cannot be used by a different user, and that the user cannot use a different device to accomplish the same task, is virtually inconceivable. Thus, user mobility can hardly serve as a distinguishing criterion for mobile applications. Finally, Pandya's definition of service mobility seems like a combination of device and user mobility, which makes it equivalent to device mobility if we assume user mobility to be always given. Specifically, service mobility does not seem to imply that the software providing the service is mobile.

In their roadmap, Roman, Picco and Murphy [7] make the distinction between physical mobility (movement of mobile hosts) and logical mobility (mobile units of code and state). From our point of view the situation here is similar to Pandya's definition: In our opinion the notion of physical mobility of Roman et al. is too coarse and needs to be refined. The same is true for the notion of mobility used by Issarny et al. [8]. Here the notion of computer and user mobility is used, but these notions lack a proper definition and hence a solid foundation.

Due to these concerns with existing classification approaches, we want to sharpen the existing definitions and thus present an alternative methodology that abstracts from concrete business and technology characteristics, but instead is based on high-level usage patterns, device capabilities, and service requirements.

3. Classification Criteria

In the following sections, we will present the three classification criteria user mobility, device mobility and service connectivity, and discuss their correlation.

Since today's e-commerce applications usually provide a range of different services to users (where a *service* shall be defined as a part of an application that supports a certain business process), it may be difficult to associate the whole application unambiguously with one category. Therefore, our criteria allow the independent classification of individual services within an application.

3.1. User Mobility

Since our goal is to deduce architectural, infrastructural and implementation aspects of a service from its classification, we strive to keep the classification criteria as non-technical as possible, and instead focus on user requirements and usage patterns. Consequently, the first criterion expresses the level of freedom of location and movement that is granted to a user while he is executing a business process (the user's location and movement while he is *not* executing a process are irrelevant, since the system is neither aware of nor influenced by them). We define four degrees of *user mobility*:

- A *local user* can only execute business processes at the application's location.
- A *distributed user* can execute business processes from a remote location.
- A *mobile user* can execute business processes from different remote locations.
- An *in-motion user* can execute business processes while changing his remote location.

Looking at the sets of all local, distributed, mobile and in-motion users (denoted by U_{loc}, U_{dis}, U_{mob} and U_{mot}, respectively), we notice that the sets of local and distributed users are obviously disjoint ($U_{\mathrm{loc}} \cap U_{\mathrm{dis}} = \emptyset$). Mobile users, however, are special cases of distributed users, and in-motion users are mobile users with additional requirements. Thus, distributed users are a superset of mobile users, which in turn are a superset of in-motion users ($U_{\mathrm{dis}} \supset U_{\mathrm{mob}} \supset U_{\mathrm{mot}}$). The distinction between the latter user groups becomes clear if we consider the differences between the sets, i.e. distributed users that are not mobile ($U_{\mathrm{dis}} \setminus U_{\mathrm{mob}}$), and mobile, yet not in-motion users ($U_{\mathrm{mob}} \setminus U_{\mathrm{mot}}$):

- A distributed *immobile user* can execute business processes from one remote location only.
- A mobile *at-rest user* can execute business processes while remaining in a static remote location only.

Note that in order to execute a business process while in motion, the user must carry the device that is used to work with the service with him (e.g. a PDA). However, if the user will aways be at rest while executing the process, he does not need to carry his own device with him, but can use any devices that are provided in locations where users may intend to work with the application (e.g. terminals dispersed throughout a trade fair center).

After defining the user's mobility, we now focus on the mobility of the device that he uses to execute business processes.

3.2. Device Mobility

Intuitive definitions of object mobility usually focus on whether it is possible to move an object physically, e.g. by defining mobile as "capable of moving or of being moved readily from place to place" [9]. From a software engineering perspective, though, this definition of physical mobility is not sufficient because it does not state how to distinguish the "places" from each other and thus deduce that the object has moved – we still need a frame of reference in relation to which objects are moving.

Communications networks provide such a frame of reference in the form of their access points (e.g. GSM cells, WLAN hot spots, etc.). Every access point has a certain coverage area that a device must enter in order to be able to connect to the network. In this scenario, we can define that *mobility is the capability of moving or of being moved readily between the coverage areas of a network's access points.* According to this definition, we distinguish four degrees of *device mobility*:

- A *local* device cannot connect to the network.
- A *distributed* device can connect to the network.
- A *mobile device* can connect to different access points.
- An *in-motion device* can connect to different access points while the user is using the device.

The sets of all local, distributed, mobile and in-motion devices (denoted by D_{loc}, D_{dis}, D_{mob} and D_{mot}, respectively) exhibit the same relationships as the different degrees of user mobility: $D_{\text{loc}} \cap D_{\text{dis}} = \emptyset$, and $D_{\text{dis}} \supset D_{\text{mob}} \supset D_{\text{mot}}$. The distinction between the network-enabled devices again becomes clearer when we look at the differences $D_{\text{dis}} \setminus D_{\text{mob}}$ and $D_{\text{mob}} \setminus D_{\text{mot}}$ that define immobile and at-rest devices:

- A distributed *immobile device* can always connect to the same access point only.
- A mobile *at-rest device* can only connect to the same access point while the user is using the device.

Note that in the presence of multiple distinct communication networks with different access point densities, a device that is mobile in relation to one network (i.e. moving into and out of the coverage areas of different access points) may at the same time be immobile in relation to another network (i.e. remaining within the coverage area of the same access point at all times). It is therefore important to consider which network to use as a frame of reference.

Since virtually every object can be moved from place to place with sufficient effort, the word "readily" introduces an important constraint both into the general and the specific definition of mobility presented above: While not specifying absolutely under which conditions an object can be considered mobile, it demands that the effort required to move an object shall be evaluated in relation to other metrics (e.g. the benefit of moving it or the effort required to move other objects). In the general definition, this effort may be determined by the object's weight or fixation. In the network-specific definition, configuring a device appropriately to connect to different access points may require additional effort, which may render the device immobile in the sense that it cannot connect *readily* to different access points.

We express devices' mobility in terms of their capability to connect readily to different access points here, because from a software engineering standpoint, small physical movements within the coverage area of one access point are undetectable and thus irrelevant.[2] However, larger physical movements that take the device out of reach of one access point and into the coverage area of another require a handover process that must either be handled transparently by the network infrastructure or explicitly by the application. Consequently, device mobility is not a characteristic of the device alone, but also of the network infrastructure, and potentially of the application.

3.3. Service Connectivity

Following the OSI reference model [10], the mobility of the service is determined by the mobility of the device that allows the remote user to execute business processes. Therefore, service mobility is not an independent criterion, but tied to device mobility. However, services must be prepared to handle a side effect of device mobility: Since the coverage areas of a network's access points may not overlap everywhere, there may be locations without network coverage. Consequently, a mobile device may be unable to connect to the network in certain locations, and an in-motion device may experience a loss of connection when passing through an uncovered area. The provisions that need to be taken by the service in order to handle these situations depend on how strongly it relies on the network connection. We define four degrees of *service connectivity*:

- An *offline service* never requires a network connection.
- A *hybrid-offline service* occasionally requires a network connection.
- A *hybrid-online service* requires a network connection most of the time.
- An *online service* requires a network connection at all times.

The sets of all offline, hybrid-offline, hybrid-online and online services (denoted by S_{off}, S_{hoff}, S_{hon} and S_{on}, respectively) are disjoint ($S_{\text{off}} \cap S_{\text{hoff}} \cap S_{\text{hon}} \cap S_{\text{on}} = \emptyset$).

One might argue that the definitions of the hybrid connectivity degrees are somewhat fuzzy, which is certainly true. Similarly to the "readiness" for movement in the previous section, the limiting ratio of connected vs. disconnected operations can hardly be specified absolutely here. Rather, the tolerable level of disconnected operation must be set in relation to other metrics such as the degree of autonomy that is allowed by the service's business process, and any given architecture or infrastructure elements.

Usually, a hybrid-offline service will allow the user to execute a business process offline, and only require a connection to the server infrequently and briefly in order to

[2] Note that we are only concerned with the impact of mobility on applications' architecture and communications infrastructure here. For location-aware applications, a small physical movement may certainly have consequences; however, those are in the realm of the business logic. An examination of the ties between device mobility and location-awareness is a topic of ongoing research, as discussed in Section 5.

Table 1. Correlations between the classification criteria.

	D_{loc}	$D_{dis} \setminus D_{mob}$	$D_{mob} \setminus D_{mot}$	D_{mot}
U_{loc}	S_{off}	S_{off}	S_{off}	S_{off}
$U_{dis} \setminus U_{mob}$	$\emptyset$	$S_{hoff} \cup S_{hon} \cup S_{on}$	$S_{hoff} \cup S_{hon} \cup S_{on}$	$S_{hoff} \cup S_{hon} \cup S_{on}$
$U_{mob} \setminus U_{mot}$	$\emptyset$	S_{hoff}	$S_{hoff} \cup S_{hon} \cup S_{on}$	$S_{hoff} \cup S_{hon} \cup S_{on}$
U_{mot}	$\emptyset$	S_{hoff}	$S_{hoff} \cup S_{hon}$	$S_{hoff} \cup S_{hon} \cup S_{on}$

transmit the process' input and/or output data. In contrast, a hybrid-online service will usually communicate frequently with the server while the user is executing a business process, but handle temporary losses of connection gracefully (e.g. by caching input and/or output data that is transmitted as soon as a connection is available, or performing trivial tasks autonomously without requiring a connection).

3.4. Correlations Between the Criteria

Considering possible combinations of the three criteria user mobility, device mobility and service connectivity in an application, we find that some combinations are feasible while others are contradictory.

For example, an in-motion user aims to work while he is changing his location. If he is using a device from the mobile at-rest category (i.e. a device that can connect to the network from any location, but not while moving), he will not be able to use an online service, because that service category requires a permanent network connection, which a mobile at-rest device cannot provide while the user is in motion. However, an in-motion user *can* employ a mobile at-rest device if the service is hybrid-online or hybrid-offline, i.e. the service does not require a network connection at all times but also allows some level of disconnected operation.

Relationships like this one are summarized in Table 1: If a user belongs to a certain group from the leftmost column and uses a device belonging to a certain group in the topmost row, then the feasible service connectivity must be from the set given in the associated table cell. For a user from the U_{mot} group and a device from the $D_{mob} \setminus D_{mot}$ group, for example, we find that the set of feasible service connectivity degrees is $S_{hoff} \cup S_{hon}$.

Further to this discussion, if an in-motion user (U_{mot}) employs a distributed immobile device ($D_{dis} \setminus D_{mob}$), i.e. one that can only connect to the network from a single, specific location), the service can only be hybrid-offline (S_{hoff}), i.e. not require a network connection most of the time (while the user is moving), and only briefly connect when the user is at rest in the specific location that the device can connect from. Conversely, if an in-motion user employs an in-motion device that can remain connected to the network even when the user is moving (D_{mot}), he can use online services that require a permanent connection, or hybrid-online services if he wants to be immune against occasional connection losses. He may even use a hybrid-offline service, even though it would not utilize the device's networking capabilities fully.

A closer look at the table suggests that with the exception of U_{loc}, D_{loc} and S_{off}, the correlation between the three criteria follows these rules:

- If a certain service connectivity is feasible for a certain user/device mobility combination, all lower service connectivities are also feasible for this combination.

- In order for online service connectivity to be feasible, the device must be in the same or a higher mobility category than the user.
- If the device is in a lower mobility category than the user, the feasible service connectivity is reduced, possibly overproportionally.

Local users, local devices and offline services do not follow these rules because their sets are disjoint from the network-capable degrees of the three criteria. If a local user only works with a service on the same device that it is running on, no network connection is necessary, so the service is classified as offline (even if the device is capable of accessing a network, that feature will not be utilized by the service). Conversely, if the user is not local, no offline service can be available on any device since a network connection is always required to contact it.

One might argue that a moving user could still use an offline service (such as a premium calculator) on a mobile device that he is carrying with him. However, since we defined user mobility as movement occuring remotely from a service and device mobility as movement occuring in relation to a network, the user, device and service in this scenario would all be local and stationary in relation to each other. From a technical perspective, the physical mobility of this closed system is not relevant. Therefore, it also belongs to the local user and device category. Note, however, that these offline services may still support the user in executing business processes on hybrid or online services.

4. Technical Implications of the Classification

So far, our methodology enables developers to deduce feasible degrees of service connectivity from the frame conditions set by the desired user mobility and the available device mobility.[3] Often, these different degrees of connectivity will require different technical provisions to be taken in the implementation of the service.

In the second step of our methodology, we therefore need to identify architectural implications of different degrees of connectivity. We are focusing on information systems with client-server characteristics here – other types of mobile computing applications (e.g. telemetry or peer-to-peer applications) [3] may be subject to different architectural implications, which are a topic of future research.

4.1. Distribution of Architectural Tiers

E-commerce systems store and process data according to the business requirements of their application domain. Their architecture usually follows a three-tier model, distinguishing presentation logic, business logic and data storage. In a client-server environment, these layers may be distributed according to different strategies. Figure 1 shows how these distribution patterns depend on the degree of service connectivity. For each set of services, the figure indicates which parts of the three layers must reside on the client, which parts must reside on the server, and what information must be communicated between both sides.

[3] Depending on the given information, the correlation table can obviously also be used to deduce the degree of user mobility allowed by a given combination of device mobility and service connectivity, or to indicate the level of device mobility required to provide a given service to users with a given mobility degree.

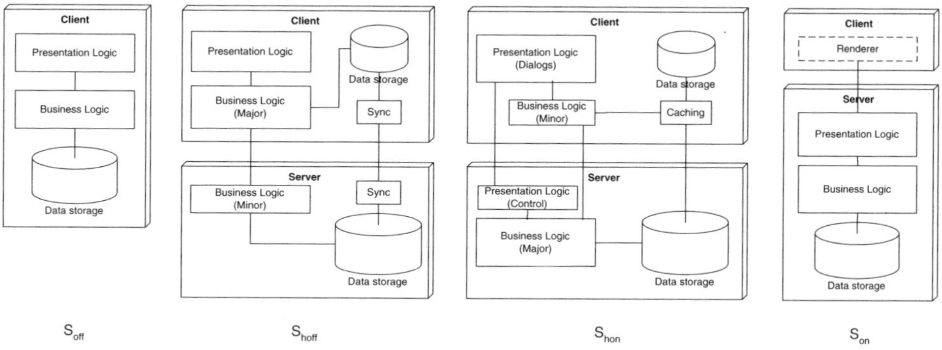

Figure 1. Distribution patterns for information systems, depending on service connectivity.

For example, a hybrid-offline service may access the network occasionally, but is used without a connection most of the time. Therefore, it must also implement the complete presentation logic and all major features of the business logic on the client side, and store all data that the user requires to execute business processes. In most information systems, this is a subset of the complete data repository stored on the server, which is synchronized when a connection is present. In addition, the server may provide some minor additional business logic features when connected.

Conversely, a hybrid-online service can rely on the presence of a network connection most of the time, and may just have to deal with temporary losses of connection. Under these conditions, most of the dialog control logic can reside on the server, however, the client should be able to display dialogs and allow basic interactions even without a network connection. This can be achieved by implementing the dialogs on the client and coupling them loosely to the server-side control logic that just needs to send "triggers" to let the client perform pre-defined dialog sequences autonomously. Similarly, most of the business logic can be implemented on the server, with just a restricted set of features being available on the client in case of a temporary loss of connection. All required data can usually be accessed over the network connection, however, a temporary storage is required on the client to cache incoming data and buffer outgoing data in case the connection breaks down. Once the connection has been re-established, the cached/buffered data can be updated from/in the server-side database.

Finally, an online service can rely on a permanent network connection, so the presentation logic, business logic and data storage can reside completely on the server. Communication is then constantly required in order to transmit a description of the user interface to display to the client. Since the interpretation and rendering of the interface description can be realized application-independently (e.g. by an existing web browser), we used a dashed box in the figure.

Note that the figure shows the *minimum client requirements* and the *maximum server requirements* for providing the associated service connectivity. For example, if more presentation logic was implemented on the client side of an online service, the connectivity degree could remain the same (in fact, it would be equivalent to a hybrid-online service for the presentation layer). However, if no data was stored on the client side of a hybrid-online service, online connectivity would be required for the storage layer. These relationships can be expressed in the following rules:

- Different layers of one service can support different connectivity degrees.
- Shifting logic from the server to the client on a layer allows a lower connectivity degree for that layer
- Shifting logic from the client to the server on a layer requires a higher connectivity degree for that layer
- A service's overall connectivity degree is determined by the highest degree of all its layers.

For example, a service that runs the complete presentation logic on the client, relies on the server for most business logic operations, and reads and writes any processed data directly from/to a database on the server can only support online connectivity.

4.2. Examples

To illustrate the classification methodology, we will now apply it to real-world examples from recent industry projects. After identifying the requirements and deducing the available architecture choices as suggested in this paper, we compare them to the architectures that were actually implemented in those projects.

As an example, we consider a dispatch system for a truckage company that constantly provides truck drivers (who are in motion most of the time and thus belong to the U_{mot} category) with current dispatch and routing information and allows them to trigger processes in the back-end through an on-board unit connected to the GSM network (e.g. an in-motion device from the D_{mot} category). This combination would allow the whole range of hybrid-offline, hybrid-online and online service connectivity. However, since parts of the system (such as the routing) still need to work while crossing gaps in the network coverage, an architecture that does not exclusively rely on the network was chosen: While the complete presentation logic and business logic required by the driver resides on the client (as for a hybrid-offline service), the system strives to always work with current data received from the server, and only uses cached data in case the connection is interrupted. Since this represents a hybrid-online connectivity in the storage layer, the whole system is considered hybrid-online (S_{hon}).

In contrast, a lottery portal that allows users to participate in lottery games with their WAP-enabled cellphone also fulfills the U_{mot} (in-motion users) and D_{mot} (in-motion devices) criteria. However, to keep the service as independent from the users' devices as possible, the system was built using a completely server-centered architecture. Only the markup for the displayed WML pages is communicated to the client, resulting in online service connectivity (S_{on}).

The same portal can also be accessed on another channel via short message service (SMS). This way, an in-motion user (U_{mot}) may type his lottery bet into a text message on his mobile phone (a D_{mot} device). The message may be composed independently of network availability and is sent out when network coverage is available. The server then generates a confirmation SMS, which is transmitted back to the device when it is connected to the network. The system is therefore still usable (i.e. messages can be composed and read) during brief network outages. However, if the network connection is lost for a longer time, it becomes more unusable since the user cannot place bets or receive the important confirmation messages. Since there is no business logic residing on the client, and client-side data (i.e. message) storage represents a kind of buffering, the service can be considered hybrid-online (S_{hon}).

5. Conclusions

In the preceding sections, we introduced three criteria for the classification of mobile information systems that allow us to deduce the possible connectivity of a service from two high-level frame conditions – coarse usage patterns (in terms of user mobility) and basic device capabilities (in terms of device mobility). Using the service connectivity for guidance, we can then decide on the more technical issue of how to distribute the implementation of the presentation, business and storage layer across the client-server architecture.

Due to the lack of space we could not show in detail how the second step may be performed, which is also still being optimizied as part of our ongoing research. In this context, we are mainly focusing on two questions: Firstly, which other application classes need to be considered? Can we use any existing application classification and apply our new criteria to it in order to examine the implications of mobile use, or are there other general characteristics of mobile applications that determine the distribution patterns of other information systems? And secondly, when a certain combination of user and device mobility allows a range of service connectivity degrees, which criteria determine which connectivity degree is actually chosen on each layer?

When looking for such classification criteria, we need to find a balance between mobile application characteristics whose nature is more that of requirements than of consequences or features (for example, high bandwidth is a feature of certain communication channels – a related requirement that could be more suitable as a classification criterion is high data volume). Also, while as software engineers, we tend to focus on technical characteristics, we should also look for relevant application domain criteria – one strong candidate for such criteria certainly is location awareness.

Further research should also go into the granularity that is possible and sensible for such a classification scheme. The criteria presented in this paper already operate on the service instead of the application level, so different services can constitute one application; and within one service, different layers can (under certain restrictions) support different service connectivities. However, we still need to examine architectural implications for applications that comprise services with different connectivity degrees.

Finally, we have only considered the mobility of users and devices with regard to physical networks so far. Ultimately, the classification criteria and rules for their architectural implications should also cover virtual aspects of mobility – i.e., mobility with regard to virtual networks, and logical mobility of code that may be exchanged between devices.

Based on the basic criteria introduced in this paper, the above questions should provide a basis for interesting research in a number of directions, helping us to understand the characteristics of mobile commerce applications better and thus develop them more efficiently.

References

[1] M. Weiser. The computer for the twenty-first century. *Scientific American*, 265(3):94–104, 1991.

[2] O. Höß, D. Spath, A. Weisbecker, A.C. Allag, U. Rosenthal, and M. Veit. Ein Klassifikationsschema für die Architektur von mobilen Anwendungen - Erläutert an einem Praxisbeispiel zur mobilen Erfassung von Führerscheinprüfungen. In *Mobile Business – Processes, Platforms, Payments*, pages 131–142. Gesellschaft für Informatik, 2005.

[3] Upkar Varshney and Ron Vetter. Mobile commerce: framework, applications and networking support. *Mobile Networks and Applications*, 7(3):185–198, 2002.

[4] J. Rice, A. Farquhar, P. Piernot, and T. Gruber. Using the web instead of a window system. In *Proceedings of the ACM Conference on Human Factors in Computing Systems (CHI '96)*, 1996.

[5] Rajiv Chakravorty and Ian Pratt. WWW performance over GPRS. In *Proceedings of the IEEE International Conference on Mobile and Wireless Communication Networks*, 2002.

[6] R. Pandya. *Mobile and personal communication systems and services.* IEEE Press, 2000.

[7] G.C. Roman, G.P. Picco, and A.L. Murphy. Software Engineering for Mobility: A Roadmap. In *Proceedings of the Conference on the Future of Software Engineering*, pages 241–258. ACM Press, 2000.

[8] V. Issarny, F. Tartanoglu, Jinshan Liu, and F. Sailhan. Software Architecture for Mobile Distributed Computing. In *Proceedings of the Fourth Working IEEE/IFIP Conference on Software Architecture (WICSA'04)*, pages 201–210. IEEE, 2004.

[9] AHD. *The American Heritage Dictionary of the English Language.* Houghton Mifflin Co, 4th edition, 2000.

[10] ISO. *ISO/IEC Standard 7498-1: Information Processing Systems – OSI Reference Model – The Basic Model.* International Organization for Standardization, 1994.

Chapter 8

Ubiquitous and Web Related Systems Software

New Trends in Software Methodologies, Tools and Techniques
H. Fujita and M. Mejri (Eds.)
IOS Press, 2005

Meme Media for the Federation of Intellectual Resources over the Web by Clipping and Combining Them

Yuzuru TANAKA [1]
Meme Media Laboratory, Hokkaido University, N-13, W-8, Sapporo 060-8628, Japan

Abstract. The publication and reuse of intellectual resources using the Web technologies provide no support for us to clip out any portion of Web pages, to combine them together for their local reuse, nor to distribute the newly composed object for its reuse by other people. Such a composition requires both a layout composition and a functional composition. Both of them should be performed only through direct manipulation. This paper shows how the meme-media architecture is applied to the Web to provide such support for us. This makes the Web work as a shared repository not only for publishing intellectual resources, but also for their collaborative reediting, and furthermore for the flexible federation of intellectual resources. Federation here denotes ad hoc definition and/or execution of interoperation among intellectual resources. We will propose a general framework for clipping arbitrary Web contents as live objects, and for the recombination and linkage of such clips based on both the original and some user-defined relationships among them. This framework allows us to define federations of intellectual resources over the Web dynamically through direct manipulation.

Keywords. Middleware, Web Technologies, Web Architecture, Software Architecture, IS integration, Knowledge Integration

1. Introduction

During the last decade, we have observed the rapid accumulation of intellectual resources on the Web. These intellectual resources include not only multimedia documents, but also application tools running on the client side, and services provided by remote servers.

The publication and reuse of intellectual resources using the Web technologies can be characterized by the schematic model in Fig. 1 (a). The Web publication uses a compound document representation of intellectual resources. Compound documents denote documents with embedded contents such as multimedia contents, visual application tools, and/or interactive services provided by servers. Such a compound document published on the Web defines a Web page. The model in Fig. 1 (a) has no support for us to extract any portion of published Web pages, to combine them together for their local

[1] Yuzuru Tanaka, Meme Media Laboratory, Hokkaido University, N-13 W-8, Sapporo, 060-8628, Japan. Tel.: +81 11 706 7250; Fax: +81 11 706 7808; E-mail: tanaka@meme.hokudai.ac.jp.

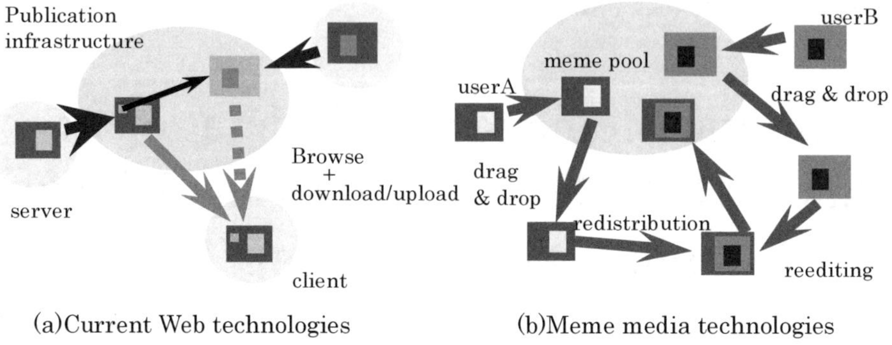

Figure 1. The publication and reuse of intellectual resources.

reuse, nor to republish the newly defined composite object into the Web. The composition here means not only textual combination but functional federation of embedded tools and services. Federation here denotes ad hoc definition and/or execution of interoperation among intellectual resources. While the integration denotes interoperation among intellectual resources with a priori designed standard interoperation interfaces, federation denotes interoperation among intellectual resources without a priori designed interoperation interfaces. We need some support to reedit and to redistribute Web resources for their further reuse and new intellectual-resource creation.

Figure 1 (b) shows a new model for the worldwide publication, reediting and redistribution of intellectual resources. As in the case of the Web, you can publish a set of your intellectual resources as a compound document into a worldwide publication repository. You can use a browser to view such documents published by other people. In addition to these operations, you can clip out any portions of viewed documents as reusable components, combine them together to define a new compound document for your own use, and publish this new compound document into the repository for its reuse by other people. This new model of publishing, reediting and redistributing intellectual resources assumes that all these operations can be performed only through direct manipulation. Meme-media technologies proposed by our group [14,20–22], when applied to the Web, realize this new model, and make the Web work as a meme pool of intellectual resources. They provide the direct manipulation operations necessary for reediting and redistributing intellectual resources.

'Meme' is a word coined by Richard Dawkins. He pointed out a similarity between genetic evolution of biological species and cultural evolution of knowledge and art, and coined the word 'meme' to denote the cultural counterpart of a biological gene. As biological genes are replicated, recombined, mutated, and naturally selected, ideas are replicated, recombined, modified with new fragments, and selected by people. The acceleration of memetic cultural evolution requires media to externalize memes, and to distribute them among people. Such media allows people to reedit their knowledge contents and redistribute them, and hence may be called meme media. They work as knowledge media for the reediting and redistribution of intellectual assets.

Web Service technologies can provide us with similar functions for the functional linkage among Web applications [1,4,16,18]. Web Service technologies enable us to interoperate services published over the Web. However, they assume that the API (Application Program Interface) library to access such a service is a priori provided by its server side. You need to write a program to interoperate more than one Web service. Meme-media technologies, on the other hand, provide only the client-side direct manipulation operations for users to reedit intellectual resources embedded in Web pages, to define a new combination of them together with their functional linkage, and to republish the result into the Web. In addition, meme-media technologies are applicable not only to the Web, but also to local objects. Meme media can wrap any documents and tools, including also any Web services, and make each of them work as interoperable meme-media object. You can easily combine Web resources with local tools and Web services.

This paper shows how the meme-media architecture is applied to the Web to make it work as meme pools. This makes the Web work as a shared repository not only for publishing intellectual resources, but also for their collaborative reediting and federation. We will propose a general framework for clipping arbitrary Web contents as live objects, and for the recombination and linkage of such clips. In our previous works, we proposed two separate frameworks for these two purposes; one works for the former [14,21,22], and the other for the latter [11]. Here we will propose a unified framework for these three purposes.

2. Wrapping Web Resources as Meme Media Objects

2.1. Meme-Media Architecture IntelligentPad

IntelligentPad is a two-dimensional representation meme-media architecture. Its architecture can be roughly summarized as follows for our current purpose. Instead of directly dealing with component objects, IntelligentPad wraps each object with a standard pad wrapper, i.e., a software module with a standard visual representation and a standard functional linkage interface, and treats it as a media object called a pad. Each pad has both a standard user interface and a standard connection interface. The user interface of every pad has a card like view on the screen and a standard set of operations like 'move', 'resize', 'copy', 'paste', and 'peel'. As a connection interface, every pad provides a list of slots that works as IO ports, and a standard set of messages 'set', 'gimme', and 'update'. Each pad defines one of its slots as its primary slot. Most pads allow users to change their primary slot assignments.

You may paste a pad on another pad to define a parent-child relationship between these two pads. The former becomes a child of the latter. When you paste a pad on another, you can select one of the slots provided by the parent pad, and connect the child pad to this selected slot. The selected slot is called the connection slot. Using a 'set' message, each child pad can set the value of its primary slot to the connection slot of its parent pad. Using a 'gimme' message, each child pad can read the connec-tion slot value of its parent pad, and update its primary slot with this value. Whenever a pad has a state change, it sends an 'update' message to each of its child pads to notify this state change. Whenever a pad receives an 'update' message, it sends a 'gimme' message to its parent pad. For each slot connection, you can independently enable or disable each of the three standard messages. By pasting pads on another pad and specifying slot connections, you may easily define both a compound document layout and functional linkage among these pads.

2.2. Clipping and Reediting of Web Resources

Web documents are defined in HTML format. An HTML view denotes an arbitrary HTML document portion represented in the HTML document format. The pad wrapper to wrap an arbitrary portion of a Web document specifies an arbitrary HTML view and renders any HTML document. We call this pad wrapper an HTMLviewPad. Its rendering function is implemented by wrapping a legacy Web browser Internet Explorer. The specification of an arbitrary HTML view over a given HTML document requires the capability of editing the internal representation of HTML documents, namely, DOM trees [15]. The DOM tree representation allows you to identify any HTML-document portion, which corresponds to a DOM tree node, with its XPath expression [9] such as `/HTML[1]/BODY[1]/TABLE[1]/TR[2]/TD[2]`. The precise definition of DOM and XPath is out of the scope of this paper. For the details, you may refer to their specification documents [9,15].

The definition of an HTML view consists of a source document specification, and a sequence of view editing operations. A source document specification uses the document URL. Its retrieval is performed by a function 'GETHTML' in such a way as

```
url = 'http://www.abc.com/index.html';
doc = url.GETHTML();
```

The retrieved document is kept in DOM format. The editing of an HTML view is a sequence of DOM tree manipulation operations selected out of the followings:

CLIP(*node*)
: To delete all the nodes other than the sub tree with the specified node as its root.

DELETE(*node*)
: To delete the sub tree with the specified node as its root.

INSERT(*node*, *HTML_view*, *location*)
: To insert a given DOM tree (HTML view) at the specified relative location of the specified node. You may select the relative location out of CHILD, PARENT, BEFORE, and AFTER.

An HTML view is specified as follows:

```
defined-view = source-view.DOM-tree-operation(node),
```

where source-view may be a Web document or another HTML document, and node is specified by its path expression. This code is called the view editing code of the HTML view. The following is an example view definition code.

```
view1 = doc
        .CLIP('/HTML/BODY/TABLE[1]')
        .CLIP('/TABLE[1]/TR[1]')
        .DELETE('/TR[1]/TD[2]');
```

After the first CLIP operation, the node `/TABLE[1]/TR[1]` corresponds to the node `/HTML/BODY/TABLE[1]/TR[1]` of the original document doc. The former path expression `/TABLE[1]/TR[1]` is called the relative path expression.

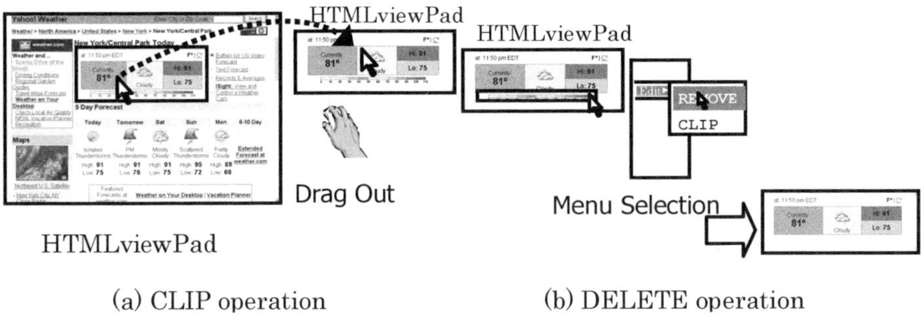

Figure 2. Direct Manipulations for extracting and removing views.

An HTMLviewPad with a view editing code can execute this code to recover the edit result when necessary. Its loading from a server or a local disk to a desktop is such a case.

2.3. *Direct Editing of HTML Views*

Instead of specifying a relative path expression to identify a DOM tree node, we will make the HTMLviewPad to dynamically frame different extractable document portions for different mouse locations so that its user may move the mouse cursor around to see every extractable document portion. When the HTMLviewPad frames what you want to clip out, you can drag the mouse to create another HTMLviewPad with this clipped-out document portion. The new HTMLviewPad renders the clipped-out DOM tree on itself. Figure 2 (a) shows an example clip operation, which internally generates the following view edit code.

```
url = 'http://www.abc.com/index.html';
view = url.GETHTML()
       .CLIP('/HTML/BODY/TABLE[1]');
```

The HTMLviewPad provides a pop-up menu of view-edit operations including CLIP, DELETE and INSERT. After you select an arbitrary portion, you may select either CLIP or DELETE. Figure 2 (b) shows an example delete operation, which generates the following code.

```
url = 'http://www.abc.com/index.html';
view = url.GETHTML()
       .CLIP('/HTML/BODY/TABLE[1]')
       .DELETE('/TABLE[1]/TR[2]');
```

The INSERT operation uses two HTMLviewPads showing a source HTML document and a target one. You may first specify INSERT operation from the menu, and specify the insertion location on the target document by directly specifying a document portion and then specifying relative location from a menu including CHILD, PARENT, BEFORE, and AFTER. Then, you may directly select a document portion on the source document, and drag and drop this portion on the target document. Figure 3 shows an

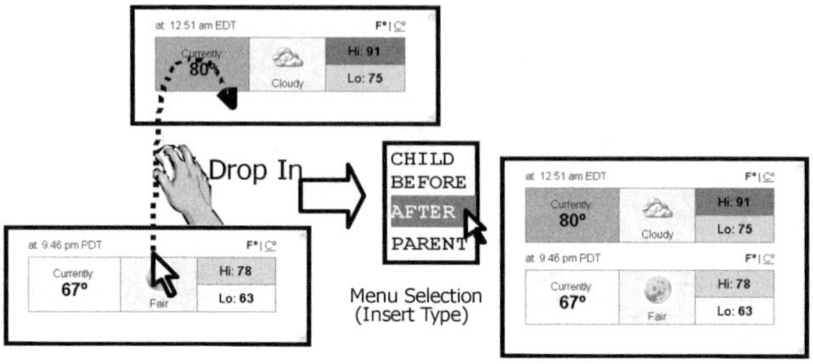

Figure 3. Direct manipulation for inserting a view in another view.

example insert operation, which generates the following code, where the target HTMLviewPad uses a different name space to merge the edit code of the dragged-out HTMLviewPad to its own edit code:

```
A::view = A::url.GETHTML()
            .CLIP('/HTML/BODY/.../TD[2]/.../TABLE[1]')
            .DELETE('/TABLE[1]/TR[2]');
view = url.GETHTML()
        .CLIP('/HTML/BODY/.../TD[1]/.../TABLE[1]')
        .DELETE('/TABLE[1]/TR[2]')
        .INSERT('/TABLE[1]', A::view, AFTER);
```

The dropped HTMLviewPad is deleted after the insertion.

2.4. Automatic Generation of Default Slots

Each HTMLviewPad has the following four default slots. The #UpdateInterval slot specifies the time interval for the periodical polling of referenced HTTP servers. A view defined over a Web document refreshes its contents by periodically retrieving this Web document in an HTTP server. This is done by periodically executing its view editing code. The #SourceURL slot stores the URL of the source document. The #ViewEditingCode slot stores the view editing code. The #DestinationURL slot is used to hold a destination URL with or without a query to access a new page. The HTMLviewPad updates itself by executing its view editing code whenever one of the following conditions occurs: (1) the #SourceURL slot or the #ViewEditingCode slot is accessed with a set message, (2) the interval timer invokes the polling, (3) a user specifies its update, or (4) it becomes active after its loading from a file.

Depending on the type of the node to clip out, the HTMLviewPad automatically generates some additional default slots.

When you clip out a general node such as a text node or a paragraph node, the HTMLviewPad automatically creates a new HTMLviewPad, defines a default text-value slot in this new pad, and sets the text in the selected node to this slot. The slot name is specified by the user when he clips this node. This slot works as the default primary slot of this clip.

If the text is a numerical string, the HTMLviewPad converts this string to a numerical value, and sets this value to the automatically created slot. This slot works as the default primary slot of this clip.

When you clip out a table node such as </HTML/···/TABLE>, the HTMLviewPad creates a new HTMLviewPad, converts the table value to its CSV representation, and generates a new default slot with this value in the new pad. The slot name is specified by the user when he clips this node. This slot works as the default primary slot of this clip.

When a clip of one of the above three types receives a set message, it sends a set message to its parent with the current primary slot value, and also sends an update message to its child pads. When it receives an update message from its parent pad, it sends a gimme message to get a new HTML view to render on itself.

When you clip out an anchor node, the HTMLviewPad creates a new HTMLviewPad, defines the following three default slots. The slot names are specified by the user when he clips this node. For example, let us consider a case in which we clip out an anchor defined as follows:

```
<A href=./next.html>
Next Page
</A>
```

The text slot holds 'Next Page', while the href slot holds './next.html' as its value. Whenever the anchor is clicked or a set message is sent to the submission slot, the destination URL is calculated, and is set to the #DestinationURL slot. Then this HTMLviewPad sends a set message to its parent pad with the value of its submission slot as its parameter value, and also sends an update message to each of its child pads if any.

When you clip out a form node, the HTMLviewPad ctrates a new HTMLviewPad, defining two default slots, i.e., an input slot and a submission slot. The #DestinationURL slot works as the default primary slot of this clip. When this clip receives a set message to its submission slot, it creates a query to the server from the input slot value, and updates #DestinationURL slot with the concatenation of the server URL and this query. Then it sends a set message to its parent with its primary slot value, and also sends update messages to its child pads. If it receives an update message from its parent, it sends a gimme message to get a new HTML view to render on itself.

For example, let us consider a case in which we clip out a form defined as follows:

```
<FORM action="./search">
<INPUT Type=txt name=keyword >
<INPUT Type=submit value="search">
</FORM>
```

The input slot holds the input keyword. Whenever we submit a form input or the submission slot receives a set message, the HTMLviewPad calculates the destination URL with a query '/search?keyword=<the input slot value>', and sets this value to the #DestinationURL slot. Then the HTMLviewPad sends a set message to its parent pad with the value of its primary slot as its parameter value, and also sends an update message to each of its child pads if any.

For a non atomic node corresponding to an internal node of a DOM tree, its clipping generates a new HTMLviewPad and its HTML slot with the current HTML view as its value. The slot name is specified by the user when he clips this node. This slot works as the default primary slot of this clip. This clip accepts no set message. When this clip receives a gimme message to this slot, it returns this slot value. When a user operation on this clip updates its HTML view, it sends the new HTML view to its parent, and also sends an update message to each of its child pads.

3. Recombination and Linkage of Web Resource Clips

3.1. Recombination of Web Clips and Their Linkage

Here we consider the clipping of more than one HTML node from more than one Web page visited through a single navigation, and their functional recombination based on the functional linkage relationship among these nodes in this navigation. Figure 4 shows a Google Web page, and the clipping of the keyword input form, and the first search result through a search navigation with 'IntelligentPad' as a search keyword. The Web browser used here is also an HTMLviewPad. We can use its node specification mode to clip out HTML nodes only through mouse operation. The HTMLviewPad internally holds a sequence of such operations as a view editing code including event operations. Event operations include the following three operations:

CLICK(*anchor_node*)
    To return the destination Web page of this anchor
SET(*form_node*, *input*)
    To set an input value to the specified form input node
SUBMIT(*submit_node*)
    To return the output page by sending the corresponding server a query specified by the current input-form values.

In this example, we first clipped out the keyword input form, and the search area selector as two new HTMLviewPads from the Google home page.

These clips have the following view editing codes:

```
Clip1  view  =  url.GETHTML()
                .CLIP(π)
Clip2  view  =  url.GETHTML()
                .CLIP(π1)
```

After these clips are clipped out, the HTMLviewPad Clip0 showing the Google home page has the following view editing code:

```
Clip0  view  =  url.GETHTML()
```

Then we input a search keyword 'IntelligentPad' on this Google home page, set a selector, and click the search button to obtain the first search result page. This changes the view editing code of Clip0 as

```
Clip0  view  =  url.GETHTML()
                .SET(π, 'IntelligentPad')
                .SET(π1, *)
                .SUBMIT(π2)
```

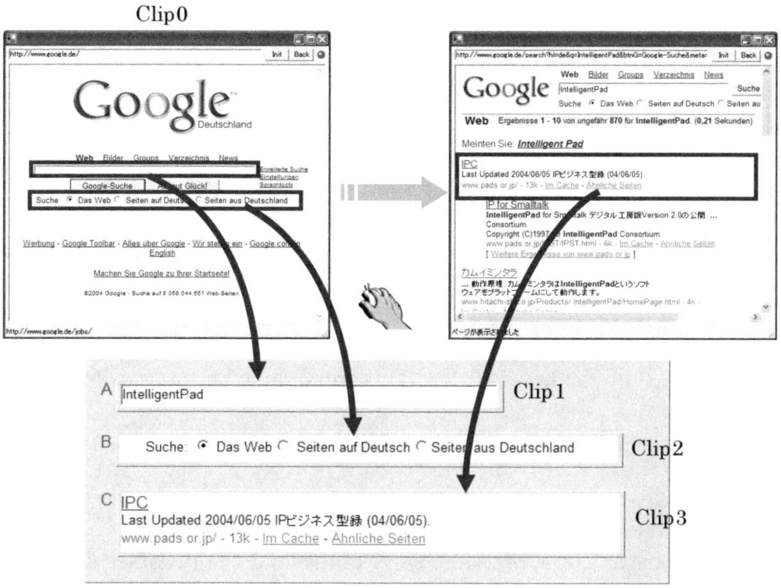

Figure 4. Clips extracted from a single navigation and their recombination on a ClipboardPad.

where .SET(π1, *) denotes that the current HTML view at node π1 is set to the node π1. This substitution may seem to be redundant. However, in the later discussion, this parameter value is connected to the Clip2, and is updated by a set message from this clip that may have changed its HTML view through user's interaction.

Now the Clip0 shows the second page. From this page, we clipped out the first search result as another new HTMLviewPad Clip3.

```
Clip3  view  =  url.GETHTML()
                .SET(π, 'IntelligentPad')
                .SET(π1, *)
                .SUBMIT(π2)
                .CLIP(π3)
```

Each of these clips is pasted on the same special pad called a ClipboardPad immediately after it is clipped out. This ClipboardPad is used to make these clips operate with each other based on their functional linkage relationship in the navigation. It holds a list of view editing codes, each of which corresponds to a single navigation. When we clip out and paste Clip1 on a ClipboardPad, it creates a new entry in the view editing code list, and puts the view editing code of Clip0 at this time. This entry value becomes as follows:

```
view = url.GETHTML();
```

The ClipboardPad associates this clip a new cell name 'A', creates a corresponding slot #A, and connects Clip1 to this slot. It associate the slot #A with the node π. This adds one more operation .CELL ('A', π) at the end of the above code using the following new operation:

CELL(*cell_name*, *node*)
To associate the specified cell with the specified node, and to return the same HTML view as the recipient.

When we paste Clip2 on the same ClipboardPad, it searches the list for an entry with such a code that is a prefix of the view editing code of Clip0 at this time. This comparison neglects all the CELL operations in the code stored in each entry of the code list. The Clip-boardPad updates this entry with the code σ, inserts all the CELL operations in the old entry code at the same positions in σ, and adds one more CELL operation to associate the node $\pi 1$ with the new cell 'B'. This entry value becomes as follows:

```
view  =  url.GETHTML()
         .CELL('A', π)
         .CELL('B', π1);
```

The ClipboardPad connects Clip2 to the slot #B.

When we finally paste Clip3, the same entry of the code list becomes as follows:

```
view  =  url.GETHTML()
         .CELL('A', π)
         .CELL('B', π1)
         .SET(π, 'IntelligentPad')
         .SET(π1, *)
         .SUBMIT(π2)
         .CELL('C', π3);
```

The ClipboardPad connects Clip3 to the slot #C.

When we input some keyword on Clip1, it sends a set massage to the slot #A with its primary slot value, which is the value of the slot #keyword, i.e., the input keyword. The ClipboardPad scans CELL operations for the slot #A, finds the associated node π, searches for a SET operation with π as its first parameter, replaces its second parameter with the input keyword, and executes this view editing code. When we select an item on Clip2, it sends a set message to the slot #B with its updated HTML view. This values is used to rewrite the second parameter of SET($\pi 1$, *). Then this ClipboardPad executes the view editing code.

Whenever the Clipboard executes a view edit code, it sends update messages to all the clips working as output devices. Each of thease clips sends a gimme message to its connection slot. The ClipboardPad searches for the node associated with this connection slot, and returns the HTML view of this node.

These mechanisms allow clips obtained during a single navigation to interoperate with each other based on their original functional relationships in the navigation.

3.2. Linkage Between Web Clips from Different Navigations

A ClipboardPad is also used to define functional linkage among different clip sets clipped out from different navigations. When we paste a clip on a ClipboardPad, the ClipboadPad automatically gives it a unique cell name such as 'A'', 'B'', 'C'', '$A1'$', '$B1'$', '$A2'$'. Like

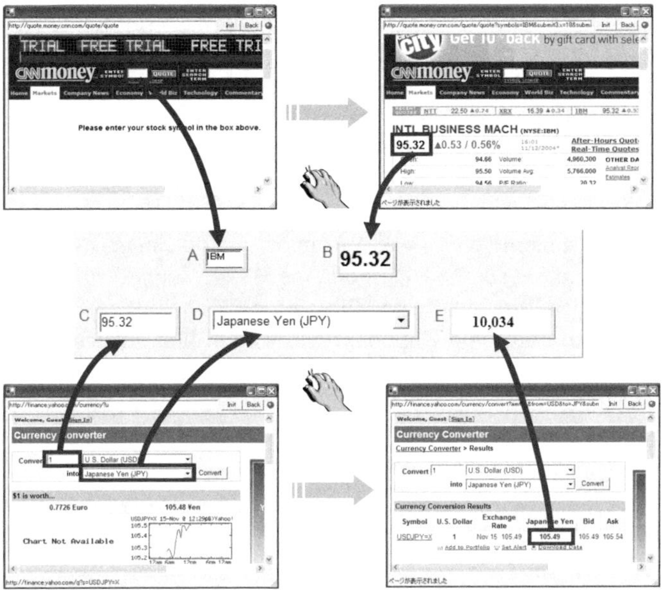

Figure 5. Clips extracted from more than one navigation and their recombination on a ClipboardPad.

a spreadsheet tool, it allows us to relate an input cell X clipped out from a navigation to other cells $Y1, Y2, \ldots, Yk$ clipped out from another different navigation just by specifying an equation $X \leftarrow f(Y1, Y2, \ldots, Yk)$, where f is an arbitrary computable function. Whenever one of the cells $Y1, Y2, \ldots, Yk$ is updated, the ClipboardPad computes $f(Y1, Y2, \ldots, Yk)$, and updates the cell X with this new value. This triggers the execution of the view editing code in which the cell X is defined, and updates all the output clips involved in this view editing code. Some of these updated cells may be linked to other cells through some equations, which may trigger further updates of the ClipboadPad.

Figure 5 shows two navigations, one starting with CNN Money Stock Quote page, and the other with Yahoo Finance Currency Conversion page. From the former, we clipped out the company code input form and the stock quote output, and put them in this order on a ClipboardPad, which associated them with two cells A and B. From the latter, we clipped out the dollar amount input, the currency selector, and the converted amount output, and put them in this order on the same ClipboardPad, which associated them with three more cells C, D, and E. Then we input a substitution expression $\leftarrow$ B to the cell C. The composite tool enables us to retrieve the current stock quote of an arbitrarily selected company in an arbitrarily selected currency.

4. World-Wide Repository of Meme-Media Objects

Meme media technologies for clipping and recombining Web resources can be applied to arbitrary Web pages, and hence, any legacy Web applications such as Google and Wiki services. They also enable us to make any legacy applications interoperable with each other just by developing their HTML view interfaces.

Here we will apply meme media technologies to Wiki service to make it work as a worldwide repository of pads for sharing and exchanging them, i.e., as a meme pool. Wiki is a piece of server software that allows users to freely create and edit Web page content using any Web browser. Wiki supports hyperlinks and has a simple text syntax for creating new pages and crosslinks between internal pages on the fly. Wiki is unusual among group communication mechanisms in that it allows the organization of contributions to be edited in addition to the content itself.

In order to make a meme pool system from Wiki, you can access a Wiki page using an HTMLviewPad, and extract the URI input, the HTML input form, refresh button, and the output page as Web clips, and paste them on a ClipboardPad. You need to paste a PadSaverLoaderPad on the same ClipboardPad, which then creates a new cell with its connection to this pad. Now, you can relate the input and output of this cell respectively to the cell for the input form clip and the one for the extracted output page clip. A PadSaverLoaderPad makes conversion between a pad on itself and its save format representation in XML. Suppose that the PadSaverLoaderPad, the extracted HTML input form clip, and the extracted output page clip are assigned with cell names A, B, and C. The relationship among them is defined as follows. We define the equation for the cell A as $\leftarrow C$, and the equation for the cell B as $\leftarrow A$. People can access any page specifying its URL, drag-and-drop arbitrary composite pads to and from the PadSaverLoaderPad on the composed pad to upload and download them to and from the corresponding Wiki server. Each page is shown by the PadSaverLoader-Pad. This meme pool system based on Wiki technologies is called a Wiki piazza. Figure 6 shows a Wiki piazza. Users may manipulate and/or edit some pads on an arbitrary page of a Wiki piazza to update their states. Another user accessing the same page can share the updated pads by just clicking the reload button to retrieve this page again from the corresponding server. For a jump from a page to another page in a Wiki piazza system, we can use an anchor pad that can be pasted on a Wiki piazza page. This anchor pad holds a URL that can be set through its #refURL slot, and, when it is clicked, sets this URL to the #URL slot of the Wiki piazza, i.e., to the #URL slot of its base ClipboadPad.

A Wiki piazza system allows people not only to publish and share contents represented as pads, but also to compose new contents by combining components of those pads already published in it. People can publish such newly composed contents into the same Wiki piazza system. The collaborative reediting and redistribution of contents in a shared publishing repository by a community or a society of people will accelerate the memetic evolution of contents in this repository, and make it work as a meme pool.

5. Related Work

Web Service technologies such as SOAP (Simple Object Access Protocol) [7] enable us to interoperate different services published over the Web. However, they assume that the API (Application Program Interface) library to access such a service is a priori provided using the WSDL. Users need to write a program to interoperate more than one Web service. Our technologies, on the other hand, provide the client-side direct manipulation operations for users to re-edit intellectual resources embedded in Web pages for the visual definition of their arbitrary new layout combination as well as their interoperation.

The Semantic Web [8] is an extension of the Web in which Web contents are associated with explicit machine-processable semantics. The Semantic Web Service tech-

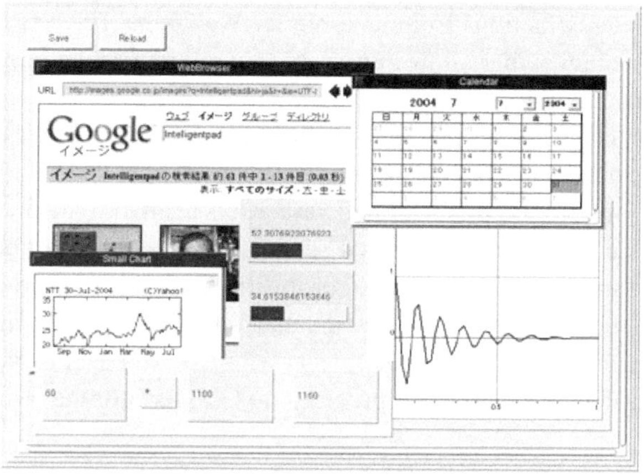

Figure 6. A worldwide repository of pads developed by applying meme media technologies to Wiki.

nologies [2], which integrate Web Service technologies and Semantic Web technologies, aim to automate Web service composition. In our approach, on the other hand, we do not aim to automate any composition of Web applications. We focus on how instantaneously users can create wrappers for Web applications when the users want to reuse them in some functional combinations with other applications.

There are a few preceding research studies that adopted programming-by-demonstration (PBD, for short) technologies on Web pages. Internet Scrapbook [19] allows us to re-edit Web documents by demonstrating how to change the layout of a Web page into a customized one. Internet Scrapbook applies the same editing rule whenever the Web page is accessed for refreshing. They enable us to change layouts, but not to extract any components, nor to functionally connect them together.

Bauer and Dengler [5,6] have also introduced a PBD method in which even naive users can configure their own Web based information services satisfying their individual information needs. They have implemented the method into InfoBeans. By accessing an InfoBox with an ordinary Web browser, users can wrap Web applications. By connecting channels among InfoBeans on the InfoBox, users can also integrate them functionally together. However, it seems difficult for users to reuse a part of composite Web applications defined by other users.

WebVCR [3] and WebView [10] provide familiar man-machine interfaces to record and replay users' actions. Users can create and update their 'smart bookmarks', which are shortcuts to Web contents and represent a series of Web-browsing actions, by pressing a record button on their Web browser. Smart bookmarks can therefore be used to record hard-to-reach Web pages that have no fixed URLs. However, WebVCR does not support the definition of I/O ports for Web applications. For example, end-users could not modify the parameter values of an input-form. WebView allows us to define customized views of Web contents. When a user records a smart bookmark, he or she can indicate whether each input form value is to be requested at the playback time or to be a priori stored at the demonstration time. However, in WebView, it seems difficult for end-users to create a new view that integrates different Web applications.

Sometimes Web applications may revise the format of their front-end HTML pages. There are lots of preceding research studies on the induction of a Web wrapper from a given set of example extractions from an arbitrary Web page. However, there are hardly any other research studies that allow end-users to wrap more than one Web application and to define interoperation among them in the same environment.

W4F [17], which is a semi-automatic wrapper generator, provides a visual support tool to define an extraction. The system can create a wrapper class written in Java from user's demonstrations. To use this wrapper class, users need to write program codes. DEbyE [12] provides a more powerful visual support tool for the wrapping of Web applications. DEbyE stores the extracted text portions in an XML repository. Users need to use another XML tool to combine extracted data from Web applications. LExIKON [13] can learn an underlying relation among objects within a Web page from a user-specified ordered set of text strings to extract. It provides no GUI tool for the join of two extracted relations.

6. Conclusion

Meme-media architectures work as the enabling technologies for interdisciplinary and international availability, distribution and exchange of intellectual assets including information, knowledge, ideas, pieces of work, and tools in reeditable and redistributable organic forms. When applied to the Web, they make the Web work as a shared repository not only for publishing intellectual resources, but also for their collaborative reediting and reorganization. Meme-media technologies allow us to reedit multimedia documents with embedded tools and services, and to combine their functions through copy-and-paste manipulations of these documents. Meme media over the Web will make the Web work as a meme pool, and significantly accelerate the evolution of memes in our societies.

Meme media technologies provide another way of defining interoperations among different Web resources, which, in *de facto* standard approach, are defined using Web Service and Semantic Web technologies. The former requires no programming but reediting of existing Web application pages for the definition of their interoperation, while the latter requires programming to define a new composition. Meme media technologies, however, do not exclude the use of these de facto standard technologies in their paradigm. We have already developed a Web-service wrapper, which, when given a Web service with its WSDL description, analyzes this description, and automatically creates a pad that works as a proxy of this Web service. This tool shows its user all the I/O functions of the target Web service, and allows him to select some of them to work as slots. Such a proxy pad can be combined with any pads. Meme media technologies add a new functional dimension to standard Web technologies without losing any of their functions.

Meme media objects composed by our clipping and combining framework are not robust against the DOM-tree structural change of source Web pages. They may need to be redefined whenever such structural changes may occur in some of their source Web pages. Meme media technologies do not aim at the automatic composition of Web resources. They aim at the flexible, instantaneous, ad hoc definition and execution of their interoperation.

References

[1] Rakesh Agrawal, Jr. Roberto J. Bayardo, Daniel Gruhl, and Spiros Papadimitriou. Vinci: a service-oriented architecture for rapid development of web applications. In *WWW '01: Proceedings of the 10th international conference on World Wide Web*, pages 355–365, New York, NY, USA, 2001. ACM Press.

[2] Anupriya Ankolekar, Mark Burstein, Jerry R. Hobbs, Ora Lassila, David L. Martin, Sheila A. McIlraith, Srini Narayanan, Massimo Paolucci, Terence Payne, Katia Sycara, and Honglei Zeng. "daml-s: Semantic markup for web services". In *"Proceedings of the International Semantic Web Workshop"*, 2001.

[3] Vinod Anupam, Juliana Freire, Bharat Kumar, and Daniel Lieuwen. Automating web navigation with the webvcr. In *Proceedings of the 9th international World Wide Web conference on Computer networks : the international journal of computer and telecommunications netowrking*, pages 503–517, Amsterdam, The Netherlands, The Netherlands, 2000. North-Holland Publishing Co.

[4] Rainer Anzböck, Schahram Dustdar, and Harald Gall. Software configuration, distribution, and deployment of web-services. In *SEKE '02: Proceedings of the 14th international conference on Software engineering and knowledge engineering*, pages 649–656, New York, NY, USA, 2002. ACM Press.

[5] Mathias Bauer and Dietmar Dengler. InfoBeans-configuration of personalized information. In *Proceedings of the International Conference on Intelligent User Interfaces*, pages 153–156, 1999.

[6] Mathias Bauer, Dietmar Dengler, and Gabriele Paul. Instructible information agents for web mining. In *IUI '00: Proceedings of the 5th international conference on Intelligent user interfaces*, pages 21–28, New York, NY, USA, 2000. ACM Press.

[7] Don Box, David Ehnebuske, Gopal Kakivaya, Andrew Layman, Noah Mendelsohn., Henrik Frystyk Nielsen, Satish Thatte, and Dave Winer. Simple object access protocol (soap) 1.1. W3C Recommendation, 2000. http://www.w3.org/TR/2003/REC-DOM-Level-2-HTML-20030109/.

[8] T. Burners-Lee, J. Hendler, and O. Lassila. The semantic web. *Scientific American*, 284(5), May 2001.

[9] James Clark and Steve DeRose. XML Path Language (XPath) Version 1.0. W3C Recommendation, 1999. http://www.w3.org/TR/xpath.

[10] Juliana Freire, Bharat Kumar, and Daniel Lieuwen. Webviews: accessing personalized web content and services. In *WWW '01: Proceedings of the 10th international conference on World Wide Web*, pages 576–586, New York, NY, USA, 2001. ACM Press.

[11] Jun Fujima, Aran Lunzer, Kasper Hornbæk, and Yuzuru Tanaka. Clip, connect, clone: combining application elements to build custom interfaces for information access. In *UIST '04: Proceedings of the 17th annual ACM symposium on User interface software and technology*, pages 175–184, New York, NY, USA, 2004. ACM Press.

[12] Paulo Braz Golgher, Alberto H.F. Laender, Altigran Soares da Silva, and Berthier A. Ribeiro-Neto. An example-based environment for wrapper generation. In *ER '00: Proceedings of the Workshops on Conceptual Modeling Approaches for E-Business and The World Wide Web and Conceptual Modeling*, pages 152–164, London, UK, 2000. Springer-Verlag.

[13] Gunter Grieser, Klaus P. Jantke, Steffen Lange, and Bernd Thomas. A unifying approach to html wrapper representation and learning. In *DS '00: Proceedings of the Third International Conference on Discovery Science*, pages 50–64, London, UK, 2000. Springer-Verlag.

[14] Kimihito Ito and Yuzuru Tanaka. A visual environment for dynamic web application composition. In *HYPERTEXT '03: Proceedings of the fourteenth ACM conference on Hypertext and hypermedia*, pages 184–193, New York, NY, USA, 2003. ACM Press.

[15] Philippe Le Hegaret Johnny Stenback and Arnaud Le Hors. Document Object Model (DOM) Level 2 Specification. W3C Recommendation, 2003. http://www.w3.org/TR/2003/REC-DOM-Level-2-HTML-20030109/.

[16] Marlon Pierce, Geoffrey Fox, Choonhan Youn, Steve Mock, Kurt Mueller, and Ozgur Balsoy. Interoperable web services for computational portals. In *SC '02: Proceedings of the Proceedings of the IEEE/ACM SC2002 Conference*, page 39, Washington, DC, USA, 2002. IEEE Computer Society.

[17] Arnaud Sahuguet and Fabien Azavant. Building intelligent web applications using lightweight wrappers. *Data Knowl. Eng.*, 36(3):283–316, 2001.

[18] Michael Stal. Web services: beyond component-based computing. *Commun. ACM*, 45(10):71–76, 2002.

[19] Atsushi Sugiura and Yoshiyuki Koseki. Internet scrapbook: automating web browsing tasks by demonstration. In *UIST '98: Proceedings of the 11th annual ACM symposium on User interface software and technology*, pages 9–18, New York, NY, USA, 1998. ACM Press.

[20] Y. Tanaka and T. Imataki. IntelligentPad: A Hypermedia System allowing Functional Composition of

Active Media Objects through Direct Manipulations. In *Proceedings of the IFIP '89*, pages 541–546, San Francisco, CA, 1989.

[21] Yuzuru Tanaka. Meme media and a world-wide meme pool. In *MULTIMEDIA '96: Proceedings of the fourth ACM international conference on Multimedia*, pages 175–186, New York, NY, USA, 1996. ACM Press.

[22] Yuzuru Tanaka. *Meme Media and Meme Market Architectures: Knowledge Media for Editing, Distributing, and Managing Intellectual Resources*. John Wiley & Sons, Inc., New York, NY, USA, 2003.

New Trends in Software Methodologies, Tools and Techniques
H. Fujita and M. Mejri (Eds.)
IOS Press, 2005

Component-Based Grid Programming Using the HOC-Service Architecture

Jan DÜNNWEBER and Sergei GORLATCH
University of Münster, Germany

Abstract. Grids are a novel class of distributed systems that allow to seamlessly combine multiple resources of heterogeneous servers on the Internet for demanding applications. We deal with the challenging task of programming grid applications which have to meet the requirements of abstraction and interoperability. We present our concept of customizable Higher-Order Components (HOCs) whose parameters may be not only data but also mobile code units. We demonstrate how applications are built by customizing HOCs using code parameters and describe the HOC-SA – a service-oriented architecture for developing grid applications by composing HOCs. We show where HOC-SA ranges in the variety of currently available software component architectures. In presenting our implementation, we explain how HOC-SA exploits modern grid middleware such as the WSRF implementation in the latest Globus Toolkit while hiding its complexity from the user.

1. Introduction

Grids are a novel class of distributed systems that allow to seamlessly combine the aggregate processing and data storing potential of multiple servers on the Internet into integrated platforms for highly demanding applications. Grids offer great potential for data- and compute-intensive applications that go beyond conventional supercomputers and local clusters. However, the heterogeneity and dynamicity of grids pose new challenges for application developers: network connections may break during a running process, security aspects are of critical importance because of the many providers and users involved, remote machines need to be located and addressed in an appropriate manner, etc. These complicated issues are often unmanageable for an application programmer.

A promising approach to hide the complexity of grids from the programmers is to use a component architecture with a certain level of abstraction from the underlying distributed infrastructure. In order to enable grid software to establish the required dynamic links between heterogeneous hosts, it is built upon loosely coupled components, i.e., components with interchangeable implementations and a high degree of interoperability. Components [26] are software building blocks used to compose applications by selection, customization and combination of them. To develop distributed applications this way, components must be interoperable, i.e., using matching formats and protocols to enable data exchange across the boundaries of heterogeneous networks, operating systems and applications.

Our approach to systematizing and simplifying the development of grid applications is based on the concept of *Higher-Order Components* (HOCs) [3] which are offered to the programmer as services within *HOC-SA* [9] – a Service-oriented Architecture for HOCs.

HOCs are partially implemented services provided to the application programmer as reusable program building blocks. Using HOCs, applications are written simply by supplying parameters (application level code) describing the missing pieces in the HOC implementation. Thereby, HOCs provide an abstraction over the underlying service setup, which can be quite complex, but remains hidden from the user.

Our work is a further development of the general approach known as Service-Oriented Architectures (SOA) [10]. Systems are composed of distributed services, network accessible entities, capable of serving requests that arise recurrently in different applications. Another significant property of services is that they have well-defined interfaces and dependencies specified in standardized, usually XML-based, formats. Currently, the most common SOA implementation technologies are either plain web services as defined by the W3C [30] or grid services as defined in the OGSA [1]. Component software, as presented in [26], focuses on compositionality. A SOA software design, in contrast, neither implies any concept for object composition nor defines a linkage to standard object-oriented or component-based technologies; SOA rather focuses on communication issues.

The novelty of HOC-SA is that it merges service-orientation with the traditional component approach into a model where components are assembled from services. The need for this new programming methodology is driven by the fact that components for grids must be both, composable on the high level of application logics and interoperable via message exchange.

The structure of the paper is as follows. In Section 2, we briefly introduce the general concept of web services and the closely related grid service standards OSGA and WSRF. Section 3 introduces the HOC-SA and the API structures for HOCs on both the server and the client side, using the concrete example of the Farm-HOC. We demonstrate the advancements of HOC-SA over plain SOA technology. In Section 4, we give a survey of current component technologies for distributed computing and discuss the advantages of the HOC-SA technology in the context of grid applications. We conclude the paper in Section 5.

2. Web Services and the Grid

Traditionally, distributed software systems have been developed by writing self-contained client and server programs. Tools for developing such systems can be based on plain RPC technologies; but also object-oriented systems using the more recent RMI and CORBA communication mechanisms often come along with a similar, monolithic architecture. Despite its topological simplicity, the client-server architecture imposes severe difficulties: clients and servers have to exhibit the same hardware properties and run the same operating system or higher-level platform (e.g., a Java virtual machine), otherwise, each data transmission would imply a time consuming process of data format detection and conversion.

2.1. Web Services

Web services, as defined by the W3C standardization consortium, are "designed to support interoperable machine-to-machine interaction over a network" [30]. Technically, this interoperability is realized by decoupling the services' functionality from the underlying support system; this allows to access services in an implementation-independent manner. A web service is a server application that can be requested to perform operations on behalf of a *consumer* that is either a client program or another web service. Contrary to traditional server applications, web services are not self-contained programs: they require a hosting environment that handles the communication between services and consumers. Server programs that can host several different services (or other application components) are called *containers*; they fall into the category of middleware as they form a layer between operating systems and applications.

According to [26], web services can be seen as a type of software components. In our HOC-Service Architecture, components can be more complex, i.e., composed of multiple services or other components, while web services are just used for communicating within or between HOC implementations. Containers extend the functionality of the components deployed (installed) therein by application-independent features which apply to complex combinations of services and other constructs like HOCs as well as to plain web services. Component extensions provided by containers, which can be very useful in the context of grid computing, may include, e.g., failover procedures or the encryption and decryption of sensible data etc. The most basic responsibility of a container supporting web services consists in the transparent marshaling and unmarshaling of parameters and return values communicated over the network. Requests to remote services in the client code and the server-sided code for processing them look like the code for local method invocations (or like a subroutine call in a non object-oriented programming language). Behind the scenes, the container converts all data transmissions into the XML-based SOAP protocol, allowing to interconnect distributed software in heterogeneous networks. The transmission of SOAP-encoded data is usually handled using HTTP as the wire protocol via the standard port 8080 and can therefore pass across firewalls and internet proxies.

Examples of middleware including (or consisting in) a web service compliant container include commercial application server programs like WebLogic [6] or WebSphere [17], the Apache Axis open source system [5] and, recently, in version 3.x or higher, the Globus Toolkit for grids [15]. These containers support web services written in C, C++ or Java with standard formats used for service interface definitions (WSDL), data exchange (SOAP) and the service configuration (WSDD).

2.2. Grid Services

Programming language independence and connectivity across internet boundaries make web services a suitable implementation technology for grid application development. Another important feature of web services in the context of highly dynamic grid environments is that they allow to build loosely-coupled systems: services depend neither on the context of the calling application nor on its state. A context-independent service may be called from a standalone application or from within a component hosted by another container. State independence means that there is no particular order in which the operations offered by a service must be requested.

However, web services also have drawbacks as compared to, e.g., CORBA or RMI. A web service is *stateless*, i.e., it cannot maintain data values outlasting a single invocation. Moreover, web services are *intransient*, i.e., once deployed to a container, they are initialized when the container is launched, and they shutdown when the container stops. As a consequence, connecting web services to data resources (e.g., a database) usually results in conflicts as soon as more than one client accesses a service.

To overcome these drawbacks, the Open Grid Service Infrastructure (OGSI) [28] defined the notion of *grid services*, a special type of web services that are stateful and *transient*, i.e., they can be instantiated and destroyed upon request. OGSI replaced common standards like WSDL and WSDD with OGSI-specific derivates. These non-standard solutions (GWSDL and GWSDD) hampered the acceptance of Globus Toolkit 3 and were abandoned in the newest Globus Toolkit 4. The Open Grid Service Architecture (OGSA) describes the concept of providing stateful and transient services for grid computing, while OGSI just specifies the way grid services were implemented in GT 3 for that purpose. Contrary to OGSI, the OGSA, and therefore the broader notion of "grid services", is still used [1], but now it refers to a web service that maintains application state data accordingly to the web service resource framework (WSRF) specification [21].

Since originally WSRF services are stateless and intransient, they are used within a *façade* [13], which is a data management abstraction composed of stateful and transient resources that can be accessed individually via services using WS-Addressing [22]. If not mentioned otherwise, in the following, we use the term "service" for any web service that is grid-aware in the sense that it maintains its own transient state, regardless of the implementation technology (OGSI or WSRF). Note that both, the OGSI- and WSRF-compliant service containers, can be run either as a plugin of a commonly used application server (such as those provided by Apache, BEA and IBM) or independently of such software.

3. Components in the HOC-SA

Our approach is to propose a novel service architecture, HOC-SA, where a component (HOC) can make use of several services with clearly defined interactions. Moreover, we suggest extensions to the web service data transmission mechanism that allow to exchange units of mobile code between services and clients. Before we describe HOCs and HOC-SA in more detail, we give some motivating remarks on the use of software components in contemporary business systems, which allow to build complex architectures in a convenient way.

The Software component technologies that are most widely used in modern e-commerce systems are Enterprise Java Beans (EJBs) [20] and the .NET framework [25]. EJBs communicate using RMI-IIOP [25], an extension of RMI where the native Java-communication mechanism is replaced by the IIOP-standard as specified by the Object Management Group (OMG). Therefore, Java and non-Java programs can interoperate in an EJB system. The .NET framework emerged from Microsoft's COM+ technology [19] and also supports multiple programming languages. Besides a programming language independent communication mechanism, both these technologies include implementations of different component types for various purposes and APIs of their own. EJB offers, e.g., three different high-level component types: 1) session beans for transient applica-

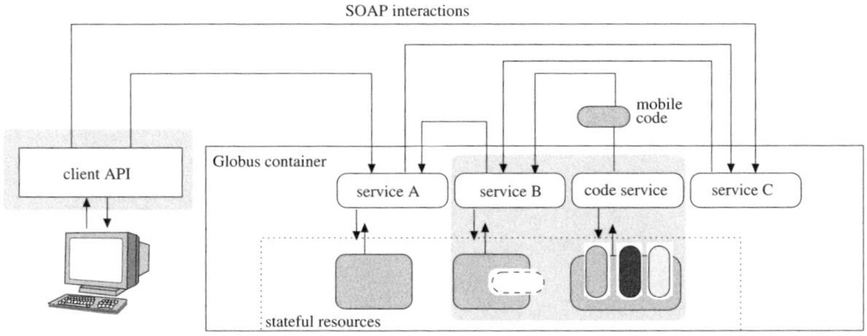

Figure 1. Interactions between services and resources in the HOC-SA.

tion entities such as shopping carts 2) message-driven beans for running activities such as inventory updates in the background, because Java multithreading may not be used in EJB implementations (thread control is taken over by the container in EJB software), and 3) entity beans for persistent objects such as customer accounts. A good description of example use cases for these component types in a realistic e-commerce system can be found in [29].

Compared to such mature architectures, it is questionable if plain web services or grid services can be equated with components as it is suggested, e.g., in [16]. Contrary to EJB or .NET, the specifications of services describe merely an access mechanism, while it is left open to the programmer what is accessed via this mechanism.

3.1. Application Level Grid Service Programming Using Mobile Code

Higher-Order Components (HOCs) aim at simplifying the programming of grid applications. Users of traditional grid middleware are confronted with a considerable amount of low-level configuration work, like writing service interface definitions, deployment descriptors etc. Moreover, the choice of XML-Schema for type declarations within a service interface, as it is required for SOAP-based communication, restricts the parameter type range to data records and primitives; so, for the transmission of executable code over the network, e.g., sending a code parameter to a HOC, we need a workaround.

HOCs solve this problem as shown in Fig. 1, where the relation between the HOCs and a Globus-based grid environment is depicted. Multiple services may be contacted from clients and may interact with each other (e.g., service `A` with service `B` and service `C`) and with stateful resources (service `A`, service `B` and the code service). The shaded pattern beneath the client API and the code service points out that these entities are specific to the HOCs. The hole in the resource connected to service `B` indicates that service `B` is only partially implemented and missing parts of the implementation must be transferred from the code service to make the service fully functional. Before we explain the enabling mechanisms for the required transfer of mobile code in service interactions, we introduce HOCs, software components that rely on this mechanism.

Candidates for HOCs are recurring patterns of parallelism, independent of concrete applications, like `farm` or `divide-and-conquer` patterns, as well as the collective operations `scan` and `reduce` known from MPI programming [12]. Such patterns are sometimes referred to as algorithmic skeletons [7].

HOCs simplify grid application development in two ways:

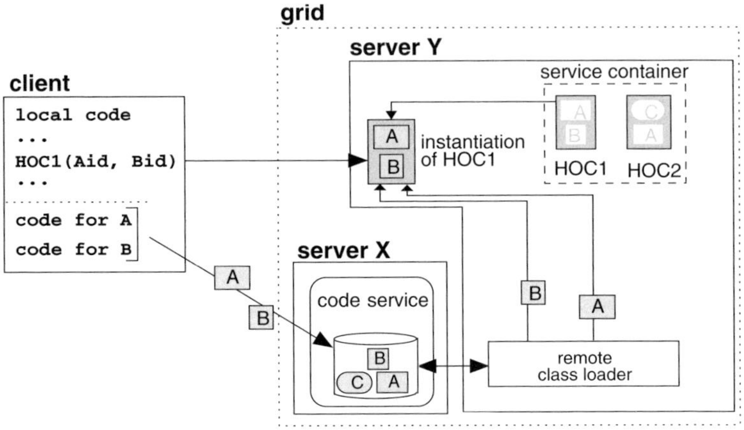

Figure 2. The code service and the remote class loader in the HOC-SA.

- HOCs hide from the application programmer all underlying middleware arrangements and distribution mechanisms of a particular application: the programmer selects appropriate components and constructs the application as a composition of HOCs;
- HOCs are reusable, *generic* components that can be customized with application-specific units of code to adapt a HOC to the needs of a particular application. The customized HOCs are then used as ordinary services to process data in a parallel, efficient manner employing multiple servers in the grid.

Our motivation for HOCs is that services composed from customizable components offer more potential for code reuse than services that have a fixed functionality. However, using HOCs in a grid setting faces two challenges: because HOCs are customized with application specific *code*, the corresponding code units must be: (1) sent from the application host to the grid server executing the HOC (i.e., *code mobility* is required), and (2) executable on the server hardware running the HOC. While the second problem can be solved by using a portable format (e.g., Java bytecode or an interpreted scripting language) to implement code units, code mobility has not yet been addressed in the grid context and is not supported by recent grid middleware, including the latest version of the Globus Toolkit.

Since a code mobility mechanism for stateful services is required for the customization of HOCs, our service architecture (HOC-SA) addresses exactly this problem. We provide two extensions to OGSA, a *remote class loader* and a *code service* (both introduced in [9]), which allow to implement a service partially and customize it by providing mobile units of code using a well-defined API.

Figure 2 shows how these extensions work together in an application. The client sends code units (labeled `A` and `B` in the client program in the figure) encoded as plain data (i.e., arrays of bytes) to server `X` hosting the code service. Server `Y` runs a service container hosting two components, `HOC1` and `HOC2` (for the sake of simplicity, each of these two components consists of a single service that is local to server `Y`). When the client requests an operation performed by `HOC1`, it sends code unit identifiers (labeled `Aid` and `Bid` in the figure) to server `Y`; they are used for the selection of the associated code units in the instantiation of `HOC1`. The standard Java class loader is replaced by the remote class loader on server Y that downloads from the code service those class definitions which are not available on the local file system, and creates instances of the classes defined therein using the Java reflection mechanism. This way, the transferred codes, that have been encoded as byte arrays during the transmission, become Java objects again. When server Y then processes a service request by performing the operation specified in the invocation, these objects perform the application-specific work.

3.2. The Structure of APIs for HOCs

The programming model for grids using HOCs aims at the following separation of concerns. The implementation of a generic parallel pattern in a distributed environment is an inherent part of a HOC and therefore statically coded into the associated service. All details of a particular application are expressed via customizing units of code that are provided to a HOC at runtime in the form of mobile code parameters. In the following, we refer to each HOC type (pattern) in singular, although it may have multiple implementations.

To illustrate the purpose of code parameters, we describe three particular HOC types:

- The *Reduce-HOC* implements the reduction pattern of computation, where an application-specific binary operation is used to combine multiple data into a single result value.The code unit implementing this binary operation (e.g., addition on numbers) is the code parameter of the Reduce-HOC.
- The *Divide&Conquer-HOC* offers the divide-and-conquer pattern and requires four code parameters: One for the divide phase, one for the combine phase, one for processing the base case and, finally, a predicate deciding when the base case is given.
- The *Farm-HOC* expresses the *farm* pattern of parallelism, where work units (tasks) are generated by a single *master* and distributed to several *workers* which process their assigned tasks. The HOC implementation manages data distribution and synchronization between master and workers in a way most suitable for the platform the HOC is running on (e.g., using a preconfigured threadpool on a multiprocessor machine). The application developer accesses the Farm-HOC via a simple, well-defined API that hides all machine-specific details. The code for master and workers is provided by the application programmer and tackles application-specific concerns, i.e., how tasks are generated (master) and solved (worker).

Let us discuss the Farm-HOC as an example in more detail. The interfaces of the Farm-HOC code parameters read as follows in Java notation:

```
interface Worker { double[] compute(double[] input); }
interface Master {
   double[][] split(double[] input, int numWorkers);
   public double [] join(double [][] input); }
```

We have chosen double arrays as the datatype for input and return values in the parameter interfaces, as this is the most generic choice that is possible for an implementation using web services (the XML-Schema type xsd:any is mapped to plain Java objects by the Globus container and does not allow for derived types, so it is not a reasonable alternative).

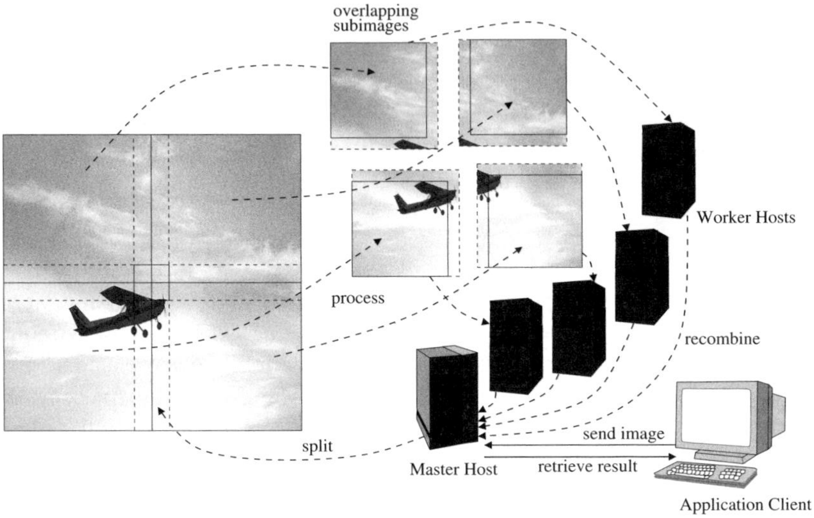

Figure 3. A compute farm for image filtering.

As an example application, let us consider an image filter which, for each pixel in a two-dimensional input picture, computes a value in the output picture, based on the pixel values in a surrounding area of the input picture. To express this application using the Farm-HOC, the programmer only has to implement the interfaces of the `Master` and `Worker` code units shown above. The `Master` splits the input image into several overlapping subimages, such that each pixel and the surrounding area needed to compute its value are contained in at least one subimage. An example for splitting a picture into four overlapping subimages is shown in Fig. 3. The `Workers` apply the actual filter operation to each pixel in a subimage, and eventually, the `Master` recombines the resulting subimages into a single image again.

The application programmer does not need to deal with concerns regarding the communication between `Master` and `Workers` and the synchronization between them, because this is already taken care of in the Farm-HOC implementation. The client program only contacts one service host (the `Master` host), sends the image and retrieves the result of the distributed computation. The dashed arrows in Fig. 3 depict communications that happen transparently to the application client.

In contrast to the application programmer, the component developer deals with the implementation of HOCs, i.e., for the Farm-HOC, he does not need any knowledge about the application-dependent codes. Instead, he only has to ensure that tasks generated by the `Master` are eventually executed by the `Workers` and results are received by the `Master`, and that this is done in an optimized way for the hardware platform the HOC is running on. The various `Master` and `Worker` hosts in Fig. 3 show one possible implementation option for the Farm-HOC that can also be realized in a way that both, the `Master` and `Workers`, run on a single host.

3.3. Role Distribution between Grid Programmers

As follows from the Farm-HOC example, the separation of concerns in grid programming with HOCs splits the community of programmers into two different groups

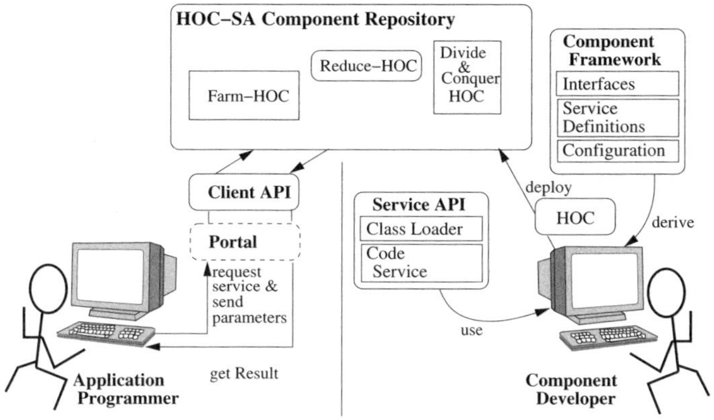

Figure 4. Developer roles and the APIs in the HOC-SA.

(see Fig. 4): 1) component developers who design and implement HOCs including the setup and configuration work required for the target platform, and 2) application programmers who use the HOC-based service architecture (HOC-SA) to compose applications by combining and customizing the available HOCs.

Application programmers work with a simple and well documented Client-API for passing code parameters, accessing services and retrieving results from remote hosts. For convenience reasons, we have also set up a special HOC-portal that allows to submit source code parameters to HOCs via a web browser, including an interactive mechanism for handling syntactic errors at runtime. The parameters supplied to a HOC are application-specific codes provided by the users who are experts in a specific scientific domain, e.g., biochemists, physicists or seismologists.

In contrast, component developers must be capable of writing efficient parallel code for the target architecture and the employed middleware system. They are also required to prepare the middleware configuration and setup files for each component. The right part of Fig. 4 shows that the component developer works with a framework that defines basic services, common interfaces and a standard configuration to derive new HOCs. The services definitions provided by the component framework include such basic arrangements as the signature of the method used to pass the hostnames of available computers for running computations. The code service and the remote class loader are included in the server-side, so-called Service API. This API frees the component developer from dealing with raw binary data when code parameters are evaluated, as explained in Section 3.1.

3.4. Building the Farm-HOC Using the Service API

We will now use the example of the Farm-HOC (introduced in Section 3.1) to demonstrate how HOCs are developed using the server-sided framework and service API. The Farm-HOC implementation discussed here consists of the following two web services: 1) a `Farm`-service executing the `Master`-parameter, and 2) a `Worker`-service executing the `Worker`-parameter.

In the following, we will take a closer look at the processing mechanisms of web services. We explain what the required setup is used for and we present HOC-SA framework utilities that simplify configuring HOCs to that effect that not every configuration file needs not be written anew for each HOC implementation.

3.4.1. Service Interface Configuration

When a service request is processed, the container handles the marshaling and unmarshaling of parameters and return values according to XML configuration files. These files must be located at a certain position within the container installation directory in a procedure called deployment that is conducted before the container is launched. This way, implementation codes are assigned to service operations and the public interface of the service is mapped out.

In a service interface belonging to a HOC, several operations and their associated parameter type definitions are always present, while others are specific to a certain HOC type. The Farm-HOC, e.g., has in common with all other HOCs that it is implemented only partially and therefore needs to be supplied with a data source to load the missing parts of the implementation at runtime.

Like all other HOCs, our Farm-HOC inherits its basic features from service definitions provided by the HOC-SA. This way, HOC-SA component developers reuse not only executable code but also declarations stored in external service configuration files: Whenever a new HOC is derived from the component framework using the `extends` declaration in the corresponding XML service interface configuration file, the newly declared service interface inherits from a parent configuration. This configuration inheritance is an enhancement of grid services over standard web services.

The most important basic features of a HOC that are defined in the HOC-SA component framework are: 1) a HOC can send and receive messages asynchronously; 2) a pool of servers can be configured and made available to the HOC for outsourcing computations; 3) every HOC has one method to initiate a new computation and one method to retrieve results.

3.5. Service Implementation

As a part of the HOC-SA, we provide shell-scripts to component developers for creating, bundling and deploying HOCs. This includes the generation of the stub code that mediates between the service implementation and the middleware, according to the interface definitions discussed in Section 3.4.1. So, what remains to be done for the component developer is to provide service implementations.

The Farm-HOC is implemented by the `FarmImpl`-class shown at the bottom of the UML class diagram in Fig. 5. The names of the four methods defined in the `FarmImpl` intuitively reflect their intended purpose. There are two types of relationships: Inheritance from concrete classes (shown as solid arrows in UML) and the derivation of abstract interfaces (dashed arrows in UML). Figure 5 clearly separates methods that are available in all HOCs (methods of `GridHOC`) from methods that are specific to the Farm-HOC (methods of `FarmImpl`). Any other HOC implementation includes its specific methods the same way, in a class that extends `GridHOC` and implements the `PortType` interface generated from its XML-description.

An important feature of HOCs is that there can exist multiple service implementations for the same HOC, each tuned to a particular hosting environment. For the Farm-HOC, one possible implementation consists of only one `Farm` service running the `Master` unit and several threads, all running the `Worker`-unit on the same server. This solution is preferable if the service host is a large multiprocessor machine which can run the `Master` and several `Workers` in parallel. A different implementation, which we

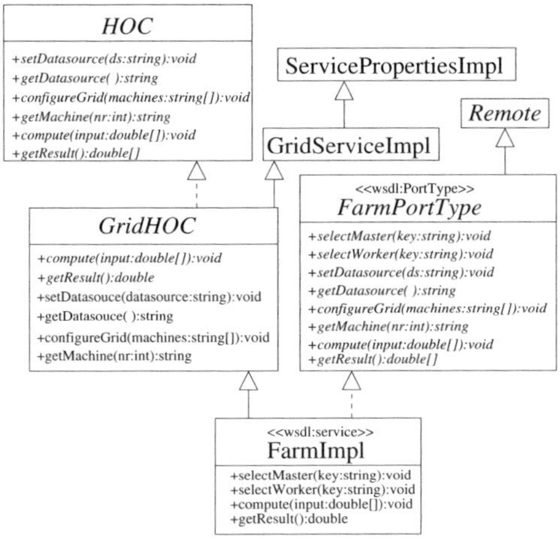

Figure 5. The Farm-HOC and its parent classes in the framework.

discuss in this paper and show in Fig. 5, is a multi-service approach, where `Workers` are services themselves, running on other hosts than the servers where the `Master` is running. This distributed implementation is more suitable, e.g., if both the `Farm` service and the `Worker` services are hosted on a cluster with a large number of nodes, each consisting of one or few processors, with low latencies of inter-node communication. Such a distributed implementation is also suitable for a network of workstations, such as a university computer pool.

Also the handling of mobile code can be managed in different ways. Either, code parameters are loaded by the remote class loader, which abstracts over the required loading mechanism and makes remote code available like local code, or the HOC loads remote code directly, e.g., directly via JDBC [11] or via the OGSA-DAI [2] framework. An advantage of the latter possibility is that the HOC programmer is in control of the kind of database and the query language used. A programmer who wants to search and reload code units without knowing their names, providing only semantic information, might prefer querying an XML-database, which allows to classify data using an ontology system [23].

So far we described the typical HOC operations of a basic service implementation, i.e., the retrieval and processing of mobile code parameters for an arbitrary HOC on the server-side. Let us now take a look at the methods that are specific to the Farm-HOC. When the `compute`-method is called, the `Worker` code will be dispatched to the `Worker` service residing on all `Worker` hosts. The UML class diagram in Fig. 6 depicts the design used for this kind of computation by delegation.

As suggested by the rationale of HOCs, the actual computations performed by a HOC are described by the code parameters, while the HOC itself only provides the underpinnings for executing these codes using a collection of distributed services. For the Farm-HOC this means that the `compute` method starts with delegating its input to an object running the `split` method of the `Master` parameter code unit. In terms of our Farm, the resulting group of subsets of the input can be combined by the `getResult` method using delegation again, after each subset has been processed by a `Worker` service instance.

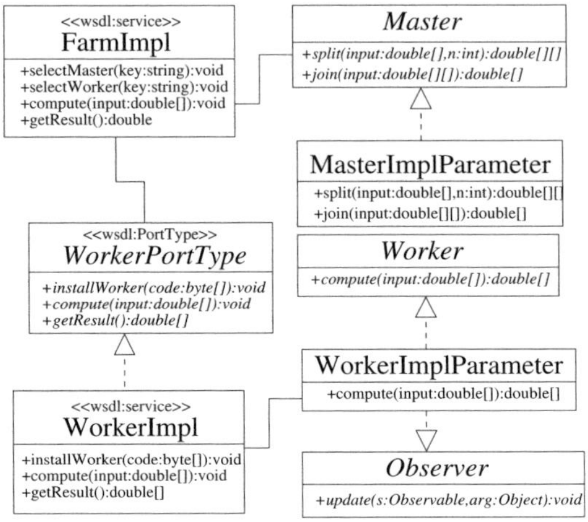

Figure 6. The design for the Farm-HOC evaluation by delegation.

3.6. The Client-Side API for HOCs

Conceptually, HOCs are generic services which are customizable for a particular application. Therefore, we need a client interface for customizing a HOC and a client interface for invoking it. In this section, we describe the client-side API that provides both interfaces.

For a simple client application, such as the image filter described above, the application developer selects an appropriate HOC, uploads the customizing code units and requests the parallel processing of the image data. The uploading of customizing code can be handled either via SOAP, such that code is encoded using a primitive array type which is quite simple, or via a more efficient data transfer mechanism that may involve a more extensive setup, such as the recently specified WS-attachments [10]. For complex applications, we need mechanisms for storing code parameters persistently in (potentially multiple) databases and combining multiple HOCs across multiple systems. Think, e.g., of a data-compression procedure applied to large amounts of experimental results scattered across multiple distributed machines. This can be realized by a Farm-HOC nested into a Reduce-HOC, with the Farm-HOC compressing single files and the Reduce-HOC using an application-specific code unit to concatenate the results into a single archive. For such applications, we provide a comfortable portal that allows to select HOCs and then upload, compile and store their code parameters using a standard web browser, see Fig. 7. By typing the IP-Address or name of any of the grid servers used for hosting HOCs, the user gets connected to the portal application. This web application first presents to the user a HTML-form that allows to choose any of the HOCs that have been deployed in the container running on this server. This GUI is based on dynamically generated HTML-forms and exploits a particular feature of the Globus Toolkit: The Java implementation of WSRF (and the former OGSI) is an extensions of the Apache Axis Servlet [5] and can be run within any standard application server. Therefore, our portal, which is based on Servlet technology, can be deployed into the same container[1] that is also ready for hosting the HOCs.

[1] Apache Tomcat 5, in our present implementation.

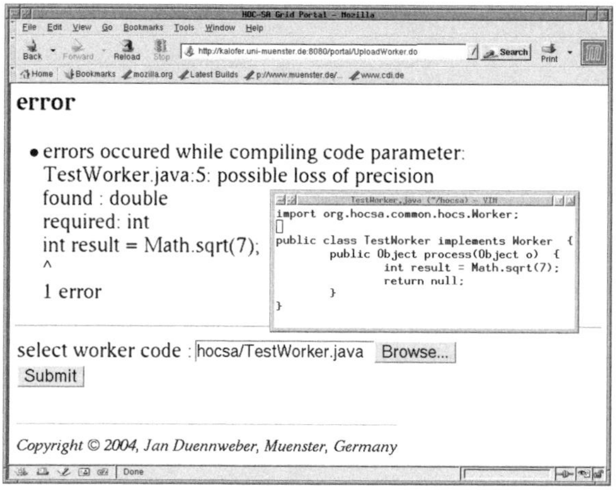

Figure 7. The HOC-SA portal and its online error handling mechanism.

Once a HOC is selected, the user can submit code parameters using an HTTP-upload, i.e., the browser will open a file selector that allows to select a local file and transmit it via HTTP, as shown in Fig. 7. As file format, we currently support Java source code and also script languages like Python or Ruby. The portal rejects incorrect submissions of code units, displaying the error message from the Java compiler or the script interpreter, thus providing an interactive online development environment for grid programming using HOCs. The only requirement to the client machine is that it provides a web browser and a standard text editor.

If a code parameter has been accepted, then the portal displays the associated code unit identifier that must be used to select this parameter in an invocation. In Section 3.1, we conceptually explained Fig. 2 containing the two example identifiers `Aid` and `Bid`. The following code fragment illustrates how the programmer can invoke the Farm-HOC and how code parameters are selected via code unit identifiers in the client code:

```
farmHOC = farmHOCFactory.createHOC();
farmHOC.setMaster("Aid");
farmHOC.setWorker("Bid");
farmHOC.configureGrid("masterHost", "workerHost1", ...);
farmHOC.compute(input);
```

The example starts by requesting a new instance of the Farm-HOC from the Farm-HOC service factory (line 1) according to the factory design pattern [13]. The programmer does not need to know what concrete implementation is instantiated on the server-side, but always retrieves just a reference of a generic interface that complies with the XML-definitions discussed in Section 3.4.1. Lines 2–3 pass identifiers referring to the uploaded code parameters (as specified by the interfaces in Section 3.2). In line 4, the hosts for both `Master` and `Workers` are selected. The HOC is then invoked to process input data on the Grid (line 5). If the uploaded parameters have been provided using a script language, the HOC internally interprets this code using the Bean Scripting Framework [4]. Script languages are very tolerant regarding assignment expressions, type conversions etc. and therefore even more simple to use than Java, and they are portable as well.

4. A Survey of Component Models

We conclude our description of the HOC-SA with a survey and comparison of the currently used component models for grid and web applications. Let us start with the term *software component* itself.

The book *Component software* [26] by Clemens Szyperski declares, firstly, that a component "is a unit of composition...". This short statement is often cited as the origin of a more extensive concept, where components capture common programming patterns as independent, composable program units and present to the application programmer a high-level API hiding platform-specific details. This interpretation implies the basic features that are common to most component models; a separation of concerns and code reuse: different applications requiring common functionality share a common component implementing that functionality.

Beyond compositionality, Szyperski's definition requires that components are software units "...with contractually-specified interfaces and explicit context dependencies only" [26]. In an implementation where components are self-contained software entities, the "context" is simply the target operating system. In this case, the system-level support for most applications is only rudimentary, because operating systems are usually designed universally, except some special cases, e.g., embedded devices. Of course, when a more specific runtime environment, e.g., a J2EE container, is used for a certain component type, the "context dependencies" increase, but the runtime environment can also provide support that is more appropriate for the application. Examples of software components that take advantage of a predefined and adapted runtime environment can be found in e-business systems. Some applications, e.g., automatically synchronize with a database, an enterprise resource planning (ERP) system or customer relationship management (CRM) software. Programmers access components via interfaces that abstract components as high-level entities, such as accounts or shopping carts, without requiring any knowledge about further implications.

Current efforts in grid middleware, like Globus and Unicore, are starting to adopt some ideas from e-commerce component systems. However, there is still no standard component architecture available for high-performance computing applications on grids.

The novelty of the HOC-SA design is including a grid-enabled web service container as a requirement in the component model. This brings the following advantages: interoperability with any technology that can access web services; a loosely-coupled infrastructure where components can easily be exchanged, which facilitates fault tolerance; and finally, the implicit usage of standardized and secure internet protocols for communication (HTTP and HTTPS). As we will see in the following, HOCs are quite closely related to the skeleton model [7]. However, the web service container of the HOC-SA introduces new aspects, such as handling component states and transferring mobile code in the grid, which have so far not been studied in skeleton research.

Let us now survey the features of different component design approaches including both the scientific and commercial area. Concluding, we will show how we integrated the most important advantages of these models in the HOC-SA.

4.1. The Skeleton Model

Our motivation for *higher-order components* (HOCs) is that in parallel computing it is often useful to parameterize a component not only with data but also with application-specific code. The idea originates from algorithmic skeletons [7], where the parallelization strategy is captured in components (skeletons) separately from application-specific tasks. A parallelization strategy may describe a distributed evaluation schema for, e.g., divide-and-conquer algorithms, pipelines or farms. An application-specific task might be coloring graphs, traversing data structures or sorting data. By parameterizing a skeleton with code units, its strategy can be adapted for a particular application. As an example, we briefly describe the divide-and-conquer skeleton which has an analogous HOC representation, introduced in Section 3.2. The divide-and-conquer skeleton is parameterized with four code units: a predicate that decides whether data is elementary, a split function to divide non-elementary data in parts, a function to process elementary data, and a join function to combine partial results. Once this skeleton is instantiated by, e.g., the typical subroutines of quicksort for applying comparisons and subdividing according to a given pivot element, it can be used for parallel sorting. The programmer provides application-specific code, while the distribution of data and computation for parallel processing is done by the skeleton implementation.

Conceptually, a HOC can be seen as a skeleton, made available via grid/web services. For a distributed evaluation of a skeleton, a code mobility mechanism, i.e., the possibility of shipping code over network connections, is required. A solution using SOAP communication is presented in Section 3.1 of this paper. Alternatively, the CORBA communication mechanism or Java-RMI allow for code mobility in homogeneous environments. PaCO++ [24] and Lithium [8] are examples of skeleton-based frameworks that rely on these mechanisms.

4.2. Component Frameworks for Web-Applications

Grid component models based on web service technologies, such as OGSI and WSRF, have their origins in component frameworks for web applications.

The most common web component technologies are CCM, EJBs and Servlets. The terminology with "containers, frameworks and deployment" stems from these technologies, so that the Globus Alliance' efforts in WSRF and the recent GT4 Release can be viewed as an approach to integrate these technologies into grid computing. In this section, we relate web technologies to Globus and HOC-SA. Finally, we also take a look at the CCA, a component architecture that originates from e-science. CCA includes a broad notion of a software component that complies with both HOC-SA and the web component models.

4.2.1. CCM: The CORBA Component Model

CCM is a component model defined by the Object Management Group (OMG) that produces and maintains computer industry specifications (e.g., CORBA, UML, XMI). The CCM specifications include a Component Implementation Definition Language (CIDL); the semantics of the CORBA Components Model (CCM); a Component Implementation Framework (CIF), which defines the programming model for constructing component implementations, and a container programming model. CCM is therefore technically quite similar to HOC-SA, although HOC-SA does not define any language of its own. A programming paradigm, such as the skeletal HOC programming model of the HOC-SA, is not specified by the CCM.

4.2.2. Enterprise Java Beans

In contrast to the HOC-SA model targeted mostly towards compute intensive tasks, Sun Microsystems' EJBs were defined for distributed e-commerce applications. Therefore, EJBs focus on transaction-, security- and database-management [20] (just like Microsoft's competing business component framework .NET [19]), instead of exploiting parallelism in a distributed environment. The Globus Toolkit for grid computing contains some scripts that allow to expose the so-called home interface of an EJB as a grid service automatically [28]. A home interface is used to create EJB-instances, so if a HOC-SA application should profit from the features of EJBs, such as high availability via pooled instances, a HOC can request an EJB-instance from the associated home interface and delegate invocations via SOAP.

Most of our HOC-implementations, such as the Farm-HOC discussed in Section 3.5, comply with the recent WSRF specifications [21], which have many similarities with the EJB model. Most notable are probably *resource homes* and *life-cycles*. A resource home is used to create resources for maintaining state within services like those explained in Section 2.2. A resource home is designed according to the factory pattern [13] and located via JNDI, just like an EJB home interface. In WSRF, a life-cycle defines the sequence of operations that are performed by the container during recurring events, such as the creation or deletion of a resource. Both WSRF and EJB allow for customized life-cycles in the form of user-defined operations that can be associated with life-cycle events.

4.2.3. Java Servlets and JSPs

Servlets and Java Server Pages, which allow to generate Servlets dynamically from tagged page-templates, process HTTP-requests by generating HTML or XML data. Both Servlets and JSPs are compositional units with explicit interface and dependency definitions and therefore, Servlets and JSPs are components as well. They also rely on a container that handles the bindings between requests and method invocations, just like Web services. The difference between Servlets/JSPs and Web Services is that Servlets are used for handling requests that were submitted by human users using web browsers, while Web services are used for inter-machine communication.

The Globus Container relies on the Java Servlet technology for maintaining grid services (internally, service requests are handled by a modified version of the Apache Axis Servlet [5]). Therefore, a full runtime-environment for Servlets and JSPs is available on every server in a Globus-based Grid. Our HOC-SA exploits this fact, which allows for the transfer of data between clients and servers via HTTP using Servlets. This way, HOCs avoid the time-consuming SOAP encoding process. This cooperation between Servlets and HOCs is enhanced in our JSP-based, user-friendly portal (described in Section 3.6) which allows a client to connect to the HOC-SA via a standard web-browser.

4.2.4. CCA: The Common Component Architecture

CCA has been defined by a group of researchers from academia and industry committed to defining a standard component architecture for high-performance computing. The basic definition of a component in CCA [27] states that a component "is a software object, meant to interact with other components, encapsulating certain functionality or a set of functionalities. A component has a clearly defined interface and conforms to a prescribed behavior common to all components within an architecture. Multiple components may be composed to build other components." Interfaces and behaviors in CCA are described by so-called *uses*- and *provides-ports*, which make components interoperable. In CCA, the systems that a component can interoperate with must support the format used to represent a component's ports. HOC-SA in contrast, implies the use of standard web service interfaces. The CCA-model gives a very broad definition of software components, which is quite similar to the definition in [26]. HOC-SA can be viewed as an implementation of CCA for the grid if we adapt some terms. But, as it is the case for CCM, also CCA does not define any specific programming model like HOCs. Current activities of the CCA forum include the definition of a CCA-specific format of component interfaces (Babel/SIDL) and framework implementations (Ccaffeine). The definition of components given in the OGSA-glossary [15] is closely related to that in the CCA-glossary, in the sense that it also requires a *uses* and a *provides*-port for every component.

5. Conclusion and Related Work

The main contribution of this paper is a novel kind of component model, Higher-Order Components (HOCs), and its implementation for Internet-based grid environments in form of the HOC-Service Architecture (HOC-SA). HOC-SA is, to the best of our knowledge, currently the only OGSA-compliant framework that allows for skeletal programming, i.e., code parameterized with other code, by offering partially implemented, customizable components. HOCs embody the skeleton concept in a distributed environment that uses SOAP for communication; therefore, HOCs are interoperable with other OGSA-compliant models, like the CCA-based XCAT3 [14]. As demonstrated by examples using the Farm-HOC, the HOC-SA is a useful architecture for a broad range of grid applications.

While this paper focuses on the concept and the design of the HOC-SA, a more elaborate description, and a detailed example of how to use HOCs from a client perspective, can be found in [3].

We have also discussed the relations between our grid components (HOCs) and the component models commonly used in Web application programming. A typical e-commerce application, the web interface is built upon Servlets and JSPs, business entities are modelled using session EJBs and the persistence issues are managed using entity-EJBs or an O/R-mapper, e.g., hibernate [18]. Our portal application shows that also in a grid architecture, Servlets and JSPs can be used to provide a web-enabled GUI. To cope with various different database types, OGSA-DAI is more appropriate than, e.g., hibernate for grid applications, since O/R-mappers can only map all data to the tables of relational databases. The computations performed in grid applications are far more complicated than that of a business application. Think, e.g., of load-balancing: Vast amounts of concurrently used shopping carts can easily be handled, as these components have no dependencies between each other. The container can automatically outsource instances of such cart components (defined in the container configuration), as soon as the customer quantity exceeds a certain limit. Contrary, computational work units that can emerge dynamically, e.g., during the evaluation of a divide-and-conquer algorithm, have causal and temporal dependencies and can therefore not be handled as easily. HOCs have been developed to cope with such problems and HOC-SA is a component architecture appropriate to the demands of distributed computational applications.

Acknowledgments

This research was partially supported by the FP6 Network of Excellence *CoreGRID* funded by the European Commission (Contract IST-2002-004265). We are grateful to Julia Kaiser-Mariani for her help in improving the presentation.

References

[1] Global grid forum (GGF), GridForge Working Group, http://www.ggf.org/ogsa-wg.
[2] UK Database Task Force, Data Access and Integration, http://www.ogsadai.org.uk.
[3] M. Alt, J. Dünnweber, J. Müller, and S. Gorlatch. HOCs: Higher-order components for grids. In V. Getov and T. Kielmann, editors, *Component Models and Systems for Grid Applications*, CoreGRID, pages 157–166. Springer-Verlag, June 2004.
[4] Apache Organization. Jakarta BSF: The Bean Scripting Framework. http://jakarta.apache.org/bsf.
[5] Apache Organization. The Apache Web Services Project: Axis. http://ws.apache.org/axis.
[6] BEA Systems, Inc. Weblogic. http://www.bea.com/products/server.
[7] M.I. Cole. *Algorithmic Skeletons: A Structured Approach to the Management of Parallel Computation*. Pitman, 1989.
[8] M. Danelutto and P. Teti. Lithium: A structured parallel programming enviroment in Java. In *Proceedings of Computational Science – ICCS*, number 2330 in Lecture Notes in Computer Science, pages 844–853. Springer-Verlag, Apr. 2002.
[9] J. Dünnweber and S. Gorlatch. HOC-SA: A Grid Service architecture for Higher-Order Components. In *IEEE International Conference on Services Computing, Shanghai, China*, pages 288–294. IEEE Computer Society Press, Sept. 2004.
[10] T. Erl. *Service-Oriented Architecture: A Field Guide to Integrating XML and Web Services*. Prentice Hall PTR, 2004.
[11] M. Fisher, J. Ellis, and J. Bruce. *JDBC API Tutorial and Reference, Third Edition*. Addison-Wesley Professional, 2003. isbn 0321173848.
[12] I. Foster. *Designing and Building Parallel Programs. Concepts and Tools for Parallel Software Engineering*. Addison Wesley, 1995.
[13] E. Gamma, R. Helm, R. Johnson, and J. Vlissides. *Design patterns: Elements of reusable object-oriented software*. Addison Wesley, 1995.
[14] D. Gannon and S. Krishnan. XCAT3: A framework for CCA components as OGSA services. In *Proceedings of the International Workshop on High-Level Parallel Programming Models and Supportive Environments, 2004*.
[15] Globus Alliance. http://www.globus.org.
[16] S. Gosain, A. Malhotra, O.E. Sawy, and F. Chehade. The impact of common e-business interfaces. *Commun. ACM*, 46(12):186–195, 2003.
[17] IBM. Websphere application server. http://www-306.ibm.com/software/webservers/appserv/was/.
[18] JBoss Network. Hibernate – persistence for idiomatic java. http://www.hibernate.org.
[19] J. Löwy and J. Osborn. *COM and .NET Component Services*. O'Reilly and Associates, 2001.
[20] R. Monson-Haefel. *Enterprise Java Beans. Developing Enterprise Java Components*. O'Reilly and Associates, 2001.
[21] OASIS Technical Committee. WSRF: The Web Service Resource Framework, http://www.oasis-open.org/committees/wsrf.
[22] A. Organization. Apache addressing. http://ws.apache.org/ws-fx/addressing.
[23] J. Park and S. Hunting. *XML Topic Maps:Creating and Using Topic Maps for the Web*. Addison-Wesley, 2004.
[24] C. Pérez, T. Priol, and A. Ribes. PaCO++: A parallel object model for high performance distributed systems. In *Proceedings of the Conference on System Sciences (HICSS-37)*. IEEE Computer Society Press, January 2004.
[25] Sun Microsystems. Java RMI over IIOP protocol specification. http://java.sun.com/products/rmi-iiop.
[26] C. Szyperski. *Component software: Beyond object-oriented programming*. Addison Wesley, 1998.
[27] The CCA Forum. Cca glossary. http://www.cca-forum.org/glossary.

[28] S. Thomas, S. Tuecke, J. Gawor, and R. Seed. Java OGSI hosting environment design – a portable grid service container framework. In *Globus online documentation*. 2004. http://dsd.lbl.gov/SGT/GlobusDocs.

[29] F. Valera, A. de Solages, E. Vázquez, and L. Bellido. Parallelism and messaging services in a j2ee-based e-commerce brokering platform. In *5th International Conference on Electronic Commerce Research*. ACM Press, 2002.

[30] World Wide Web Consortium, W3C. Web Services, XML Protocol Recommendations. http://www.w3.org/2002/ws.

New Trends in Software Methodologies, Tools and Techniques
H. Fujita and M. Mejri (Eds.)
IOS Press, 2005

Design and Implementation of an Agent-Based Middleware for Context-Aware Ubiquitous Services

Hideyuki TAKAHASHI [1], Yoshikazu TOKAIRIN, Takuo SUGANUMA and Norio SHIRATORI
Research Institute of Electrical Communication, Graduate School of Information Sciences, Tohoku University

Abstract. In ubiquitous computing environment, different kinds of system components including hardware elements, software components and network connections are required to cooperate with each other to provide services that fulfill user requirements. This paper proposes an agent-based middleware for ubiquitous environment that consists of computers and home electric appliances. The middleware, called AMUSE, can take QoS (quality of service) in ubiquitous environment into consideration by coping with not only user context but also resource context, using agent-based computing technology. In this paper we describe concept, design and initial implementation of AMUSE. Simulation results of experimental ubiquitous service using AMUSE has been shown to prove the effectiveness of our proposed scheme. Additionally, we show the initial implementation of multimedia communication application based on AMUSE to confirm the feasibility and effectiveness of our scheme.

Keywords. Ubiquitous Computing, Agent, Context-aware, QoS, Service construction

1. Introduction

In recent years, researches on ubiquitous computing [1] environment and service provisioning on the environment has been greatly accelerated. There are two mainstreams in researches on ubiquitous services; one is research on user context in the environment, and the other is for service construction scheme. In user context researches, advanced methods for obtaining user's physical location and finding appropriate services from the locating information and user profile are mainly investigated [2]. On the other hand, in researches on service construction, superior frameworks and schemes are actively challenged for dynamic cooperation among many kinds of system components, i.e., entities in ubiquitous environment, to provide user-oriented services [3–8].

[1] Hideyuki Takahashi, 2-1-1 Katahira, Aoba-ku, Sendai 980-8577, JAPAN. Tel.: +81(22)217-5454; Fax: +81(22)217-5411; E-mail: hideyuki@shiratori.riec.tohoku.ac.jp.

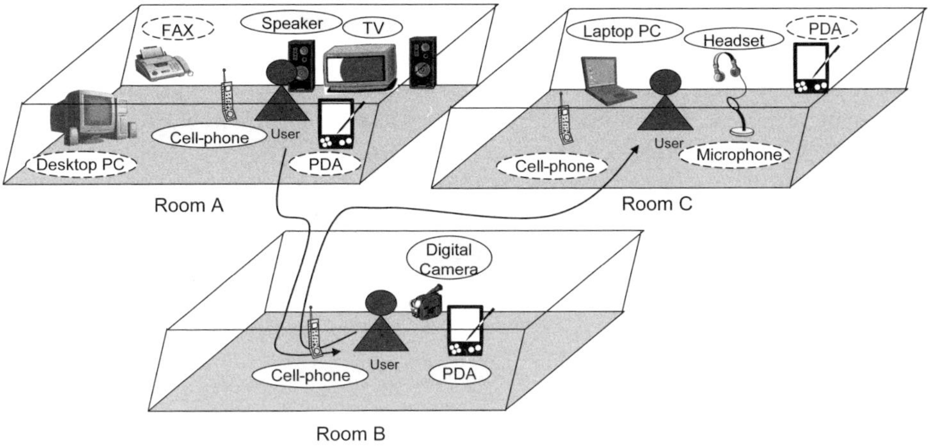

Figure 1. An application of ubiquitous service provided by multimedia home electric appliances.

The discussion on actual applications of ubiquitous services have been mainly focused on remote control of home electronics appliances from portable devices and information delivery system based on user's locating information. In the future, user demands on these ubiquitous services will move into much richer applications such as multimedia communication services. Thus, we are promoting research and development on fundamental technologies aiming at post ubiquitous computing environment, including multimedia service provisioning by cooperative behavior of audio-visual home electronics appliances. For instance, we are targeting at the services such as video streaming or videoconferencing constructed from coordination of computers and home appliances as shown in Fig. 1.

To provide necessary and sufficient QoS that satisfies user requirement is an intrinsic problem to realize such ubiquitous services. To address this, we have to consider not only from user context, but also resource context of hardware, network and software. This is because resource availability tends to be poor and unstable in ubiquitous environment. In addition, multiple users would be given the ubiquitous services simultaneously, thus problems of effective resource sharing and assignment should be addressed.

In this research, we are aiming at investigating ubiquitous service construction scheme in order to provide QoS-aware and stable services against changes of resource status and user's situation. We proposed an unique idea of effective handling of multiple contexts including user context and resource contexts. To accomplish the objective, we apply agent-based middleware approach.

The remarkable feature of this approach is agentification of each entity in overall ubiquitous environment. We embed context management ability and cooperation ability for conflict resolution on multiple contexts to each agent. Furthermore, we give maintenance mechanism for long-term context to accumulate and reuse history and experiences of past cooperation among agents. The individual behavior and the cooperative behavior of agents would make the QoS-aware service provisioning possible. The primary contribution of our work is that it enables provisioning rich services such as multimedia communication services in anytime and at anyplace with comfortable quality.

In this paper, we propose a multiagent-based middleware for ubiquitous computing environment, called AMUSE (Agent-based Middleware for Ubiquitous Service Environment). Moreover, we describe design of AMUSE focusing on the service construction scheme for QoS-aware service provisioning considering the multiple contexts. We evaluate our proposal from results of simulation experiments. Furthermore, we illustrate the initial implementation of multimedia communication application based on AMUSE to confirm the feasibility and effectiveness of our scheme.

The rest of this paper is organized as follows. In Section 2 we present the motivation and concept of AMUSE. In Section 3 service construction scheme in AMUSE is described. The simulation results are presented in Section 4. Moreover an application of AMUSE is illustrated in Section 5. Finally we conclude this paper in Section 6.

2. Concept of AMUSE

2.1. Related Work

Our work on the context-aware middleware is related to many other researches in this field. CARMAN [2] considers Mobile News Service(MNS) for mobile users. It provides service based on user mobility, device's performance and user's preference. When the service is provided by a single mobile device, performance of the device is most important for the service. Therefore there are various kinds of works for providing high quality of web service within the limits of device's performance [9]. These works are focusing on provisioning individual user-centric service using a single mobile device. To provide multimedia service by utilizing the available resources, we found it will be more efficient if multiple devices around the user can be used at the same time, instead of using only a single mobile device.

In other similar works, service is provided by coordination with any devices around user. For example, there are frameworks like STONE [6] and Ninja [8]. These frameworks construct the service based on service template which is requested by user. It means they search appropriate function to the requests and cooperation between various devices. In addition, Ja-Net [3] focuses on emergent service based on user preference.

The purpose of these works is same as our proposed work in terms of providing the service by coordination with heterogeneous entities. Moreover these works are providing superior mechanism of useful naming system, service description language, and service emergence.

However, we suppose existing service construction schemes are based only on user context and functional components, and they are concentrating on guaranty of coordination and operation or standardization of the specifications. Because it is important for ubiquitous environment to satisfy a particular requirement and limitation including network and computer resources. In case of rich service provisioning such as multimedia communication services in ubiquitous environment, we suppose it is much more important to consider QoS. For instance, there are ever-changing situations like user mobility, device's performance around user, and resource condition. Therefore, there would be a possibility that devices that are physically very close to the user can't provide the service due to lack of the resources, even if the devices potentially have good performance. Moreover it's necessary to provide the service considering cooperation problem of unexpected devices, softwares, and network.

From analysis of these previous works, we concluded that it's required to achieve service construction scheme which considers not only user context but also other contexts, in effective and integrated manners.

2.2. Target Issues

Following three technical issues need to be addressed to provide QoS-aware services on ubiquitous computing environment that consists of computers and audio-visual home electric appliances.

(P1) Resource context maintenance

Here we define "context" as situation of target entity at time t and temporal changes of the situation after/before time t. The situation of target entity is represented as internal representation model of the entity. Previous works for context awareness have been mainly focusing on user context acquisition scheme including locating information of the user. However, in terms of resource of entity, it was treated as only a value of the target resource parameter at time t, not as "context". In ubiquitous environment that consists of many kinds of entities in different level of functionality and performance, it is important to consider resource context efficiently as well for proper QoS control.

(P2) Multiple context coordination

In ubiquitous environment on which heterogeneous entities coexist, QoS should be maintained in the range from entity level to overall system level. To do so, we have to consider not only input/output specification of the entity, but also multiple context coordination including user context and resource context.

(P3) Non-deterministic property of service construction

Furthermore we need to cope with problem of mutual dependency and interoperability among entities that are not resolved deterministically from analysis of static specifications of entities. This is because each entity is basically designed to work by itself, not designed to work with other entities cooperatively. Thus, services constructed from the entities would not work properly in accordance with the specifications.

2.3. AMUSE Framework

In AMUSE, we solve the technical issues P1 to P3 described in the previous section with the following two approaches.

(R1) Agentification of each entity

"Agentification" is a process to make a target entity workable as an agent by adding knowledge processing mechanism to the entity. In our proposal, we agentify each entity respectively. Also we add context management ability and cooperation ability to resolve context conflict to the agents. Moreover, we embed long-term-context maintenance ability to the agents to accumulate cooperation history and experiences. Thus we can overcome the issues related to P1.

(R2) Multi-context-based Service Construction scheme

To realize QoS-aware ubiquitous service construction considering multiple context, we propose contract-based service construction scheme of agents, to solve the problem of P2. Agents make organization based on CNP (Contract Net Protocol [10]). Moreover, we model heuristics and dependency information on cooperation history in past among agents as long-term context among agents. This kind of context is also managed by the

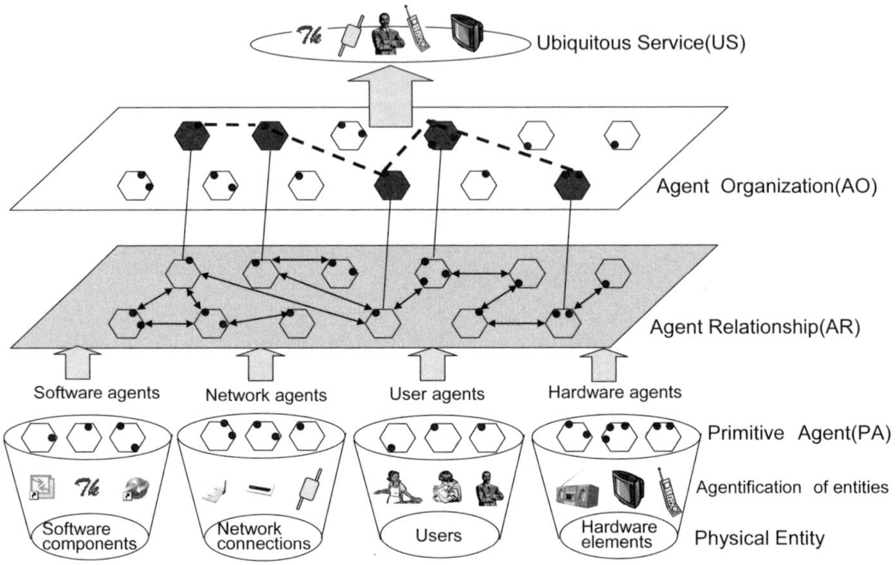

Figure 2. Framewrok of AMUSE.

agent. By using this context, agents can construct more advanced services employing lessons learned. This would be a solution to P3.

The fundamental framework of AMUSE is shown in Fig. 2. AMUSE consists of four layers, i.e., Primitive Agent layer (PA), Agent Relationship layer (AR), Agent Organization layer (AO), and Ubiquitous Service layer (US), based on concept of symbiotic computing [11]. PA makes physical entities to agents. In PA, context of each entity is managed by corresponding agent. In AR, inter-agent relationship based on long-term context among agents is created and maintained. In AO, agent organization is constructed based on the context in PA and AR, when user requirement to specific service is issued. On the top layer US, actual ubiquitous service is provided to users.

2.4. Service Provisioning Process in AMUSE

Service provisioning process in AMUSE framework is shown in Fig. 3. This process consists of the following six steps.

(1) Entity agentification

Each entity is rebuilt as agent by adding domain oriented knowledge representation model that is suitable for classification of the entity. Details of agentification mechanism are illustrated in Section 2.5.

(2) IAR updating

We define long-term context among agents as Inter-agent Relationship (IAR). Each agent has different IARs to all other agents with which it has cooperated in past time. Each agent updates their IAR after its service provisioning by itself or by cooperation with other agents. More details of IAR are described in Section 3.2.

(3) User requirement acquisition

Agent acquires user requirement, and analyzes the requirement from user's profile, locating information, and behavior in the ubiquitous environment. Agent has to choose

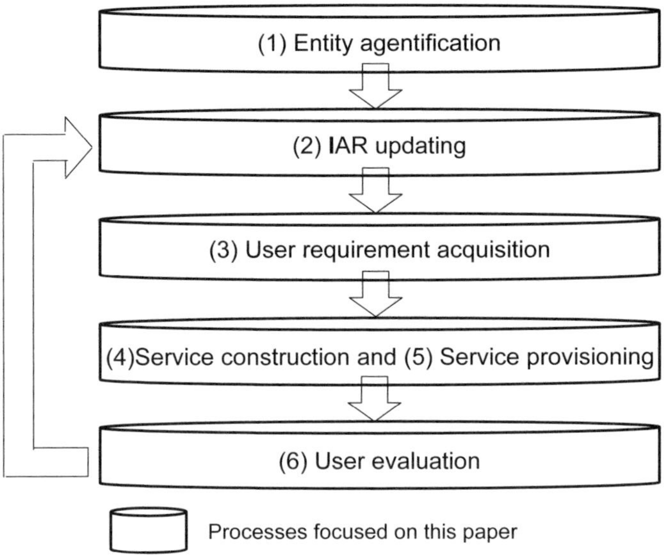

Figure 3. Service provisioning process based on AMUSE framework.

in the most suitable manner to get the requirement, because useful input devices may not be available in everywhere. This remains an open problem and is not treated in this paper.

(4) Service construction and (5) Service provisioning

After user requirement is acquired, agents construct its organization using CNP to provide service. In this scheme, we apply hierarchical CNP, i.e., task announcement is propagated in order of hardware agents, software agents and network agents. The agent organization is created based on context managed by each agent, and actual service is constructed and provided with combination of entities controlled by agents. Details are discussed in Section 3.

(6) User evaluation

When the service provisioning is finished, the agent organization receives user's feedback concerning the quality of provided service. To measure the evaluation, we introduce us-effectivity(E) referring Ja-Net [3]. In AMUSE, when E value changes, each agent informs the update to all other agents that have relationship to it. That is, the evaluation result is propagated to all related agents, and it effects to service construction subsequently. Details are illustrated in Section 3.3.

2.5. Agent Architecture for AMUSE

The basic architecture of agent in AMUSE is shown in Fig. 4. Here Cooperation Mechanism (CM) is a mechanism for exchanging messages among agents. Domain Knowledge (DK) is a knowledge-base system to store and activate various domain knowledge concerning the target entity. Based on the knowledge, agent monitors and controls the target entity, and makes actions to other agents. Entity Processing Mechanism (EPM) is an interface between DK and target entity. It passes events from entity to DK such as exceptions, and directs control instruction from DK to entity.

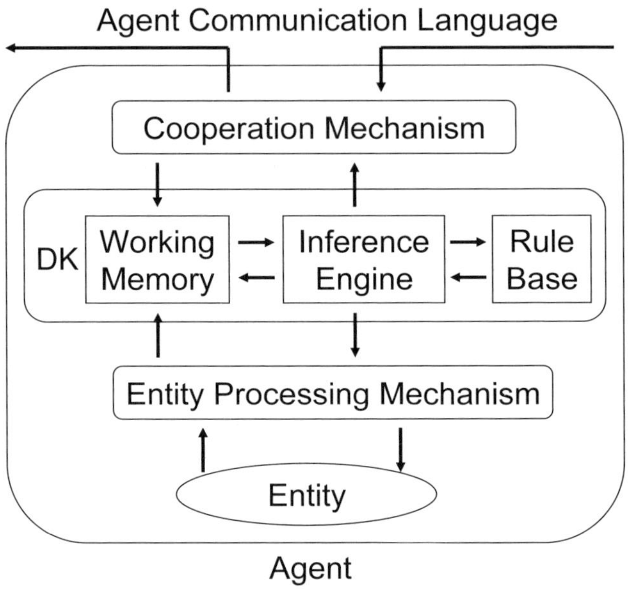

Figure 4. Basic agent architecture.

DK consists of three subsystems, i.e., Working Memory, Inference Engine and Rule Base. In Working Memory and Rule Base, set of Facts and Rules are stored respectively. Inference Engine refers to the Rules and Facts, and works as production system. By employing this inference mechanism, agent performs interaction with other agents and controls the target entity.

Figure 5 shows management functions for service construction in AMUSE. These functions are implemented as Rule set and related Facts in DK. IAR Management is module for maintenance of IAR such as creating, updating and deleting of it. Context Management is module for monitoring and recognizing context of the entity. Moreover Contract Management is module to maintenance contract conditions and contract status in case that contract relation is created with other agents.

3. Service Construction Scheme in AMUSE

3.1. Creation of IAR

IAR consists of three kinds of relationships. They are, Tight-Relationship (TR), Group-Relationship (GR) and Competing-Relationship (CR) like shown in Fig. 6.

(a) Tight-Relationship(TR)

TR is created among agents that provide some services by constructing organization of the agents. By using this relationship, it is possible for the agent to have past cases of successes and failures in cooperation.

(b) Group-Relationship(GR)

GR is given to group of agents that have some potential dependencies. For instance, there is GR among hardware entities such as desktop PC, speakers and PC displays. By

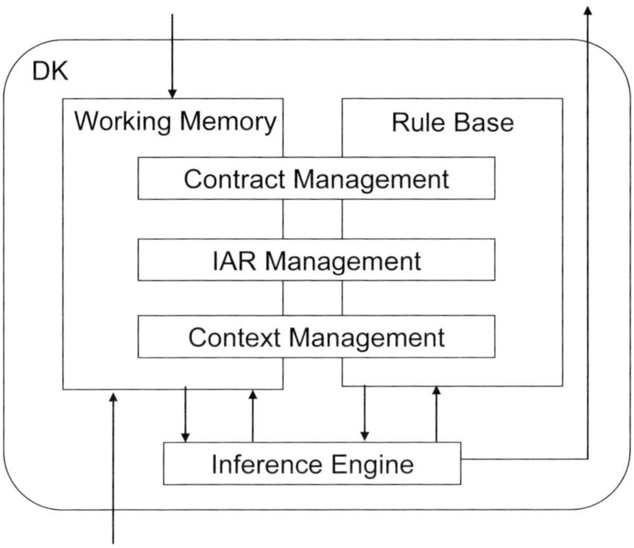

Figure 5. Management modules in DK for AMUSE.

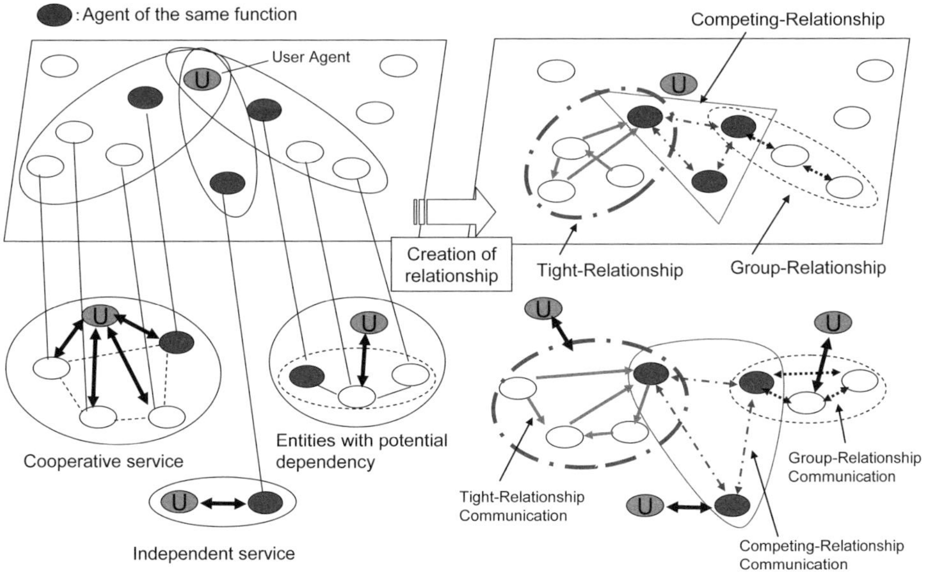

Figure 6. Creation of Inter-Agent Relationship.

using GR, it is possible that agent informs changes in their states frequently to the agents within the group.

(c) Competing-Relationship(CR)

CR is formed among agents that have same function. Why this relationship is introduced is that these agents would compete when task announcement of the function is

```
IAR ::= {iar}*
iar ::= < id, name, func, relationship, state, availability, shared values >
id ::= int
name ::= string
func ::= {type}*
type ::= audio-output | audio-input | image-output | image-input | ...
relationship ::=  TR | GR | CR
state ::= running | online | offline
availability ::= < acceptability, us-effectivity, ... >
shared values ::= < operating rate, ...>
```

Figure 7. Knowledge representation of IAR.

issued. By using CR, the competing agents routinely inform their status to each other, and they can make good organization effectively when CNP-based negotiation runs.

3.2. Knowledge Representation of IAR

Figure 7 shows knowledge representation of IAR. IAR is represented in set of `iar` which is an individual relation. The `iar` consists of `id`, `name`, `func`, `relationship`, `state`, `availability`, and `shared values`. The `id` is an integer value to identify each agent. The `name` is a name of agent against which the `iar` points. The `func` is an expression of functionality of the entity such as specification of I/O. It is a set of `type`. The `type` represents each function. For instance, the agent that has I/O function of the voice has `audio-output` and `audio-input` in `type` variable. The `relationship` indicates type of relationship such as `TR`, `GR` and `CR`. The `state` indicates present state of agent. Here, `running` means state of service is being provided, `online` means state of standby, and `offline` means state of service cannot be provided, respectively. The `availability` indicates degree of effectiveness of the agent. It consists of `acceptability`, `us-effectivity`, etc. The `acceptability` (A) indicates acceptance ratio to task announcement or bid of the agent.

$$A = b1/t \text{ (or } a/b2)$$

Here, $b1$ is number of times that agent has been received bid, t is number of times that agent has sent task, a is number of times that agent has been received award and $b2$ is number of times that agent has sent bid. The `us-effectivity` (E) indicates metrics of evaluation that agent receives after providing user with service.

$$E = p/n$$

Here, p is the total number of times of good evaluation, and n is the total number of times of good and bad evaluation based on strength value of Ja-Net [3]. The initial values of p, n and E are set to 1. The `shared values` is referred as common index used by each agent. For instance, there is `operating rate` (O) that indicates how often agent is usually used.

$$O = u/l$$

Here, u is number of times in which it is used. The l is fixed period which is decided by user. It can be used to understand trend of changes in the preference of the user according to the `shared values`.

3.3. CNP-Based Service Construction with IAR

Our scheme which is based on CNP builds agent organization using three kinds relationship. CNP is a mechanism to make contract relationship among agents by exchanging messages such as task announcement, bid, and award, shown in Fig. 8. Here, we explain features of service construction scheme with IAR.

(1) Case of Tight-Relationship(TR)

In Fig. 8(1), we assume that agent A has a relationship of type TR with both agent B and agent C whereas no relationship exists between B and C. `TR` between A and B indicates that trouble was occurred when they had cooperation in the past, and `TR` between A and C indicates no trouble in the past. When B and C receives the task announcement from A, they refer to each IAR. Here, B does not send bid because `TR` against A is bad. That means the trouble in cooperation would occur this time too. On the other hand, C sends bid because C judges from `TR` that it would contribute to the task announced. In fact, it is possible to reduce trouble in cooperation by agent considering coordinated relationship in the past.

(2) Case of Group-Relationship(GR)

In Fig. 8(2), we assume that agent A has no relationship with both agent B and agent C whereas relationship of type GR exists between B and C. Here, C recognizes that `GR` against B exists when C judges the task announcement from A. Then C sends bid if C judges that B can provide service by referring to `state` in IAR. On the other hand, C ignores the task announcement if B can not provide service. In fact, it is possible to reduce the trouble in cooperation by agent considering dependency of the agents.

(3) Case of Competing-Relationship(CR)

In Fig. 8(3), we assume that relationship of type CR exists between agent B and agent C whereas agent A has no relationship with both B and C. B and C receive the task announcement. Each agent checks IAR of type CR if it can process the task. When agent has `CR`, it refers to state of the `CR`. For instance, B sends bid in case that B judged the value of `us-effectivity` on this task is higher than that of C. On the other hand, C ignores the task announcement in case that it judged `us-effectivity` of B is higher than C. In fact, it is possible to efficient construction of service by consideration of state of same function agent.

4. Simulation and Evaluation

4.1. Implementation

We implemented agents based on AMUSE to perform simulation. In the implementation, we employed agent-based programing environment DASH [12] that is based on multiagent programing framework ADIPS [13]. We also performed simulation by IDEA [14]. IDEA is interactive design environment for Agent system. We used DASH programing environment because agent which is developed for simulation can easily be reused when we build the real-world system in future.

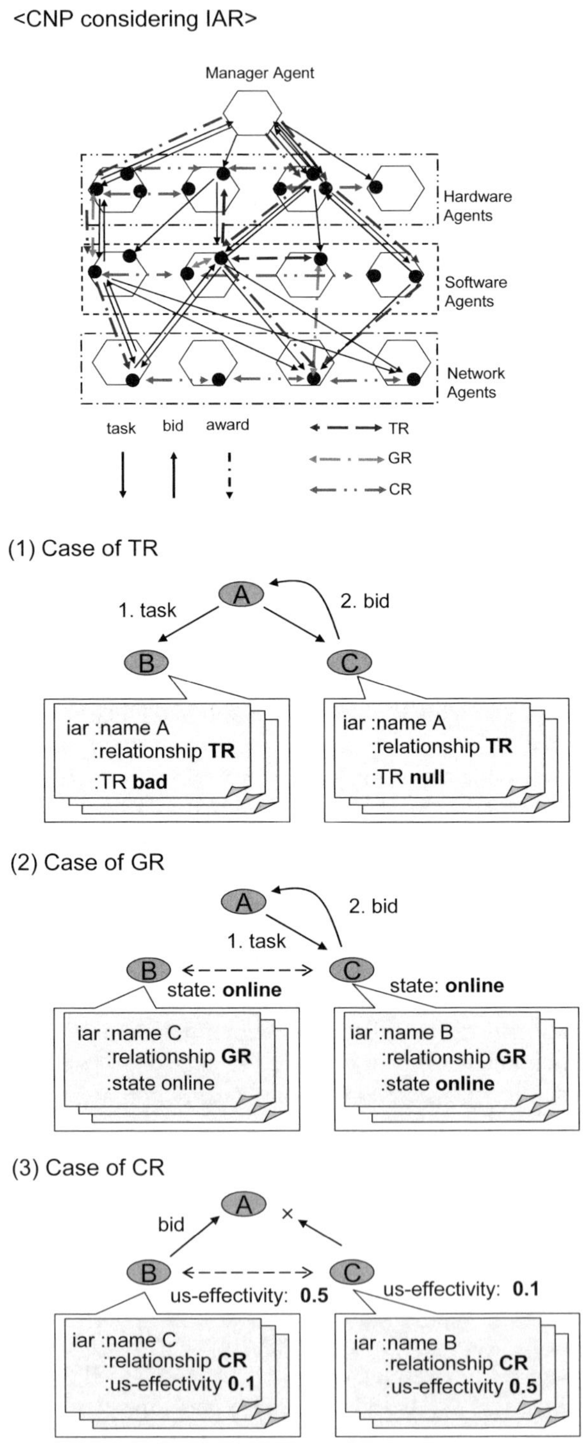

Figure 8. Characteristic of CNP by IAR.

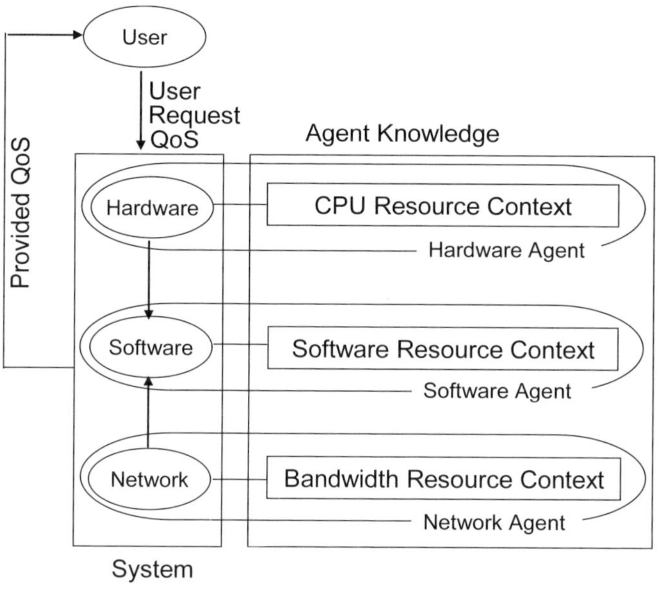

Figure 9. Behavioral situation representation of the system.

4.2. Evaluation Method

We performed simulation of system behavior based on AMUSE. In this simulation, QoS awareness of the system is measured and we investigate how much the QoS awareness is improved by introducing AMUSE. To measure the QoS awareness, we apply User Request Achievement (URA) level. Using these metrics, we can measure how much the user requirement is fulfilled with provided quality of service by the system. Details of URA are described later.

Figure 9 shows the behavioral situation representation of the system. Here, three entities including a hardware entity, a software entity and a network entity are making organization and providing service to a User. The user issues "User Request QoS" and the system provides service with "Provided QoS". Hardware Agent (HA) monitors CPU resource context and Network Agent (NA) monitors bandwidth resource context. On the other hand, Software Agent (SA) has knowledge concerning mapping from resource availability onto actual user level QoS.

The QoS evaluation of service is based on URA. URA is calculated by comparison between User Request QoS RU and Provided QoS SV. We defined the range of URA is from -1 to 1. Here, ru_i is an element of RU and it represents User Request QoS on service element i. Also sv_i is an element of SV and it represents Provided QoS on service element i. The value of ru_i and sv_i is from 1 to 10. Here, URA on service element i, i.e. URA_i is represented as follows:

- $SV = \{sv_1, sv_2, ...\}$
- $RU = \{ru_1, ru_2, ...\}$
- $URA_i = \frac{sv_i - ru_i}{10}$

This means that, if URA_i is above zero, the user requirement is fulfilled and if it is below zero, the requirement is not satisfied.

In this evaluation, the number of service elements is assumed to be two ($i = 1, 2$) and URA indicates the total URA, that is, a mean value of URA_1 and URA_2 for simplification.

We performed simulation of service construction with the above conditions for 500 times. The agent constructs CR immediately after simulation beginning. When SA constructs service, it refers to NA's bid and IAR. If SA judges that other agent is suitable, it disregards the task even if the task is acceptable. And if agent receives bid by two or more agents that can fulfill user requirement, agent sends award to agent with the highest value of E of IAR after referring to the value of E. In the actual simulation, we use only the strength of Ja-Net for the value of E. The simulation receives a assumed user evaluation each time of service construction. The user evaluation is reflected to E. User evaluation is assumed good if sv_i is within from 120% to 100% when ru_i is regarded as 100%. In this case value E is set to 1. It is assumed bad in case that sv_i exceeds 120% or is below 80%, and the value is set to -1. Otherwise it is regarded as usual, and the value is set to 0.

We compare three patterns of agent behaviors, i.e., our proposal (IAR-based approach), the case considering only user context (User-request approach), and the case considering only the maximum QoS value of agent for QoS without consideration of resource context (Maximum approach). For the simulation, resources of HA and NA are assigned random values in every service construction. Also we give tendencies of user request in three patterns, which is high quality (7∼10), middle quality (4∼7), and low quality (1∼4).

4.3. Simulation Results and Evaluation

Figures 10–12 shows the variation of the value of URA. Figure 10 is a comparison where RU is always in high, Fig. 11 shows the comparison where RU is always in middle, and Fig. 12 depicts the case where RU is always in low.

Figures 13–15 shows the frequency distribution concerning URA. Figure 13 is a comparison for case that RU is always in high, Fig. 14 is a comparison for case that RU is always in middle, and Fig. 15 is a comparison in case that RU is always in low.

From analysis of Fig. 13 in case that RU is always in high, our approach could achieve the user requirement with higher frequency than User-request approaches. From this result, in case that user requirement is higher than the service environment, it can be understood that the requirement can not be fulfilled even if only user context is considered. Moreover, in case that agent considers only the user request and the maximum value that can be selected, URA generally is lower than our approach, when user requirement is not fulfilled. It is understood that some conflict on resource context is occurred. Also it is understood that our approach decreases bad service construction by considering IAR. This is because that IAR decreases the conflict of resource context. From these results our approach is rather effective in this kind of case.

From analysis of Fig. 14 in case that RU is always in middle, URA of User-request approach often closes to zero much more times than other approaches. On the other hand, compare to the User-request approach, IAR-based approach could fulfill the user requirement frequently. Moreover the case that URA of our approach is higher than

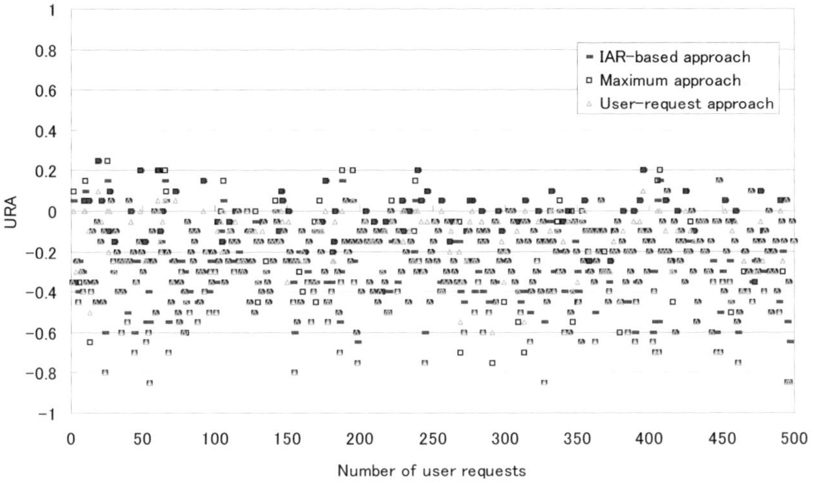

Figure 10. Variation of value of URA in case that RU is always in high.

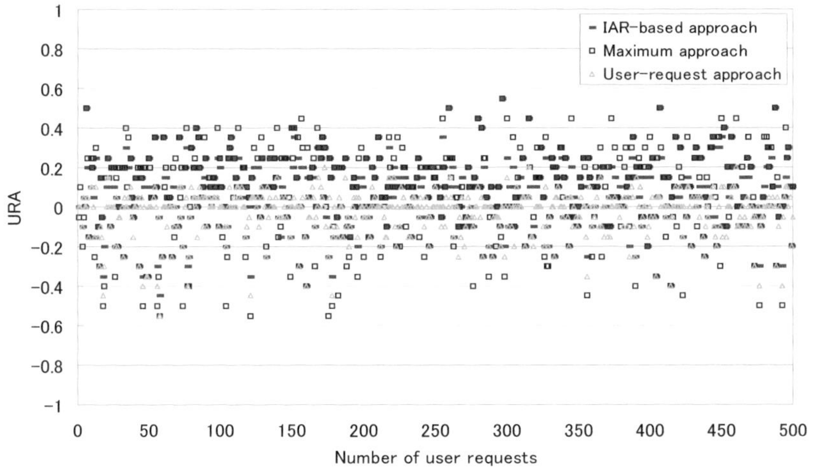

Figure 11. Variation of value of URA in case that RU is always in middle.

that of Maximum approach is a little. From this result we conclude that, if resources are available, our approach can provide a slightly better service than the original user requirement. It is also understood that our approach considerably reduce bad service construction than other approaches such as in Fig. 13.

By analyzing Fig. 15 where RU is always in low, URA of User-request approach often extremely close to zero more frequently than other approaches. In our approach and Maximum approach, the case that URA closes to zero is not frequent. But, our approach closes to zero much more times than Maximum approach. Moreover our approach and

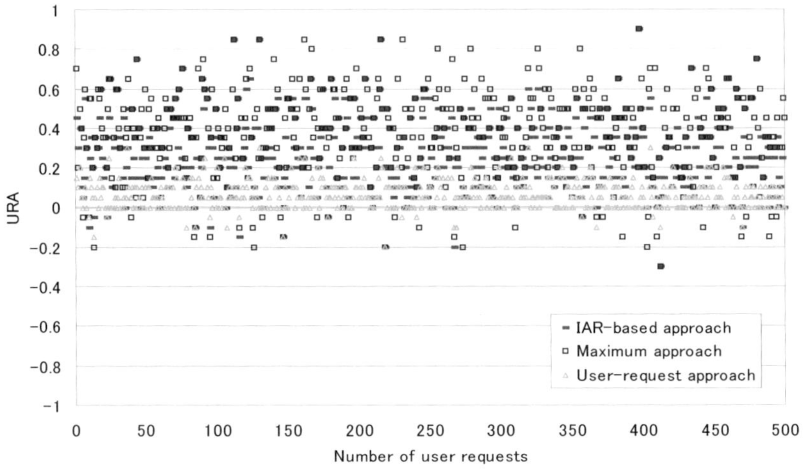

Figure 12. Variation of value of URA in case that RU is always in low.

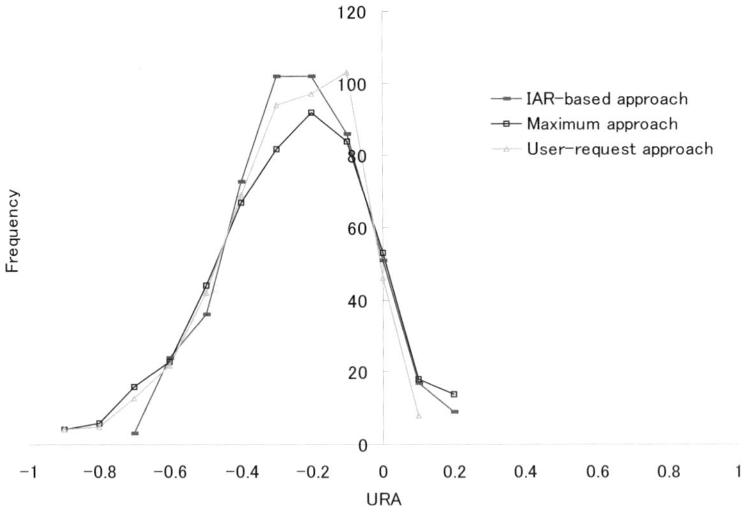

Figure 13. Results of comparison in case that RU is always in high.

User-request approach reach much closer to zero than Maximum approach. Thus, we can find that the agents construct organization considering user requirement and IAR effectively. However, in this case, our approach is thought to be meddlesome service for user who does not want excessive quality.

From these simulation results, it is understood that our approach is most effective under unstable environment with high-level user requirement. Additionally, it should be considered whether user requirement or relationship between agents which has the higher priority, when agents construct service. That is, user requirement can be fulfilled

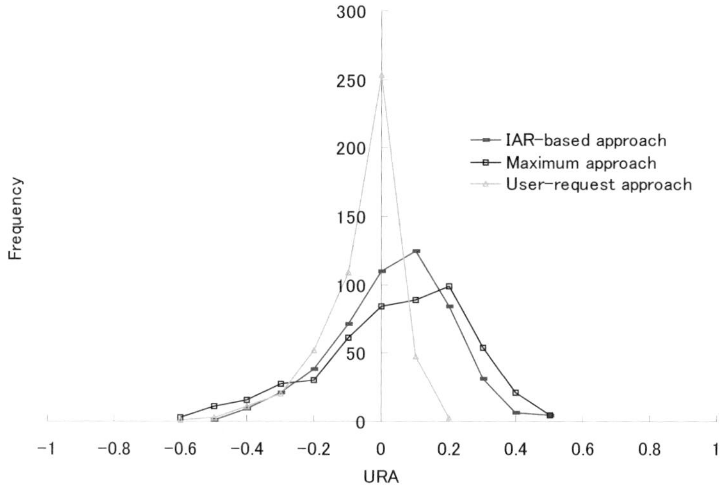

Figure 14. Results of comparison in case that *RU* is always in middle.

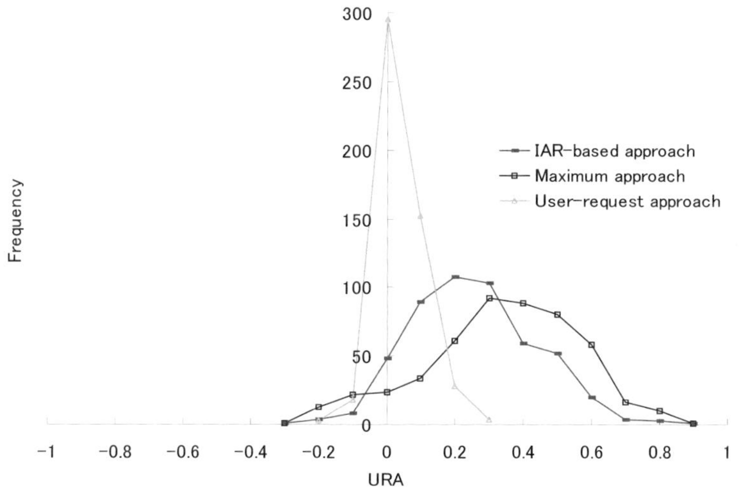

Figure 15. Results of comparison in case that *RU* is always in low.

by mainly considering IAR rather than user requirement in the environment with high user requirement and instable resources. However, in the environment with suitable user requirement and stable resource, user requirement should be mainly considered rather than IAR. Therefore, we suppose that it is necessary to consider top priority between user requirement and IAR so that it matches to the situation when service is constructed in ubiquitous environment.

5. C-QUSE: An Application of AMUSE

5.1. Multimedia Communication System C-QUSE

To evaluate feasibility and effectiveness of our scheme, we implemented an application of multimedia communication system based on AMUSE, that is, C-QUSE (Context and QoS-Aware Ubiquitous Service Environment). Multimedia communication is one of the resource sensitive application domains. Thus it would be a good example to confirm the effectiveness of AMUSE. C-QUSE can consider multiple contexts and provide QoS-aware multimedia communication service. This system can provide user with the live streaming service, for instance video stream or videoconferencing, whenever I/O devices such as PC, television, audio system, etc., are available near to the user. Moreover this service can control user request and quality according to user's situation including physical position. User would be provided with live video stream of distant place at anytime and anywhere. We suppose this system has a wide range of application. Especially, support of telework, teleconferencing, and content delivery for amusement which includes music, movie, sport casting, home movie, etc. are adequate applications of this system. We are targeting at the services that always stay close to user's movement and provide live contents. Thus we suppose that it is most important that the system can extemporarily provide such services employing available devices at that location in ad hoc manner.

5.2. Implementation of C-QUSE

This application has been implemented by using IDEA and reusing of part of agents which are developed for simulation experiments described in Section 4. The positional information of user that is one of the user contexts is tracked by IS-600 [15]. We use Java Communications API to acquire the positional information from IS-600 into Java environment. We connected a DV camera and a USB Web camera to the PC that has a role of live streaming server. The streaming server agent resides in the server, and manages the streaming service. If the streaming server agent receives the other agent's request, it can provide for the different quality of service based on the agent request. We use DVTS [16] and JMF(Java Media Framework) [17] for sending streaming of different quality. As the home electric appliance, we used a television set. Therefore we converted digital DV stream to analog signal by the DV converter.

5.3. Empirical Study with C-QUSE

In this experiment, we evaluate feasibility and effectiveness of AMUSE focusing on its ability of multiple context management. This experiment consists of the following three scenarios and we observed the system's behavior according to the scenarios.

(1) User-location-oriented behavior

Here, we check that our system based on AMUSE can provide the user location-oriented service like the existing ubiquitous services.

(2) User-request-oriented behavior

In this case, we check that our system can provide the service based on user requests. From this scenario, we prove that AMUSE can provide the service in consideration of not only user location but also user requests.

(3) Multiple-contexts-oriented behavior

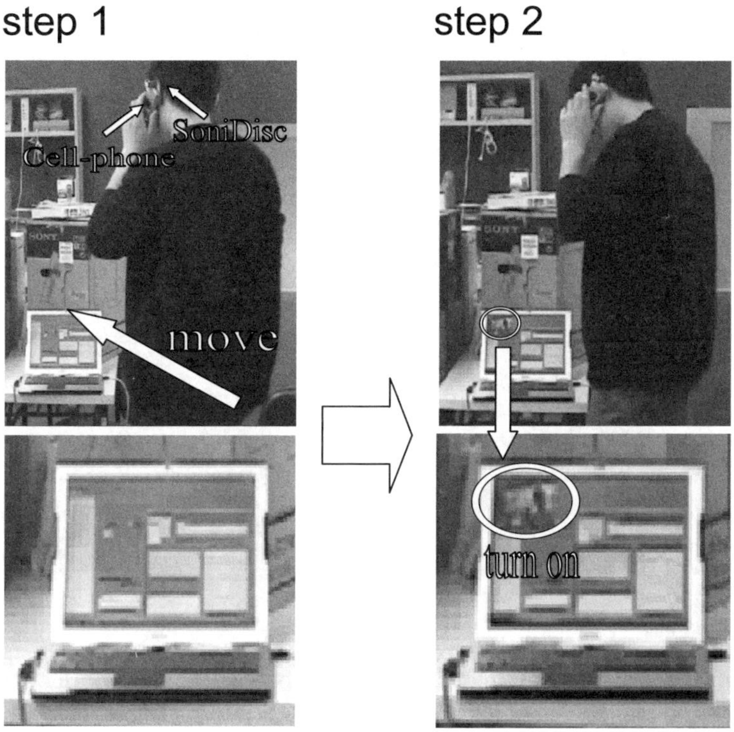

Figure 16. User-location-oriented service provisioning by C-QUSE.

In this case, we check that our system can provide context-aware service in consideration of QoS by cooperation among agents. From this case, we prove that our framework have a potential and beneficial effect on ubiquitous multimedia communication services.

Figure 16 shows the user-location-oriented service provisioning of C-QUSE. In this case, we employed SoniDisc of IS600 attached to the cell-phone to track the user's positional information. The laptop PC which can provide I/O of video services is managed by an agent. When user approached the laptop PC (Fig. 16 (step 1)), the agent recognized the user and started the service. Managing the laptop PC, the agent checked the available software for receiving the video stream and it required the streaming server agent of the video stream by using JMF. The streaming server agent received the request, then it delivered the video stream to the laptop PC (Fig. 16 (step 2)). From this case, we can check that our system based on AMUSE can provide the service as in the case of the existing user-location-oriented ubiquitous services. However, QoS is not considered in this case, thus the comfortable service that satisfies the user requirement can not be available.

Figure 17 shows the behavior in case of user-request-oriented service provisioning. In this case, we employed SoniDisc attached to the cell-phone same as in the case of Fig. 16. We used television and desktop PC for providing I/O of video service. These hardware devices are managed by TV agent and Desktop PC agent, respectively. When the user approached the television and the desktop PC, these agents referred to the user request of quality from user contexts. In case of Fig. 17 (step 1), user requested only

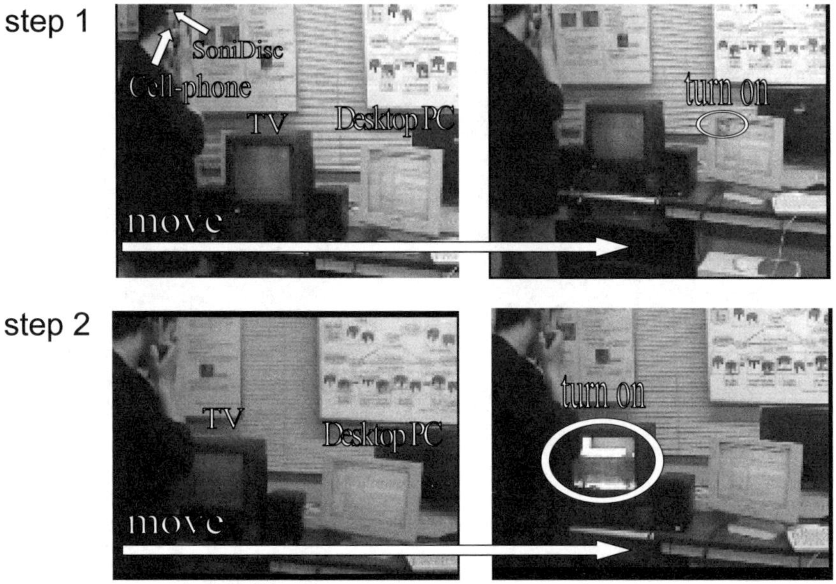

Figure 17. User-request-oriented service provisioning by C-QUSE.

video stream service and the request of quality is none. Then, the Desktop PC agent required the streaming server agent of the video stream by using JMF. This stream can not consume huge network resource. In case of Fig. 17 (step 2), user requested high quality service. Then, the TV agent required the streaming server agent of the video stream by using DVTS, and the TV agent provided the high quality video stream service. From this case, we confirmed that our system can provide user with the service based on user requests other than user location.

Figure 18 shows the behavior in case of multiple-contexts-oriented service provisioning. In this case, we used three hardware devices, they are, a television, a desktop PC, and a laptop PC for providing I/O of video services. This time, we assume that user brings a portable terminal device like PDA and has SoniDisc attached to the laptop PC. User moves with the laptop PC and the user request remains high quality. Each one of these hardwares is managed by the TV agent, the Desktop PC agent and the Laptop PC agent, respectively.

In step 1 of Fig. 18, the laptop PC is the only hardware that can provide user with the service from location of user contexts and hardware contexts. Therefore, the laptop PC agent provided user with the stream by using JMF because the laptop PC agent size up the available function as a maximum quality. In step 2 of Fig. 18, the TV agent and the Desktop PC agent recognized that user approached their range of service area. They referred to user request from contexts and the other agents' contexts from their own IAR, and they knew the Laptop PC agent was providing user with the service. They compared the available quality with the laptop PC agent since user requests of quality was high. The TV agent made judgments that it is possible to provide much higher quality than anyone else, and it requested stopping the service with the Laptop PC agent. Then, the TV agent required the streaming server agent of the video stream by using DVTS after the Laptop PC agent accepted the TV agent request. In step 3 of Fig. 18, when user got

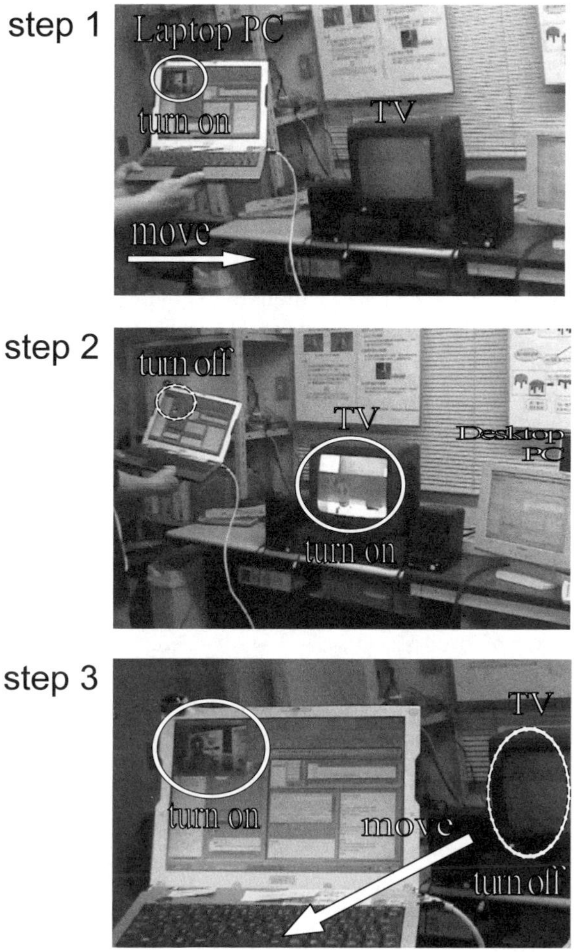

Figure 18. Multiple-contexts-oriented service provisioning by C-QUSE.

away from the TV which was providing the service and the Desktop PC, the TV agent informed stopping the service with other agents. And the Laptop PC agent started the service for the nearest device from user. From this case, we can check that individual agents based on AMUSE can provide the service while controlling quality by considering other agent's contexts.

From these three experiments, we have confirmed the remarkable features of our scheme compare to the traditional ubiquitous system. Agents that have competing functions can cooperate with each other by effective use of IAR. For instance, when the streaming server's resource is low, the streaming server bogs down if any agents request DVTS and JMF by only considering user contexts.

6. Conclusion

In this paper, we proposed AMUSE, a multiagent-based middleware for Context-aware ubiquitous service. We described design of AMUSE focusing on the service construction scheme for QoS-aware service provisioning considering the multiple contexts. We also evaluated our scheme with some simulation experiments and confirmed its remarkable usefulness in ubiquitous environment, particularly for multimedia services. Moreover we implemented an application as a first step towards practical use of AMUSE and performed some empirical studies with prototype system concentrating on evaluation of the effectiveness of multiple contexts management.

In future, we will evaluate prototype system using various actual hardware devices such as PC and home electric appliances to confirm the feasibility, effectiveness and basic performance in real-world environment. As a future goal of our research, we are planning to consider various agent status more dynamically to improve the updating and deletion mechanism of IAR with more extensive simulation.

References

[1] M. Weiser, "The Computer for the Twenty-first Century," *Scientific American*, vol. 265, no. 3, pp. 94–104, 1991.

[2] P. Bellavista, A. Corradi, R. Montanari, and C. Stefanelli, "Context-Aware Middleware for Resource Management in the Wireless Internet," *IEEE Trans. software Eng.*, vol. 29, no. 12, pp. 1086–1099, 2003.

[3] T. Itao, T. Nakamura, M. Matsuo, T. Suda, and T. Aoyama, "Adaptive Creation of Network Applications in the Jack-in-the-Net Architecture," *Proceedings of IFIP Networking*, pp. 129–140, 2002.

[4] M. Minoh and T. Kamae, "Networked Appliance and Their Peer-to-Peer Architecture AMIDEN," *IEEE Comm. Magazine*, vol. 39, No. 10, pp. 80–84, 2001.

[5] T. Iwamoto and H. Tokuda, "PMAA:Media Access Architecture for Ubiquitous Computing," *Journal of IPSJ*, vol. 44, no. 3, pp. 848–856, 2003.

[6] M. Minami, H. Morikawa, and T. Aoyama, "The Design and Evaluation of an Interface-based Naming System for Supporting Service Synthesis in Ubiquitous Computing Environment," *Journal of IEICEJ*, vol. J86-B, no. 5, pp. 777–789, 2003.

[7] J. Nakazawa, Y. Tobe, and H. Tokuda, "On Dynamic Service Integration in VNA Architecture," *IEICE Trans*, vol. E84-A, no. 7, pp. 1624–1635, 2001.

[8] S. Gribble, M. Welsh, R. Behren, E. Brewer, D. Culler, N. Borisov, S. Czerwinski, R. Gummadi, J. Hill, A. Joseph, R. Katz, Z. Mao, S. Ross, and B. Zhao, "The Ninja architecture for robust Internet-scale systems and services," *Special Issue of Computer Networks on Pervasive Computing*, vol. 35, no. 4, 2001.

[9] W.Y. Lum and F.C.M. Lau, "User-Centric Content Negotiation for Effective Adaptation Service in Mobile Computing," *IEEE Trans. software Eng.*, vol. 29, no. 12, pp. 1100–1111, 2003.

[10] R. G. Smith, "The Contract net protocol: High-level communication and control in a distributed Problem solver," *IEEE Trans. Comput.*, vol. 29, no. 12, pp. 1104–1113, 1980.

[11] K. Sugawara, N. Shiratori, and T. Kinoshita, "Toward Post Ubiquitous Computing-Symbiotic Computing-," *IEICE Technical Report*, vol. 103, no. 244, pp. 43–46, 2003.

[12] K. Sugawara, H. Hara, T. Kinoshita, and T. Uchiya, "Flexible Distributed Agent System programmed by a Rule-based Language," *Proceedings of the Sixth IASTED International Conference of Artificial Intelligence and Soft Computing*, pp. 7–12, 2002.

[13] S. Fujita, H. Hara, K. Sugawara, T. Kinoshita, and N. Shiratori, "Agent-based Design Model of Adaptive Distributed Systems," *The International Journal of Artificial Intelligence, Neural Networks and Complex Problem-Solving Technologies*, vol. 9, no. 1, pp. 57–70, 1998.

[14] A. Takagaki, T. Uchiya, H. Hara, T. Abe, and T. Kinoshita, "Interactive Development Support Environment for Agent Systems," *Information Technology Letters*, vol. 2, pp. 143–144, 2003.

[15] IS600: IS-600 Mark 2 Precision Motion Tracker. http://www.isense.com/products/prec/is600/.

[16] A. Ogawa, K. Kobayashi, K. Sugiura, O. Nakamura, and J. Murai, "Design and Implementation of DV based video over RTP," *Packet Video Workshop 2000*, May 2000.

[17] JMF: Java Media Framework. http://java.sun.com/products/java-media/jmf/.

Chapter 9

Software Design for Creative and Interactive Users

New Trends in Software Methodologies, Tools and Techniques
H. Fujita and M. Mejri (Eds.)
IOS Press, 2005

Computation, Interaction and Imagination: *Into Virtual Space and Back to Reality*

Ernest EDMONDS and Linda CANDY
Creativity and Cognition Studios, Faculty of Information Technology, University of Technology, Sydney, POBOX123 Broadway, NSW, Australia
ernest@ernestedmonds.com

Abstract. The main aim of the research from which this paper arises is to identify requirements of computer support for creative work by investigating the work of artists and exploring the potential of new creative technology in this field. The paper reports upon an experimental artists-in-residence on the campus of Loughborough University during which events were recorded and analysed. The nature of the interchanges between artist and technologist as well as the artists' perspectives upon the use of the technologies and what they gained from it are described. One significant conclusion is that the influence of using computers on the artists' thinking is quite as significant as any direct outcome in terms of product. The enabling of creative transformations is a key aspect. The paper poses three questions and tries to find an answer to each by exploring the modelling of the results of the study in the context of what we know so far about computational approaches to understanding creativity. The results demonstrate that one aspect of VR may be understood in relation to previous studies of emergence.

1. Introduction

This paper is concerned with software that encourages human creativity. Where the creative person is working deeply and seriously in their domain we have found that, when using computers, they frequently need access to programming systems rather than packaged applications. Hence, the software systems that are of concern here are, typically, end user programming environments. The focus of the discussion is in the creative deployment of Virtual Reality programming by artists.

The modeling of creative practice is complex to the extent of extreme difficulty. Our approach to this problem is to look in parallel at creative practice by human experts, the interactions between experts and computer-based tools and media and the computational models that, at this stage, can be partially generated. In this paper the concern is understanding creative steps that occur in relation to the use of computational systems. The idea is to try to gain that understanding in a way that might illuminate the computational modeling of the complete creative design process. Within one paper only small steps can be made, but the step forward presented here is to show how design strategies can be employed that enable tractable, and hence perhaps computable, creative acts.

The notion of emergence has been discussed frequently (Edmonds and Moran, 1997). This is the notion of a new unexpected concept appearing during a process. Much of the work has looked at drawing. In such cases, a shape that was not employed or thought about in the construction of a drawing is seen in the result and proves interesting. The acts of drawing and looking at the result are seen to be as important as pure thinking (Soufi and Edmonds, 1996). This paper extends this fundamental idea into the use of virtual reality (VR) systems.

VR provides, in its simplest interpretation, a way of looking at reality that avoids us having to either actually be there or construct the specific artifacts to be considered. Even in its most normal usage it covers more concepts and, although we do not have the space to discuss the broad issues, it is clear that the implications are much deeper than that. Turkle, for example, studied computer-mediated communications in virtual realities. As a result she argues that these systems provoke self-reflection and simulated thought, the emphasis being on social and cultural issues. "Watch for" she says "a culture that leaves a new amount of space for the idea that he or she who plays, argues, and builds is a machine" (Turkle, 1996). Mowshowitz, on the other hand, has looked at the organisational and political implications and effects. He has considered the enabling of the development of virtual organisations and argues that "In the long term, the social changes will crystallize in virtual feudalism, a system of political authority centered in private, virtual organizations and based on the management of abstract forms of wealth" (Mowshowitz, 1997). From a different, but related, point of view Cicognani has argued for a linguistic perspective. She sees a parallel development between "cyberspace", the ways that we use language and the ways that we can construct new worlds (Cicognani, 1998). This paper picks up just one implication of VR that arose in the exploration by a sculptor and uses it to explore the creative opportunities, beyond visualisation of the non-existence, that exist in VR.

The Creativity and Cognition 1993 symposium (Candy and Edmonds, 1993) encouraged intersections between art, science and technology. This has continued in a series of lively meetings, most recently in April 2005 (Candy, 2005). The 1996 symposium (Candy and Edmonds, 1996) included artists who were users of new technology as well as those using more conventional methods. A residency was held which enabled established artists who had not previously used computers in their art, to work in multi-media laboratories. The processes that the artists went through, including the appropriateness of the technologies employed, were studied. The results indicated that no existing applications matched all the needs of the artists and the available technology needed to be modified using research tools. Nevertheless, both artists and technologists benefited as subsequent work has indicated. This later work has formed part of the study that is included in the report below. Using computers in the Arts is now well known (Moser and MacLeod, 1996; Schwartz, 1997) but the main aim of the research programme being undertaken is rather different, in that it is to identify certain future requirements of computer support for creative work by investigating the work of established artists and exploring the potential of new creative technology in this field. This single case provides initial results and an indication of the direction in which the work is likely to proceed.

The paper poses three questions and tries to find an answer to each by exploring the modeling of the results of the study in the context of what we know so far about computational approaches to understanding creativity.

2. Creative Interaction

2.1. Creative Scope

Creativity is often concerned with the emergence of new concepts as a result of interaction with existing ideas, models and people. What distinguishes this view from others in the exploration of the nature of human creativity is the recognition of the role of interaction with the world. This is, therefore, to be differentiated from focusing on 'creativity in the head' without reference to the impact of external factors. A clear and significant example of this is the externalisation process that is involved in emergence seen in design (Schön and Wiggins, 1992). For a discussion of the cognitive modeling of emergence see Soufi and Edmonds (1996).

The idea of *collective creativity* is worth exploring in this context. The word 'collective' on its own suggests that the creativity may be a combined effort between one or more party. If we take the view that the externalising of ideas is significant to creativity, then it can be argued that so is the manner of that externalisation and this brings us to the interaction process (Edmonds, 1993). It is suggested that computer devices and applications may have special qualities that distinguish them from other artifacts that humans interact with in creative work.

The potential for the creativity of every human being is shaped by factors that are both outside our control and within it. Factors such as genetic makeup, geographical location, climate, economic resources, health, education and formative and lifelong experiences contribute in different ways to the scope for creativity that the person enjoys. *Creative scope* can be summed up as: how we interact with what we have at our disposal within the context in which we live and work.

In most cases, research issues relating to creative scope are studied independent of one another. Some studies of creativity have investigated small-scale problem solving abilities and lateral thinking skills, and have attempted to extrapolate the results from those examples into real world situations or as general purpose models of creative thinking. Case studies of individuals of outstanding creative scope have shown, by contrast, that a combination of factors may contribute to the success or otherwise of the creative effort. Thus, Creative Scope is affected by multiple factors and, if we are to understand how it works, we need to take a wider view of how creativity takes place. In relation to the discussion therefore, contextual issues point to *interaction* with the world, and hence, are a collective contribution to creativity. We, therefore, need to consider both the actors and the artifacts that define the context within which creative thought occurs.

2.2. Actors and Artefacts

Actors represent the roles played by people and their different combinations that drive the activities. The set of actors includes: individual designers, the design team, and the organisation. If we take the artifact, as an example of a Contributor to the Interaction process and try to envisage how it contributes to concept formation in creative work, it becomes clear that the different roles of the human actor influence how it is used. For each artifact, there are different actor roles and, therefore, different kinds of interaction.

The kind of actor role may be different according to the nature of the artifact. The creativity of the user depends upon the kind of interaction that takes place and this in turn depends upon the aims of the actor. A designer may not be particularly creative in the outstanding sense but, in making modest changes to an existing design, will derive concepts that are new to him or her. The creative role may be integrated with the other roles of user and builder but this depends upon the kind of artifact and the level of complexity involved in designing and constructing it.

2.3. Interaction Processes for Creativity

If interaction of one kind or another is important in creative knowledge work, then it is worth looking more closely at the word itself and the different ways it can be defined. The word 'inter-act' refers to a reciprocal process, that is, something from one party that acts upon the other and vice versa. Thus, 'Interaction' is always two way. It may imply, too, a form of exchange which is not necessarily of the same quality or type in both directions. It implies that *transformations* of the exchanged information may occur.

We usually refer to the act of *using* tools or information or ideas, rather than interacting with them. And yet, it is true to say that we experience different kinds of interaction with artifacts that is characterised by the purpose to which we put them and the design of the artifact itself. The act of drawing combined with looking at the paper on which the drawing exists provides an important example of interaction, simple as it might appear to be (Schön, 1983). A traffic management system that guides us towards the best route involves interaction with the device. It also requires a level of skill that is thought to be achievable for most people and which requires an ability to handle a high degree of complexity. The point is that there are many computer systems embodied in the vehicle only some of which are apparent to the driver and, even fewer of which require interaction, as distinct from action or reaction. If there is no interaction, is there any potential for collective creativity? In this case, the answer is likely to be no.

The nature of interaction is often conceived in rather simplistic terms: but interaction with knowledge and artifacts that results in creative concept externalisation is more than simply putting in and taking out. We speak of human-to-human interaction but to capture the richness and variety of this phenomenon requires more precision. Terms may instead be selected according to the nature and circumstances of the exchange: e.g. communication, sharing discussion, argument, persuasion, exchange, etc. There are ways of characterising interaction that might usefully be considered in relation to the interactive process.

Creativity in the interaction with artifacts, such as computers or musical instruments, is strongly influenced by the actor roles. Composing music and performing it are very different processes. The concert pianist may be highly skilled and more so than the composer but the degree of creativity that he derives from the artifact is not the same. Does a composer interacting with a particular kind of musical instrument derive creative benefit? If he did not use an instrument, would he compose in his head as well or with the same kind of result? In what way is the interaction different whether a piano, computer music generator or pencil on a score sheet is used?

In looking at these issues in the specific context of VR and the support of human creativity, three key questions are posed:

1. Is VR able to provide support for creative interaction and if so, how?
2. What, in contrast with other tools, is special about the computer and VR in relation to creativity?
3. Which interaction processes, between humans and computers, most support creativity?

In the next section we will focus upon one instance that has been studied in some detail. This will help provide insight into the answers to these questions.

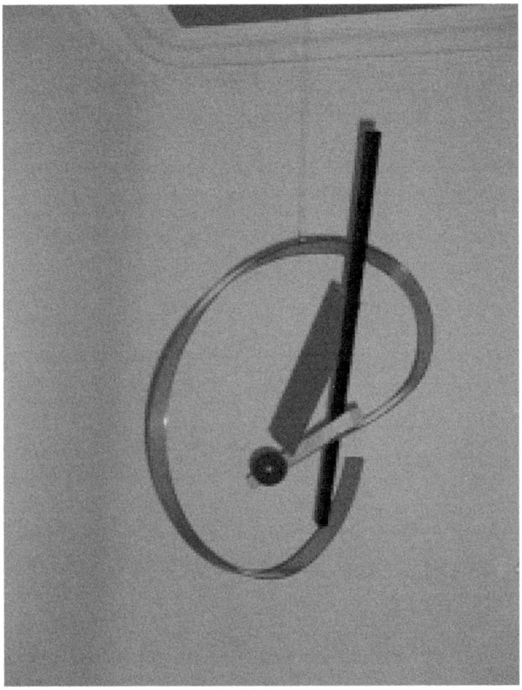

Figure 1. Mobile.

3. A Study of the Use of VR by a Sculptor

3.1. The Artist

Fré Ilgen is an artist who is exploring his perception and understanding of 'reality' in its various aspects (Ilgen, 1997; 2004). He studies the simulation of complex movements in three dimensional objects to which he applies a complex combination of forms and colors. Most of his work is in sculpture, much of it in suspended forms (see Fig. 1). He used his experiences with these dynamic objects for exploring the potential of Virtual Reality during Creativity and Cognition 1996. His first request was that the VR system should not impose gravity and that the representations of physical space should be removed. He wanted a black space without the constraints of gravity in which to create sculptural objects, move them about in relation to one another and determine combinations of outcomes.

The following quotations by him are illustrative of the issues explored during the interviews.

- *Structure and Order*
  "I am looking for the structure at a deeper level of nature, if you like."
  "Our search for understanding wholeness can be translated as a search for structure on a deeper level – although it is hard to speak of *the* structure. A structure which makes it apprehensible how everything and ourselves are interrelated in the whole."

- *Process and Product*
  "... you are known as an artist for your next piece, you have an urge to create another one, which doesn't make the former piece unimportant but it explains that your desire is not so fulfilled that you never want to make anything new."
- *Materials and Tools*
  "material is not that important in my work"
- *On the Use of Virtual Reality*
  "In my work I have to emulate the struggle with gravity ... I never will be able to create real motion which I simulate in my normal art work which I can create and explore in VR.
  "'By hand' I defined a relative complex rotation-movement of every shape around the sphere. This sphere functions quite well as fixed point of reference in the described infinite black space. ...The movement of these few forms make an extremely strong impression of depth and enough sense of orientation. The result was intoxicating. I finally could see the movement I imagined for years!"

3.2. Outcomes

The outcomes from the artists in residence were different in each case. However, one factor in common was that none of the artists felt able to use a computer system exactly as it was offered to them. In each case, they had needs which could not be dealt with by a ready-made solution. Nevertheless, artwork was conceived and carried through to completion albeit with considerable support from other people. Ilgen had created a Virtual Reality sculpture system. Most significant in his work were the facts that he removed gravity and had his piece float in a void. His virtual reality was not reality as we know it.

3.3. Subsequent Developments

In Ilgen's case, the role of VR technology as a stimulus to the thinking and practices of this artist was clearly apparent. He was convinced that the VR enabled him to escape from the constraints of physical objects and freed him to consider structures but that was to change later. During the following year he underwent a change of direction from creating mobile structures made of wood and metal to painting on large canvasses using conventional methods. He has sought out special pigments and become deeply involved in the realization of 'true' color in his works. The experience with VR inspired him to develop a kind of painting that visualizes the simulation of the color space: he calls these 'Virtual Paintings', see Fig. 2.

Thus we see that, whilst the VR experience was both a promising line of development for Ilgen and a very rich experience in itself, a major outcome occurred in his practice. In his view, this could not have occurred without the VR stimulus.

Figure 2. Virtual Painting, Lazy.

4. Towards a Computational Model of Creative Interaction

4.1. Reality, Computed Reality and Imagined Reality

The work of Ilgen discussed above illustrates the three interacting realities at play. One could outline his process in terms of *reality*, the physical world, *imagined reality*, the model of the world that he holds and manipulates in his head, and *virtual reality*, the model of the world held in the computer system and experienced by Ilgen. A simplified description of the process that he went through can be given as follows.

He considered and manipulated the *reality* of his sculptures in his studio. Knowing of his opportunity at Loughborough, he created a new *imagined reality*, which was the basis of his first steps into *virtual reality*. There followed considerable moves between the *imagined and virtual realities* until he created his new piece in the VR system. Later, whilst thinking over his experience and reflecting upon its implications he manipulated his new *imagined reality* until he found a way of creating a version or view of it in *reality*, but without the computer VR system. Figure 3 illustrates the exchanges between the three realities.

An important question that arises is that of what kind of transformations were at play and how were they performed? In order to do this, let us consider the model of each reality and consider just one aspect of the models that Ilgen transformed.

We can consider the initial model of *reality* to be **M1** and note that this includes laws of physics as well as the particular design constructs, such as cuboids, that were used in the existing sculptures. For the sake of simplicity, let us assume that the first VR system constructed was, as far as practical, a copy of the sculptures, which we can represent as **V(M1)**. Thus, for the most part, **V(M1)** contains a subset of the properties of **M1**. For example, the former does not model tactile experience. The exceptions are where the scientist had to make changes in the interests of implementation, such as using 2.5D or making a gently curved surface flat.

Now, in working with **V(M1)**, we know that Ilgen made several radical changes. For example, he turned gravity off. Hence he created, let us say, **VM2** which now bore little resemblance to earth bound physics in an important respect. Let us call his model in *imagined reality* of **VM2**, **I(VM2)**. Now, he carried **I(VM2)** away with him from the Loughborough experience.

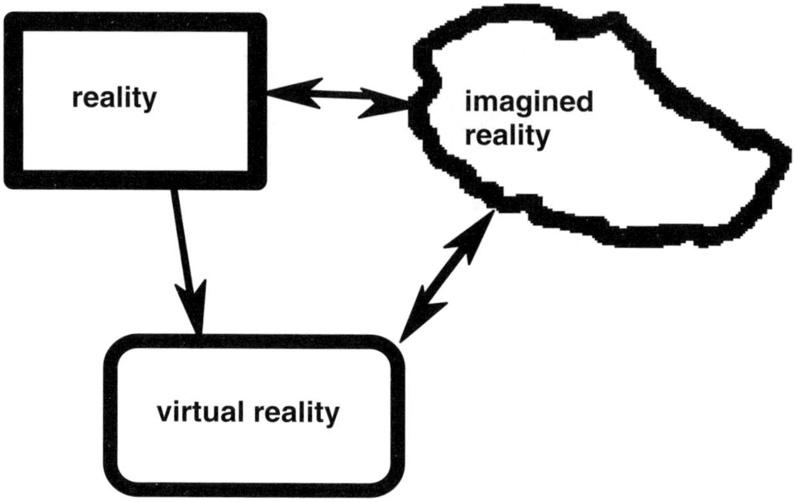

Figure 3. The Three Realities.

Back in his studio, he was able to work with **M1** but, at the same time, think about **I(VM2)**. What followed was a transformation of **I(VM2)** into something in his imagined reality, say **IM3**, that he could construct in reality without the VR computer system. In fact, as we noted above, he made paintings. Thus he moved back to a new *reality* in his studio, which we can call **M3**. It is worth noting again that he claims that he would never have made these paintings if it had not been for the VR experience. Hence the transformations that we are considering must be seen to be important steps in the creative process observed.

So what were the key steps in this creative process? They are of a number of types but the ones that seem to have been most significant are those that moved the models between the different realities and imagination itself: the transformations within *imagined reality*.

4.2. Creative Transformations

As the main subject of the paper is creativity, it is appropriate to consider imagination itself first. It is beyond our scope to try to describe the imagination process directly. Instead we will try to illuminate it by discussing the influences upon it in the case in hand. Thus, the question is, what stimulated Ilgen's imagination to operate as it did? Two particular steps can be observed.

Firstly, moving from his observation of **M1** to **V(M1)**, he did not only see the common, or similar elements. Indeed, the interest was in considering the differences. Whilst the explicit nature of **(M1-V(M1))**, was not uninteresting, the most important trigger to imagination was the realisation that certain invariables in **M1** had become variable in **V(M1)**. In particular, whilst both included the constraints of gravity, **V(M1)** need not have.

One mechanism for the generation of creative designs is the introduction of new variables, or the making of a constant a variable (Gero and Maher, 1993). In the application of such mechanisms we always have the problem of the selection of the element to act on; which constant to make variable. In the related case in point we can see at least part of an answer.

The knowledge and observation of the two versions of reality, **M1** and **V(M1)**, focused Ilgen's attention upon a small number of elements that could be changed. The selection process of what to change was bounded in a way that imagination could cope with. Thus, with the sculptor's experience and motivation for exercising his imagination, we can see that it was not so surprising that, in the context of the interactions at play, he imagined **VM2**. The interactions between the models created the scoping context that made the application of his imagination both possible and fruitful.

The next creative action took his imagined picture of **VM2**, **I(VM2)**, and led to the creation of **IM3**. This is more difficult to explain but it is clear again that it was not a matter of the imagination allowed to run free unencumbered. **I(VM2)** was only realisable within the VR system but Ilgen wanted to continue with his successful artistic development *without* the VR. What followed was an interaction process between *imagined reality* and *reality* in which **I(VM2)** had transformations applied to it that moved it into line with physics. As is so often the case, the solution of **IM3**, a work conceived as painted on a canvas, looks obvious in retrospect. The fact is, however, that the constraints placed upon imagination by the specifics of the problem were what made this, rather than some other random and less satisfying solution tractable. As Ilgen asserts, the **M3** paintings would never have been made had it not been for the creative transformations that we observed.

As well as imagination itself, transformations within *imagined reality*, we mentioned above the significance of transformations that moved models between the different realities. The point here is that the sculptor's decision to make such a move, e.g. from **M1** to **V(M1)**, is a deliberate act. It was not a random event, nor was it made in an attempt to simply re-create **M1**. Making this transformation was specifically intended to trigger the imagination. It was an application of a specific creative design *strategy*. Thus, although Ilgen had no idea of the outcome, he knew exactly what he was doing.

Creative transformations are scoped and constrained acts taken in order to stimulate creativity. That stimulation, however, is directed in a way that limits possibilities in order to provide tractable scenarios. Thus, we see, in creative transformations, an example of strategic design knowledge applied to assist in concept formation (Candy and Hori, 1997), i.e. in creative design.

5. Implications and Conclusions

Earlier in the paper, three questions were posed:

1. Is VR able to provide support for creative interaction and if so, how?
2. What, in contrast with other tools, is special about the computer and VR in relation to creativity?
3. Which interaction processes, between humans and computers, most support creativity?

We considered the case of a specific artist's work. This artist did not wish to use VR to simulate "real" reality. Rather, he used it to create movement in a void without gravity. This example points to the main issue that is at the heart of the concern of this paper.

Computers can be very helpful to us by performing tasks on our behalf. For example, they are very good at performing calculations, storing information and producing visualizations of "real" objects that do not yet exist as a made artifact. Increasingly, however, a different role is being found for the computer. This role is that of a catalyst, or a stimulant, to our own creative thinking. In such cases the computer is not primarily performing a task for us and generating an answer within itself, rather it is helping us to generate answers within ourselves. The computer helps us think. Ilgen's experience is an example of how using new technologies does not necessarily lead to a dependence or focus upon the technology but rather to a change in understanding.

We have also shown how we can understand the use of VR by the artist in terms of creative transformations. This has demonstrated how strategically selected actions can drive or enable creative thought in ways that may be computationally tractable. The interactions seem to be a significant part in the computation of creative results. It was also noted that we may see VR in the context of emergence. The artists or designer may build virtual models in the same way that they draw as part of the creative process.

So, the answers to our questions might be:

1. Yes, VR is able to provide support for creative interaction, as a reality into which and within which creative transformations may be made.
2. What is special about VR is its ability to flexibly represent models, including models closely relating to what Ilgen terms "real" reality.
3. Transformations and the manipulation in and changes to models of the world are the interactions with VR that most support creativity.

The implications for the design of VR end user programming environments that support creativity are implicit most strongly in the third answer. Creative transformations may be key in creative practice. We hypothesise that this result is of general applicability well beyond the domain of VR and well beyond the set of users represented by artists.

Acknowledgments

Thanks are due to Fré Ilgen for working with us in this research. Loughborough University and Loughborough College of Art and design made significant contributions towards the Artists-in Residence event. Roy Kalawsky made the work with virtual reality possible.

References

Candy, L. *Proceedings, Creativity and Cognition 2005*. ACM Press, NY. 2005.

Candy, L. and Edmonds, E.A. (eds.). *Proceedings, Creativity and Cognition 1993*. LUTCHI Research Center, Loughborough University, UK. 1993.

Candy, L. and Edmonds, E.A. (eds.). *Proceedings, Creativity and Cognition 1996*. LUTCHI Research Center, Loughborough University, UK. 1996.

Cicognani, A. On the Linguistic Nature of Cyberspace and Virtual Communities. *Virtual Reality*. 3 (1) pp. 16–24. 1998.

Edmonds, E.A. and Moran, T. Interactive Systems for Supporting the Emergence of Concepts and Ideas. Proc CHI'97 ACM Press. NY. p. 233. 1997.

Edmonds, E.A. Knowledge-Based Systems for Creativity. Gero and Maher (eds.). *Modelling Creativity and Knowledge-Based Creative Design*. Lawrence Erlbaum. NJ. Pp. 259–271. 1993.

Gero, J.S. and Maher, M.L. Introduction. Gero and Maher (eds.). *Modelling Creativity and Knowledge-Based Creative Design*. Lawrence Erlbaum. NJ. pp. 1–6. 1993.

Ilgen, F. *Oscillations of Color and Change*. Foundation for the New Arts, NL. 1997.

Ilgen, F. *Art? No Thing! Analogies between art, science and philosophy.*. PRO Foundation, NL. 2004.

Moser, M.A. and MacLeod, D. (eds.). *Immersed in Technology*. MIT Press. Cambridge, MA. 1996.
Mowshowitz, A. Virtual Feudism. Denning and Metcalfe (eds) *Beyond Calculation*. Copurnicus, Springer Verlag. NY. pp. 213–232. 1997.
Schön, D.A. *The Reflective Practitioner: How Professionalls Think in Action*. Basic Book. NY. 1983.
Schön, D.A. and Wiggins, G. Kinds of Seeing and Their Functions in Designing. *Design Studies*. 13 (2). pp. 135–156. 1992.
Schwarz, H.-P. (ed.). *Media-Art-History*. Prestel, Munich. 1997.
Soufi, B. and Edmonds, E.A. The Cognitive Basis of Emergence: Implications for Design Support. *Design Studies* 17 (4) pp. 451–464. 1996.
Turkle, S. Constructions and Reconstructions of the Self in Virtual Reality. Druckerey (ed.) *Electronic Culture*. Apature, NJ. pp. 354–365. 1996.

New Trends in Software Methodologies, Tools and Techniques
H. Fujita and M. Mejri (Eds.)
IOS Press, 2005

GUIDE: Games with UML for Interactive Design Exploration

Jennifer TENZER [1]
Laboratory for Foundations of Computer Science, School of Informatics
University of Edinburgh

Abstract. In this paper we present our design tool GUIDE, which allows the user to explore a design in UML interactively by playing a game. The game incorporates both the design model and a specification of what it means for the design to be correct. The central idea of this approach is that the designer can increment the game during a play and gradually add more detail to it. Specification and design are refined by repeated plays of the game. The designer stops playing when design and specification are detailed enough for his purpose and fit to each other. The interactive game approach helps to cope with incompleteness and informal definition of UML models, which make strictly formal verification techniques difficult. The designer may resolve these problems when they arise during a play or let the GUIDE tool determine how the play should proceed.

Keywords. Interactive software design, UML, Formal games

1. Introduction

The Unified Modeling Language (UML) [21] is a standard language for modelling the design of object oriented software systems. There exists a variety of UML tools, most of which focus on support for drawing UML diagrams and generating code from them. None of the currently existing UML tools provides much support for experimentation and evaluation of different design options. The hard tasks of deciding whether a design fits to the specification, improving it and comparing it to other solutions still has to be accomplished by the human modeller without much guidance from a tool.

Our design tool GUIDE (**G**ames with **U**ML for **I**nteractive **D**esign **E**xploration) [5] aims at filling this gap. The foundation for this tool are *exploration games* which are an extension of two-player games as used in formal verification. The GUIDE tool supports the user in defining an exploration game, playing it in different roles, and incrementing the game definition.

An exploration game involves four different participants: two players called Verifier and Refuter who compete with each other, a Referee, and an Explorer. The game contains the design model of the system under consideration and a specification of what it means

[1] Correspondence to: Jennifer Tenzer; Tel.: +44 131 650 5146; Fax: +44 (0) 131 667 7209; E-mail: J.N.Tenzer@sms.ed.ac.uk.

for the design to be correct. The objective of Verifier is to show that the design fits to the specification, while Refuter tries to find a flaw in the design. All moves are performed in several stages. The responsibility for each stage can be assigned to one of the players or the Referee. The responsibility assignments allow the game participants to resolve non-determinacy during a play when they are faced with incompleteness or informality of the UML model. The Explorer has the power increment the game definition at any point during a play. The incrementations can affect both the design and the specification of the system and may improve the chances of winning for one of the players.

The exploration game framework can be applied to UML in many different variants. A game variant has to specify how exactly the exploration game is defined, i.e. what its positions, moves, and winning conditions look like, which parts of the UML model are used for the definition, how the responsibilities for the players are assigned and how the Explorer may increment the game. Game variants can either be used to check one design solution with respect to desired or undesired properties, or to compare two different designs.

The GUIDE tool does not expect the user to have any knowledge of formal games or verification and helps him to set up a game on the basis of a UML design model. Once the game is defined the modeller can start a play. The part of the Explorer always has to be played by the human designer, who may play any number of the other game participants in addition. Taking on the role of Verifier or Refuter provides the modeller with a specific perspective and goal for the design exploration. As Refuter he will concentrate on detecting flaws in the design, as Verifier he will attempt to demonstrate that the design is correct. GUIDE makes the moves for all game participants that are not played by the user, evaluates the winning conditions and guides the user through a play.

GUIDE is itself a framework which can be extended in various ways. Additional game variants can be implemented, new kinds of expressions for winning conditions and responsibilities may be defined, and alternative algorithms for computing the moves that are made by the GUIDE tool can be integrated.

The remainder of this paper is organised as follows. Section 2 gives an overview on related work. In Section 3 we argue that games are a suitable foundation for an interactive UML design tool like GUIDE which supports design exploration. Section 4 contains an informal summary of the exploration game framework and a description of an example game variant. The core functionality of the GUIDE tool is presented in Section 5. In Section 6 we explain the architecture of GUIDE and some of the technical solutions that have been chosen. Section 7 provides a brief insight into how the GUIDE tool can be extended and customised. In Section 8 we conclude and discuss possibilities for future work.

2. Related Work

The idea of using games as basis for a tool that allows design exploration has first been introduced in [16] on a general level. Exploration games are extensions of two-player verification games as introduced in [4] and [19]. A precise definition of the formal exploration game framework will soon appear in [18]. An application of exploration games to UML activity diagrams has been presented in [17].

On a very abstract level the whole software development process can be regarded as an interactive game. In [1] agile software development is considered as a "cooperative game of invention and communication". The software developers play the game with two goals in mind. The primary goal is the delivery of a working software product, and the secondary goal is to prepare the next game. Non-cooperative games can be used as metaphor for design reviews [8] or inspections [3], where one player defends the design, and the other players try to find a flaw in it. An adversarial attitude has also been successfully adopted by the Black Team [2] for testing software systems. As far as we know games have not yet been applied in a more formal way to the software design process or used as foundation for tools. In particular there exist no approaches where games are used to explore a UML model as introduced in this paper.

The work of Harel et. al. on "play-in play-out scenarios" [6,7] has a similar flavour to our work, and is motivated by similar concerns about the interactivity of tools to support design. Play-in scenarios allow the capture of requirements in a user-friendly way. The user specifies what behaviour he expects of a system by operating the system's GUI – or an abstract version thereof – which does not have any behaviour or implementation assigned to it yet. A tool which is called the play-engine transforms the play-in of the user into live sequence charts (LSCs), which are used as formal requirements language. The user does not have to prepare or modify the LSCs directly but only interacts with the GUI. This approach differs form ours in that its focus is on capturing and testing the requirements while we are mainly interested in helping the user to design a system which fulfils the requirements. Thus play-in play-out scenarios do not aim to help in defining intra-object behaviour, as our exploration games do, but remain on the higher level of interaction between objects and user.

When UML tools are considered, the commercial tools Rhapsody [15] and Real Time Studio [14] are most related to our work, because they allow the designer to "play through" and examine state machines by animation. However, these tools require very precise design models. They do not permit informally specified constraints or interruptions of the animation process in order to add more information or change the design. There is also no notion of a system specification in these tools against which the design is checked. The user merely observes the animation and decides on his own whether the system behaves as he expected.

The tools HUGO [9] and vUML [10] allow the designer to check general properties of UML state machines, such as the possibility for deadlocks. HUGO additionally verifies whether desired (or undesired) behaviour specified by UML interaction diagrams can be realised by state machines. Both tools translate a UML model which has been created by an external tool into a formal model which is then used as input for the model checking tool SPIN. They differ from our GUIDE tool in two respects. First, they require a UML model as input which is precisely defined. Informal guard conditions, undefined object attributes and non-deterministic state machines are not permitted. Second, they concentrate on the evaluation of a UML model, while our exploration games are focused on interactive modification of the design.

3. Motivation

Games have been chosen as foundation for GUIDE because they offer several advantages. First, playing a game does not require background knowledge in formal methods and is fairly intuitive. The basic idea of two players Verifier and Refuter who compete against each other to prove the correctness of the design or detect a flaw in it is easy to grasp. Since the GUIDE tool is targeted at mainstream software designers, this has been an important factor for choosing the tool foundation.

Another advantage of games with respect to tool support is that they are an *interactive* technique, which allows the modeller to influence a play. The progress of a play is determined by the decisions of the players who react to each other's moves, and by the Referee. These roles can be played by the designer, who may also increment the game definition as Explorer during a play.

Such an incremental development of a game is the central idea of this work. Since the design and the specification of the system are both incorporated in the game, the designer can increment each of those parts. For example, suppose that the design model is complete, but that there is only limited understanding of what it means for the design to be correct. Perhaps it has not yet been understood how the informal specification of overall system requirements should be translated down into precise requirements; or perhaps the informal specification is itself incomplete or incorrect. In mainstream business software development, which is our main focus of concern, both are likely to be the case. The game as initially defined by the modeller may incorporate only a small amount of information about what it means for the design to be correct: it may be "too easy" for Verifier to win the game. The modeller should be able to improve the game to make it a better reflection of the correctness of the design. This might include, for example, changing the winning conditions so that plays which would have been won by Verifier are won by Refuter in the new game. At the same time, it is likely that the design itself is too incomplete to permit full verification. The modeller should also be able to change the game by adding more information about the design.

This idea fits very well to iterative and incremental software development processes where the specification is updated along with the artifacts describing the system design. Thus games are a very natural choice with respect to how software is usually developed. The designer increments the game while it is being played and has to ensure that the game is challenging for the two players. A sequence of such incrementations, which may be part of different plays, is an exploration of the design and its specification. Even though the incrementations of the game may be beneficial for one player, the modeller is not necessarily biased. For example, during one play the designer may first increment the game such that it becomes easier for Refuter, and later explore a different part of the game which increases Verifier's chances of winning.

The advantage of permitting game incrementation during a play is that the designer does not have to start a new play from the beginning but can continue the improved game from the current position. However, the disadvantage is that an incrementation may invalidate the play. For example, moves of the old game may not be part of the incremented version anymore. Even if all moves of the play still exist after the exploration, there is no guarantee that the players will select the same moves as before when the play is repeated from the beginning. Thus a winning strategy for the old game does not necessarily work in the incremented game and may have to be adapted.

Figure 1 illustrates how different plays of game *G0* initiate different explorations. The new versions of the game are further improved which leads to new variations and combinations of design and specification. Incrementing the game will in most cases correspond to adding more detail to its parts. That means both specification and design become gradually more precise. Hence this approach provides a smooth progression from

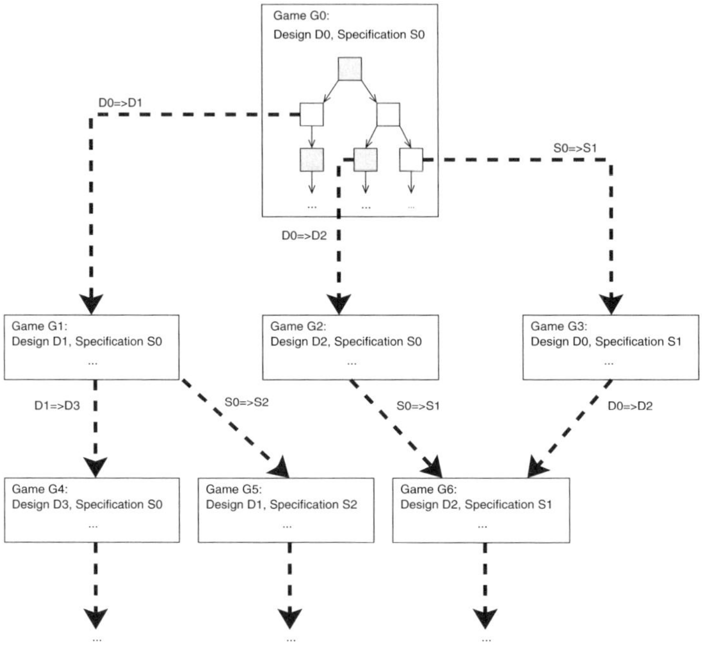

Figure 1. Repeated game incrementation.

informal exploration of decisions to full verification. This has the potential to lower the commitment cost of using formal verification. The designer can stop exploring if he believes that design and specification are precise enough for his purpose. Playing the game again from the beginning without further incrementations verifies the current design against the current specification. The designer may still have to provide information during the verification process if the game is too incomplete at some points, which is very likely with UML design models as basis. However, it is not necessary to improve the game so far that the complete system can be verified formally without the help of the designer.

Finally, games may have another advantage: games which people play in their free-time are played for fun. The question is whether games that are played with the purpose of exploring design decisions are also to some extent entertaining. If so, a game-based design tool like GUIDE may actually make the work of software designers more enjoyable.

4. Exploration Games

In this section we describe exploration games informally and introduce an example variant which is based on UML state machines. However, the concepts of exploration games are very general and can easily be applied to other UML diagram types or combinations thereof. A full formal definition of the exploration game framework and several applications to UML is to appear in [18].

An exploration game is defined by a game arena, an initial position, responsibility assignments for the different stages of each move, game settings, winning conditions for the players, and possible incrementations by the Explorer. The game arena consists of positions and moves. It draws information from particular parts of a UML design model – in our example from UML state machines and class diagrams. A move may have a precondition and parameters. The preconditions of the move do not have to be specified formally. If they are based on constraints in the UML model they are very likely to be formulated in natural language. The participants in an exploration game are the two players Verifier and Refuter, the Referee and the Explorer. A move is selected in the following steps:

1. Precondition evaluation. The set of legal moves from the current position is determined by declaring which informally specified preconditions are assumed to be true.
2. Choice of move shape. A move shape is a set of moves which have the same source position, name, precondition and parameter signature. The moves belonging to a move shape only differ in their parameter values and target positions. Only legal move shapes may be selected in this move step.
3. Parameter provision. The move shape is reduced by fixing the parameter values for the move. If only one single move is left, the next move has been selected and the last step is obsolete.
4. Resolution of non-determinism. There may be more than one move which belongs to the selected move shape and has the chosen parameter values. These moves only differ in their target positions and one of them has to be picked as next move.

In contrast to formal models that are normally used as basis for verification games, the UML model is most unlikely to define a unique system, complete in all detail. In the exploration game framework the game participants resolve any kind of non-determinacy during a play. The responsibility for performing the four different move steps are assigned to Refuter, Verifier or the Referee. In contrast to the players the Referee does not benefit from decisions about the progress of the play.

The game settings can be general or specific for one variant. They are used for two purposes. First, they fix an interpretation of the UML semantics where necessary. UML contains "semantic variation points" for some of its features which provide a degree of freedom in its interpretation. Since the possible moves in a game depend to a great extent on the UML semantics, the designer has to decide how such semantic variation points should be treated. Second, the game settings may impose restrictions on how the game is played and incremented. For example, the game settings can specify a move limit and thus determine the maximum length of a play. Furthermore the game settings define whether the Explorer may increment the game in a way that violates the play history.

The Explorer's goal is to make the game more precise and keep the balance between Refuter and Verifier. He is allowed to adjust the difficulty of the game for the players by incrementing the game definition during a play. Apart from incrementing the game the Explorer may also backtrack in the play history or change the current position. The role of the Explorer is always played by the human designer who has enough knowledge about the system to choose sensible incrementations and make the model more precise. Additionally the modeller may take on other parts in the game, such as, for example, the role of one of the players to examine the design from a particular perspective.

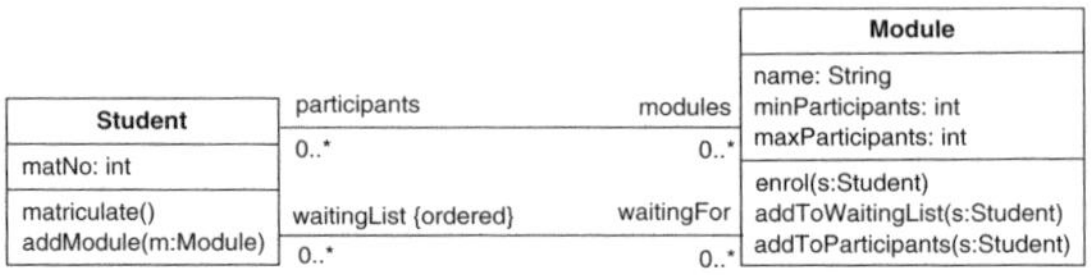

Figure 2. Example class diagram.

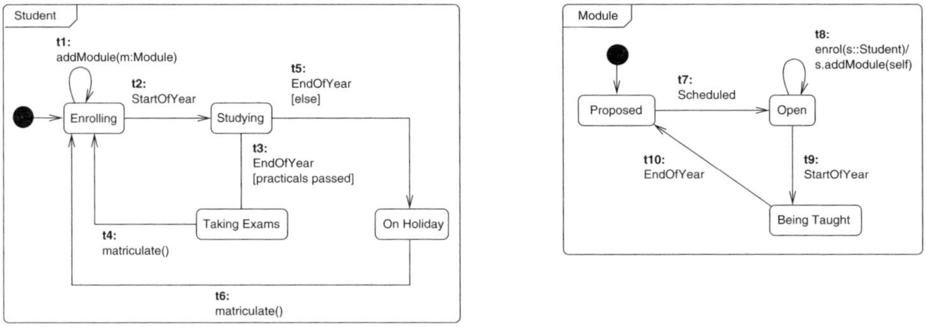

Figure 3. State machines for *Module* and *Student*.

Incrementations are defined with respect to the UML model for all parts of the game where this is possible. Thus the designer does not work with the game definition, but increments the game indirectly via changes in the UML model. After he has performed such an incrementation as Explorer, the play is continued according to the new game definition.

4.1. Example of an Exploration Game

For our example game variant we assume that a UML model for a university course registration system consisting of the class diagram in Fig. 2 and the two state machines shown in Fig. 3 is given. Notice that the guard conditions in the state machines are informally specified. Whenever we refer to one of the players we use the female form for Verifier and the male form for Refuter.

During a play of this game a collection of objects is observed with respect to state changes. The objects constitute the system which is verified. Here we consider a student *Joe* and a module *CS1*.

Positions: A position represents a snapshot of the system and consists of the following parts:

- For each object
  - $*$ a state configuration,
  - $*$ and an event pool.
- A set of parameters which are in scope at the position.

The positions where all event pools are empty belong to Refuter, all others to Verifier. At the initial position all objects are in their default states and the event pools are empty.

Moves: In this example the moves from Refuter's positions correspond to generating events. All events which refer to an operation in the class diagram are regarded as call events and are targeted at a specific object. When a call event is generated a target object has to be specified and the event is put into its event pool. The call events in our example are *matriculate*, *addModule*, *enrol*, *addToWaitingList* and *addToParticipants*. All other events that occur in the state machines are considered as signal events. They are broadcast to all objects and put into their event pools when generated. If an event is parameterised, suitable parameter values have to be provided for it.

A move from one of Verifier's positions corresponds to firing a set of state machine transitions according to the UML semantics. For each object the first event in its pool is dispatched and an enabled state machine transition is fired, if there is any. An event which does not trigger any transitions is discarded as specified in the UML standard [21, p. 492]. Whether a transition is enabled or not depends on the evaluation of the guard condition at the time when the event occurs. Thus the legality of a move is determined by the evaluation of the guards, which are considered as preconditions of the move.

If a transition is fired and an effect is attached to it, another event is generated. The new event is put into the appropriate event pool and the object completes its transition. This corresponds to the idea of *asynchronous* actions in UML, where the object does not have to wait until the new event has been processed before it reaches the next stable state.

Figure 4 shows some of the positions and moves of our example game. Refuter's positions are shown in grey-shaded rectangles and are labelled by "R", Verifier's are labelled by "V". The position shown as *p0* is the initial position.

Winning conditions: Refuter wins a play if a position is reached where *CS1* is in state *Open* and *Joe* is in state *Taking Exams*. He also wins all plays which end at a position belonging to Verifier because no further moves are possible. Verifier wins all other plays.

Because of the informally defined guard conditions at the transitions it is unclear for some of the moves whether they should be regarded as legal or not. For this example we assign the responsibility for deciding about the legality of moves to Verifier. Furthermore we assume that the players select move shapes at their own positions. They also provide parameters and resolve non-determinism for all moves emerging from the positions belonging to them.

Responsibilities:

- Verifier decides whether an informal precondition of a move is assumed to be true.
- Verifier and Refuter fulfil all other tasks at their own positions and for the moves emerging from these positions.

Game settings: According to the UML semantics an event is always discarded if it does not trigger a transition. Here we introduce a setting which specifies whether this solution should be applied to call events. For this example game we assume that discarding call events is forbidden.

Incrementations:

- Add or delete a state transition.
- Add or delete a state. If a state is deleted, all transitions which emerge from or lead to it are also deleted.
- Add or delete an event or operation.

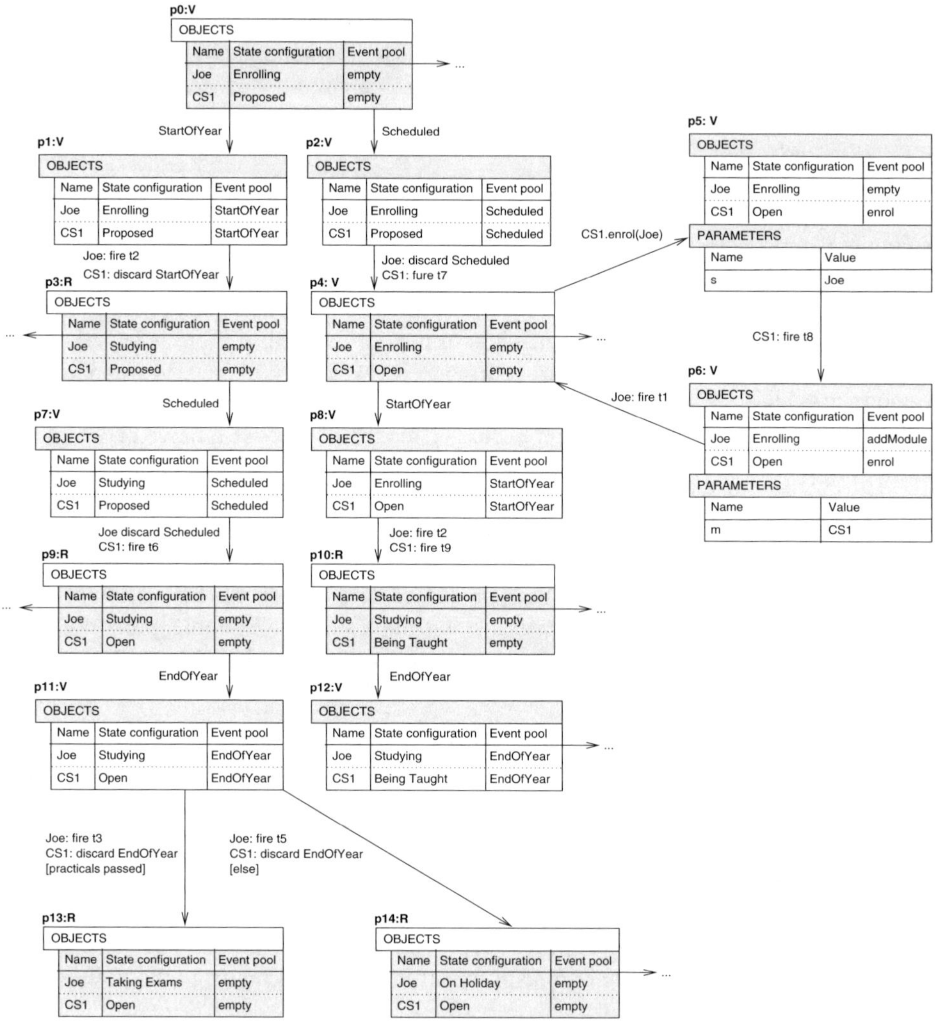

Figure 4. Positions and moves in the example game.

- Change the guard condition at a transition.
- Change the winning conditions.
- Change the responsibility assignments.
- Change the game settings.

Notice that the first four incrementations all operate directly on the parts of the UML model which have been used as basis of the game definition for our game variant. The last three incrementations are more general and transferable to other game variants which do not use UML state machines and class diagrams as foundation.

The game variant which has been introduced here is a simple example of an application of exploration games to UML in order to illustrate the approach. We have abstracted from details, such as, for instance, how exactly the winning conditions and responsibilities are defined. Since the positions of the game only record the abstract states of the objects, it is difficult to evaluate sophisticated guard conditions. For example, it is not possible to decide whether the number of students who are enrolled in a module exceeds the maximum number of participants. In order to evaluate a precondition like this we would have to define a more complex game variant whose positions contain the objects' attribute values and links. For our example game preconditions whose evaluation is undefined because the positions do not contain enough information are treated as if they were informally defined. The game participants have to decide whether their evaluation is assumed to be true or false.

4.2. Example Plays without Exploration

We examine some example plays of our game, consisting of the positions shown in Fig. 4. Here we only consider plays which do not involve incrementations by the Explorer. Assume that Refuter challenges by *StartOfYear* at position *p0*. Verifier has only one choice to respond to this challenge and moves to *p3*. From there Refuter's next moves are *Scheduled* and *EndOfYear*. Again Verifier has only one possibility to react to these events and the play continues from *p3* via *p7* and *p9* to *p11*. Here Verifier has for the first time the chance to actually select a move. Before she can do this she has to decide which of the moves are legal. The guard condition *else* at transition *t5* indicates that exactly one of the transitions triggered by *EndOfYear* must be enabled, i.e. the guard conditions are mutually exclusive. That means only one move emerging from *p11* can be declared as legal. Verifier realises that she will lose the play if she moves to *p13*, because this position fulfils the winning condition for Refuter. Hence a rational choice for Verifier is to declare that the move to *p14* is legal. If she selects this move, she can avoid losing the play. In fact, if Verifier applies this strategy every time position *p11* is visited, she can win all plays. That means Verifier has a winning strategy and the design is is considered to be correct with respect to the specification under the current game definition.

Verifier wins this variant of the game so easily because she can always avoid firing transition *t3*. At an early stage of the design phase, it may be useful to give Verifier so much power. This game variant is suitable for playing through the desired scenarios of the system without being forced to consider preliminary parts of the design or special cases. A variant of the game which is maximised for detecting flaws is to allow Refuter to decide about the validity of informal preconditions. In the example play described above Refuter will then declare that the move to *p14* is illegal. Thus Verifier is forced to move to position *p13* where Refuter wins the game. If the Referee is responsible for evaluating informally defined preconditions, the outcome of each play is uncertain. None of the players has a safe winning strategy because the decision of the Referee at *p11* determines who wins the play.

4.3. Example Plays with Exploration

In this section we use the example game from Section 4.1 to show how a game is repeatedly changed by incrementations. During the explorations the state machine for *Module* will be altered. The resulting state machine after all explorations considered here is shown in Fig. 5. In the descriptions of the example plays we will again refer to positions which are part of the arena excerpt shown in Fig. 4.

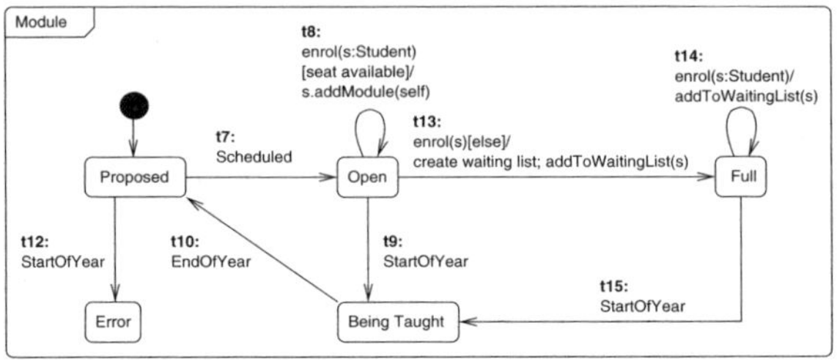

Figure 5. State machine for *Module* after exploration.

Assume that Refuter challenges by *StartOfYear*, *Scheduled* and *EndOfYear* from the initial position. Verifier applies her winning strategy and moves to *p14*. At this point the designer realises that the game is too easy for Verifier. This discovery urges him to increment the game as Explorer such that the disadvantaged player has a better chance of winning. The Explorer backtracks to position *p11* and changes the responsibility assignments such that Refuter is responsible for the evaluation of all informal preconditions. The play is continued with these modifications and Refuter declares that the critical move to *p14* by which Verifier can avoid losing the game is illegal. Now Verifier has no other choice except to move to *p13*, where Refuter wins the game.

The designer decides to play the incremented game again from the beginning to see how the players move under the changed circumstances. It becomes obvious that it is now Refuter who can always win the game easily by declaring that the move to *p14* is illegal. The modeller realises that Verifier loses because she cannot respond adequately when Refuter raises *StartOfYear* before *Scheduled*. There are several alternatives of how he can improve the game as Explorer such that Verifier has better chances of winning. Here we consider the following three possibilities:

1. Backtrack to *p1*, add a new state to the state machine for *Module* and add a transition *t11* from *Proposed* to the new state which is triggered by *StartOfYear*. With these changes Verifier must fire *t11* for *CS1* in response to *StartOfYear*. The state of object *CS1* changes to the new state and the critical state combination is avoided as the play continues.
2. Backtrack to *p1*, add a new state *Error* and add a new transition *t12* from *Proposed* to *Error* with trigger *StartOfYear*. Then change the winning conditions such that Verifier wins the game if state *Error* is reached. Verifier must fire *t12* for *CS1* in response to *StartOfYear*. After that move the winning condition holds and Verifier wins the play.
3. Backtrack to *p7* and change the winning conditions such that Verifier wins if Refuter challenges with *Scheduled* immediately after *StartOfYear*. With these changes position *p7* becomes a winning position for Verifier, because the two events have been generated in the forbidden order.

The first two options indirectly extend the set of moves for Verifier in the arena of the game. If the first solution is chosen, Verifier has the chance to circumvent a position which leads to a win for Refuter in the old game by using one of the new moves. The last two possibilities involve changes of the winning conditions such that Refuter is discouraged to make the critical sequence of moves which causes problems for Verifier. Here we assume that the Explorer chooses the second alternative. If played without exploration, the improved game is always won by Verifier.

We can continue in various ways, with the designer gradually improving both the system design and its specification. A way of incrementing the game which has not been considered yet is to alter the guard conditions at transitions. For example, the designer can refine the conditions under which *t8* may be fired by adding a guard condition *seat available*. When Refuter challenges by *Scheduled* and *m.enrol* from the initial position, Verifier now loses the play if Refuter declares that *seat available* does not hold. Verifier cannot find a transition which is triggered by *m.enrol* and the game settings forbid her to discard call events. That means there are no moves possible from the current position which belongs to Verifier, and Refuter wins the play.

A simple way to improve Verifier's chances of winning the game is to change the game settings such that call events may be discarded. Another approach which preserves the strictness of the game settings is to add more detail about what should happen if there is no seat available when a student attempts to enrol to the model. One solution is to add the student to a waiting list. In order to follow this approach the Explorer adds a new state *Full*, and transitions *t13*, *t14* and *t15* as shown in Fig. 5 to the diagram. After this exploration Verifier has again a winning strategy for the current game.

4.4. Significance of Explorations

Explorations can be regarded as possible answers to design questions. Sometimes very concrete design questions arise during a play. For example, the fact that Verifier loses the game at position *p13* after the first incrementation leads to the following questions;

- What should happen if the year starts before the module is scheduled?
- Is the sequence *StartOfYear*, *Scheduled* legal or out of the system's scope?

Often it may be enough that the play evolves in a way which was not expected by the designer to make him think about certain design issues. For example, the designer may realise during a play that a feature which he assumed to be part of the system is missing both in the specification and the design. The designer discovers this flaw because he misses corresponding moves in the play. In our example the designer could for instance ask himself whether a module can be cancelled at any time.

In other cases the idea for a new exploration is not triggered directly by a play, but comes up when the designer thinks about how to improve the game for one of the players. For example, attaching a guard condition to *t8* is just one possibility to improve the chances of Refuter that the designer decided to follow.

It is also possible to think of Explorer's incrementations as independent proposals for system changes which are not inspired by plays of the exploration game at all. On this more general level exploration games can for instance be used to explore the evolvability of a system. In this case the incrementation is hypothetical and serves to show that a game can be extended as desired without breaking functionality that was present in the initial design.

5. Playing a Game with the GUIDE Tool

GUIDE is a prototype tool written in Java which is based on the exploration game framework. Before a game can be set up with GUIDE, a UML model has to be created. GUIDE

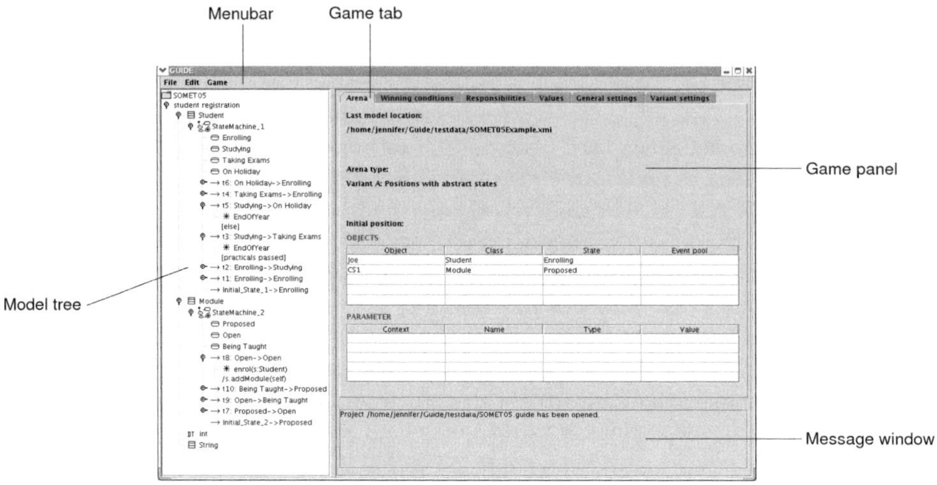

Figure 6. GUIDE main window.

does not contain a visual editor and requires an .xmi file which is compliant to the UML1.4 metamodel [20] from an external UML tool as input. We have chosen an old version of the UML metamodel, because most UML tools still use this version. The test models for GUIDE have been created with the community edition of the Poseidon tool [13].

Figure 6 shows the main window of GUIDE after a project with the example game of Section 4.1 has been opened. There is a menubar on top of the window, a model tree which displays the UML model on the left hand side, a game panel with six different views on the right, and a message window at the bottom. The views in the game panel are controlled by the game tabs on top of the panel. Each view shows a particular part of the game definition. The definition of a new game in GUIDE consists of the following steps using the menubar:

1. Open the UML model game by *File→Open Model*, which displays a file dialogue.
2. Set the arena type by *Edit→Arena type*, which opens a dialogue where the user can select one of the types that are currently available in GUIDE. The arena type specifies the game variant and determines which parts of the UML model are used within the game. Once the user has performed this step, the model tree is displayed.
3. Set the initial position by *Edit→Initial position*. The dialogue which is invoked by this operation is customised for the arena type that has been selected. For the example game variant which is considered in this paper the designer first enters object names and then selects classes from the UML model for them. After that he chooses a state from the appropriate state machine for each object. Since the user cannot enter arbitrary class and state names, the initial position is always valid. The user can also specify parameters which are known at all positions of the game and their initial values. The parameter values have to be updated manually during a play and allow additional information about the system to be recorded.

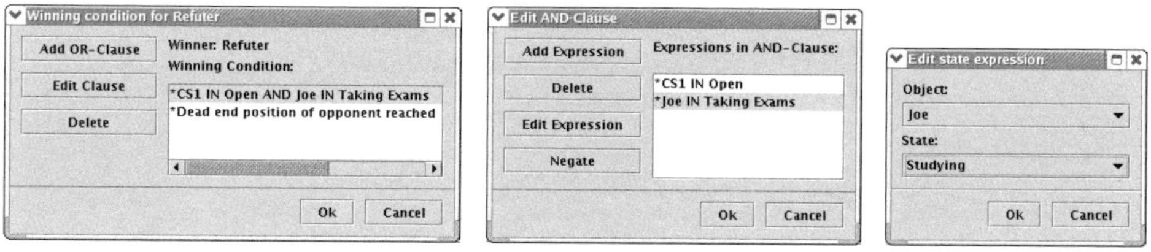

Figure 7. Dialogues for editing an expression in Refuter's winning condition.

4. Define the winning conditions for the players by *Edit→Winning condition Refuter* and *Edit→Winning condition Verifier*. Most of the dialogues which are displayed on selecting these menu items are the same for each variant because GUIDE contains a general expression framework. A typical sequence of dialogues is shown in Fig. 7. A winning condition consists of one or more AND-Clauses. Each AND-Clause is a conjunction of expressions, which can be applicable to all variants, such as for instance *Dead end position of opponent reached*, or to just one game variant. The only dialogue that is variant specific in Fig. 7 is the last one in the sequence where the state expression is defined. This expression may be part of a winning condition because it "fits" to the selected arena type.

GUIDE uses default values for all other parts of the game definition which can be changed by the user. The responsibilities of the two players and the Referee are edited via dialogue sequences that are very similar to those for the winning conditions. Moreover the game settings may be modified directly in the corresponding game tabs. The tab for the general game settings, which are the same for all game variants, is shown in figure 8. The same figure also shows a context menu in the model tree which pops up when the user clicks on a node representing a state machine with the right mouse button. The model tree contains context menus like this for all other node types. Each item of the context menus opens a dialogue which allows the user to increment the corresponding part of the UML model at any time. In the *Values* view the user can specify which values should be used for parameters that are not objects but primitive data types. This is a mechanism to enforce finiteness of the number of moves that emerge from a position, which we do not consider further here.

Notice that a game cannot be defined in arbitrary order. For example, it does not make sense to define a winning condition before a UML model, which serves as foundation for the game, has been opened. Therefore some of the menu items in GUIDE are not always enabled and the user is forced to perform the different steps of the game definition in a reasonable order.

Once the user is satisfied with the game set up, he can start to play by *Game→Play*. A dialogue as shown in Fig. 9 appears and asks the user for the distribution of tasks during the play. After that the play window which contains the current position and play history is displayed and the players start to move. Figure 10 shows one of the plays that was discussed in Section 4.2 in the play window of GUIDE. When the last position of this play is reached, GUIDE discovers that Refuter's winning condition holds. The play is finished and GUIDE announces that Refuter is the winner.

Each move consists of the four stages that were explained in Section 4.1. The algorithm for GUIDE moves, which is selected in the general settings tab, computes how

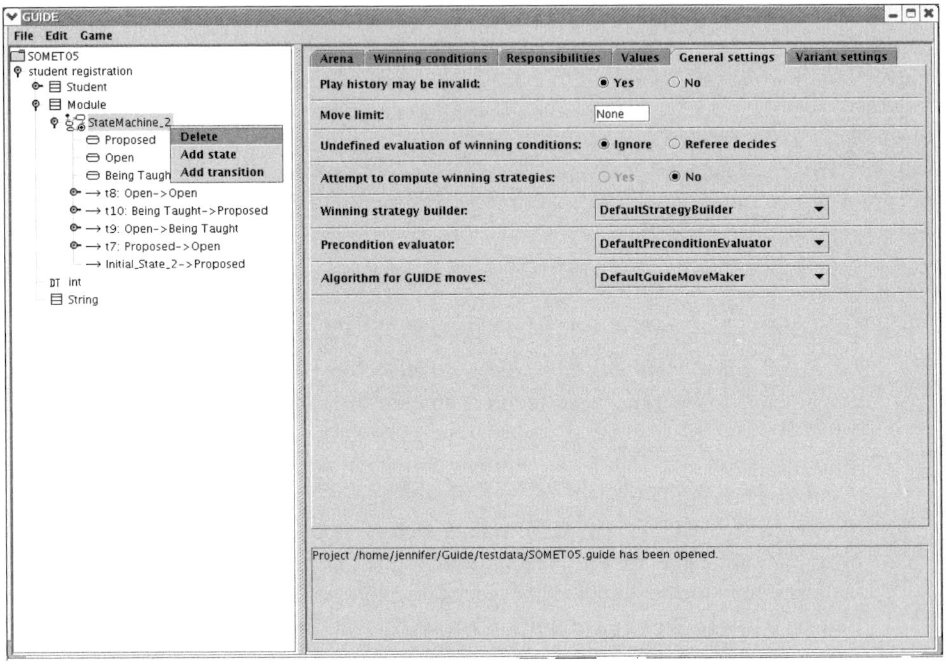

Figure 8. GUIDE main window with general settings tab and a context menu for a state machine node.

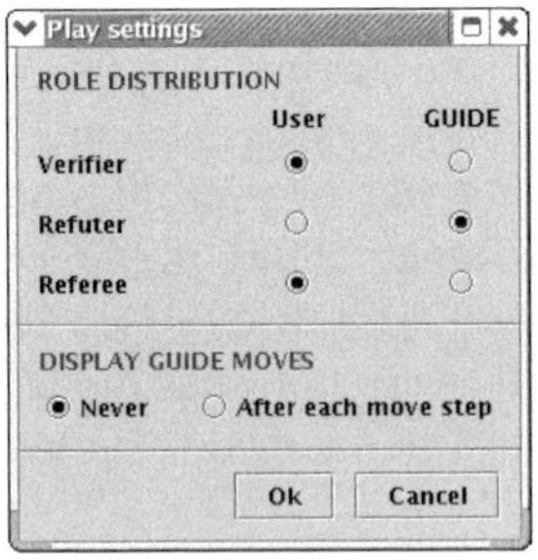

Figure 9. Preparation of a play.

GUIDE performs these move steps in the role of the players or the Referee. If the settings specify that GUIDE should attempt to compute winning strategies for the players, the algorithm can use these strategies during its computation. The user can choose in the dialogue for the preparation of a play whether the move steps that are made by GUIDE should be displayed. If the user has to perform a part of the move, he is asked for input by different dialogue windows. Figure 11 shows a sequence of move steps in the example game where the user plays both Refuter and Verifier.

At any time during a play the user can increment the game definition as specified by the formal exploration game framework. He is not forced to answer the dialogues that are displayed immediately and can use the context menus in the model tree, the

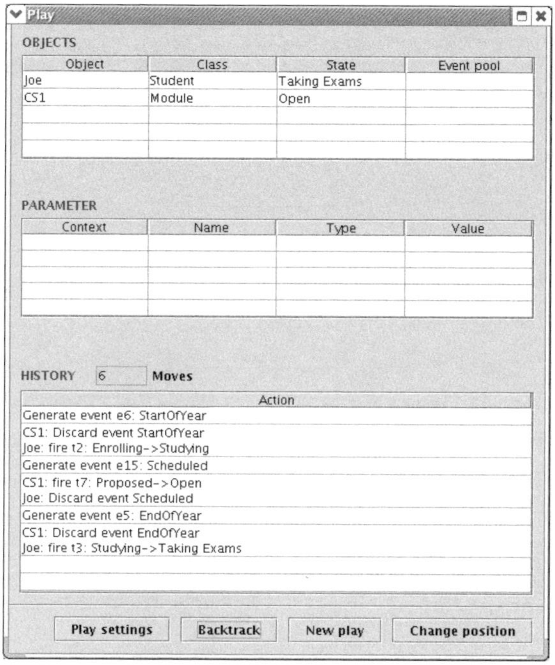

Figure 10. Play window showing a play without exploration.

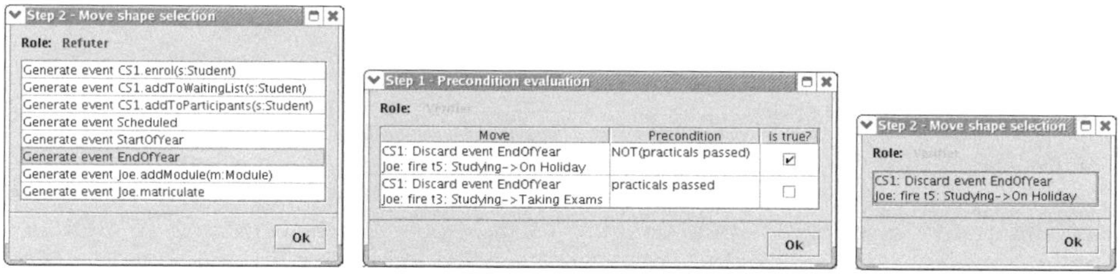

Figure 11. Dialogues for move steps.

items of the *Edit* menu and the features in the game settings tabs to increment the game. Furthermore the *Change position* button in the play window permits modifications of the current position during a play. Each change of position results in an incrementation of the game arena because the new position becomes the target of the last move. Whenever the modeller performs an incrementation, a short description is displayed in the play history. Figure 12 shows the history of the example play in Section 4.3 during which incrementations have been performed.

The *Backtrack* button in the play window allows the modeller go back to an earlier position of the play which can be selected in the history. Backtracking includes the incrementations of the game, i.e. the game definition is also changed back to an earlier version. For example, clicking the *Backtrack* button in the play window shown in Fig. 12 would restore the old version of Refuter's winning condition and remove transition *t12*

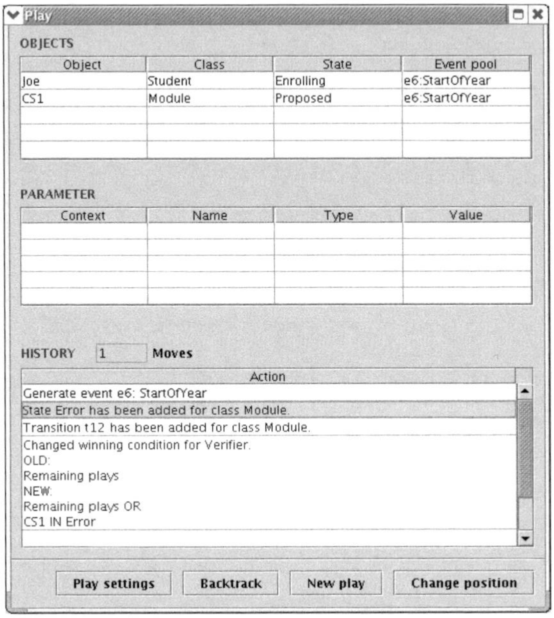

Figure 12. Play window showing a play with exploration.

from the UML model. After backtracking the play would continue at the second item of the play history, which is selected.

6. GUIDE Architecture

This section is intended as an overview on GUIDE's architecture and concentrates on the most important classes and methods. Figure 13 shows the package structure of GUIDE.

Package *io* consists of classes for saving and loading GUIDE projects and UML models. As storage mechanism for the UML model we have used the Metadata Repository (MDR) by NetBeans [11]. The MDR project is aimed at persistent storage and manipulation of metadata. It is based on the Meta Object Facility (MOF) standard [12]. The solution based on MDR has two main advantages. First, different UML tools can be supported because MDR is not bound to a particular XMI version or tool-specific saving format. That means the XMI output of any UML tool that is compliant with the UML1.4 metamodel can be read into GUIDE. Second, MDR's interfaces for accessing and manipulating the UML model have reduced the amount of code that had to be written.

The classes in *event* specify the actions which are invoked via the GUI, and package *ex* contains exception classes. The *uml* package provides classes for the UML elements that appear in the model tree. The classes in the *gui* package are Java Swing components, such as for instance a file dialogue, which are customised and used by different parts of the tool. The main frame of the GUI is also located in the *gui* package. All other GUI components are stored further down in the package hierarchy in subpackages of the *game*, *expression* and *algorithm* packages.

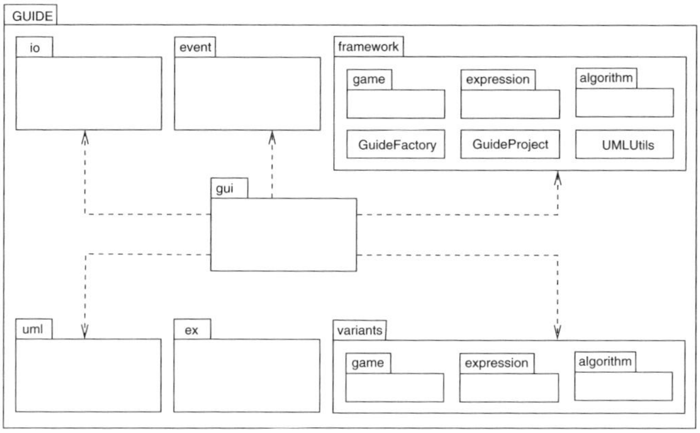

Figure 13. The package structure of GUIDE.

The most interesting packages in the context of this paper are the *framework* and *variants* package. As shown in Fig. 13 they both have the same structure. The *framework* package provides general classes and interfaces which can be refined and realised in the *variants* package. The class *GuideFactory* consists of methods for finding classes in the *variants* package which implement particular interfaces or are subclasses of *framework* classes. Java's reflection mechanism is used for this purpose. The relation between the *framework* and *variants* package is further discussed in Section 7.

Figure 14 shows the part of GUIDE which contains the game structure. As in the formal exploration game framework, a *Game* consists of an arena, an initial position, winning conditions, responsibility assignments and game settings. The UML model of a game is given by a *UmlPackage* which is a class in MDR. The abstract classes *Arena*, *Settings* and *MoveComponent* are specialised by concrete classes in the *variants* package. The concrete subclass of *Arena* for the game variant which we have considered in this paper is based on UML state machines. As in the example game discussed in Section 4.1, the *Settings* subclass refers to the UML state machine semantics. The concrete subclasses of *MoveComponent* for the game variant considered here stand for generating events, firing transitions and discarding events.

The part of GUIDE's framework package which is essential for playing a game is shown in Fig. 15. The *GameEngine* is invoked by the GUI and controls the play. It is linked to a *Play* which consists of *ExplorationPosition* instances. Each exploration position is a tuple of a *Position* and an *Incrementation*. If a move is made during a play, an exploration position with *null* as incrementation and the target position of the move is added to the history. In case the game is incremented, a concrete instance of the abstract *Incrementation* class and *null* as position constitute the new exploration position.

There already exist all necessary concrete subclasses of *Incrementation* in GUIDE, which represent incrementations of the model, winning conditions, responsibilities, and game settings, respectively. They all implement the abstract *undo* method which restores the game that is provided as parameter to the state before the incrementation has happened.

The general expression framework of GUIDE is shown in Fig. 16. Both *Winning-Condition* and *ResponsibilitySet* are associated with collections of *AndClause* instances.

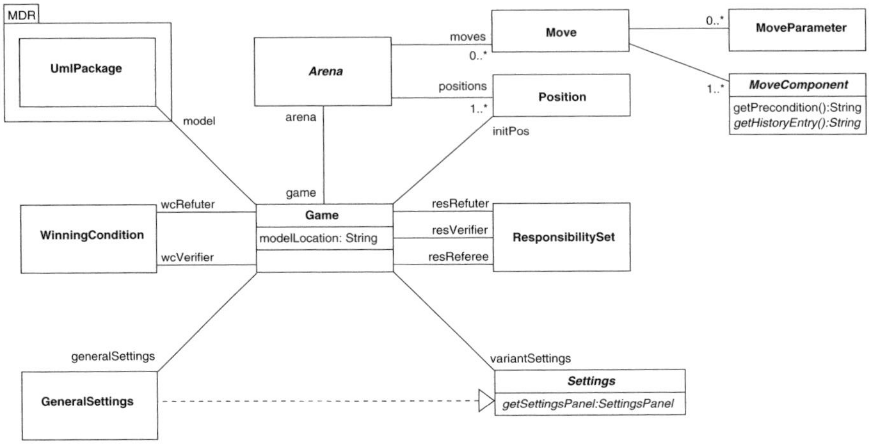

Figure 14. GUIDE game framework – Game structure.

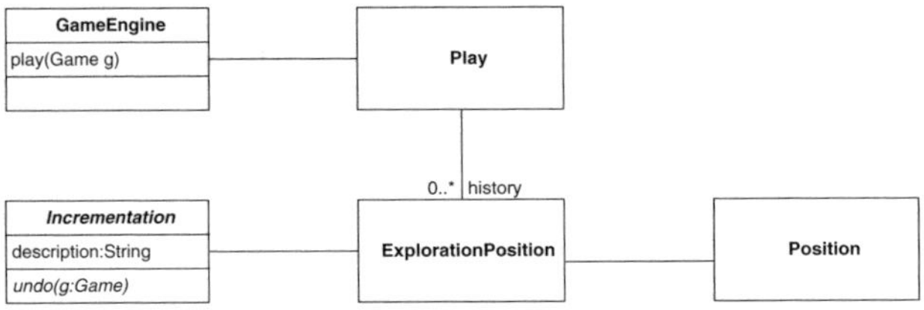

Figure 15. GUIDE game framework – Playing a game.

When a winning condition is evaluated, the result is true if one of its AND-Clauses is true. The *evaluate* method of *AndClause* which has a play, general settings, and variant specific settings as parameters is invoked for each AND-Clause to perform the evaluation. Within this method the expressions that constitute the clause are cast to *Winning-conditionExpIF* and evaluated. The GUI ensures that an AND-Clause which is part of a winning condition only consists of expressions which implement this interface and are suitable for the arena of the game. If all expressions are evaluated to true, the evaluation of the AND-Clause and of the winning condition also return true.

Instances of *ResponsibilitySet* are evaluated in similar fashion, but make use of two different evaluation methods. Which one is chosen depends on the type of responsibility that is evaluated. A *ResponsibilitySet* consists of four different AND-Clause collections, which correspond to the four responsibilities in the exploration game framework. The responsibilities for precondition evaluation and move shape selection are evaluated over positions, while the ones for parameter provision and resolution of non-determinism are evaluated over move shapes.

GUIDE provides several subclasses of *Expression* which implement the interfaces of the expression framework and define expressions that are usable in all game variants. An example of a general winning condition expression is *Move limit reached*, which refers to the move limit that may be set as part of the general settings. This expression is represented by a constant in a subclass of *Expression*.

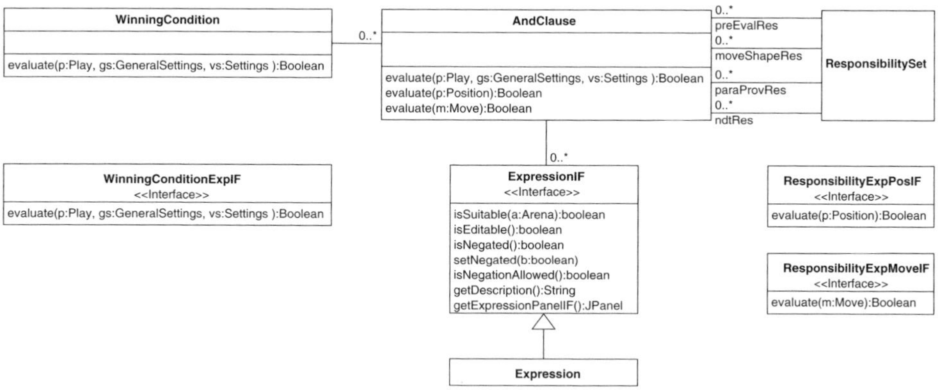

Figure 16. GUIDE expression framework.

Further subclasses can be created for variant specific types of expressions. For the variant which is based on UML state machines, a class *StateMachineExp* has been added to the *variants* package. The class implements all interfaces except for *ResponsibilityExpMoveIF* in Fig. 16. Hence an object of this class can be used in winning conditions and for the definition of responsibilities which are based on positions, but not for responsibilities referring to moves.

Notice that there is no separate class which represents move shapes in GUIDE. A move shape is simply a move whose parameters and target position are ignored. Another important point is that the *evaluate* methods in the expression framework return *Boolean* values. That means they can return true, false or a *null* object. The latter is used to indicate that the evaluation has been undefined.

The contents of the algorithm package are shown in Fig. 17. Two interfaces and one abstract class are associated with *GeneralSettings*. They define the algorithms that are used by the tool to make moves and evaluate preconditions during a play, and for computing winning strategies. There are two methods for computing a winning strategy in *StrategyBuilderIF*. The first one computes a fresh winning strategy, while the second method adapts an existing winning strategy during a play. The latter is needed to react to game incrementations and decisions by the game participants. The *evaluate* method in *PreconditionEvaluatorIF* uses a return value of type *Boolean* to cater for undefined evaluations.

Most of the methods in *GuideMoveMaker* require a parameter that specifies which role GUIDE should play. The only exception is the last method which refers to the undefined evaluation of winning conditions. It is used to determine whether the play may be continued or one of the players wins in case the game settings specify that the Referee is responsible for this decision and GUIDE acts as Referee. For the provision of parameter values by method *provideParameterValues* a mapping from types to possible values has to be specified.

GUIDE provides simple default implementations of the interfaces and abstract class in the *algorithm* package. The default precondition evaluator always returns *null* to indicate that the evaluation is undefined and has to be performed by the responsible game participant. The subclass of *GuideMoveMaker* which is used by default computes GUIDE's moves on the basis of the associated winning strategies if there are any. Otherwise

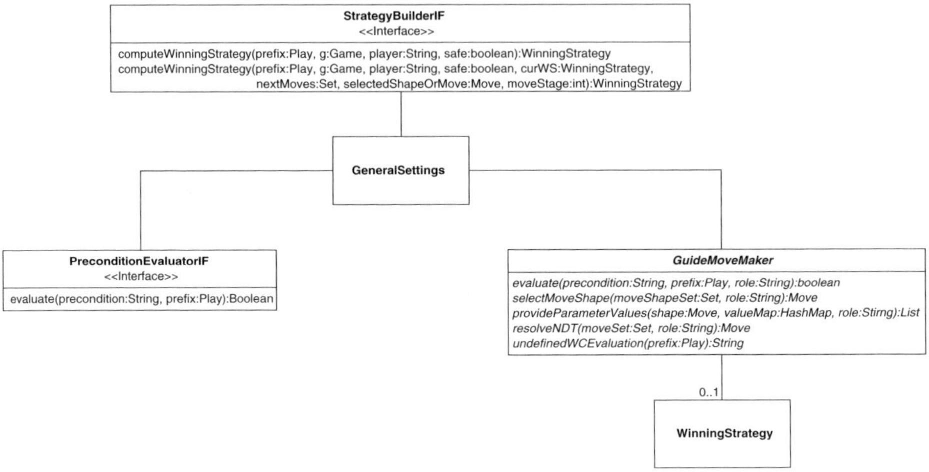

Figure 17. GUIDE algorithm framework.

GUIDE performs the different tasks which it is responsible for randomly. The default strategy builder only attempts to compute a winning strategy if a move limit has been set for the game. It searches for a winning strategy by building the arena up depth first until the move limit is reached.

7. Extensions of GUIDE

The *GuideFactory* class is used to search the *variants* package for realisations of interfaces and subclasses of the *framework* classes while GUIDE is running. The classes that are found are instantiated, and can be selected to be part of the tool via the GUI. This solution permits extensions of GUIDE by adding new classes to the *variants* package. Since the *GuideFactory* attempts to instantiate the classes in this package, new classes should always have a default constructor with no parameters.

In order to define a new game variant, a subclass of the abstract class *Arena* has to be created within the *game* subpackage. The definition of a new variant also requires new subclasses of *Position* and *MoveComponent*, and a panel for displaying and editing positions belonging to the new arena. Moreover methods which compute the next moves emerging from a position and customise the model tree are left abstract in *Arena* and have to be implemented. Any user-defined game variant which follows these rules becomes available for selection in the dialogue that is displayed by *Edit→Arena type*.

Another part of GUIDE that can be extended is the *expressions* package. A new kind of expression should be implemented as subclass of *Expression*, and realise at least one of the interfaces for winning conditions or responsibilities shown in Fig. 16. The interface *ExpressionIF* contains a method for deciding whether an expression is suitable for an arena and one which yields a panel for editing expressions of this type. The *Expression* class provides default implementations for these methods which should be overridden by its subclasses. The solution for the implementation of the first method in class *StateExpression*, which is part of our example variant, was to define another interface

StateExpressionIF. This interface specifies which methods should be provided by a suitable arena. The *isSuitable* method in *StateExpression* checks whether the arena implements this interface. All expressions which are suitable for the arena of the game become available for selection in the expression dialogues of the GUI.

It is also possible to define customised algorithms which specify how the GUIDE tool evaluates preconditions, makes moves and computes winning strategies. Classes which contain new algorithms should implement at least one of the interfaces shown in Fig. 17 or be subclasses of *GuideMoveMaker*. They must be put into the *algorithms* subpackage of *variants* to be found by GUIDE and are then displayed as options in the general settings panel, where the user can select which algorithms should be used.

8. Conclusion

In this paper we have introduced our tool GUIDE, which is an implementation of the exploration game framework. By repeatedly playing an exploration game, the designer gradually adds more detail to the design and specification in the role of the Explorer. While a game is being played, the designer may resolve non-determinacy by interaction with the GUIDE tool. He can take on the roles of other game participants to examine the design from a particular view and to perform parts of the moves in the play.

At the moment GUIDE supports the example game variant, expressions and algorithms which have been described in this paper. The tool is a proof-of-concept prototype which needs further testing with more complex examples than presented here. Probably the most important task for future work is to give users the opportunity to exercise our tool and to analyse their feedback. Thereby it would be possible to identify which parts of the approach presented here are most interesting in practice and where improvements are necessary. Experiments with students could be used as first step for testing GUIDE more thoroughly before advertising it to a wider community. More advanced investigations could focus on the comparison of exploring a design using the GUIDE tool with traditional reviewing techniques such as design reviews.

Another possibility for future work is to extend GUIDE's capabilities, and in particular its algorithms. For the evaluation of preconditions GUIDE could be coupled to a tool that can evaluate OCL (Object Constraint Language) constraints, such as for example the USE tool [22]. If the designer commits himself to use OCL in the UML model, some of the move preconditions may then be evaluated automatically and do not require interaction with the game participants during a play.

There are also plenty of opportunities for improving GUIDE's move algorithm and strategy builder. Heuristics and "looking ahead" in a play can help GUIDE to move reasonably on behalf of the game participant during a play. These techniques would also be useful for computing winning strategies in an infinite arena. We have enforced finiteness by requiring a move limit for our strategy builder and restricting the number of parameter values that can be provided for moves. An algorithm which can handle infinite arenas would make these restrictions obsolete.

In this paper we have assumed that it is always the designer who plays the Explorer and increments the game. It is undoubtedly fascinating to imagine that the tool could perform the exploration of the design. However, the exploration generally requires knowledge about the system and design skills. We expect that building a tool which performs the tasks of a designer to a certain degree would involve a large amount of research in the area of artificial intelligence. The GUIDE tool does not aim at substituting the designer, but at supporting him in using his skills. A very advanced version of GUIDE could try to give the designer feedback about which kind of incrementation is beneficial for a player in specific situations. However, it is then still the designer who has to make a concrete incrementation according to the tool's suggestion.

Acknowledgements

The author would like to thank the anonymous reviewers and her supervisor Perdita Stevens for useful comments on this paper, and the DIRC (Interdisciplinary Research Collaboration in Dependability – GR/N13999/01) project funded by the UK Engineering and Physical Sciences Research Council for its support of this research.

References

[1] A. Cockburn. *Agile Software Development.* Addison-Wesley, 2002.
[2] T. DeMarco and T. Lister, editors. *Peopleware – Productive Projects and Teams.* Dorset House Publishing, 1987.
[3] M. Fagan. Design and code inspections to reduce errors in program development. *IBM Systems Journal*, 15(3), 1976.
[4] E. Grädel, W. Thomas, and T. Wilke, editors. *Automata, Logics, and Infinite Games: A Guide to Current Research*, volume 2500 of *LNCS*. Springer, 2002.
[5] GUIDE – Games with UML for Interactive Design Exploration. The first release is planned for summer 2005 and will be available from the author's homepage at `http://www.lfcs.informatics.ed.ac.uk/jnt`.
[6] D. Harel. From play-in scenarios to code: An achievable dream. *IEEE Computer*, 342(1):53–60, January 2001.
[7] D. Harel, H. Kugler, R. Marelly, and A. Pnueli. Smart play-out of behavioral requirements. In *Proceedings of Formal Methods in Computer-Aided Design, FMCAD'02*, pages 378–398, 2002.
[8] W.S. Humphrey. *A Discipline for Software Engineering.* Addison-Wesley, 1995.
[9] A. Knapp and S. Merz. Model checking and code generation for UML state machines and collaborations. In *5th Workshop on Tools for System Design and Verification, FM-TOOLS'02*, Report 2002-11. Institut für Informatik, Universität Augsburg, 2002.
[10] J. Lilius and I. Paltor. vUML: A tool for verifying UML models. In *Proceedings of Automated Software Engineering, ASE'99*. IEEE, 1999.
[11] NetBeans Metadata Repository (MDR). Website at `http://mdr.netbeans.org`.
[12] Meta-Object Facility (MOF). Available from the OMG at `http://www.omg.org`.
[13] Poseidon for UML, version 3.0. Available from Gentleware at `http://www.gentleware.com`.
[14] Real Time Studio professional, version 4.3. Available from Artisan Software at `http://www.artisansw.com`.
[15] Rhapsody, version 5.0. Available from I-Logix at `http://www.ilogix.com`.
[16] P. Stevens and J.Tenzer. Games for UML software design. In *Formal Methods for Components and Objects, FMCO'02*, volume 2852 of *LNCS*. Springer, 2003.
[17] J. Tenzer. Exploration games for safety-critical system design with UML 2.0. In *Proceedings of the 3rd International Workshop on Critical Systems Development with UML, CSDUML'04*, Technical Report I0415, pages 41–55. Technische Universität München, September 2004.
[18] J. Tenzer. *Exploration games for UML software design.* PhD thesis, University of Edinburgh, School of Informatics, 2005. Submission expected in July 2005.
[19] W. Thomas. Infinite games and verification. In *Computer Aided Verification, CAV'02*, volume 2404 of *LNCS*. Springer, 2002.

[20] OMG Unified Modeling Language Specification, version 1.4, September 2001. Available from the OMG at http://www.omg.org.
[21] UML 2.0 Superstructure Final Adopted Specification, August 2003. Available from the OMG at http://www.uml.org.
[22] USE – a UML-based Specification Environment. Website at http://www.db.informatik.uni-bremen.de/projects/USE.

New Trends in Software Methodologies, Tools and Techniques
H. Fujita and M. Mejri (Eds.)
IOS Press, 2005

A Grounded Theory Study of Programming in Artist-Programmer Collaborations

Greg TURNER, Alastair WEAKLEY, Yun ZHANG and Ernest EDMONDS
Institute for Information and Communication Technologies, Creativity and Cognition Studios, Faculty of IT, University of Technology, Sydney, PO Box 123, Broadway NSW, Australia

Abstract. This paper presents findings from a grounded theory study of the social and technical roles of programmers in art-technology collaborations. The process of 'attuning' between the actors and artefacts involved is a recurring theme in our study and one that we think is central to transdisciplinary collaboration and for non programmer-focussed software development. We reflect on the use of grounded theory to study software engineering social processes and conclude that the methodology can bring designers and researchers rich theoretical understandings that can be used to develop new tools to support different types of software engineering.

Keywords. Grounded theory, interactive art, collaboration, end-user programming, creativity support

1. Background

1.1. How We Think About Interactive Art

From a technological perspective, computer-mediated interactive art involves a computer system with some form of input from the audience-participant, some form of output to the audience-participant, and, most interestingly from a programming perspective, some form of processing in between. However, interactive art is in practice quite a complex field, involving various creators, producers and audiences, not just a set of computational artefacts with an 'optimal', or easily formally-defined configuration. When we think about any of the entities situated within these art systems [5], we should not lose sight of that very situatedness.

1.2. How We Think About Programming

The authors adopt the view that any reasonable definition of programming (for example, that programming is a specification of a computation [3], or that programming is taking actions with the objective of creating an application that serves some function for the user [20]) can describe *all* uses of a computer. There is no particular ontological distinction between programming a computer and using it. This is not to say that all languages are the same – we do not ignore the obvious technological and cognitive differences between, for example, the language of Direct Manipulation [23] and Assembly Language. These differences to suggest a continuum between two poles, which we call 'gentle programming' and 'deep programming'. For the sake of simplicity, the term 'programming' will from now on be used to refer to the *entire* continuum of styles between gentle and deep. So, by 'ability to program', we mean 'ability to deep program when necessary'.

1.3. Why is Programming Important to Art?

Computers allow us to think thoughts and to experience things that would be impossible without them, particularly in aid of entertainment and scientific discoveries, but what is it about the tool that allows new thought? An examination of the important developments in computing (and particularly programming) history indicates following four technological strengths, which we call the four Ss: *speed*, *slavery*, *synaesthesia* and *structure*. Other significant developments (such as the Internet and digital artworks), exploit one or more of these, and programming tools which provide access to these strengths are presumably to be desired.

Treated briefly here, with particular reference to applications in interactive art, 'Speed' refers to the computer's ability to do certain things quicker than we can. We use computers to think thoughts that would otherwise require too much time. In interactive art, the goal is often to generate the response 'in real time'.

'Slavery' is descriptive of both the incredible cheapness and unquestioning obedience of computation, and it is what allows artists and programmers to create massive and wide-ranging programmatic edifices. However, this pedantic obedience carries with it the danger of genie-in-the-bottle or sorcerer's apprentice-style mishaps.

'Synaesthesia' is another way of describing Negroponte's 'formless bits' [21] – that all a computer does is perform operations on collections of 1s and 0s. Inside a computer, video is the same stuff as audio is the same stuff as text is the same stuff as time, which means it is possible, for example, to combine them and convert between them. Synaesthesia is itself strongly exploited in interactive art, probably as a consequence of this quality.

'Structure', that mysterious descriptive power of computing, is the hardest quality to nail down, perhaps because it has no direct analogue in the physical world. Abstracting situations into structures is the current distinctive speciality of programmers and systems analysts, and may be an important reason why artists employ them. Understanding the potential of abstract structure is the key to fully engaging with the computing medium. As a result there are people who advocate that everyone should learn to program (e.g. Kay and Goldberg [16], Flanagan and Perlin [9]), and people who advocate that artists who make computer art must learn to program (e.g. Maeda [18], though he has since revised this opinion [19]). However, since many artists make good computer art without deep programming (by getting a programmer to do it for them), we have to assume that programming is not always necessary. Although many artists do indeed find the requisite level of engagement by learning the necessary technical skills from scratch, many others find it vicariously, by delegating the work to a programmer.

2. Desirable Support for Creative Activities and Technological Implications Thereof

2.1. Creativity Support

There is a need for an interactive art programming environment to support the creativity of artists. It is worth emphasizing that our interest here is to *support* creativity—not to replace any of an artist's creativity with computer code, nor necessarily to have the artist transfer 'complete' creative knowledge to either programmer or computer. The computer is a particularly special tool for potentially realising creativity, and we wish to better present the capabilities of that tool to enhance that potential for a wider population. Earlier work [27] reviewed the work of creativity support researchers, in particular the generalised operations which they had identified as being useful for creative workers. Ben Shneiderman lists eight specific operations that should "help more people be more creative more of the time": Searching (for knowledge and inspiration), Visualising, Consulting, Thinking, Exploring, Composing, Reviewing, Disseminating [22]. In the digital art domain some of these tasks would be highly interrelated (for instance, visualisation, exploration and composition). Michael Terry and Elizabeth D. Mynatt highlight the need for support of Schön's theory of reflection-in-action: near-term experimentation (previews of the results of actions), longer-term variations, and evaluation of actions [26]. In our own study, empirical evidence was used to identify some examples of aspects of creative exploration: Breaking with convention, immersion in the activity, holistic view and parallel channels of exploration [7]. These activities highlight that artists are rarely content to use an existing tool solely in the way it was intended by its creators, nor is the workflow straightforward and linear.

An important issue to consider when making creativity support tools is language expressivity (expressivity presumably being valued in tools for artists, for example). Metaphorically speaking, gentle programming languages allow us to make "big brush strokes" with benefits in terms of effort and limitations in terms of fine control and extensibility. Deeper programming languages, on the other hand, are equivalent to not just making "smaller brush strokes", but even to making new paint and brushes, and this means that it is difficult to construct large systems from small articulations. Gentle programming languages each impose an aesthetic which is so easily linked with a corresponding artistic subgenre that it becomes increasingly hard to avoid cliché: The visual and interaction hallmarks of Flash and Director for net art and CD-ROMs and of Max/MSP for performance-based electronic sound art are recognisable, and it can be difficult for creative practitioners to work around these aesthetic restrictions. Deeper programming languages suffer less from this problem, but at the expense of ease of learning and obviousness of use. Neither gentle nor deep languages are very expressive – a truly expressive language would allow both large and small computing granularity, both obvious gestures and subtle nuances.

One way of achieving this expressivity is to have the entire computer system built around a *homogeneous, universal,* concept that can be used at both microscopic and macroscopic levels of systems, and everywhere in between, a bit like glass lenses in microscopes and telescopes. A homogeneous universal computing concept means that a) the environment will be built in itself and b) there would be no technological distinction between programming and using the system, to match the ontological nature described in Section 1.2. Any single Turing-complete system would do for such a concept, but of particular power is Squeak Smalltalk [15], which is attractive for our purposes because it is written in itself (beyond fundamental logic and some hardware calls), which means that the language and environment itself can be modified, and because it has a large set of ready-made (and of course modifiable) libraries for achieving complex tasks. Single universal systems in general present security and intellectual property issues, and currently the Squeak environment has usability, visualisation, multimedia and aesthetic problems which makes it less than ideal for artistic expressivity, but there is potential for these to be developed by interested parties.

2.2. Social Support – Communication and Collaboration

Collaborations take place within two styles of communities; one is 'Communities of Practice' (CoPs) [20] and the other is 'Communities of Interests' (CoIs). In a CoP, people work together who come from similar backgrounds, e.g. programmers who are producing software. In CoIs, (which are also 'communities of communities' [2]), people who come from different backgrounds concentrate the same project, e.g. art-technology collaborations. Communication between collaborators in CoIs is difficult because they come from different backgrounds and therefore use different languages and different knowledge systems. The fundamental challenge which faces CoIs is to build a shared understanding of the task at hand. This shared language rarely exists at the beginning, but is evolved incrementally and collaboratively and emerges in people's minds and in external artifacts [8]. Boundary objects [24] are important artefacts in CoIs, because they have meaning across the boundaries of individual knowledge systems. Boundary objects allow different knowledge systems to interact by providing a shared reference that is meaningful within both systems and they serve to communicate and coordinate the perspectives of various constituencies [29].

Our earlier studies have reported on the use of the visual programming language Max/MSP in close collaborations, partly by supporting such shared references. As well as being a popular programming environment for interactive art, it is suggested that Max/MSP can also contribute to the social interaction between collaborators. Weakley et al. [28] suggest that the developing Max/MSP program can be regarded almost as a working sketch of the finished artefact. In the same way that one may work collaboratively using sketches to explore, explain and develop ideas, the expressive and accessible nature of the visual program encourages collaboration. Edmonds et al. [6] report seeing "... a radical shifting and sharing of responsibility" with both parties able to contribute to the other's domain of interest. Of course, this is not to say that such visual programming languages (VPLs) are a panacea. For instance, Green and Petre [14] identify a number of areas where, in terms of usability, VPLs appear to be worse than text-based languages. In the VPLs that they studied, they identified notable shortcomings in the two areas of 'viscosity' (the diagram editor associated with the VPL makes it difficult to change the developing program) and 'secondary notation' (the readability and clarity of text-based programs is typically enhanced by such secondary notations as whitespace or commenting, and the VPLs that Green and Petre studied tended to constrain the ways that objects could be arranged or highlighted). Max/MSP shares such constraints to a lesser extent than the VPLs examined in Green's and Petre's study. It is often desirable and necessary, to spend some time tidying up the program, particularly if it is to be easily understood by another person. This is, however, also true of text-based languages (and, it might be said, of any human endeavour!) and, in comparison with text-based languages, Weakley et. al. report on MAX/MSPs particular ability to allow the programmer to deliberately make the program more self explanatory (by colour-coding, highlighting or quickly adding live visual elements to the code to indicate the status of processes), and how that ability assisted the artist-technologist collaboration that they studied. Max/MSP also supports real-time interaction between collaborators by allowing the program to be modified while it is actually running and therefore it supports synchronous collaboration. This is in contrast to a more traditional approach where an artist might seek help from a programmer who would work largely alone, successive iterations of the program being tested from time to time; a much more disjoint process.

Max/MSP is an instance of technology which supports close collaboration, but the technical system was not specifically designed for this purpose; instead the support for collaboration arose from use of the tool itself. Although there are many tools available to support *communication*, we do not yet have dedicated tools which explicitly support *collaboration* in the development of interactive art.

3. The Supportive Role of the Programmer

As outlined in Sections 2.3 and 2.4, not much is known about what precisely it is that programmers do in the context of producing interactive art, besides writing programs. Similarly, little is known about the way that artists prefer to specify their requirements to programmers – for example, how expressive is the specification language used, and what sociologically is the process of transforming this language into less expressive computer code? Section 1.3 shows the artistic and technological rationale for working with programmers, but the question remains: how good are programmers at living up to the need for them? Specifically, which facets of the programmer's role are supportive to the artist, and which are obstructive? How can technology enhance the support and ameliorate the obstruction? To answer these questions, we carried out a social study on the role of the programmer in art collaborations.

3.1. Methodology

An approach based upon grounded theory was adopted for this study. Grounded Theory [12,13,25] is an approach where the theory emerges from the data itself, and is thus grounded in it, rather than being an approach which tests existing theories. The theory's emergence from the data is good for discovery of the important issues in a field, because it provides a way to discover the commonalities in the views of many and disparate experts, with the added advantage that any biases or preconceptions held by the researcher should have minimal impact.

There are two main schools of grounded theory analysis, those of Anshelm Strauss [25] and Barney G. Glaser [12], erstwhile colleagues of each other, and the two originators of the approach [13]. The two disagree on whose version is most correct. We have chosen to follow Glaser's approach, since it appears to be more elegantly simple, and his critique of the partiality of Strauss and Corbin's question-asking process is convincing.

The first iteration of grounded theory analysis is the open coding stage, which begins with no preconceived codes, and produces codes from the asking of neutral questions of the data. Glaser then advocates several iterations of gathering more data, comparison and selective coding in order to establish categories and super-categories of codes, and to situate the most important categories within a framework that shows the overall picture. Categories that get 'saturated' with data points are more important to a theory than categories that do not.

The preliminary source for open coding was the collected Case Reports for the COSTART (Computer SupporT for ARTists) project—which centred round seven intensive artist-technologist collaborations. Artist, technologist and observer statements, from recordings, interviews and diaries, for seven projects, and is a good collection of case-study material—were coded by hand, and arranged to produce a list of categories.

More codes were taken from primary data – transcripts of interviews with artists and technologists from the larger and more meticulous COSTART 2 project [4], which involved 9 further residencies, bringing the total to 16 artists, 6 technologists and 4 observers. These were coded using NVivo software [11]. At this point there was a list of categories indicating the many and various issues that arose and were recorded during the collaborations.

It was decided that an appropriate way to gather some of the data needed to saturate some of these categories was to conduct a series of qualitative interviews with artists and programmers who had been involved in collaborations. In order to distinguish the feelings and actions of people in the artist role from the feelings and actions of people in the programmer role, and to explore the issues facing non-programmers, initial subjects were selected who were interactive artists who do not program, and programmers who program for such artists.

The interviews were conducted in December and January 2005, face-to-face (with one exception where iChat was used), were recorded and, for the first iteration, transcribed for coding in NVivo. Six subjects were chosen—four programmers and two artists who had worked with these programmers.

The interviews were semi-structured and qualitative, with questions designed according to best practice (as described in [10]), based upon the concepts that were popular, but as yet unsaturated. The lengths of the interviews ranged from 30 minutes to 1 hour 45 minutes.

After the several iterations of selective coding and data gathering, a hierarchy of about 200 codes and categories of codes emerged, with associated memos describing the relationships between codes according to grounded theory analysis.

To present the findings for this paper, we selected out several irrelevant codes, such as those pertaining to ownership and quality issues, and issues which seemed to be particular to specific artworks.

To avoid repeating ourselves, we also selected out incidents that further validated what has already been discussed in Section 2. This left us with categories and memos from which we can form a grounded theory about the core social values, rather than those dictated by technology, in the relationship between artist and programmer.

3.2. Findings and Analysis

The memos from the study were collected to form the theory that follows. Broadly speaking, our theory contends that of fundamental importance is the process of *attuning* between humans, and between artist and programmer-attuned computer. The programmer's role is to attune the computer to the artist, through either 'intimate iteration' or 'toy-making'. Ideally the attuning happens to the extent that the artist no longer needs the programmer, yet this does not always happen in practice because of the extra work involved. Technological development of art systems starts with an artistic description which is transformed into a technological description by the programmer, starting with fundamental technological choices, which are tested with the artist for appropriate artistic meaning, then abstracted and built into higher-level structures.

We will now explore the theory in detail.

3.2.1. Collaboration Context

Artists work with programmers for several stated reasons, given that a need was established for a computer system beyond the capabilities of the artist his or herself to create.

With non-programming artists, there is a definite hierarchy, albeit, a complex and contested one. Briefly, the perception is that programmers are *craftsmen* who are engaged as assistants, consultants and teachers, depending on the artist's expertise, willingness to learn and skills of others in the project. Yet artists must at the same time *trust* programmers to estimate and lay out the work plan, and make thousands of other decisions about the project.

Mamykina et al. used the COSTART data to discern types of artist-technologist collaboration (technologist as assistant, full partnership with artist control, and full partnership) [21]. Although our findings align with that theory, we didn't find an explicit example of a "full partnership" that involved non-programming artists.

Ability to trust the programmer comes from valuing the programmer's *personality, expertise* and *sensitivity*. Expertise (which is particularly valued with *agility*, or willingness to reach beyond expertise) is interesting, because artists will often want to challenge expertise, by testing their own hunches, or requiring extensions to or re-evaluations of the expertise. An example in the data is of an artist requiring non-realistic lighting from a VR expert. Sensitivity refers to the programmer's ability to respond to the artist's needs, both explicit and, importantly, implicit, making it a prerequisite for *attuning*.

We found that programmers work with artists for different sets of stated reasons, primarily *satisfaction* (fulfilling goals, such as earning money, technical challenge, ownership) and *enjoyment* (with no well-defined goals, for example creative urges, 'soulfulness', to teach, friendliness). When programmers are motivated by learning (technical and aesthetic skills), they seem to derive both satisfaction and enjoyment.

The level of *dependency* of the artist on the programmer, combined with the motivations of each, has a strong influence on the passivity of the programmer – their level of comfort with, for example, suggesting changes for either technical or aesthetic reasons. However, there appears to be less which influences the ability of the programmer to suggest changes for pragmatic reasons.

There was some evidence of *subversive* or *passive-aggressive* behaviour amongst programmers who made changes without consulting the artist, or made disingenuous suggestions, because it was technically easier, or because they preferred one aesthetic course over another. It was difficult to get information in retrospect about the effects of this behaviour without breaching confidentiality, though the artists in the study were generally not shy of suggesting even 'pedantic' changes, and any dissatisfaction with programmers was due to 'inflexibility' or 'grumpiness'.

3.2.2. Approach to Problem-Solving

In all cases where it was mentioned, artists presented, or were characterised as initially presenting, what to a technologist sounds like very imprecise descriptions of the systems they envisaged. The form of these descriptions ranged from using 'vague language' through describing it 'in terms of effect' to consciously communicating a 'metaphorical understanding'. There was some evidence of dissatisfaction at this approach amongst programmers who wanted more specificity, logic and sequencing. However, this artistic meaning needs to be understood by the programmer – it is the first stage of the *attuning* process.

What then appears to immediately take place is a process of transforming this conceptual description into technological terms. This was mainly achieved by *question asking* on the part of the programmer – about critical detail, what-if scenarios, and so on. Rather than the traditional requirements gathering process of 'breaking down' a 'top-level' description into 'low-level' terms, this process seems to be more a way to informally map the artistic expression of the piece into a technological expression, at all levels of expression. We speculate, with two data points in support, that this is also a comfort-bringing process of changing the problem domain from an open world into a 'hermetic' system.

In order for the programmer to check that his mapping of the artistic expression to the technological expression is appropriate, it becomes necessary for him to test fundamental technological components with the artist, beginning with the most fundamental, to see if the artistic meaning these components create is appropriate. In our studies, the first result of the mapping is often a perception of what technology will be used, or what potential technology needs to be researched, first in terms of hardware, then programming environment, then fundamental algorithms (a reversal of this process was found in one collaboration where the piece was based upon an algorithmic process described by the artist – the initial development was characterised as 'an engine' around which input and output could be added). As these fundamental things are chosen, the artist in turn asks the technologist several questions about this low-level technology. The artist and technologist begin to get *attuned* over the low-level technology.

Out of all cases, there was only one example of a formal top-down approach to design, when the artist was able to be quite specific about required features (in this case the system was explicitly a toolkit).

Both artist and technologist seem to agree that 'knowing the rules' for the system allows the system to be developed. But here arises a dilemma: the programmers in the study indicated a greater level of comfort with and satisfaction from achieving set rules and goals within a design, whereas it was difficult to get these rules from the artists, and the artists indicated a need to 'play' in order to discover what the system should do. This is essentially the dichotomy between *analysis* and *synthesis*.

3.2.3. Developing Subsystems

Bottom-up development was used in all of our studies. Small programs are developed by the programmer to test each of the fundamental technologies. One respondent likens the process to sketching, as a way of finding out more about the sub-problem: "I make things up as I go along, usually, I think. But I think that's more my designery [sic] training because with that you have a vague idea, then you, like, draw it and then look at that and discover something new in the drawing."

Many of the programmers exhibited a particular preoccupation at this point with the input and output technologies system. This appeared to be for a variety of reasons: chiefly, that these are the lowest-level technologies; also that they are the hardest thing to get right (input is characterised as being technologically harder than output, partly because of the human-controlled element, partly because computer technologies have greater bandwidth for output than input so output is easier to model, and partly because interactive art often involves unfamiliar sensor hardware). As one respondent puts it, "usually I want everything to talk to everything else before I start working on how decisions are made … invariably you'll make the brain wrongly if you don't have the right shaped skull for it".

Simultaneously and separately, in cases where it was applicable, the artist works on his or her material ("the content") then presents it to the programmer. This can be seen as a process of attuning between the artist and his or her material, and also between the artist and programmer. There was one case where this approach helped the artist feel as if she had something to do. There is no evidence of a particular methodical approach here, which is attributable to the uniqueness of the artists' practice.

Once sufficient understanding of the sub-problem has been acquired, the programmer begins to generalise and to build up the sketch: "small parts of the system [are] being experimented with and you see really how they operate and you, as in the artist, or me, as in the programmer, are having to think about how these things fit into the system, then that's where the ideas of generality and structure and abstractions start to come in. It's an interesting thing."

3.2.4. Intimate Iteration vs. Toy-Making

At all stages of development, there will be facets of the technology that the artist will want to make decisions about, and facets that are not of interest. Reports about the level of engagement that artist had with the system varied from being interested in everything (itself associated with desire to learn programming), to being interested only in 'front-end' facets, i.e. those aspects which would have an effect on the audience. Decision points for artists can be triggered by any of the artist, programmer or computer (via the programmer). The artist's decision-making process was described by one programmer as a way of adding the 'character' to the system.

In many cases, the artistic decisions were made by working intensively with the programmer, who makes small changes to test different outcomes. This 'intimate iteration' seems to work well enough in some cases, and may save time, but there was at least one case of an artist saying she did not feel she was 'hands-on' enough.

A more encouraging approach, in terms of the goal of creating a supportive environment, was for the programmer to build a technological 'toy' for the artist. We found this to be useful for several reasons. Firstly, concept of a toy directly aligned with the oft-reported behaviour of artists 'playing' with systems, data, mappings and algorithms, in order to discover both the necessary rules for the system (remember the earlier concept that finding the rules would allow the problem to be solved), and exploring what one artist called 'probabilities and tendencies' within the data. Secondly, producing the toy is a way for the programmer to take himself 'out of the loop'; this means that, as one programmer put it, 'by taking myself out of the loop it makes it really clear what the dynamics of the system are as opposed to what my interpretation is'.

Thirdly, and crucially, as one artist stated, "instead of [the programmer] just doing it and you saying 'can it be more squiggly?' and him going back and changing parameters, I found I *understood the language of the algorithm* just by playing with the parameters and understanding what the software developer, how they had broken down this organic thing" (our emphasis, edited for repetition and anonymity). The artist was not referring to the language in which the algorithm was implemented (Python, incidentally), but rather the language necessary to communicate meaning to and from the algorithm itself. This attuned manipulation of an algorithm's language produces meaning *both technically and aesthetically*.

To recap, 'playing' with technological 'toys' is crucial to the development of interactive art systems, for six reasons:

1. finding rules,
2. developing the 'character' of the system,
3. intuitively learning the 'language' of the algorithmic system (which is distinct from the less-intuitive language in which the program was written),

4. making the toy's place within the system apparent,
5. producing technical and aesthetic meaning simultaneously (which also assists transdisciplinary collaboration), and
6. making the artist feel more comfortable and empowered.

These toys, then, are boundary objects that embody a language for creating meaning between artist and technologist, and artist and computer, and perhaps less necessarily, technologist and computer. (There is also scope for these toys to become boundary objects for other communities, such as audience members, other artists and technologists, researchers and curators).

4. Implications for Software Methodologists

4.1. Use of Grounded Theory to Understand Software Methodology

As Kautz et al. relate, "The literature on [Information Systems development methodologies] is extensive and wide-ranging. It consists however largely of prescriptive and normative textbooks and work that is based on anecdotes, but there is limited scientifically collected and analyzed empirical documentation…" [17]. Kautz et al. go on to provide an illuminating grounded theory study of actual use of development methodologies in one large company, to counter this state of affairs.

Grounded theory is a methodology that can produce surprisingly rich theories to explain social phenomena, from little more than repeated careful observation (imagine conducting a scientific experiment where no hypothesis pre-exists, and no variables are controlled). It was developed by Strauss and Glaser to help form an understanding of the awareness of dying in hospitals [13], but it has since been employed in a variety of social contexts, including this one.

The particular advantage of grounded theory is that every aspect of a resulting theory can be split into multiple sub-aspects, and finally to actual observations. This provides for great richness and concreteness of theory, usefully systematic comprehension of data, and as such makes it harder for the researcher to insert his or her preconceptions.

We have conducted a grounded theory study because we felt it important to study the social interactions across and between two disciplines during art-software development, so that methodologies and tools can be developed to support those interactions. As a result, we were able to discover a rich theory about the correspondingly rich methodologies used in interactive art development. By testing the theory, through production and evaluation of tools which support it, we can then form methodological recommendations for practitioners. There is no reason to suspect that social study, and grounded theory in particular, would be any less useful in developing useful methodologies and supportive tools in other software engineering contexts.

4.2. Comparing 'Creative' Software Development with 'Commercial' Software Development

We can draw some comparisons between the commercial software development in the Kautz grounded theory study and the non-commercial software development in this. The Kautz study identified five categories which affected the practical use of systems development methodologies: *universality* (there is no universally applicable methodology), *confidence* (in the work's progress as shown by the methodology), *experience* (means a programmer is more likely to pick and choose specific techniques from methodologies rather than follow them all), *co-determination* (choosing the methodology created a feeling of responsibility to use it) and *introduction* (providing appropriate training in and transition to a methodology).

Except for in one of the cases in our study, we found no cases of plan-centric (or 'engineering-style') software development methodologies being used. (The exception was in the case where the artist was able to specify precisely what he wanted, and a requirements analysis and UML diagrams and so forth were produced.)

We found Kautz et al.'s categories to be in alignment with this study, but the small scale of the communities, and the high expertise and autonomy of the programmers means that *introduction* category becomes virtually irrelevant, and conversely that the *expertise* category becomes highly relevant. The *confidence* category is also diminished in importance, because the artists (the equivalent of customers or managers) are closely involved in the development process, and trust of programmers is valued. *Co-determination* becomes sometimes inaptly named, as usually the programmer is the only individual with a stake in the methodology choice. In the large collaboration we studied, *co-determination* seems an important factor in methodology adoption by individuals concerned, but the details of this would require further investigation.

Universality is interesting. The approaches taken by programmers working with artists could all (with the single exception mentioned above) be characterised as being forms of agile programming, and indeed a form of agile programming was explicitly adopted as the methodology for the large project in the study. One of the artists from that project said: "I continue to be attracted to the philosophies and some of the techniques of agile programming, principally because I see it as a means of operating whereby you do have a holistic understanding of the eventual delivery but you address immediate and evolving needs rather than fantasising that you can describe a project in the brief right at the start". Agile methodologies are characterised by their ability to accept changing situations, rather than trying to predict what they might be. They also tend to place themselves in subordination to the people using them, rather than being processes or frameworks in which people must operate. These things make it eminently suitable for developing artwork, since the technological requirements are often imprecise throughout the project, and also that part of creative practice is breaking with the convention of processes and frameworks. However, agile development methodologies used in isolation would result more in the 'intimate iteration' style of development, identified in this study to be limiting in terms of artist engagement with the computing medium. We are currently producing and evaluating tools and methodologies which support our theory that 'toy-making' is a more effective style of development.

4.3. Further Work

Our own work will test the theory by evaluating implementations of the ideas in this paper. The result will be design guidelines for implementers of future, more complete systems and methodologies for making interactive art.

It is worth considering briefly the potential of the intuitive language-conveying abilities of toys to encourage more abstract thinking about the computer medium itself than would necessarily be involved in engaging with a particular system. We can take one pointer from linguistics: Boroditsky and Ramscar claim that abstract knowledge can be built up from experience-based knowledge [1]. They write: "To properly characterize abstract thought, it will be important to look not only at what comes from innate wiring and physical experience, but also at the ways in which languages and cultures have allowed us to go beyond these to make us smart and sophisticated as we are." – we have found evidence to show that learning the language of an algorithmic system takes place as a result of toy-using, but the ways in which we can use such new languages to go technologically beyond the experience of playing with the present algorithmic system are not yet clear.

Software engineering methodologists should look into whether toy-making is beneficial to other kinds of interdisciplinary software development communities, and into ways that the toy-generation process can become a formal part of methodologies for these communities.

As reviewers of this paper noted, we have not touched upon mathematical formalisation of the processes described here, principally because we decided to look closely at the vagaries of human-level interaction before leaping into implementation of a potentially inappropriate system. At the moment, we have made high-level recommendations for systems and methodologies; to make recommendations specific and detailed enough to construct a mathematical formalisation would require intensive study in several sub-areas—for instance, how to identify parts of code which are useful as parameters for toy-making—that could only usefully take place once a broad and simple system has been implemented. So although the terms we use (e.g. 'expressivity') are currently ambiguous in terms of programming language definition, we suggest that those wishing to construct formalisations take pointers from formalisations of the programming systems we have cited. We also suspect that a mathematical formalisation may only be completed in retrospect after iterative evolution of such a system in conjunction with real-world human use.

We recommend that grounded theory studies are conducted in these sub-areas and other main fields of software development, and compared and contrasted with ours and Kautz's. The beauty of grounded theory is that all the separate concepts and codes can eventually be built up into 'super-theories', providing a rich and complex understanding of the general human practice of making software.

References

[1] Boroditsky, L. and Ramscar, M. The Roles of Body and Mind in Abstract Thought. Psychological Science, 13 (2). 185–189, 2002.

[2] Brown, J.S. and Duguid, P. Organizational Learning and Communities-of-Practice: Toward a Unified View of Working, Learning, and Innovation. Organization Science, 2 (1). 40–57, 1991.

[3] Campbell, J. Lessons in Object-Oriented Programming, 2003.

[4] Candy, L. and Edmonds, E.A. Explorations in Art and Technology. Springer, 2002.

[5] Cornock, S. and Edmonds, E. The Creative Process Where The Artist Is Amplified Or Superseded By The Computer. Leonardo (6). 11–16, 1973.

[6] Edmonds, E., Candy, L., Fell, M., Knott, R., Pauletto, S. and Weakley, A., Developing Interactive Art Using Visual Programming. in HCI International 2003 Proceedings, (Crete, Greece, 2003), Lawrence Erlbaum Associates, 2003.

[7] Edmonds, E.A. and Candy, L. Creativity, Art Practice and Knowledge. Communications of the ACM, 45 (10). 91–95, 2002.

[8] Fischer, G., Communities of Interest: Learning through the Interaction of Multiple Knowledge Systems. in IRIS'24, (Norway, 2001), 2001.

[9] Flanagan, M. and Perlin, K., Endpapers: collaboration, process and code. in ISEA2004, (Helsinki, Tallin, 2004), 2004.

[10] Foddy, W.H. Constructing questions for interviews and questionnaires: theory and practice in social research. Cambridge University Press, Cambridge, England; Melbourne, 1992.

[11] Fraser, D. QSR NUD*IST Vivo: Reference Guide. Qualitative Solutions and Research Pty., Melbourne, 1999.

[12] Glaser, B.G. Basics of Grounded Theory Analysis. Sociology Press, 1992.

[13] Glaser, B.G. and Strauss, A.L. The Discovery of Grounded Theory: strategies for qualitative research. Aldine Publishing Company, Hawthorne, N.Y, 1967.

[14] Green, T.R.G. and Petre, M. Usability Analysis of Visual Programming Environments: A 'Cognitive Dimensions' Framework. Journal of Visual Languages and Computing, 7. 131–174, 1996.

[15] Ingalls, D., Kaehler, T., Maloney, J., Wallace, S. and Kay, A., Back to the Future: The Story of Squeak, A Practical Smalltalk Written in Itself. in OOPSLA'97 Conference, (Atlanta, Georgia, 1997), 1997.

[16] Kay, A. and Goldberg, A. Personal Dynamic Media. Computer, 10 (3). 31–41, 1977.

[17] Kurtz, K., Hansen, B. and Jacobsen, D. The Utilization of Information Systems Development Methodologies in Practice. Journal of Information Technology Cases and Applications, 6 (4), 2004.

[18] Maeda, J. Design By Numbers. MIT Press, 1999.

[19] Maeda, J. and Burns, R. Creative code. Thames & Hudson, London, 2004.

[20] Nardi, B. A Small Matter of Programming. MIT Press, Cambridge, MA, 1993.

[21] Negroponte, N.P. Being Digital. Alfred A. Knopf, New York, 1995.

[22] Shneiderman, B. Creativity Support Tools: Establishing a framework of activities for creative work. Communications of the ACM, 45 (10). 116–120, 2002.

[23] Shneiderman, B. Direct Manipulation: A Step Beyond Programming Languages. IEEE Computer, 16 (8). 57–67, 1983.

[24] Star, S.L. The Structure of Ill-Structured Solutions: Boundary Objects and Heterogenous Distributed Problem Solving. in Gasser, L. and Huhns, M.N. eds. Distributed Artificial Intelligence, Morgan Kaufmann, San Mateo, CA, 1989, 37–54, 1989.

[25] Strauss, A.L. and Corbin, J. Basics of qualitative research: Techniques and procedures for developing grounded theory. SAGE Publications Ltd., Thousand Oaks, CA, 1998.

[26] Terry, M. and Mynatt, E.D., Recognizing Creative Needs in User Interface Design. in Creativity and Cognition Conference 2002, (Loughborough, UK, 2002), ACM Press, 38–44, 2002.

[27] Turner, G. and Edmonds, E.A., Towards a Supportive Technological Environment for Digital Art. in OzCHI 2003: New directions in interaction, information environments, media and technology, (Brisbane, Australia, 2003), 2003.

[28] Weakley, A., Johnston, A. and Turner, G., Creative Collaboration: Communication Translation and Generation in the Development of a Computer-Based Artwork. in HCI International, (Las Vegas, 2005 (to appear)), 2005 (to appear).

[29] Wenger, E. Communities of Practice – Learning, Meaning and Identity. Cambridge University Press, Cambridge, England, 1998.

New Trends in Software Methodologies, Tools and Techniques
H. Fujita and M. Mejri (Eds.)
IOS Press, 2005

Acting Interactively in a Digital World

Roman DANYLAK and Ernest EDMONDS
Creativity and Cognition Studios, University of Technology, Sydney
rdanylak@it.uts.edu.au, ernest@ernestedmonds.com.au

Abstract. The virtual world that computation now presents to us and involves us in, otherwise known as digitisation – collapses the 'self'; personal identity to which we have become accustomed to in the last four hundred years, is challenged by the illusion of many selves, transforming our experience of the usual. Digital technology predicates this change; we are no longer happy with just being John Smith, our namesake, and the technology allows, even encourages this; it presents us with the possibility of playing in an infinite game where we can be many other beings, other types of people, rather than staying as 'who' we are. The combination of separate, unique, historically evolved representational technologies, best stated as counterfeit, production and simulation, distinctions established by Baudrillard [1] allows this diversity of self to evolve in a digitised environment. This paper will focus on Spielberg's film *Catch Me if You Can*, the narrative describing the **actions** of its game playing protagonist, Frank Abagnale – who exemplifies digital man - adopting many personas but in a pre-digital world. This study offers a clear understanding of the nature of interactivity and its relationship to representation and human action. Semiotic analysis of these distinctions will be included.

Keywords. Self, counterfeit, production, simulation, action, multimodal, game, interaction, semiotic, metaphor, metonymy, utterance

The confusions which occupy us arise when language is like an engine idling, not when it is doing work.

Wittgenstein [2]

The ordinary world generally demands of us to be one person and one person only, so our credit cards, bank statements and birth certificates tell us. In Arthur Miller's play *The Crucible* [3], its hero, John Proctor, declares passionately, having being forced to falsely sign his innocence away as a party to witchcraft and then awaiting execution, that 'I have given my soul; leave me my name'. This is a statement of fixed individuality as a final value, the internal and external being one and the same and having enduring currency for at least four hundred years in the West, of course till now. Multimodal interactivity is akin to a mask – changeable, archetypal, not really personal – allowing us to be other characters in such places as chat rooms, digital videos, altered photographs, ghost authored documents, games and similar, making something else other than a single-self experience real and very accessible.

At the core of this change is a fundamental shift resulting from the fluidity of digitisation; morphing data from one form into another is seamless as is reproduction, perfect copy after perfect copy of sound, image and text. The physics of communication has also been altered [4]: the instantaneous nature of communication collapses geographical divisions giving the communicator a new space to play in, an interactive live, infinitely spacious new theatre.

To elucidate this phenomenon of the multiple self in interactive environments this writing will focus on a recently produced film *Catch Me If You Can* [5], played by Leonardo De Caprio and Tom Hanks, directed by Steven Spielberg. It is a particularly useful film in that the action of its protagonist, Frank William Abagnale Jnr (De Caprio) exemplifies the mobility of multiple selves in the information age and the technology by which they are produced. The film is set in the very early stages of modern mass electronic

communication, 1963, and is based on the true story [6] of Frank William Abagnale Jnr, who having adopted a number of false identities, was able to defraud several millions of dollars by firstly posing as an airline pilot, then acting as a surgeon and then as an a associate attorney general, roles he played convincingly, living an accompanying extravagant lifestyle.

Frank acts as a new type of man in the information age, using three modes of representation simultaneously, these being *counterfeit*, *production* and *simulation*: to counterfeit is a classicist, renaissance, representational concern; production an industrial modernising concern; simulation, the contemporary practice of coding used in computing [7]. These modes of representation follow one another historically in Western culture and most significantly the three now exist concurrently in multimedia interactive environments. Frank, in this respect, is the inventor of multimodal interaction; his behaviour, the techniques he employs, model such technologically advanced interaction. What allows him to do what he does i.e. fool the system by advancing within it beyond its own design capacity, is to use the three modes of representation – counterfeiting, production and simulation concurrently – coordinating their communication as tools and media at his disposal.

The plot is as follows: Frank Abagnale, at age sixteen, finds himself in the middle of his parents emotion filled divorce inducing a crisis in his life. To satisfy his need for money and security he attempts to pass off bad cheques, attempting it many times, succeeding eventually with a forgery. To do this he must also 'play a role', charming young women to surrender critical information to him on how cheques are processed. At this point two of the three representations have begun: he has counterfeited the cheque and simulated a personality. Their combination is a winning combination getting him a new simulation impersonating a Pan Am airline pilot, flying the skies for free. His second incarnation is then as a doctor in charge of some twenty doctors and nurses in an emergency ward. The third incarnation is as a lawyer serving as an associate district attorney. In between them there is a James Bond persona with fast cars and glamour, and finally a return to the airline pilot to elude capture. All of these transformations require the combination of the three representational techniques previously mentioned.

As counterfeiter, ink, pen, different paper types, typewriters, photos, identification badges, the removal of critical corporate logos from objects such as model planes required to create authenticity of cheques, are all a part of Frank's art of counterfeiting; these are his first tools and materials for creating the fakes of the real. He exudes the skill of a 16th century Dutch painter, setting up his studio in hotel rooms around the world, the artefacts are intimate and personal, stored in boxes, capable of altering minute artistic detail.

Production then ensues: a linear manifestation of the counterfeited art form. Frank goes from inspecting the authenticity of his first forgery to shuffling a handful of cheques desiring more of the same. Eventually, Handratty (Tom Hanks), the FBI agent chasing Frank, lays out twenty or so of the cheques on a desk in disbelief, the theft now escalating exponentially. Frank's concern is for the mechanical reproduction of his art. He buys his first typewriter at an auction because he needs machinery; art becomes process as he fills a bath tub full of model planes from which he has removed the transparency logo of the Pan Am corporation, ceasing to make 'originals' but replacing the activity with mass reproduction instead.

The third representation is simulation: the adoption of personalities by Frank. Voice, composure, vocabulary and lifestyle need merely be desired then witnessed by Frank to adopt them, initiated by *action*. Frank treats the world of information as his database, a place where like digital computation, there is random entry and exit points, a key characteristic of digital technology [8]. It's a cut and paste life for Frank and like digital data the reproduction is easy and transmutable. The world is a new stage and he lives out life like a storybook, taking on fictional roles, but always in combination with counterfeiting and production. The world of information surges around him like a virtual set. Television, which is everywhere, is Frank's tutor; there he can witness how doctors talk, dress and associate, which he translates back into a performance; episodes of Perry Mason, the Hollywood television series lawyer tutors Frank in the superficialities of acting like a lawyer. This surface he pulls away bringing it into three dimensions through his will to act, to 'be' these people.

A semiotic analysis illuminates some universal facts about Baudrillard's distinctions of counterfeit, production and simulation. There are three semiotic terms of particular use here, these being: metaphor, metonymy, and utterance. Metaphors are the image element of language, for example if one says 'dog' we see a dog in our mind's eye; metonymy is the linear explication of language, that is, the way in which words form chains; whilst utterance is the expression of language in the 'now', its sonic nature that establishes our experience of events being unique [9].

With these distinctions in mind, the three elements of reproduction have parallels in natural language, as organised in the following table.

Figure 1.

Semiotic term	Reproductive technology
metaphor	counterfeit
metonymy	production
utterance	simulation

Metaphors are counterfeits in that they represent the image likeness of the object signified; metonymy resembles production in that it is the sequential manifestation of images or text, the machine of language; whilst simulation is like utterance in that is a perfect 'now' – a total perfect representation of an entity and its qualities.

This concurrence points to a profound fact about the development of communication technologies: that they are extensions of the fundamentals of our language functions. Anthropomorphism then dominates in digital technological manufacture – the reproduction of what humans are themselves in their artefacts. These artefacts of language are coordinated by Frank enabling him to transform himself, defining himself as never before because human cultural definition is through language. This combination of media is unique to digital multimodal interaction, where sound, image and text can manipulate and coordinate a vast range of communication artefacts regardless of their point of evolution in human history.

Where writers like Barthes in his work The Death of The Author [10], were signalling the end of the individual literary talent, Frank signals the birth of the multimedia actor, the world as fiction, pure language constructing itself as system of signs and symbols which can be acted in, the world truly as a multimodal stage. The book is now supplanted by the electronic and all its simulacra. When one role no longer suits Frank or when he is close to detection, as is the case with his Pan Am pilot disguise, all he need do is receive the words and images to change character again as if changing programmes. A central, fixated self is of no use to Frank in his process of constant metamorphosis.

Frank's signature behaviour is the appropriation of signs and symbols; the first shot we see of Frank in his happy past life is him ripping the label from a wine bottle, a sort of violent prelude to 'cut and paste'; this is his signature as Handratty learns, who on seeing a wine bottle with a detached, torn off label, deduces that rank is close by. Such signs/labels to Frank are mobile; they can change place, be put elsewhere at his desire like a digitised file. In 1963, technology does not have such mobility but Frank makes it mobile, learning how to create perfect fakes, which of course brings him however much money, travel, consumption he desires. He adds the fluidity placing and recontextualising these symbols with the effect of giving him power. The sign and the signified are separated and reassigned to mean what Frank chooses them to mean interrupting the established codes of mass communication with his chosen processes and representations.

The ripping off of the wine label by Frank, is oddly enough, the act of interaction. Interaction, which, if understood as a dialogue, is the exchange of information that then alters the code by which the exchange occurred. This is communication with the object altering what the bottle label now signifies. The label upon a bottle no longer means 'wine' but ripped label upon bottle means 'Frank was here' and also whatever else Frank will deign it to mean.

Furthermore, in this interactive world invented by Frank, he not only reads, but he also builds, a fundamental potential of coded simulation. The simulation allows him to make worlds, which he can inhabit as long as he plays according to the rules of the environment. At all times Frank must use the necessary passwords and codes to gain access to the various chambers of the world, communicating according to the norms of function, representation and building, arranging more codes as he goes along. The parallel here is with contemporary computer games such as Sim City 3000 [11]which allow users to build housing complexes, mountains, volcanoes, zoos, dams, sports fields and so on. It is just that for Frank he is actually in the program, setting up interactivity as he goes along and evolving environments not on screen but in the real world.

Frank is homo digitalis, a new kind of being, one that the world had not seen the likes of; he is a congregated hyper-elite of one. Endless simulations are happily and skilfully performed by him, manifested as a personal, albeit surface-only transformation. The hero has a thousand faces and Frank is willing to try on at least a few of them. Just as Renaissance man, at worst, a Machiavellian, left the fixed medieval man behind for individual, internalised, mobile war-faring ambition [12], Frank leaves his unsuccessful, personally and historically ascribed identity for a number of new lives. He sees the personal potential of coordinating the artefacts of past and present representations and disregards the social penalties of this behaviour because there are no ready barriers, no detection devices in place, and the power is so seductive. The system can only detect what it knows, and what Frank's activity – an analogue multimedia shuffle – is so new, without precedent, without definition. Similarly, Handratty is a new man; when attempting to explain the nature of the crime to fellow FBI agents he is laughed at and belittled, misunderstood, as these types of crime were novel, as much as cheques, telephones, television and commercial air travel were.

The film's final climax shows Frank being caught by Handratty in a printery in France, attempting to forge more cheques in vast quantities; the printing press is the ultimate artistic tool for Frank, mechanical and semi-electronic, endless reproduction of what he requires at the press of a button; he is the king of the industrialised process. It can produce as much value as Frank wants, and of course as an 'artist', a maker of fakes, he is at home in France, where some of the world's most significant images, the fakes of nature, have emerged from. Interestingly this is the end of the simulations; Frank has no costume, playing no character at all, but is instead dressed only in a plain singlet. Handratty has caught him out of disguise and found the core personality behind all of the representations for the purpose of imprisonment.

The significant motivation portrayed throughout the film is that of chasing fuelled by a fugitive shape-shifting multiple personality: that really is the game. And gaming of course is one of the single largest manifestations of multimodal interaction [13]. This aspect of Frank is part of what generates his creativity in that as a young man he can play with the world of information, changing it, moulding it, doing what he likes, not fearing consequences at all. Who can I be next? Where can I go now? How far can the truth be stretched? These are the notions that inform the game that Frank plays, allowing him the imaginative capacity to experience 'being' other people, empowered by his version of multimodal interaction, transforming an otherwise ordinary world.

These games of illusory multiple selves do however have a finish; finally truth emerges, that which the masks have been hiding. The running, the disguises are simply the manifestation of Frank's fear; he is finally captured looking into his estranged mother's new home on Christmas eve; he can no longer hide from himself, showing what he is really pursuing. The question of truth is constantly restated between Handratty and Frank, Handratty also coping with estrangement from his own family. As such the illusions of identity that he plays in a multimedia world only bring the truth of Frank's being into sharper contrast on his journey to find himself, to admit truly what is inside of him.

Multimodal interaction then has transformative power. Abagnale's real life activities as portrayed in Catch Me if You Can show that the instantaneous combination of historically separate representative media offers a cultural navigation that has powerful personal significance as well as being fun. The recombination is the effect of the manipulation of the sign and the signified in a variety of representative dimensions: this defines interaction. The pre-emptive nature of this activity points to interactive multimodality being a significant innovation.

The world that such interaction encapsulates, steered through the actions of newly created persona, is a world of glittering, mobilising, often invisible potentials that we are only beginning to see and experience, shaking the foundations of historically established notions of who we in fact are. The example of Abagnale's biography via Speilberg's film, is the story of an individual who has made the first imaginative leap to combine these unseen potentials, creating a new world of experiences and travelling on new trajectories. As Wittgenstein stated, language is a problem when it is idling and not working; Frank Abagnale Jnr showed how language and its representative media can in fact work differently when connected electronically. This illuminates the more intimate and potential realities of a machine that is the hands of millions of people everyday.

Acknowledgements

Parts of this text have appeared in: Mesh, vol. 18, 2005 New Media Journal, Swinburne University of Technology, Melbourne, Victoria, Australia.

References

[1] Baudrillard, J., *In the Shadow of the Silent Majorities, or, The end of the Social, and other essays.* Semiotext(e), 1983.
[2] Wittgenstein, L., *Philosophical Investigations*, ed. B. Blackwell. 1988. p. 51e.
[3] Miller, A., *The Crucible*. 1953: Penguin. p. 124.
[4] McLuhan, M. and McLuhan, E., *Laws of Media; The New Science.* 1988: p. 94.
[5] Spielberg, S., *Catch Me if You Can*. 2002: Parkes MacDonald Production.
[6] Abagnale, F.W., *Catch Me If You Can.* 2000. New York Broadway Books.
[7] Baudrillard, J., *Selected Writings*. Stanford University Press. 2001. p. 138.
[8] Manovich, L., *The Language of New Media.* MIT Press Cambridge Mass., 2001: p. 218.
[9] Barthes, R., *Elements of Semiology*. 1964, New York: Hill and Wang. pp. 58–60.
[10] Barthes, R., *Image, Music, Text.* New York: Hill and Wang, 1977.
[11] Zvenigorodsky, A., *Sim City 3000 http://simcity.ea.com/*. 2005.
[12] McLuhan, M. and McLuhan, E., *Laws of Media; The New Science.* 1988: p. 50–60.
[13] Chesher, C., *How to tell apart video games and new media art.* in Interaction: Systems, Theory and Practice, Creativity and Cognition Studios Press, Sydney, 2004: p. 225–227.

H. Fujita and M. Mejri (Eds.)
IOS Press, 2005

Author Index

Book, M. 281
Candy, L. 353
Chatzigeorgiou, A. 54
Chua, B.B. 111
Danylak, R. 401
Denis, K. 103
di Sciullo, A.M. 207
Dünnweber, J. 311
Edmonds, E. 353, 388, 401
Ekenberg, L. 173
Feuerlicht, G. 263
Fujita, H. 83
Funyu, Y. 144
Godbout, D. 83
Gonzalez-Perez, C. 252
Gorlatch, S. 311
Graham, M. 18
Gruhn, V. 281
Gustas, R. 235
Henderson-Sellers, B. 252
Hülder, M. 281
Koch, G. 224
Kof, L. 126
Ktari, B. 83
Litke, A. 54
Lohmann, D. 33
Malyshkin, V. 194
Meesathit, S. 263
Mejri, M. 83
Mitsui, K. 144
Negoro, F. 67
Oudshoorn, M.J. 18
Pizka, M. 126
Rolland, C. 3
Sandhu, P.S. 156
Sasaki, J. 144
Schäfer, C. 281
Shiratori, N. 330
Singh, H. 156
Spinczyk, O. 33
Stephanides, G. 54
Suganuma, T. 330
Takahashi, H. 330
Tanaka, Y. 295
Tenzer, J. 364
Tokairin, Y. 330
Turner, G. 388
Urban, M. 33
Verner, J.M. 111
Weakley, A. 388
Yoneda, T. 144
Zagorulko, Yu. 194
Zhang, Y. 388
Zotos, K. 54